Literary Life in German Expressionism and the Berlin Circles

Studies in the Fine Arts
The Avant-Garde, No. 25

Stephen C. Foster, Series Editor

Associate Professor of Art History
University of Iowa

Other Titles in This Series

Literary Life in German Expressionism and the Berlin Circles

by
Roy F. Allen

UMI RESEARCH PRESS
Ann Arbor, Michigan

Produced and distributed by
UMI Research Press
an imprint of
University Microfilms International
Ann Arbor, Michigan 48106

Library of Congress Cataloging in Publication Data

Allen, Roy F., 1937-
    Literary life in German expressionism and the
Berlin circles.

    (Studies in fine arts. The avant-garde ; no. 25)
    Revision of thesis (Ph.D.)–University of Wisconsin,
1972.
    Bibliography: p.
    Includes index.
    1. German literature–20th century–History and
criticism. 2. Expressionism. 3. German literature–Berlin
(Germany)–History and criticism.   I. Title. II. Series:
Studies in the fine arts. Avant-garde ; no. 25.

PT405.A47 1983   830'.9'1   82-4762
ISBN 0-8357-1315-6   AACR2

Table of Contents

List of Illustrations

Illustrations follow p. 255

1. Program for the April 3, 1912, performance of "Der Neue Club" in memory of Georg Heym (masthead: woodcut by Karl Schmidt-Rottluff, 1911)

2. Kurt Hiller (1930)

3. Portrait in oil of Herwarth Walden by Oskar Kokoschka (1910)

4. Poster by Oskar Kokoschka for *Der Sturm*

5. Herwarth Walden and Oskar Kokoschka in the offices of *Der Sturm* (1916)

6. Title page for an August, 1911, number of *Der Sturm* with drawing by Ernst Ludwig Kirchner

7. Title page for the October 4, 1913, number of *Die Aktion* with portrait of Alfred Lichtenstein by Max Oppenheimer

8. Woodcut portrait of Franz Pfemfert by Georg Tappert (1920)

9. Alfred Richard Meyer (1928)

10. Title page for Book 6 (Sept. 1, 1913) of *Die Bücherei Maiandros* with drawing by Ludwig Meidner

11. Gottfried Benn (Brussels, 1916)

12. Title page for Gottfried Benn's *Söhne* (1913) with drawing by Ludwig Meidner

Preface

The "Expressionismus-Boom" (Richard Brinkmann, 1980) which began some twenty years ago still shows no signs of abating. In such a climate of sustained interest the publication of a study originally complete as a doctoral dissertation in 1972 is perhaps not out of place; its approach—largely very factually and historically oriented—has, at any rate, helped it to date less rapidly than it otherwise might have amid the plethora of methodologies since World War II.

Neither time nor the context of the series in which this study now appears made it possible to undertake a complete revision of the original; nothing short of a total revamp of both the style and content would have been desirable in light of the development of both my own approach to scholarly studies and of Expressionism research in the last ten years. It was, in particular, not possible to update the Introduction without radically altering the basic thrust of the original.

However, besides subjecting the original version to a fairly thorough facelifting to remove the more objectionable excesses of "dissertationese," I was able to take some limited advantage of recent strides in our understanding of Expressionist literary life. Thus, factual errors in the original have been corrected. Factual additions to our knowledge of Expressionism since 1972 pertinent to this study are reflected in the text, the notes, and the bibliography. In response to criticism of reviewers and other readers of the original, an index of names, titles, and subjects has been added to enhance its usefulness as a reference work.

To make the study accessible to a larger readership, the passages quoted from German texts have been translated into American English. Readers with little or no German should be forewarned: the axiom "translation is interpretation" is seldom so patently true as it is of renderings of German Expressionist language. The translations, unless otherwise identified, are my own; they were executed, first and foremost, with readability and, only secondarily, with adherence to the letter of the original in mind; they are meant to be utilitarian aids to readers in need and should, at all times, be compared with the originals in the notes.

I wish to thank many of those same reviewers and readers for their helpful suggestions for improving the original manuscript which I was able to implement in the present version; I would have liked to have done them greater justice had it been possible. I would especially like to express my gratitude to Professor Jost Hermand of the University of Wisconsin, Madison, whose inspiration, advice, and encouragement helped produce the original version of this study. I am also indebted to Professors Klaus L. Berghahn, Reinhold Grimm, and Ian C. Loram of that same institution for their valuable help in improving the original manuscript. Finally, I am grateful to Professor Stephen Foster of the Fine Arts Archive/Dada Archive and Research Center at the University of Iowa for his encouragement and assistance in preparing this study for publication in this series.

Roy F. Allen
Spring, 1983

Introduction

The concept of "Expressionism" applied to a certain body of German literature produced during the first approximate quarter of this century has often been a source of considerable vexation, almost a bugbear, for literary historians. One annoying thread runs through most of the studies of Expressionist literature from the recent past: repeated reference is made to the failure of literary scholars both to develop a precise and widely accepted definition of the essence of Expressionism and to establish definitive standards for judging the degree of propriety of applying it to a given author's work. The latter fact is especially true of studies published since the appearance in 1959 of Richard Brinkmann's report on Expressionism scholarship from the period 1952-59.[1] Brinkmann had many a bone to pick with this research; but he punctuated in particular that major failure of scholars just mentioned.[2] In March, 1960, he put out a postscript to the report in which he reviewed several new studies, including most notably Walter Sokel's *The Writer in Extremis: Expressionism in Twentieth-Century German Literature* (Stanford, 1959). Again, this time confronted with Sokel's work, Brinkmann is forced to underscore the discrepancy between the scholar's liberal use of the term "Expressionism" and his simultaneous failure to face squarely the crucial problem of defining it. Brinkmann now insists that the question of whether the conventional use of the term to designate a style or epoch in German literary history should be retained is one which scholarship can no longer put off.[3]

In the few years that followed the appearance of the Brinkmann reports two more attempts at a comprehensive view of Expressionism in German literature came out: Walter Muschg's *Von Trakl zu Brecht: Dichter des Expressionismus* (Munich, 1961) and Egbert Krispyn's *Style and Society in German Literary Expressionism* (Gainesville, 1964). In an apparent response to Brinkmann's criticism of Sokel and others, both Muschg and Krispyn attempted once more to come to terms with the concept of "Expressionism" and to redefine it. Neither study is extensive enough, neither delves deeply enough into the literature so as to be able to be considered definitive, and not surprisingly, therefore, neither has met with wide endorsement.

To the present date the state of research on the broad question of a definition has remained unchanged. John Willett's recently published *Expressionism* (Toronto, 1970) is, to be sure, extensive in scope; but it was clearly written as a popular survey of expressionistic trends in art as well as literature in this century as a whole rather than as a systematic study of the concept of "Expressionism" in German literature applied to the central period from about 1910 to 1920. A large number of full-length studies of specific aspects or authors of Expressionism have also come out since 1960, and at fairly regular intervals up to the present day. However, while they have contributed much to our understanding of the particular topics they investigate, such studies have all failed to clear up the most troublesome issue. In the studies of authors the problem of defining Expressionism itself was either skirted or, at most, touched upon indirectly. In the studies of aspects of the movement the problem was resolved by summarizing, on the whole uncritically, the findings of past research (Horst Denkler, Annalisa Viviani),[4] by resorting to Sokel's approach (Armin Arnold, *Die Literatur des Expressionismus*)[5] or, the scholar seemingly despairing of the possibility of defining the concept, by simply opting to postpone an attempt at a definition and use the term "Expressionism," at least for the interim, as little more than an arbitrary label for the literature being discussed (Peter Hohendahl, Gunter Martens, Armin Arnold, *Prosa des Expressionismus*).[6] Thus, with research on the truly crucial issue having reached the stage of a stalemate, Brinkmann's insistence on a decision on the use of the term seems more urgent, more demanding of a direct response now than ever before.

In my view there is only one direction which a response to Brinkmann can follow. Proposals to abandon the term and, as suggested most prominently by Wolfdietrich Rasch, Wilhelm Emrich, Herbert Lehnert, and Helmut Kreuzer, to consider the period in modern German literature in the few decades or more since approximately 1890 as one continuous and uniform literary revolution have not been widely accepted.[7] Such proposals generally argue for replacing the terms "Naturalism," "Impressionism," "Neoromanticism," "Neoclassicism" and "Expressionism" with a term like "Die Literatur der Jahrhundertwende" (Rasch, Kreuzer)[8] or "Jugendstil" (Lehnert)[9]; their approach illuminates, often quite convincingly, common features of those literatures, but it ignores significant differences. Moreover, such proposals are unable to explain away satisfactorily three very obtrusive facts. First of all, the current use of the term "Expressionism" was not established by literary historians, but by the bulk of those authors generally subsumed under it. Secondly, once the currency of the term had been established (after about 1914),[10] the same authors rallied beneath it as a banner and proclaimed their support of it in a vast body of programmatic statements. Finally, such authors also felt that the term best signified what they stood for; they, therefore, made repeated efforts of their own to define it, both in programmatic statements made during their "Expressionist years" and in memoirs published in the ensuing decades. In view of these facts, it seems clear that we are forced to find a proper place for the term in our conception of the history of twentieth-century German literature. It seems equally clear that such a place is not to be found by ignoring or trying once again to rule out the factor of divergence in style and themes which so many readers of Expressionism have noted: this divergence, especially in style,[11] has been all too conclusively established by scholarship over the past almost half a century to leave much room for further disagreement.

We must search therefore for a unity of Expressionist literature on an alternative level to that of style and themes. Such an alternative is suggested by certain very prominent omissions in past research on Expressionism, which we can bring into focus if we briefly survey its development over the past several decades. Expressionism scholarship has been treated in detail elsewhere: in reports, such as Brinkmann's, in introductions to numerous studies of Expressionist literature and in reviews in scholarly journals. For the purposes of the present discussion, therefore, I need only sketch in here the basic direction which that scholarship has taken. I will also limit myself here to a survey of only the major, full-length studies that have appeared in print; they will suggest the general outlines and direction of other studies, such as those published in journals or in symposium volumes.

The earliest major works on Expressionism, completed between the middle of the 1920s and the middle of the next decade, are also the first attempts at a comprehensive view of the literature. The second volume of Albert Soergel's *Dichtung und Dichter der Zeit: Im Banne des Expressionismus* (Leipzig, 1925) is not a systematic study of the concept of Expressionism but a sweeping survey of some of the basic tendencies in the literature, some of their background in the intellectual and social history of their times and a discussion of some of the more prominent aspects of the work of selected representatives of the literature.[12] Ferdinand Josef Schneider's *Der expressive Mensch und die deutsche Lyrik der Gegenwart* (Stuttgart, 1927), on the other hand, concentrating on the Expressionist lyric in the early phase (1910-14) in the work of Iwan Goll, Georg Heym, Ernst Stadler and Franz Werfel, is an attempt at a definition of the essence of Expressionism, more specifically of the Expressionist approach to life. Schneider sees this approach as manifested in an ecstatic or "expressives Legensgefühl" found in other periods of history as well and embodied in the similarly timeless figure of the "expressiver Mensch." Wolfgang Paulsen's *Expressionismus und Aktivismus: Eine typologische Untersuchung* (Bern and Leipzig, 1935) was the most penetrating analysis of Expressionist literature to appear before the Second World War. In a thesis that was to have considerable impact on subsequent scholarship, Paulsen advocates dividing Expressionism into two distinct and contradictory directions: Expressionism, which is metaphysically oriented and looks to intangibles for the reform of contemporary life, and Activism, which is politically oriented and seeks to change the social and political structure of the contemporary world. The last major work to appear in this early phase of the scholarship was Willi Duwe's *Deutsche Dichtung des 20. Jahrhunderts: Die Geschichte der Ausdruckskunst* (Zürich, 1936). Duwe studies Expressionist literature as it was manifested in the three genres of the lyric, the drama and prose fiction. For Duwe, the literature is best understood as a reaction to Naturalism: as part of a modern rebirth of mysticism and religion, which stretches from the end of the last century to Duwe's time, and with its emphasis on the expression of the inner world of man, Expressionism is the counterpole of Naturalism and its emphasis on materialism and the representation of external reality.

The interpretations of Expressionism in all of the major studies published during the period from the late 1930s to the mid-1940s were colored in a very conspicuous way by the political conditions of their era. In varying degrees, they all treat Expressionism as a moot point and—in the manner (and no doubt under the direct influence) of Georg Lukács's essay " 'Grösse und Verfall' des Expressionismus" (1934)[13] and of the 1937/38 polemical exchanges in the Moscow-based German exiles' journal *Das Wort*[14]—attempt to discover in Expressionism affinities with National Socialism. Wilhelmina Stuyver's *Deutsche expressionistische Dichtung im Lichte der Philosphie der Gegenwart* (Amsterdam and Paris, 1939) investigates Expressionist literature, as the title of her book itself indicates, in relationship to such contemporaneous philosophers as Nietzsche, Dilthey, Bergson, Klages, and Heidegger. *Expressionism in German Life, Literature and the Theatre* (1910-24), completed the very same year by Richard Samuel and R. Hinton Thomas, is largely a restatement of some of the ideas already put forth in past research on Expressionism. Samuel and Thomas deal with the basic aspects of the intellectual and sociopolitical background of the literature and with its major themes and stylistic features.[15] The impact of the political turmoil of the period comes through most strongly in M.F.E. van Bruggen's *Im Schatten des Nihilismus: Die expressionistische Lyrik im Rahmen und als Ausdruck der geistigen Situation Deutschlands* (Paris and Amsterdam, 1946). In a broad sample of the Expressionist lyric, van Bruggen attempts to define Expressionism as the manifestation of a nihilistic crisis in German intellectual history and, therewith, as an ideological forerunner of National Socialism.

It was not long after the end of the Second World War that scholarship began what might be called a rehabilitation of Expressionism, i.e., a revival of a much more receptive interest in the literature than had been entertained during the era of Nazism. The revival is characterized by a concentration on the work of specific representatives, most often the early lyricists, rather than by attempts at a more comprehensive view of the literature. It is also preoccupied with metaphysical or existential themes and certain structural and formal features in the works of the lyric poets, again, preferably of the early phase (Alfred Mombert, Theodor Däubler, Georg Trakl, Else Lasker-Schüler, Ernst Stadler, Georg Heym, et al.). The period of the postwar revival comes to an end around the beginning of the 1960s.

The rehabilitation was initiated by Fritz Martini's *Was war Expressionismus?* (Urach, 1948). The first half of his book is a discussion of the basic world view of the Expressionist and of the basic features of Expressionist language; this is followed by a selection of lyric poetry of the movement. Although Martini questions the possibility of interpreting Expressionism as a unified movement, he reads it, nevertheless, as manifesting a new attitude towards life which required a new language, new themes and new images. *Der bildhafte Ausdruck in den Dichtungen Georg Heyms, Georg Trakls und Ernst Stadlers* (Heidelberg, 1954) by Karl Ludwig Schneider attempts to determine the essential features of the Expressionist metaphor through an analysis of the lyrical poets of the early phase which the author considers representative of Expressionism as a whole. A second book by Schneider on the movement, *Zerbrochene Formen: Wort und Bild im Expressionismus* (Hamburg, 1967) is a collection of essays, some old, some new; in spite of its publication date, it reflects the dominant interests of the period we are now discussing. Schneider studies a variety of features of imagery and form in the Expressionist lyric of especially Heym and Stadler. Another collection of essays, *Expressionismus: Gestalten einer literarischen Bewegung* (Heidelberg, 1956), coedited by Hermann Friedmann and Otto Mann, attempts in the overt arrangement of the volume to give a comprehensive and systematic view of the literature; but it remains basically a symposium volume, made up of the only superficially coordinated work of a large body of contributors, with emphasis on the lyric; it, therefore, understandably fails to provide a uniform answer to the key question: What is Expressionsim?[16] That question is, for the same reasons, also left unanswered by the new, totally revised and expanded edition of the latter work, *Expressionismus als Literatur,* edited by Wolfgang Rothe (Bern and Munich, 1969). Nonetheless, the new edition is a much more penetrating introduction to the study of Expressionism than was its predecessor. It is more up-to-date and gives a much more balanced survey of the literature by adding several new chapters on very important, yet, until recently largely neglected, aspects of the movement: "Das Ich und die Welt: Expressionismus und Gesellschaft," "Der Mensch vor Gott: Expressionismus und Theologie," "Impressionismus und Expressionismus," "Die Prosa des Expressionismus," etc. The last major study from this period, Kurt Mautz's *Mythologie und Gesellschaft im Expressionismus: Die Dichtung Georg Heyms* (Frankfurt am Main and Bonn, 1961), coming as it does on the threshold of a shift in direction in Expressionism scholarship, reflects the interests of the past and points to the new interests of future research. Thus, as later scholars often will, Mautz investigates the Expressionist view of contemporary society; but his use of the lyric poetry of one of the early Expressionists (Heym) as his primary source places him in the period of the postwar revival of Expressionism.

The new direction just referred to follows upon, and is to some extent prepared for by, a series of new attempts at a comprehensive view of Expressionism, all of which appeared in quick succession just before or just after the year 1960. The first and most impressive of the new attempts is the study by Walter Sokel mentioned earlier.[17] Although Sokel, as we have already stated, does not really confront the issue of defining Expressionism head-on, he does give us the most penetrating analysis to date of the relationship of the literature to European intellectual history, to the society of its times and to modern literature in general. The other two comprehensive studies from this period have also been mentioned before: Walter Muschg's *Von Trakl zu Brecht* and Egbert Krispyn's *Style and Society in German Literary Expressionism.*[18] Both of the latter monographs (in Muschg's case in the long introductory chapter to a series of essays on individual authors in his book) are concentrated attempts at a redefinition of the concept of "Expressionism"; but both works suffer from relying too much on source material already selected for them by past scholarship and from being too selective in the numbers of authors against whose work they test their definitions.

The last approximate decade of this scholarship has seen a decided turn towards the investigation of some of the long-neglected, yet very basic, aspects and sources of German Expressionist literature. In a clear effort to complete our only partial view of Expressionism in the past, scholars have finally begun in recent years to study some of the facets of the movement that had seldom, and never in depth, been faced squarely by scholars before: e.g., the whole spectrum of drama and prose, the political literature and the general question of political commitment, the large body of theoretical writings, and the various periodical publications of the Expressionists. This new development, as with the special interests of the preceding period, parallels and stimulates a similar development in the printing and reprinting of Expressionist literature: in the last decade or so, a much broader sampling of the literature has begun to appear in reprint, including now not only the work of the lyricists and other perennial favorites, but also of the dramatists, the authors of imaginative prose, the theoretical writings and even a very representative selection of the periodical publications of the movement.

Armin Arnold's *Die Literatur des Expressionismus*[19] is the first of the major studies of this period. In the first half of his book, Arnold investigates Expressionist language (especially as it relates in the work of the much-neglected figure of Stramm to Futurism) and then, in the second half, takes a new look at some common Expressionist themes (especially that of the New Man). The second half of the book remained, by nature of its selectivity, inconclusive; but the author was able to establish quite convincingly in the first half that there is no single, unifying style in the works of the Expressionists. The year 1967 saw the appearance of two monographs focusing on the Expressionist drama. Peter Hohendahl's *Das Bild der bürgerlichen Welt im expressionistischen Drama*[20] checks the image of the middle class in Expressionist drama against the contemporary social conditions that contributed to, or helped condition, that image. Horst Denkler's *Drama des Expressionismus*[21] compares Expressionist drama with the programmatic texts and theater of the movement, in an attempt to arrive at certain basic "typological" features of Expressionist drama. A third book on the Expressionist drama appeared in 1970: Annalisa Viviani's *Dramaturgische Elemente des expressionistischen Dramas.*[22] Viviani elucidates the nature and function of basic dramaturgical elements of the Expressionist drama (dialogue, light, color, time, space, costume, gesture, etc.) as manifested in the stage directions of plays published by representative authors of the movement. The same year in Stuttgart appeared Eva Kolinsky's *Engagierter Expressionismus: Politik und Literatur zwischen Weltkrieg und Weimarer Republik*, a long-overdue investigation in depth into the political literature of Expressionism. Kolinsky deals with the political commitment of the Expressionists, as the title of her book suggests, only as expressed in their writings at the very end of the First World War. Gunter Martens' *Vitalismus und Expressionismus*[23] illuminates, in a detailed analysis of both philosophical (Nietzsche, Bergson, Simmel) and literary (Dehmel, Wedekind, Lasker-Schüler, Schickele, Stadler, Heym, Kaiser) texts, the close ties between philosophical and literary vitalism and Expressionism. Finally, most recently, Armin Arnold has contributed in the second of his books on the movement, *Prosa des Expressionismus*, the first full-length study devoted exclusively to a seldom-explored genre of Expressionist literature.[24] Arnold offers here what he admits to being only a "preliminary attempt" to shed some light on some of the features and sources, and on a few of the (in Arnold's view) exemplary (Jung, Artzybaschew, Corrinth) and not-so-exemplary (Edschmid, Flake) authors, of the prose.

I will also attempt in this study to help round out our fundamental understanding of Expressionism. At the same time, I will attempt to point, from a new perspective, to a unifying principle in the movement. All of the research I have surveyed here has contributed invaluably to our understanding of Expressionism; yet, some very basic aspects of the movement still remain unilluminated. Furthermore, I believe the lack of a full grasp of some of these aspects has contributed significantly to the failure of scholarship to find a unifying principle in Expressionism.

First of all, all of the studies discussed in the preceding pages, as our survey has attempted to indicate, approach Expressionism from a largely ahistorical standpoint in relation to the development of both the movement itself and the authors who are believed to have represented it in the period from about 1910 to 1920. Scholarship has often attempted to relate Expressionism to the general social, political, and intellectual history of its times (cf. the studies of Stuyver,

Sokel, Mautz, Hohendahl, Viviani). Yet, except for Kolinsky's work, which, as noted, concentrates only on a brief segment of the time covered by the movement, no serious and detailed investigations have been made to date into the progression and development, the changes and shifts of emphasis and interest in Expressionism throughout the movement. Secondly, with a few minor exceptions, represented by an occasional reference in the studies by Sokel and Samuel/Thomas or by a brief section in the study by Hohendahl,[25] there has been no careful consideration of the social history of the Expressionists, i.e., of the nature, structure, and activities of the groups or circles which, as several of the scholars interested in this period have recently begun to recognize, played so prominent a role in the lives of the Expressionists.[26]

With only a few dissenters (especially the "New Critics"), literary scholarship has generally been receptive to the contribution which an author's biography can make to the understanding and appreciation of his literary work, recognizing, nonetheless, the restraint that must be exercised (in light of the excesses of Positivism) in drawing conclusions about the relationship of the literary work to the author's life. Literary scholarship, especially in the recent past, has also come to accept widely the value of the study of a literary work in relationship to its social and political matrix in a broad sense (the so-called "sociological approach" to literature). Seldom, on the other hand, have literary historians been prepared, or even able, to appreciate fully the contribution which can be made to the understanding of a literary work, or a body of literature, by a study of the biography or social history of groups of writers working to some degree in concert in the interest of literature. This fact, of course, has often been due, at least in part, to the paucity of information on group activities of writers. A writer's memoirs will deal, in most instances, in detail only with his personal and individual experiences; and, if the circle of writers he might have been involved with in some capacity was exclusive and functioned for the most part in the private sphere, then outsiders can offer little record of the group's existence, its nature and activities.

In the case of Expressionism the state of information of the latter sort is exceptional in certain respects. The circles of writers who represented Expressionism in the central period were also largely private bodies. However, their public activities were usually very extensive as well. In addition—and this must be read as a significant testimony to the extent to which these circles were felt by those who have chronicled them to have played an important role in their lives—both the public and private activities of the circles have been documented in great detail in an astonishingly large body of memoirs, reminiscences and other reports by former Expressionists, most of which have been published in approximately the last two decades. In addition, a further record of the activities of the circles has been preserved in the form of the journals which they usually edited in concert and supported with contributions as a group: all of these journals have recently been recovered from the obscurity of private collections and made available for researchers in libraries, such as the Deutsches Literaturarchiv of the Schiller-Nationalmuseum in Marbach a.N.; many of them have also been reprinted in the last few years. Thus, with the help of reports on the circles of Expressionism, of the journals they sponsored, of the literature which emanated from them, it is now possible to reconstruct in astonishing detail their origins, structure, development, and activities so as to be able to assess the importance and the extent of potential influence which they may have had on the lives and work of their members.

I will attempt just such a reconstruction in the present study by investigating the literary activities of the circles active between about 1910 and 1920. This then is a study of the "Expressionist movement" in the fullest sense of that term. The term "movement" has most often been somewhat loosely applied to Expressionism in the sense of certain stylistic and thematic trends or tendencies in the literature. Neither the English term nor its German equivalent ("Bewegung") have been glossed to date in any of the standard handbooks to literature.[27] However, the dictionary definitions of those terms alone suffice to make clear that, applied to literature, they would have to connote not only certain trends or tendencies in style or themes in a given body of literature, but also, even before all else, the concerted activities of an organized group or groups of individuals working or tending towards some goal in behalf of that same literature.[28] As just defined, the term "movement"—to demonstrate this fact is a major aim of the present study—applies especially well to Expressionism in the central period, and, so applied, helps to illuminate its unifying principle.

Because of the potential breadth of a study of this kind—as will become obvious in the course of the following chapters, it could easily fill several volumes if the attempt were made to exhaust the subject—the present study will emphasize the Berlin circles and their activities; they were, taken as a group, the most active and influential of the circles in the central period of the movement. In addition, this study will proceed in a strictly historical manner in relation both to the development of the circles and to their sociopolitical matrix, so as to be able to appreciate fully the importance of such development in the context of the individual circles as well as in the broader context of the whole movement. Literary scholarship has traditionally been sensitive to the importance of the factor of change and development in an author's work; it therefore follows that such a factor can be of significance in the work of groups of writers who are affiliated with one another in some manner, or in the work of a whole movement of writers.

The nature of this investigation would make it possible for each of the following chapters to stand alone; each one, however, acquires its full measure of meaning only when it is read in the context of the whole. The reader should keep this in mind while reading through the following pages; this will help to give a sense of the synthesis which provides the real message of this study. The concluding chapter ("Some Conclusions") will offer some assistance in achieving this synthesis, but only after the reader has made his or her own effort.

1

The Expressionist Era (1910-20)

The Expressionist movement in literature and the arts was the cultural child of the age of William II in Germany; but more than being only an unconscious reflection, it was simultaneously a purposeful rejection of that age in form and spirit. On the fundamental level, Expressionism mirrored what was probably the most pronounced quality of the Wilhelminian age, its great optimism; it repudiated, on the other hand, virtually the entire ideological and cultural base on which the optimism was established.

The artists and writers who were associated with Expressionism, and subsequently wrote reflections on their youth and early manhood in the approximate half a century that lies between 1870/71 and the end of World War One, have left behind a fairly detailed picture of Wilhelminian Germany and of their double-faced response to it. As Walter Sokel, Peter Hohendahl, Egbert Krispyn, and Kurt Mautz have conclusively shown in their studies of its literature[1] and as I will further demonstrate in this history of its circles, Expressionism bore more conspicuously and directly than many such literary movements a most crucial relationship to its society. Given the crucialness of this relationship, it is imperative that I begin with a brief discussion of the Expressionist's view of Wilhelminian Germany, as he has recorded it most directly in his many reports and memoirs on the period, so as to place the movement, specifically the Expressionist revolt, in proper perspective before its ideological and cultural background.[2]

Blending nostalgia with a large portion of irony, the Expressionists who have chronicled their age have baptized the pre-World War One era "die goldene Zeit," "die Zeit unserer Unschuld," or even more simply, using a proverbial catchphrase, "die gute alte Zeit."[3] Read in the context of the Expressionist chronicles, these labels, and some of the very similar ones offered, are all more meaningful and accurate than such period tags as a rule tend to be. The image which these chroniclers draw for us of the era is unanimously, in fact, that of a relatively serene, secure and untroubled time, not unlike the blissful, but also—as the Expressionists were often quick to stress—naive, innocence of childhood. A large percentage of Germans of that age were optimistic about the future and confident about the present.[4] This was particularly true of the new middle class which at least morally and materially, though not yet politically, dominated the age.

The Wilhelminian burgher looked with satisfaction into the recent past, for his sense of security was grounded on a long preceding period of peace and prosperity. The peace, consistently taken so much for granted by most members of society up to the very outbreak of war in the summer of 1914, had commenced forty-three years before that date with the victory of Germany over France in 1871. Its beginning had marked simultaneously the unification of Germany under one central ruling political body and subsequently fostered a surge in industrial and overall economic growth which was unparalleled anywhere else in the world of the time. These developments filled the members of especially the dominant new middle class not only with a feeling of great confidence and national pride, but, as the Expressionists felt, also with a sense of complacency.

Complacency implies by definition resistance to change, and change was one thing which this society seemed to fear most, at least change of a radical or fundamental nature. Such change would have been looked upon as a threat to the status quo; thus, the Wilhelminian establishment protected itself from forces it considered disruptive, especially in politics and morals, from unrestrained criticism and undesirable foreign influence, through a watchful censorship of the press and other public forums. Because of this society's overall assumption of such a self-protective posture, the Berlin Expressionist Kurt Hiller, for one, looked back upon it as an antiintellectual, anticosmopolitan society, one categorically intolerant of any form of complication or nuance.[5] Its adversity to change, however, was not allowed to conflict in its mind with progress. Progress had almost assumed the force of a shibboleth for the middle class; but it was understood to be a gradual and slow progress, not a radical upheaval; its additive nature seemed, therefore, to blunt and disguise its inherent insurgent quality for the middle-class mind.[6] Most importantly in the view of the Expressionist, this progress was one which was being registered on the material level alone and not on the intellectual or spiritual levels as well.[7] For many of the Expressionists, therefore, the image of Wilhelminian burgher, with his concentration on material needs, came to be most tangibly associated with the "Plüschmöbel" that was the fashion of the day in middle-class homes.[8]

The Wilhelminian burgher protected and preserved the status quo morally through an emphasis on such ideals as order, restraint, resignation, and discipline.[9] These ideals applied equally to all areas of life, to business and social, to private and public life. As the dissident Expressionist interpreted the basic moral position of the Wilhelminian, it amounted, in the end, to the repression and suppression of not only the disruptive but also the benevolent and salutary qualities of human character. When the Expressionist assumes an antiestablishment posture in his revolt, he is directing this posture first and foremost against what he saw as the repressive-suppressive aspect of middle-class morality. Thus, the Wilhelminian in stereotype was stridently criticized as much for his general lack of deep, human feeling and compassion as he was for his crass materialism and lack of social conscience. The phrase "Trägheit des Herzens"—taken from the subtitle of Jacob Wassermann's novel *Caspar Hauser* (1908), which portrays the destruction of primeval innocence by a soulless society—was to become, in constant variation, almost a motto thrown accusingly into the face of the Wilhelminian establishment for its spiritual sloth and insensibility. One of the many Expressionist journals gave its variation on the phrase as part of its program: "Our goal is the rebirth of the heart."[10] Karl Otten echoes the concept in the title and preface of a collection of poems published in Franz Pfemfert's Expressionist series "Der rote Hahn": *Die Thronerhebung des Herzens* (Berlin and Wilmersdorf, 1918). Max Krell, who had close contacts with Expressionist circles in Berlin and Munich and was a frequent contributor to Expressionist publications, wrote of the Expressionist protest:

> Our protest was directed at the torpidity and superficiality of conventional society which by the second decade of our century was still acting as though everything in our world were in good order and "safely protected by our weapons." The man of letters in particular sat back complacently in the plush easy chair of good society.[11]

The dominant society of Wilhelminian Germany seemed to be so protective of its security that it feared to look directly in the face of those unappeased elements beneath the surface glitter of reality whose latent presence was, none the less, betrayed by such key phenomena as poverty and prostitution.

The phenomenon, the issue of prostitution, was central to the Expressionist revolution on the moral level. The flourishing of prostitution in the Wilhelminian era, as the Expressionist viewed it, most sharply gave the lie to the effectiveness of the Wilhelminian approach to morality, particularly to sexual conduct. As one of the strongest expressions of the subsurface and most basic side of man's nature in the mind of the Expressionists, sexuality was a decisive issue for them and the cast of their cultural revolt, particularly in the early or prewar phase of the movement. Sexuality was the factor in human character which, as Otten was to write many years after the end of the era, had arrested and engrossed his thinking as well as that of all his fellow Expressionists.[12] The Wilhelminian middle class, however, as submitted by the Munich Expressionist poet and painter Richard Seewald, confronted sexuality with the attitude signified by the word "Tabu."[13] For the Expressionist, this attitude advocated sexual repression, and exemplified for him what he saw as the general repressive-suppressive nature of the whole moral structure of the Wilhelminian middle class. Stefan Zweig, whose close connections with Berlin artist life and literature can be traced back to the beginning of the century and then forward into Expressionism as well, wrote in his noted portrait of this era, *Die Welt von Gestern*:

> Our century...felt that sexuality was an anarchical and therefore troublesome element which could not be permitted to express itself openly, because every form of free, extramarital love was inconsistent with middle-class "propriety."...If sexuality could not simply be gotten rid of, then it was at least not supposed to be visible in the world of morality. Thus, it was tacitly agreed that the whole aggravating complex would not be mentioned either in school, in the family circle, or in public and that everything that might remind one of its presence would be suppressed.[14]

Women in Germany were felt to suffer more suppression of this sort than were the men. They were expected to avoid the expression of their sexuality both in and out of marriage.[15] Zweig again sums up well the thinking of the Expressionist on this point: "'Well brought up'at that time for a young girl was synonymous with 'remote from life.'"[16] Although men were considered freer, since the presence of sexual drives in their nature was at least tacitly granted, they were, nevertheless, forced to seek satisfaction of these drives *extra muros* of "good society," and this usually meant by means of prostitution. Thus, prostitution was felt to provide the sole foundation for erotic life outside of marriage.[17] In spite of this fact, however, the phenomenon of prostitution was relegated by the middle-class mind to the arcane corners of his world and the whole issue of it thereafter shunned. On ground which they saw staked out for them by Nietzsche and then by Freud and his disciples (who had just begun to publish the results of their investigations into human sexuality shortly before the beginning of the Expressionist era), and under the impact of such elder recusant poets as Frank Wedekind, Heinrich Mann and August Strindberg, the Expressionists were to lay particular stress in their literature on the role played by sexuality in human life. In laying this stress, they lent their posture a more defiant aspect opposite established moral canons by consistently glorifying and idealizing the prostitute as an example of the individual liberating himself from the straitjacket morality of contemporary society. George Grosz, typifying the latter tactic, even chose the figure of the prostitute—as he stated in his own interpretation of the work—to symbolize the "revolution" in the painting "Deutschland, ein Wintermärchen" (1918).[18] Richard Huelsenbeck, writing in a letter to a friend during the Expressionist era, maintained that the "free life style" of prostitutes made them "the real human beings": "Thank God for the whores and their free life style; they are the real people."[19]

In the early phase of the movement as a whole, the entire spectrum of politicoeconomic questions raised by the central phenomenon of poverty played only a secondary role. In the circle around Franz Pfemfert's *Die Aktion* (1911-32)[20] and in the pages of Paul Cassirer's and Alfred Kerr's *Pan* (1910-15),[21] there was, as will be described later, some very definite and direct interest in what were considered to be certain politicoeconomic injustices—again, as exemplified most poignantly by the existence of poverty—inherent in the structure of the Wilhelminian capitalist monarchy. However, the great emphasis in this period, as will become clear in the course of this study, was placed on the inner, the metaphysical and aesthetic needs of man, rather than on his concrete politicoeconomic needs. This fact is even illustrated implicitly by those relatively few Expressionists who were politically aware or committed in prewar years, for they tend to lean in most cases (see especially *Die Aktion;* and Erich Mühsam's journal *Kain,* 1911-14, 1918-19[22]) towards anarchism. Anarchism, especially in the nonmilitant form advocated by Expressionists at this time, is only a *quasi*-political ideology, since it seeks to do away with *all* forms of government, aiming solely at the attainment of total liberty for the individual; by definition, therefore, it is ultimately (i.e., particularly once the ideal state of existence is realized) apolitical and, so to speak, a form of "nongovernment."

Before the war, the vast majority of Expressionists shared with the Wilhelminian, although for other reasons (see above), his overall lack of interest in political issues. Spiritually buttressed by what the Expressionists portray as his complacent serenity (and, of course, cognizant of his very limited political role as a citizen under the Wilhelminian monarchy), the Wilhelminian burgher was persuaded to ignore, even to disdain politics. The subject was simply not considered worthy or needful of concern. Heinrich Mann, therefore, recalled: "Anyone who took up intellectual politics in 1910 might truly have doubted the seriousness of his undertaking; such a thing had never been, and would never again be, as incomprehensible as it was then in Germany."[23] War on his native soil in particular was something which the representative German of this era rarely contemplated; and, above all, it was something which he would scarcely consent to discuss. In his mind, that Progress in which he believed so contentedly had simply rendered war obsolete and anachronistic. Herbert Jhering, the noted Berlin theater critic and frequenter of Expressionist circles in the period, wrote:

> It was a time of peace. Our hearts stand still when we hear this word. Peace. People were at peace in their beliefs, in their consciousness, and in their imaginations. At peace also in their blindness. Because they had faith, they did not see. They were convinced that the progress of civilization had to be progress in all forms of thought, that it had also to permeate all areas of life, even the social and political, and to destroy or to channel into productive endeavors the dark forces of violence and the savage passions.[24]

War was familiar to most only through romanticized descriptions of it in fiction, patriotic songs or the tales of the veterans of 1870/71.[25] Warning signs of imminent war which began clouding the political skies towards the summer of 1914 were shrugged off lightheartedly until the very day of mobilization and the declaration of war that immediately followed in August of that year.

Political crises, such as the Boer War, the Balkan conflicts, the pre-World War One troubles in Russia, which would have unsettled any thoughtful individual's confidence in another age, were blithely put out of mind by the average Wilhelminian German. Jhering wrote of the reaction at home to the German Boxer campaign of 1900:

> The false sense of security of that era is illustrated also by the fact that the so-called Boxer Campaign in China was depicted in the middle-class press with patriotic pride as an adventure, rather than as a war or a warning against any such form of agitation.[26]

If not thus taken lightly, such crises, to cite the view of another chronicler, then simply did not strike the consciousness of the mind of these citizens, but seemed to occur somewhere beyond the fringes of their own world.[27] As a result of such political obliviousness, when the realities of the conflict of a world war were finally brought roundly home to this society in the second half of 1914, the shock it caused and the impression it left were all the more acute.

The effects of the war and the revolution that followed it were especially acute on the Expressionists, for those two events were instrumental in transforming the major thrust of ideological thinking in their movement from a concern with aesthetic, metaphysical and moral questions to a desire to change the political and economic structure of Germany. The original ideals, concerned mostly with man's spiritual needs, are still sounded in the literature of the movement after 1914 and after November, 1918, but they now, in most instances, appear in the context of proposals for certain governmental reforms which lean decidedly away from the monarchy and capitalism of Wilhelminian Germany towards political and economic ideas found on the opposite end of the political spectrum, especially in socialism and communism.

The stress of opposition in the Expressionist revolt on the social level was directed at the concept of authority; thus, Seewald, who had offered the word "Tabu" as the keyword for opening the "backdoor" to Wilhelminian society, offers the word "Autorität" as the keyword for opening the frontdoor.[28] The concept of authority circumscribes in the Expressionist mind the basic orientation of the whole spectrum of Wilhelminian social life, for what this society demanded of the individual above all else seemed to be total deference to authority. There was a whole hierarchy of authority, beginning at the highest echelon with the Kaiser, followed by the military, the police and the courts, and concluding with the schools and the father as head of the family circle.[29] The last two named members of the hierarchy had the major responsibility for inculcating in the individual in his crucial formative years respect for authority. The pedagogy of the schools has been depicted by the Expressionists as the most unadulterated manifestation of the ideals of the middle class mentioned earlier: authoritarian, regimented, and militaristic. The painter and poet Karl Hirsch, one of the founders of the Expressionist "Novembergruppe" in Berlin during the Revolution and a member of the circle around *Die Aktion,* recalled his school days in Hannover with typical bitterness:

> And then I started school. I was not induced to go to school by a light-hearted desire to learn, as every child actually should be, but solely because I was forced to.... However, attending school was one of the duties to which a German citizen had to submit. My brother and I attended the Lyceum II, which later was known as the Goethe Gymnasium. This was a perversion of the name of the greatest German poet so as to make it appear that humaneness in the Goethean sense were at home here. That was not the case.[30]

The Expressionist view of the German university was no less bitterly critical; this fact explains the popularity amongst Expressionist circles before the war of a small volume by Ludwig Hatvany, himself associated with the Expressionist camp in Berlin, entitled *Die Wissenschaft des Nicht Wissenswerten* (Berlin, 1908; 2nd ed. 1911).[31] In this diatribe, written in the form of university lecture notes and very much under the impression of Nietzsche's attacks upon the philologists, Hatvany condemns university learning in Germany as fossilized, lifeless and antihumanistic.

The middle-class family structure of Wilhelminian Germany, in particular as it represented a medium for paternal authority, was denounced with equal acrimony by the Expressionists. Since paternal authority was also both the first and the most tangibly felt arm of authority in this society to be encountered by them as they began to come of age, it often became the first bulwark of authority to be stormed in their revolt. The clash of parent and child, again especially of father and son, has been much written about in studies of Expressionism as one of the archetypes (the "Father-Son Conflict") of revolt in this literature; but its presence in the literature was frequently an echo of its very real presence in the lives of many of the composers of that literature. The traumatic experiences of this sort of Franz Werfel, Walter Hasenclever, Johannes R. Becher and Otto Gross were four of the more notorious examples.[32]

With the vast majority of the members of this society, however, the demand of obedience to authority seemed to have met with virtually total success. That is the view of Heinrich Mann, whom the Expressionists looked up to as a leader and confederate; Mann called the Wilhelminian era, because of its abiding devotion to authority, the "Age of Innocence" in his autobiography *Ein Zeitalter wird besichtigt* and concluded:

> The Germans had an unshakeable faith in a force which was called the "Reich"—even though shocks had been felt in the foundation of the "Reich" for 20 years; anyone who had his feet planted firmly on the ground had to feel it trembling. No one noticed it.
>
> They imagined that everything was in order, after for so terribly long a time the fateful decisions had been left to a monarch who, though constantly restless, lacked self-confidence.[33]

The features of Germany under William II described in the preceding pages represent, of course, only a small part of the whole and only the Expressionist view of that same part.[34] These features were, nonetheless, those which the Expressionists, in reflections on the period, have separated from the whole as being, by implication or direct statement, most decisive in determining or conditioning their response to society. Wilhelminian Germany was the society in which all of these artists, were born, with the sole exception of Else Lasker-Schüler, and in which all, now including the latter poetess, were raised and educated.[35] Their view of Wilhelminian Germany was, in most instances, first set down in similar terms in the literature which they composed during the period: most notably in Carl Sternheim's series of plays "Aus dem bürgerlichen Heldenleben" and in the plays of Georg Kaiser; in most detailed form in the trilogy of novels by Heinrich Mann, brought together as *Das Kaiserreich (Der Untertan, Die Armen, Der Kopf:* 1914-25).[36] The Expressionists were naturally not alone in their particular assessment of this society; but they clearly stood wide apart from such a literary defender of the conservative German middle class tradition as the Thomas Mann of *Betrachtungen eines Unpolitischen* (1918).[37] The Expressionists were, on the other hand, to be distinguished from the other detractors from Wilhelminian Germany not only by the special combination of features of it which they particularly opposed but, most importantly, by the form which their alternatives assumed in literature and in life style.

The Early Phase

The initial reaction of the Expressionists to William II's Germany characteristically took the shape of a withdrawal from it. The paternalism, regimentation and demand of deference to authority of this society amounted in their minds to the suppression of the individual in favor of the state and to the repression of man's essential nature in favor of the norms of the middle class; they thus sought a freer, less restricted life style.[38] This life style, as they were eventually to feel, they discovered in the close circles of poets and painters which around 1910 began crystallizing into the movement later to be called (by them and literary historians alike) "Expressionism."[39] These coteries of artists had by this time established their center in a given city in and around the café which had assumed the role there of a "Künstlercafé" or "Literatencafé."

The Expressionists had originally been attracted to, and then loosely held together in, these circles by a fairly nebulous disenchantment with Wilhelminian society. However, gradually a widespread uniformity of opinion on the sources of their discontent and on the means for alleviating it began to acquire an increasingly distinct form by about 1910; what had been at first a retreat from their society was at last reversed now and transformed into a stridently critical opposition to it. The activities in the circles were simultaneously growing more intense and more organized, as the circles themselves became more tightly knit and more governed by a common spirit and a common attitude. Their adherents had begun to meet on a fairly regular and more or less official basis; having been consistently rejected by the established press, they had in concert begun founding their own journals and other series publications, and, in addition, often their own publishing houses, all of which subsequently functioned as their own literary tribunes. The general program of such groups, besides being reflected in the contributions to their journals, was usually announced as well in a foreword or afterword to the first issues. The editors of the new journals acted as a rule as the leaders or at least as the pivotal figures in the circles. In some instances, as happened in the case of Herwarth Walden of *Der Sturm* and Franz Pfemfert of *Die Aktion,* such editors had helped to found the groups' new journals after having bolted from their positions as assistant editors of established periodicals in protest over the chief editors' resistance to the publication of those same writers who were soon to be associated with Expressionism.

The founding of their own journals is one of the series of decisive steps to be encountered in the course of this study which were made by the Expressionists in the direction of bolstering and of making concrete the feeling of backing a movement or of being united behind a common cause or mission. Although the contributions to the publications of a given circle came primarily from the sponsor-group, the fact that contributors from other circles identified with Expressionism were also frequently represented had the effect of unifying the circles as a whole in mutual opposition to what Wilhelminian Germany stood for in their minds and in mutual support of certain solutions to it. In this sense especially, writers, such as Kasimir Edschmid, René Schickele, Kurt Pinthus and C.F.W. Behl, all of whom were once representatives of Expressionism, are justified in describing the movement as having constituted in a body a single, unified community or "Gemeinschaft" of artists.[40]

The circles which became most conspicuous around 1910 were located in the cities of Berlin, Munich, Dresden, Strassburg, Leipzig, Vienna, Prague and in the city of Paris, where a partly variable circle of German artists existed until the war. These were the cities which functioned as centers of Expressionism before the war. Amongst all of them Berlin was far and away the dominant one. The various reasons for its preeminent position will be covered in the next chapter; at this juncture it will suffice to point out that most crucial was the fact that the circles which backed two of the three (the third being *Die weissen Blätter:* 1913-21) most influential and esteemed periodicals in the movement were located in this city: the circle around Walden and *Der Sturm* (1910-32) and that around Pfemfert and *Die Aktion* (1911-32). Also stationed in Berlin was the group attached to Alfred Richard Meyer, who was editor of the earliest of the Expressionist publications, the series *Lyrische Flugblätter* (1907-15, 1919-23), and coeditor of the short-lived journal *Die Bücherei Maiandros*

(1912-14). Here were located as well the circle around Paul Cassirer, publisher of the journal called *Pan* (1910-15), and the more formally organized group around Kurt Hiller which called itself "Der neue Club" and whose journal *Neopathos* had gotten no farther than the stage of galley proofs when it was nipped in the bud by the outbreak of war in August, 1914. All of the groups just mentioned foregathered mainly in the Café des Westens in Berlin.

In Munich at the outset of the Expressionist period there were concentrated a number of important groups, most prominently those centering in the Café Stefanie around Erich Mühsam, Heinrich F.S. Bachmair, Hugo Ball, Otto Gross, Franz Blei and Wilhelm Herzog. All of these leaders in Munich were, at one time or another during the period, editors of periodicals which supported the movement. The group of painters known as "Der blaue Reiter" and headed by Wassily Kandinsky and Franz Marc also had its home base in Munich; it participated, if only to a limited degree and primarily through theoretical writings, in literary Expressionism as well. In Leipzig the circle around Kurt Wolff and Ernst Rowohlt came together in Wilhelms Weinstube and managed to survive the split between its leaders that led to Rowohlt's departure from their publishing firm in late 1912; the major tribune of the Leipzig group before the war was the series *Der jüngste Tag* (1913-22). Anchored in Strassburg was the circle dominated by Ernst Stadler and René Schickele, which had its roots in an earlier circle active at the beginning of the century around the student journal *Der Stürmer* (1902-3). Although the latter group turned out no such literary organ of its own during the Expressionist era, its leader René Schickele went on to become editor in 1914 of the important Expressionist monthly *Die weissen Blätter*. In Dresden, where the Expressionist painters of "Die Brücke" were also situated, the poet Paul Adler and the publisher Jakob Hegner together attracted Expressionists, although usually on a temporary basis only, to their community in Hellerau from other centers throughout the decade. The circles around Ludwig von Ficker's *Der Brenner* (1910-14, 1919-54) in Innsbruck and around Karl Kraus's *Die Fackel* (1899-1936) in Vienna were not identified exclusively with Expressionism, but they, nevertheless, attracted and brought together Expressionists from time to time before the war. The group around Max Brod in the Café Arco in Prague, which produced the almanac *Arkadia* of 1913, had a similarly tangential relationship to the movement. In Greifswald, Oskar Kanehl, also a member of the circle around *Die Aktion,* gathered a small group of supporters around his periodical *Wiecker Bote* (1913/14) for a brief year or so until it was cut short by the war. Also just prior to the war, a circle associated with both literature and painting developed around August Macke and Karl Otten in Bonn; and another group, having a somewhat ambivalent relationship to the literary movement, developed in Heidelberg around Ernst Blass and the monthly *Die Argonauten* (1914-16, 1921). Finally the Café du Dôme in Paris, where most notably the painters Rudolf Levy and Hans Purrmann presided over discussions, was a favorite stopping place of German Expressionist poets and painters when on visits to Paris in this period.[41]

The adherents of these circles represented a radically unorthodox attitude towards life and aesthetic and moral values in the framework of Wilhelminian Germany; in the case of not a few, they were equally unorthodox in their overt behavior and style of dress. In many respects, the Expressionists in these circles exhibit features commonly associated with the bohemian artist as he has appeared in societies dominated by the middle class in the last approximate century and a half; and it will help to fix the image of the Expressionist if we compare him briefly with that more perennial figure.

The most extensive and definitive study into the figure of the bohemian artist to date has been done by Helmut Kreuzer in his book *Die Boheme: Beiträge zu ihrer Beschreibung* (Stuttgart, 1968). As Kreuzer has been able to establish, the modern bohemian artist is both the antithesis and the product (i.e., the "antagonistic complement") of the middle class; he represents a programmatic form of individualism which is emancipated from the conventions of life style and of aesthetic, moral or political judgment, and he stands in opposition to the monetary system and to a scale of values, power and social opportunities which are based upon economics, materialism and utilitarianism.[42] The more specific features of bohemians, as outlined by Kreuzer, include: (a) they are composed of informal groups which live or gather in artist and student quarters of large cities or of "picturesque" suburbs and meet in public places, studios, private apartments, editorial offices, book stores, galleries; (b) they experience, or interpret in retrospect, their joining of the bohemia as their liberation from conventional society, as a conscious break with the milieu of the "authoritarian" school, the family circle, the middle-class professions, the academies; (c) they express their opposition to conventional society through provocative or aggressive actions, behavior, dress; (d) they oppose the "philistine" conventions and "bourgeois" values of society with a life style based upon the principle of spontaneity; (e) they demonstrate their opposition to the materialism of the dominant society by exhibiting a disregard for the value of property and profit; (f) they sympathize with the "humbled" and "offended," the underprivileged races, nations, classes; (g) and, when they express themselves politically, their strongest affinity is to anarchism.[43]

If we recall the description of the nature of the Expressionist revolt and life style as described in the first pages of this chapter, then it is already clear that the Expressionists can, in a broad sense, be identified with the figure Kreuzer describes, the degree of this identification depending upon the individual Expressionist or the circle involved. Like the bohemian artist, the Expressionist also set himself in direct opposition to the basic values and standards of the middle class on many levels and looked upon his participation in the Expressionist revolution as a break with the conventional structure of that class. The Expressionists were also inclined to gather in larger cities and therein to prefer the same kind of meeting places as those preferred by the perennial bohemian. While most members of the movement were basically conventional, sometimes almost elegant (e.g., Carl Sternheim, Gottfried Benn) in dress and seldom disposed to provocative behavior except as expressed literarily, there were, nonetheless, a number who, like the bohemian, expressed their antagonism towards the middle class in extravagant behavior (most notably the Dadaists of Berlin, described in the last chapter of this study) and dress (e.g., John Höxter, Else Lasker-Schüler). Most tended to sympathize with the poor, even before the war (see especially the articles on the plight of the poor and the worker in *Die Aktion*); and, although, as we have stated, only a small number expressed themselves in a specifically political manner in the early phase most of those that did so leaned most strongly, like the bohemian, in the direction of anarchist ideas.

Beneath the surface of these parallels, however, there is a significant distinction to be made in the structure of the two life styles; and this distinction on the Expressionist side is, moreover, crucial to the development of the unity within the movement which the present study has set out to demonstrate. There is a distinct tendency in the Expressionist circles, not found to a marked degree in those of the bohemian artists, towards structuring and organizing the pattern of life and of their literary activities and, therewith, towards enduing their literary life with a degree of regularity and permanency. This tendency is manifested in a variety of ways which will be treated in detail in the course of this study: in the formal (e.g., "Der neue Club") or semiformal organization of the membership of the circles both physically (e.g., by recognizing a specific director, fixing meeting times) and ideologically (by recognizing a group program); in the sponsoring of permanent or semipermanent literary organs of the circle which appear at more or less regular intervals (literary journals, series publications, etc., many of them lasting well over a decade); in the sponsoring of literary cabarets, recital forums, and theater groups as public media for the circles' members; and in the organization of a variety of other projects and activities related to literature (exhibitions, book stores, demonstrations, balls, etc.). The same tendency we are outlining here is also remarked indirectly in the great artistic productivity which came, on a relatively regular basis, from the circles in a collective form (through their publishing activities) and from the individual members (the sizeable body of literary work produced by such Expressionists as René Schickele, Else Lasker-Schüler, Franz Werfel, Max Brod, Franz Jung, Kasimir Edschmid, Walter Hasenclever, Johannes R. Becher, Carl Sternheim, et al.). Finally, manifesting this same tendency, the great majority were to distinguish the pattern of their life and thought most clearly from that of the bohemian artists when, during the course of the war and the November Revolution, they were to become involved in a generally very formally organized and, in great part, very pragmatically oriented political movement, seeking change in the direction of greater equity in the social, economic and political structure of contemporary society. This tendency towards structuring and organizing, towards regularity and permanency, as it contrasts with the emphasis on informality and spontaneity in the more typical bohemian artist's life style, described by Kreuzer, highlights the seriousness of purpose and the fervor of commitment in the Expressionist revolt.

Throughout the era, we will discover the Expressionists continuing to convene, like the related bohemian artists, in the private apartments, the homes or the hotel rooms of the members, in editorial offices, galleries and, in rare instances, in the more conventional literary salon; but, during the early phase of the movement, the focal or converging point for the movement as a whole was to remain the artist or literary café. The significance of this particular focal point as an indirect indicator for the existence of the movement is suggested by the fact that, when the café begins to lose its power of attraction for the Expressionists at the end of the first World War, then we will begin to remark the simultaneous dissolution both of the movement as a whole as well as of the individual circles. In the early phase especially, the artist or literary café happened to be the social institution of the era which combined convenience with the degree of freedom in manners, conversation, and thought that the Expressionists required. The family home was apparently too often marked with the stigma of parental authority; and the existing literary clubs, organizations and salons were too much dominated by tradition or a conservative literary bias to allow sufficient freedom of expression. Moreover, the kind of friendships they sought, candid and unceremonious ones, could also, as the Expressionists felt, only be found in a society that otherwise seemed stiff and formal to them inside the café. Iwan Goll gives expression to the latter feeling in a poem, entitled appropriately "Café," which appeared in *Die Aktion* in 1914:

All my fellow men of the city
Were only dusty, pale lanterns,
Teeming with alien light.—
Only here did I find friends,
Natural forests still, bethorned and deep,
Or plains
With wind-pure senses.
Here was the instinct of noble animals,
Hands had the gesture
Of blossoming roses.

Like music,
What they said hovered
Above the roar of the cyclopean city.[44]

A few of the circles, such as "Der neue Club" of Berlin, were actually formed by a group of artists immediately upon seceding from a traditional literary club or organization in protest over its stultifying and outmoded conventions and tastes. The artist café was, therefore, almost the only place where these artists felt they could meet in order to freely and democratically discuss and share their ideas as well as their work, since both their ideas and their work tended to be radical and unorthodox no matter the theme or form of expression. The café came to assume a unique and decisive threefold function in their lives: it became at once a home-away-from-home, a studio in which to work and a place to develop their thoughts or further their education. It was here at their regular table that they spent a majority of their time and did a significant share of their creative work, often on a collective basis. It was also here that they made many important, new acquaintanceships; and, most importantly, it was also in the constant, hours-long, often heated discussions in which they were incessantly submerged in the café, especially before the war, that they developed and polished their ideas and were educated, or at least guided, in a variety of subjects, foremost among them being, naturally, literature and the arts. Stefan Zweig, therefore, called the café "our best place of education for what is new"; and Ferdinand Hardekopf, a key figure in the early phase, once declared himself in agreement with the Anglo-Irish poet George Moore that the way to promote art was through the establishing of cafés.[45] Many of the members of these circles have defined this role of the café in broader terms and asserted that they received their sole higher education in the humanities through the discussions held here in the general period in question. It was in this broader sense that Wolfgang Goetz, a regular in Berlin artist cafés before and during the era, called the Café des Westens a "school":

> The [Café des Westens] was a school, and a very good one at that. We learned to see here, to perceive and to think. We learned, almost in a more penetrating way than at the university, that we were not the only fish in the sea and that one should not look at only one side of a thing but at least at four.[46]

Oskar Maria Graf and Leonhard Frank, to cite but two of the more outstanding examples, came into the café with only a very limited formal education and were later to pay tribute to the broad education which they claimed to have received here in artist circles.[47] In a few cases, budding young artists went, or might even have been sent by the more liberal parent, to the artist café with the conscious aim of obtaining an education. Hans Purrmann once overheard Paul Cassirer giving related advice to a widow concerning her son's education:

> The place where many received their education was the café. This fact is illustrated sufficiently by the advice Paul Cassirer once gave, in my presence, to the widow of a respected Munich graphic arts dealer who was concerned about her son's education: "Rather than to a university, send him to an artist café for three years, for example, to the Café du Dôme, and have him try to establish contacts with modern artists." That must have been

what a certain Munich art dealer had in mind when he sent his son Justus to join us in the "Café du Dôme" for a few years.[48]

Max Krell, who has described his involvement in the movement in *Das alles gab es einmal,* calls the café in this era the "exchange-office of ideas and plans":

> The cafés were our home. The cafés had an additional function then which has since been lost. Whether we were sitting in the Café du Dôme in Paris, the Griensteidl in Vienna, the Merkur in Leipzig or the Greco in Rome, they served as our exchange-offices of ideas and plans, of intellectual interchange, even of ruin. Here we debated and attacked with our critical swords.[49]

Finally, as Krell remarked above, the cafe's functioned as a kind of "home" for these artists. Lasker-Schüler, who was an inveterate habitué of the artist café for over three decades, expressed how important a part of her life it was when she claimed in a letter to a friend that she had herself "carried" to the café if too ill to go on her own.[50] Similarly, Hugo Ball, when short of money once—as he was so often in his life—regretted most having to give up temporarily his daily session in the café. He wrote from Munich on that occasion to his sister: "It's a lousy situation. I don't leave my hole anymore. As a result, I've given up going to the café, although it's very important to me. For that's where my friends, newspapers, and new ideas are."[51] Hardekopf, in whose poetry the café was a salutary balm ("I quickly took refuge in the café."[52]), echoed the sentiments of Lasker-Schüler and Ball in an ode to the café published in *Die Aktion:* "We can do without everything—except, of course, / our coffee (enchanting olive ink, ringing the interior) and our café."[53]

The circles, meeting in the cafés, were educative, too, and in two major ways. First of all, they provided a framework in which the members could share and mutually evaluate their work and ideas. Secondly, the discussions in this framework aroused, at least encouraged, the interest of the participants in the figures who were to come to be looked upon, by the Expressionists and literary historians both, as having had the greatest impact on the movement. Participants in the daily exchanges in the circles report that the writers most often discussed included Oscar Wilde, Strindberg, Baudelaire, Rimbaud, Wedekind, André Gide, Dostoievski, Heinrich Mann, Jules Laforgue, Alfred Kerr, Karl Kraus, and Walt Whitman.[54] The major thinkers whose ideas they bandied about their regular tables were Nietzsche, Freud, Jung, Georg Simmel, Wilhelm Windelband, Heinrich Rickert, and Henri Bergson.[55] Of the latter, the consensus of the reports designates Nietzsche and Freud as most prevalent in these discussions and, as literary historians also agree, they were eventually to be the most influential for the development of Expressionist literature as well.

Nietzsche's works helped in particular in the break with traditional mores; and his ideas were frequently first discovered by the Expressionists in the discussions in their circles. Benn, who was a regular in the circle around *Die Aktion*, credits Nietzsche with having provided the whole foundation on which the thinking of his generation was constructed. He writes in retrospect in the essay "Nietzsche—nach fünfzig Jahren":

> Actually, everything that my generation discussed, dissected in its deepest thoughts—one can say: suffered through; one can even say: enlarged upon—all of that had already been expressed and explored, had already found its definitive formulation in Nietzsche; everything thereafter was exegesis. His treacherous, tempestuous, lightening manner, his feverish diction, his rejection of all idylls and all general principles, his postulation of a psychology of instinctual behavior as a dialectic—"knowledge as affect," all of psychoanalysis and Existentialism. They were all his achievements. As is becoming increasingly clear, he is the great giant of the post-Goethean era.[56]

Franz Jung, a member of the same circle, singles out Freud, on the other hand, as, more than any other one figure, having been responsible for the attenuation of "die gute alte Zeit" through his assertion that sexuality constitutes the great driving force of human character in the unconscious mind.[57] The Nietzsche-cult in these and other artist circles in Germany had a long tradition which antedated the Expressionist period by almost two decades; there were numerous followers of him in every one of the movement's centers.[58] Freud's discoveries were much more recent and were only beginning to spread beyond the borders of Vienna by 1910. Their dissemination in the Expressionist camp, however, was facilitated directly by the presence in circles, first in Munich and then in Berlin and Zürich as well, of one of Freud's own students, the "enfant terrible" of the world of psychology of the time, Otto Gross.[59] Gross had studied under Freud in Vienna at the beginning of our century and was soon considered by his teacher as one of the only two "truly original minds among his followers."[60] During the Expressionist decade, he assumed the self-assigned task, much to the consternation of his former mentor, of spreading Freud's theories abroad in order to assist with them and his own particular interpretation of them in the cultural revolution launched by the Expressionists.[61] Some of his much-publicized exploits during this decade will be commented on later.

In the fine arts, it was van Gogh who stood out in strongest relief in conversation when the Expressionists came together. His impact on both writers and painters was reportedly of equal intensity. Leonhard Frank, who himself began as a painter and only later turned, with much greater success, to the writing of literature, records that van Gogh's art caused a virtual "earthquake" amongst the habitués of the Café Stefanie in Munich before the war.[62] Ernst Blass observed a similar response at the other end of the country in the circles meeting in the Berlin Café des Westens.[63]

The unending dialogues and debates in the circles were, in most cases, augmented at fairly regular intervals by more formal recitals in private and public, the so-called "Autoren-Abende" or "Vortrags-Abende." They were usually held in the cafés as well and were, with few exceptions, sponsored by the circles. At these gatherings, members of the host circle or guest authors from other groups read from their works or gave programmatic lectures before the general public or invited guests. The recitals became an important means for disseminating the Expressionist view and one more means for uniting the circles in a body through the exchange of ideas and literary techniques. Many of these readings before the war are reported to have on occasion attracted literally hundreds of spectators. The majority of the circles held such recitals during the decade; most notable were those given under the auspices of *Der Sturm, Die Aktion, Das Forum,* "Der neue Club," "Das Gnu," and the circles around A.R. Meyer and Paul Cassirer. The most famous and probably the most singly influential of these events, judging from the many reports of contemporaries, was held by *Der Sturm* in the spring of 1912 within the frame of an exhibition of Futurist painting.[64] The featured speaker was the Italian literary agitator and iconoclast of all vestiges of the European cultural past, Filippo Marinetti. Marinetti had been noisily storming the capitals of Europe with his message since 1909 when his first Futurist manifesto appeared in French in the Paris newspaper *Le Figaro.*[65] At his performance in Berlin in 1912 he read from his Futurist manifestoes and poetry, and in conjunction with it rode through the streets of Berlin in a taxi, throwing copies of his manifestoes onto the sidewalks and attaching them to sign posts—until he was ordered to desist by the Berlin Chief of Police Jagow.[66] He gave repeat performances in Berlin in early, and then again in late, 1913; they, like the first, called forth many responses (most of them positive) from the Expressionist press.[67] Other recitals which were also vividly recalled were the readings on repeated occasions by Georg Heym of his nightmarish poem "Der Krieg" and by Jakob van Hoddis of his equally apocalyptic poem "Weltende" at meetings of various circles in the prewar phase.[68]

No matter where in a given city these artists congregated, whether in the café, in a private residence or studio, or in the offices of their editors and publishers, their gatherings were always shot through with a spirit of unity and comradeship, with a great willingness and desire to share their views and discoveries and to assist one another artistically and otherwise. A typical description of this communal spirit is given by Lothar-Günther Buchheim in reference to the early Expressionist group of painters in Dresden who called themselves "Die Brücke":

> The desired unity of life and art was completely realized among the bohemians in Friedrichstadt. They worked with unremitting dedication, pushed each other to the heights of inspiration, helped each other with mutual, unvarnished criticism. They immediately shared with each other the discoveries they made. They made use of every hour of the day and often even worked during the night, most of the time in frenzied excitement.[69]

The results of such a collective style of literary life proved to be as fruitful in the other centers of the movement as it was in Dresden, a fact testified to, for example, by the almost two hundred periodicals, series, anthologies and almanacs of Expressionism, most of which were planned and executed by the concerted work of a circle of artists.[70]

In the inchoate stage of Expressionism being described here, the major topics of discussion in the circles were literature and the arts. Their artistic zeal had led the Expressionists to an almost total disregard of social and political issues, a situation which prevailed with few exceptions until the late summer of 1914.[71] Until this time their conversations had been interlarded with criticism of the Wilhelminian bourgeoisie, especially of its materialism and spiritual inanition, but such criticism had rarely been made from any but an aesthetic, moral, or metaphysical standpoint, rather than from a concretely social or political one. Alfred Döblin's description of the predominant attitude amongst these artists before the war is typical: "Politics had no value then. It was something for the philistines. It was no match for music and literature."[72] The one exception of significance to this kind of thinking in the early phase was to be found in the group which flocked to Pfemfert and *Die Aktion:* the sociocritical and political bias of this journal was announced without equivocation (along with a determined and outspoken sponsorship of "modern impulses" in literature and art) in the programmatic afterword to the first issue (February 20, 1911).[73] Hiller, a leading member of the group, even made an outright attempt on behalf of the journal early in its first year to revindicate an interest in political issues; but it was a solitary gambit against the mainstream and few of his cohorts rallied to the cry.[74] With only isolated exceptions, again, there was also no talk of war and no sense of political crisis in these groups. Beyond occasional vague and ambivalent romantic longings for war as a break from the drabness and impotency of contemporary life (Heym, Stadler), or beyond a few equally obscure warnings of some kind of impending catastrophe (Hoddis, Heym), it was evidently only in the small circle of Rhenish Expressionists around August Macke and Karl Otten in Bonn that a genuine foreboding of imminent war was both clearly felt and articulated in the movement.[75] Max Brod characterizes the attitude of most members of his generation prior to August, 1914, in his autobiography *Streitbares Leben* in this way:

> Who would have thought of the possibility of a war in 1914!... War was thought of as something historically obsolete, as odd, as something in which earlier generations (the unfortunate ones!) had believed—but not we realists endowed with the faculty of reason.[76]

The main concern of those young dissidents in the early phase was with the liberation of the individual from the ideological yoke of Wilhelminianism. The great majority at this time saw this as realizable through a change in the inner self of the individual, i.e., by overcoming the restrictions imposed upon him by this society on an individual basis. It was not until he had felt the impact of the war that the Expressionist finally began to become pointedly aware of the need for changing society as a whole and for directing his attention to the needs of the community as well. For the present, he remained basically inner-directed, more concerned with his private self than with his social self. This attitude was in more than one regard an unwitting legacy of the Wilhelminian bourgeoisie. The Expressionists were like their self-chosen adversary in their indifference to social and political issues; but, in addition, their self-interest was, paradoxically, conditioned in large degree by the very same segments of their society against which their self-interest was redirected once it had been reinterpreted. The leading circles of Wilhelminian Germany had, after all, demanded all along little else of this youth, as of its other subjects, but deference to authority; the rest of their lives belonged to themselves. Karl Hirsch illustrates this fact in explaining in his reminiscences on the era his own apolitical self-centeredness:

> I was the victim of a middle-class education which at that time demanded nothing more from children than that they obey the laws of the class to which they belonged.[77]

Wilhelminian Germany was an authoritarian, not a totalitarian, regime; and, in delimiting its demands on the individual in the above manner, it can be said to have sown the seeds itself of the adversity which came eventually from the Expressionist corner.

The inner-directed tendency of the movement at this time is reflected in the predominant position of the lyric in the group activities of the early phase. The lyric is the genre traditionally most commonly associated with a literary content that looks inwardly on man, and was, therefore, most appropriate to early Expressionism's overriding concern with man's subjective needs. Stefan Zweig, in the influential essay "Das neue Pathos," which was first published in 1909 in *Das literarische Echo* and then in 1913 in the Expressionist journal named after the essay itself, heralded the dawning of a period that would see the revitalization of the lyric.[78] The lyricist, Zweig claimed, as testified to by the new flourishing of public poetry recitals, was beginning once again to establish an intimate and vital relationship to his public, similar to that entertained by poets before the advent of the written word. This development was restoring to the lyric its former "pathos" and was thereby revivifying it.[79] Zweig's prediction had soon proven itself to be true; by 1913, when a paroxysm of artistic activity had been attained not only in the Expressionist circles in Germany, but in artistic circles throughout Europe and America, Peter Scher in *Die Aktion* was, with justification, characterizing the contemporary era as "ein Zeitalter der Lyrik."[80] The drama, according to Scher, had been outstripped by the lyric as the preferred genre. The following year his words were echoed in the same periodical by another lyricist from Pfemfert's circle, Hugo Kersten.[81] Concrete support of the claims of these two poets is found in the fact of the predominance of the lyric, within the area of imaginative literature, in the vast majority of the Expressionist anthologies and almanacs, issues in series as well as in the contributions to Expressionist journals during this prewar period.[82] Moreover, while public recitals at which the reading of lyric poetry dominated, flourished in these years, the first significant involvement of the Expressionists in the organizing of theater groups representing their movement was not to begin until the last half of the war.

Regardless of what activity was involved and regardless of the subject matter being treated, whether literature, art, philosophy or, as in later years, politics, one force always determined the form and style of intercourse within the circles and between them and their audiences: the desire to arouse and goad the listener or reader into participating in the implementation of a change in the nature of contemporary life under the prevailing society. The doctrine of "l'art pour l'art," which had defined the character of the literature, and in its broader, philosophical implications the general thinking, of the preceding generation, was repudiated by all of the circles. As made unmistakably clear by the programs of the periodicals, the new literature was collectively polemical in orientation; it was a "littérature engagée," even though at first only to a very limited extent in a political sense.[83] Paul Raabe sees the essence of Expressionism, in fact, in this attempt to use the word as deed and through the poetic word to change the world.[84]

Since these artists were critical of the contemporary world and sought change, their movement was by implication founded on deep discontent. A glaring paradox is, however, characteristic of such movements: while such malcontents are driven by their unrest into a position of opposition to the established order, the vitality and zeal with which they throw themselves into the search for change expresses, on the other hand, an intense exhilaration and optimism in life. The Expressionists in particular felt a strong sense of mission which buoyed them up and allowed them to resist any form of pessimism and despair. As Ball suggests, they were fighting as much against the lethargy of the society around them—a spirit which they felt was a natural consequence of the Wilhelminian middle-class acceptance of the determinist-positivist view of life—as against its repressiveness.[85] Their sense of mission and its attendant high-pitched intensity of experience was a decisive factor in the cohesion of their circles, for it could readily infect any young artist who came under its sway and then draw him into the movement. It, therefore, accounts in large part for the development of a feeling of community in the circles. This was the experience of Johannes R. Becher who was especially close to the circle around Heinrich Bachmair in Munich:

> We were passionately dedicated to our cause, only satisfied by it and it alone; yes, we were
> obsessed. In cafés on the sidewalks and squares, in our studios, we were "on the move" day

and night. We set out at a furious pace to fathom the unfathomable, to create—united as poets, painters, composers—the "art of the century," the incomparable art which would tower timelessly above the arts of all previous centuries. We thought we could do it—our age, the twentieth century! We were stepping up to the forum of the centuries, challenging them to a contest. And we thought, "it's a joy to be alive"; our desire to live was so sanctified by our cause that we would not have hesitated a minute to put a bullet through our heads because of this splendid beginning of life, as a sign that we were dispensing with all other forms of "being alive" if we could not live this life of *ours*.[86]

Their vitality and sense of mission in particular set them off from their coevals and senior contemporaries, such as Gerhart Hauptmann, Stefan George, Thomas Mann, Rainer Maria Rilke, Hermann Hesse, Hugo von Hofmannsthal and others, who took a more somber view of life in the twentieth century. Beneath the angry flow of cultural, social and political criticism on the surface of most Expressionist literature was always a strong undercurrent of optimism about the possibility of realizing an ideal world. This spirit was, as stated at the outset of this study, one of the important legacies of Wilhelminian Germany which the Expressionists did not seek to discard; however, there was a clear distinction to be drawn in favor of the Expressionist brand: theirs was a buoyant, ambitious form of optimism which stemmed from a unique vision of man's potential future. The Wilhelminian burgher's more somber optimism was based on his smug confidence in the additional fruits which past accomplishments would yet bear in the course of an even, gradual "progress."

The War Years

The beginning of the Great War was a brutal shock. It dampened the hopes and exhilaration of most of the Expressionists, for a time at least. They were numbed by the reality of something which they had scarcely been able to envision before without the help of the imagination of a Heym. Hans Arp describes this state of mind in a brief reminiscence on the period:

> The people who had not taken part directly in the outrageous madness of the world war acted as if they did not understand what was going on round about them. They had the glassy look in their eyes of lost sheep.[87]

The intellectual community, as many of the Expressionist chroniclers admit, having been so totally unprepared for the war, were in particular left stunned and baffled by it.[88] They had been so preoccupied with art and philosophy and with the metaphysical threat to man from a stultifying culture that they had overlooked the imminent and equally serious threat from the more tangible, insidious social and political conditions under William II. Brod writes:

> Never before has a generation been so brutally overwhelmed by the facts of life. We were simply ignorant; without giving it much thought, we considered everything we had learned at the *gymnasium* and read in histories of the world as fairy tales.[89]

Like most of her fellow-artists, Hannah Höch, a painter who was a member of the Berlin Dada group after the war, had sensed the collapse of a whole "well-tempered" world view in that fateful summer of 1914.[90] Now the subject of politics came to dominate their lives and their thoughts and their conversations.[91] They had snubbed politics earlier; they now wrote about it, talked about it and eagerly read about it. Ball had been submerged in work for Expressionist literature, art, and theater all through the prewar phase and was still enthusiastically making plans for a series of literary matinées and art exhibitions in Munich just three days before Germany declared war on Russia, on August 1, 1914.[92] Yet, by the time he writes his sister on August 7 of that same summer (four days after Germany's declaration of war on France), he can report that he has already volunteered for military service; he records, in closing the letter, an astonishing reversal of attitude:

> Art? I'm finished with all that; it all looks ridiculous now. Cast to the winds. It's all meaningless now. I can't begin to tell you how I feel. And I really can't foresee the consequences of it all yet.... Let's hear from you often, please. I shudder to think of the future. The only thing I still find enticing is the war. Too bad, that will also not be completely fulfilling.[93]

Ball passes through the second stage of politicization, i.e., from political awareness to pacifism, more quickly than many; this development takes place as a direct result of a visit to the Belgian front where he viewed the mass decimations of soldiers on the battle field; herewith his enthusiasm for war abruptly left him.[94] Having put down his copies of his former favorites, Kandinsky's *Über das Geistige in der Kunst* and Carl Einstein's *Bebuquin,* he was beginning to read in November, 1914, as a member of Pfemfert's circle in Berlin, Krapotkin, Bakunin, Mereschkowsky.[95] His abandonment of art was not to be permanent; but it was to leave an indelible impression on his subsequent work. As a phenomenon affecting the artist and intellectual community as a whole, the change in attitude with the coming of the war exemplified by Ball was so conspicuous when it occurred that it did not have to wait for historians of a later era in order to be recorded. Wilhelm Herzog had already remarked it within the first year of the war, for example, in an article published in his journal *Das Forum* and dated February 16, 1915.[96] Herzog is taking a stand on the then-current theory of the antithesis of civilization and culture:

> For a large proportion of the intellectuals, culture, until August 4, 1914, involved being little concerned about the political life of one's nation, being easily disgusted by the parliamentary conflicts, so that one could devote oneself completely to one's business dealings or—with famous predecessors in mind—dedicate oneself to painting the surfaces of one's canvases or executing a short story, without being disturbed. Not only the greatest share of our artists, but the majority of those with a refined sense of aesthetics lived within our nation remote

from any public interests. In fact, it was simply the done thing to take no interest in politics. One read good books, collected good pictures, went to good concerts; one became a bibliophile, considered several magazines an expression of our culture and related topics, associated with scholars and artists; in short, one was cultured.

To fight for more just forms of existence? Social Democrats were already taking care of that issue all too boisterously. "They're right about a lot of things. But, after all, everything will eventually take care of itself.... "

Then the war overtook us. Cultured, egoistic aesthetes became politicians, worshippers of the people. Now they foreswore their individualism and wanted only to be a member of the masses.[97]

Under the specter of the war the Expressionists as a whole remained optimistic; their concern with the nature of contemporary life, none the less, now began to assume a far more serious aspect. The lightheartedness which had characterized life in their circles quickly vanished now.[98] The war was clearly destined to be the most influential event of the whole decade in their lives and art; it was something which they interpreted as more than just a sign of political crisis; it seemed rather to be an apocalyptic symptom of a far graver crisis that was rooted in the very foundations of contemporary Western civilization.

This event could, of course, at the same time, not fail to have some very concrete effects upon the movement that were perhaps even more far-reaching than the intellectual and psychological ones. First of all, in converting large numbers of Expressionists to political interest, it redirected much of their energies and interests outside literature per se. Many were made into political activists—sometimes only temporarily—and into authors of literature which began to reflect sharply this new political commitment; others—and there were few exceptions to this trend—at least began to reveal through their literary work a new understanding of the importance of social and political issues. Secondly, literary life in the circles was greatly disrupted as the war physically broke them up—sometimes permanently and otherwise for the duration of the war—and scattered their adherents throughout Europe. Only very few of the original circles managed to survive, and when they did, they could not avoid drastic alterations in their membership. With the groups thus largely dispersed, a hush very quickly settled over their former haunts, the literary cafés.[99] Only in the few instances when Expressionists happened to be stationed at the same post or when they managed either to avoid induction or to secure a premature release from military duty did group activities continue, as occurred most noticeably in circles in Berlin, Munich and Vienna. It is evident that such activities ceased totally in at least the cities of Bonn, Heidelberg, Greifswald, Strassburg and Paris.[100] Some from the ranks of the circles never were allowed to return from the battlefield; and among these unfortunates were some of the young poets and painters, such as Alfred Lichtenstein, Ernst Wilhelm Lotz, August Macke, Franz Marc, Gustav Sack, Ernst Stadler, August Stramm, Georg Trakl, who were esteemed most highly by members of the movement.[101]

Two new centers of Expressionism, on the other hand, were the incidental byproducts of the dislocations arising out of the war. Switzerland, to which increasing numbers of Expressionists exiled themselves in the course of the war, came to function primarily as a place where earlier relationships could be reestablished, although Zürich did see the appearance of a few relatively stable and cohesive circles. The latter groups converged most regularly on the Café la Terrace and the Café Odéon. Most prominent of these was the one around Schickele and *Die weissen Blätter,* which Schickele had brought to Zürich late in 1915 because of difficulties with the censor in Germany over the journal's pacifist leanings.[102] Also, in Belgium, during the German occupation, a new circle developed in Brussels out of a small number of Expressionists, most of whom were stationed in the city on military duty. This group included Benn, Otto Flake, Carl Einstein, Friedrich Eisenlohr, Carl Sternheim and others.[103] As was to be expected, these two new centers all but completely disappeared from the literary scene with the approach of the end of the war.

The literary periodicals of Expressionism had to suffer losses similar to those suffered by the circles for which they usually served as literary organs. Many of their editors were inducted into the army, therewith forcing the cessation of publication. The few who managed to continue their work were now able to draw on fewer contributors at a given time, since most of their original supporters were now in the service and only able to contribute from their military posts at irregular intervals. At the beginning of hostilities in 1914, a total of sixteen such journals were still being published; only five of that number were able to survive the first year of war.[104] Added to these difficulties were two others to make the future look yet grimmer for the remaining journals and for prospective editors of new journals which might want to fill the gap left by those lost to the war.

First of all, the controls on the press and theater were intensified to the extreme as the military authorities took over the office of censor right after the start of the war. Reflecting the earlier priorities in Expressionist literature, the numerous conflicts with the censor before the summer of 1914 had been over moral, rather than political issues, as a rule.[105] What the Expressionists were to encounter in the early phase had been forecasted by the experiences of an author whom they looked up to as one of their mentors. Frank Wedekind's troubles with the censor over the moral implications of his plays throughout the prewar period in Germany were notorious and helped to increase the sympathy which came to him from the Expressionist camp.[106] In the early phase there had been many such incidents. There had been, for example, the famous cases involving charges brought against Cassirer's *Pan* in 1911 and against *Die Aktion* in early 1914 for publishing allegedly obscene literature.[107] In the theater there had been the much publicized case involving similar charges lodged by the Berlin Chief of Police Jagow against the Reinhardt production of Sternheim's *Die Hose* in 1911.[108] Ball and Klabund had even been planning an anthology of literature censored and confiscated on such grounds just prior to the war.[109] When the Expressionists began to turn their concerns in a political direction after the outbreak of the war and then to oppose the war, they at first enjoyed a brief respite from rigid censorial controls; as Wieland Herzfelde observes, the government had been long accustomed to a politically noncommittal attitude on the part of the majority of the intellectual community and, therefore, little expected opposition to come from this quarter.[110] The government soon spotted the shifted political stance of the Expressionists, however, and the remaining literary organs of the movement were forced to either camouflage their opposition to the war, as did *Die Aktion* by relegating such sentiments to letter-columns or marginal glosses, or they had to move their editorial headquarters to more hospitable territory, which is what Schickele was doing, as already mentioned, when he took *Die weissen Blätter* to neutral Switzerland in late 1915. For Herzog, who refused to hedge on his criticism of the war and of the government, this kind of military surveillance of the press brought at first, from mid-1915 on, repeated deletions in the issues of *Das Forum* and finally, in September of the same year, the total ban of his periodical for the duration of the war.[111] The Expressionist antiwar, antiestablishment drama was also soon barred from German and Austrian stages; this was the fate, for example, which, long overdue, finally overtook Schickele's *Hans im Schnakenloch* in the summer of 1917 after ninety-nine performances in Berlin's "Kleines Theater" and productions in numerous other cities of Germany.[112] Max Reinhardt's theater "Das junge Deutschland" was established in the latter half of the war in part to circumvent the severity of censorship by producing plays for invited guests only.[113]

In addition to the application of stricter censorship, the government gained greater control over the press through the enactment of a law which forbade the initiation of any new periodicals for the rest of the war without the explicit license of the military authorities. This restriction was obviously designed to permit the government to stifle potential opposition, but it could also be circumvented, as Herzfelde and his associates were to prove by acquiring in 1916 the title and publication rights of a journal which had been voluntarily discontinued by its original editors in the fall of 1914.[114]

Besides in print, opposition to the war was expressed by the Expressionists through public demonstration. An antiwar spirit was the one which gave rise to a "Conzil" attended in Weimar on New Year's Eve 1914/15 by Kurt Pinthus, Walter Hasenclever, Ernst Rowohlt, Rudolf Leonhard, Albert Ehrenstein, Paul Zech, Heinrich Eduard Jacob and others; and such was the spirit which prompted the protest held that same night in Berlin by Ball and some friends on the balcony of the apartment of Else Hadwiger.

Opposition to the war, nevertheless, did not go unchallenged in the Expressionist circles; patriotic sentiments were, at least at the outset, quite noticeably widespread, and the number of Expressionists who enthusiastically enlisted as mobilization began was not insignificant.[116] Some poets from their ranks also did not hesitate to voice their patriotic, and often bellicose, sentiments in print. One of the more prominent expressions of this position is in the lyrical broadsheet *Der Krieg* which was published by the A.R. Meyer Verlag in late September, 1914; it collects patriotic and prowar verse by Klabund, Rudolf Leonhard (N.B. his participation, just remarked, at the Weimar antiwar "Conzil" just a few months later; cf. below in this chapter for a discussion of this conversion), Alfred Lichtenstein, Alfred Richard Meyer and Peter Scher.[117] Such division of opinion on the war had unavoidably to result in the eventual rupture of many friendships. Thus, the critic Alfred Kerr, to cite a more prominent example, had originally been looked up to by many Expressionists as a model, and he had made many friendships in the same camp before the war; but Kerr's particularly conspicuous support of the German effort in verse, which began appearing shortly after the start of hostilities, caused many of his earlier admirers and friends to denounce him.[118] Public and private skirmishes between the prowar and antiwar factions in the Expressionist community were also apparently not uncommon. The most notorious of these clashes occurred in the Café des Westens on May 7, 1915, between Leonhard Frank and an unidentified journalist, in the course of which Frank slapped the journalist in the face for cheering the announcement of the sinking of the "Lusitania" that day.[119] This was the event which forced Frank the very same night to flee to Switzerland, where he sat out the rest of the war.[120]

Gradually, with the unexpected and sobering prolongation of what had been anticipated as a repetition of the brief campaign of 1870/71, the patriotic fervor began losing ground to the opposition in many quarters. This development became more and more prominent in especially the ranks of the Expressionists. The change was, for at least the Expressionists, a predictable consequence of the sudden awakening of social and political awareness and the often concomitant turn to political activism which was described earlier. The earlier advocacy of change in the ethical and cultural structure of society was blended more and more now with a call for social and political change as well. A movement which had been predominantly inner-directed thus began now to exhibit clear tendencies towards outer-directedness, too.

What is probably the most blatant example of a radical switch in position on the war, accompanied, perhaps instead preceded, by a new awareness of the politics behind it, is offered by the experience and poetry of Rudolf Leonhard. Leonhard, by his own admission largely apolitical in attitude until the summer of 1914, had volunteered for military service at the very outset of the war and in the first two months of it had authored a small volume of some of the most fanatically jingoistic verse to come out of the Expressionist camp in the period.[121] The verse, which appeared in the *Lyrische Flugblätter* of Alfred

Richard Meyer in October or November, 1914, under the title *Über den Schlachten,* is not inclined to hedge on the expression of nationalistic sentiments. Its general tone is illustrated by the poem "Landsturm auf Wache": "Immer wieder wird 'Deutschland, Deutschland über alles' gesungen / Ich hätte die Worte fast vergessen / nun geht mein Herz, vom Hass besessen / so hat mich nie ein Gedicht bezwungen." "'Germany, Germany before all else' was sung again and again / I had almost forgotten the words, / but now my heart is possessed by hatred; no poem has ever moved me that way before." Nor does the verse collected here incline even to disguise a preference for war over peace, as exemplified by the closing lines of the poem "Soldaten": "In our wounds we learned a peaceful mien / There is no paradise down here on earth, / but for us it is better to have war than peace."[122] Leonhard was sent into the field of battle in the first year of the fighting and produced there two new series of war poetry. The first, entitled "Aus den Schlachten," was written during the winter of 1914/15 and the battle of Masuren; the second, "Das neue Leben," came out of the fighting in the summer of 1915.[123] The sentiments which had dominated "Über den Schlachten" are suddenly absent from these two new series; Leonhard's first-hand experience of the war in the meantime had presumably provoked a turnabout in his mind, as it did in the minds of so many of his fellow Expressionists. The emphasis in the new poetry is no longer placed upon the glories of battle, but on death, the loss of life in the fight, on suffering, and throughout there echoes now a recurrent longing for peace.[124] The motto for the second cycle, "Aus den Schlachten," hints at the change which has taken place:

> I have descended into battle
> and have sought out horror:
> my heart has not remained silent even in the wildest clamor,
> it has raged and cried and cursed—
> and if I am allowed to live on after peace,
> then I will bear witness every more loudly to what must be said!
> (on the march in Poland, February, 1915.)[125]

Leonhard, as confirmed by Fritz Max Cahén who saw the poet during the war and noted with great surprise the change in his friend's philosophy, had suddenly become a pacifist.[126] Leonhard describes for us himself the reversal of position on the war which he had undergone and points up its relationship to a concomitant political awakening in the foreword to *Das Chaos.* This book appeared shortly after the German November Revolution and brought together in one volume the three cycles of poetry just discussed so as to represent, in Leonhard's own words, "ein europäischer Weg."[127] He admits here his "bad conscience" in respect of the first cycle in the book and then continues:

In one respect I thought what I had done was not unpardonable: until then a sentimental skeptic, I had only rarely taken an interest in politics. When war broke out I did not know the political situation; I assessed it incorrectly and was not impressionable but gullible. I have since learned that it is wrong not to be politically informed. But how was I to know that then. How many were in a different situation? I was not reeducated then because—this was already bad enough—I had not yet learned anything. When the war broke out I lived only in the overwhelming feeling engendered by it; nothing else mattered; I did not know what was good and what was evil. I felt—as the first poem expresses—it was evil; but I believed it was therewith a revolution against a more evil world which deserved it. I believed everything; I also believed—as the second expresses—that nations, not people, were responsible for the war. I was deluded into thinking that the rotten state of the previous peace would have been worse for those who were suffering than the war—and I then wrote the poem "Soldaten." I had no doubt discussed the war with friends academically; yes, I had committed the unjust act of assuming the psychological perspective, failing, in doing so, to face the horrible thought of its reality. That is why my beliefs were so wrong—until I began to see. A short time later I could not have seen it that way nor believed it: now, for the first time, I understood the relationship between war and peace.[128]

After the war Leonhard was to become a follower of Karl Liebknecht and a member of the revolutionary "Rat geistiger Arbeiter" in Berlin in 1919.[129] We must imagine for ourselves for the most part the various stages of development which lay between his original political indifference and his later revolutionary activism, for these stages are not recorded anywhere by Leonhard himself; but we can follow the successive stages of this same kind of development in the lives of Oskar Maria Graf and Leonhard Frank, as documented in their autobiographies.[130] The narratives of these two volumes, written in novel form, both commence in time before the advent of Expressionism and both conclude sometime in the postwar era. In the course of their lives, the two protagonists are converted to political commitment or activism, and in both instances it is a conversion which derives most directly from their experiencing of the war and its ramifications. Graf had come under the influence of anarchist circles in Munich (e.g., "Die Gruppe Tat") well before the war, but the first decisive changes in his thinking began taking place, gradually and more or less on an unconscious level, only after the summer of 1914.[131] Although Graf did volunteer for military service at the outset of the war, it was done more in a spirit of an aimless drifting with the tide than of a real commitment to the cause.[132] In addition, during his brief term in the army he pursued a consciously "Schweikian" approach to military duty.[133] Towards the end of the war, after an early release from the service on psychological grounds, Graf established contact with the Independent Socialists in Munich and, as a result, eventually participated directly in the Bavarian Revolution in 1918.[134] Frank's similar conversion is more abrupt, occurring almost automatically with the very beginning of hostilities; and it is more radical, in the sense that it comes to the surface immediately as pacifism.[135] He had easily resisted the initial wave of high-spirited patriotism which had induced many of his fellow poets to enlist; from the very start and before most others, as his autobiography portrays it, he had seen the "insanity" which underlay what was taking place all over Europe.[136] While Frank apparently did not become as politically active as Graf was to (Frank spent most of the war in Switzerland and did not return to Germany until after the Revolution had already begun), the stories which he published collectively in mid-1918 as *Der Mensch ist gut* added significant flame of inspiration to the revolutionary fire that flared up at the end of the war. The last story in the volume ("Die Kriegskrüppel") concludes, in fact, in a prophetic prologue to the November Revolution.[137]

Another well-defined illustration of this spread of politicization of thought and literature as a direct outcome of the war is offered on a much broader scale by the developments towards the end of the war in German Dadaism, an offshoot of Expressionism. In its origins in Zürich in 1916, German Dadaism had sprung in great part from the escapist inclinations shared by what were mostly self-exiled German artists who had come to Switzerland in retreat from the effects of the war; the movement, as Raoul Hausmann has written, was accordingly cultivated as an "artistic game."[138] Two years later, in the first half of 1918, Dadaism was transplanted, under the leadership of Huelsenbeck, to Berlin where it acquired fresh supporters, such as Raoul Hausmann, Walter Mehring, Herzfelde and others. Here Dadaism could hardly avoid having to confront face to face the issues of the war and the various other political developments which were still largely unfelt in the quiet isolation of Zürich; it was thus invested with strong, patently political overtones now.[139] An unequivocal indication of this quality of Berlin Dadaism is the unshrouded endorsement of Communism or of socialist reforms in the manifestoes published by its members.[140] Huelsenbeck is always careful in his essays and memoirs on Dadaism to draw a distinction between its manifestations in Berlin and Zürich; similarly, Franz Jung asserts that, because of its political tendencies, Dada as practiced in Berlin had little more than its name in common with the earlier Zürich movement.[141]

An important role in at least furthering, if not also in actually laying the ground for, the development of social and political awareness amongst the Expressionists was played by Pfemfert's *Die Aktion* and the circle which backed it. Due in large part to the fact that *Die Aktion* was the only major periodical of Expressionism which before, and well into, the war showed a deep and consistent interest in social and political issues, it came to overshadow the other journals in the second half of the Expressionist years. Such an interest had, of course, been a programmatic part of Cassirer's *Pan* before the war— especially during Kerr's editorship; and the Munich-based periodical *Kain*, although less widely circulated than most Expressionist journals, revealed a pronounced political orientation.[142] However, *Pan* lacked in particular the editorial continuity which accounted for much of the potency of *Die Aktion*, since *Pan* had changed editors several times, and publishers twice, before the end of its brief life. In addition, *Pan* as well as *Kain* lacked the support and force behind them of a group of regular contributors; in the case of *Pan* this was due mainly to the lack of editorial continuity and with *Kain* to the fact that it was both edited and penned by one hand alone, that of the self-styled anarchist Erich Mühsam. Finally, *Pan* began to hang fire after the middle of 1913, putting out, haltingly, only five issues between June 1, 1913, and April 1, 1915, when it then became totally inactive. *Kain* suspended publication in August, 1914, by the editor's own admission to avoid having to take an explicit position in print on the war, and did not return to the newsstands again until the conflict was over.[143] The only other prewar Expressionist journals which might be considered in this context were *Revolution* (1913) and *Das Forum* (1914-29).[144] *Revolution*, however, was in essence an offshoot of *Die Aktion*, as Paul Raabe states, since its editors and many of its contributors had been schooled in Pfemfert's approach; furthermore, it had little time to make much of an impact on its readership since it lasted through only five issues (three months) of publication.[145] *Das Forum*, which was edited by Herzog, was, as, again, Raabe points out, a continuation of Herzog's editorial policy established in his earlier position on *Pan* in 1910.[146] It was also, like *Revolution*, begun much too late to have a sizable influence on Expressionism in the decisive years and, in addition, was banned in August, 1915, for the rest of the war after little more than a year of publication.[147] *Die Aktion*, on the other hand, remained fully active throughout the whole Expressionist period; and even during the war, although in much more subdued form than before, it continued to give expression to political views.[148] The extent to which it and its editor had been able to determine the basic direction of thinking of the members of its immediate circle in the prewar phase is reported, amongst others, by Jung. He claims that a young poet who joined this group was educated, whether he willed it or not, by especially the leader to think in terms of social criticism with strong political accents.[149] During the war *Die Aktion* was widely read in the trenches by young soldiers, to whom Pfemfert made a special effort to send free copies.[150] Erwin Piscator, who was one of these readers-in-the-field, attests to the journal's circulation there and adds that it not only brought home to these soldiers the brutal truth of the senselessness of the war, but, more importantly, aroused in them an awareness of the crucial role of politics in shaping civilization.[151]

On the Barricades

The long-awaited end to the hostilities finally came in early November of 1918; but it did not bring with it the peace which had been anticipated. Even before the signing of the armistice had taken place on November 11, 1918, a revolution inspired by democratic and socialist forces had erupted, fostering new conflicts and violence. Although the Kaiser very soon abdicated and the new Republic was proclaimed almost at once, struggles broke out between the two leading factions of the new government, the Social Democrats and the Independent

Socialists, which prevented the nascent Republic from firmly establishing order for several months. Germany was also crippled by an inflation which had begun during the war and, soon after its end, had reached staggering proportions.[152] The fate of the Expressionists and the next stage in the development of their movement were intimately bound to these events. The inflation, which was not finally slaked until the mid-1920s, was alone to be responsible for the demise of more than one of the Expressionist journals; for those that persevered it increasingly inhibited their potentialities. The general political chaos of the postwar period filled most of the people, including most of the Expressionists, with a feeling of confusion and uprootedness. Ottomar Starke echoes many other chroniclers in his description of the general state of mind during this period:

> People lived in those days in a strange state of limbo. People only came to their senses after the war was over and very slowly. For forty years they had lived in a state of total peace. A splendid, untroubled, paradisical period of youth lay behind us. Now, all of existence had suddenly become extremely problematical; people felt insecure, threatened, perhaps spied upon and informed against. There was little to eat. People felt they were not free, as if they were being pushed about, but did not know from which side nor in which direction. They would have liked to put their minds in order but got no place attempting it. I began then to feel that my existence was like that of a person who was rooted in the familiar soil of traditional, established, and gratifying facts, but was being forced now to lead a nebulous, shadowy existence. I felt I no longer had a past or a future. There was also no longer any trustfulness, only a kind of expeditious cynicism, a dangerous form of passiveness which destroyed many of my contemporaries.[153]

Nevertheless, as though seeking a way out of such disconcerting feelings and aiming to demonstrate conclusively their heightened social and political awareness, the Expressionists in overwhelming numbers threw themselves actively into the maelstrom of postwar political life and lent their full support to the Revolution. The Revolution promised them a means of accomplishing in a very tangible and concrete manner the mostly metaphysical ideals of Expressionism which had been expressed earlier programmatically in, for example, the desire for the realization of man's true, essential nature, for the establishment of a brotherhood or community of mankind, the permanent end of all war, the revitalization of life, and for the deposition of the reigning materialist-positivist philosophy of Wilhelminian Germany.[154] They not only participated in the Revolution directly, but also wrote politicoliterary manifestoes and pamphlets in support of it, defended it in their journals and glorified it in their poetry.[155] They set up their own organizations to give it formal backing and to integrate into it their own artistic movement.

The pattern for these organizations was set by the revolutionary councils, such as the "Rat geistiger Arbeiter" in Berlin. The latter council was brought together by intellectual supporters of the Revolution on the day it converged on Berlin (November 9, 1918).[156] The council's membership was broad and the

Expressionists were strongly represented in it; its goals coincided closely with the spirit of Expressionism at this stage.[157] One of its members from the Expressionist camp reports on the demands the council made at the first meeting, held in the old "Reichstag" in Berlin: the abolition of all academies, the socialization of all theaters, the nationalization of all free professions, the abolition of all titles and the immediate creation of a world parliament.[158] Similar demands were made public in the manifestoes issued by the Expressionist organizations. The earliest of these and the most active was the Berlin "Novembergruppe" which was formed at the outset of the Revolution by a group of painters and sculptors, some of them poets, too, including Karl Hirsch, Max Pechstein, Ludwig Meidner, Otto Mueller, George Grosz, César Klein.[159] They were soon joined by representatives of literary Expressionism. In their announced policy, like that of other similar organizations throughout Germany, they accomplished a fusion of Expressionism with the goals of the Revolution: they vowed to support the latter while documenting the former as a "Weltanschauung."[160] The slim volume *An alle Künstler!* (1919) was almost exclusively a product of the "Novembergruppe"; it combined illustrations by artists of the group with poetry, essay and manifesto, in all of which, as so typical in Expressionism as a whole in this phase, political program is inseparable from the literary and aesthetic content: the artistic goals advocated in its key manifesto depend upon the realization of a Socialist Republic in Germany which will unite art and the masses.[161] Expressionists in other cities quickly followed suit: in Dresden appeared the "Gruppe 1919," in Halle the "Künstlergruppe," in Magdeburg the "Vereinigung für neue Kunst und Literatur," in Bielefeld "Der Wurf," in Karlsruhe the "Gruppe Rih," in Düsseldorf "Das junge Rheinland."[162] The occasion of the November Revolution, they all felt, bestowed upon them a much greater license than ever before to knock down the barriers of the traditions of the past and to forge ahead unrestrictedly towards new horizons in all spheres of activity. Pechstein declared in the manifesto just cited: "The revolution had brought us the freedom to express and realize wishes we had harbored for years."[163]

Few could resist the call of political involvement. Even the editor of what had been the most esoteric and most aesthetically oriented periodical in the prewar phase, Herwarth Walden, became infected by the new, dominant spirit now. His dictum had originally been: "Art and politics have nothing to do with each other." Under the pressure of the postwar political upheaval he gradually discovered he could no longer maintain that distinction.[164] Like most Expressionists, Walden also felt most drawn to the political left, and before the early 1920s were out he had already embraced Communism wholeheartedly.[165] The political commitment of Pfemfert's *Die Aktion*, which had always been marked, could only be intensified to the extreme now; and that it was. During the war, Pfemfert's circle had clandestinely organized its own political party, "Die Antinationale Sozialistenpartei Gruppe Deutschland."[166] The sponsorship of this party, as well as of the "Spartacus League" and the Russian and German Revolutions, were all finally made public in the pages of *Die Aktion* early in November, 1918.[167] Just a few months prior to that date Pfemfert was already writing that literature itself, no matter the direction it took, was no longer of any interest to him.[168] *Die Aktion* and its ancillary publications began reflecting this new perspective, shared by editor and contributors from his circle alike, by becoming increasingly dominated by political essay at the expense of literature in succeeding years. Finally, in 1927, the subtitle of the journal was belatedly changed from "Wochenschrift für Politik, Literatur, Kunst" to "Zeitschrift für revolutionären Kommunismus."[169]

Accompanying the surge in political activity, and closely related to it, was a great resurgence in Expressionist literary life. There had already been signs of such a tendency towards the end of the war as increasing numbers of Expressionists, new and old, began returning from exile in Switzerland and elsewhere or were managing to secure an early release from active military duty for various reasons.[170] The sharp increase in the number of Expressionist periodicals about this time was one of the clearest indicators of a change: while only seven had been going to press at the beginning of 1917, the last year of the war, from the end of 1917 to the early part of November, 1918, saw the establishment of a total of twenty new journals.[171] Also, the final year of the war witnessed an event of major importance for the Expressionist drama: on December 23, 1917, Max Reinhardt's new experimental theater "Das junge Deutschland" opened in Berlin. This event represented the first real breakthrough for the Expressionist drama, until this time little performed, for "Das junge Deutschland" was in practice to be devoted with few exceptions to the production of Expressionist plays throughout its years of activity.[172]

By the end of the war, artistic activities amongst the Expressionists had again reached a high pitch of intensity, rivaling that of the years just before the war. Max Krell recalls:

> The armistice brought a sigh of relief. The silencing of the cannons was already a relief. We wanted to make a clean sweep of things, not only the rules of war but also those that had led us into it. In spite of the restricted circumstances, we had the feeling that the freedom of the word, the arts which were supposed to enrich our lives, of the theater, of poetry, had been saved.
>
> With unparalleled energy, we set about demonstrating that the defeat had in no way broken our intellectual and moral vigor.
>
> Indeed, the cultural life of the country put on a great show before the backdrop of destiny which was being increasingly shaken by the storms of turmoil.[173]

These activities manifested themselves for the most part along the earlier lines, although there were some important differences. First of all, the Expressionists were again to be seen in large numbers in the favorite literary cafés; yet, the café no longer seemed to dominate their lives to the extent it had before the war, a fact which can be read in part as an overt indication of their more serious and practical concerns now. Some of the circles which had developed out of the artist café, such as those around *Der Sturm* and *Die Aktion,* were now to be spotted here only very rarely in a body. Some individual figures, such as Benn, tended to avoid now at least the more popular cafés of the artists, foremost of which after about 1920 was Das Romanische Café in Berlin.[174] On the other hand, even Benn and others similarly inclined, did continue to maintain close contacts with fellow Expressionists as a rule.[175] Many had found other, more convenient meeting places now, such as the offices of their publisher or of the editor of the periodical with which they were most closely associated. Secondly, the evidence which is available indicates that most of the circles which had been completely broken up by the war did not reassemble after it. These included in Berlin the circle around Alfred Richard Meyer, "Der neue Club" and its splinter group led by Hiller which called itself "Gnu," all of the circles which had met in Munich and the one centered in Leipzig around the Kurt Wolff publishing company. In addition, none of the smaller groups which had been active in Heidelberg, Bonn, Greifswald and Paris materialized again. Finally, one other important element missing in great part from the postwar scene were the "Autoren-Abende" which had flourished in the early phase but now occurred only sporadically outside of the Walden circle.

There were certain things lost to the war; but on the whole the enthusiasm, the persistent sense of mission (now, of course, with altered goals) and the feeling of community amongst the Expressionists recalled the era before the so-called "Great War." Moreover, the appearance of several new circles towards, or just after, the end of the war gave positive testimony to a renewal of vigor in Expressionist literary life. The original centers which had survived the war (although not without many changes) were Berlin, Munich, Dresden, Vienna, Innsbruck; there was also still some activity in Zürich which, as already mentioned, had not become a focal point of the movement until the war years. New groups now appeared in some of the latter cities as well as in Konstanz, Darmstadt, Hannover, Hamburg and, on a smaller scale, in Frankfurt am Main.[176] New publishing companies which favored the movement were formed, such as Der Malik-Verlag and the second Ernst Rowohlt Verlag (both in Berlin).[177] The literary market was very soon flooded with new periodicals. Harry Graf Kessler, with such journals particularly in mind as *"Jedermann sein eigner Fussball"* (1919), put out by his friend Herzfelde, and Anselm Ruest's *Der Einzige,* entered in his diary for February 19, 1919: "Publications, some of them interesting, were sprouting up like mushrooms."[178] Most of these new publications, espousing Expressionism programmatically, emanated from the circles, new and old: forty-four were being put to press by the end of 1919, more than double the number established in the entire prewar phase.[179] Compilations of Expressionist literature began to be printed now in much larger numbers than previously: twenty new series, devoted in name or by implication to the publication of this literature, were initiated in the few years following the war.[180] Most of the older series which had been started before 1918, such as *Lyrische Flugblätter* and *Der jüngste Tag,* now more than doubled the number of their listings.[181] This was also the period which saw the appearance of the vast majority of the almanacs and anthologies which are generally considered to be the major documents of the movement: *Die Erhebung* (1919-1920), *Der Anbruch* (1920), the last three volumes of *Das Ziel* (1919, 1920, 1923), *Kameraden der Menschheit* (1919), *Die Gemeinschaft* (1919), *Menschheitsdämmerung* (1920), *Die Entfaltung* (1921), *Unser Weg* (1919, 1920) and many others.[182]

The Expressionist experience was also broadened at the beginning of this phase of the movement considerably as the theater began to play a much greater role in it than previously. This development had been foreshadowed by the founding of "Das junge Deutschland" towards the close of the war. Once the war was over and the censorship restrictions had been lifted, theaters all over Germany began opening their repertoires to Expressionist plays. One of these theaters, called "Die Tribüne" and opened in Berlin on September 20, 1919, gave its total support to the Expressionist drama, both in the style as well as in the content of its productions.[183]

The lyric had dominated the group activities of the movement in the early phase. Between 1914 and 1918 it had easily been able to hold its own alongside the other genres, in particular in the form of the vast body of poetry sent to journals from the trenches of battle—a body of poetry which gave expression, predominantly by far in a gloomy or negative vein, to the individual's intimate experience of the war.[184] By the beginning of the third phase of the movement the lyric was, on the other hand, quickly eclipsed by the drama. The drama is traditionally a far less subjective form than the lyric poem; it, therefore, no doubt seemed to many authors of late Expressionist literature much more suited to a broader treatment of the new sociopolitical themes which could only be (and were only) dealt with in outline or abstract form in the lyric.[185] The new theaters mentioned above reflected, and encouraged, this change. Now, although the Scandinavian dramatists were still popular, the German stage for the first time in decades unequivocally came under the control of German playwrights, especially Expressionist playwrights of Germany, with Georg Kaiser and Carl Sternheim in the forefront of popularity.[186] This was a natural development, for the German playwright could, of course, most directly reflect the specific and concrete contemporary concerns. The hypersubjective Strindberg of *Nach Damaskus* and *Gespenstersonate* had met with little competition on the same ideological plane before the war and had, therefore, been able to dominate the German stage, so long as the audience remained subjectively oriented in equal degree; in revolutionary Germany he was out of step with the "spirit of the times."

By the end of the war, as Huelsenbeck wrote from Berlin at that time, Expressionism had become the official movement in the arts.[187] The public and the press, from which noisy antagonism had come before the war, were gradually becoming more and more amenable to it. The works of both poet and painter were suddenly in public demand. This was especially noticeable in painting, in which field the art dealer, for example, who in the earlier years of struggling for recognition had served the artist as patron and collector and only lastly as intermediary between the artist and the public, was now reduced to fulfilling the role of mere merchant.[188] He no longer had to fight to get the works of the artist he represented accepted by the public; buyers now flocked to his galleries. In the drama this trend was reflected in the not-so-desirable fact that the box office was said to have gained control over the repertoires of the flourishing theaters and was, pursuing only its current whim, demanding Expressionist plays.[189] The attitude of the Expressionists themselves changed, too, in many instances: they had formerly ignored, scorned and defied public opinion; they now, in contrast, not only enjoyed, but often, as many of their contemporaries complained, even seemed to court, public approbation.[190]

Well before the middle of the 1920s had been reached, Expressionism as a phenomenon in literature and the arts was still alive, but clearly as a *movement,* in the fullest sense of the term, it was moribund. The reasons for its demise and the swiftness of it are suggested by the Expressionists themselves in statements which began appearing in print already at the end of the First World War; all of the reasons they offer relate to the events following the outbreak of the war which were described above and to the effects which these events had upon the Expressionists. It was pointed out that the majority of these artists had gradually, and primarily under the impact of the war, become more socially and politically cognizant, and then more pragmatically reformist. This development meant for large numbers of them active participation in the November Revolution, and, out of necessity or desire, identification with a particular political movement or party. With few exceptions, the political direction taken was towards the left, i.e., towards socialism or communism. Many participated in the Communist movement in Germany, and, although they rarely carried this involvement to the point of joining the Communist party, many supported the far left-wing Spartacus League. This tendency was represented most blatantly by Pfemfert, Walden, Max Herrmann-Neisse, Jung, Johannes R. Becher, Oskar Kanehl, Rudolf Leonhard, Ludwig Rubiner, Otten, Otto Freundlich, Herzfelde, Carl Einstein, et al. There were many, including again some of the latter, who were attracted for a time or longer to the related German Independent Socialist Party (USPD). Expressionist supporters of this party were, to name a few, Klabund, Herzog, Becher, Döblin, Leonhard Frank, Hiller, Leonhard, Pinthus, Alfred Wolfenstein, Piscator, Schickele, Otten, Pfemfert, Ernst Toller. Most of the remaining Expressionists, while perhaps not as active in their support of a political party or movement to the extent others were, at least sympathized with socialist ideas in this period. Into this group fall such authors as Edschmid, Carlo Mierendorff, Rudolf Kayser, Sternheim, Kaiser, Franz Werfel, Erich Mühsam, Friedrich Eisenlohr, Franz Blei, Otto Flake, Oskar Maria Graf, Robert Müller, Iwan Goll, Paul Zech.

Very soon, the Revolution and the government of the new republic fell under the control of the more moderate parties, in particular the Social Democrats and the Center Parties, which consistently resisted radically socialist reforms. The socialist Revolution had therefore failed; the bourgeois Revolution (Restoration) had triumphed.[191] Most of the Expressionists, having identified with the socialist side, subsequently came to look upon the November Revolution in its entirety as a failure and, more precisely, as a betrayal of their ideals. The most immediate impact which this turn of events made on their lives was to cause a new note to begin to be sounded in their statements and their creative work now. It was a note of cynicism and pessimism, one totally foreign to the original optimism and exuberance on which most of Expressionism had been founded before the war.

Walter Hasenclever claims he had already foreseen "the impossibility of realizing political ideals in Germany" as early as 1917; just prior to that year he had completed works, such as the play *Der Retter* and the poem "Der politische Dichter," which had bespoken the directly opposite point of view.[192] Most of his fellow artists, however, had to witness the "failure" of the Revolution before coming to such a realization; and, significantly, Hasenclever's direct statement of loss of political faith was not put into print until some time (1924) after the latter event had taken place.[193] One of the first to publicly recant his original political hopes for Germany in this period was Schickele. He had recorded his sanguine feelings about the Revolution and his concomitant vision of a new world in the essay "Der neunte November," which was finished in manuscript in December, 1918: "The new world had commenced. Behold: mankind liberated . . . Now! Let's begin, freed of the burden of the Middle Ages, the march into the new age! Now!"[194] Yet, even as this essay was finally going to print in Edschmid's series *Die Tribüne der Kunst und Zeit* in 1919, Schickele was forced to add a "Nachwort" which was informed by a distinctly ominous mood. He begins here:

> Today, not even a year later, I would have to confess to an indescribable sense of disappointment if the inner conflicts which I settled during the war had not prepared me for disappointment.[195]

Schickele's loss of faith in the Revolution, as he records it in that "Nachwort," was due more than anything to an abhorrence of the violence and brutality which it had fostered.[196] This was also the factor which gave rise to Toller's similar disclaimer a year after Schickele's. Toller had given sufficient proof of his revolutionary zeal and activist optimism just after the war, first in his direct participation in the Kurt Eisner government of the new Bavarian Republic, and then again, a few months later, in his somewhat more cautious collaboration with the Bavarian Soviet Republic, proclaimed in April, 1919.[196] By 1920, on the other hand, he is discovered writing in a letter to a friend from prison of the state of despair he finds himself in and branding in the same letter as his "Lebenslüge" what he had originally espoused as "die erlösende Kraft des Sozialismus."[198]

The Expressionist anthologies published around this time mark the change of spirit, too. They had conventionally been opened or closed by the editor with an assertion of faith in what the future could bring in the way of a better world through the efforts and inspiration of the poets represented in the volume at hand.[199] This was still true of anthologies which came out almost in the midst of the Revolution, such as *Kameraden der Menschheit* and *Die Gemeinschaft,* both edited by Ludwig Rubiner during 1919.[200] Then, just one year later, in the summer of 1920, appeared an anthology of Expressionist poetry entitled *Verkündigung.*[201] Its editor, Rudolf Kayser, closes the book in his afterword in a strikingly somber spirit:

> This period—it is the fall of 1920 and the atmosphere is very spent and stale—is anything but one of ascendancy and completion.... After years of youthful storming, passionate cries and revolutions, we must confess today: our hopes have not been realized; we are the hunted and the searching, biding our time between our youth and our paternity.... For the first time in our age a new generation has appeared which is not guided by an overweening optimism.[202]

In disillusionment over their failure to realize the high-set and often very utopian ideals which they had brought with them to the Revolution from Expressionism, they quit the new Republic and usually quit political involvement in general as well. They despaired of the possibility of ever attaining their original aims, so they simultaneously began to turn their backs on the literary movement which had inspired their political involvement. The main burden of guilt for their failure was not charged, however, to Expressionism, but to German society at large. Sternheim, a member of the circle around Pfemfert since before the war, exemplifies this fact. He had been one of the first to announce his support of the then incipient Revolution in Germany in the essay "Die deutsche Revolution," which appeared in the November 30, 1918, issue of *Die Aktion.*[203] In 1920, in the long essay *Berlin oder Juste milieu,* he had to admit sadly the Revolution's defeat, but made use of the same opportunity to write a bitter indictment of the whole of German society for sowing the seeds of this defeat through its conservative compromises.[204] Goll, in a similar vein, had reacted to the betrayal of the Revolution by the moderate forces by washing his hands of both Germany and of Expressionism. In a letter written to a friend on October 31, 1919, from the train which was taking him to Paris, he expressed his relief at leaving Germany behind him and also vented his disgust ("Vor ganz Europa spucke ich aus") ("I spit in the face of all of Europe.") at Europe as a whole.[205] A year later, now settled in Paris, he described in more detail in an essay, written for the eyes of all to read back in his former country, the reasons for his deep sense of despair. The essay is appropriately entitled "Der Expressionismus stirbt":

> As has been rumored, smiled about and suspected in all quarters: another art movement is being killed by the age which betrayed it. Whether it is the fault of the art or the age is immaterial. If one wanted to be critical one could prove that Expressionism is being killed by the carcass of the revolution which it wanted to serve as high priestess....
>
> Expressionism was a fine, good, great thing. The solidarity of the intellectuals. The deployment of the guardians of truth.
>
> But the result is, unfortunately and by no fault of the Expressionists, the German Republic of 1920....
>
> Yes, indeed, my fellow Expressionist: the danger today is taking life too seriously. Fighting for a cause has become grotesque. Intellect, in this era of the profiteer, has become ludicrous....
>
> The "Good Man" steps off into the wings with a bow of desperation.[206]

The demise of Expressionism was equated by others as well with the failure of the Revolution; for many the two exploits had become so completely intertwined and inseparable that the collapse of the one had to signify at the same time the identical fate for the other. This attitude is expressed by Pinthus in the gloom-filled "Nachklang" added to the 1922 edition of *Menschheits-dämmerung* (first edition dated 1920)—in which he also now describes his anthology as "ein abschliessendes Werk."[207]

While virtually all Expressionists abandoned the movement, if not the phenomenon, too, in the early 1920s, not all repudiated either immediately or totally their more recently established political affiliations. There were a few notable exceptions to the widespread shuffling or total eschewal of political ties. One such exception was Walden. As already mentioned, he became active in the Communist movement after the war, and was to remain so committed long after the heyday of Expressionism had passed. In the late 1920s, as had Pfemfert a few years before him, he began devoting increasing space in his journal *Der Sturm* to articles sympathetic to Communism, especially the Russian form, and to articles advocating very concrete social change.[208] In 1932, his political convictions induced him to emigrate to Russia, from where as late as 1938 he was still producing evidence of his adherence to those same convictions.[209] Mierendorff, Hans Schiebelhuth, Armin T. Wegner, Jung, and Becher were some of the other former Expressionists who also remained active in some way in politics after the close of the revolutionary period. However, in the course of this continued political involvement, most such activists, following the pattern of Pfemfert, soon gave up Expressionism in exchange for the ideology of their newly chosen political movement or party.

There was also a nonpolitical factor which made a major contribution to the decline of Expressionism. This factor issued, ironically enough, directly from the movement's attainment of popularity on a broad scale. Its success resulted inevitably, as many Expressionists have claimed, in the movement's commercialization and vulgarization. It began to attract numerous *epigones* who ground out crude imitations in the Expressionist manner in order to share in what had become a lucrative enterprise for author and publisher alike. This situation caused Pfemfert to turn his back on the movement even before he had become so completely preoccupied with political activities in the Revolution. He wrote in July, 1918, in *Die Aktion:*

> When it seemed necessary to force the public to provide a place for the new generation of German writers, everyone in whom I thought I detected even just a spark of talent found a forum in this journal. It does not matter that I was at times wrong, that *Die Aktion* was only a stepping stone for many "young writers" into journalism. I simply got rid of such fellows quietly and had the pleasure of receiving "refusals" from the rejected. I did not take offense, because they were only products of their times. Only the complete lack of culture in our literature made a frequent phenomenon possible: a juvenile imitator like Hasenclever was allowed to pass for a dramatist; a gross outrage like *Seeschlacht* could be declared a theatrical sensation; an Edschmid, a Kornfeld, et al., could be referred to as poets. It is a humiliating affair, of course, but it has only been dangerous since August, 1914. "Young Germany" hid behind the golden back of the bourgeoisie so as to make a good living. Youth has become a business; but business was never an intellectual affair. At present I can do nothing to oppose this consortium but to chase them, mercilessly, from my doorstep so that they cannot compromise us.[210]

Pfemfert's judgment here is colored by personal feuds and differences of opinion which were unrelated to literature, and, in the most literal sense, i.e., to the point of completely excluding Expressionist literature from his journal, his judgment was not lived up to immediately; but the general import of it was soon to be echoed by many other spokesmen of the movement in the next few years. Even one of the authors singled out by Pfemfert above for criticism, Edschmid, was to complain in 1920 that Expressionism had become popular reading on the lowest intellectual levels of the reading public.[211] Becher lamented in May of the same year in a letter to a friend: "I am expecting without emotion the complete collapse and the shameful bankruptcy of everything that wrapped itself in the label 'Expressionism.'"[212] Jung concluded that the movement was no longer directed by the artists themselves now: "Expressionism had become trite, had come under the control of the editorial staffs of the big publishing houses."[213]

There is concrete proof of at least Jung's claim. In the earlier years, the Expressionists had been able to find acceptance for their works in most instances through only the publishers who came from their own ranks, through innovators like Heinrich F. S. Bachmair, Kurt Wolff, Alfred Richard Meyer, Hermann Meister, Ernst Rowohlt, Richard Weissbach, Pfemfert, and Walden.

Now—a clear sign of success—even the larger and the more conservative publishing houses, such as the S. Fischer Verlag and the Gustav Kiepenheuer Verlag which had almost totally eschewed this literature for a decade, were also eager and willing to sponsor it and—this is most significant—to do so under the name of "Expressionism."[214] Walter Mehring's experience with *Die neue Rundschau* illustrates this reversal in publishing policy well. This journal, an S. Fischer publication and thus up to this time relatively conservative editorially, had earlier, when admitting a discussion of the issue into its pages, published mostly critical, or at best fairly cool and dry, appraisals of Expressionism.[215] Now, however, it was prepared to "let the youth take the floor" and print a defense of the movement by Mehring ("Die neue Form"), the very same defense (except for very minor changes) which the journal, under the same editor then as now (Oscar Bie), had rejected years before.[216] This kind of recognition was interpreted by some as final literary success, but most agreed with Pfemfert, Jung, Edschmid, Schickele, that it signified the decay and end of the movement.

Thus, some on political grounds, some on aesthetic grounds, many were arguing that Expressionism in literature and the arts was dead; still others were speaking as loudly of its long-last victory—and all of these voices were mingling discordantly in the same period, between about 1919 and 1921.[217] By the approach of the mid-1920s, however, the dominant voice was without question the one which was heard to say: "Expressionism is dead."[218] As far as such a pronouncement was applied by its author to the *phenomenon* of Expressionism, it was certainly wrong, for expressionistic *tendencies* were to be remarked in literature and the arts for many decades after. However, for the *movement*, the obituary of Expressionism could be written with full certainty by the middle of the 1920s.

2

Expressionism in Berlin

At the turn of the century, Munich unquestionably ranked first before all other cities of Germany as a center of the latest developments in literature and painting.[1] Berlin was, of course, not without its circles of poets and painters. While it had become relatively quiet by now in and around Friedrichshagen just outside the city where the former Naturalists and some of the Neo-Romantics (Gerhart and Carl Hauptmann, the Hart brothers, Arno Holz, Johannes Schlaf, Bruno Wille, et al.) had established their own artist colony around 1890, at the beginning of the following century Julius and Heinrich Hart had moved on to the South-West suburb of Berlin-Schlachtensee and there had founded "Die neue Gemeinschaft."[2] The members of this new circle of strongly anarchistic orientation included Mühsam, Peter Hille, Gustav Landauer, Lasker-Schüler and many others.[3] In the same period, and also overlapping in some instances in membership with the latter group, a number of poets, calling themselves "Die Kommenden," had begun to meet once a week in the popular Nollendorf-Casino in Berlin proper.[4] Mühsam, himself a member, has claimed that "Die Kommenden" represented a transition between the earlier Naturalism and the Expressionism soon to come.[5] Amongst the group's regular members, besides Mühsam and the founder Ludwig Jacobowsky, were Hille, Lasker-Schüler, Peter Baum, Margarete Beutler, Heinz Lux, Stefan Zweig and the head of the group after Jacobowsky's death (1900), Rudolf Steiner.[6]

Such groups as "Die neue Gemeinschaft" and "Die Kommenden" may have laid a part of the foundation for the later circles of Expressionists in Berlin and have also provided one of the important links between the Expressionist generation and the earlier bohemian artist tradition in the city; they did not, nevertheless, constitute an equivalent of the artistic high life which was flourishing in and around the many secessionist journals, the cafés and the ateliers of fin-de-siècle Munich. Berlin could take most pride in those years in being the political capital of the new "Reich"; and the city also best embodied the empire's essence, for the spiritual core of Berlin, as one of the city's Expressionist literary critics wrote on the eve of the November Revolution, was a mixture of "Gründerjahre" capitalism and Prussian officialdom.[7] Since the heyday of Naturalism over a decade before, such qualities had, side by side, eventually succeeded in making Germany's first modern metropolis inhospitable ground for new attitudes in art. That same Berlin critic evaluated the situation in this way:

> It emerged as a European city on the border between two worlds, neither of which have any relationship to the intellect: the proper sober-mindedness of old Prussia and the boundless lust for profit of the new industrialists. That is why the new Berlin lacked unequivocalness, a clear set of values and style. The resident of the city became a grotesque mixture of loutish bureaucracy and daredevil speculation. The city, which towered up around him, seemed to be a product of police ordinances, businesses, and operettas. The people in Berlin were void of love, devoted to their private aims, not even subject to any of the storms of political passions.[8]

Munich, for historical and cultural reasons, and primarily through the appearance of the satirical journal *Simplicissimus* (1896ff.) in the city, had become a main source of criticism of the prevailing spirit of Wilhelminian Germany. Gradually, however, resistance to that spirit had grown in strength and numbers even in the immediate vicinity of the Kaiser's residence: developing in Berlin in large part at first "underground" in the backrooms of West Side cafés—where, as Mehring felt, once one had entered "Prussianism" had forever been left behind[9]—Expressionism became the major front of resistance to Wilhelminianism throughout Germany, when it finally surfaced around 1910; it subsequently turned "die Stadt mit dem Asphalt-herzen" (Lasker-Schüler[10]) into the focal point of the new German artistic avant-garde. Although it can be argued that the revolution in literature and painting which in Germany was later called "Expressionism" neither originated in, nor first hit, Berlin, none the less, the city very soon assumed the leading position in all activities of the movement after the first signs of it had appeared.[11]

Throughout the Expressionist period Berlin maintained its supremacy and served, in addition, as a converging point for Expressionists and representatives of related tendencies from all over Europe. There were several reasons for this fact. First of all, the greatest concentration of periodicals of Expressionism was to be found in the city: during the period 1910-20 a total of thirty-two such journals were published and edited here, a number almost twice that of the closest rival (Munich) which managed to father only eighteen.[12] More significantly, two of the three most influential, comprehensive and long-lived of the Expressionist tribunes, *Der Sturm* and *Die Aktion,* along with the extensive circles which backed them, were stationed in Berlin for the entire span of their publishing life. Even the third member of this triumviral elite, *Die weissen Blätter,* which was originally founded by Erik Ernst Schwabach in Leipzig in 1913 (two years after *Die Aktion* and three years after *Der Sturm*) and then moved to Switzerland during the war, was finally brought to Berlin for its last three years in print (1919-21).[13] A majority of the publishing houses which gave substantial or total support to Expressionism had their home offices in this city, such as those of Cassirer, Erich Reiss, *Der Sturm, Die Aktion,* Der Malik-Verlag, Rowohlt (1919ff.), Meyer and others.[14] Thus, Berlin could easily dominate not only in the publication of journals but also of individual volumes representing Expressionism; the latter included the important issues in series, the anthologies and the almanacs, all of which, as suggested before, in functioning as a form of defense or at least documentation of this literature, helped to stamp it with one of the earmarks of a literary movement. Added to the above factors, but at once closely interconnected with them, were the many circles which regularly convened in Berlin cafés and private residences in the city and which together were active, stable, influential and cohesive on a scale unmatched by any other center of the movement. In the prewar phase, the Berlin circles which were most prominent were those around *Der Sturm, Die Aktion,* Meyer, Cassirer, Meidner, *Neue Jugend,* and those which were known as "Der neue Club," "Das Gnu," and "Die feindlichen Brüder."[15]

Mehring of the Walden circle and the Berlin Dadaists claims that the international revolution in art which was manifested in Germany as "Expressionism" did not reach Berlin until 1912 with the first Futurist exhibition held in the gallery of *Der Sturm* concurrent with an appearance of the poet Filippo Marinetti.[16] Mehring's estimate must be considered fairly conservative, since there is evidence which clearly demonstrates that the movement had gotten its official start in Berlin at least two years before. "Der neue Club" had, for instance, been founded in the fall of 1909 and had opened its "Neopathetisches Cabaret" in June of the next year; and March of 1910 had seen the debut of *Der Sturm,* which was to be followed in February of the very next year by the first issue of *Die Aktion.*[17]

Nevertheless, two phenomena which tend to overshadow in implications the events just named, and similar ones, focus most sharply on the year 1912 and speak very strongly in Mehring's favor. That year was, firstly, one of the merging and converging, in an especially tangible and conspicuous form, of more or less endemic Expressionist tendencies in Berlin (e.g., Benn, Hoddis, Heym, Hiller, Walden, Pfemfert, Döblin, Lasker-Schüler, Meidner) with national and international related tendencies, such as Fauvism, Cubism, Futurism. A description of this eclectic and restless climate in Berlin about this time is given by Otto Flake, who himself had just moved to the city and had very soon begun frequenting regularly the Café des Westens:

Arp had been in Paris and reported on the experiments in painting; a mood of unrest passed through the artistic and intellectual world. The exotic was rediscovered and not only, as had been the case a hundred years before, because of its romantic charm; it also embodied now new ideas and new perceptual motifs. The European's conviction that his was the dominant race and that he had simply created civilization, was shaken. There were cultures not based on his ideas, not based on progress, consciousness, an increase in technological energy; they perhaps know more than he about the nonmaterial world, about the significant realms of experience. European man did not seem more noble than the primitive races; the literati were even prepared to rank Negro sculpture ahead of all of Greek and Roman antiquity.[18]

Marinetti's visit in 1912 was only the most prominent and scandalous of many happenings of like consequences in that year and the next. In the winter of 1912/13, when Robert Delaunay's "Orphic Cubist" works were being shown in *Der Sturm,* he and his interpreter-spokesman, the poet Guillaume Apollinaire, visited Berlin together, with the latter giving a public lecture during their stay on new developments and concepts in art.[19] As happened with Marinetti, Apollinaire's programmatic statements on the new art, especially that of the Cubists, were published in *Der Sturm* so as to correspond with the author's appearance in Berlin.[20] *Der Sturm* was sponsoring its first exhibitions in 1912, bringing before the Berlin public the work of not only the Italian Futurists, but also the innovative canvases of the French Fauvists (called in the fifth *Sturm* exhibition "Französische Expressionisten") and of many other non-Germans (Picasso, Herbin, Ensor, Wouters, et al.), while at the same time giving extensive exposure to new German art, such as that of the Munich "Blauer Reiter."[21] The former Dresden group called "Die Brücke," which had just moved, practically *en masse,* to Berlin in 1911, had its first group showing in the city in 1912 in the "Galerie Gurlitt."[22]

German-speaking poets of Expressionist tendency from other cities of Europe had already begun to demonstrate a special attraction to Berlin at the beginning of the Expressionist period. Friedrich Burschell has recalled that rumors circulating in Munich artist circles around 1910 to the effect that more could be learned in Berlin than elsewhere were convincing enough to induce him, for one, to gravitate towards that city during the next few years.[23] Burschell thus began spending winters in Berlin and summers in Munich, with the most immediate result that he soon became a very active contributor to numerous Expressionist-aligned publications; following the war he was also to become editor of two journals of his own creation in Munich: *Revolution* (1918) and *Neue Erde* (1919).[24] Grosz, having begun his art studies at the Dresden Royal Academy of Art, responded to the pull of Berlin in 1912: "Berlin at that time was becoming a main center of activity. Even in art it was replacing the old centers of Munich, Düsseldorf and Dresden."[25] This gravitation from other cities of Europe towards Berlin had become especially marked by 1913, so much so that Jung, for example, was able to report of that year that most faces which had been seen earlier in Munich's meeting place, the Café Stephanie, were now cropping up in similar locales of Berlin.[26]

A second phenomenon supporting Mehring's date is the unmistakable surge in intensity of collective activities between 1912 and 1913. The number of journals put out in Berlin doubled.[27] The recitals given by the various circles in the city also increased noticeably in incidence; through invitations for guest readings, these events contributed significantly to the commingling of national and international Expressionist tendencies in providing an impetus for visits to Berlin by sympathetic artists from other centers. *Die Aktion* held only two such "Autoren-Abende" in 1911, but in 1913 sponsored eight and in the first half alone of the next year a total of seven.[28] The *Sturm* exhibitions, inaugurated in 1912, have just been mentioned; between their inception and the outbreak of the war no less than twenty-eight of them had already been held in Berlin, with some of them becoming travelling exhibitions shipped out to other cities throughout the world.[29]

There was, moreover, no quiet in Berlin before the storm; the intensification of activities here approached frenzied proportions in the year or so before the outbreak of the war. Ball was struck by the excitement in the city at this time; he had come up from Munich in July, 1914, to meet, in particular, with the circles in the Café des Westens and described his impressions on the visit in a letter to his sister: "Life here is magnificent and surprises me with new impressions."[30] His description could be applied not only to the literary avant-garde, but equally to life on virtually all levels of Berlin society. The city had developed into a metropolis bustling by day with the activities of business, industry, and politics and bursting at the seams after dark with the wild excitement of a full-scale night life which could rival that more perennially famous one of Paris. The appropriate gesture to accompany this excitement was provided by a dance craze which hit the city in this period. Dance halls were opening all over the city, with some, most notably the new one in the "Lunapark" in Halensee, becoming rivals of the literary cafés amongst the Expressionists.[31] *Die Aktion* organized its own balls, four of which, advertised as "Revolutions-Bälle," were held between 1913 and 1914.[32] Expressionist literature reflected the cult of the dance in this period, most conspicuously in the poetry produced by members of the Meyer circle.[33] Tilla Durieux, the actress-wife of Paul Cassirer, characterizes the general state of mind of Berliners about this time as "delirium":

In Halensee they had converted the Lunapark, which I could look down on from the windows of my modest apartment, into a spectacular amusement center with all the necessary surprises and contrivances. There was shouting, laughter, and gaiety everywhere. There was a large dancehall which every evening was swarming with people who preferred to dance in their street clothes. This was the meeting place of the bohemians, the painters, and writers; here you met the worthy bearers of well-known names who suddenly started having such great fun that they were able to dance through the night with a pretty girl without getting tired. The bars and the "Palais de Dance" made other demands on one's external appearance and one's pocketbook. The one-step had just appeared; and they danced the "Wooden Leg" to the hit "Bobby, where's your hair," i.e., they hopped across the dancefloor with one lame leg. Berlin had been seized by a delirium of joy....

A joy in one's work and in life filled Berlin to the bursting point, and nobody suspected that the menacing specter of war was participating in our mad dance. There were, no doubt, a few voices raised in warning, but our ears were deaf to them. It was as if everyone were being urged by an unconscious fear to enjoy life, to laugh, and make merry before a nightmare descended on us.[34]

The outbreak of war in August, 1914, had the same sobering and benumbing effect on the "delirium" in Berlin as it did on most life elsewhere in Germany and Austria. The Berlin circles suffered the same consequences of mobilization and declaration of war as did the circles of other centers: most members very soon enlisted or were inducted; publications were slowed down and stopped; group activities were terminated. The high spirits and the lightheartedness which had characterized life in the cafés had left with the first official reports on the war; and shortly thereafter little else was left behind but the quiet of relative desertion as most habitués departed for the front or went into exile in Switzerland.[35] All of the Berlin circles and the literary tribunes which they had sponsored had become completely inactive before the first year of war was out, with the sole exceptions of the two circles and journals around Walden and Pfemfert. Six journals had still been appearing in 1914 before the war had started: *Der Sturm, Die Aktion, Pan, Die Bücherei Maiandros, Das neue Pathos, Neue Jugend.*[36] By April, 1915, only the first two of the latter remained. Except in the Walden circle again, the literary recitals also came to an abrupt end.

Thus, Berlin Expressionism clearly did not come out of the opening of the war unscathed; yet, while all other centers of the movement ceased to show any overt signs of life not long after the start of this phase, Berlin at least was able to continue the tradition uninterrupted in the circles around Walden and Pfemfert. These two groups were not, of course, totally unaffected: the ranks of their memberships were severely reduced and the physical size of their journals was also noticeably abbreviated. In addition, the shadow of the censor hung heavy over especially *Die Aktion* now, which could only have been expected, given the fact that it had been the most politically oriented of the prewar Expressionist publications.

Outside of activities of the Walden and Pfemfert circles and two literary evenings organized in the first half of 1915 by Ball and Huelsenbeck just prior to their departure for Zürich, Berlin remained relatively quiet on the Expressionist literary scene throughout that first year of hostilities. Then, as early as the end of 1915, there appeared a first foreshadowing of a break in the lull. As a result in part of the early release from military duty of Franz Jung, a new, even though modest-sized, Expressionist journal began to appear under the heading of *Freie Strasse* (1915-18).[37] The publication was the combined effort of Jung and his friends—dating mostly from Jung's Munich days— Gross, Georg Schrimpf, Richard Oehring, and Oskar Maria Graf, and each of the first five of the slim, fifteen-page volumes in the series was edited in turn by one member of the group. Jung claims that the series had a general editor as well: Claire Jung (née Otto, the wife of Oehring and later of Jung), who was allegedly assisted by Pfemfert; but there is no official indication of this fact in the journal itself.[38] The series totaled six volumes, spread out over a period of three years, the last number coming out in 1918. This last volume was to be of historical note, for it was edited by Huelsenbeck, just returned from Zürich, and provided Dadaism with its first literary forum in Berlin.[39]

The repetition of Jung's military fate in the lives of ever increasing numbers of other Expressionists over the next few years stimulated a steadily growing regeneration of literary life in Berlin as it did in other cities of Germany; and the climax of this revival was not finally to be reached until after the Revolution. By 1916 it is even more noticeable with the establishment of two more journals: *Der Bildermann* and *Neue Jugend*.[40] The first of these lasted through only nine months (April-December, 1916) and was not the product of an active, cohesive company of contributors: its publisher, Cassirer, was no longer surrounded by a close circle of associates and supporters and was himself soon to leave Berlin, moving more or less permanently to Switzerland for the remainder of the war in the winter of 1916/17.[41] *Neue Jugend* (1916-17), on the other hand, betokened much more. It emanated from a more substantial source, being the concerted work of a group of artists which had begun assembling in Berlin around Herzfelde, himself just returned from the Belgian front. This circle, newly constituted, was eventually to provide the nucleus for the "Club Dada" shortly after the addition to it of the former Zürich Dadaist Huelsenbeck in 1917.[42]

During the last approximate year of the war, from the middle of 1917 to the beginning of November of the next year, the rejuvenation of the movement becomes an unmistakable fact in especially Berlin. Two new circles appear here now: the just-mentioned "Club Dada," comprising the Berlin school of Dadaism—the only substantial and well-organized branch of this direction on German soil—which, once a calm had settled over the city in the Revolution, was to sponsor several journals of its own; also the circle around Wolf Przygode and Hermann Kasack, whose journal, however, was initially to appear in Munich through the Roland-Verlag from 1918 to 1920.[43] Both of these groups held literary recitals in Berlin to promote their ideas, those sponsored by the Dadaists attracting considerable public attention. The Dadaists were of additional note in being associated with a very active publishing company which was directed by the original leader of the group, Herzfelde.[44] In this same period, six new Expressionist-aligned journals were also founded: *Marsyas* (1917-19), *Sturm-Bühne* (1918/19), *Eos* (1918-20), *Das junge Deutschland* (1918-20), *Berliner Romantik* (1918-25), *Diogenes* (1918-21).[45] The new *Sturm* publication just listed points to the recoupment which Walden was accomplishing at this time as well. The Pfemfert circle was enjoying the same kind of times, as testified to by the four new series which it inaugurated between April, 1916, and the summer of 1917.[46] *Das junge Deutschland* was the organ of a new theater group of the same name which, as already mentioned, represented a major breakthrough for Expressionist drama.

As Heinz Herald, the group's leading spokesman and one of its directors, wrote in a programmatic statement summing up the first year of work, "Das junge Deutschland" was established by Max Reinhardt as a "tribune for the young generation," i.e., to produce the plays of the new, young dramatists whose drama was unrecognized and seldom performed:

> What was the aim of "Das junge Deutschland"? To be a tribune of the young generation of dramatists who were beginning to bestir themselves but were encountering resistance everywhere, who were being ridiculed and not taken seriously precisely because they wanted to be taken seriously, because they were—and had to be—different from the generation of their fathers. This young generation wanted to cast off the passivity of the dominant view of art; they wanted breadth of perspective, freedom, results. They wanted to realize their ideals.[47]

So as to be uninhibited by the tight wartime censorial controls, the group was set up as a private organization, with admission to performances limited to members only.[48] The group made its debut in Reinhardt's "Deutsches Theater" in Berlin on December 23, 1917, with the theatrically provocative (great attention was paid to realism and detail in the props, but the enclosing walls in interior scenes were absent!) première production of Reinhard Sorge's *Der Bettler.*[49] During the three seasons it remained active, from 1917-20, "Das junge Deutschland" staged almost exclusively Expressionist plays by such authors as Kaiser, Werfel, Friedrich Koffka, Hasenclever, Kokoschka, and others.[50] Its immunity to censorship even permitted the group to give one of the first productions—before the war's end!—of Reinhard Goering's "tragedy" *Seeschlacht* (March 3, 1918), which, although not directly antiwar, creates a decidedly disturbing ("tragic") image of war.[51] Herald was to write many years later that with the first production organized by "Das junge Deutschland" Expressionism was "born" on the stage.[52] This statement is certainly true in the sense that this group, as Herald had originally set out to accomplish, brought to the Expressionist drama, particularly the more technically unconventional manifestations of it (Sorge, Goering, Unruh, Kokoschka, Kornfeld), its first great successes in Germany at the close of the war, making it respectable fare for most any theater's repertoire in the years that followed.[53]

In opening "Das junge Deutschland" Reinhardt must have been motivated in part by a perception of the growing popularity of Expressionism in the broader public towards the close of the war. Another semipublic event, which had preceded the latter one by just ten days, bespoke the same trend because of its taking place before a similarly less restricted audience than had events associated with Expressionism in earlier years. This event was, at the same time, one of broader significance for Expressionism since it involved the movement as a whole, rather than the drama alone. The event in question was

Edschmid's reading of his now famous essay "Expressionismus in der Dichtung" on December 13, 1917, before "Die deutsche Gesellschaft 1914" in Berlin.[54] "Die deutsche Gesellschaft 1914" was at that time, according to Edschmid, "the most prominent club in Berlin"; it had been organized at the beginning of the war as a patriotic organization representing for the world the unity of the German people behind the nation in the fight; and although the unity was, as Edschmid maintains, found to be unattainable, nevertheless, all classes of society were brought together in the organization: "die Wilhelmstrasse," the parliament, the Supreme Command of the army, the Social Democrats, General Moltke and Philipp Scheidemann, Max Reinhardt and Maximilian Harden, the Chancellor of the "Reich" and the Prussian Prime Minister Count Georg von Hertling.[55] Edschmid, furthermore, was not invited to speak before this group by one of its Expressionist members, but by a representative of the Foreign Office.[56] His talk found only a tepid reception here; however, it was to receive wide circulation in print, beginning with its appearance the following spring in *Die neue Rundschau* and continuing two years later with its publication in book form in the series *Tribüne der Kunst und Zeit* (1919). It was to remain, in the minds of Expressionists and literary historians alike, one of the major programmatic statements on the movement, establishing in content and style a pattern for numerous, similar statements in the years to come.[57] In the first half of 1918 Edschmid gave his program international exposure when he took a related lecture ("Über die dichterische deutsche Jugend") on a tour of three Swedish cities.[58]

The air in Berlin literary circles began to fill with excitement in this last year of the war as more and more soldiers already were returning from the field. One of these was the poet-novelist-essayist Otto Flake, whose experience on his return illustrates the conditions in the city. Flake's relationship to Expressionism as a whole can be summarized as having been until this time a position of detachment. He had spent 1916 and the first half of the next year in military service in Brussels and, then, in the second half of 1917, was able to go back to Berlin where he had lived until the war had broken out. This time he was no longer able to remain aloof from his immediate surroundings. The tow of the turbulent and animated atmosphere in the city was too strong to resist and, as he reports in his autobiography, he was thus, for the first time, induced to begin writing—consciously—in an Expressionist prose style. He says that he was living in the city now "in a nexus of tensions" (in his case some of these "tensions" stemmed from his personal life as well) and continues:

> There were not only annexationists: the Socialists split up; feelings ran high among the intellectuals. No matter how the war ended, the old days would not return. We grasped the change in our subconscious; we could not yet give it a name.
> I myself felt a strange compulsion to decompose language, to condense sentences, to look for new forms of expression. Expressionism had started these developments; for the first time I felt caught up in and swept along by the contemporary currents.[59]

His literary activities in the next few years clearly reflect this change, as he describes it himself, in thought and style.[60] Thus, as Flake makes clear, the times were unsettling in Berlin; but everywhere on the literary scene they were stimulating as much productivity as with Flake.

In the final days of the war Berlin became a center of major political developments in Germany which were to lead up to the November Revolution. At the beginning of November, 1918, there were demonstrations in the streets of the city calling for the abdication of the Kaiser. On November 9 the Revolution, which had been picking up momentum throughout Germany and the occupied territories for months, finally reached Berlin; the next day William II crossed over into Holland. The new Republic was immediately proclaimed. The Expressionists were flocking back into the city and were actively involved in large numbers in these political events as they were in other cities of Germany. Given the fact that much of their energy was thus being absorbed by political activities, and given the attendant political chaos and the growing inflation, one should, as Will Grohmann has said, have expected nothing less than a stagnation of all intellectual and artistic endeavors.[61] The direct opposite was, in fact, what did occur all over Germany, as already described in the previous chapter: the resurgence which had begun shortly before this date was not only continued, but sharply intensified; the intellectual and artistic fields, to use Grohmann's characterization again, behaved as though for them "a new spring" had begun.[62] With the lifting of censorship restrictions and the flood of returning soldiers, there was a blossoming of publishing activities especially in Berlin, for this city again led the way in every respect. In the prewar phase a total of eight Expressionist journals had appeared in Berlin; during the course of the postwar period the number was more than tripled to twenty-five.[63] In Munich (again the closest rival), in contrast, only thirteen such journals came out during this phase.[64] In series publications it was the same: nine had their home base in Berlin, only four in Munich.[65] Berlin also had the largest concentration of publishing houses showing special favor to the movement, most notably now *Der Sturm, Die Aktion,* Reiss, Cassirer, Fischer, Rowohlt and Der Malik-Verlag. The latter two were new. Der Malik-Verlag was the creation of the circle of Berlin Dadaists and was to publish primarily the literary production of the same group until the approach of the mid-1920s, by which time the company's listing was international and showed a clear preference for literature of a far left-wing political orientation.[66] The Berlin Dadaists and their publishing activities will be discussed in detail later.

The Ernst Rowohlt Verlag represented Rowohlt's first independent effort since his break with Kurt Wolff in Leipzig before the war.[67] Rowohlt was amongst the many returning to Berlin from military duty on November 9; and, as he recalled later, in the midst of the throng and tumult of the Revolution on the Potsdamer Platz he stumbled upon Hasenclever who was full of "new plans."[68] The two immediately moved together into the "Hotel Koschel" where they were joined in the next day or two by another old Leipzig friend and associate, Pinthus.[69] Encouraged largely by Lasker-Schüler's almost constant residence there, the "Hotel Koschel" had been turned into a "kind of headquarters of the Expressionists" in Berlin in those first days of the Revolution.[70] Other guests during Rowohlt's stay were Kokoschka, Theodor Däubler and Albert Ehrenstein.[71] Here, as Rowohlt says, "the most unheard-of plans were made"; and, in fact, it was here, according to Pinthus, that the idea came to Rowohlt for establishing a new home for especially Expressionist literature which was now being both created and acknowledged on a broader scale than ever before.[72] With the advice and assistance of his Leipzig friends, Rowohlt officially established his new publishing company on January 7, 1919, and already on the first day of the following month moved into his new offices in the Potsdamer Strasse to begin work.[73] Partial financial backing for the company was solicited by Pinthus from a businessman whom he had met at the beginning of the same year while staying, again with Hasenclever and Kokoschka, in the "Hotel zum Drachenfels" on "Der weisse Hirsch" in Dresden.[74] The first publications were originally conceived by Pinthus and then planned by him and Rowohlt while vacationing in the "Erzgebirge" in the spring of 1919: the first issues of the series of Expressionist broadsheets which appeared under the allusive heading *Umsturz und Aufbau* and the major anthology of Expressionist poetry, outlining the whole decade past, *Menschheitsdämmerung.*[75]

Berlin also became the focal point of the Expressionist drama in this phase. The city already had Reinhardt's "Das junge Deutschland" which strongly favored the Expressionist drama and was entering its second season during the Revolution. Then, the following year, what Pinthus has justifiably called the first actual Expressionist theater opened its doors to the public in Berlin on September 20, 1919.[76] This theater, called "Die Tribüne," was, indeed, established by its director Karlheinz Martin for the express purpose of producing only Expressionist plays and, in a much more determined and consistent manner than in Reinhardt's theater, with the intention of staging these plays in a style appropriate to them and analogous to the literary style they represented.[77] The design of the stage alone of the small theater on the "Charlottenburger Knie" in which the group produced its plays was unique and antitraditional; the aim of its design, like that of each production as a whole, was to communicate "Geist" in the Expressionist sense. To achieve this, greater depth of communication was sought between actor and audience, and this, in turn, called for a break with the still dominant traditions of the naturalistic theater of illusion: a theater-in-the round was constructed with footlights, prompter's box, curtain and wings omitted.[78]

"Die Tribüne" premièred with two plays by Hasenclever: *Der Retter* (1915) and *Die Entscheidung* (1919).[79] The selection involved a curious combination thematically, but one which was, none the less, most befitting the political confusion of those times (i.e., 1919ff.): the first play was a product of Hasenclever's most politically committed and politically optimistic period, while the second (subtitled "Komödie"!) gives a disparaging picture of revolution and of revolutionaries and came of his "mystical period" (Pinthus's label) which followed upon a loss of faith in seeking political solutions to man's problems.[80] The first production was not a complete success with the critics. Herbert Jhering, for example, although in agreement with the theater's aims and of the opinion that they best suited the demands of the times, was critical of the production, in part because of the thematic clash of the two plays, and in greatest part because he sensed an absence of a necessary degree of conviction and intensity of feeling in the poet, the director and the actors.[81] The success of the next production, however, was undisputed: Toller's *Die Wandlung,* staged on October 3, 1919, was the sensation of the season and a triumph for both the Expressionist drama and the techniques of Martin's theater; even Jhering was enthusiastic now.[82] In spite of this success, "Die Tribüne" was forced to close at the end of the year; its impact was, even so, long-lasting and its innovative stage techniques were adopted, even for the staging of the classics of the world drama, by many other directors and theaters, most prominently by Leopold Jessner at the Berlin "Staatstheater" and "Schiller-Theater."[83]

The fate of "Die Tribüne" and then, in close proximity in time, the closing of "Das junge Deutschland" at the end of its third season (August, 1920) were both symptomatic of a trend which was discussed in the previous chapter: the rapid decline of Expressionism as a *movement* immediately after as rapid an attainment of broad popularity after the war. Another sign of, or perhaps even a contributing factor to, this trend in Berlin was the city's failure to become again after the war the kind of dominant and cohesive center of the movement that it had been before this time. While there had been several very active and collectively productive artist circles here in the first phase of the movement, there were in the latter phase in point of fact only two: the Berlin Dadaists and the circle around *Der Sturm.* Cassirer had, of course, once more gathered a group of supporters around himself and his reactivated publishing company after his return from Switzerland, but the main interest of the group, as of the publishing company, was now predominantly political and not literary.[84] This was also the nature of the partially new circle around Pfemfert's *Die Aktion,* as well as of the journal itself and of its ancillary publications.[85] Furthermore, the profusion of periodicals which were appearing in Berlin in this period was misleading, for only ten of these twenty-five Expressionist organs were actually founded in the city after the war; and that small a number could almost be matched squarely by Munich now. Most of the twenty-five were either continuing from an earlier phase of the movement or had been transferred to Berlin from another center during the final phase.[86] In addition, only three of the journals actually founded in Berlin in this period were the collective creations and tribunes of a cohesive circle of contributors stationed in the city: *"Jedermann sein eigner Fussball"* (1919), *Die Pleite* (1919-20, 1923-24), *Der Dada* (1919/20), all three emanating from the same circle (the Berlin Dadaists).[87] *Der blutige Ernst* (1919) and the originally Halle-based journal *Der Gegner* (1919-22) eventually became tied to the latter group, too, but only subsequent to their founding by editors outside the group and after the appearance of several issues.[88] The great majority of the Berlin journals of this phase and of the journals appearing in other cities were drawing on the movement as a whole for their contributors rather than on a smaller coterie of associates: this fact was both an indication that Berlin was no longer the dominant center it had been previously and that ties amongst the Expressionists were now broader and more evenly spread throughout the movement. Finally, most of the Berlin journals, new and old, lasted only a year or two beyond the end of the war. Few survived the beginning of the 1920s and still fewer until the middle of the new decade, by which time only five remained active; of the five only one, *Der Sturm,* had by then retained adequate signs of adherence to Expressionism so as to warrant still being classified as an "Expressionist" journal.[89]

The end of the movement had come fast. The "Club Dada" had dissolved before the end of 1920 after only two years of activity. Cassirer's circle had already become negligible in importance and in extent of membership by the time of Cassirer's suicide in 1926. By about the same time there were similarly few signs left of a circle of associates around Walden and *Der Sturm* or around Pfemfert and *Die Aktion.* At the end of the present decade, Mühsam was able to report of seeing only a few "remnants of the old Bohemia" in the cafés of Berlin.[90]

Expressionism was, therefore, dead as a movement in Berlin as elsewhere by the middle of the 1920s. The city itself, however, did not, as a result, lose the cultural supremacy in Germany which it had originally derived from the latter movement; if anything, it now was strengthened. Berlin had become in the meantime the major center of such post-Expressionist tendencies in art and literature as the "New Objectivity" and "Socialist Realism." The twenties were to come to be known popularly in retrospect as "die goldenen Zwanzigerjahre" because of their frivolity and the frenzy of activity in them, and, culturally, this tag was to be embodied most completely, most representatively by Berlin before all other cities of Europe.[91]

3

The Artist Cafés of Berlin

In Germany or Austria in the Expressionist decade there existed few literary salons in the broad sense of an established drawing room where artists could regularly find social intercourse with their kind, could preview their works, find encouragement and patronage and exchange ideas. In the salons that were active in this period the Expressionists were at most, if at all, only sparsely represented. Berlin was no exception. Here the closest approximation of such an institution, and the only one of any prominence, was situated in the home of the publisher Samuel Fischer; it was open almost exclusively to the former Naturalists and to the more conservative writers from the generation of which the Expressionists came. Flake, who began frequenting Fischer's salon in the two years before the first World War when he was residing in Berlin, lists some of those he met here: Gerhart Hauptmann, Walter Rathenau, Thomas Mann, Arthur Schnitzler, Hugo von Hofmannsthal, Stefan Zweig, Franz Blei, Bernhard Kellermann, Jacob Wassermann, Annette Kolb, Lovis Corinth.[1] Of the latter and other artists who came, Flake, Norbert Jacques and Blei were the most noted of the few authors who had a close personal and literary association with Expressionism; significantly, however, only Blei's relationship to the movement was extensive and ran uninterruptedly throughout the Expressionist era, while Flake and Jacques were both Fischer authors during most of that same period and only sporadically in contact with the Expressionists.[2] The established literary and art societies and organizations clearly offered no alternative to the salon; they were also dominated by conservative or classical tastes and, thus, when not excluding the younger, unrecognized and unorthodox artist from their circle, they could grant him small encouragement and little freedom, artistically or socially. The Expressionists, therefore, as stated earlier, were forced to retire to the artist or literary café, to the private residence or studio of a fellow artist or to the offices of their publisher in order to find the amenities traditionally associated with the salon or artist society. Of the latter alternatives, the café became the primary focal point of the Expressionists and their circles and of their activities in the various cities of Europe where they came together.

The café, of course, had a tradition as a "waiting room of literature" (Hermann Kesten)[3] well before the Expressionists discovered it.[4] According to Emil Szittya, ubiquitous habitué of cafés all over Europe, the modern Bohemian artist café in Germany had the roots of its traditions in the Berlin tavern owned by Julius Türke, nicknamed "Zum Schwarzen Ferkel" and made famous by the group that had foregathered there around August Strindberg in the mid-1890s.[5] With Strindberg, the group's "Zentralstern" as Carl Ludwig Schleich put it, had sat here Richard Dehmel, Paul Scheerbart, Carl Ludwig Schleich, Edvard Munch, Stanislaw Przybyszewski, Julius Meier-Graefe, Otto Julius Bierbaum, Otto Erich Hartleben and others; their "unofficial" literary organ had been the journal *Pan* which members of the group had founded in 1895.[6] At least a partial confirmation of Szittya's claim can be seen in the fact that most of the members of the "Ferkel" group had, a few years later, around the beginning of our century, close contacts with circles which included a number of the subsequent elder Expressionists; in addition, Paul Scheerbart, Carl Ludwig Schleich and Julius Meier-Graefe entered, still later, into direct associations with the Expressionists apart after about 1910.[7]

In Berlin there were several cafés or similar establishments which were popular amongst the Expressionists during the era of their movement, but only a few of them were important enough to be worthy of separate mention here. Two of these, the Café Austria and the Café Sezession, had been occasional meeting places of artists for a short time prior to 1910. The Café Sezession (later known as the Café Kutschera) became a recognizably popular meeting place of artists in Berlin for a short time between about 1904 and 1906 as a result of the remodeling of the Café des Westens which had caused most of its regular guests to make a temporary exodus and establish their purlieu elsewhere.[8] A circle of friends around Schickele and Hardekopf, to which Mühsam belonged, was one of the groups that preferred the Café Sezession over the Café des Westens during that brief period.[9] The latter group will probably have also included some of the other artists and poets who are known to have been amongst Schickele's closest friends in Berlin at the time: Lasker-Schüler, Walden, Lotte Pritzel, Baron Friedrich von Schennis, Leo Kestenberg, Balder Olden, et al.[10] During the early phase of Expressionism two public recitals were given in the Café Sezession by "Das Neopathetische Cabaret" of "Der neue Club": at the first, held on November 16, 1911, the audience heard Heym, Hardekopf, Rudolf Blümner, and others read; at the second, on December 16, 1911, the performers included Hoddis, Carl Einstein, Walden, and Rudolf Kurtz.[11]

The Café Austria was a favorite meeting place of Frank Wedekind and a small circle of friends prior to Wedekind's move to Munich in 1907.[12] Before 1910, Mühsam and his friends Donald Wedekind (brother of Frank Wedekind), Franz Flaum, Peter Hille and Edvard Munch often met here.[13] In the Expressionist era this café was the scene of numerous recitals sponsored by the circles. Most of the "Autoren-Abende" sponsored by *Die Aktion* between 1911 and 1914, at which Expressionists, as guest performers and spectators both, came together from all over Europe, were held here.[14] Two evenings of the "Neopathetisches Cabaret" took place here in 1911.[15] After Hiller and Blass had seceded from "Der neue Club" and formed "Das Gnu," they continued to make use of the same café for performances of their own cabaret. One of these was attended by Lasker-Schüler, who reported an audience present that evening which numbered in the "thousands."[16] It was at another of the meetings of "Das Gnu" here, according to Meyer, that Hoddis read his famous poem "Weltende" and Heym read his equally noted ballad "Der Krieg."[17] There was clearly still some tendency to make use of the Café Austria for artistic activities as late as 1918, for in June of that year the "Club Dada" held a matinée here, at which Hausmann recited "the first phonetic poems" in German literature.[18]

Dalbelli's Italienische Weinstube is of general historical note in literary annals for having been the site of one of the first literary cabarets opened in Germany: Max Tilke's "Zum hungrigen Pegasus," at which about 1901/02 the stage could be taken by any artist who wished to read from his work.[19] The year following the demise of Tilke's cabaret, Mühsam and Hille founded in the same room the cabaret "Zum Peter Hille."[20] These events were a reflection of the popularity which Dalbelli's was enjoying amongst the younger artist bohemia in Berlin in those years.[21] It was, for example, the favorite locale of an unincorporated or independent literary group of Berlin University students ("Finken") during the time it was presided over by Döblin (around 1904).[22] Also at the beginning of our century, it was the occasional meeting place of the circle of friends around Walden and Lasker-Schüler, which included Hille and Döblin and which entertained close contacts with Richard Dehmel, Wedekind and Paul Scheerbart.[23] The core of the latter group was later to form the basis for the *Sturm* circle which was to be discovered convening at Dalbelli's on occasion in the years just prior to the war.[24]

One more café is worthy of mention in the present context: the "Zeitungscafé" called Café Josty. This establishment became of special importance for the history of Expressionism when the key meeting place of the circle around *Der Sturm* was shifted here from the Café des Westens shortly after Walden's marriage to Nell Roslund in November, 1912.[25] In the spring of 1913, the same group sponsored one of the more important events of the prewar phase of the movement in the "Choraliensaal" of this café: Marinetti's second public lecture in Berlin, which, like his first in the city, attracted great attention in the Expressionist press and public.[26] Around 1912 or 1913 a small circle of friends around Lasker-Schüler, which seems to have included, amongst others, Paul Zech and Franz Lindner, also moved their meeting place here—but only temporarily—when they were thrown out of the Café des Westens for allegedly "not eating enough."[27] Paul Boldt, a member of the circle around *Die Aktion,* immortalized this café in a poem entitled "Auf der Terrasse des Café Josty": the contents of the poem and Boldt's literary affiliations may indicate that he came here with some of the other supporters of Pfemfert.[28]

None of the cafés mentioned thus far could begin to rival the overwhelming favorite of the Expressionists and other bohemians in Berlin, the Café des Westens, whose tradition and importance in the history of modern German literature as an artist café antedates the Expressionist decade by at least ten years. It was here that Ernst von Wolzogen, sitting amongst his friends at his regular table in 1901, had planned Germany's first literary cabaret, "Die bunte Bühne," and it was here that the various performers would meet after having danced, sung, or recited on the stage of that cabaret.[29] By the beginning of the following decade, the Café des Westens was fast becoming not only the meeting place of all of the Expressionist circles centered in Berlin, but also a magnetic pole drawing artists to itself from all over Europe. Upon arriving in Berlin in these years, whether on a brief visit or for an extended sojourn, the first stop for a young artist associated with Expressionism was invariably this café. So important a role was played by this particular café in the development of Expressionism that Schickele, one of the acknowledged leaders of the movement, would say of himself and his fellow Expressionists as a whole: "Outside our circle, we were the mob from the Café Grössenwahn [=Café des Westens]."[30]

This "garden amongst the streets of Berlin," as one of its perennial guests liked to think of the Café des Westens, was located on the Kurfürstendamm, Berlin's most fashionable street in that period, where it meets the Joachimsthaler Strasse.[31] The café itself was situated on the ground floor, while on the second floor guests could play chess or billiards.[32] The overt appearance of many of the members of the regular clientele represented a stark contrast with the average passers-by; many of the men wore the traditional coiffure of revolutionary youth: long flowing locks and beard; both men and women were frequently conspicuous by their highly individual style of dress.[33] One partly tongue-in-cheek, eyewitness account describes how the doings here will have looked to the unassuming burgher timidly scurrying past this "inferno":

> The simple burgher scurries shyly and nervously past this inferno. The respectable merchant, the frugal pensioner, the brave officer, the pensive scholar, the competent theater director, the class-conscious actor, the unhurried craftsman, the conventional painter, the classical poet, the frantic wagon driver, the loyal dramaturgist, the social-climbing tennis fanatic, the spinster with suitcase in hand, and, last but not least, the unassuming ragman, all cast a timid glance through the revolutionary window panes and commend their souls to Wildenbruch and all the other good spirits of the great art exhibitions. A faint shudder ripples through their normal bodies, through their healthy blood. They saw demonic forms sitting there in the depths: men with long hair, snake-like curls, long, extravagant cravats, secessionist socks, and nonalcoholic underwear are living it up.[34]

The account appeared originally in *Der Sturm* in October, 1911, and is a more-than-slight exaggeration of fact, for it as written in response to a protest published in the established press against the Café des Westens in particular and against similar ones in Berlin in general. The controversy had originated in a trial heard before a Berlin magistrate, in the course of which it was alleged that the West Side of Berlin was being turned into a "den of infamy" ("Sumpf") by certain "undesirable elements" living there.[35] The extravagant dress and eccentric behavior of its clientele had earned for it, from the same shocked Berlin middle class, the nickname Schickele used above: "Café Grössenwahn," a nickname which the bohemians, however, transvalued and defiantly adopted themselves.[36]

According to Krell, the Café des Westens was already full by late morning with artists who sat working silently and alone at their regular tables, many of which bore beneath their glass tops drawings and sketches by these same or earlier guests.[37] During these early "working hours" the artist clientele would object vigorously to being disturbed; but later, towards evening, and especially just before and after the theater, the café became filled with the noisy excitement of lively conversation, debate and incessant "table-hopping."[38] The beginning of each week was marked by the appearance of the current issues of *Der Sturm* and *Die Aktion* which were anxiously awaited by all in the café in the evening. Meyer describes the high pitch of excitement generated by the anticipation of this event:

> It is very difficult for someone today to imagine the excitement with which we sat in the evening in the Café des Westens or out in front of Gerold's next to the Gedächtniskirche, quietly drinking our evening beer and awaiting the appearance of *Der Sturm* or *Die Aktion.* It was not so much the excitement of seeing ourselves in print as the keen anticipation of possibilities: of being attacked with words which could produce an effect like that of a powerful acid.[39]

Poets, painters, critics, philosophers, actors and directors packed the café in the evening, all intensely involved in discussions on literature, art, and related subjects. Politics, as in the other centers of Expressionists, did not as a rule become a matter for serious concern until the war.[40] The general remarks about the nature and atmosphere of life in the literary café in the first chapter apply in the most representative way to the Café des Westens: the discussions and debates, as well as other activities conducted here, in spite of the unavoidable factional disputes that will always arise in such close quarters, were outstanding for their pervasive spirit of comradeship. Blass confesses to not having begun to write seriously until after he had started to keep company with the poets who met in the Café des Westens: amongst them he found encouragement, guidance, and inspiration in his craft.[41] Here, too, as he wrote in one of the earliest (1928) memoirs on this café, he shared the sense of belonging to a literary movement, participated in the mutual edification, and felt regenerated:

> It was the café of my sorrows and inspirations, of my unsociability and my desire for fame, of my friends and my contemners, and later also of my first passion. The sorrows I shared there were those of a literary movement, the battle against the colossal philistine.... Yes, it was, indeed, a deep-felt battle against the uneventfulness, the dullness, the lethargy, the baseness of the world of the philistine. In the café the spirit of man was still of some value. Yes, you were taught to be an artist in this institution; I think back on it as on a severe school and not without a feeling of pride in having participated in it.
>
> It was a place of refuge and an unparliamentary parliament. Even the timid and reticent learned to speak and express themselves. You learned to recall to mind the things that were very important to you. It was an education in sentient truth.[42]

Like other literary cafés, the Café des Westens was both a clearing-house of ideas for the Berlin branch of Expressionism and the office in which much of its business was transacted: periodicals, such as *Der Sturm* and *Die Aktion,* were founded and planned here; recitals and similar activities were organized here; contributions to Expressionist publications from Berlin and other centers were solicited here.[43] The Café des Westens was, in short, an indispensable ingredient of daily literary life for the Berlin Expressionists. Lasker-Schüler wrote to a friend in a letter from 1910: "You know, the [Café des Westens] is our stock exchange; you have to go there because that is where you make your deals. All the dramaturgists, painters, poets go there..."[44]

The "Café des Westens" maintained its crucial role in the life of the Expressionist circles throughout the early and middle phases and into the beginning of the postwar phase.[45] Then, sometime around the beginning of 1921, the owner of the café decided to remodel and seek to attract a more distinguished clientele. The Bohemians who had monopolized it for two decades were subsequently forced out and are reported to have moved, practically *en masse,* to a café located just a short distance away, at the corner of Tauentzienstrasse and Budapesterstrasse.[46] These new headquarters were officially called "Das Romanische Café," but, as it assumed the characteristics of the older café, it very quickly inherited into the bargain the older café's nickname of "Café Grössenwahn."[47]

While this event thus interrupted a long tradition in Berlin artistic life, it came, nevertheless, at an appropriate time for the current ministers of that tradition, the Expressionists, since their movement was about this same time abruptly drawing to a close.[48] Also symptomatic of different times was the decision of the older café's proprietor to pay court to the new prosperous class of Berlin, the nouveaux riches or, as one chronicler put it, the "Kurfürstendammschieber."[49] The sole reminder of the bohemian period of the Café des Westens after the removal of the Expressionists was the "Kabarett Grössenwahn," which was installed here by the proprietor under the direction of the veteran actress Rosa Valetti and with the financial backing of Dr. Eugen Robert, a director for "Die Tribüne."[50]

Although the café by this time was no longer the unchallenged center of Expressionist literary life that it had been before the war, still, Das Romanische Café performed much the same function for these same artists which the older café had: again heated debates on a variety of subjects are conducted here far into the night, and again collective activities, such as the founding of periodicals, are carried on at the respective "Stammtische."[51] The circles active in Berlin following the war were already beginning to dissolve by this time and relationships between the Expressionists as a whole were becoming less close and more desultory: this fact might explain why there are few references in reports on Das Romanische Café to specific circles by name. However, many individual faces familiar from the older café are spotted here again: Nell Walden, John Höxter, Theodor Däubler, Silvia von Harden, Meidner, Frank, Mühsam, Lasker-Schüler, Rudolf Levy, Blei, Otten, Huelsenbeck, Schreyer, Salomo Friedlaender, Benn and many others.[52] The presence of guests, such as the latter, might indicate the presence as well of the circles with which they were affiliated.

Two circles not sighted earlier in the Café des Westens are reported meeting in the new café in the 1920s. The first of these centered around the older painters Emil Orlik and Max Slevogt; they were often joined by the painter Max Oppenheimer, the poet Däubler and the humorist Alexander Roda Roda.[53] The second group was made up mostly of contributors to the journal *Die neue Bücherschau,* which in primarily its first publishing year, under the editorship of Hans Theodor Joel (1919-22), had close ties with Expressionist literature.[54] Members of this group appear to have included Egon Erwin Kisch, Max Herrmann-Neisse, Becher, Leo Lania and the Dutch newspaper correspondent Nico Rost, who, while stationed in Berlin in this period, became a close friend of Benn and Carl Einstein.[55]

Das Romanische Café remained an artist café well beyond the demise of Expressionism, becoming the meeting place of writers and painters representing more recent tendencies in art and literature. At the end of the 1920s, however, a few of the adherents of the former movement are still to be seen sitting here amongst the many newcomers.[56]

4

"Der Neue Club"

About 1907 Hiller was joined by Hoddis in a non-fencing student fraternity, "Die Freie Wissenschaftliche Vereinigung," which was affiliated with Berlin University.[1] The activities and interests of Hiller, Hoddis, and a few other friends in the fraternity were predominantly intellectual, while those of the other members, Hiller says, were "feuchtfröhlich."[2] It was thus not long before Hiller and his friends had formed a distinct, radical and intellectual faction within the fraternity.[3] After several frustrating clashes with the other members, Hiller's faction finally seceded and in March, 1909, founded its own organization, appropriately named "Der neue Club."[4]

The new group immediately began meeting every Wednesday evening in the "Fledermauszimmer," a restaurant located in the Nollendorf-Kasino on the Kleiststrasse in Berlin; here the members held long discussions on art and contemporary society and shared with one another the products of their latest literary efforts.[5] At their first organizational meeting that spring, Hiller was elected permanent president; in attendance already, besides Hiller, were Erwin Loewenson, Hoddis, John Wolfsohn, Erich Unger, Robert Majut.[6] They were already by this time united to a man ideologically by their mutual opposition to the prevaling social and cultural conditions in the Wilhelminian era, and, because they aimed also to actively oppose these conditions now, they were anxious to recruit more supporters in their battle.[7] At the beginning of the winter semester 1909/10 a notice was attached to the student bulletin board in Berlin University announcing the first public meeting of "Der neue Club" for November 8 that fall and including a general appeal for a broader audience.[8] The already strong programmatic spirit in the group was further amplified and given more concrete form at this first public meeting in the polemical and philosophical statements with which Loewenson and Hiller opened the evening.[9] The most tangible outcome of this and subsequent gatherings in the next few months was the addition of several new members, until the regular membership totaled sixteen; besides those mentioned so far, they were: Friedrich Schulze-Maizier, Wilhelm S. Guttman (Ghuttmann), Armin Wassermann, Ernst Engert, Heym, Blass, David Baumgardt, Arthur Drey, Robert Jentzsch, and Friedrich Koffka.[10] Three other young poets of similar literary and philosophical bent, Armin T. Wegner, Heinrich Eduard Jacob and Rudolf Kurtz, were closely associated with this circle and were frequent participants in its activities, but they were evidently not regular members.[11]

It has been reported variously that Hiller's circle met as a group regularly in the Café des Westens, i.e., in addition to the Wednesday sessions in the Nollendorf-Kasino; although the specific members involved in this context are not mentioned by name in the reports, it can be assumed that most, if not all, of the regular members of the group were usually present.[12] Those individual members who are definitely known to have been habitués of the Café des Westens, at least during its heyday from about 1910 to the beginning of the war, were Hiller, Loewenson, Hoddis, Guttmann, Heym, Koffka, Blass, Baumgardt, Jentzsch, H.E. Jacob, Wegner, and Kurtz.[13]

The circle in "Der neue Club" was dominated over by the personality and intellect of Hiller.[14] He was best remembered by those that were close to him in this period for the sharp logical turn of his mind, for his mastery of the art of debate, as a skillful composer of polemical pamphlets (usually written in defense of the new literature) and as a propagator of the so-called "fortgeschrittene Lyrik," a prewar term for what was later called "expressionistische Lyrik."[15] Hiller's influence was to extend gradually deep into Expressionism as a whole and he was eventually to play a pivotal role in the movement by reason of both his ideas and his person. Edschmid has written of him, for example:

> No matter how one might judge him from a distance, Kurt Hiller is an indispensible part of pre-World War One literary life. The literature of the previous generation groaned under the hailstorm of attacks which he launched with a freshness and audacity, with a shrewdness and maliciousness that squarely hit their marks.[16]

Hiller was a rarely absent and not easily ignored member of the literary life in the Café des Westens from 1910 on and into the war. His friendships and activities there were not restricted to his own particular circle; his contacts reached into most of the other circles that met there and to many of the individuals who came there before the war, especially the circles around *Der Sturm* and *Die Aktion* and the poets Wegner, Benn, Lasker-Schüler, Hardekopf, Zech, Ludwig Rubiner, Hasenclever and Werfel.[17] Hiller was one of the most gregarious of those associated with Expressionism, and this fact, combined with his very aggressive personality, will have borne a large share of the responsibility for the spread of his own influence as well as of that of "Der neue Club." His store of political and sociological knowledge was extensive, as attested to by his contemporaries and by his writings, such as his large compendium on prewar literature and society entitled *Die Weisheit der Langenweile*.[18] It was especially in those areas, politics and sociology, that his impact was most strongly felt in his own circle and in others. Schulze-Maizier, to cite a most patent example, later recalled the leading role which Hiller played in his political education after he had joined "Der neue Club."[19]

Another leading and very influential figure, but in a more strictly literary sense, in the club and in Expressionism was Hoddis. Hiller wrote of Hoddis that he considered him "the poetically most powerful representative" of the views espoused by the club.[20] As have Pfemfert, Pinthus, Becher, and others, Hiller has also credited Hoddis with creating not only the style of lyric that became characteristic of the poets in "Der neue Club" who called themselves "Neopathetiker," but with contributing as well, in a major way, to the creation of the Expressionist style of lyric in general, a style associated with conciseness and concentration of language, with stark and unexpected images and the use of the technique of "simultaneity."[21]

Judging from the statements of contemporaries, Hoddis's influence would appear to have been based almost solely on the impact of one single poem: "Weltende."[22] This now famous poem of just eight short lines, with which Pinthus's *Menschheitsdämmerung* opens, was reportedly able to exercise a powerfully disturbing effect on the reader or listener of its day.[23] The poem was first published on January 11, 1911, in *Der Demokrat* (at that time under the editorship of Pfemfert), although it had long before that date become known to Hiller's circle and had probably been recited already by Hoddis for the general public in the club's cabaret.[24] Becher has acknowledged his debt to the poem for contributing to his early development as a poet.[25] He describes in a memoir on Hoddis the effect of it on himself and his fellow poets when it appeared as hypnotic and haunting:

> I do not have the literary talent to recreate the effect of the poem I want to talk about now. It would stretch even the wildest dreams of my readers to breaking-point were I to attempt an account of the magic there was for us in that poem by Jakob van Hoddis, "End of the World." These two stanzas, these eight lines, seem to have transformed us into different beings, to have carried us up out of a world of apathetic bourgeoisie which we despised and which we did not know how to leave behind. These eight lines helped us escape. We kept discovering new beauties in these eight lines; we sang them, we hummed them, we murmured them, we whistled them to ourselves. We went to church with these eight lines on our lips and we sat whispering them to ourselves at the cycle races. We shouted them to each other across the street like catchwords; we sat together with each other so that the hunger and cold ceased to exist. What had happened? In those days we did not know the word: metamorphosis.[26]

Many others in Becher's generation drew on the poem as a model for their verse, particularly Blass and Lichtenstein.[27] Lichtenstein first made the break with traditional forms in the lyric and began to turn towards new modes of expression after his contact with Hoddis and with Hoddis's style in "Weltende."[28] Lichtenstein's poem "Dämmerung," written and published shortly after this experience, most clearly illustrates his indebtedness to Hoddis: it is composed of the same short, paratactic lines, the same abrupt vaulting with each successive line from one stark, unconventional image to the next; each image and the poem as a whole call forth the same forboding of impending catastrophy (cf. the frequently recurring, related motif of "der jüngste Tag," the Day of Judgement, in Expressionism in general); even the titles of both poems are alike in their evocation of the arrival of a time of radical transformation.[29] As Kurt Mautz points out in his study of Heym, Hoddis's "Weltende" also no doubt inspired Heym's treatment of the same motif in a similar style in such poems as "Der Gott der Stadt," "Umbra vitae" and "Der Krieg."[30]

Of an influence equal to that of a Hoddis or a Hiller, as members have claimed, was the general atmosphere created within "Der neue Club" by the membership as a whole. The clearest testimonial to this fact is given by Hiller's closest friend and associate in the group, Blass. Blass had been introduced to the club by Jacob in the first half of 1910, shortly after Blass had become a regular in the Café des Westens.[31] Like Hiller, Blass was to establish broad associations on the literary scene in Berlin, having most frequent intercourse before the war outside "Der neue Club" with the Walden and Pfemfert circles and with the writers Hardekopf, Schickele, Leonhard Frank, Einstein, Döblin, Rubiner, Herzog, Kurtz, Leo Matthias, and Alfred Wolfenstein.[32] Blass himself later admitted, however, that the decisive turn in his development as a writer did not come until after his introduction to "Der neue Club" and the beginning of a close association with its members. From this point in time dates the real commencement for Blass of a serious concern with literature; in this circle, before the background of the "Café des Westens," Blass found himself as a writer:

> The Club members frequented the Café des Westens, called Café Megalomania by the philistines. I went there too now, sat with the others, was invited by Dr. Hiller to become a member. I accepted gladly, although I felt very young and insecure and regarded the others as older, more qualified to judge, better versed in philosophy, perhaps because they were, perhaps only because they spoke authoritatively.
>
> How I came into my own I scarcely know. I was encouraged, made to write poems and reviews. Things began to snowball. People asked: Have you written anything new this week? Blass poems appeared, at first playful and imitative, then with more feeling, more self-consciousness. But of how it all came about I have as little awareness as the Baron in *The Lower Depths*. It came to pass, I did it timidly, just to see how it would turn out.[33]

Loewenson has described in detail the equally decisive role played by the club in the development of the fourth major figure to come out of this circle, Heym.[34] Heym was introduced into "Der neue Club" around March, 1910, by Wilhelm Guttmann, shortly after he had responded to an advertisement placed by Guttmann in the *Berliner Tageblatt*.[35] Guttmann was at that time in the process of establishing a new theater group, called "Neue Bühne," as a tribune for the plays of new, young dramatists, and had placed an advertisement in the

Berlin paper soliciting manuscripts. Heym submitted the manuscript of his one-act tragedy *Die Hochzeit des Bartolomeo Ruggieri.*[36] Although Guttmann was not interested in producing Heym's play, he took the young, unrecognized poet instead to a meeting of "Der neue Club."[37] Heym was in this way drawn out of a literary isolation which traced back to his earliest literary efforts.[38] Like the others who joined the club, he found encouragement, guidance and appreciation and became involved in the constant discussions on literature and related topics.[39] He was thus brought into contact with both the thought and works of philosophers of the day and with the whole main stream of Expressionist literature and literary life in Berlin; he subsequently established close contacts with the circle around Walden and especially with the one around Pfemfert.[40] The very first publication of poetry by Heym issued from a contact he made within the club shortly after joining. On July 6, 1910, he made his first appearance in the club's "Neopathetisches Cabaret."[41] Jacob, who had also read in the cabaret on that same evening, began taking a personal interest in Heym the following day when he noted on a stroll with him through the park how downtrodden he was because of his lack of notoriety.[42] Jacob was at that time theater critic for the Berlin weekly *Der Herold,* and, after several unsuccessful attempts to get Heym's poetry accepted by Berlin journals of greater note, he used his influence to have two of his peoms brought out in the October 1, 1910, issue of his own small paper.[43] Heym's contacts with Pfemfert bore similar fruit: Pfemfert threw his support behind Heym, first in *Der Demokrat* (November 23, 1910) and later in *Die Aktion,* the very first issue of which (February 20, 1911) contained verse by Heym.[44] The appearance of his poetry in *Der Demokrat* brought him to the attention of Ernst Rowohlt in Leipzig who published the first full volume of his poetry the following year.[45]

As his contemporaries and his confederates in "Der neue Club" have interpreted him—and a similar impression is gathered from a careful reading of his journals—Heym came to the club as a very ingenuous, uncerebral, basically intuitively oriented individual, "healthy" in his instincts but lacking in intellectual depth.[46] Hiller, for example, wrote of him:

> He was in every respect a very instinctual type. It was precisely the Faustian element in the Goethean sense which his personality lacked. Of course, as I have already said, he had a soul, as square-shooting as it was physical; always open and honest, often gruff but never scheming, a thoroughly straightforward fellow. But he was in no respect philosophical; in spite of all the—if you like—profundity of his visions, he was basically unintellectual, at least as remote as any burgher from the logicistic, conceptual form of intellectuality. He was unproblematical.[47]

Heym did not need to alter his character in the above respect in order to find acceptance in the club, for it was largely because of the qualities outlined by Hiller above that he exercised an especially strong attraction on those members who—again Hiller is our interpreter—were notably "hyperintellectual and crippled in their instincts," i.e., those who were never able to come to proper terms with either their sexuality or with their philosophy.[48] His closest friends in the club, therefore, became Baumgardt, Loewenson, Guttmann, Hoddis, Jentzsch, and Schulze-Maizier.[49] Hiller and Blass, while they, like all the members of the club, both "loved and admired" Heym, were not able to identify completely with the type of poet he represented, for they advocated a form of lyric poetry that did not exclude, as they felt his did, "the experiences of philosophical man," the thinking man.[50]

Within the broader circle, Heym, Baumgardt, and Schulze-Maizier constituted a smaller, yet more intimate, band of their own. Soon after the trio had been completed by the addition of Heym and Baumgardt, both in early 1910, they began taking lengthy trips together into the outskirts of Berlin, all during which they continued the discussions begun within the confines of the club.[51] Baumgardt has recorded the subject of their long conversations on these excursions; it reflected the extent to which the concerns of the club pervaded the members' lives as a whole:

> The theme of our conversations was in particular our outrage at the lack of intense feelings in contemporary poetry and in contemporary middle-class thought, our solidarity with Loewenson's program, the "phalanx of a new, a second pathos" after the intellectual satiety and skepticism of our elder contemporaries.[52]

The effect on Heym's character and on his work of this new, intimate association with an enthusiastic circle of poets dominated by a programmatic spirit was expectedly marked. Loewenson has pointed especially to the circle's role in helping Heym, on the model of the program of the club, to achieve a total expression of his own particular personality and to cast off the restraints of convention.[53] There was a great, reciprocally fructifying camaraderie in the club, which even extended into the members' personal associations with one another outside the club meetings; soon after his reception into the club, Heym began to respond to its atmosphere:

> Heym was accepted into the club immediately. His quick reflex reaction changed the content and form of his poetry, and changed him, too. The "mask" of the "robust fellow," with which he entered the club and which he saw greeted with a happy smile, ceased to be merely a mask: his ostentatious robustness, tempered by an air of self-irony, becomes second nature to him.[54]

Thus, as in Blass's case, the club essentially helped Heym find himself— Loewenson at another point in his study calls the change "a breakthrough of his self"—and his own individual style, by effecting the filling out of his character and style with a quality which had formerly been only a pose. Loewenson emphasizes that this change was only made possible because Heym found himself surrounded by a group of enthusiastic, confident, optimistic, and independent young poets.[55] Loewenson justifiably sees this change reflected most clearly in entries made by the young poet about this same time in his diary, especially in the more optimistic and cheerful opening of the third volume, dated June 17, 1910 (i.e., about two months after joining the club), which contrasts sharply with the predominantly morose tone of the previous volumes:

> I began my third journal perhaps under more favorable prospects. I intend, in fact, not to start another one....
>
> In general, I am now happier, calmer than in the past. I am adopting the robust style of personality which surrounds me like a fortress.[56]

It is noteworthy also that in the same entry, in the paragraph that follows the ones just cited from, Heym thinks he is now for the first time able to define the source of the unhappiness that has visited him for so long, an unhappiness he had sought in vain to explain to himself in an entry in the previous volume of his journal (July 20, 1909). The source, he feels, lies in the "complete uneventfulness," in the lethargic spirit of the times, and he asks: "Why not start a revolution?"[57] Here and in the entries of like import in the weeks to come, he may very well be reflecting the similar content of the discussions in the club and those he was beginning to have about this time, as noted above, with his friends Baumgardt and Schulze-Maizier on their excursions together. Gunter Martens has pointed out that it is also around this time that a new development appears in Heym's poetry. His poetry now begins to reveal marked features which are eventually to be associated with Expressionism: his language becomes more concise, more concentrated and more figurative, his subject matter becomes more contemporaneous as he turns to a concern with, for example, modern urban life and to a preoccupation with the theme of a premonition of imminent doom, which Loewenson calls the "basic theme" in "Der neue Club" as a whole.[58] Furthermore, he hits his stride now and begins to turn out the poems which will establish his fame: the sonnets on the French Revolution, the poems dealing with the dead and, in April, 1910, the first Berlin poems.[59]

Jacob Picard, who was a member of the Heidelberg circle around Blass and *Die Argonauten* (January, 1914-December, 1916; December, 1921) just prior to the war, has suggested that the programmatic spirit which was characteristic of Expressionism was exemplified best by "Der neue Club."[60] Schulze-Maizier noted some very tangible signs of this spirit already at the very first public meeting of the club on November 8, 1909, at which Schulze-Maizier was most struck and attracted by the high degree of enthusiasm generated mutually by the participants.[61] The foundation of the program and aims of the club was, in fact, laid down at that meeting in the talks given by Loewenson ("Die Dekadenz der Zeit und der 'Aufruf' des Neuen Clubs") and Hiller ("Das Wesen der Kultur").[62] At the core of the program was the concept of "neues

Pathos," a term which the club adopted from the essay of the same name published shortly before the meeting in question by Stefan Zweig in *Das literarische Echo.*[63] Loewenson defines the concept as a state of heightened emotion, but one which was not to be carried to the extreme of frenzy or mental imbalance, rather was to be a state of heightened emotion under the control of the intellect, a synthesis of both body and mind, feeling and thought:

> Our "new pathos" was, to begin with, like any state of profound excitement, but not only of the emotions, like the old, intellectually dependent and therefore all the more hollow-sounding "pathetics".... But a new form which neither excluded the intellect nor found a place for it as we had learned as students, only within the framework of theory and a complicated, historically well-founded doctrine.
>
> We faced life itself, as we encountered it in more or less pleasant forms in all fields, with the self-assurance of youthful vivacity.[64]

This new attitude was to be manifested in the activities of the club and spread abroad by its members in a "regenerative movement" ("Regenerations-bewegung") directed against what they saw as the apathy and decadence, the general lack of vitality in contemporary society.[65] Through the vehicle of their literature, of which the lyric was to be held in highest esteem, the members of the club avowedly aspired to arouse their audiences and readers from their lethargy, before what these poets foresaw as an impending apocalypse could become a reality. In the broadest sense, therefore, "Der neue Club," like all of the Expressionists, sought to change the world through the instrument of the poetic word.[66]

Nietzsche's thought provided much of the foundation for Expressionism, and "Der neue Club" was certainly no exception. The philosopher's name was consistently displayed on the club's banner: he was often cited as an authority, as in that announcement of the first public meeting posted at the University of Berlin, and there were readings from his works at recitals sponsored by the club. Members of the group have acknowledged the debt owed him by the club.[67] The central concept of the club, "neues Pathos," parallels itself a concept likewise central to Nietzsche's thought. Hiller drew this parallel himself in the talk "Das Cabaret und die Gehirne" which he gave at the first performance of the club's cabaret (June 1, 1910).[68]

Having first defined the concept of "neues Pathos" here in a way synonymous with Loewenson's definition, Hiller cites a passage from Nietzsche's *Ecce Homo* to demonstrate the philosopher's agreement with the club's interpretation of the phenomenon:

> ... ich schätze den Wert von Menschen, von Rassen danach ab, wie notwendig sie den Gott nicht abgetrennt vom Satyr zu verstehen wissen.
>
> (*Ecce Homo,* Chap. 4)

I measure the value of people, of races, according to how unnecessary they think the separation is of god and satyr.

Hiller's reference is defensible, for the satyr in Nietzsche's mind is associated with Dionysus (in *Die Geburt der Tragödie aus dem Geiste der Musik*, Chap. 7, he calls this figure "der dionysische Choreut") and "god," at the other extreme, is equated with Apollo. Nietzsche's famous dialectic of the Apollinian and the Dionysian coincides, in a narrow sense (Nietzsche's poles are actually much more encompassing), with Loewenson's poles of "feeling" and "intellect"; and Nietzsche, like the members of "Der neue Club," saw the ideal condition, which for him was realized in Greek tragedy, as lying in a synthesis of the two poles.[69] In *Die Geburt der Tragödie aus dem Geiste der Musik* Nietzsche describes the synthesis as a "confraternity" formed by the two deities of Dionysus and Apollo (chap. 21) and summarizes, at the end of that work, their mutually beneficial relationship in the ideal condition:

> Dabei darf von jenem Fundamente aller Existenz, von dem dionysischen Untergrunde der Welt, genau nur so viel dem menschlichen Individuum ins Bewusstsein treten, als von jener appollinischen Verklärungskraft wieder überwunden werden kann, so dass diese beiden Kunsttriebe ihre Kräfte in strenger wechselseitiger Proportion, nach dem Gesetze ewiger Gerechtigkeit, zu entfalten geötigt sind.
>
> (Chap. 25)

> At the same time, an individual's consciousness can only accomodate as much of the foundation of all existence, of the Dionysian substratum of the world, as can be subdued in turn by that Apollinian transfigurative force, so that these two artistic impulses are forced to develop their energy in strict, mutual proportions according to the law of constant equity.

Ernst Blass cites the writings of Sigmund Freud as another important source of the circle's thinking. An incident reported by Loewenson demonstrates that Freud at least was the subject of discussion within the club.[70] In literature, the club members reportedly admired in particular Heinrich Mann, Kerr, Karl Kraus, Stefan George, Wedekind, and Brod.[71] The club's admiration for Brod led to the sponsorship of an evening in his honor on November 19, 1910, at which Brod read from his play *Die Höhe des Gefühls*.[72] A great stimulus to the work of the club, according to Blass again, was provided by Blei's journals *Der lose Vogel* (1912/13) and *Hyperion* (1908-10).[73]

"Der neue Club" differed from most other Expressionist circles in that it sponsored no periodical, yearbook, or other continuing publication as a forum for its program and literature. There had, however, been plans for such a publication which were beginning to materialize in 1914. Loewenson was leading an effort at this time to found a tribune for the circle under the name *Neopathos*. The first number had been put together out of contributions by members of the club and was to have included illustrations by artists from the

"Brücke" group, with which the club, primarily through the mediation of Guttmann, had established close contacts after the painters' move to Berlin from Dresden.[74] As that first number reached the stage of galley proofs, the war broke out and the plans for the journal were quashed altogether.[75]

Loewenson's abortive effort had probably been the outcome of plans for a journal of the club in which Zech reported having participated as early as 1910 and 1911.[76] Zech's home in that period was in Elberfeld, but he had begun corresponding by mail with Heym about a new journal and had then arranged to meet him in a Berlin café in the course of a trip east which would take him through Berlin. Zech was met that day in the café by Heym, Hoddis, Jentzsch and by Heym's close friend Ernst Balcke. The project was further discussed and planned during that meeting; titles for the journal were proposed: Heym suggested *Neopathos* and Jentzsch *Neue Jugend;* contributors were decided upon, including, besides those present, Lasker-Schüler, Blass, Mynona (=Salomo Friedlaender), Paul Scheerbart, Alfred Mombert, and Schickele.[77] After Zech's return to Elberfeld, the discussion was continued by mail; but Heym's untimely death in January of 1912 put an abrupt end to the correspondence.[78] Zech eventually moved permanently to Berlin; and in 1913, as he was to claim in a memoir written four decades later, that earlier plan was finally realized when he began to coedit with Hans Ehrenbaum-Degele, Robert Schmidt, and Ludwig Meidner a periodical called *Das neue Pathos* (1913-14; 1920).[79]

Loewenson must have been involved in, or at least privy to, the earlier plans for a journal of the club; and so it would appear that both the Zech journal and the one being put to press by Loewenson in the next year were the products of the same original plans. If that was indeed the case, Zech's *Das neue Pathos* was, nonetheless, an independent effort and cannot be considered to have been a tribune of "Der neue Club," for, although its title and to some extent its program were related to the club, only two of the club's members were represented in its pages.[80]

The club's sole public organ as well as its main collective activity remained the literary cabaret which it established in the summer of 1910.[81] At the series of performances held in "Das neopathetische Cabaret" between June 1, 1910, and April 3, 1912, members of the club, and guest artists of a similar literary tendency, read from their works, presented talks of a philosophical or programmatic nature, or gave musical recitals.[82] Loewenson states that the club intentionally chose the "almost frivolous" form of a literary cabaret as its platform because of the medium's inherent combination of audacity and colorfulness through which, with the spirit of "neues Pathos," the club could best combat both the "central apathy" and the "hollow pathos" of contemporary culture.[83] The adjective in the title of the cabaret was important, Loewenson states, for it was to indicate a unity of the performers under the concept of "neues Pathos" and, at the same time, was meant to reflect the intention of manifesting in every piece recited that synthesis of intellect and feeling which "neues Pathos" connotes:

> A synthetic fusion of artistic-intuitive intentions and those which acknowledge and desire centrality was to be present in every product in this "Neopathetisches Cabaret."[84]

The cabaret was ultimately conceived of as a means through which a broader audience could be reached and additional supporters recruited for the club's "regenerative movement."[85] It proved to be a very successful venture, in at least the first regard, for, while the crowds were reportedly at times hostile, reviewers wrote of seeing extremely large audiences at the performances.[86] The cabaret also attracted leading Expressionists both as guest artists (e.g., Lasker-Schüler, Walden, Rudolf Blümner, Hardekopf, and Carl Einstein) and as regular spectators and supporters (e.g., Benn, Lasker-Schüler, Friedlaender, Meyer, Alfred Wolfenstein, Zech, Ernst Wilhelm Lotz, and Pfemfert).[87] There is at least one definite testimony to direct literary influence stemming from the performances in the club's cabaret. C.F.W. Behl, a writer and critic associated with Berlin Expressionism, reports that his first encounter with the movement was made here in the readings given by Heym in 1910; and Behl immediately sensed that the "neues Pathos" manifested by Heym's verse represented a "decisive turn," "ein Umbruch und Aufbruch," in literary tradition.[88]

Initially, the members of the club were united in a body by the high pitch of enthusiasm with which they rallied to the support of the club's program and its activities; their enthusiasm permitted them to overlook or suppress disagreements that might otherwise have arisen on certain details in the further elaboration of the program. That was the situation at least in the beginning. However, in time cracks began to appear in the foundation of the club, especially after Heym's entrance and the subsequent division of sentiment amongst the club's members on him and his work.[89] By the early part of 1911, Hiller says, over differences which were in part personal and in part intellectual in nature, the club had been split into two factions, with Hiller and Blass ranged on the one side and Loewenson, Heym, Hoddis and most of the others posted on the opposing side.[90]

Hiller has reported that on the intellectual level the division of the circle was directly related to the specific divergence of opinion on the figure of Heym which was discussed above.[91] It was essentially a matter of an imbalance of interest, for, as Hiller phrased it, the excessive attraction which Heym had been able to exercise over certain members of the club had meant the neglect of the intellectual side of man and insufficient communication between the philosophical and the athletic types of man.[92] It was, in other words, a difference in *practice* and not, as Gunther Martens has claimed in his essay on Heym and "Der neue Club," one in *theory*.[93] Martens has asserted that the schism in the club can be traced back in origin to the divergence in world views as expressed by Loewenson and Hiller in their talks opening the first public meeting of the club on November 8, 1909.[94] According to Martens, Loewenson in his talk put forth a basically irrationalistic world view which was determined not "intellectually" but "voluntaristically," while Hiller in his talk delineated a rationalistic direction of mind, pinnacling the "ideational" ("das Ideeliche").[95] In Martens's view, therefore, the positions of Loewenson and Hiller were diametrically opposed from the start and had inevitably to lead in the end to a break within the club. This view amounts, of course, to inferring the absence of any ideological unity within the club. Since it is the claim of the present study that such a unity did in fact exist, specifically behind the concept of "neues Pathos," it is necessary to consider in more detail the positions of Loewenson and Hiller, both of which revolve around the concept of "neues Pathos."

Loewenson's original talk, from which Martens was able to cite in manuscript, is as yet still unpublished. However, Martens's interpretation of Loewenson's position is not borne out by Loewenson's statements on "neues Pathos" in either his study of Heym or in his short essay "Bemerkungen über das 'Neopathos'"; nor is Martens' interpretation of Hiller's philosophy borne out by a close reading of Hiller's essay "Über Kultur," which, since when published for the second time in *Die Weisheit der Langenweile* it was dated "November, 1909" (the month and year of that first public meeting), can safely be assumed to be the published (and no doubt expanded) version of his original talk.[96]

Loewenson's definition of "neues Pathos" as a synthesis of "intellect" and "feeling" has already been cited from his study of Heym.[97] He states further in the same work that what Heym was confronted with upon joining the club in the spring of 1910 was, ideologically, a viewpoint of "totality."[98] As defined by Loewenson, "totality" represents the ideal condition of being which encompasses and unites all sides of man's character and establishes a center within him from which all inclinations and impulses proceed; this condition is opposed to one in which the individual's body and mind are divided, whose impulses, having two possible sources, may, therefore, conflict:

> He [Heym] discovers a new type of aspect of totality as a program and criterion for standards, both in weekly debates and in poetic and theoretical offerings. It is an aspect of totality which derives from productive vitality, does not shy away from an uninhibited expression of feeling, which includes a humor of vital affirmation, which combines the uncanny and the grotesquely tragicomical features of existence. He discovers a striking uniformity of values and wills in the turbulent, light-heartedly serious and polemical medley of the 'Neopathetisches Cabaret'.... He feels motivated to effect a centralizing fusion of his poetic, republican-political, and his innately religious inclinations.[99]

In the essay "Bemerkungen über das 'Neopathos'" Loewenson labels the "totality" a "total synthesis" which, once having become second nature ("instinktiv- und organisch-werdend") to man, will restore to him the "centrality" of character which he has lost in our age:

Even the new pathos manifesto aimed to initiate a regenerative movement which for once would be thought through objectively and be methodically implemented and which would transcend personal and intellectual concerns. The necessary precondition for this movement was a total synthesis which would gradually become instinctual and organic and, in manifest phenomena, even provide rational convictions with access to the super-rational. Only with the help of this total synthesis can the "centrality" ruptured by our age be made operative again.[100]

Heym, according to Loewenson, became a leading example of this "total synthesis" or "totality" of character following upon his entry into the club and the changes it wrought on his personality.[101]

Hiller's position on these questions is seen, on close examination of his statements of his own world view, to be the exact equivalent of Loewenson's. Hiller stated in an epistolary report on Heym, written in 1946 for Carl Seelig, that at the time of Heym's entry into the club Hiller also nurtured the longing for the "Hellenic ideal of harmony," or synthesis of the physical and intellectual sides of man's character:

Even then, although it was largely unconscious, I harbored the *hellenic* ideal of harmonious balance of physical and intellectual perfection. At any rate, the (let's say) *athletic* type of man was at that time, *au-delà de la littérature,* not an object of resentment but of sympathy. How could he have seemed objectionable to me within the framework of literature, provided only the philosophical channel communicated with the athletic![102]

Hiller's memory was not in error; that the "Hellenic ideal" did play a crucial role in the formation of his world view around the time of the inception of "Der neue Club" is unmistakable. Since, on the other hand, this ideal was largely subconscious at the time, as Hiller says above, his expression of it in his writings from the same period cannot be expected to have been in as explicit terms as those used by Loewenson.

In the essay "Über Kultur" from November, 1909, Hiller, by way of agreeing with Georg Simmel, postulates in terms of an imbalance in contemporary man between his objective and subjective life what Loewenson called the "lost centrality" of modern man.[103] When a culture is at a low level or early stage of development, Hiller states here, man's objective and subjective life coincide or are in equilibrium, i.e., man is able to subjectively assimilate, readily and fully, the externals (what Simmel called the "objects") of his particular culture. When, in contrast, a society, such as Wilhelminian Germany, becomes hyperrefined to the point that it overwhelms man with its external complications, then man is unable to achieve a proper balance between his subjective and objective life.[104] Hiller sees this latter condition as a major problem in his day:

The acute alienation of objectified intellect and individual culture seems to me to be one of the most reprehensible failings of our age. What good does all the ostentatious display of differentiation and abundance if no one can partake of it.[105]

Rejecting as unrealistic any Rousseauistic wishes to return to a simpler, more natural life, Hiller sees the solution to the contemporary malaise in the individual's striving to absorb into his nature not the contents of this hyperrefined culture, which Hiller considers impossible to absorb, but the form or manner of it, i.e., to absorb its quality rather than its quantity.[106] This solution and the process it involves is subjective; but culture, he contends, is something which can only be grasped subjectively through feeling and not through logic:

> Thus, "culture," that so often and so terribly misused expression, remains the name for a degree of refinement of movements and functions which are scarcely comprehensible logically and yet emotionally quite specific.[107]

Having once integrated the manner or form of his culture into his personality and fused it with the self "organically" so that it becomes a "universal" determinant of his behavior, i.e., so that it becomes second nature to him—we are reminded of Loewenson's "instinktiv- und organisch-werdende Gesamtsynthese"—then man will have regained a "totality" of character in which all of his powers—those of the nonintellectual side, such as "art," "experience," "feeling," and those on the intellectual side, such as "knowledge," the "problematical," "thought"—are brought together in harmony:

> The formula "culture" will be transformed into the highest form of praise, besides that for creativity, which we can bestow on someone, if the idea of the "cultured" individual is realized by adding to the ethos of refinement the requirement that this refinement become a characteristic of all experience, of all activities, that it permeate one's personality, that it be *universal* instead of being limited only to thought, feeling, sociological behavior or some other particular capacity....
>
> Art and perception, experience and problem solving, feeling and thought blend, embrace, and permeate each other with such feverish intensity, with such chemism, that the "classicistic" requirement—as imposed in especially clear terms by Leonard Nelson (in volume two of *Die Fries'sche Schule*)—that both functions be developed in strict separation, in peaceful coordination, without "incursions" of the one into the territory of the other, seems like a constraint, because its intention is to regress one stage in our psychic and anthropological development, to transform a condition of complexity and refinement into one of simplicity and robustness, to substitute poverty for wealth.[108]

Hiller makes it clear that he rejects any excess emphasis on the intellect, for he attacks in "Über Kultur" those thinkers, especially scientists and scholars, who rely solely on the extreme form of intellect, i.e., logic, who cultivate a "hypertrophische Zerebralkultur."[109] He emphasizes that a proper cultural life in his view is "die synthetische Verfeinerung der Gesamtheit eines geistigen Daseins" ("geistig" here in the sense of "subjective" or "inner" and not "intellectual").[110]

It was stated earlier in connection with a discussion of Nietzsche's influence on the club that Hiller, in a talk given at the first performance of "Das neopathetische Cabaret," defined the concept of "neues Pathos" in a way synonymous with Loewenson's definition of the term. Hiller said in that talk:

> This is the distinctive feature of a more aspiring vitality and of the new pathos: being always passionately informed by a commitment to ideas, by the desire for knowledge and the dedication to art and the amazing delights that lie between. The new pathos is nothing more than: an increased psychic temperature.[111]

Martens, citing the phrase "das lodernde Erfülltsein von unserem geliebten Ideelichen," attempted to suggest that it demonstrated Hiller's emphasis on the intellect, placing him in opposition to Loewenson.[112] In the light of Hiller's remarks in "Über Kultur," however, the same phrase would appear rather as a restatement of Hiller's desire for a balance between emotion—suggested in the first part of the phrase ("das *lodernde* Erfülltsein")—and the intellect—suggested by the last part of the phrase ("das Ideeliche"). This seems to be the same insinuation behind the concluding part of Hiller's definition of "neues Pathos," the phrase "erhöhte psychische Temperatur," in which the first adjective connotes emotion and the second the mind.[113]

Hiller and Loewenson may have been guilty of misunderstanding each other's respective world views; but in theory, as it was interpreted in the preceding pages, their philosophical positions were in accord on the major questions. Moreover, a similar viewpoint is reflected in statements on "neues Pathos" published in *Der Sturm* in the early years of the club by another member and later leader of the group, Erich Unger.[114] The conflict which divided the club must, therefore, have stemmed on the philosophical level from a failure to maintain in practice the balance between "feeling" and "intellect" which both Hiller and Loewenson had claimed they were seeking in theory. Hiller, as reported, claimed the failure was the work of the other side, of Loewenson and his followers.[115] Brief statements on the reason for the split in the club have also been published by representatives of the opposing faction, by Loewenson and Baumgardt; while they do not agree with Hiller's explanation of the schism and place the blame for it on his shoulders, they do imply, with Hiller, that the disagreement related to practice, not theory.[116]

No matter how much the conflict might have been related to intangibles in theory or practice, it was real enough, for when it first came to a head in the early part of 1911 it caused the cancellation of the performance of "Das neopathetische Cabaret" which had been scheduled for February 27.[117] At a meeting of the club around this time Hoddis reportedly led a move to unseat Hiller as president.[118] Although the move was unsuccessful, the following announcement, which appeared in *Die Aktion* at the beginning of the following month, indicates the ultimate consequences of the attempt:

> Our contributor *Dr. Kurt Hiller* informs us that he has just recently withdrawn from "Der Neue Club," which he had directed since its founding, bored by the tactless behavior of some

of its members. He considers it important that he not be held responsible for the future actions of this organization.[119]

Hiller did not make his exodus alone; he was joined by Blass and Armin Wassermann.[120] The three secessionists now establish their own club, called "Der literarische Club Gnu," and, to rival the Loewenson group, initiate their own program of cabaret evenings in the fall of 1911.[121] Complete data on the performances of the cabaret, which were held in the bookstore of Reuss and Pollack and in the Café Austria, are as yet unavailable; advertisements which appeared in *Der Sturm* and *Die Aktion* indicate that at least four evenings were sponsored by "Gnu" in the 1911/12 season and at least five in the following season of 1912/13.[122] These announcements indicate that, as with "Das neopathetische Cabaret," Hiller was able to recruit as performers many key members of Expressionism, such as Blümner, Walden, Hardekopf, Zech, Pfemfert, Einstein, Wolfenstein, Becher, Lichtenstein, and Rubiner.

One of the "Gnu" recitals was of some importance for Expressionism: at the one given on November 23, 1911, Max Brod, on a visit to Berlin from Prague, introduced a new poet to his audience, Franz Werfel, by reading samples of his poetry.[123] Up to this time Werfel had been unknown outside Brod's small Prague circle; this recital from his work, however, combined with a second one by Brod on December 15 that same year and followed shortly thereafter by the appearance of *Der Weltfreund* (pub. in Berlin at the end of December, 1911), were to establish for Werfel a wide reputation of note almost overnight.[124]

The break with "Der neue Club" had not been all-inclusive, for some of those who had held to Loewenson's faction in the schism were to appear in Hiller's new cabaret. Thus, Meyer, for example, could report of hearing Heym unsettle his listeners in "Gnu" with a reading of his poem "Krieg" and could recall the similar effect which Hoddis's reading of the poem "Weltende" had on the audience at another performance.[125] Lasker-Schüler's report on a meeting she attended in 1911 in the Café Austria is of note, in that it indicates a very large audience in attendance, numbering in the "thousands."[126]

Disputes seemed to follow Hiller everywhere, as a concrete confirmation of his alleged contentious nature: about the middle of 1913 some trouble developed in "Der Club Gnu" when Hiller and Blass broke off their friendship.[127] What caused this split is not reported, but Blass's break with Hiller coincided with what was to be for him the beginning of a break with the whole movement represented by the habitués of the Café des Westens in Berlin. About this same time, he quit Berlin and moved to Heidelberg where he established his own monthly, *Die Argonauten,* and commenced to turn away artistically by degrees from Expressionism towards a more "classical" style under the influence of Stefan George.[128] "Der Club Gnu" survived the break; and soon after Blass's departure Hiller gained a new follower in the young

Hasenclever. Hasenclever was at that time working on his play *Der Sohn;* and Raabe states that postcards written by him from this period and preserved in the Schiller-Nationalmuseum (Marbach a.N.) demonstrate the strong influence which Hiller had on the political sections of the play.[129] Shortly after its completion, Hasenclever read from the play at a performance of "Gnu" given in the spring of 1914.[130] The report on that particular recital was the latest on "Der Club Gnu," whose dissolution was probably forced soon after by the outbreak of the war.

Hiller himself was able to remain in Berlin throughout the Expressionist period, maintaining always close contacts with the artist circles in the Café des Westens.[131] Throughout the period he continued to be one of the most influential contributors to a wide range of Expressionist publications.[132] His own series of *Ziel-Jahrbücher,* which he edited between 1916 and 1923 in five volumes, played a major role in laying the foundation for the Activist program adopted by the majority of Expressionists during the German Revolution.[133] He was also an active participant in the Revolution and made an abortive attempt to establish an Activist Party in Berlin in 1919.[134]

After the departure of the Hiller faction, "Der neue Club" had remained intact, with Unger replacing Hiller as the leader of the group. The performances of "Das neopathetische Cabaret" were soon resumed and continued in the same manner as previously. As mentioned earlier, it was subsequent to the split in the club that the efforts to establish a journal of the club began to materialize; one of Loewenson's motives in organizing this effort was to use the journal as a means of reuniting the original members.[135] Even before much progress had been made on the journal, a reconciliation of sorts had evidently been achieved, if Lasker-Schüler's reference to such an occurrence between members of the two factions involves the rift which has been described in this study: in one of the letters which make up the volume *Mein Herz,* she reports to Walden, the alleged recipient of most of the letters, that she was surprised to note on entering the Café des Westens recently (ca. early fall, 1911), that Hiller, Blass, Hoddis, Loewenson, and Kurtz were all sitting together at one table and again "reconciled."[136] The reconciliation, if it did indeed take place, was no more than a renewal of contact; Hiller's "Gnu" continued its activities and, while Hoddis and Heym were to read at performances of the new cabaret, Hiller, Blass, and Wassermann did not again participate in the performances of "Das neopathetische Cabaret" held in the following months.[137]

The gradual demise of "Der neue Club" over the next two years appeared prepared for by the death of Heym. He had become the focal point of the group after the secession of Hiller's faction; but then, on January 16, 1912, while skating on the frozen Havel river in Berlin, he and his friend Ernst Balcke both fell through the ice and drowned.[138] The next meeting of "Das neopathetische Cabaret," which was held in Heym's memory on April 3, 1912, was the final one.[139] The preparations for the meeting and the coeditorship of a selection of poetry from Heym's literary remains, which was published the same year as *Umbra Vitae,* were the last collective acts of the club's membership, outside of the necessary degree of collaboration which will have been required by the continuing plans for *Neopathos.*[140] The ranks of the club had already begun to thin as early as 1911, however. In that year, Jentzsch and Schulze-Maizier had moved to Munich. Schulze-Maizier was, nonetheless, kept informed there on developments in Berlin in the club by correspondence with Baumgardt, while Jentzsch remained in contact by mail with Heym who also paid Jentzsch a visit in Munich in 1911.[141] Hoddis began to drift away from the club about the same time, as he began to travel frequently away from Berlin; he spent much of 1912 in Munich and then for the remainder of his life was constantly in and out of mental institutions.[142] Baumgardt moved to Heidelberg not long after the club ceased to be publicly active in 1912.[143]

Later plans to revive "Das neopathetische Cabaret," like the preparations for *Neopathos,* indicate that the spirit, if not the body, of "Der neue Club" was still alive up to the middle of 1914; the outbreak of war at that point finally put a conclusive end to any hopes for such a revival.[144]

5

Herwarth Walden and *Der Sturm*

Even before the onset of the Expressionist era, Herwarth Walden's activities in behalf of new, unrecognized and revolutionary art, reaching back to the first few years of our century, had already begun to earn him the loyalty and friendship of many of the young and aspiring creators of that art from all over Germany and parts of the Austro-Hungarian Empire. With the founding of his own journal, *Der Sturm,* in the first months of 1910, the conclusive step was finally made in coalescing behind him and his efforts in support of what he was very soon to call "Expressionism" a close and cohesive circle of confederates with relatively distinct outlines. The Walden circle was destined gradually to grow and then to undergo many alterations during the Expressionist era. However, with its frame thus established by that important publishing event just mentioned, it was to constitute throughout the period the key source on which Walden was to draw for most of the regular contributions to *Der Sturm* as well as for the regular participants in the other activities sponsored under the journal's name. The Walden circle was less formally organized as a whole than "Der neue Club," in the sense that it did not meet at specific and regularly scheduled times and had no general and official program. However, there were certain fundamental attitudes and ideas which reverberated consistently through statements made public by the members of the group in its various artistic tribunes, as will be discussed later. In addition, the circle did gather on an unofficially regular basis around Walden—initially at his table in the Café des Westens where the group was encircled by the other Expressionists in Berlin—in order to discuss and share their ideas and latest artistic efforts.

As with Expressionism as a whole, in the development of the Walden circle three separate phases must be distinguished, all of which correspond to an equal number of related phases in the development of *Der Sturm* itself. The first phase of the circle covers the prewar years or the period of early Expressionism, during which the most constant members, besides Walden himself, included Rudolf Blümner, Alfred Döblin, Salomo Friedlaender, William Wauer, Peter Baum, Paul Scheerbart, and Gottfried Benn.[1] Walden's friendship and literary association with Döblin, Blümner, Scheerbart, and Baum reach back to the first few years of this century; they had all been, from

the start, staunch supporters of Walden's "Verein für Kunst" (1903ff.) which
will be discussed in the pages below.[2] Friedlaender had begun an association
with Walden on journals he edited just prior to the establishment of *Der Sturm;*
and Wauer joined Walden's following, at the latest, around the time the latter
event took place or just shortly thereafter.[3] Peter Scher, in a memoir on the
early Oskar Kokoschka, includes Benn in Walden's circle of friends as early as
1910; Benn did not, however, begin to appear in *Der Sturm* until January,
1913, and even then his role in the journal remained quite negligible.[4]

During the same prewar period, there were also a few less permanent
members of the group and some latecomers to it. Else Lasker-Schüler had, of
course, been Walden's most constant companion as well as his closest literary
associate since their marriage about 1901; and she continued to play this dual
role in Walden's life until their divorce in 1911.[5] The following year her place
was taken by Walden's new wife, Nell Roslund.[6] Kokoschka, coming up to
Berlin from Vienna, worked in close association with Walden from March,
1910, to the spring of 1911, during which time he shared a room with Blümner
in abject poverty.[7] From October, 1910, to September, 1911, Kokoschka was
Walden's official editor on *Der Sturm* for Austria-Hungary; in this capacity
and as a contributor of illustrations and poetry, Kokoschka left a decisive
imprint on the journal in especially its formative years.[8] Although he returned
to Vienna in the spring of 1911, he continued to maintain contacts with Walden
in the years to follow and to contribute to *Der Sturm*.[9] Albert Ehrenstein, also
from Vienna and a close friend of Kokoschka, had been contributing to *Der
Sturm* from that city since the journal's first year of publication; he then joined
the circle in Berlin sometime during 1912 after Kokoschka had completed the
illustrations for Ehrenstein's novel *Tubutsch* (1911).[10] The last to join the circle
in this prewar phase was August Stramm. He had sought in vain for a publisher
who would accept his highly unorthodox poetry, until he sent his play *Sancta
Susanna* to Walden at the end of 1913.[11] Walden enthusiastically accepted the
play for publication; and shortly before Stramm's poetry first began appearing
in *Der Sturm* (April, 1914) he and Walden began a personal association whose
consequences for both parties, especially for Walden and the future course of
Der Sturm, were much more far-reaching than could have been anticipated on
the basis of the length of the association.[12] Since Stramm was an officer in the
reserves, he was called into active service at the very outbreak of the fighting in
August, 1914. He was killed on the Russian front the next year, on September
1, 1915.[13]

Besides the members of Walden's closer circle, there were a number of
writers who were friends and frequent guests of the circle, although apparently
not regular adherents. These included Alfred Richard Meyer, Peter Scher,
Ernst Blass, Carl Einstein, Alfred Kerr, Walter Mehring, René Schickele,
Rudolf Kurtz, Theodor Däubler and, when on visits to Berlin from Vienna,

Karl Kraus and the architect Adolf Loos. These are, for the most part, names which appear again in prominence in other Expressionist circles.[14]

John Höxter reports on a gathering of the Walden circle in the Café des Westens about 1910, at which Walden, Lasker-Schüler, Döblin, Einstein, Mynona, Baum, Kokoschka, Kraus, and Loos were in attendance.[15] Most such reports, telling us that the circle convened here, mention few names specifically, outside of Walden's and Lasker-Schüler's; but it has been widely recorded that all of the members and frequent guests of the group, with the sole possible exception of Kerr, did frequent the Café des Westens on a regular basis.[16] Here the main focal point of the circle around *Der Sturm* remained through about the first three publishing years of the journal. In the winter of 1913, however, an event occurred which forced a change. One morning during that winter, Lasker-Schüler, driven almost insane by jealousy, made an attempt on the life of Walden's new wife of one year, Nell Walden.[17] As a result of this incident, the Waldens had to avoid Lasker-Schüler, and this meant her favorite spot, the Café des Westens. Shortly before this, Walden had already completed the move of all facilities of *Der Sturm* (offices, exhibition rooms, etc.) from the Katharinenstrasse and Augustastrasse to the Potsdamerstrasse.[18] The new favorite café and "center of the *Sturm* movement" was, therefore, found near by on the Potsdamer Platz in the "Zeitungscafé" called Das Café Josty.[19] Until the demise of the group in 1924, the meeting place of Walden and his friends alternated between this café and the new facilities of *Der Sturm*.[20]

Most of the changes in the *Sturm* circle which together create the outlines of a second phase in its development were precipitated, directly or indirectly, by the outbreak of war in 1914. Baum, Benn, Ehrenstein and Stramm entered the military at the outset; before the end of the first year of hostilities they had also been joined by Döblin.[21] An additional loss to the group occurred in October, 1915, when Paul Scheerbart died, of natural causes.[22] Thus, of the regular membership only the Waldens, Blümner, Wauer, and Friedlaender remained.[23] Of the frequent guests of the circle listed earlier, only Däubler and Mehring were able to maintain a noteworthy degree of personal contact with the group during the war.[24]

Nevertheless, in spite of the unsettled conditions in the country during the period, several new faces were added to Walden's list of associates in this phase. The poet Adolf Knoblauch and his wife Anna joined the circle at the beginning of this phase.[25] In 1915, together with the poetess Sophie van Leer, who remained Walden's secretary until 1918, the circle's ranks were increased by the painters Georg Muche, Georg Schrimpf, and Maria Uhden.[26] The following year saw the addition of a young poet who was thereafter to play a key role in the activities of the circle until its final dissolution: Lothar Schreyer.

Schreyer's induction into the army had been delayed because of his health; and before this event had finally taken place his attention was brought to

Walden's journal by a friend while Schreyer was still residing in Hamburg. Schreyer, as he wrote many years later, had already begun writing in the style he found represented now in the literature of *Der Sturm;* this discovery inspired him with enough confidence to submit his highly unorthodox play *Die Nacht* to Walden's equally unorthodox journal.[27] The manuscript was immediately accepted and it appeared in *Der Sturm* in the July issue of 1916.[28] About the same time, on the occasion of a visit with Walden in Berlin while on his way to Leipzig to assume his first military post, Schreyer was asked to join Walden's circle.[29] As it happened, he was able to comply with Walden's wish much sooner than expected, for just three weeks later, in September, 1916, he received an early release from active military duty for the duration of the war.[30] In August, 1917, Schreyer was made Walden's assistant editor ("Schriftleiter") on *Der Sturm,* which position he held officially until the end of the publishing year 1924, and thereafter, according to Schreyer, mostly *in absentia* until 1928.[31]

Also in 1916, Kokoschka was once again in close personal contact with the Walden circle in Berlin for a period of several months while recuperating from an injury sustained in battle.[32] During this stay, Nell Walden recalled, Kokoschka came to the *Sturm* offices every day; he left his imprint on *Der Sturm* this time primarily in the form of the series of portraits of poets and friends of the Walden circle (Nell Walden, Blümner, Knoblauch, the poet Hermann Essig, the actresses Gertrud Eysoldt and Claire Waldoff) and other drawings published in the journal in the last three months of 1916.[33] Finally, during the course of the war, there were five more additions to the group: the painter Fritz Stuckenberg and his wife; a lawyer friend of Walden, Kurt Neimann, and the subsequent director of the "Sturm-Bühne" (1917ff.), John Schikowski, with his wife Lina.[34] A frequent visitor to the circle during the war was the German-American painter Lyonel Feininger. As an "enemy alien" during these years, Feininger had been put into an internment camp near Berlin; but Walden was able to arrange for regular leaves from the camp which permitted him to come to the *Sturm* circle in Berlin.[35]

As thus constituted, the membership of the circle around *Der Sturm* remained fairly stable throughout the rest of the war. The only disruptions occurred in 1917 when Muche was finally called to active duty (February, 1917) and when Schrimpf and Uhden moved to Munich shortly after they were married.[36]

The final stage in the development of the *Sturm* circle, which covers the postwar years until 1924, sees the gradual falling away of much of the support and loyalty which Walden had formerly enjoyed from his adherents. Of the members of the closer circle from the previous phases, only Nell Walden, Blümner, Wauer, and Schreyer continued their associations to the end of this phase.[37] Shortly after the close of the war, they were joined by two new associates: Kurt Schwitters and Otto Nebel. Schwitters, who was a Dadaist and the creator and theorist of what he called "Merzmalerei" and "Merzdichtung," was residing in Hannover in this period, but made frequent trips to Berlin to participate in the activities of the *Sturm* circle.[38] Nebel, a painter and poet, joined the group in 1920 and became a student of Blümner in the art of recitation and a major exponent of the "Wortkunstwerk" of *Der Sturm*.[39]

Walden was not the official president of the circle over which he presided, as Hiller was in "Der neue Club," but all of his biographers agree that he was the indisputable leader and spokesman for the group.[40] He was a much more versatile and multitalented individual than most of his counterparts in the other circles; he was at once editor and publisher, poet, composer and musician, theoretician-polemicist-critic of literature and art, patron of, and dealer in, the arts, and, in the end, political journalist. All of these talents and professions, including the latter one, he put in the service of the "new art" (his original term, and later his synonym, for "Expressionism"). For the artists who represented this tendency and clustered around him, he became both mentor and patron, critic and spokesman.[41] Nell Walden, in an essay on Walden the man, emphasizes, as do his other biographers, the aggressive and dynamic qualities of his very "complicated" personality, especially where art was involved:

> It is also not easy to understand this complicated personality which was composed of so many elements: severity, brusqueness, defensiveness, aggressiveness, and the fighting spirit. At the same time he was, however, timidly reclusive, inwardly sensitive, and sentimental. His limits were sharply drawn: dark or light—there were no shades in between; always uncompromising as he was in life. Walden was a fighter; of course, not in the military but in the intellectual sense. He defended his opinions and ideas aggressively and untiringly. Dynamic and full of energy, restless, in a certain sense limitless, he was only interested in the fight. His weapons were polemics and propaganda.[42]

He was intractable and intransigent in his ideas on art and literature, but, as Mehring recalls, he would quickly suppress his own aesthetic position when, as often happened, waxing ecstatic over a work of art which his keen critical eye told him possessed originality.[43] Such intense qualities of character as those described by Nell Walden and Mehring, brought together in one individual, had the potentiality of making Walden's relationship with others problematic; and, indeed, as Nell Walden relates in another memoir on him, he seemed only able to either attract or repulse others, but not to leave them lukewarm.[44] He thus acquired enemies—even in the Expressionist camp—but the attraction, on the other hand, which he was able to exercise on many leading Expressionists was, according to Schreyer, like that of a magnet.[45] Many talented writers and painters, especially the young, were drawn into his sphere of influence, as we have already seen; they came seeking his counsel and patronage; they all had a great respect for his person and his views on art. Walden's relationship to his circle, as Mehring suggests, was that of teacher to disciples.[46]

Walden's intimacy with the Bohemian artist community of Berlin can be dated as early as the time of his marriage to Lasker-Schüler in 1901, shortly after which the new couple reportedly began virtually "living" in the Café des Westens.[47] Since, as just remarked, Lasker-Schüler subsequently played a key role in Walden's life up to about 1911, it is worth considering briefly her association with Berlin literary life from the beginning of her literary career to the end of the Expressionist years. With a summary view of her career in mind, it will be possible to appreciate better the potential benefits which could accrue to Walden from it.

Lasker-Schüler was one of the most gregarious members of the Expressionist camp and one of the most colorful and omnipresent figures of the German artist bohemia as a whole in the first two decades of this century.[48] Her association with the Berlin artist bohemia was perhaps older than Walden's, beginning about 1900, shortly after her marriage to her first husband, the Berlin physician Berthold Lasker, had come to an end. At this time she began dividing her time between her furnished rooms in the city and the Café des Westens.[49] Already in the same year she is discovered to be a member of the artist society founded by the Hart brothers, "Die neue Gemeinschaft," and also, still in the same year, a member of the related group called "Die Kommenden."[50] It was the original head of the latter group, Ludwig Jacobowsky, who, in fact, arranged for her première in print as a poetess by publishing (1899ff.) some of her poems in Michael Georg Conrad's journal *Die Gesellschaft,* of which Jacobowsky was coeditor at the time.[51] After her marriage to Georg Levin, whom she gave the new name Herwarth Walden, she was his constant companion in the Café des Westens. While Walden generally restricted himself here to his own circle, Lasker-Schüler established close contacts with virtually all of the circles and artists that came to the café in the years to follow. Thus, during the Expressionist era she associated with members of Meyer's circle in the café, and often sat here with the circle around Pfemfert and *Die Aktion.*[52] About 1910/11 she was a regular member of the circle that convened in the Café des Westens at the table of the Berlin lawyer Hugo Caro, who was a friend and legal counselor of many Munich and Berlin artists in the prewar period.[53] Besides Lasker-Schüler, Caro's regular table companions in the café included the poets Döblin, Victor Hadwiger, and Lasker-Schüler's close friend Hans Adalbert von Maltzahn.[54] After her divorce from Walden in 1911, her presence in the Berlin artist community was often interrupted by travels, especially to the artist centers in Leipzig and Munich; when back in the Café des Westens in the last few years before the war, she sat most frequently with Benn.[55] About the beginning of 1913 she was also a member of the group, which appears to have included, amongst others, Zech and the singer Franz Lindner, thrown out of the Café des Westens for allegedly "not eating enough"; they all moved to the Café Josty after the incident.[56] During the war she appeared in the circles of exiled Expressionists in the artist cafés of Zürich.[57] She returned to the Café des Westens in that period as well, however, and was close there now to Herzfelde and the circle of Berlin Dadaists around him, who named their publishing company after her novel *Der Malik*.[58]

Because of her wide-ranging literary friendships, therefore, Lasker-Schüler was no doubt to a significant degree instrumental in helping Walden establish literary contacts, as she was also known to have been for her other friends.[59] In addition, she was one of the most widely admired poets in the Expressionist camp throughout the decade.[60] She was frequently invited to participate in recitals sponsored by the movement, not only in Berlin by *Der Sturm, Die Aktion,* "Der neue Club," but also by groups in Munich, Leipzig, Vienna, Zürich and Prague.[61] Her writings, many of which are important sources of biographical information on Expressionism, were well represented in most of the major publications of the movement.[62] She had always been well represented in the journals edited by Walden prior to 1910, and in *Der Sturm* her poetry was given more space than that of any other single poet published in the journal in its first two years.[63] According to Nell Walden, Lasker-Schüler's verse formed the model for one of the two basic styles of the lyric represented in *Der Sturm,* with Stramm's poetry, as will be discussed later, being the model for the second major style.[64]

To return to Walden's career—almost from the very start of his active involvement in the literary life of Berlin, he identified with the unorthodox, antitraditional tendencies in literature. This fact is documented by Döblin, whom Walden met and began associating with shortly after the turn of the century.[65] Döblin described in a late literary memoir the activities and literary sympathies of himself and Walden in the first years of their friendship: "Wir mokierten uns über die damaligen Götzen der Bourgeoisie, Gerhart Hauptmann und seinen unechten Märchenspuk, über die klassizistische Verkrampfung Stefan Georges."[66] Walden's circle of friends in that early period, as Döblin tells us, already included, besides Döblin and Lasker-Schüler, also the arch-bohemian poet Peter Hille, and entertained close contacts as well with Richard Dehmel, Wedekind, and Paul Scheerbart.[67]

Shortly after Walden and his bride had established a regular table for their circle of friends in the Café des Westens, he made his first move to organize active support of the artists whom he had befriended or with whom he sympathized: in 1903 he founded the "Verein für Kunst," an organization designed to provide a framework within which poets and other artists and writers could read from their work or hold lectures.[68] The major thrust of support from the organization was directed towards unrecognized talent representing new trends and new values in literature and art; this fact is emphasized by Walden's frequent literary associate prior to the *Sturm* period, Hardekopf. Hardekopf's comments on Walden's work in the "Verein für Kunst" were made in the context of a general defense of his character and talents which was published in pamphlet form by his many friends in 1909.[69] Hardekopf maintained in his contribution to the pamphlet:

> He created the "Verein für Kunst," whose organizational and aesthetic achievements will be carefully recorded in cultural history: as an unrelenting documentation of aristocratic intellectuality within the "contemporary" age's idiocies, as the declaration of war by European artists on Germany's pitiful delight in urban, materialistic banalities or the trite sentimentalities of regional art (at its best: Sunday church bells ringing across the wheat fields). The "Verein für Kunst" enjoyed the luxury of having taste and of loving fanatically the new, unapproved values. "Selectivity" always reigned supreme: that aristocratically sparing critical perspective, that self-discipline which does not react to all enticements, only to the unforeseen, the dangerous ones, to the mastery of minds which have ventured forth boldly into new territory.... This cadre was pure; its performances were not invaded by the instincts of the rabble. And with a few waves of his hand, Mr. Walden provided each poet who appeared here with an appropriate setting.[70]

The predominantly modernist preferences of the group, to which Hardekopf alludes above, are also demonstrated by a list of some of those who appeared before it from 1903 on: Peter Altenberg, Hermann Bahr, Baum, Dehmel, Döblin, Peter Hille, Arno Holz, Lasker-Schüler, Heinrich and Thomas Mann, Alfred Mombert, Scheerbart, Wedekind, Adolf Loos, and others.[71] "Der Verein für Kunst" remained very active throughout the *Sturm* period, its evenings eventually being renamed "Sturm-Abende."

In the few years just prior to the beginning of the Expressionist decade and the founding of *Der Sturm*, Walden was the editor of a series of literary journals; his activities on these were to demonstrate, more concretely than his work for the "Verein für Kunst," not only his consistent ability to attract the support of the young, revolutionary artist, but also the kind of innovativeness and discerning artistic judgement that was to make *Der Sturm* one of the leading journals of Expressionism. The editorial policy and artistic position which he was to apply in the latter journal are already evident in his previous editorships.[72]

In the first half of 1908 he was made editor of the very old Berlin monthly (founded in 1831) *Das Magazin für Literatur des In- und Auslandes.*[73] He retained that post just three months, editing only an equal number of issues; but in that short span of time he left his imprint indelibly on the journal, transforming both its face and its contents radically.[74] He began with the masthead, modernizing it by using a very bold Roman type with cleaner, rounder edges and more simple form for the title than his predecessor had; he then replaced "...für Literatur des In- und Auslandes" with the subtitle "Monatsschrift für Literatur/Musik/Kunst und Kultur."[75] The next important change bespoke in turn a change in the content, for Walden added a second subtitle: "Organ des Vereins für Kunst zu Berlin."[76] *Das Magazin,* which had become a relatively conservative literary review, devoted mainly to semischolarly literary criticism under the previous editor (Dr. Eduard Loewenthal), became under Walden a progressive publication of mainly avant-garde literature and criticism by the mostly very young authors either associated with, or favored by, Walden's "Verein für Kunst": Hille, Lasker-Schüler, Döblin, Peter Baum, Schickele, Otto Freundlich, Blümner, Flake, Rubiner, Mühsam, et al. The line connecting *Das Magazin* with "Der Verein für Kunst" under Walden was drawn more sharply by publishing announcements at the end of each of the issues he edited of the forthcoming events sponsored by his organization.[77] It is not known why Walden left his position on *Das Magazin;* but his successor in April, 1908, Eugen Dreyer, continued much of Walden's new format: retaining Walden's masthead, with the omission, of course, of the second subtitle, and continuing to give a more balanced coverage to literature (contemporary, but definitely not avant-garde literature) and literary criticism.[78]

Later that same year, Walden assumed the new post of assistant editor on the somewhat more distinguished literary journal *Morgen: Wochenschrift für deutsche Kultur.*[79] This publication had only been founded the previous year in Berlin by Werner Sombart and had as its head editors Richard Strauss, Georg Brandes, Richard Muther, "with the assistance of Hugo von Hofmannsthal."[80] As had been the case with *Das Magazin,* under Walden's editorship some authors are published who were soon to figure prominently in Expressionism: Schickele, Friedlaender, Hardekopf, Rubiner, Scheerbart, Brod.[81] His tenure lasted a little longer on *Morgen,* through seventeen issues, but then came to an end at the beginning of 1909 when the journal was merged with *Nord und Süd.*[82]

Walden's troubles with the directors of the next two journals on which he worked were a foretaste of the kind of response he was to have to expect from the established press during the era of *Der Sturm.* On January 24, 1909, he was engaged by the "Genossenschaft Deutscher Bühnenangehöriger" as editor of its public organ *Der neue Weg,* reportedly with the agreement that the journal continue to publish material relating to the theater and the journal's sponsor group, but that, in addition, the new editor be permitted to use the remainder of each issue to raise the journal's literary level and make it of interest to a broader readership.[83] The style of literature to which Walden planned to open up *Der neue Weg* was the same as that which he had recruited for *Das Magazin* and *Morgen,* namely literature of a mostly avant-garde tendency. This intention is already hinted at in its new programmatic foreword:

> *Der neue Weg* is the organ of free spirits, of good Europeans. No other prefatory declarations shall be made here. Our actions shall reveal what we want and whether we can accomplish it. German actors had the courage to act. They will travel the new road, which they have set out upon, with the free spirits of all the arts and cultures. The pages of this journal are dedicated to their interests.[84]

The list of contributors which Walden was able to put together this time includes, besides the names of many authors of general literary prominence at that time (Hermann Bahr, Dehmel, Arno Holz, August Strindberg, et al.), the names of most of those poets who were to be his closest associates during the *Sturm* period: Baum, Blümner, Döblin, Friedlaender, Kurtz, Lasker-Schüler, Scheerbart, and Schickele.[85] Walden was permitted to edit only three issues of *Der neue Weg* (January 30, February 6 and February 13, 1909), and then was summarily dismissed by the president of the "Genossenschaft Deutscher Bühnenangehöriger," Hermann Nissen, who had reacted adversely to the avant-garde literary direction which the journal had begun to follow.[86] This event moved Walden's many friends to publish a declaration of support for him and his activities in behalf of literature; it was signed by Baum, Blümner, Friedlaender, Hardekopf, Kurtz, Scheerbart, Schickele, and contained statements by the latter and by Peter Altenberg, Brod, Dehmel, Holz, Paul Leppin, Heinrich Mann, Norbert Jacques, Julius Meier-Graefe, and others.[87]

Walden's experience on *Der neue Weg* and its repercussions were repeated in almost every detail when, the following September, he became editor of another theatrical journal, named by Walden himself *Das Theater*.[88] He was able to hold this position through ten issues; but again his attempts to update the literary content of the journal by the inclusion of the work of many of those same revolutionary contributors he had brought with him from his previous editorships met with the strong disapproval of his employers. His refusal to change his editorial policy led to dismissal from this post as well, in January of 1910.[89]

This brings us up to the time of the founding of *Der Sturm*, for Walden had become convinced by his experiences on *Der neue Weg* and *Das Theater* that there was little hope of converting established journals to his literary views; he now, therefore, decided to found his own publication with the assistance of his friends. The first issue of the new journal, with the militant title of *Der Sturm*, came off the press just two months after Walden's dismissal from *Das Theater* and contained another declaration of support of him by his friends, this time in reaction to the treatment he had received from the owners of the latter journal. The signatories of this new declaration were Walden's associates of long standing: Blümner, Döblin, Friedlaender, Hardekopf, Kurtz, Lasker-Schüler, Rubiner, and Schickele.[90] The pattern of Walden's life and work for the next decade and more was now already firmly established: his work was to revolve around *Der Sturm* and its affiliated activities and his life was to center around his circle of friends and supporters. He was to be found henceforth most often seated at his regular table, at first in the Café des Westens and later in the Café Josty, constantly engrossed, like the other café's habitués, in lively discussions with his circle.[91] For Walden in particular the sharing and exchanging of ideas and work in these discussions was to be a necessity; he used them especially as a means of previewing his essays, critiques, and other writings that were intended for publication in *Der Sturm*.[92]

Walden and *Der Sturm* regularly elicited a hostile reaction from the established press throughout the Expressionist decade, but such attacks only accomplished each time what Walden's troubles with the directors of *Der neue Weg* and *Das Theater* had: the knitting together of his circle, more tightly than before, behind him in support of his work.[93]

A short statement prefacing the first issue of *Der Sturm: Wochenschrift für Kultur und Künste* made it clear that Walden and his followers intended to continue the same revolutionary artistic position which had been manifested in the four earlier journals Walden had edited:

> For the fourth time we are entering the public forum with a new journal. Three times before, through the most flagrant breaches of contract, attempts were made to hinder our activities because they embarrassed too many readers. We have decided to be our own publisher. For we are still fortunate enough to believe that art and the arts can take the place of journalism and popular literature.[94]

Der Sturm was to represent more than just a continuation of that earlier position, however, for it was to intensify the earlier opposition to established art and literature by making it more explicit and by carrying it through in a much more consistent and radical manner than before. The title of the journal, which was conceived by Lasker-Schüler, was itself already meant to be a signal for the revolt and to connote the "purging, extirpating, and destroying" action of a storm, directed in this instance against the artistic residue of the cultural past. That is the way in which the meaning of the title is explained by Schreyer in a memoir on *Der Sturm:*

> Everything that of necessity took place now bore the mark of this symbol. A storm purifies, uproots, destroys. But it also sweeps across the land like the Holy Ghost. It is unceasing transformation, total rejuvenation, a signal in which the spiritual reality of perfection confronts the frailty and hope of earthly existence.[95]

This same general aesthetic direction is also set forth at the outset in the first issue of *Der Sturm* in the contribution signed by Kurtz, whose title and context of publication, Kurtz's qualifying footnote to the article notwithstanding, would endue it at least with pretensions to being a statement of the journal's program.[96]

Kurtz's philosophical position in this manifesto, entitled "Programmatisches," parallels very closely that espoused by the spokesmen of "Der neue Club," with which, it will be recalled from the previous chapter, Kurtz was also allied. He sets out here "to demolish" the reader's "slothful, sublimely grave world view."[97] This world view, whose most pronounced quality is "gravity" ("Ernst"), amounts for Kurtz and his partisans to that "spiritual sloth" ("Lebensträgheit") and "insensibility" ("dumpfes Herz," "Unempfindlichkeit") which long ago was defined by Nietzsche.[98] This attitude, which Kurtz associates with the middle class in the course of his essay, rejects through its "ethics of brutal insensibility" ("die Moral der brutalen Unempfindlichkeit") all complication, all paradox.[99] It "blindly" relies solely on the intellect, shunning instinctual life; its vehicle of expression is, therefore, the classical style, well proportioned sentences which develop their thought content "gravely," step by step.[100] As Kurtz interprets it, this approach narrows man's sphere of experience, stinting his freedom of movement, and "violates reality."[101] For this conventional world view Kurtz would substitute one which would remove all restrictions on experience and make it possible for man to know once again that feeling of freedom of movement which had been achieved by the Romantics through a fusion of the logical and intuitive faculties in their concept of irony. Again Nietzsche is an exemplar, this time as intermediary between the Romantics and the present generation:

> In that fortunate age of our past, when logical inspiration was shot through with a profound, aesthetic-intuitive sense, this feeling was reflected in the concept of irony, and one of the few worthy successors of that generation, Nietzsche, preached the glad tidings of the "dance" to no avail to somber minds.[102]

Kurtz advocates an art that expresses a world view in which intellectualism is subdued by an emphasis on the instincts, on the "dark forces" of life; the role of the intellect is to be reduced to employing its regulative powers to place the "dark forces," to which it has lost all connections, in the service of life:

> Intellectualism can only be subdued by a noisy emphasis on the instincts, the dark forces, which the intellect ought to organize and place in the service of life, but to which it has long since lost all ties.[103]

Such a reorientation of perspective would expand man's range of experience to encompass all aspects of life and thus grant him that "exuberance of being" ("Fülle des Daseins") and "cheerful" spirit which had been a property of the Romantics.[104] It would check the conventional falsification of life which derives from oversimplification of it; once again paradox and irony would be restored to their place in man's vision.[105] Finally, such a reorientation would require a new literary style consonant with the new perspective; it would have to represent a break with the classical manner, allowing for a less analytical, logical structure and involving (as Kurtz seems to be suggesting here) such devices as abrupt shifts from parataxis to hypotaxis and an acute condensation of language.[106] He closes his manifesto with a final stress on the aggressive posture with which he, and his like-minded partisans, will confront any statement by the established culture disposed to the retention of its own conventions instead of to the "full appreciation of existence":

> With our most provocative measures, we will flout every manifestation of this culture which aims at the preservation of its conventions instead of the full enjoyment of life. We will pluck out with painstaking care every sign of liberal diffidence, all meaningless customs.[107]

Kurtz added a footnote to his essay in which he says that his statements were meant to characterize his own position and that of his close friends only and not the opinions and aims of the contributors to *Der Sturm*.[108] Nevertheless, his essay was to function as a program of the journal in a broad sense; elaborated upon and added to over the years, it was to reverberate throughout *Der Sturm*. His overall opposition to established cultural conventions was, of course, broadly delineative of the position to be maintained by the journal in its support of revolutionary art and literature. His more specific espousal of a more all-inclusive world view than that manifested by the established culture, with its excessive dependence on the logical faculty, reappears again and again: in Hiller's and Unger's essays which advocate a unity of feeling and intellect in human character; in the essays of Friedlaender which offer a recovery of man's lost centrality through the assumption by the individual of a neutrality of vision opposite the polarities of reality; in the Futurist manifestoes which sponsor the destruction of conventional grammar and syntax and a reorientation of vision under (Crocean) intuition in place of logic; and especially in the theory of the "Wortkunstwerk," as set forth by Walden, Blümner, Schreyer, and other *Sturm* contributors, which, through a form of poetry shunning the conventional restrictions of logic, aims ultimately at restoring to man the unity with the cosmos lost him by the dominance of the logical faculty.[109]

In spite of the continuity of program in *Der Sturm* described above, the total image of the journal from beginning to end went through three successive stages of development. The first of these stages, from 1910 to roughly the beginning of the war, was one of organization and crystallization. From the start, the typography was progressive for its time in its use of antique boldface type and a bold masthead similar to the one used by Walden for *Das Magazin*. The earliest graphic artworks illustrating the journal are caricatures ("Karikaturen") in the art nouveau style that still could be found also in *Simplicissimus* and *Jugend* in the same period. Then, very soon, beginning in the twelfth issue of May 19, 1910, the series of radically unconventional drawings by Kokoschka is initiated.[110] Kokoschka's work is mixed with the caricatures and other drawings of art nouveau and similar styles throughout the remainder of 1910; then, in January of 1911, he is joined by Pechstein and shortly thereafter by the other "Brücke" artists Kirchner, Heckel, Schmidt-Rottluff, and Mueller and by that group's former friend, Emil Nolde.[111] The first woodcuts, by Kirchner, appear in the second half of 1911; and in the course of that period and the next year the work of numerous other Expressionists begins to appear: Artur Segal, Moriz Melzer, Jules Pascin, César Klein, Wassily Kandinsky, Wilhelm Morgner, Franz Marc, Heinrich Richter-Berlin, Georg Tappert, et al.[112] By the end of 1913 illustrations in pre-Expressionist styles have completely disappeared from the journal, with the Expressionist woodcut now rapidly becoming the distinctive component of the journal's pictorial image. The pictorial image which *Der Sturm* was to retain until the early twenties, that of an esoteric and avant-garde journal of literature and art, was completed when Walden announced in the September, 1912, issue the cessation of all nonfactual, illustrated advertisements for business firms in the journal's pages.[113]

As the pictorial image of *Der Sturm* was crystallizing in this early phase, so was the literary one. In the first two years of the journal, essays on broad cultural and philosophical themes are liberally mixed with literature, art criticism, and theory; but the journal's interests very soon narrow, centering almost exclusively on literature and the arts. The latter development coincides in time with the German première in *Der Sturm* (March, 1912ff.) of the first manifestoes of the Italian Futurists which were to be of decisive importance for the future radical literary theory and style of many of Walden's associates.[114] The dominant literary contributions throughout the first phase, however, are only mildly revolutionary in nature, in the manner of the leading poet of the phase, Lasker-Schüler. Her work, like that of the other major literary contributors before the war (Döblin, Blass, Ehrenstein, Lichtenstein, Scheerbart, Zech, Meyer, et al.) is characterized by a strongly solipsistic bias in content and by a style frequently unconventional in its use of imagery and language but with only some slight tendency towards the kind of hypercondensation or abstraction in language and asyntactic structure achieved later in the "Wortkunstwerk." In the course of the third year (1912/13), as Walden's support of Expressionist painting in the journal noticeably intensifies and the *Sturm* exhibitions of avant-garde painting are initiated, art criticism and theory begins to assume a dominant place alongside the literature; Walden himself, from 1913 to almost the end of the war, is writing almost exclusively on Expressionist painting.[115]

The beginning of the second phase in the journal is marked by the outbreak of the war. Almost immediately after that event, Walden is forced to reduce *Der Sturm* to a monthly, beginning in October, 1914.[116] The pictorial image of the journal remains unchanged in this phase, however; its support of Expressionist painting, as of Expressionist literature, continues unabated. Most of the contributors of graphic artwork to the journal of the first phase continue in the second, in spite of the absence of some of its artists from Berlin. In addition, reflecting the changes in Walden's circle in this period discussed above, the work of a few new graphic artists begins to appear: Uhden, Schrimpf, Feininger, Muche, and Fritz Stuckenberg.[117]

The greatest changes in the image of *Der Sturm* in this phase occur in the style of its major literary contributions. By the end of 1915, most of the major poets of the first phase were no longer represented; these included Lasker-Schüler, Blass, Döblin, Ehrenstein, Lichtenstein, Scheerbart, Zech, Meyer, and a few others. A few new names of poets, writing in the kind of relatively restrained style represented by the above, become prominent during the war: Isidor Quartner, Adolf Knoblauch, Wilhelm Runge, Kurt Heynicke, Sophie van Leer and, to a lesser extent, Thomas Ring.[118] Taken as a whole, however, the work of the latter was very soon overshadowed—not so much in space as in editorial and programmatic patronage—by the development of a much more unorthodox style which was to become the equivalent of the official literary style of *Der Sturm;* this new style was the one termed by Walden, and the other expounders of it from his circle, the "Wortkunst." The "Wortkunst" was much more than just a theory of poetics; it was, in addition, the outline of an ideology, for it defined not only the principles of a specific style of composition but also the "spiritual" benefit which was to accrue to the reader of the work composed in it.

The "Wortkunstwerk," i.e., the poetic work composed according to the principles of the "Wortkunst," was to provide the reader with a "spiritual experience" ("das geistige Erlebnis") rather than with an aesthetic one.[119] The central feature of this experience was to involve the restoration to the reader the sense of oneness with the world or cosmos which, the "Wortkunst" theorist claimed, had existed before the modern age, before the "Aufklärung," and which had been destroyed by the dominance of the logical faculty.[120] Walden stated of art which conforms to the concept of "Wortkunst": "Kunst greift über Menschheit hinaus, ballt Menschheit zusammen. Kunst kreist die Menschheit in ihrem All." ("Art reaches out beyond mankind, brings mankind together. Art encircles mankind in his totality.")[121] Schreyer wrote similarly:

> The "Wortkunstwerk," the work of art, integrates us into the cosmos. He who has been thus integrated is the cultured man of today. The culture of the past is dead. Let us do away with dead culture so that there will be room for the vital integration of the one into the all, of man into the world.[122]

Otto Nebel claimed of the same poetry: "The LOT of poetry is a FESTIVAL in the ALL, and all that is pure is *poetry* in light."[123] The frustration of this "spiritual experience" in conventional poetry derives principally from the impositions of logic upon content and language.[124] These impositions encourage the use in poetry of analogies, which are products of the logical mind and which, because of their nature as indirect comparisons with reality, are "substitutes" for reality rather than manifestations of it.[125] The "Wortkunstwerk," on the other hand, attempts to communicate directly with the reader, rather than indirectly through the logical faculty, by presenting an image ("das Bild") which *is* the reality, the "spiritual reality" ("eine geistige Wirklichkeit").[126] Thus, as Walden illustrates, the "Wortkünstler" does not write "I am as sad as autumn," but "I am autumn."[127] In this way, the factor of the ego or personality of the poet is eliminated which, represented by the logical connective "as" or "like," would intervene between the reader and the poetic image, preventing the unity of reader and poem that makes possible in turn the desired "spiritual experience."[128] The "Wortkunstwerk" is, therefore, not the communication of certain feelings or thoughts of the poet, as Schreyer claims, but is the "manifestation" of a reality ("Kunde einer Offenbarung").[129] In addition to the use of the image in order to break the traditional control of logic on the poetic word, the "Wortkünstler" also shifts the traditional emphasis from the meanings of words in sentences to the rhythm and sound values of the words.[130] This shift is accomplished primarily by a rejection of the conventional logic of syntax and grammar; the new structural devices, replacing the old and constituting the modes for the creation of the rhythm, become, as Schreyer termed them, "concentration" and "decentration."[131] "Concentration" denotes the condensation of content and form (the use of one word to convey what might otherwise have been conveyed in several; the omission of declensional endings, articles, etc.). "Decentration" denotes various forms of repetition of words and groups of words, parallelisms, word associations and inversions of word order.[132] In the "Wortkunstwerk" the "logic" which binds all parts together into a unified whole is not meaning, syntax and grammar, but rhythm.[133]

Ideologically, the "Wortkunst" was highly theoretical and intangible, of course; stylistically, however, the concept was fairly concrete, being equivalent in a broad sense to a theory of "abstract poetry"—some of the interpreters of the "Wortkunst" in *Der Sturm* actually used "abstract poetry" as a synonym for "Wortkunst"—as it has been defined by Richard Brinkmann in an essay on the Expressionist lyric: a form of poetry which does not adhere to the general grammatical-syntactic-conceptual continuity of its chosen language, which does not adhere as a medium of experience to the system of selection of that language.[134] The major source for the theory of the "Wortkunst" of *Der Sturm* can be traced, and was traced by its interpreters in Walden's circle, back to the Futurists.[135] There is much in the program of the "Wortkunst" which is reminiscent of that of the Futurists: the rejection of conventional grammar and syntax, the advocacy of condensation of language (omission of the adjective, adverb, conjunctions), the opposition to the intrusion of the poet's ego and to the restrictions of logic in poetry.[136] The circle around Walden looked as a model for the "Wortkunst" especially to Stramm, who had in turn been greatly influenced by his contact with the theories of the Futurists through their appearance in *Der Sturm* and possibly also through Stramm's presence at Marinetti's lectures in Berlin.[137] Stramm himself also acknowledged his indebtedness to Walden for his poetic development.[138] Stramm's own poetry in the "abstract" style began appearing in *Der Sturm* shortly after his first meeting with Walden at the beginning of 1914.[139] The poet's work appeared in Walden's journal regularly from April, 1914, through almost the first full year of the war, and then intermittently, culled from his literary remains, after his death at the front (September 1, 1915). During the war, the theory of "Wortkunst" began to be developed and elucidated by Walden and his associates, and the work of the first practitioners of the style, after Stramm, began to appear in *Der Sturm:* the "Wortkünstler" of this period include Schreyer, Franz Richard Behrens, Adolf Allwohn, Kurt Liebmann, Mehring, and Günther Mürr.[140]

The verse of Günther Mürr, which first began appearing in January, 1912, offers one very patent illustration, within the journal's pages, of a development towards the "Wortkunst" style. His verse here is markedly progressive only in content before the war (e.g., the series of poems entitled "Hamburg" is in the genre of the "Grossstadtlyrik" popular in early Expressionism). It then reveals a decided turn towards condensation of language when it reappears, after a four-year absence from the journal, in the first half of 1918 (April and July issues). Finally, in its last installments ("Wir" in the September, 1918, issue and "Raumfahrt" in the October (?), 1919, issue) it veers sharply into line with the hypercondensation and "decentration" typical of Stramm and the "Wortkünstler."[141]

Der Sturm remained politically neutral on the subject of the war throughout its entire duration. The subject was, in fact, scarcely broached at all. Editorially, it is acknowledged only indirectly and without comment in the announcements of the deaths on the battlefield of artists who had been connected with *Der Sturm.*[142] In the imaginative literature published in the journal in this phase, the war forms the background for the poems, later collected as *Tropfblut,* which Stramm wrote at the western and eastern fronts of the fighting and sent almost immediately to Walden for publication in *Der Sturm;* but again, even here no clearly discernible political position is taken on the war, for, although Stramm's image of it in these poems is certainly not positive, he emphasizes each time only the purely human side of the conditions perennially fostered by war: death, grief, misery, etc.[143]

The lineaments of *Der Sturm* established in the course of the war continued unbroken into the immediate postwar period. Both the end of the hostilities and the German November Revolution had come and gone, without either event being acknowledged in the pages of the journal or leaving a noticeable mark. It was not until the following year, 1919, that significant changes began to take place. The support of Expressionism in the graphic arts through reproductions continues in this phase at the same level as before, up to the final year of the journal, 1932, when such illustrations vanish completely from its pages. Many of the major names in this department, familiar from the earlier two phases, still have their work represented here now: Kokoschka, Jacoba van Heemskerck, Paul Klee, Muche, Gino Severini, Marc Chagall, Hans Arp, Fernand Léger, et al. In addition, the work of a number of artists new to *Der Sturm* is reproduced in this last phase: Alexander Archipenko, Laszlo Moholy-Nagy, Josef Peeters, Johannes Itten, Béla Kadar, Ludwig Kássak, Schreyer, Edmund Kesting, and many others.

The cultivation of the "Wortkunst" style maintains a dominant place both in the literature published in the journal and in the journal's pages as a whole until the middle of the 1920s; although after that time it yielded first place to a new department which will be discussed shortly, poetry in the "Wortkunst" style was never to be absent from a single issue through the final year of publication.[144] A changeover in the "Wortkünstler" does begin to take place in 1919, on the other hand, in which year three poets, Allwohn, Mehring, and Mürr, drop out and many new practitioners of the style begin to join forces with the journal: Willy Knoblauch (1919ff.), Kurt Schwitters (1919ff.), Otto Nebel (1920ff.), Kurt Heinar (1922ff.), Ingeborg Lacour-Torrup (1923ff.), Franz Hoffmann (1923ff.), Iwan Heilbut (1924ff.), Waldemar Eckertz (1925ff.), Alexander Mette (1925ff.), Erich Arendt (1926ff.), et al.

What can be interpreted, at least in principle, as an extension of the "Wortkunst" style appeared briefly in the pages of *Der Sturm* in the 1920s. The extension was a radicalization of the direction of the "Wortkunst" towards pure sound, i.e., towards a break not only with the conventional grammatical-syntactic-conceptual continuity of the language but also with the established phonic configurations of words. It is the literary equivalent of total abstraction in painting: the tendency in a literary composition to avoid the use of groups of sounds, as in abstract painting to avoid the representation of shapes and forms, whose reference in reality is preestablished. It was the form of poetry cultivated earlier, during the war, by members of the Zürich Dada circle, one member of which, Ball, claimed to have invented it: Ball termed verse in this form "Lautgedichte."[145] The two practitioners of this form of poetry in *Der Sturm,* Blümner and Nebel, referred to it as "absolute poetry" ("absolute Dichtung"); it is represented here by Blümner's noted poem "Angolaina" (1921) and by sections of Nebel's "runic fugue" "Unfeig" (1924, 1925).[146]

Of the major poets from the previous phase who wrote in a less radical style than that of the "Wortkünstler," only Heynicke and Ring are still contributing to *Der Sturm* somewhat frequently during this phase; but even their verse clearly comes now under the influence of the stylistic tendencies represented by the "Wortkunst."[147]

The most fundamental change in *Der Sturm* in this last phase occurs on the ideological level. In remaining aloof from the contemporary political events in Germany and other parts of Europe since before the beginning of the war, *Der Sturm* had eventually been drawn out of what, by the time of the November Revolution, had become the mainstream of the Expressionist movement and its literature. However, as it developed, the almost ivory-tower aestheticism of *Der Sturm* was not able for long to resist the sobering effects of the harsh realities forced upon the consciousness of the German mind by the political chaos of the revolutionary period and the Weimar Republic, by the hard times of the postwar inflation, by the hue and cry from the Expressionist camp about the basic politico-economic needs of mankind. The first concrete indications of the beginning of a shift in the ideological posture of *Der Sturm* comes in two essays by Walden, published in the journal as the first Constituent

National Assembly is meeting in Weimar to draw up the constitution of the new republic (February-August, 1919).[148] The titles of these two essays, "Kunst und Leben" and "Künstler, Volk und Kunst," already suggest a new concern with a very realistic question: the relationship of art to life and the people.

Walden is essentially outlining here the responsibility of the artist, as Walden now views it, opposite life and the people. The artist, Walden maintains, has no higher station in life than any other of his fellow countrymen, and can, therefore, demand no more rights for himself than anyone else.[149] Furthermore, art is the property of the people; thus, the artist is not to indulge himself in his work, turning away from life (i.e., reality), but is to face life squarely and serve it.[150] The artist, and those interested in art as well, fulfill this responsibility of serving life by learning to answer the only questions which are of significance in the real world: the economic questions.[151] The artist does not, however, provide his own answers to these questions, for they have already been made ready at hand by Karl Marx and Friedrich Engels; the artist's task is rather simply to render the answers to the economic questions perceptible, in other words to express them artistically.[152] The style of this artistic expression was still, as Walden implies, to be Expressionist, but it was now to have a clear political cast to it:

> We do not wish simply to engage in politics, we wish to engage in politics so that life will assume a more humane form. We want to engage in an objective and sober brand of politics. For art, too, is objective and sober, that is, organic.[153]

Schreyer continues this new direction taken by Walden in the very next issue in the essay "Der neue Mensch."[154] Defining the current social system as the manifestation of "suffering," he attacks those features of contemporary German society which contribute to this condition: exploitation of the worker, excessive division of labor, separation of the members of society into the rich and the poor, perpetuation of the system of private property, bureaucracy, etc.[155] In removing these ills from society, thereby eliminating the necessity for the "struggle for survival" ("der Kampf ums Dasein"), man will be made free, society will form a "community" and the "New Man" will be born.[156] The "community" and with it the "New Man" derive from practicing "goodness" ("die Güte"), which act Schreyer defines as involving essentially that union of the self with the cosmos—here it is called the "submission of the self to the cosmos" and has strong political overtones—advocated earlier by the theorists of the "Wortkunst" in *Der Sturm:* "It [goodness] is the submission of the one to the all."[157]

An official declaration of the politicization of *Der Sturm* could be read between the lines of an announcement which appeared in the journal towards the end of the following publishing year: the announcement stated that with the commencement of its twelfth year (1921),[158] in addition to continuing to bring graphic arts, poetry and imaginative prose, *Der Sturm* would begin to carry a new department devoted to essays of a polemical, critical, or satirical and of a scholarly and investigative nature.[159] The editor was promising more than he was going to give, however; in the next two years there actually appeared only a few contributions which could be assigned to the new department: Wauer's anticapitalist essay "Gold, Währung, Kapital: Eine Studie" is one of the few bold exceptions to the rule.[160] The factors that had prevented the journal from holding to the plan were the same ones, as a note signed by Blümner and added to the last issue of 1923 explained, that were forcing it to begin its fifteenth year (1924) as a quarterly instead of monthly publication.[161] The first factor Blümner refers to simply as "external," by which he no doubt means to suggest primarily the effects of the inflation that had already in the recent past been forcing *Der Sturm* repeatedly to raise the price of its issues.[162] The second factor mentioned involved the paucity of contributions of a high quality artistically, for *Der Sturm* would continue to refuse, Blümner declares, to publish the "false Expressionists," the artists who are nothing less than mere imitators of the literature which has been appearing in *Der Sturm.*[163] The similar paucity of outstanding writers of political essay in contemporary Germany, Blümner continues, has also prevented *Der Sturm* from expanding its field of interest as had earlier been planned.[164]

Der Sturm is thus forced to continue for the next few years to be what it had been from the start: a journal devoted predominantly to literature and the arts, with the only addition now being an occasional editorial or essay with obvious political orientation to remind the reader of the journal's new ideological posture. The journal's editor was becoming more and more deeply committed politically all the time, however, and a radical shift in emphasis in his journal was thus inevitable.[165] The shift finally came, abruptly, immediately upon Walden's return from a visit in the summer of 1927 to Russia, when he initiated in September of that year a series of sociopolitical articles on the Soviet Union.[166] The series began with an eyewitness account based on his visit, entitled "USSR 1927."[167] By 1930 Walden's enthusiasm for the new Russian regime had enduced him to put out a special "Sowjet-Union" issue of *Der Sturm,* consisting exclusively of articles from the pen of Walden on various aspects of Soviet Russian politics and society.[168] Walden had in the meantime begun to devote whole issues to the literature and art of other Slavic nationalities ("Junge slovenische Kunst," "Junge bulgarische Kunst," "Rumänische Literatur").[169]

The culmination of this development towards sociopolitical commitment in *Der Sturm* is reached in the journal's last year (Vol. 21, 1932), when it is merged with *Der Durchbruch.* As Walden explains in his announcement of the merger, *Der Durchbruch* was a periodical devoted primarily to supporting new ideas and individuals that were seeking especially to help better the lot of the physically ill and infirm.[170] With the merger a new assistant editor is added—

André von Kún—and a new subtitle as well in line with the journal's already obvious geographically broader political and artistic scope: "Internationale Monatsschrift." The product of the transaction was an odd amalgam: the bulk of each issue subsequently was to consist of sociopolitical commentary, written mostly by Walden, and of articles advocating specific reforms in medicine and the care of the physically ill and infirm, written mostly by Walden and professionals in the field. Only sparsely scattered amongst those very pragmatic and largely very pedestrian treatises were a few short literary or philosophical pieces and art, drama or literary critiques, most of which were contributed by the few writers and poets who had remained loyal to Walden to the very end (Heynicke, Liebmann, Blümner, Nebel, Schwitters, Mynona).[171]

A part of the success of *Der Sturm* in its earlier years had unquestionably stemmed from its directing its appeal at a definite audience, namely the supporters and young representatives of the "new art." However, at what sort of audience this new version of the journal was aimed was far from clear. Was it addressing itself to medical men, to political revolutionaries, or to devotees of literature? Nowhere in the journal itself is there made an appreciable attempt to synthesize its new motley interests; and a sufficiently extensive and regular readership which would do this for the journal, and without its help, would certainly have been at least difficult, if not impossible, to come by. It was thus understandably a brief experiment that managed just three issues, one for each of the first three months of 1932; and then *Der Sturm* became history.

Brief mention has already been made of what was apparently the earliest of Walden's many ambitious projects for the support of literature and the arts, "Der Verein für Kunst," established in 1903. Its purpose was to provide the unrecognized representatives of especially the avant-garde with a public forum for their work and ideas; by the time it was one year into the Expressionist decade it had sponsored a total of ninety-five readings or lectures.[172] Throughout the rest of the prewar phase and into the war years, such performances continued to be sponsored under the name of "Der Verein für Kunst"; the speakers featured during this period included Lasker-Schüler, Döblin, Blümner, Adolf Loos, Karl Kraus, and Walden himself.[173] In the second half of 1916 they were reorganized and renamed "Sturmkunst-Abende" and henceforth scheduled more regularly for Wednesday evening of each week.[174]

The first recital in the new series, a memorial evening in honor of August Stramm, was held on September 1, 1916; it was followed that winter (1916/17) by sixty-six more such evenings.[175] The performers at the "Sturmkunst-Abende" were to come exclusively from Walden's immediate circle of associates now; one of these associates, Blümner, his most steadfast supporter from the time of the beginning of "Der Verein für Kunst" to the very end of *Der Sturm*, became the dominant figure by far and the official host at these evenings.[176] Blümner, who had been an actor and a director under Reinhardt in

Berlin, directed much of his dramatic skill to the development of the art of recitation at the "Sturmkunst-Abende," and soon after the inauguration of the new series of recitals was to teach the art of recitation at the "Sturm-Kunstschule."[177] He occasionally read his own works at these evenings, but most often drew his material from the works of the poets published in Walden's journal.[178]

The "Sturmkunst-Abende" were held primarily in Berlin in the *Sturm* gallery, but occasionally were also sent abroad to other cities of Germany and Europe, including Hamburg, Frankfurt a.M., Cologne, Jena, Dresden, Leipzig, Hannover, Halle an der Saale, Dortmund, Erfurt, Essen, Munich, Breslau, Budapest and Copenhagen.[179] They thus obviously constituted a potentially effective medium for disseminating Expressionist literature, as represented by *Der Sturm*, not only throughout Germany but also to other parts of Europe. For the Walden circle itself, besides providing the members' work with added exposure to the public, the recitals had the additional function of creating yet another setting in which the circle and its friends were drawn together, for each Wednesday evening after the performance Walden, his closest friends and invited guests would repair to their reserved room in the "Weinstube Huth" on the Potsdamer Platz, where they carried on, as Nell Walden reports, "extremely lively" discussions until late in the evening.[180] There is no exact information available on all of the recitals in "Der Verein für Kunst" and at the "Sturmkunst-Abende," but some idea of the total number held can be gained from a report on Blümner's activity: Schreyer claims that Blümner performed at approximately three hundred of the "Sturmkunst-Abende" in Berlin and other cities of Germany and Europe.[181] Announcements of the recitals in *Der Sturm* indicate that they were still taking place in Berlin on a more or less regular basis on Wednesday evenings as late as the spring of 1927.[182]

As Schreyer wrote, Walden excited greatest public notice during the Expressionist period through the exhibitions of avant-garde art which he organized and sponsored under the name of his journal from 1912 to close to the end of *Der Sturm*.[183] While the response from the public and established press in the early years of the "Sturm-Ausstellungen" was seldom positive, it was certainly always large.[184] The exhibitions, which involved group ("Der Blaue Reiter," "Expressionisten," "Futuristen," "Französische Expressionisten," "Die Pathetiker," "Die Neue Sezession," "Kubisten," etc.) and one-man (Kokoschka, Kandinsky, Gabriele Münter, Marc, Gino Severini, Alexander Archipenko, Macke, Klee, etc.) showings of the work of avant-garde artists from all over Europe and other parts of the globe, took place several times a year during the Expressionist decade, initially only in Berlin in the *Sturm* gallery and then, beginning in February, 1914, also in major cities throughout Europe and in key cities of Japan (Tokyo, Kyoto) and the United States (Detroit, Denver, Kansas City, New York).[185] The major function of these exhibitions was, of course, to bring broad public recognition to the representatives of the new avant-garde.[186] They had, however, a second function, in providing a stimulating and apposite framework within which to hold the equally progressive recitals before "Der Verein für Kunst"and later at the "Sturmkunst-Abende."[187] Three of the most sensational and influential of those recitals, the one given by Marinetti in the spring of 1912 during the exhibition of the Italian Futurists and the two he gave in November of 1913 during the "Erster Deutscher Herbstsalon," were held before just such a provocative backdrop of heretically executed canvases and sculpture.[188]

An important byproduct of the "Sturm-Ausstellungen" was the direct contact which they fostered between the *Sturm* circle and artists and writers of related tendency from every quarter of Europe. The impetus for Marinetti's three visits to Berlin listed above and for his visit in February of 1913 had been given by this means: his Futurist compatriots were being shown in the *Sturm* gallery on all those dates.[189] In the same way Apollinaire, accompanied by Delaunay, had been drawn to Berlin in January, 1913, where he lectured on that visit on the subject of Cubism, represented by the paintings of his compatriot Delaunay which were decorating the walls of the *Sturm* gallery as he spoke.[190] The Walden gallery, according to Schreyer, eventually became a meeting place of poets, painters, scholars and politicians from many countries.[191] Herwarth and Nell Walden reinforced and widened this sort of contact through their extensive travels to the art centers of Europe, gathering material and making arrangements for exhibitions or making appearances at the opening of traveling exhibits, at which Walden sometimes gave an introductory lecture.[192] This activity is best exemplified by the preparations in 1913 for the most comprehensive of the early *Sturm* shows, the "Erster Deutscher Herbstsalon," modeled after the celebrated avant-garde comprehensives of the annual Paris "Salon d'Automne" (1903ff.), at which the closest French equivalent of the German Expressionists, the Fauves (shown at the fifth *Sturm* exhibit in August, 1912, in fact, as "Französische Expressionisten"), had their first group showing (1905).[193]

The Waldens began their preparations at the end of January of that year by journeying to Vienna, where they spent a few days visiting with Kokoschka in his studio and participating in lengthy discussions on art in the Café Central with Karl Kraus, Ehrenstein, Arthur Holitscher, Kokoschka, and Loos.[194] Then they went to Budapest to meet with artists residing there and visit the current art exhibitions. Travelling always at "express speed," as their friend Marc described it, the Waldens were in Hamburg in February and in March in Barmen, Elberfeld, Düsseldorf and Cologne.[195] Next came Paris, where they spent eight days, almost constantly in the company of painters and poets sympathetic to the artistic and literary direction supported by *Der Sturm,* including Blaise Cendrars, Delaunay, Apollinaire, Juan Gris, Fernand Léger, Marc Chagall, and others. Each afternoon in Paris they spent discussing art with such artists, as Nell Walden recalled, and then, in the evening, they would all go to the favorite artist locales of the Latin Quarter and Montmartre, in particular to the Café Rotonde and the Café du Dôme, where the discussions begun earlier in the day were often continued. Then the Waldens returned quickly to Berlin in order to prepare the next number of *Der Sturm* for publication. In March, 1913, they went to Munich, where they were met at the station on arrival by the whole "Blauer Reiter" group and taken directly to the Café Odéon. During this trip they saw Kandinsky and Gabriele Münter in Schwabing and also visited Franz and Maria Marc in nearby Sindelsdorf. The next cities on their itinerary were Frankfurt a.M. and Wiesbaden; here, again, they met with artists and visited art dealers and art organizations. In April they were in Scandinavia. At the beginning of May they were back in Berlin to see another number of *Der Sturm* through the press and to move their residence and the *Sturm* gallery to a new address in the city. Next they visited Frankfurt a.M. again and then went on to Mannheim, Strassburg, and Colmar, on their way to Switzerland. After stopping off in Basel, Bern, Fribourg, Lausanne, Geneva, and Lucerne, they headed for Weggis, where they made contacts with the painters Walter Helbig and Oskar Lüthy and no doubt at the same time with Lüthy's close friend Hans Arp, whose work also appeared in the large exhibition of *Der Sturm* that fall.[196] Finally, they returned to Berlin by way of Lucerne, Zürich, Munich, and Leipzig.[197] According to Nell Walden, all of the artists who exhibited in the "Erster Deutscher Herbstsalon" from September to November of that year also visited the *Sturm* gallery in person during the showing.[198]

As early as the first part of 1914, Hugo Ball, with the help and counsel of some of his Munich friends (in particular Kandinsky), had conceived the idea of what he called (even before the use of the adjective was firmly and widely established) an "Expressionist Theater."[199] This theater was to have been a "modern" and "experimental" theater which would have applied to the drama the same principles of style and thinking already well manifested then by the "new direction" (Ball's term again) in music, painting and poetry.[200] The theater alone, Ball felt at that time, would have been capable of forming the "new society" envisioned by the "new direction" in literature and painting.[201] His theater was to have represented a new conception of the "Gesamtkunstwerk" and a radical break with the recent realistic or naturalistic dramatic tradition of the West, i.e., the notion of a "theater of illusion," by making use of some of the techniques and of the music of Asian (Japanese) theater, by restoring the use of stilts or cothurni, masks, megaphones and nonrealistic sets.[202] By using such techniques, the attempt would have been made to affect the "subconscious" of the spectator, in contrast to the established theater which was "impressionistic" and addressed itself solely to the "rational faculty" ("Verstand") of the audience.[203] Ball was seriously working on the implementing of his ideas and had already selected a theater in Munich for the productions in the new style.[204] He was also preparing a volume, which at one point was given the tentative title *Expressionistisches Theater,* and which would have included contributions by himself, Kandinsky, Marc, Klee, Kokoschka, Alfred Kubin ("Expressionismus und Bühne"), and others, all outlining the new style.[205] These plans, however, like so many amongst the Expressionists at that time, were all abruptly quashed and never allowed to reach fruition by the outbreak of war in the summer of that year.

During the very time that Ball was hard at work on his attempts to establish an "Expressionist Theater" and edit a book on the subject, he met with Walden in Berlin (July, 1914) and arranged to direct the appearance of the *Sturm* exhibitions in Munich, beginning September 1, 1914.[206] Although these plans, too, were cut short of fruition by the outbreak of the war, Ball, nevertheless, was able to accomplish, three years later in Zürich, much of what he had set out to do in Munich. Thus, from March to April, 1917, he succeeded in arranging for the appearance in the "Galerie Dada" in Zürich of a series of *Sturm* exhibitions and organized in conjunction with them a four-part series of "Soirées," the second of which was officially titled "Sturm-Soirée."[207] Ball recorded in an entry in his diary from that April that these soirées realized "an old favorite plan" of his—he is, of course, referring to the one he drew up in Munich in 1914 for an "Expressionist Theater"—for they were a manifestation of "Gesamtkunst," pulling together in one performance painting, music, dance and poetry.[208] The soirées, framed in the gallery by the paintings of Kandinsky, Klee, Heemskerck, Kokoschka, Muche, Uhden, and many other Expressionists, featured recitals of Expressionist and related poetry, "abstract" and "Expressionist" dances, avant-garde musical and dramatic presentations (including a production of Kokoschka's "Curiosum" *Sphinx und Strohmann*) and, finally, intermittent programmatic statements and lectures.[209] The performers included members of the Zürich circle of Dadaists, German and Austrian Expressionists, and poets representing similar tendencies from France and Italy.[210] One of the performers at the second soirée on April 14 was Walden himself.[211] This intimate association with Ball, which stretched throughout the period Ball was working on his conception of an "Expressionist Theater," obviously provided Walden with liberal opportunity to be exposed to Ball's ideas directly. Indirectly, this exposure could have come by way of Ball's Munich friends Kandinsky, Klee, Marc, with whom Walden was in regular contact in the same period.[212]

Whether independently, or, as is more likely, through his connections with Ball, Walden also began calling for the establishment of an "Expressionist Theater" in February of 1915, which, although not yet outlined in detail, already agreed with Ball's ideas on the surface.[213] The first tangible moves towards creating such a theater were not made by the *Sturm* circle, however, until significantly, the very same month and year (March, 1917) that Ball's "Sturm-Soirées" got under way. In the issue of *Der Sturm* for that date appeared the announcement of the creation of a "Sturm-Schule" for "instruction and training in Expressionist art."[214] This was largely the product of the meeting of Blümner and Schreyer, both of whom had had prior training in the theater; and instruction in the dramatic arts was to be the most active division of the school.[215] Besides the dramatic arts—i.e., stage techniques, acting and recitation, which were taught by Blümner and Schreyer—the school also taught the art of Expressionist painting, poetry and music.[216] The list of teachers for the school in that first announcement is impressive in retrospect; they included, besides Blümner and Schreyer, Rudolf Bauer, Heinrich Campendonk, Jacoba van Heemskerck, Klee, Muche, Münter, and Walden.[217]

To what extent the school was active in the divisions of painting, poetry and music is not recorded; in the dramatic arts, however, it quickly bore fruit. To utilize the talents developed in the latter area a "Sturm-Bühne" was established in September of the same year.[218] The director of the new theater was Dr. John Schikowski, who had earlier been associated with Otto Brahm's "Freie Bühne."[219] This event had been prepared for, ideologically, by the publication of a series of essays in *Der Sturm* from August, 1916, to March, 1917, and by a series of lectures at the "Sturm-Abende" from April to June, 1917, in all of which their author, Schreyer, formulated in detail the theory and techniques of what he termed the "Bühnenkunstwerk."[220] In basic conception, the "Bühnenkunstwerk" of *Der Sturm* paralleled very closely Ball's "Expressionist Theater" (the "Sturm-Bühne" was alternately also called an "Expressionist Theater" or "Theater of the Expressionists" by Walden's group): it, too, was to constitute a "Gesamtkunstwerk," fusing all art forms into one total production or "unified work of art" (for this reason Schreyer preferred to call the "Bühnenkunstwerk" an "Einheitswerk" so as to distinguish it from Wagner's creation which, according to Schreyer, was not a fusion but merely a "juxtaposition" of the various art forms), and it was to represent a break with the traditional "theater of illusion" by employing techniques similar to those proposed by Ball (e.g., masks, sometimes larger than life size, non-Western music, nonnaturalistic style of acting).[221] In addition, the "Bühnenkunstwerk" was conceived of as the dramatic counterpart, both philosophically and stylistically, of the "Wortkunstwerk" of *Der Sturm*.[222] The stylistic theories of the "Wortkunst," centering on "concentration" and "decentration," applied equally to the dramatic composition.[223] Also, the same "spiritual experience" which the reader was to undergo through the "Wortkunstwerk" was to be enjoyed by the spectator of the "Bühnenkunstwerk": he was to experience the same kind of restoration of a sense of unity of being and of unity with the cosmos.[224] This philosophical aspect is emphasized in Schreyer's essays on the subject and is put forth in the original announcement in *Der Sturm* of the founding of the "Sturm-Bühne":

We know that the contemporary individual longs for a spiritual reality in which he can experience unity of being. This spiritual reality is manifested in art. The artistic experience satisfies our longing.[225]

Like the "Wortkunstwerk," the "Bühnenkunstwerk" produced on the "Sturm-Bühne" was aimed at creating a "community" of men, both amongst the performing actors and actresses as well as amongst the spectators, and thereby, as Schreyer interpreted, to the making of the "New Man" who would embody the condition of unity with the cosmos:

We were interested in the individual in the community and, creating and performing the "Bühnenkunstwerk" which aimed at being a cosmic mirror of the unity of life, in the possibility of propagating the community of natural-supernatural life as a form of experience of unification. This was to be accomplished by realizing this unification ourselves and giving it a tangible form in the symbolism of the work of art created out of all artistic means.[226]

Thus, in the ultimate philosophical function of the "Sturm-Bühne" Ball's earlier plan for an "Expressionist Theater" is met again, for, it will be remembered, Ball also intended his theater as a means for forming a "new society."

The performances of the "Sturm-Bühne" were closed to the general public and were given only for the members and invited guests of the "Verein der Sturm-Bühne."[227] The first production, August Stramm's play *Sancta Susanna* (published in *Der Sturm* in May, 1914), premièred on October 16, 1918.[228] Berlin, as Schreyer recalled, was already "living in the convulsions of the approaching revolution" on that date, so that the performance could only take place with police protection.[229] It was also no doubt due to the heightening of the political ferment in Berlin in the weeks that followed that prevented the other performances originally planned for that same fall from being carried out.[230]

As a special forum for expounding the theory of the "Bühnenkunstwerk" and as a vehicle of support for the productions of the "Sturm-Bühne," Walden founded in January, 1918 the periodical *Sturm-Bühne: Jahrbuch des Theaters der Expressionisten.*[231] *Sturm-Bühne* published programmatic essays on the "Bühnenkunstwerk," plays by the poets of *Der Sturm* and drama criticism.[232] Like most of the Expressionist periodicals established towards the end, or just after, the war, and for the same reasons, *Sturm-Bühne* was short-lived, lasting through just eight issues, put out between January, 1918, and October of the following year.[233]

The Walden theater also had difficulty surviving those chaotic postwar months. Although it did manage to remain active periodically, most of the practical work done for it in the "Sturm-Schule" had to be transferred to Schreyer's home in Hamburg right after the close of the war because of the conditions in Berlin.[234] In Hamburg, independent of the "Sturm-Bühne,"

Schreyer very soon established, with the support of Walden, the "Kampf-Bühne."[235] Conceived along the very same lines, both philosophically and artistically, as the "Sturm-Bühne," Schreyer's "Kampf-Bühne" also produced primarily Expressionist drama by the poets of *Der Sturm;* the two exceptions to this repertoire were much older works, which, nevertheless, have much in common with Expressionism.[236] The performances of the Hamburg theater were also limited exclusively to members of its supporting organization, who eventually numbered about three hundred.[237] The "Sturm-Bühne" in Berlin apparently produced only one more play, which premièred in 1920, after that first production in October, 1918. Schreyer's troupe in Hamburg, on the other hand, did a total of eight productions in less than two years: Stramm's *Die Haidebraut* (*Der Sturm* 5, 1914, 74-76) and *Kräfte* (*Der Sturm* 5, 1915, 150-56); Friedrich Hölderlin's *Der Tod des Empedokles* (second version); *Ein Krippenspiel* from 1589; Walden's *Sünde* (Verlag Der Sturm, Berlin, 1918); and Schreyer's plays *Kindsterben* (*Der Sturm* 11, 1920, 148-52), *Mann* (Verlag Der Sturm, Berlin, 1918) and *Kreuzigung* (*Der Sturm* 11, 1920, 66-68).[238] Each of these productions was prepared for by innumerable discussions and work sessions in Schreyer's home and a minimum of one hundred stage rehearsals.[239] Walden paid visits to the Hamburg troupe; and Blümner also came occasionally.[240] The "Kampf-Bühne" also made one guest appearance in Berlin, for which Walden rented Reinhardt's "Deutsches Theater."[241] The performance, of Schreyer's *Mann,* was also for invited guests only; one of the guests was Reinhardt himself, whose comments afterwards, according to Schreyer, were "cautiously and respectfully appreciative."[242]

Both the "Sturm-Bühne" and the "Kampf-Bühne" were disbanded when Schreyer responded to a call to join the "Bauhaus" in Weimar in 1921.[243] The "Sturm-Schule," however, out of which both of the *Sturm* theaters had developed, continued to be active; in the twenties, probably in an attempt to bring it into line, at least in name, with the more practical orientation of *Der Sturm* in that period, it was renamed the "Sturm-Hochschule."[244] This practical bias within the school, as it was in the journal, is particularly prominent in its last year, which is also the last year of *Der Sturm;* at this time the school announces the establishment of a division for training in the field of fashion ("Modeschule Berlin") under the direction of Richard Dillenz.[245]

Before the war *Der Sturm* and the other activities sponsored under its name had had to contend with much angry adversity from the censor, the public, and the established press; however, this condition was more than counterbalanced by the large support which came to *Der Sturm* from the Expressionist camp.[246] During the war, the former condition not only persisted but was also intensified, on the one hand because of Walden's continued support of non-German artists who were now labeled "enemies," and on the other because most of Walden's former supporters were now preoccupied with the question of the war and politics or with military duty.[247] Thus, at the beginning of the war *Der Sturm* fell on bad times financially. Nell Walden, however, was able to more than pull the journal and its other activities through, since her command of her native tongue, Swedish, was much in demand for translating, reporting, writing, and secretarial work.[248] In the last couple of years of the war, with Nell Walden's help and the return of much support to Walden as the literary life amongst the Expressionists began to revive, *Der Sturm* once more prospered.[249] The postwar years should have been expected to bring to *Der Sturm* even greater prosperity than before with the attainment of popular success in that time by the movement which Walden's group had supported all along with great vigor; but the popular success of Expressionism, as pointed out earlier in this study, was unexpectedly brief, and the Expressionists were soon discovered to be turning to other interests and in other directions in their lives. The peak of the enthusiasm of support for, as of the popularity of, *Der Sturm* and its ancillary activities had been reached by 1923, according to Lothar Schreyer.[250] By the following year the ties which had held Walden's circle together had already reached a sufficient stage of advanced deterioration for a special effort to be felt necessary in order to try to hold the group together. This effort, Schreyer reports, was made by Wauer with the organization which he established with the support of both Walden and Schreyer and named "Internationale Vereinigung der Expressionisten, Futuristen, Kubisten und Konstruktivisten."[251] The move came too late, however. The support which was to come from Walden's old circle to the activities sponsored after the mid-1920s was to be only a token of what it had been earlier; Walden himself was to begin assuming a conspicuously larger role in the years that followed in the only one of his projects still exhibiting strong signs of life by then, his journal *Der Sturm;* he was often to write in these last years—perhaps as much by choice as by necessity—a large percentage, once even all, of the contributions to a given issue.

The postwar inflation, as Nell Walden suggests, played its part in destroying *Der Sturm* and the other activities sponsored under its name; where it did not severely hamper those activities, it crippled them completely.[252] However, the change in interest and direction on the part of the members of Walden's circle was clearly the dominant factor in its dissolution. Schreyer, for example, was one of Walden's most important associates right after the war; but in 1921 he nevertheless accepted an appointment to the "Bauhaus" in Weimar, and was beginning shortly thereafter, as Schreyer himself wrote, to move in a new artistic direction, away from the subjectively oriented approach to art of his past work towards a greater objectivity.[253] Although he continued to maintain his association with Walden and especially with Walden's journal for a few years after joining Walter Gropius in Weimar, he obviously could no longer bring the same amount of enthusiasm to such work as he had in previous years. Three other important collaborators on *Der Sturm* had preceded Schreyer to the "Bauhaus": Feininger (1919), Klee (1920), Muche (1920).[254]

Many other contributors to *Der Sturm* followed the same, or a similar, pattern in the early twenties.

Walden's own ideological development after the war was also a factor in the break up of his circle: it drove a wedge between him and at least two, perhaps more, members of his circle. Contributions to *Der Sturm* in the postwar phase by members of the circle demonstrate clearly that some shared Walden's sociopolitical interest, if not as well his leftist leanings, in that period; but few were apparently willing to carry this interest quite as far as Walden did.[255] Schreyer, in particular, could not follow Walden all the way in his new commitment. Although, as we saw in the discussion of the development of *Der Sturm,* he did manifest in the journal itself a limited interest in the sociopolitical factors of contemporary life after the war, he could not make politics a way of life as Walden was to do; in the course of the twenties he eventually embraced fully the Christian church.[256] In the end, Schreyer and Walden parted friends, as Schreyer wrote later, but by then all that had remained of common ground between them was their friendship.[257] Nell Walden states that Walden's ideological development after the war was also responsible for the deterioration of her relationship with him; their split over political differences led directly to their divorce in 1924.[258] The latter event, as Schreyer and Blümner felt at the time it occurred, marked the beginning of the end for the *Sturm* circle.[259]

Walden's postwar endorsement of, first, the political left and, then, of Communism specifically, was described above in tracing the politicization of his journal in the same period. Prior to that time he had staunchly rejected out of hand any mixing of politics and art; he had always held: "Art and politics have nothing to do with each other."[260] The *Sturm* circle had also abided by this position in the earlier phases, Nell Walden claims, for its members had shown no interest in politics prior to the war; and after some sporadic signs of such an interest in the pages of Walden's journal in its first approximate year of publication, none could be remarked again until after the November Revolution.[261] Nell Walden reports—and Walden's essays which appeared in *Der Sturm* about the same time bear out her chronology—that the change in Walden's thinking began to take place shortly after the end of the war, when he began to show an intense interest in the politics of the left.[262] The war and the November Revolution no doubt were important influences on his turn to politics. His looking to Soviet Russia and his conversion to Communism were, according to Nell Walden, determined in part by his contacts with Russian artists who appeared in Berlin after the war.[263] He and his circle had become acquainted soon after the war with the Russian troupe of the cabaret "Der Blaue Vogel," which performed often in Berlin in that period.[264] He soon became a close friend of the director of the troupe, Jushny, and then began seeking out, more and more, the company of other Russian artists who came to the city.[265] His interest in Russian culture led him to an interest in Russia and

Russian politics—at least this is the order in which these interests are evidenced in his contributions to *Der Sturm*.[266] He eventually became a member of the German Communist Party.[267] In 1927 he made his first trip to Russia, on which he reported enthusiastically in *Der Sturm*.[268] This enthusiasm is given artistic expression, too, about that same time, as, for example, in Walden's workers' play ("Sprechchor") entitled "Auf!" which climaxes on a line prophetic of Walden's future: "Im Osten glüht das Licht / Dort ist das Leben geboren." ("A light glows in the east / There is the origin of life.")[269] He responded to the call to Russia which was implicit in his play just three months after the demise of his journal: in June of 1932 he finally moved his place of residence permanently to Moscow.[270] He was heard from most regularly from Russia thereafter through his contributions to the Moscow-based journal of German exiles *Das Wort*.[271] One essay contributed by Walden to that journal in 1938, entitled "Vulgär-Expressionismus," manifests unequivocally his continued support of both Communism and Expressionism and his persistent desire—a desire which had been very much on his mind at his last meeting with Schreyer shortly before his departure for Russia—of consolidating the one with the other.[272] Walden is believed to have been arrested by the Russian State Police on March 31, 1941; he was never heard from since.[273]

Excursus on the Walden-Pfemfert Polemic

Kurt Pinthus wrote of Expressionism in a late memoir:

> It will someday be difficult to write the history of the literary groups which, between 1910 and 1920, developed simultaneously in Prague, Berlin, Vienna, Leipzig, Dresden, Munich, and other cities. They often developed in conjunction with similar efforts in the fine arts, and in spite of their individual differences felt they together represented common interests, a community.[274]

One of the purposes of the present study is to demonstrate that the Expressionists did indeed constitute the "community" Pinthus recalls; but the "individual differences," which Pinthus did not forget, also must not be overlooked. No community made up of so extensive a number of individuals, as that of the Expressionists was, can be expected to have contained no examples of divergence or dissent. Thus, such differences appear in the literature of the movement, where they have thwarted again and again the efforts of students of this literature to arrive at a widely accepted definition of Expressionism which is all-inclusive; and these differences appear from time to time in the literary life of the movement, where they take the form of disagreements, rifts, rivalry and even polemics between members of the movement.[275] We have already seen how the latter kinds of personal differences led to a schism in "Der neue Club." An illustration of this side of Expressionist literary life on a broader scale, a dispute which cuts across two circles, is provided by the relationship between the Walden circle and the next one to be described here, the circle around Pfemfert and *Die Aktion.*

A few contemporaries have reported on the "state of war" which existed in Wilhelminian Berlin between Walden's *Der Sturm* and Pfemfert's *Die Aktion.*[276] Their enmity was made public in a polemic which was fired up just two months after *Die Aktion* began appearing and was still hot in the summer of 1918. The polemic grew out of the Kerr-*Pan*-Jagow affair (February, 1911f.), in the course of which Kerr was taken to task for his handling of the affair by Karl Kraus in *Die Fackel.*[277] Pfemfert reacted to Kraus's attack by taking the side of Kerr in an article entitled "Der kleine Kraus ist tot," in which he reversed his earlier support of Kraus.[278] Walden then countered in *Der Sturm* the same month with a mocking attack upon *Die Aktion.*[279] In the subsequent exchanges between Walden and Pfemfert in May of the same year the original impetus to the dispute largely receded into the background, with Pfemfert calling Walden "der ausgebleichte Somali" and accusing him of a lack of sound aesthetic judgement and with Walden countercharging Pfemfert with being a Walden-*epigone* who publishes the manuscripts rejected by *Der Sturm.*[280] After two attacks (by Blei and Lasker-Schüler's son, Paul Lasker-Schüler) upon Walden in *Die Aktion* in 1915, both of which remained unanswered by *Der Sturm,* there was another brief series of exchanges between the two editors in the summer of 1918.[281]

The Walden-Pfemfert polemic and the schism in "Der neue Club" are exceptional incidents in the Expressionist camp. Most representative by far of the relationships in Expressionist literary life are, rather, the close associations which existed between all of the circles in Berlin and between them and the other circles throughout Germany and other parts of Europe. Even in the case of the Walden and Pfemfert circles the antagonism between them appears to have been confined almost exclusively to their leaders, for it did not prevent members of either group (e.g., Benn, Friedlaender, Scher, Lichtenstein, Hiller, Blass, and Hardekopf) from publishing in both *Der Sturm* and *Die Aktion* concurrently, although certain recorded remarks by Scher and Benn suggest that such crossing over was generally discouraged by Walden in particular.[282] Also, in spite of the fact that the antagonism between Walden and Pfemfert came vociferously to the surface on occasion in the Café des Westens—where the two sat, just tables apart, surrounded by their supporters—there was, nevertheless, also fraternization on a personal level between the two groups: Benn, Einstein, Friedlaender, Blass, and Schickele are known to have had close personal contacts with both circles during most of the prewar phase of the movement; and just prior to the appearance of the Walden-Pfemfert polemic in print in their respective journals, Blümner and Scheerbart, both close friends and associates of Walden at the time, participated in the "Paul-Scheerbart-Abend" sponsored by *Die Aktion* on March 22, 1911.[283] Finally, the feud also did not noticeably infect Expressionists from other circles, for both *Die Aktion* and *Der Sturm* are reported to have been received by such circles with equal enthusiasm—at least until the war, when the long-standing political commitment of *Die Aktion* began to earn it the greater sympathy of the Expressionist readership.[284]

6

Franz Pfemfert and *Die Aktion*

It was around the time that *Die Aktion* began publication (February, 1911) that the outlines became especially distinct of a more or less fixed circle of followers and supporters around Franz Pfemfert. Just as the establishment of *Der Sturm* had acted as the catalyst in the consolidation of the Walden circle, so also the founding of *Die Aktion*, in providing a segment of the poets representing the incipient movement of Expressionism with an exclusive and independent forum for their work and ideas, simultaneously coalesced these poets in a tangible as well as in an intellectual way behind the editor. The Pfemfert circle was also to be seen henceforth regularly in the Café des Westens, its members plunged there in constant discussions and debates; and it was to continue to convene here on into the war.[1]

There was an extensive number of artists who maintained a close personal and literary association with Pfemfert during the prewar phase of Expressionism. In addition to his wife and most important associate, Alexandra Ramm, they included Carl Einstein, Jakob van Hoddis, Anselm Ruest, Ludwig Rubiner, Max Oppenheimer, Kurt Hiller, Maria Ramm, Ernst Blass, Grete Meisel-Hess, Ferdinand Hardekopf, Claire Otto, Alfred Lichtenstein, Richard Oehring, Paul Boldt, Alfred Wolfenstein, Hellmut Wetzel, Franz Jung, Gottfried Benn, Oskar Kanehl, Henriette Hardenberg, Karl Otten, Hugo Kersten, Carl Sternheim, and Gustav Landauer.[2] The less regular members or occasional guests of Pfemfert's circle included, most prominently, Franz Blei, Peter Scher, René Schickele, Max Brod, Else Lasker-Schüler, Georg Heym, Salomo Friedlaender, Heinrich Mann, Johannes R. Becher, Walter Hasenclever, Otto Gross, and Iwan Goll.[3]

Einstein, Hoddis, Ruest, Rubiner, Oppenheimer (pseud. and nickname "Mopp") and Pfemfert's wife were amongst those who were directly involved in the founding of *Die Aktion* at Pfemfert's table in the Café des Westens at the beginning of February, 1911. Einstein, Hoddis, and Rubiner, along with Hiller, Heym, and Friedlaender, had been amongst the contributors to the Berlin weekly *Der Demokrat* while it was under Pfemfert's editorship during the year prior to the beginning of *Die Aktion* (January, 1910, to February, 1911).[4]

Heym had even personally hawked copies of an issue of *Der Demokrat* in December, 1910, in the metropolitan railway in Berlin in order, as Heym himself put it in his diary in his inimitably ingenuous way, to "make propaganda" for himself, since the issue contained some of his own verse.[5] It was to Heym that Claire Otto owed her introduction to the Pfemfert circle in the summer of 1911; and the following year she could already have made her first contacts with her future husband Jung when he moved to Berlin from Munich and began what was to be a very long personal and literary association with Pfemfert.[6] When Benn's likewise long-standing friendship with Pfemfert was begun is not clearly known; however, statements made by Benn in published letters to friends and the date of his first contributions to *Die Aktion* both point to the year 1912.[7] Becher first appeared in Pfemfert's circle early in 1912, after having joined his Munich friend and later publisher Heinrich F.S. Bachmair in Berlin at the beginning of the previous fall to study for the winter semester at Berlin University.[8] Becher returned to Munich just before Easter of 1912; but he was to see Pfemfert periodically during the next couple of years when on visits to Berlin.[9] From the same Munich circle as Becher Gross came to Berlin in 1913 where he was directly introduced to the *Aktion* circle by his Munich friend Jung.[10] However, Gross's personal connections with Pfemfert's group, as with the Berlin artist community in general, was permitted to last only a few months: he was arrested in late 1913 and interned in an insane asylum in Troppau at the instigation of his professor-father. This incident immediately touched off a storm of protest in the Expressionist camp, in particular in the pages of *Die Aktion* and in the special Gross issue (no. 5, edited by Jung) of *Revolution.* The Expressionists seized upon the incident, exploiting its potential for being interpreted as a classical example of the tyranny of the Wilhelminian father (read: father-state) over the son.[11] Largely under the pressure brought to bear on the authorities and on Gross's father by the Expressionist protest, Gross was released from the Troppau asylum in the early part of 1914, but apparently thereafter returned to Munich instead of to Berlin.[12] One of the last to join forces with Pfemfert and *Die Aktion* in this early phase was Sternheim. Sternheim had already been a close friend of two of the major contributors to the journal before he himself also began a personal and literary association with Pfemfert around the time of the outbreak of the war: he had been a friend and sometime associate of Blei since 1908 when they had coedited the Munich avant-garde semimonthly *Hyperion* (1908-10), in which a number of the painters and poets later to be associated with Expressionism had appeared (Brod, Einstein, Heckel, Norbert Jacques, Franz Kafka, Heinrich Lautensack, Heinrich Mann, Meyer, Wilhelm Michel, Jules Pascin, and Schickele); and since 1913 he had been a friend of Ernst Stadler, who had frequently visited Sternheim in his home outside Brussels.[13]

The beginnings of a personal and literary association with Pfemfert in the case of the remaining members and friends of this circle can only be dated in a somewhat approximate manner, primarily from the time of their first appearance in *Die Aktion* or their first participations in functions sponsored under the journal's name. 1911: Maria Ramm (the sister of Alexandra Ramm and the wife of, first, Einstein and, secondly, of Heinrich Schaefer, a later associate of Pfemfert also), Blass, Meisel-Hess, Hardekopf, Blei, Scher, Schickele, Brod, Lasker-Schüler; 1912: Lichtenstein, Oehring, Boldt, Wolfenstein, Wetzel, Heinrich Mann; 1913: Kanehl, Hardenberg, Hasenclever, Goll; 1914: Otten, Kersten, Klemm.[14] The essayist and self-proclaimed socialist Gustav Landauer, who was an important political influence in Expressionism and an active participant in the government of the Bavarian Soviet Republic after the war, was never a contributor to *Die Aktion;* but he is reported by Jung to have, nevertheless, been a member of Pfemfert's "closer circle."[15] The context of Jung's report implies that the period of Landauer's association with Pfemfert included at the least the latter prewar years.

Ideologically, *Die Aktion* and the circle backing it were not materially affected by the outbreak of the war; as already remarked on more than one occasion in this study, by the time of that event *Die Aktion* had long been almost a lone island of political commitment in the main current of Expressionism. Had the physical conditions attendant upon war not made it impossible, *Die Aktion* would no doubt have been overwhelmed now by literary supporters to match the greater interest of the readership in the journal in the years that followed. Pfemfert's circle, however, was only a little less disrupted physically by the effects of the war than were the other circles of the movement. Up to this date only a few, although none the less important, supporters had left Pfemfert's circle.

Heym's collaboration had been lost to *Die Aktion* as it had to "Der neue Club" by his accidental death in January, 1912.[16] The following year another, more intimate associate of Pfemfert from "Der neue Club," Hiller, split with the editor over personal as well as ideological and moral differences; this was a break whose significance for Pfemfert is punctuated by his devoting an eight-column-long lead article of an *Aktion* number to a vitriolic diatribe against Hiller in December, 1913.[17] That same year, Hiller's three-year-old friendship with Blass came to an end, and Blass moved to Heidelberg where he soon lost contact with both *Die Aktion* and Expressionism as a whole.[18] Scher's contributions to *Die Aktion* abruptly halted in the fall of 1913; this was the year in which he moved to Munich, and although there is no public sign of a break between him and Pfemfert at this time, he was later, in 1916 and again in 1918, to be attacked by Pfemfert in his journal for ideological reasons.[19] Hoddis, as mentioned in connection with "Der neue Club," began drifting away from the Berlin Expressionists in 1912, at first because of his travels, and then because of mental illness.[20] Finally, Meisel-Hess's association with Pfemfert appears to have also come to end sometime during the immediate prewar years.[21]

The outbreak of the war not only very soon caused the curtailment of the activities of Pfemfert's circle (e.g., the "Autorenabende," the "Revolutions-Bälle," the size of the issues of *Die Aktion*), but, in addition, quickly robbed Pfemfert of the physical presence, if not also the literary support, of most of the remaining members of his circle. Only Pfemfert's wife, her sister Maria Ramm and Claire Otto, Wetzel, Lasker-Schüler, Friedlaender, Oehring, Landauer, and Boldt appear to have been able to maintain regular contact with Pfemfert in Berlin throughout the war.[22] Lichtenstein was one of the first from the Expressionist camp to die on the field of battle. He was just completing the conventional one year of voluntary military service when the war broke out; he was forthwith inducted, shipped off to the Western front (August 8, 1914!) and scarcely more than a month later was killed in France (September 25)—but not before he was able to send back to Germany by field-post to his friends Pfemfert, Scher, Meyer, and Kurt Lubasch some of the very first war poems composed in the trenches of World War One.[23] Klemm, Benn, Kanehl, and Einstein spent the entire war at assigned military posts in the field, except perhaps for brief leaves; and Sternheim, Becher, Blei, Heinrich Mann, and Brod, although not serving in the military, were restricted in their mobility by wartime conditions and similarly only able to visit Berlin occasionally now.[24] Otten reports that his undisguised opposition to the war resulted in his arrest at its outbreak; spending a part of the time in prison and a part as "Arbeitssoldat," he was held in protective custody until the winter of 1917/18.[25] Rubiner and Goll exiled themselves for the duration of the war to Switzerland, where they joined the other German Expressionist exiles.[26] They were followed to Switzerland in 1915 by Oppenheimer and in 1916 by Hardekopf.[27] Schickele took *Die weissen Blätter* to Switzerland in the latter part of 1915; he thereafter lost contact with Pfemfert and was later taken to task on several occasions during the war in Pfemfert's column in *Die Aktion*, largely on political grounds.[28]

Pfemfert dissociated himself from several other former friends during the war, as well as from most of the other representatives of Expressionism. Amongst his own associates, he also broke off with Ruest for ideological reasons in 1915, and, as already noted, in 1916 with Scher.[29] On similar grounds he parted company with Blei at the end of 1917; and, in the same period, also severed ties, for reasons that are not clear, with Wolfenstein and with Wolfenstein's bride of one year, Henriette Hardenberg, a year following the couple's move to Munich and just months after Pfemfert had paid homage to the poet by devoting a special number of *Die Aktion* to him.[30] Finally, Hasenclever, who had served in the army from 1914-16, was added to the list of those fallen out of favor with Pfemfert in the latter half of the war, for what appear to have been both aesthetic and political reasons.[31]

The renewal of the ranks of Pfemfert's personal following in Berlin by additions during the course of the war was small by comparison with the losses.

One of the first to join Pfemfert in Berlin following the outbreak of the war was Hugo Ball. Ball had contributed mostly poetry to *Die Aktion* from Munich under his own name from the summer of 1913 to the summer of the next year.[32] With his Munich friend Hans Leybold, Ball had also coauthored for *Die Aktion* a series of poems, whose form shows strongly the influence of Jakob van Hoddis's "Weltende"-style and whose content, often verging on the absurd, foreshadows Ball's Zürich Dada period; these poems appeared in *Die Aktion* between March and August, 1914, under the pseudonym of "Ha.Hu.Baley."[33] Ball had met with Pfemfert on at least one occasion in Berlin before the war; this was in July, 1914, in connection with Ball's arrangements for a series of matinées in Munich for "Der neue Verein," one of which was to have been an *Aktion*-matinée.[34] The plans for the series were quashed by the outbreak of the war, but Ball was able to reestablish his association with Pfemfert on a personal level when he came to Berlin in the winter of 1914/15 for an extended sojourn.[35] Although his work did not again appear in *Die Aktion* after August, 1914, his contacts with Pfemfert in Berlin that winter and during part of the following spring were intimate and, as he reports in his diary, had a decisive effect on his political development then and in the years that followed.[36] His experience in Pfemfert's sphere was shared by the poetess Sylvia von Harden. She came into contact with Pfemfert in Berlin in 1915 through her very close friend in that period, Hardekopf.[37] Von Harden never became a contributor to *Die Aktion;* yet, like Ball, she reports that her acquaintance with Pfemfert had "immense" meaning for her.[38] The young poetess was in Berlin for only about a year; she moved on to Munich in 1916 and later joined Hardekopf in the circles of German exiles in Switzerland.[39] Her poetry was eventually to appear in a number of Expressionist publications.[40]

The year 1915 also saw the return of one of Pfemfert's earlier associates: after a brief stint in the army in the first months of the war, Jung was able to rejoin his friends in the Expressionist camp in Berlin.[41] For the rest of the war, in addition to contributing generously to Pfemfert's publications (*Die Aktion, Das Aktionsbuch, Aktions-Bücher der Aeternisten,* etc.), Jung also put out with a circle of friends in Berlin, that included Gross, Schrimpf, Oehring, and Oskar Maria Graf, a periodical series in broadsheet format under the heading *Freie Strasse* (1915-18).[42] Jung was living at this time with Claire Otto, whom he was also soon to marry (she was apparently still married to Oehring at the beginning of this period); and it was Claire Otto, according to Jung, who was the general editor of the series, enjoying in the task the assistance of Pfemfert.[43] The painter and poet Karl Jakob Hirsch also had close contacts with the Pfemfert circle in Berlin during the war.[44] He had already associated on a personal basis with Munich Expressionist circles in the Café Stephanie from about 1911 to 1913, while studying art in the city; then, from the spring of 1913 through the first half of 1915 he had been painting and studying art, first in the Worpswede colony, next in Paris, and finally in Worpswede again.[45] Around the middle of 1915 he decided to move to Berlin; and about this same time he also began contributing to *Die Aktion*.[46] Although Hirsch was inducted into the army on September 15, 1916, he was very soon stationed near Berlin in Adlershof and permitted to live in his own apartment in Charlottenburg; he was thus able, as he wrote in his autobiography, to frequent the Café des Westens regularly in this period.[47] His association with Pfemfert and *Die Aktion* in the meantime had been intensifying: in June, 1916, Pfemfert dedicated a special number of his journal to the young artist and in January, 1918, sponsored a one-man showing of his work in the exhibition rooms of *Die Aktion*.[48] At the end of the war, as will be discussed later, Hirsch was active in the Revolution. Hugo Kersten's work had been strongly represented in the pages of *Die Aktion* from the beginning of 1914 through most of the first year of the war; however, the number of his contributions had fallen to a trickle by the beginning of the spring of 1915, the same time in which he had gone to Zürich and there, in March of that year, cofounded and coedited with Emil Szittya the first two issues of the very short-lived "Literarische Kriegszeitung" *Der Mistral*.[49] Kersten finally returned to Berlin in 1917, but did not reappear in the pages of *Die Aktion* until 1919, after a three-year absence from the journal (his last contribution, the only one for the year, had appeared in October, 1916). Kersten suddenly died, an accidental death, in Berlin in 1919.[50]

The Silesian poet Herrmann-Neisse had been a regular contributor to *Die Aktion* from his home in Neisse since the journal's first year of publication.[51] Since 1905 he had been a close friend of another Neisse-born poet and also later associate of Pfemfert, Jung; and it had been Herrmann-Neisse, as Jung was later to admit, who had provided Jung with his real introduction to the literary world, while he was still a "Gymnasium" student, through the circle of aspiring young poets that was gathering at that time in Herrmann-Neisse's home.[52] Jung was later able to return the favor, for it was he, as Herrmann-Neisse's biographer-interpreter Rosemarie Lorenz tells us, that brought Herrmann-Neisse's attention in the summer of 1911 to two books—Schickele's collection of verse *Weiss und Rot* (1911) and his novel *Der Fremde* (1907)—which sparked the decisive turn in his literary development, the turn in a new direction towards the tendencies represented by his young contemporaries in the Expressionist camp.[53] Unlike his friend Jung, however, before the war Herrmann-Neisse had established only superficial personal contacts with Pfemfert and other Berlin Expressionists on his few brief visits to the city between November, 1912, and the outbreak of the war.[54] For the next three years he was isolated in his home town, prevented by wartime conditions from continuing his trips to Berlin. Then, in March, 1917, he is finally able to fulfill a long-held wish of moving his permanent residence to the capital of Expressionism, where he immediately begins what is to be a very long friendship and intimate association with Pfemfert.[55]

In spite of the support Pfemfert was thus receiving from home during the war, the bulk of the contributions to his journal during these years, as opposed to the prewar period, was coming from abroad, from artists who, because they were either stationed out in the military field or virtually isolated in other cities of Europe for the duration, were able to give Pfemfert little or no personal support. The latter artists included such major contributors as Paul Adler, Ludwig Bäumer, Blei, Ehrenstein, Otto Freundlich, Goll, Klemm, Otto Pick, Heinrich Schaefer, and Werfel.[56] Nevertheless, *Die Aktion* survived the war years well, and in the last two there even appeared signs that indicated that the circle around the journal was beginning to prosper and to expand its activities again.

In the spring of 1916 Pfemfert began expanding the publishing activities of the Verlag der Wochenschrift *Die Aktion.* In April, 1916, he initiated the series *Aktions-Bücher der Aeternisten* (1916-21), for the publication of prose by primarily major contributors to his journal.[57] The programmatic statement of the series, "Erste Proklamation des Aeternismus," was composed by Hardekopf under a pseudonym he occasionally used, "Stefan Wronski." In this stylistically unique manifesto, Hardekopf, defining the literature of what he calls the "Aeternists," sets forth some basic artistic principles which echo many other Expressionist and Futurist programs: it is (a) antibourgeois, antitraditional and extremist literature ("Here on one promontory, bold experiments will be made. Our books will be incomprehensible to the middle class.") (b) with a primarily urban background ("We have explored the insides of the great metropolises and of phosphorescing souls. We are cheerfully at home at macabre masquerades and at scabrous routs, in painted catacombs and chiaroscuro cafés, in subcutaneous bars and on ogival-style summits, at roadhouse taverns and at Eusapia séances, in syndicalist café concerts and detective Pullman cars, with somn- and noctambulists, at bistros, with excavators and deputies, in morphinic boudoirs and corrupt automobiles, in gambling houses and in bed, in discipline and in caprice.") (c) composed from a perspective of "Simultaneity" ("In us all past is present and future. Everything has to pass through us."), and conceived without regard to conventional logic, syntax and grammar ("Our psychology will shock you. Our syntax will asphyxiate you. We will smile at your confusions, abstractly and augurally. Sublime subjunctives will be reduced to dust, futures will evaporate narcotically, and frothy balls of quintessential fragrance, à la *je m'en fiche,* will disperse in the air.").[58] All but one (Péguy) of the authors published in the series were members of Pfemfert's circle at one time: Hardekopf, Einstein, Jung, Benn, Heinrich Schaefer, and Charles Péguy.[59]

In October, 1916, Pfemfert began putting out two other series: *Die Aktions-Lyrik* (1916-22), again primarily as a forum for poets from *Die Aktion;* and *Politische Aktions-Bibliothek* (1916-30), for the publication of political essays and manifestoes by socialists and communists from Europe.[60] In the summer of the following year the last of these series was opened: *Der rote Hahn* (1917-25), which published both imaginative and political literature by writers frequently met with in the pages of *Die Aktion* and by others.[61] Finally, in the fall of 1917 Pfemfert expanded his support of Expressionist graphic arts, which to that time had been restricted to illustrations in the issues of his journal. On November 1 he opened a bookstore and art dealership in the Kaiserallee in Berlin, and in these rooms a series of exhibitions was held between December, 1917, and October, 1918, featuring the artists whose work had previously decorated the pages of *Die Aktion:* César Klein, Josef Capek, Otto Freundlich, Oppenheimer, Heinrich Richter-Berlin, Karl Schmidt-Rottluff, Hans Richter, Georg Tappert, Hirsch, et al.[62]

The changes which took place in the Pfemfert circle at the close of the war were radical, and affected not only the constituency of the circle but also its ideological position in a broad sense. With the political events of this period in German and general European history, especially the Russian Revolution which preceded it and the German November Revolution which accompanied it, coincides the intensification of the political commitment of the Pfemfert circle and *Die Aktion* to the extreme. Pfemfert's interest in, and support of, literature of any strain or direction began to wane in favor of political literature and political activities. A foreshadowing of this development had already appeared as early as 1915 when, within the framework of the group of artists around *Die Aktion,* Pfemfert and his supporters clandestinely organized their own left-wing political party, the "Antinationale Sozialistenpartei (A.S.P.) Gruppe Deutschland."[63] Shortly after the Revolution hit Berlin, the existence of the A.S.P. was made public, as was Pfemfert's and his journal's support of it. A public appeal by the party was published in *Die Aktion* and over 100,000 copies of a separate printing of the appeal were put out for distribution at meetings, at train stations, in the streets; the signatories of the document were all past contributors to *Die Aktion,* all poet-politicians: Bäumer, Ehrenstein, Julius Talbot Keller, Otten, Pfemfert, Schaefer, Hans Siemsen, and Carl Zuckmayer.[64] Public meetings and functions in the name of the A.S.P. and under Pfemfert's direction were initiated after November 9, 1918, and before the year was out no less than five of them had taken place in Berlin.[65]

Little published information is available on the activities of Pfemfert or his circle of supporters behind the scenes of the publishing ventures sponsored under the name of *Die Aktion* in this postwar period. Outside of his wife and her sister, Pfemfert's regular and intimate circle of friends in Berlin now is only known with certainty to have included Otten (pub. in *Die Aktion* 1914-19); the teacher and poet Schaefer (pub. in *Die Aktion* 1914-19), who moved to Berlin in 1919 and married Maria Ramm; Herrmann-Neisse (pub. in *Die Aktion* 1911-27) and Kanehl (pub. in *Die Aktion* 1913-31; d. in Berlin May 28, 1929.)[66] Pfemfert is also known to have had frequent contacts in the 1920s with

Sternheim (pub. in *Die Aktion* 1914-24) and with Sternheim's close friend in this period, Conrad Felixmüller, one of the cofounders of the Berlin-based "Novembergruppe" (pub. in *Die Aktion* 1917-28).[67] Both Sternheim and Felixmüller were residing in Dresden in the 1920s; and the Sternheims welcomed on frequent occasions as their house guests both Alexandra and Franz Pfemfert, who came with typewriter in order to work on pieces for *Die Aktion*.[68] Outside of the original Expressionist camp, Pfemfert now entertained a personal association with a noted Berlin journalist whom he had esteemed professionally for a number of years and who had occasionally contributed to *Die Aktion* before the current phase: Maximilian Harden (pub. in *Die Aktion* 1912, 1915 and 1920-24; the editor of the weekly *Die Zukunft* from its beginning to its end, 1892-22; d. November 30, 1927 in Switzerland).[69] Harden had given only tenuous approval to republican ideas before the war, but then in later years had become a supporter of a radical form of socialism, which fact would explain his friendship with Pfemfert in this period.[70] Consonant with Pfemfert's political affiliations now, he was also in frequent personal touch with the Spartacist leaders Karl Liebknecht (pub. in *Die Aktion* 1919-28) and Rosa Luxemburg (pub. in *Die Aktion* 1918-28) until their deaths in Berlin in 1919.[71]

Besides those already mentioned, there was a large number of former and current major contributors to Pfemfert's journal who were residing in Berlin in the immediate postwar years and who may or may not have had some personal connections with Pfemfert at this time. The latter included Einstein (pub. in *Die Aktion* 1912-17), Rubiner (pub. in *Die Aktion* 1911-18; d. in Berlin on February 26, 1920), Hardekopf (pub. in *Die Aktion* 1911-16; res. in Berlin 1921/22), Claire Otto (pub. in *Die Aktion* 1919; in this period married to Jung), Oehring (pub. in *Die Aktion* 1912-15, 1923; in Berlin until 1922), Boldt (pub. in *Die Aktion* 1912-18; d. March 16, 1921, in Freiburg im Breisgau), Jung (pub. in *Die Aktion* 1912-21; made frequent trips to Russia 1922ff.), Benn (pub. in *Die Aktion* 1912-17, 1922), Kersten (pub. in *Die Aktion* 1913-16, 1919; d. in Berlin in the fall of 1919), Blei (pub. in *Die Aktion* 1911-17, 1919; res. in Berlin 1923-33), Lasker-Schüler (pub. in *Die Aktion* 1911-16), Friedlaender (pub. in *Die Aktion* 1911-16), Becher (pub. in *Die Aktion* 1912-16, 1919), Gross (pub. in *Die Aktion* 1913; d. in Berlin in 1919), Hirsch (pub. in *Die Aktion* 1915-19), Ehrenstein (pub. in *Die Aktion* 1915-29), Richter-Berlin (pub. in *Die Aktion* 1913-21, 1926; cofounder of the "Novembergruppe"), Tappert (pub. in *Die Aktion* 1913-17, 1921; cofounder of the "Novembergruppe").[72]

Like Walden in his group, Pfemfert, as editor of his circle's literary forum, was the dominant and strongest unifying force within the circle around *Die Aktion*. The careers of Walden and Pfemfert bear a number of other, even more striking, similarities which point up certain qualities of character and certain talents that, taken together, help to explain why they were sponsors of the two leading journals of Expressionism. Pfemfert, like Walden, was many-sided in his talents, being at once poet, literary and political essayist, publisher, art patron and art dealer and, finally, as Walden was to be some time after Pfemfert, radical political activist. Both had very strong individualistic strains to their personalities, especially as editors, and Pfemfert, asserting this side of his character on one occasion in the same way Walden had almost a year before him, also established his first entirely self-initiated and self-governed journal in order to break free of the controls of a senior editor over him (see below). However, indicative of one very important difference between these two antagonists of the established press and art, Walden had been frustrated in his work under previous editors primarily by constant encounter with resistance to his own avant-garde literary tastes, while Pfemfert had been most disconcerted under his chief editor by his lack of success in asserting editorially his own political views. This was a difference of basic orientation and was, thus, to be decisive for their development in the Expressionist era, for it was to set them and their journals wide apart ideologically—Walden and *Der Sturm* aesthetically esoteric and Pfemfert and *Die Aktion* highly pragmatic. It was also largely because of this difference, as it has been claimed before in this study, and no doubt as well because Pfemfert was a far more gregarious, aggressive and extroverted individual than Walden, that Pfemfert's and his journal's influence eventually penetrated deeper within his own group and further beyond its borders than did the influence of Walden and *Der Sturm*. For this reason, Schickele, who had been at home in many Expressionist circles, could state, in looking back over the previous decade from the vantage point of the year 1920, that Pfemfert's *Die Aktion* had been the "central force" of the movement.[73] In a similar vein, Otten called *Die Aktion*, in a retrospective memoir, the "Urquell expressionistischen und geistesrevolutionären Ausdrucks."[74]

Pfemfert's sociopolitical orientation was already deep-seated by the time of the founding of *Die Aktion;* it is traceable at least as far back as his very early manhood when, having to educate himself because he was not able to finish his studies at a Berlin "Gymnasium," he was studying poetry and politics and regularly reading the politically oriented, anti-Wilhelminian Berlin journal edited by Maximilian Harden, *Die Zukunft*.[75] Around the turn of the century he began frequenting political gatherings and was brought into contact with advocates of left-wing politics and anarchists in Berlin.[76] His earliest writings are reported to have already included political poems alongside political and literary essays; and the first of his early works to be published appeared significantly in 1904 in the literary-anarchist periodical *Kampf,* which was founded and edited by the anarchist Senna Hoy (pseud. for Johannes Holzmann) in 1904/1905.[77] Pfemfert's company in the pages of *Der Kampf* was prophetic of things to come, both for him and the decade of 1910-20: other contributors to the journal included Else Lasker-Schüler, Herwarth Walden, Erich Mühsam, and Peter Hille.[78] Senna Hoy was himself later to be a contributor to *Die Aktion;* and Pfemfert was to dedicate a special number of his journal in 1914 to the thirty-one-year-old writer on the occasion of his tragic death in a Russian prison.[79] Shortly after her arrival in Berlin with her sister from Russia, Alexandra Ramm met Pfemfert; she is said to have had a guiding influence on Pfemfert's subsequent literary and political interests.[80] In 1909 Pfemfert was contributing both political and literary essays to Heinrich Ilgenstein's weekly *Blaubuch;* he continued to cultivate these two genres side by side during his editorship of *Der Demokrat* from 1910 to 1911 and again in his own journal *Die Aktion* during the Expressionist years.[81] Pfemfert perhaps best expressed the strong political bent to his thinking, pointing at its source in an equally strong moral and humanitarian commitment, in a letter dated April, 1915, and addressed to the wife of his associate Wilhelm Klemm:

> The "great," the "public," the "social" life is only evil, petty, mad. It can only be opposed with work and merciless battle. I wish I did not have to do it, that is to say: our lives would suffer less provocation from the outside world if I did not. But mine has suffered such provocation as long as I have thought in political terms.[82]

Even in the beginning of *Die Aktion,* as Alexandra Ramm wrote, when Pfemfert's support of Expressionism was most enthusiastic, it was not clear which of the two, politics or literature, was foremost in his mind.[83] Nevertheless, Pfemfert's support of the one was never, until the end of the Expressionist era, to be easily separated from the other; during this period, he was always allied with Expressionism, not only because he provided its representatives with an exclusive forum in his publications and other professional ventures, but also because his own politics was in accord with the basic aesthetic aim and with many of the basic ideological values of Expressionist literature. All of the literature, political and imaginative, from his pen and that of his associates, which he admitted to the pages of his journal and to his other publications had, in Pfemfert's mind, the aesthetic function of arousing the reader to a critical attitude towards contemporary culture and society. This was, for example, to be the stated purpose of *Das Aktionsbuch* (pub. February, 1917), an anthology of poetry, prose and sociocritical, political, and literary essays by contributors to Pfemfert's journal.[84] Pfemfert declared in the short afterword to the anthology:

> This *Aktionsbuch* is not the advertising almanac of a publishing operation.
> I do not publish books as a business venture, but in order to make business dealings difficult, just as I use the technological means of the press in the publication of my completely unpopular, oppositional weekly in order to oppose the publishing business. I have put this *Aktionsbuch* together and published it under the worst conditions imaginable so that you might have something interesting to read. I was guided by one wish alone: that this book might teach you to cast off your sacred German indolence concerning human affairs.[85]

The causes espoused in his own political writings and in those of others published by Pfemfert were shared as well by Expressionist literature as a whole: he, too, espoused freedom of mind and action, political and economic equity, the new and revolutionary in contemporary culture; he, too, opposed especially the stagnated and irrelevant remnants of the cultural past, those features which he referred to in one *Aktion* editorial as "der alte Wust der Gestrigen" and which in his mind were exemplified by Heinrich Mann's Wilhelminian "Professor Unrat."[86]

For many of the young representatives of Expressionism, Pfemfert's artistic forums were, as Claire Jung and others have written, a steppingstone to recognition and public notice.[87] To such burgeoning artists, admittance to Pfemfert's circle of associates and friends was, in addition, equivalent in their minds to admittance to the literary world itself. Becher thus said of his initial establishment of connections with Pfemfert's circle in Berlin in the winter of 1911/12: "Von der Warschauer Brücke stiess ich schüchtern bis ins Café des Westens vor, und alsbald machte ich die Bekanntschaft von Franz Pfemfert, dem Herausgeber der *Aktion.* Damit hatte ich den eigentlichen Anschluss an die Literatur gefunden."[88] Pfemfert's role in the development of many of the members of his circle went much further than giving them recognition and gaining for them public notice; for many he was also mentor and model, critic and patron. In especially a sociopolitical sense, as would be expected, Pfemfert's impact on these poets was brought to bear. Franz Jung claimed that through Pfemfert's example members of his circle were induced to write from a sociocritical or political perspective.[89] As suggested at the outset of this chapter, the uniting of the Pfemfert circle in a concrete sense was accomplished primarily by the founding of *Die Aktion;* the uniting of the group in an ideological sense and the setting of it apart from other circles of Expressionists, as again Franz Jung suggests, was achieved by its sociopolitical orientation and the fusion in the pages of *Die Aktion* of sociopolitical and imaginative literature.[90]

Pfemfert's impact upon the political-literary development of Ball and Piscator has already been cited.[91] Jung's memoirs on Pfemfert and *Die Aktion* amount to a testament to the same kind of impact on his development as a writer and individual.[92] Sylvia von Harden, as pointed out earlier, was in Pfemfert's sphere of influence for only about a year at the beginning of the war; however, according to her, this was long enough for Pfemfert to make a strong impression on her and in particular in a political sense. She wrote in a memoir on this period:

> When I think back on the distant past I think of the great impression made on me by Franz Pfemfert, whose friendship I also owe to Hardy [Ferdinand Hardekopf]. Pfemfert—the tenacious man with the sparkling, inquisitive eyes, the pointed nose on a headstrong face, with the singing voice, but above all Pfemfert the political personality—meant an awful lot to me.[93]

If the political development of other such poets is not traceable in a tangible way to Pfemfert's influence, it, nevertheless, usually seemed to revolve around, or coincide with, an association with Pfemfert, his journal, and his circle's activities. The poet-painter Karl Hirsch is an illustration of this fact. Hirsch states in his autobiography *Heimkehr zu Gott* (1946) that in spite of the outbreak of the war, and even as he was setting up residence in Berlin and beginning his association with *Die Aktion* in the second half of 1915, he had remained, as he had always been in the past, too absorbed by his artistic interests to take politics seriously.[94] By the end of the war, however, Hirsch had undergone an almost complete reversal of attitude, so that his political activities at this time appeared to dominate his day: he became an active participant in the Revolution from its very inception in Berlin as a member of the revolutionary council "Rat geistiger Arbeiter" and a cofounder of the Revolution-aligned, Expressionist artists' organization "Novembergruppe."[95] Hirsch does not tell us in his autobiography to what extent his turn to a concern for political issues and to political activism at the end of the war was determined by his contact with Pfemfert, although we can sense Pfemfert's presence in the background at all times. This presence is made most tangible in a description by Hirsch of his politico-artistic activities in the "November-gruppe" which appeared in a publication commemorating the group's tenth year (1928). Pfemfert, his publications, even his offices in the Kaiserallee in Berlin are seen to be an indispensable and major part of the setting for Hirsch's political involvement:

> The storms of November. "Novembergruppe." It started when we were still running about gloomy Berlin in our tattered army overcoats, as we stood on a ladder in the rain, painting the inflammatory word "Aktion" in red-white-blue letters above the new bookstore in the Kaiserallee, until a policeman with spiked helmet rushed up and forbade it because, as he said, it was illegal to post bills in an "elegant street." It was during the time the nocturnal quiet of the Office of the Royal Air Force Inspectors was ruptured by a classified telegram which read: "Threat of revolution—All troops confined to their quarters." It started in the studiolike Office of the Royal Air Force Inspectors, where painters, dressed up as soldiers, had to make sketches of airplanes, while under their tables lay revolutionary drawings done on royal Prussian paper in royal Prussian ink for courageous Franz Pfemfert's *Die Aktion.* That was when *Die schöne Rarität* and several issues of *Der rote Hahn* came into being. That was the time when, with a cautious wink of the eye, we declared our support of the workers who were demonstrating in the streets in January, 1918, when we sat waiting for our day of liberation, for a light was shining in the East![96]

Finally, also noteworthy is the large number of past *Aktion* poets and painters who followed Pfemfert, not only into political cognizance—something which, of course, characterizes the development of the vast majority of the Expressionists, as stated at the beginning of this study—but also into political activism. This is a tendency which, if not indicative of the impact on these artists of Pfemfert and *Die Aktion,* then at least of a quality of mind which was practically a requisite one for membership in Pfemfert's circle. The political activists who had, prior to their turn to such commitment, been closely associated with Pfemfert included Hirsch, Felixmüller, Einstein, Becher, Kanehl, Oehring, Rubiner, Otten, Hiller, Wolfenstein, Jung, Freundlich, Bäumer, Richter-Berlin, Tappert, Schaefer, and several others.

The first issue of the key literary tribune of Pfemfert's circle, *Die Aktion: Wochenschrift für freiheitliche Politik und Literatur,* appeared in print on February 20, 1911. This was just eight days after Pfemfert had unceremoniously walked off his post as assistant editor ("Schriftleiter") on the Berlin weekly *Der Demokrat* in protest over the refusal of the chief editor (Dr. Georg Zepler) to permit the appearance in the journal of an article by Hiller on the radical philosopher Max Steiner, an article which Pfemfert had already accepted.[97] All of the contributors recruited for *Der Demokrat* by Pfemfert— they included Einstein, Rubiner, Friedlaender, Hiller, Heym, Hoddis, Robert Jentzsch, Simon Ghuttmann, and Erwin Loewenson—immediately declared their solidarity behind Pfemfert's action and transferred their support from Zepler's journal to *Die Aktion.*[98] There had been some noteworthy moments in the history of Expressionism to come out of *Der Demokrat* while it was under Pfemfert's editorship: the "Marseillaise of the Expressionist rebellion," as Becher has called Hoddis's poem "Weltende," first appeared here in print; and the appearance of Heym's verse here brought him his important discovery by the publisher of his first full volume of verse, *Der ewige Tag* (Leipzig: Ernst Rowohlt, 1911);[99] but there were to be infinitely more such events to issue forth from *Die Aktion.*

Die Aktion was over the years to be largely Pfemfert's creation; yet, the original, hurried planning of it, during those eight short days after Pfemfert's sudden break with *Der Demokrat,* had been a joint effort of the friends that had already rallied to his support by that time. The title for the journal had, according to Alexandra Pfemfert, finally come to her husband in bed one night during those same eight days, after they had searched in vain for one for hours that evening at Pfemfert's table in the Café des Westens with their friends Einstein, Rubiner, Oppenheimer (who designed the masthead), Ruest, Hoddis, et al.[100] The title itself was programmatic, for it already implied the aggressive posture which the journal was to assume opposite contemporary culture, especially opposite the established press, much as the title of Walden's journal had done; it was a title whose proper interpretation could be found in that "fight" ("Kampf") outlined by Pfemfert in his April, 1915, letter to Erna Klemm cited earlier.[101]

This "action" against contemporary culture was to be waged both in radical sociopolitical essay and in imaginative literature published by the journal. The radical quality of the two literary forms was underscored in the brief "Note" which appeared at the end of the first issue of *Die Aktion* and in numerous issues through the first year, and which defined the program of the journal in more explicit terms.[102] Pfemfert declares in this statement the political direction to be followed by *Die Aktion* as left-wing, although he emphasizes that it will side with no specific political party: "Without assuming a specifically partisan position, *Die Aktion* supports the ideas of the Great German Left."[103] The literary direction which *Die Aktion* was to support was to be clearly Expressionist; and this fact was to be stated explicitly, in retrospect, in the years that followed. In this programmatic note, however, it is more *implicit* in the statement that the journal will favor the "newer trends" in literature, those which the established press eschews: "In artistic and literary matters *Die Aktion* aims to represent a counterweight to the lamentable habit of the pseudoliberal press of assessing new impulses only from a commerical standpoint, in other words, to ignore them."[104] The closing statement of the "Note" makes it clear, nevertheless, that both the literature and the politics of this publication will be radical in nature: "The ambition of *Die Aktion* is to be an organ of forthright radicalism."[105]

The kind of literature and politics which *Die Aktion* espoused thus made it revolutionary; but perhaps even more revolutionary for its time, as Paul Raabe points out, was its simultaneous endorsement of both a revolutionary literature and a revolutionary politics in one journal: "This is what was new. *Die Aktion* became the forum for a new literature emerging before the background of a set of radical political values."[106] This mixture was, of course, implied by the initial subtitle of the journal; but that subtitle was one of the holdovers from *Der Demokrat* and had, like the others, eventually to be shed, i.e., at least in form, if the break with the past was to be virtually complete. This break did not begin to take place markedly until towards the end of the first year of publication. At this time, beginning with the October 9 issue (no. 33), a larger type is adopted, although it remains within Old English ("Fraktur").[107] In the following month, Pfemfert began printing frequently examples of the new lyric—the one genre in imaginative literature he had favored in *Der Demokrat* and was to favor strongly in *Die Aktion*—in a separate type, a bolder type, but also still Old English. Finally, *Die Aktion* opens the second quarter of its second year (no. 14, April 1, 1912) with a much sharper turn towards a modern typography. A totally new type is now adopted: the antique boldface already in use on Walden's *Der Sturm*. Simultaneously a separate cover-title page is added, permitting Pfemfert to achieve a much cleaner masthead by dropping the table of contents to the center of the new cover and removing most other information to the second masthead on page one of each issue. That same quarter was opened with a new subtitle: "Wochenschrift für Politik, Literatur und Kunst."

As the changes in typography were taking place, the contents of *Die Aktion* was also breaking more strongly with the past. Politics had clearly dominated the journal's pages through most of the first year; but very soon thereafter a greater balance between political and literary contributions gradually began to develop. Contributors of a more conventional stamp—and mainly sociopolitical essayists—were soon dropped (e.g., Otto Corbach, Ludwig Gurlitt, Max Jungnickel), as were, even before the middle of the first year, the regular reports from two sociopolitical organizations closely allied with *Die Aktion* in its first months of publication, "Das Komitee Konfessionslos" and "Die Organisation der Intelligenz," to which Pfemfert had been allotting separate space at the end of each issue.[108] The latter two changes in content helped to give *Die Aktion* the stamp of a more singular editorial purpose. A third such change, which occurs in the first approximate year and a half of publication and attests to an increased interest in imaginative literature on Pfemfert's part, reinforces this purpose most strongly: at this time the work of a large number of (mostly very young) poets associated with the new movement in literature begin to appear in the pages of *Die Aktion*. They include especially Becher, Benn, Blei, Boldt, Brod, Herrmann-Neisse, Einstein, Kurtz, Lichtenstein, Hardekopf, Scher, Schickele, Ernst Stadler, Otto Pick, Wolfenstein, Lasker-Schüler, Meyer, and Heinrich Eduard Jacob.[109] The next year and a half brought many more young supporters of similar tendency.

From about 1912 on Pfemfert was to limit the contributors in all departments of his journal, with only relatively few exceptions, to the young, largely unrecognized talent of the Expressionist generation, as he had promised he would in his original programmatic statement. Within the department of imaginative literature, he would occasionally favor Expressionist prose by, for example, publishing a complete novel in several installments in *Die Aktion* (1912: Einstein's *Bebuquin oder die Dilettanten des Wunders;* 1912/13: Schickele's *Der Fremde*[110]); but overwhelming preference, throughout the remainder of the Expressionist decade, was to be given to the Expressionist lyric. Thus, in this prewar phase of *Die Aktion* he initiated the series of "Lyrische Anthologien," each installment of which consumed the entire issue of the journal for that date. The series was opened with the January 8, 1913, issue, dedicated to the memory of Pfemfert's former associate Heym (d. January 16, 1912), and was continued into the war.[111] It was also in *Die Aktion* that the declaration of the contemporary era as the "age of the lyric" was made by Scher and Kersten; and in the case of Scher this declaration was given programmatic force by putting it in the prominent position of the introduction to the second "Lyrische Anthologie" (no. 27 for July 5, 1913).[112]

The support of the graphic arts of Expressionism by Pfemfert and *Die Aktion* did not begin until the latter half of this prewar phase, at a time when such support in the Walden circle had begun to intensify greatly. Pfemfert's support of this side of Expressionism also was never to approach the degree of Walden's at any time. Just three months after Walden initiated his exhibitions of Expressionist art in 1912, the first of the prints, in the same style, appeared on the pages of *Die Aktion:* Oppenheimer's drawing of August Strindberg in the May 22 issue (no. 22, pp. 643/44). The prints which appeared in the journal throughout the rest of that year were (as had, interestingly, been the case with the earliest Expressionist drawings, by Oskar Kokoschka, to be printed in *Der Sturm* in its first year) predominantly portraits of Pfemfert's contributors, drawn in most cases by Pfemfert's close associate Oppenheimer.[113] The first Expressionist woodcut to appear in the journal was by Franz Marc and was printed in the June 11 issue of the following year; in the course of 1914 this artistic medium was to become a regular and distinctive feature of *Die Aktion,* as it had of Walden's *Der Sturm.*[114] The title page drawing, another distinctive ingredient of the journal's pictorial image, became firmly established in the second half of 1913.[115] There was some critical treatment of the graphic arts and of exhibitions in *Die Aktion,* but this occurred only sporadically throughout the journal's first decade; and Pfemfert's own sponsorship of exhibitions of Expressionist art, as noted earlier, did not commence until the last year of the war.

By the time the prewar years of *Die Aktion* were drawing to a close, Pfemfert could justifiably declare that his journal had become an organ of both a new politics and—he is now able to be more specific on the kind of literature and art he favors—of some of the leading representatives of "jüngste Literatur" and of "jüngste Kunst" (both, like the other term he uses in the same declaration—"das Junge Deutschland," terms commonly used especially before the war, but also in later years, to designate the literature and art which during the war became *widely* known as "Expressionism").[116] Pfemfert made this declaration in his now famous open letter of May, 1914, to the public prosecutor in which he angrily protested the confiscation of an issue of *Die Aktion* (ostensibly on moral grounds, but without question mainly for political reasons):

> Listen, Mr. Public Prosecutor. *Die Aktion* is a weekly journal of politics, literature, art. Of the most humane form of politics. For (forgive me, readers and contributors) the new first-rate literature.... What has been published in my journal in the last three years is so valuable, so full of vibrant life, so (my God, another popular word!) stunning that future historians of literature, art, politics will not be able to write the history of contemporary Germany without having studied *Die Aktion.* Literary historians will then discover, for example: the most important, most spirited, most courageous, most moral weekly of the new literature around 1910 was *Die Aktion* of Berlin. The best minds of the new generation (the historians will say) fought their first battles here...[117]

The clearest proof of his claim is provided by a list of the major contributors to his journal during the bulk of the prewar years; they were, with but a few exceptions, members of his personal circle of friends and associates in Berlin in the same period: Blass, Blei, Brod (residing in Prague), Einstein, Friedlaender ("Mynona"), Max Brod (res. in Prague), Hardekopf, Hiller, Kanehl, Kersten, Lichtenstein, Marie Holzer (res. in Prague), Paul Mayer, Oppenheimer, Rubiner, Ruest, Schickele, Stadler (res. in Brussels), Alexandra Ramm, Otto Pick (res. in Prague), Meisel-Hess, Hellmut Wetzel, Wolfenstein, Rudolf

Kayser, Herrmann-Neisse, Hans Leybold (res. in Munich), Scher, and Kurtz.[118]

Pfemfert opened the first war-issue of *Die Aktion*—which came off the press one week late, on August 15, 1914—with the following announcement:

> Friends of *Die Aktion,* readers, contributors!
>
> *Die Aktion* will publish only literature and art in the coming weeks.
> As far as it lies in my power and my will, our journal will continue to appear without interruption.[119]

This statement, which was dated just two days after Germany declared war on France (August 3, 1914), was deceptively terse, for the changes which the effect of it was forthwith to produce in the pages of *Die Aktion* were to be the most extensive of the following four years. The major implication of the statement was immediately clear to the intimate reader of the journal: the political department of *Die Aktion* was to be dropped, except where contributions to it were not to be directly concerned with the political issues being fought out on the battle fields of Europe.[120] This change was, furthermore, not to be effective for merely "the next few weeks," but for the duration of the war. At this premature date, Pfemfert was obviously already anticipating the tightening of censorial controls under the military authorities which was to ensue very shortly and, therefore, foresaw the need for circumspection if he wanted to bring his journal through the war years unscathed, i.e., without having either to suffer the fate of *Das Forum* (deletions and then total ban of publication) or to resort to the tactic of the editor of *Die weissen Blätter* (removal to Switzerland).

His decision to delete direct political commentary on the war from *Die Aktion* was to be labeled by some of his critics as moral deviousness; however, it was eventually discovered to have been a shrewd maneuver, issuing from as strong a moral commitment as ever, and clearly not from moral compromise. Ironically enough, he was essentially seeing to the preservation of the political voice of *Die Aktion,* for this voice was, indeed, not to be muzzled, just disguised during the war years. Thus, his own political comments, which had in the past usually opened each issue, were now relegated to the last pages of each issue and given expression to there, mainly through the use of innuendo and irony, in the journal's letter column with accompanying glosses ("Kleiner Briefkasten") or in a column created in April, 1915, for this particular purpose and given the cryptic rubric "Ich schneide die Zeit aus."[121] The new column, as the title of it and as Pfemfert in his note introducing it indicated, was to publish clippings culled from the current (established) German press, whose statements of patriotic sentiment and support of the war were, when transferred from their original context to the context of this column, to be transformed—unless already self-evidently so—into tasteless manifestations of jingoism and bellicosity.[122]

The political voice of Pfemfert's collaborators was also not to be silenced completely in this period; it was to be prominently heard now in the more indirect form of the imaginative literature published in *Die Aktion.* The source of inspiration for much of this literature was to be the war, the issue of it, the experiencing of it, life in the trenches and on the battlefield. Pfemfert continued in this period his preference within literature for the lyric, in particular now for the war poem, which was given a conspicuous place in the pages of the journal in a new, continuing section of each issue inaugurated in October, 1914, under the heading "Dichtungen vom Schlachtfeld" (also: "Verse vom Schlacht-feld").[123] The contributors to the series were to be soldiers in the field, who had written their verse in the trenches or in the barracks, verse in which the sights, sounds, and sensations of battle dominated and in which nationalism or militarism were notes never struck. The dominant tone of the series, as just described, was set by the first installment in it, "Schlacht an der Marne," written by the most frequent contributor to the series throughout the war, Wilhelm Klemm. The poem's concluding lines not only shun nationalism, they also stop just short (in the first two lines quoted below) of directly espousing its antithesis:

> My heart is as large as Germany and France together,
> Pierced by all the bullets of the world.
>
> The lion's voice of the battery is raised,
> Six-fold across the land. The shells howl.
> Silence. In the distance the infantry's fire rumbles,
> For days, for weeks.[124]

Other soldiers in the field whose work could often be read in this period in "Dichtungen vom Schlachtfeld" included Kanehl, Lichtenstein, Walter Ferl, Jomar Förste, Piscator, Kurt Adler, Otto Steinicke, Hans Koch, Alfred Vagts, and Wilhelm Stolzenburg.[125]

Some prose, drawing upon the experience of the war, also appeared in *Die Aktion* after August, 1914; and, occasionally, a drawing, depicting the horrors of battle (as in Ludwig Meidner's drawing "Schlachtfeld" for the title page of the December 5 issue of 1914), would lend additional force to the implicit opposition of *Die Aktion* to the conflagration.[126] This position of *Die Aktion* and of its editor was, if in no other way, made evident at least in the consistency with which those works of art were selected for publication whose image of the war or of the times was most grim and unsympathetic.

That the position of *Die Aktion,* as manifested in Pfemfert's marginal columns and in the poetry, prose and graphic arts in its pages, was, in fact, sufficiently clear to speak with *political* force to the soldier out on the field of battle (who was often receiving copies of the journal at Pfemfert's expense in this period), is reported first hand by one such reader and contributor, Erwin

Piscator.[127] An indirect corroboration of Piscator's claim that many soldiers were, like himself, influenced in their political thinking by their reading of *Die Aktion* in the field is the sizable number of poets who first began contributing to Pfemfert's journal during their term of active military service; if not an acknowledgment of the political impact of *Die Aktion* on them, then, just as significantly, their joining forces with him at this time, contributing to his journal and other publications the kind of literature represented by the "Dichtungen vom Schlachtfeld" and, in the case of some, eventually becoming politically involved, has to be read at least as a declaration of solidarity with the political position defended by Pfemfert and *Die Aktion*. Besides Piscator, this new segment of contributors included Julius Talbot Keller, Walter Ferl, Otto Steinicke, Alfred Vagts, Rudolf Fuchs, Georg Kulka, and Edlef Köppen (whose appearance in *Die Aktion* caused him difficulties with the army staff).[128]

The war years also had some physical effects on *Die Aktion*. They considerably reduced the length of each quarter of the journal from the end of 1914 on. This was the result of Pfemfert's issuing double numbers semimonthly, beginning with the very first issue put out in the war, without noticeably increasing the size of each new number.[129] In spite of this change, the subtitle remained intact as "Wochenschrift für Politik, Literatur, Kunst" until the end of the war. There was also considerable change in the makeup of Pfemfert's list of contributors. Most noticeable is the increase in the number of painters represented with art work in the journal; this change was a reflection of Pfemfert's greater interest in Expressionist art in this period and the greater prominence of graphic arts in the pages of his journal now. The major contributors during the war included Kurt Adler, Paul Adler, Pick, Herrmann-Neisse, Einstein, Tappert (graphic arts), Klemm, Jung, Freundlich (mainly graphic arts), Sternheim, Schaefer, Rubiner, Oppenheimer (graphic arts), Bäumer, Otten, Josef Capek (mainly graphic arts), Däubler, August Brücher (transs. only), Goll, Blei, Hans Richter (graphic arts), Wolfenstein, Werfel, Richter-Berlin (graphic arts), Ehrenstein, Hardekopf, Hirsch (graphic arts), Hans Koch, and Viktor Fraenkl.[130] Most of the latter were, as stated earlier, not present in Berlin through most or all of the war.

As had been the case at the outbreak of the war, the changes in the image and editorial policy of *Die Aktion* which occur at the close of the war are a direct and immediate response to very tangible, current political events; they are spontaneous changes, too, which take place largely and quite literally overnight, i.e., from one issue of the journal to the next. The very first number of *Die Aktion* to come out in the postwar period, out of the first week of the Revolution, embodies the full spectrum of changes in the journal in this phase. The macabre title page woodcut of this issue (no. 45/46, November 16, 1918) already plunges *Die Aktion* into the thick of the most hotly disputed issues of the Revolution—the issues involved in the clash of left and right wings of the revolutionaries—with its caption: "Capitalism, which disenfranchised the working people and forced them to the slaughter, is calling for the National Assembly so that it can continue to exploit and disenfranchise."[131] The immediacy and literalness of this woodcut's political message, both through its artistic content and its caption, was to be representative for *Die Aktion* for the remainder of its publishing life. A telling forecast for the future of the journal was also the total absence of any poetry or imaginative prose in this and in the next postwar issue (no. 47/48, November 30, 1918).

The first postwar issue contained only political manifestoes and commentary centering around the issues of the Revolution directly. It opened with the first public appeal of the "Antinationale Sozialisten Partei (A.S.P.) Gruppe Deutschland," the party established by Pfemfert and certain of his associates on *Die Aktion*.[132] This appeal and the other contributions to the same issue fix sharply the basic political direction which *Die Aktion* as a whole was to follow until the end: it was to oppose most vigorously what Pfemfert called the "holy trinity" of imperialism, militarism and capitalism—the three factors which, for Pfemfert, accounted for the recent war, and it was to espouse most consistently pacifism and the Socialist Revolution.[133] The enforcing of this position is continued in the next issue, which opens with a second attack by Pfemfert on the call for a National Assembly, which he, like the other representatives of the far left-wing parties at the time, interpreted as a middle-class and capitalist conspiracy to undermine the Socialist Revolution.[134] Pfemfert's attack is followed by Carl Sternheim's warning against similar middle-class and capitalist infiltration of the Revolution.[135] The second postwar issue closes with a declaration of solidarity with the ideals and leaders of the Spartacus League.[136] With the appearance of the complete text of the constitution of the new Russian Socialist Republic in the next issue (no. 49/50, December 14, 1918), the outline of the full range of the journal's political sympathies in this phase is completed.[137]

Increasingly in the years that followed, as the divisions between right and left in the ill-fated Weimar Republic were becoming entrenched, *Die Aktion* was both to function as the political organ for Pfemfert's own party and, in a broader sense, to assume the character of a communist political "Agitationsorgan."[138] Imaginative prose and poetry, on the other hand, no matter the direction it might represent, was to be thrust further and further into the background of interest in *Die Aktion* in the same period, and, towards the end, was to be lost sight of completely.

The latter development was a predictable outcome as much of Pfemfert's intensified commitment to politics after the war as to his wide-ranging blacklisting of Expressionist poets both from within and without his circle which he had begun undertaking during the course of the war. He declared in *Die Aktion* in April, 1918: "If I could only once and for all drive it into the heads of the unsuspecting that I am not interested in literature, whether new or old!"[139] That statement was still couched in ambiguity, since it appeared in the context of an introduction to poems by three young poets; but such was not the case two months later when he announced in his column that he was turning his back on the literature of Expressionism (here referred to as "Das junge Deutschland"), because, in his view, it had begun to degenerate by selling out to the middle-class book market.[140] Even though the spurning of that literary movement was not to be carried out as abruptly as Pfemfert's announcement seemed to want to suggest—it was to be, rather, a gradual process taking place over the next several years, still, the dropping of the journal's subtitle ("Wochenschrift für Politik, Literatur, Kunst") altogether with the first issue put out after the war freed *Die Aktion* of all overt obligations to specific media of expression, rather than to certain issues, and tended as well to give added stress to the more fundamental political connotations of the main title.[141] Thus, at the beginning of the immediate postwar period, a time when Pfemfert could have sunned *Die Aktion* in the light of the literary triumphs being enjoyed at that time by Expressionism, he chose to give this literature, even where it might express quite discernibly the same political convictions, short shrift in favor of political essay and commentary. At the end of the war the journal also discontinued the series of special numbers devoted or dedicated to an individual poet associated with the journal.[142] This also happened to the series of special numbers dedicated to *Aktion* painters which had been begun during the war, for the Expressionist woodcut or drawing also became increasingly less a part of *Die Aktion* in the journal's last decade of publication.[143] By the end of 1921 only a small number of the older contributors of imaginative literature or graphic arts were still represented with any degree of frequency; they included Ehrenstein, Herrmann-Neisse, Kanehl, Mühsam, Schaefer, Freundlich, Sternheim, and Felixmüller. In the course of the next few years most of the above stop contributing, so that, by the time the new, long overdue subtitle "Zeitschrift für revolutionären Kommunismus" is given *Die Aktion* in 1928, only Ehrenstein, Kanehl (d. 1929), and Felixmüller are left.

None of these changes in the content of *Die Aktion* in the postwar period, in particular the reduction in the space alloted to imaginative literature, could have been of any surprise to the regular reader of the journal at the time. As Paul Raabe has written, long before that new subtitle had been added to *Die Aktion* in 1928 the journal had begun being read by workers in the factories in place of artists in the cafés.[144] In its last few years of publication, *Die Aktion* slowly and gradually ground to a halt, averaging less than a half dozen issues for each full year; and the content of those same issues, which the financial and other troubles of the journal permitted to appear from 1929 to 1932, was taken up almost exclusively by discussions and polemics centering around communist ideological theory and party politics.[145]

The other literary and artistic forums sponsored by Pfemfert and his circle were all outgrowths and ancillary activities of *Die Aktion*. One of them, the exhibitions of the work of the *Aktion* painters, was described earlier. Most important of these secondary activities were the literary evenings inaugurated a few weeks after the founding of *Die Aktion.*[146]

The function of these recitals, as defined in the prenotice for them in *Die Aktion,* paralleled the stated function of the journal: they were intended to give support and public exposure chiefly to poets whose talents were not being "properly recognized by public and press."[147] The directors of the readings, again as stated in that original announcement, were drawn from Pfemfert's circle of close associates before the war; besides Pfemfert himself, they were Ruest, Hiller, and Meisel-Hess.[148] In a brief note in his column in *Die Aktion* in 1916, Pfemfert reported that a total of nineteen literary evenings had been held by the outbreak of the war; only seventeen, however, have been substantiated.[149] The performers at these evenings were also, with only rare exceptions, members of Pfemfert's circle in Berlin.[150] Pfemfert and Einstein were the most regular participants; others who appeared at several evenings were Boldt, Lichtenstein, Oehring, Wetzel, Wolfenstein, Oppenheimer, and Hoddis.[151] Three readings were devoted completely to special favorites of the *Aktion* circle: the "Paul-Scheerbart-Abend" on March 22, 1911, which opened the series, the "Max-Brod-Abend" on December 15 of that year and the evening featuring Blei on March 28, 1913.[152] The recital in Brod's honor, at which Brod read from both his own work and from the poetry of his Prague friend Franz Werfel, was especially noteworthy for having contributed to Werfel's growing reputation amongst the Berlin Expressionists.[153] The May 16, 1914, recital was held in memory of Pfemfert's former friend and literary associate Senna Hoy, who had died the previous month in a Moscow prison where he had been interned since 1907 for engaging in revolutionary political activities in Russia.[154] The Senna Hoy evening featured Pfemfert and Lasker-Schüler, who had also been a close friend of the deceased poet and, although it was seriously doubted by Pfemfert at the time, is now known to have, indeed, visited him in Moscow in November, 1913, in an effort to get him released.[155] One of the *Aktion* recitals, the last one documented before the war, was held in Leipzig on June 18, 1914; the others were held in Berlin, most often in the lecture hall of the Café Austria, which enjoyed a certain degree of popularity among Expressionists in the city before the war.[156] Pfemfert had hopes of reviving these evenings during the war within the frame of the *Aktion* art exhibitions, but this plan apparently never materialized.[157]

There had been a movement before the war led by supporters of *Die Aktion* to organize a private theater group for the production of plays outside the control of the censor. The idea for the theater had first been formulated in *Die Aktion* in January, 1912, by Lautensack, a former member of the Munich cabaret group "Die elf Scharfrichter."[158] Lautensack proposed for the theatrical organization the name "Das Heimliche Theater" and for the first production *Totentanz* by his friend and former associate from "Die elf

Scharfrichter" Wedekind. To avoid the interference of the censor more effectively than had other such organizations in the past, Lautensack suggested eliminating altogether the entrance fee.[159] Lautensack's ideas immediately attracted the support of several members of the Expressionist camp and were shortly put into action by the Pfemfert circle.[160] A meeting was held in conjunction with the plan on February 26, 1912, in Berlin to "demonstrate against the censor," and funds were solicited through *Die Aktion* to finance the first production.[161] That first production was scheduled for the end of March, 1912; on the same day a "Wedekind-Abend" was also to be held, at which Ferdinand Hardekopf was to give a talk on the guest of honor, Ludwig Hardt was to read from the dramatist's work, and Wedekind himself was to sing some of his songs.[162] Both performances had to be postponed just before they were due to take place when it was learned that Wedekind would be unable to come to Berlin on that date.[163] For unknown reasons the plans were never able to be revived.

The series and other secondary publications which appeared in the Verlag der Wochenschrift *Die Aktion* reflect the development of Pfemfert's journal and the circle around it. Until the end of the war, the great bulk of these publications was devoted to Expressionist prose and poetry, most notably in the mainly prose volumes of *Aktions-Bücher der Aeternisten* (1916-21) and in the poetry series *Die Aktions-Lyrik* (1916-22).[164] Two other series were begun during the war: *Politische* (later: *Kommunistische*) *Aktions-Bibliothek* (1916-22, 1930), *Der Rote Hahn* (1917-25).[165] The first one published leftist political essays, and in the second the same kind of essays are generously admixed with Expressionist poetry and prose of patently similar political persuasion; significantly, these were the only two series to survive the immediate postwar years.[166]

By the middle of the 1920s, at the latest, it was no longer possible to speak of a circle of supporters around Pfemfert and *Die Aktion*. By this time, as we have seen, all but a very few of his older supporters had ceased appearing in *Die Aktion*. In some cases the loss of these supporters will have stemmed from literary reasons, in other cases from political factors. Pfemfert had himself, of course, withdrawn much of his own support from Expressionism, a fact which forced many writers to seek greater opportunity for publication elsewhere. Most of the members of Pfemfert's original circle had, on the other hand, become closely associated with other journals, groups, even movements, during the war and after; their literary sympathies were thus divided to a degree after the war. Most decisive in the break up of Pfemfert's circle, however, must have been the political development followed by Pfemfert and *Die Aktion* in the postwar period.

Pfemfert, both as a writer and as a person, was totally committed to politics of radical tendency after the war. He was not only actively involved in the Revolution and political events which followed it, he was also engaged in organizing meetings of his own party, the A.S.P. In addition, he was an active supporter of other parties and political activities. He was a cohort of Karl Liebknecht and Rosa Luxemburg and of their Spartacus League; and he fought on their side in Berlin in the ranks of the "Red Troops" against the Government troops led by Alfred Noske during the general strike called by the Spartacists and the Independent Socialists in Berlin in January, 1919; it was during this incident that his friends Liebknecht and Luxemburg were murdered.[167] Pfemfert was also following closely the course of the new Russian Soviet Republic during this period and supporting it, as we saw, as a writer and publisher.[168] His own overt political activism in these years was prominent enough to lead to his repeated arrest by the authorities of the Weimar Republic.[169] He no longer saw his task now, even in part, to lie in helping to gain recognition for representatives of the newer trends in literature and art, but to lie in the education of the proletariat and the workers in the communist idea as he interpreted it, an undoctrinaire, Trotskyite form of communism.[170] His opposition to the middle class was now strictly political, and only literary or artistic in an indirect way, i.e., as a result of his political position.

Thus, the very nature of Pfemfert's commitments after the war was unpropitious and unconducive to coalescing behind him and his journal of a coterie of supporters. The base of his involvement now lay well outside of the activities of the kind of close circle of writers he had gathered around him before the war; and the base of this new involvement could no longer be contained, nor its demands for expression fully appeased, within the pages of a journal. Pfemfert's ties, as were those of his similarly inclined associates, were much broader now, linked with an international movement; and the fight he was now engaged in was concentrated on overt political action, not on the printed page. It is, therefore, not surprising that there is no evidence of Pfemfert or a circle around him frequenting any of the favorite literary cafés in Berlin after the war; in so far as he might have had meetings with associates, as he had before the war, they will have been restricted to his editorial offices or to political gatherings, such as those of his A.S.P. Pfemfert in particular, of all of those who had been associated with *Die Aktion* until the close of the war, seems to have absented himself in subsequent years from the literary scene in Berlin. Finally, while most of Pfemfert's former associates on *Die Aktion,* as already mentioned, had come under the same, or a similar, political persuasion in the course of the Expressionist period, only very few were willing either to carry that persuasion as far as Pfemfert was or to remain by that persuasion for as long as or as steadfastly as Pfemfert did. Einstein, Hiller, Wolfenstein, Jung, Otten, Sternheim, Schickele, Ball, and Hirsch, to name only a few of Pfemfert's original associates who are relevant to this context, were all supporters of the Socialist Revolution after the war, but none of them were willing at any time during the Expressionist era or after to endorse communism unreservedly; nor were any of those named inclined to abandon imaginative literature to the extent Pfemfert did. A typical view of the latter years of *Die Aktion* by a former Pfemfert associate is expressed by Erwin Piscator. As Piscator saw it, the political extremism of Pfemfert and of *Die Aktion* in the postwar period "destroyed" the journal.[171]

Pfemfert's ultimate fate in Germany at the end of the Weimar Republic is virtually a copy of that of most other political activists from the left of center. Just a short half year after *Die Aktion* had ceased publication permanently (August, 1932), the total collapse of the Weimar Republic was made official by President Hindenburg's emergency decrees following the fire in the Reichstag (February 27, 1933) and by the passing of the crucial "Ermächtigungsgesetz" (March 23, 1933) by the newly elected parliament, therewith surrendering to Adolf Hitler dictatorial powers. In the midst of these events, which were accompanied by the suppression of all political parties, except for the NSDAP, Pfemfert and his wife fled from Berlin to Karlsbad on March 1, 1933; from there, still dodging the Nazi wrath, they moved on to Paris in 1936.[172] Pfemfert's antipathy to the doctrinaire Stalinist brand of communism no doubt induced him and his wife ultimately to seek refuge in the west. Journeying by way of Lisbon and New York, they finally landed in Mexico City in 1941. There was a covert appropriateness, if not significance, to this choice of residence, for Leon Trotsky, whose writings Pfemfert had often published after the war and with whose form of communism Pfemfert had been able to sympathize most throughout these years, had preceded the Pfemferts to Mexico City and had there established the base of his "Fourth International" group.[173] A year before the arrival of the Pfemferts, however, Trotsky had been murdered by a man alleged to be a Stalinist agent. After his own flight from Europe, Pfemfert himself is not known to have ever returned to any form of political activism, nor even to have ever taken up the pen again—except to write his memoirs (the manuscript of which was reportedly lost). Until his death on May 26, 1954, Pfemfert worked in Mexico City as a photographer, as he had in Karlsbad, and as he had part-time much earlier in Berlin while struggling through the financially difficult postwar years there.[174]

7

Alfred Richard Meyer

At the beginning of the summer of 1907 a young, little-known poet and reader for the Otto Janke Verlag in Berlin, Alfred Richard Meyer, took the first, modest steps towards establishing his own publishing company; he commissioned in that season, under the new imprint of the Verlag A.R. Meyer, Berlin-Wilmersdorf, the printing of two very slim volumes of verse, each volume a mere four sheets in length and in a unique variation on the traditional broadsheet format. The first of the two volumes was composed by a then equally obscure and now almost totally forgotten poet, Ernst Bartels; the second was from the pen of Meyer himself and bore the title *Ahrenshooper Abende.*[1] One evening later that same summer, in one of the favorite night spots of the Berlin artist bohemia, Dalbelli's Italienische Weinstube, Meyer made the acquaintance of the Munich cabaret poet and noted Wedekind-devotee, Heinrich Lautensack.[2] During that first meeting, Meyer showed Lautensack a copy of his just published *Ahrenshooper Abende* and convinced Lautensack to allow him to put out, in the same format, five of Lautensack's poems under the new Meyer imprint.[3] Lautensack, in turn, put Meyer in touch with another South German writer, Hans Carossa, from whom Meyer was able to obtain the publishing rights to Carossa's "first poetic work," *Stella mystica.*[4] Before the year was out, Meyer had managed to add to the four volumes just mentioned three other installments in what was eventually to develop into a continuing series of broadsheetlike volumes appearing under the rubric *Lyrische Flugblätter.*[5] Thus, by the end of the first half year of business, Meyer had made a solid beginning as a publisher; at the same time, with the undertaking of this new enterprise and the friendships it was securing for him, beginning with Heinrich Lautensack, the foundation had been laid for the subsequent development of a circle of literary associates and supporters centering around Meyer, his publishing firm and his other literary activities.

By about the middle of the early phase of Expressionism, when a journal, *Die Bücherei Maiandros,* founded and edited by Meyer and his friends Lautensack and Anselm Ruest, was added to Meyer's literary enterprises, the major thrust of Meyer's patronage of literature was being directed towards the work of writers closely associated with Expressionism—in particular writers involved in the Berlin branch of that movement. The Meyer circle, on which there is especially detailed information for the same general period, i.e., the middle of the early phase of Expressionism, reflects in its membership at this stage the dominant sympathies of Meyer's editing and publishing activities. In this period, besides the popular cabaret performer Resi Langer, whom Meyer married in 1908, and in addition to Heinrich Lautensack and Anselm Ruest, Meyer's circle of friends and literary associates is known to have included most regularly the poets Rudolf Leonhard, Rudolf Kurtz, Gottfried Benn, Paul Erkens, Fritz Max Cahén, René Schickele, Oskar Kanehl, Felix Lorenz, Ernst Wilhelm Lotz, and the writer-translators Otto Buek and Else Hadwiger.[6] Occasional visitors to the Meyer circle in this period were Max Herrmann-Neisse from Neisse and Ernst Stadler from Brussels.[7] Meyer is further known to have entertained close contacts just before the war with the poets Ferdinand Hardekopf, Hanns Eppelsheimer, Max Brod, Klabund, Else Lasker-Schüler, with the painter-poet Ludwig Meidner and the Munich publisher-poet Heinrich F.S. Bachmair; of these figures, at least Klabund, Lasker-Schüler, and Bachmair made appearances before the war in the circle as well.[8]

The Meyer circle contrasted to a degree in general spirit with the other Expressionist circles active before the war, in the sense that it would appear to have been a much merrier, much more lighthearted group of artists, more given to reveling and frolicking in its literary life than the other circles. Its mood seemed often to border on the frivolous, in spite of Meyer's contention that this mood had its roots in a profound metaphysical experience, which had issued, in turn, from a new perspective on the universe in the twentieth century acquired through such landmarks of science as Albert Einstein's theory of relativity, the aeronautic feats of the Wright brothers, etc.[9] A spirit of gaiety, almost frivolity, was, at any rate, the dominant mood which the Meyer circle expressed overtly, as recorded, for example, in the large body of light and humorous verse written by Meyer himself, but as manifested no where so tangibly as in the prominence assumed in the social life of this circle by dance halls, bars, and similar night spots, rather than by the usual artist café, which in this group had to assume a secondary place. Meyer has given a degree of immortality to several of these night spots popular among his friends by recording them in his own verse; he has also described a number of them in his important memoir on the Expressionist era *die maer von der musa expressionistica.*[10]

As members of the Meyer circle "abandoned" themselves to the dance—the most popular form of which amongst them in that era was the "Castle Walk," called in Berlin dialect "Der Wrotzen"—they could be found Thursday evenings in the Parkrestaurant at the south end of Berlin, Saturday evenings in the Türkisches Zelt in Charlottenburg and Sunday evenings in the Forsthaus Schmargendorf; then, Wednesday evenings, they would begin the dizzy round of their revelry again either in the Gesellschaftshaus Schmargendorf or in the Altes Ballhaus in the Joachimstrasse near the Alexanderplatz.[11] The last named locale is described in more detail by Meyer, for it was recorded by the group for posterity in a broadsheet of the same name, published by the Verlag A.R. Meyer in 1912.[12] The segment of Meyer's circle of friends that frequented the "Altes Ballhaus" before the war gave itself the name "Unser Klub" (later "Der schwarze Klub") and included, besides Meyer himself, Leonhard, Kurtz, Erkens, Cahén, Schickele, and, again, when on visits to Berlin, Herrmann-Neisse and Stadler; with the exception of Erkens, all of these poets—as well as several other poets and one painter not mentioned by Meyer specifically as participants in the gatherings of "Der schwarze Klub" (Blass, Brod, Hanns Eppelsheimer, Friedlaender, Victor Hadwiger, Hardekopf, Holz, Lasker-Schüler, Rolf Wolfgang Martens, Ruest, and Walter Roessner)—made contributions to the broadsheet anthology *Ballhaus.*[13]

Cahén had begun his association with Meyer by correspondence while he was in Paris.[14] Cahén had gone to the French city in October of 1912 to study and had also establshed many contacts with French and German poets and painters residing there at the time. He had associated, for example, with Paul Fort, Blaise Cendrars, and Archipenko, and in a bistro called Au Cocher Fidèle with the German Expressionists Ludwig Rubiner and Friedrich Eisenlohr. He had also met and talked with the habitués of the Café du Dôme, including Einstein and Hoddis, and had seen in the same café Marinetti and Gino Severini, who were then visiting Paris briefly.[15] In the summer of 1913 Cahén moved to Berlin, immediately looked up Meyer and was shortly thereafter introduced by Meyer into his circle of friends.[16] As Cahén remembered this group, from the time he joined it in the summer of 1913 to the outbreak of the war, there were five different places where its adherents, in various combinations determined by the particular meeting place, would gather and engage in discussions and revelry.[17] Two of these meeting places were private residences, the one the apartment of Meyer and his wife, located near the Bayrischer Platz, and the other the apartment of Else Hadwiger, the widow of the Prague Neo-Romantic poet Victor Hadwiger, whom Meyer had also known personally.[18] Else Hadwiger's apartment was located near the Südwestkorso and not far from the studio of Ludwig Meidner; the role of the host at the gatherings here was assumed by Ruest, who, according to Cahén, had been Victor Hadwiger's closest friend before his death and had edited the small selection of poetry taken from Hadwiger's literary remains and published by Meyer in 1912 under the title *Wenn unter uns ein Wandrer ist.*[19] In addition to the more regular members of the Meyer circle, a frequent appearance was made at Else Hadwiger's by the writer Kristian Krauss.[20]

Cahén also records three "Stammtische" around which the circle gathered before the war, one of them being the Altes Ballhaus referred to earlier.[21] Most important of these tables, according to Cahén, was the one baptized by Meyer "Paris" and situated in a tavern (Kutscherkneipe) on the Bayrischer Platz.[22] Members of the circle met here several times a week; and these meetings, Cahén claims, were chronicled in a lyrical broadsheet of the same name.[23] Such a publication no longer appears to be extant; however, a poem written by Meyer with the title "Paris," which appeared in the August, 1913, issue of *Der Sturm,* would seem to be identical with the broadsheet referred to by Cahén.[24] The poem, dedicated to Meyer's friend Apollinaire ("avec mille remerciments pour 'Zone'"), describes, in symbolic terms, the merrymaking of certain residents of "Paris," which, as the author carefully points out at the beginning of the poem, is not to be found on the Seine but "on the Bayrischer Platz in Schöneberg."[25] In this "Paris" in Berlin, each of whose boroughs are represented by a different bottle of liquor and given names borrowed from verses by Apollinaire, the office of prefect is filled by Karl Scholz, the Rue de Rivoli is to be found in the life line of the hands of Trudchen Scholz and the Louvre in Resi Langer's purse. The Arc de Triomphe is replaced by Rudolf Leonhard's nose and the sounds of the animals in the Zoological Gardens are provided by the verse of Ernst Wilhelm Lotz (cf. *Und schöne Raubtierflecken... Ein Lyrisches Flugblatt,* 1913), the blue doves of Luxembourg Gardens nest in the hair of Cahén and, lastly, overseeing the "city," the Eiffel Tower is portrayed by Meyer.[26] Cahén's recollection of this table differs in part in the list of participants from Meyer's record of it in the poem "Paris": Cahén remembered Rudolf Leonhard presiding, surrounded by the revelers Meyer, Kurtz, Benn, Cahén himself and, less regularly, Erkens, Lorenz, and Kanehl.[27]

In a tavern located in the center of Berlin near the Kurfürstendamm was to be found the third table around which members of the Meyer circle met, drank and conversed and debated in Cahén's time.[28] This meeting place, according to Cahén, was the domain of Ruest, whom Cahén remembers especially for his extensive acquaintance with the writings of the philosopher Max Stirner.[29] Besides Cahén himself, Ruest was most often joined here by Leonhard and by Otto Buek, who was at that time working on the edition of Kant's works published by the Ernst Cassirer Verlag.[30] On occasion, Else Hadwiger would also appear.[31] Ruest and his table companions in this tavern often "broke a lance" with another group that occupied a second corner in the room and centered around Ernst Rowohlt, who had recently dissolved his partnership with Kurt Wolff in Leipzig and moved to Berlin to become business director of the S. Fischer Verlag.[32] Following the sessions here, the Meyer group often took nocturnal strolls together in the nearby Berlin Zoological Gardens, where they continued their discussions begun earlier that evening.[33]

Cahén also tells about going on pleasure strolls alone with Meyer, which usually ended "over beer and amidst tobacco smoke" in a locale near Unter den Linden or in Dalbelli's Italienische Weinstube."[34] Cahén at this time (fall, 1913) was working especially closely with Meyer, gathering material for a Hermann Fürst Pückler-Muskau edition planned by Meyer and completing his translation for Meyer of Apollinaire's "Zone."[35] Lautensack, Cahén reports, was seen only when one was invited to his home.[36]

Meyer himself was a regular habitué of the Café des Westens before the war; and this is also known to have been the case with all of the other members of his circle of literary associates, with the exception of Buek, Lorenz, Leonhard, and Erkens.[37] For Cahén in particular his contacts in the Café des Westens with other writers, outside of the Meyer circle but during the time of his association with the group, were of singular importance in his development as a writer. He made many new acquaintances here, encountered Einstein again, and through him met Pfemfert, with whom Cahén had political debates here.[38] Cahén wrote in his autobiography *Der Weg nach Versailles,* with the Café des Westens in particular in mind: "My real Berlin experience that was of decisive importance for my later development was, however, the café."[39] Cahén, therefore, would seem to have considered his connections with Berlin cafés, such as the Café des Westens, of more decisive importance in his career than his association with the Meyer circle. For the Meyer circle as a group, however, the latter café, according to Cahén, formed only a kind of "remote backdrop" to its other meeting places.[40]

Although the Meyer circle was to cease to exist as a group almost immediately after the outbreak of the First World War and its publications were to be halted about the same time or shortly thereafter, with the result, as we shall see later, that the circle's close association as a group with Expressionism was to have covered a mere two years. Nevertheless, this circle and its activities were to leave their own indelible and not insignificant mark on the development of the movement. This importance of its role in Expressionism was in greatest part the product of the efforts of the circle's mainstay, Alfred Richard Meyer. Meyer's significant contribution to Expressionism is not, on the other hand, as might be assumed, to be sought in his own, prolific literary output; his own literary work, most of which was written in a light, humorous vein and published under the pseudonym he used for such work, "Munkepunke," had little relationship in themes or style with, and found small reverberation in, the Expressionist camp; his work was even on occasion severely attacked in journals closely allied with this movement.[41] Meyer's importance for Expressionism is rather to be discovered in his work as publisher and editor.

Born in a relatively small North German town (Schwerin), Meyer established very close ties, both as an author and as a citizen, with the life in the metropolis of Berlin very soon after arriving here in 1905 from university studies in Marburg, Würzburg, Göttingen and Jena.[42] As it does in much of the work of the Berlin Expressionists (most notably in the work of Döblin—and this is probably the feature which, more than any other, relates Meyer's work to that of the Berlin Expressionists—Berlin provides an irreplacable and everrecurring backdrop, almost always identified very directly, in a large measure of Meyer's poetry. This city already figures prominently in the latter way in one of Meyer's earliest published works, a (thematically and structurally true) cycle of fifteen sonnets, each of them dealing with a particular segment of life in Berlin ("Unter den Linden," "Am Alexanderplatz," "Im Tingeltangel," "Nachtredaktion," "Im Nachtcafé," etc.), which was published in 1907 under the appropriate title *Berlin: Ein impressionistischer Sonettenkranz* (Berlin: Verlag Neues Leben, Wilhelm Borngraeber). Even the unique language of the city's native population echoes through Meyer's poetry. Meyer's close personal ties with the city focused, during most of his long residence here, on its avant-garde literary life. He was one of the most gregarious adherents of the Berlin bohemian literary scene, challenged in this distinction perhaps only by Lasker-Schüler; he was at home, as Raabe has stated, in all of the cafés and clubs of the city.[43] In addition to having close ties with most of the Berlin circles of Expressionists, he also maintained contacts with artists of the same, or of a related, tendency in other cities of Europe, including Leipzig, Munich, Prague, and Paris.[44]

Meyer had a broad acquaintance with, and a deep understanding of, the most recent trends in literature in the first approximate quarter of our century, as attested to by his contemporaries and by Meyer's own reflections on the Expressionist era in his book *die maer von der musa expressionistica,* which is still considered one of the most important books on the subject although published more than two decades ago.[45] He was amongst the first to give publisher's recognition to one of those new trends, Expressionism, before the First World War, at a time when literature of this direction was profitable for neither publisher nor author. Because of such unprofitability, Meyer was forced to support himself, throughout his own publishing career, as a publisher's reader and as a journalist.[46] His support of Expressionist literature was not, on the other hand, either promiscuous or undiscerning. Ruest claimed in a contribution to *Die Aktion* in 1911 that Meyer published only those works "to which he felt some personal affinity."[47] Proof of Meyer's discrimination as a publisher is offered by his description of the outcome of his exposure to the poetry of Jakob van Hoddis, which will be discussed shortly. That Meyer's literary taste was both discriminating and more often than not also astonishingly astute is illustrated best by his discovery for the reading public of the Gottfried Benn that was to make literary history.

At the beginning of the year 1912, having concluded his medical studies at the Kaiser-Wilhelm-Akademie in Berlin, Benn had just entered upon a career as a military doctor; he was, at that time, without any measurable literary reputation outside of a small circle of friends.[48] Before this date only two of Benn's poems ("Rauhreif" and "Gefilde der Unseligen") and a short philosophical dialogue ("Gespräch") had found their way into print; but, in all three instances, this had been two years before and there seemed to be no indication of a possible recurrence.[49] In addition, those first published pieces had been examples of Benn's early work, before his clear break with conventional themes and styles; they had, therefore, all appeared in a journal of a conservative stamp. Then, at the beginning of the spring of 1912, Adolf Petrenz, the editor of the Berlin *Tägliche Rundschau,* gave Meyer for perusal an "unorganized manuscript" from the pen of the young Benn.[50] As Meyer recalls, on beginning his reading of the manuscript he soon became bored and was about to clap it shut without finishing it when he came upon a cycle of poems at the end, which Meyer describes as "inconsistent" with the main body of the manuscript.[51] Meyer immediately sensed the original, revolutionary qualities of the verse in this cycle and rushed it to the printer.[52] Just eight days after Meyer's discovery, in March, 1912, the cycle appeared in the series *Lyrische Flugblätter* under the now famous title *Morgue und andere Gedichte.*[53] The established press was outraged and rejected out of hand the poet and his verse as both perverse.[54] Some twenty years later Benn himself recalled of this reaction with irony:

> This first collection of poetry already acquired for me in the public mind the reputation of a degenerate rake, of a devilish snob and of the typical—today they would say of the typical Jewish half-breed, in those days they said of the typical—coffee-house poet. All the while, I was executing regimental exercises on the potato fields of the Uckermark and, at the Division Commander's headquarters, crossing the pine-covered hills of Döberitz at an English trot.[55]

Even some of the Expressionists found it difficult to come to proper terms with the macabre visions with which they were confronted in Benn's verse; but they were, none the less, largely enthusiastic.[56] Stadler, for example, in a contemporary review of the broadsheet, wrote of one poem in it ("Mann un Frau gehn durch die Krebsbaracke"): "Wer Lebensvorgänge mit solcher Knappheit und Wucht zu gestalten und in so schicksalsvollen Gesichten auszuweiten vermag, ist sicherlich ein Dichter." ("Anyone who can create life with such conciseness and force and enlarge upon it in such fateful visions is surely a poet.")[57] One fact was certain, no matter the reaction in the press, Benn's poetic career was positively launched by this publication; and he owed this breakthrough into the literary world in great measure to his new publisher.[58]

Besides Benn, Meyer was also amongst the earliest publishers of a number of other Expressionists, often just after their debut in *Die Aktion* or *Der Sturm,* including Goll, Lichtenstein, Leonhard, Lotz, Heym, Herrmann-Neisse, Zech, Lasker-Schüler, Blass, and Cahén.[59] Finally, Meyer—and this, as Cahén observed and best illustrated in his own literary life, held true of Meyer's circle of associates in general as well—cultivated earlier and more consciously than did other publishers of similar direction in Berlin close ties with the most recent trends in French literature before the First World War.[60]

In the summer of 1911 Meyer visited Paris and there made a number of contacts with representatives of the younger generation of French poets. In the Closerie des Lilas Meyer encountered the group that had already established the café's fame in the annals of the French artistic avant-garde by the wild soirées they had been holding here since shortly after the turn of the century: the circle around Paul Fort and his review *Vers et Prose*.[61] In the same café he also made the acquaintance of the *poète maudit* Léon Deubel, which Meyer was to consider later to have been an acquaintance of "decisive" importance for himself.[62] Finally, also worthy of mention were Meyer's contacts on this Paris trip with the poet whom one historian of French literature has called the "impresario of the avant-garde" of that time, Guillaume Apollinaire.[63] Meyer was to continue his friendship with Apollinaire in the following years by correspondence; this friendship, and the one with Léon Deubel, were to bear most notable fruit for Meyer in his publishing activities on his return to Berlin.

Strong ties with French literature were also entertained in Meyer's circle of friends and associates by two poets who owed the origins of these ties to their ethnic background, the Alsatians Schickele and Stadler. Schickele had studied in Paris and had worked in the city for an extended period of time (1909-11) as a journalist, during which time he had contacts with French and German poets living in the city.[64] Schickele's interest in French culture in general is widely reflected in his writings.[65] Stadler was a professor of German language and literature at the Université Libre in Brussels from October, 1910, to the middle of 1914, a position which he had taken in part because of his desire to deepen his knowledge of the French language.[66] His interest in contemporary French literature was manifested most prominently in his translations of the poetry of Francis Jammes, a poet who enjoyed considerable favor amongst the Expressionists at large and, most often in Stadler's German, in Expressionist publications.[67]

Meyer's most significant work as a publisher remained throughout his career the series of small volumes with which his firm had been opened, the *Lyrische Flugblätter* (1907-15, 1919-24).[68] The volumes in the series, as mentioned earlier, all appeared in Meyer's own, unique variation on the conventional broadsheet format. They were always slim, unbound volumes, without separate cover and consisting most often of from four to eight octavo sheets (i.e., eight to sixteen pages). Most bore a title page drawing, and all were printed in editions of very limited number. With few exceptions, they contained lyric poetry.[69]

In the first approximate four years, from 1907 to the end of 1911, the series and the Meyer company in general revealed no clear tendency to become identified with a specific literary style or movement. With the exception of the work of Lautensack, Zech, and Meyer himself, no other poets were represented in the *Lyrische Flugblätter* in that initial phase who were at any time to be closely associated with the Expressionist camp or prominently represented in publications of the movement.[70] However, punctuated by the appearance of Gottfried Benn's *Morgue und andere Gedichte* at the beginning of the year, 1912—that crucial year in many respects in the development of Expressionism as demonstrated in the course of this study—marks a sharply pronounced turning point in the literary sympathies of the Verlag A.R. Meyer. This change in direction, according to Meyer, was undertaken consciously and derived from a very concrete literary experience which Meyer had met with the previous year.

Sometime during the first half of 1911, Meyer became familiar with Hoddis's poem "Weltende." The effect which these eight lines had upon Meyer was as intense as it had been and was to be for many other young poets of that era.[71] Meyer, as he recalled later, was immediately seized by the conviction that his publishing firm as on the wrong track; he felt quite consciously that the major thrust of his support of literature as a publisher should be rechannelled towards the new literary direction which he sensed was represented by Hoddis's verse—i.e., as Meyer was able to specify many years afterwards in retrospect, towards Expressionism.[72] Meyer felt so unsettled by Hoddis's poem that, shortly after being exposed to it, he went on a vacation trip to France, in order to "escape" his feeling of "unrest."[73] It was on the Paris leg of this journey in the summer of 1911 that Meyer encountered Léon Deubel and Apollinaire; and these contacts, most tangibly those with Apollinaire whose work is closely related to German Expressionism, will no doubt have reinforced in Meyer's mind the conviction that had sent him to France.[74]

Shortly after his return to Berlin from France, Meyer was given the first conspicuous opportunity to change the basic direction of literary support in his publishing activities when he discovered the manuscript of Benn's *Morgue und andere Gedichte* in the early part of 1912. Meyer's connections with the Expressionist community had by this time already grown much more intimate. This fact is demonstrated, first of all, by the make up of Meyer's close circle of friends in this period, as represented in the broadsheet which came out after *Morgue und andere Gedichte* in the same year, the small anthology entitled *Ballhaus* and based on the Meyer "Stammtisch" in the Altes Ballhaus in Berlin. Secondly, Meyer's own participation in Expressionist publications increased noticeably after the summer of 1911. Prior to that date his work had appeared only twice in such publications: the first instance involved a poem, published in *Der Sturm* in February, 1911; and the second, also a poem, published in *Die Aktion* just about the time Meyer would have been leaving for France, at the end of May, 1911.[75] From the second half of 1911 to the beginning of the war, however, Meyer made numerous contributions to both *Die Aktion* and *Der Sturm,* in addition to being represented in two other important Expressionist journals, each of which was edited by a poet who had established personal ties with Meyer's circle in Berlin: Kanehl's *Wiecker Bote* (1913/ 14) and Bachmair's *Die neue Kunst* (1913/ 14).[76]

Thus, aided by his own closer ties with Expressionism in the second half of its early phase, Meyer was able in the same period to publish almost exclusively the work of representatives of that movement. The only poet published in 1912 in the *Lyrische Flugblätter* who clearly deviates in literary tendency from the rest was the Neo-Romantic Victor Hadwiger, who had died just the year before.[77] Besides Benn and the many poets who contributed to *Ballhaus,* two other important additions were made to Meyer's list of authors that same year. At the end of 1912 Meyer published the first collection of verse by Lichtenstein under the title *Die Dämmerung;* this was a significant addition in light of Meyer's "Hoddis experience," for Lichtenstein represents, more obviously than any other writing at that time and most tangibly in the poem which opens the Meyer broadsheet and gave it its name, the influence of the poet who had originally caused Meyer to want to seek a change in his publishing interests.[78] The second important addition to the Verlag A.R. Meyer in 1912 was a contribution to the dissemination of Italian Futurism in Germany, which had just had its debut in Berlin under the sponsorship of *Der Sturm.*

In November, 1912, just a few months after Filippo Marinetti's Futurist manifestoes had begun appearing in Walden's journal and after the Italian theorist's first public screeds against the "passatisti" of Berlin in conjunction with the première of Italian Futurist painting in the city, Meyer sponsored the publication of the first significant sampling in German of Marinetti's poetry. The volume, which came out in the *Lyrische Flugblätter* under the title *Futuristische Dichtungen* with a title page portrait of the author by the Futurist painter Carlo Carrà, was largely the work of the Meyer circle: the translation was done by Else Hadwiger and the appreciative foreword by Kurtz.[79] Kurtz's introductory remarks interpret Marinetti's poetry for the German reader implicitly in relation to Futurist theory, with much of which Kurtz was in a position to sympathize readily, given his own contemporary theoretical statements.[80] He emphasizes here the primal vision of the Italian poet ("He is ... a eulogist of the eternal sea, of the glorious sunsets, of valiant deaths."), the lyrical sentiments which his poetry expresses before the unshunned and unabused backdrop of the technological twentieth century ("From the combustion engines of the twentieth century, from the steam clouds and electrical vortices, a melancholically white moon rises up vertically. It is the moon of Jean Jacques Rousseau, the moon of Jules Laforgue. . . . He is fervent, looking down from the highest promontory of his age; he has discovered the beauty of steel constructions and is not in the least afraid to write hymns to the automobile."). He emphasizes also the synthesizing perspective sought by the poet through the intuitive faculty and the use of the technique of "simultaneity" ("The incomprehensible totality of the moment must be reflected."), and, finally, points to Marinetti's rejection of the cultural legacy of the past in his verse ("Three thousand years of art retire silently into Orcus.").[81]

In 1913 and 1914, Expressionists and poets of related tendency again stand almost completely alone in the new listings of the *Lyrische Flugblätter;* besides additional volumes by, for example, Zech, Benn, and Lasker-Schüler, Meyer also published in this period Scher, Lotz, Döblin, Heym, Goll, and others.[82] Once more there is only one poet included in the series who is clearly out of place amongst the rest by reason of his major literary ties: the Impressionist poet Max Dauthendey.[83]

In 1912 Meyer had helped to introduce the Italian literary avant-garde into Germany; the next year he did the same for a representative of the French equivalent.

In 1912, just before Meyer had begun throwing almost total support behind German Expressionism, he had brought out in the original French a small selection of verse by Léon Deubel, to which Meyer had obtained the rights from Deubel personally when he saw him in Paris the year before.[84] In November, 1913, Meyer added a second French work to his series, this time in a German translation (by his friend Cahén), and this time a work of much greater importance in literary annals: Apollinaire's manifestolike poem "Zone."[85] Goll suggested the significance of this poem, as he saw it, already in 1919 when he claimed that it would someday be used to mark the beginning of twentieth century literature: "Man wird einmal die Geschichte der Literatur des zwanzigsten Jahrhunderts von der Dichtung 'Zone,' Apollinaires Meisterstück, datieren." ("Someday the history of twentieth-century literature will be dated from the appearance of Apollinaire's poetic masterpiece 'Zone'.")[86] Meyer was publishing the poem in Germany, however, at a time when the French poet was known to only a very few members of the Expressionist camp who were able to read him in the original; and the appearance of "Zone" under Meyer's imprint was, of course, a product of Meyer's friendship with the author, kept alive by mail since 1911 and no doubt renewed on a personal basis when Apollinaire visited Berlin at the beginning of 1913 at the invitation of Walden.[87] Whether the appearance of "Zone" in German had any appreciable influence on German Expressionism is yet to be established; but the poem bears many features in common with much of the poetry of the movement, most notably in its consciously urban backdrop, its use of the technique of "simultaneity" and in its break with conventional logic in grammar and in the structure of its content.[88]

In the early years of the *Lyrische Flugblätter*, the graphic art reproduced most often on the title page was executed by artists who represented pre-Expressionist styles (especially Art Nouveau).[90] After 1911, however, with the predominance of Expressionist literature, artwork by Expressionist painters also began making frequent appearances in the series. Meidner's work decorates the covers of several broadsheets published between 1912 and 1915, including the memorable *Das schwarze Revier* by Zech (pub. February, 1913), whose title page drawing—depicting, in the style of sharply contrasting patches and strips of black and white perfected in the Expressionist woodcut, the wizened faces of tired workers standing before the soot and smoking machinery of the mine—has often been reproduced since.[90] The pages of one entire issue in the series in 1913 were devoted to the printing of eight original woodcuts by

Artur Segal; and the subtitle of the volume ("erstes der graphischen Eine-Mark-Flugblätter") would suggest that Meyer had had plans at the time of putting out a special series of broadsheets of similar contents.[91] However, only one other volume published in the series before the war, a short story by Döblin with five woodcuts by Kirchner, devotes significant space to the graphic arts.[92] Two of the painters just mentioned, Meidner and Segal, and a third painter who is now usually associated by historians with the same style (although he had few personal or professional ties with Expressionism during the decade of the movement), Max Beckmann, had examples of their work reproduced alongside the literary work of numerous Expressionist poets in the pages of a journal established by Meyer and two of his associates in the fall of 1912.[93]

The bimonthly journal *Die Bücherei Maiandros,* which made its first appearance on newsstands on October 1, 1912, was the outcome of discussions had by Meyer with his friends Lautensack and Ruest shortly after his return to Berlin from his trip to Paris.[94] Although the journal did not appear under the Meyer imprint, but under that of a publisher who had printed several of the *Lyrische Flugblätter* for Meyer, nevertheless, the editors of it—Meyer, Lautensack, and Ruest—were key figures in the Meyer circle. In addition, the journal was, according to Cahén, financed by Meyer himself and, finally, the majority of the space on the journal's pages was devoted to the work of members of the same group.[95] *Die Bücherei Maiandros* should, therefore, be looked upon as essentially a literary forum for the Meyer circle.

Like almost all of the journals identified with Expressionism and founded after *Der Sturm* and *Die Aktion, Die Bücherei Maiandros* made use of the same general typographical format which the former two journals had established by their example as most appropriate to an avant-garde or progressive content: antique boldface type with a bold, clean masthead. The issues of the journal were put out in the form of six books or volumes, each of which was devoted in full to one, specific theme. To each of the books, which were published at irregular intervals between October 1, 1912, and September 1, 1913, were appended supplements or "Beiblätter." The supplements occasionally contain the forewords to the main books, but in most cases are devoted to book reviews and commentary of various sorts, written, with few exceptions, by members of the Meyer circle. The supplements were continued alone, after the appearance of the sixth book of the journal, and issued in three installments, on November 1, 1913, and on February 1 and May 1, 1914.[96]

Book One of *Die Bücherei Maiandros* (pub. October 1, 1912) put out the first edition of a *novelle* by Samuel Lublinski, entitled "Therese und Wolfgang."[97] Lublinski, who had died in December, 1910, had been one of the first to write literary criticism about the German post-Naturalist literary avant-garde of the turn of the century (*Die Bilanz der Moderne,* Berlin, 1904; *Der Ausgang der Moderne,* Dresden, 1909); he had also entertained personal contacts with numerous representatives of it in Berlin, many of whom later figured prominently in Expressionism, including Scheerbart, Mühsam, Walden, Döblin, and Lasker-Schüler.[98]

The second book of the journal (pub. December 1, 1912) is in two parts, the first contributed by Meyer and the second by Lautensack; both parts, as suggested by the subtitle of this book, "Ekstatische Wallfahrten," portray instances of a "pilgrimage," each undertaken by the protagonist in his particular kind of "ecstasy."[99] Meyer's contribution to the volume, "Semilasso in Afrika," depicts poetically the earthly, hedonistic "ecstasy" of an adventurer in the Near East; it is a series of poems based upon the published journals of the nineteenth-century professional traveller Fürst Pückler-Muskau.[100] Lautensack's work, a libretto for cantata entitled "Via Crucis," reads in context as the spiritual counterpart of Meyer's Semilasso poems; it is a modern poetic treatment of the theme of the Crucifixion.[101]

The third book of *Die Bücherei Maiandros* (pub. February 1, 1913), which is taken up by a long expository dialogue by Ruest, and the fourth and fifth books (pub. May 1, 1913), which were published together as one volume and devoted to an anthology of contemporary German verse, are, as Meyer himself suggested in his memoir on Expressionism, the two volumes of the journal of greatest significance for the history of the movement; they are, therefore, worth considering here in greater detail.

Ruest's "Apollodorus: Über Lyrik ein Dialog" is at one and the same time a literary critique and a philosophic-aesthetic treatise in dialogue form; it is both a critical discourse on the most recent German poetry (on "allerjüngstes lyrisches Schrifttum," as Ruest specifies in the foreword to the piece[102]) and a statement of a program for the same. Befitting the classical origins of the genre, the dialogue takes place between the Greeks Apollodorus and Cebes, identified as "former pupils" of Socrates, who meet again in the nether world in the early twentieth century.[103] They set forth in their exchange what they consider to be the ideal philosophic-aesthetic foundation of poetry, and Apollodorus tests against this ideal certain contemporary manifestations of the lyric; he is guided in his survey by a young, recently deceased poet called "Oikos," whom we are soon able to identify as Heym.[104]

Apollodorus derives the ideal philosophic-aesthetic foundation of poetry from the thinking of his former mentor who directed all of his efforts, Apollodorus claims, at attempting to attain the "golden mean," the synthesis or "marriage" of "passion" and "cognition": "All of his [Socrates'] efforts, as he often said, were directed at achieving the finest blend possible, the mean, the mathematical marriage of sensuality and reason."[105] Socrates had originally relied for guidance in life upon "reason" and the "conceptual faculty"; but Apollodorus would see in his mentor's sudden conversion to the worship of Apollo and the cultivation of the Muses in his last days a final testimony to the unique capacity of poetry for manifesting the ideal "mean":

And is it not reported that on the day of his [Socrates'] death he wanted to bear witness to the fact that he no longer conferred the role of guide through this obscure life upon the sober powers of reason and the conceptual faculty, but thought that possibly the words of poetry were alone capable of achieving the so remorselessly sought mean of life?[106]

Only the highest form of poetry, "true poetry," possesses this unique capacity for manifesting the ideal, however. Such poetry seeks, first of all, to express the essence or "nucleus" ("Kern," "Mittelpunkt") of the object selected for poetic treatment, as distinguished in the contemporary era from the poetry of the Naturalists, which seeks to reproduce the totality of only the external features of the object, and from the poetry of certain post-Naturalists, which gives expression to only the inner qualities of the object.[107] The essence expressed by "true poetry" is, in turn, arrived at through a "synthesis" of the "conception" of the poetic object ("Vorstellung eines Dinges") and its "emotive property" ("Gefühls- oder Empfindungston"), for, in accordance with Socrates' "mean," the poetic word must speak with equal force to both the mind and the emotions of the reader, as Apollodorus explains to Cebes:

...I see, my dear Cebes, a much more far-reaching, powerful potential of such an art of words in the very fact that it can initiate a more special and distinct activity of the conscious and conceptual mind. Thereby it can also call into play in unexpected ways the thousands of shades of feelings and sensations which perhaps have never before been aroused and are already linked to the smallest particles of the conceptual world![108]

Thus, the poet must avoid overemphasizing either the phonic or musical qualities of the poetic word, which speak only to the emotions, or overemphasizing its connotative values, which address themselves primarily to the mind or the conceptual faculty; rather the poet must exploit the full potential of the poetic word, its "Wort-Gesamtgehalt," which is its own kind of "synthesis" of the poetic object as perceived by the senses ("Sinnending") and of the "idea" ("Idee") with which the object is associated.[109]

Having established the above criteria for "true poetry," Apollodorus, with the help of his "authority" Oikos-Heym, seeks to determine whether such poetry is still being written in the contemporary era. He must take issue, as he surveys the era, with the work of poets such as Hugo von Hofmannsthal (here identified as "Loris") and Stefan George (here identified as the poet called by some "der Meister"), for their verse too seldom realizes the complete synthesis of "conception" and "sound" ("Bild und Klang").[110] Confronted with the work of Heym, Lautensack, Schickele, and Benn, on the other hand, Apollodorus' praise is unqualified; their work in his view combines the best traditions of the past with the most salutary revolutionary development of the present.[111] Their work not only satisfies the ideal form of poetry, for which Apollodorus has drawn the standards from the past in his dialogue with Cebes, but, like the work of other representatives of the youngest generation ("die wirklich Jungen und die Jüngsten"), has broken free of the conventional limitation on poetic themes.[112] This limitation has deep cultural roots, according to Apollodorus, for it derived from a mode of thinking which had renounced the "flesh"—and hence also any preoccupations with it, and especially with its baser aspects, in poetry—in favor of an "'incorporeal' spirit."[113] Now the youngest generation of poets has overcome this "curse" by rejecting conventional notions of "good" and "evil" and of "beauty." Just as this generation is able to bring together both sides of human character in the ideal "mean," it is able as well, in a related sense, to embrace fully and face squarely all aspects of human experience, from an acknowledgement of spiritual values in life, which bring hope and renewal, to an acceptance of life's most fundamental human qualities and origins, which often bring suffering and despair:

> Slowly, slowly the more recent and younger poets are extricating themselves from a curse which for thousands of years has made their *bodies* seem disgusting to them. However, it is only the truly young and most recent generation that is completely free and untouched by any perverse, traditional notions about the "good" or "evil" of their bodies. They also confront its abjectness, which is offensive to one's "feeling for beauty" (this great idol, not god, of the ages!), as true poets, as poets who are just discovering and honoring their *god!* They also see the newborn child, in the trite language of those who worship only the intellect the "tender hope of the future," the "gift of love," etc. But the new poets look more closely and see more clearly; they see its origins, its delivery from the womb again, and they say: that is the way we are when we are born—"bluish and small, covered with urine and defecation"; and they also see the rough-handed men with the forceps who were present at the birth. They also do not merely attend the horrible operations of the physicians like the curious; because they realize profoundly the terrible necessity of the hands and instruments which cause pain, they do not call on the false god of compassion and pity who would only disconcert those hands and could make them lethal; they notice suddenly, as though incidentally, at the critical moment when the patient breathes and sighs, a single, mitigating, divine sign of blossoming hope, regeneration. . . . [114]

Ruest's dialogue ties in with Expressionism in two, quite obvious respects. Firstly, and most obviously, it holds forth as exemplary the work of poets from the Expressionist camp; and secondly, and more significantly, it agrees, in its espousal of a philosophy and an aesthetic involving the ideal of a "synthesis" of intellect and emotion and the cheerful and forthright acceptance of all varieties of human experience, with key features of the programs of "Der neue Club," the *Sturm* circle and with a large body of similar theoretical statements penned by writers associated with the same artistic community.[115]

Books Four and Five of *Die Bücherei Maiandros* are subtitled "Der Mistral."[116] Both the subtitle and the motto for this anthology of verse are taken from Nietzsche's "An den Mistral" (a poem appended to *Die fröhliche Wissenschaft*).[117] The motto has more than just occasional significance, for the "dialectical monism" of its author, which was discussed briefly in connection with the program of "Der neue Club" earlier and which underlies the sentiment expressed in the lines borrowed from Nietzsche for the motto ("Tanzen wir gleich Troubadouren/Zwischen Heiligen und Huren/Zwischen Gott und Welt den Tanz!") ("Let us dance the dance like troubadours / Amongst Saints and whores / Between God and World!"), recall the similar philosophical position espoused by one of the editors of this anthology in the dialogue "Apollodorus."[118] Yet, although the motto may indicate a specific philosophy endorsed by the editors, there was no apparent programmatic underpinning editorially in the main body of this publication. The literary sympathies which had dictated the overall selection in "Der Mistral" were clearly not as narrow as, for example, those behind another anthology which, just the year before, had also emanated from the Berlin Expressionist community: *Der Kondor* (pub. May, 1912), whose editor, Kurt Hiller, had introduced it as a "manifesto," a "secession of poets," a collection of "radical stanzas" by the youngest generation of poets.[119] "Der Mistral," as Meyer stated in the foreword to the volume, was, more broadly, a sampling of "modern verse," whose selection and purpose had both been determined by "aesthetic reasons alone."[120] Thus, while the clear majority of the hundred-odd poets who had contributed were closely associated with the Expressionist movement in Germany, there were not a few included who very clearly had other ties, such as Dauthendey, Dehmel, Hofmannsthal, Holz, Thomas Mann, Johannes Schlaf, and others.[121] If, on the other hand, the main body of the text of "Der Mistral" did not make clear that the real literary ties and sympathies of the editors did in fact, in their own minds, lie in the direction of the generation of the Expressionists rather than that of Hofmannsthal, Dehmel, or Dauthendey, then Meyer states this fact for the record in his foreword to the collection as he outlines plans for continuing this volume of *Die Bücherei Maiandros* separately as a yearbook series. The future installments in the series, Meyer forecasted here, would have been devoted, by implication to an even greater degree than the present one was, to the work of the youngest generation of poets: " 'Der Mistral' is to appear as a regular yearbook; it will in future be, first and foremost, a champion of youth, and, to a lesser extent, a presentation of the literary relationships of the generations of 1862 and 1882."[122] That Meyer, moreover, had especially aesthetic and stylistic, more so than chronological, factors in mind when he used the word "youth" above, is enunciated in the next sentence: "Today our invitation is extended to all who know they have the strength to infuse poetry with genuinely new values."[123]

The sixth and last book of the Meyer journal (pub. September 1, 1913) came off the press a little over two months after the premature death of Meyer's friend Deubel and was dedicated to his memory; it includes tributes to the French poet written mostly by his compatriots.[124]

During the early phase of Expressionism, the Meyer circle also sponsored several public recitals featuring authors of the Verlag A.R. Meyer. Since documentation on these evenings is as yet very incomplete, it is not possible to estimate how many were held, nor to gain more than a very sketchy picture of the proceedings at most of those few recitals known to have actually taken place. A review of the first recital sponsored in name by the Verlag A.R. Meyer, which was penned by Ruest and published in the December 4, 1911, issue of *Die Aktion,* provides the only detailed report on a Meyer recital in a readily available source.[125] The date of publication of Ruest's review would place the meeting at the end of November or the beginning of December, 1911. The evening took place, Ruest reports, in the Architektenhaus in Berlin and featured readings from their own works by Lautensack (from his plays *Der Hahnenkampf* and *Die Pfarrhauskomödie*), August Vetter (from his poetry), Meyer (from his then unfinished novel *Der Leichenhochzeiter*), and Friedlaender (a "Groteske" entitled "Der geflügelte Ottokar und die betrunkenen Blumen"); Langer, the last and most lauded of the performers for her elocutionary skill in Ruest's review, recited from the works of several Meyer authors.[126]

To the November 31, 1912, issue of *Die Aktion* Ernst Blass contributed a review in poetic form (in Wilhelm-Buschian stanzas!) of a "Meyer-Abend" at which Lautensack, Meyer and Zech read selections from their own work and Langer again recited poetry by other Meyer authors, including, this time, Herrmann-Neisse, Ernst Schur, Ruest, Lichtenstein, et al.[127] Blass is most critical here of Meyer's contribution to the evening ("Seine 'Semilasso'-Dichtung / Passt nicht sehr in meine Richtung.") ("His 'Semilasso' poetizing / misses the mark of my poetic striving."); but Blass had some positive remarks to make, too, and, like Ruest in his review of the first evening, as most appreciative of Langer's performance.[128] Blass's review was, no doubt, a reaction to the "Verlagsabend-A.R. Meyer," which was advertised in both *Der Sturm* and *Die Aktion* for October 7, 1912, in the bookstore of Reuss and Pollack in Berlin.[129] The Walden journal announced this evening as the "second" (of that particular season?) of the recitals of the Meyer publishing company and identified the performers scheduled to appear only in a general way as "authors" of the same firm.[130] The announcement in Pfemfert's organ is more detailed; it schedules Meyer (reading from "Das Fürst Pückler-Muskau-Buch"), Zech (reading from his then unpublished verse in *Die Brücke* and *Zwischen Russ und Rauch*), Else Hadwiger (reading translations of the Futurist poetry of Marinetti), Langer (reading Wedekind's "Schäferspiel" *Felix und Galathea*), "and others."[131]

Herrmann-Neisse participated in at least two recitals held in Berlin before the war, the first given sometime in November, 1912, and the second at the end of 1913 or the beginning of the next year; but only the first of these can be definitely assigned to the sponsorship of the Meyer group.[132] Benn is reported by Paul Raabe to have recited his verse in "Der schwarze Klub" of the Meyer circle during the time of his association with it; and Schickele is known to have given a similar reading before the Meyer circle sometime in 1913.[133] Finally, the many recitals given by Langer during this prewar period in the bookstore of Reuss and Pollack, such as the very successful "Klabund-Abend" held on April 24, 1914, appear to have taken place in name independently of at least the Meyer publishing company, if not also outside the framework of the Meyer circle.[134]

In the last year or so before the outbreak of the First World War, there already appeared signs which seemed to indicate that the ties holding Meyer's circle together were loosening. A major contributing factor was without a doubt Meyer's inability in this period to offer his associates sufficiently attractive opportunity for publication. Cahén claims that Meyer had taken on too great a financial burden with the publication of *Die Bücherei Maiandros*.[135] The journal, as remarked earlier, had been appearing sporadically since its founding, rather than bimonthly as promised in the subtitle; and by the time of the appearance of the sixth volume, on September 1, 1913, word had apparently already gotten out that the journal was on the verge of folding, for Benn wrote to Zech just one day later, on September 2, 1913: "So *Maiandros* is already retrenching."[136] Benn's opinion would seem to have been based on a reliable source, for after that sixth volume only three more thin supplements came out over a period of eight months, as if the editors were only delaying the inevitable official termination of the journal. The lack of vitality in *Die Bücherei Maiandros* left Meyer and his associates with only one very active forum, the series of *Lyrische Flugblätter*. The limited format of the series, whose expansion would also have been hindered by Meyer's straitened finances, however, could offer the Meyer circle little public exposure. It is thus not surprising that many members of this circle soon began drifting away after the end of 1913, attracted to more propitious literary opportunities elsewhere. At the end of 1913—that year which, according to Pinthus, marked a "turning point" in the development of the German film as it and the movie theater both, "rather suddenly," became "socially, literarily and artistically acceptable"— Cahén became busily employed by the Berlin film industry writing film scenarios. Cahén retained this position until the outbreak of the war, and was on this account, as he wrote, not able to join Meyer as often during this period as he had before.[137] During that last year before the war, Kurtz also began working (as a "Dramaturg") for the Berlin cinema and no doubt found his other activities similarly restricted.[138] Kanehl was spending much of his time, from the summer of 1913 to the summer of the next year, in Greifswald north of Berlin on the Baltic Sea, where he was editing amongst his friends there his own periodical, the monthly *Wiecker Bote*.[139] Meidner moved his permanent residence from Berlin to Dresden in the early part of 1914, in order to join his friend, another Meyer associate, Lotz, who had preceded Meidner there shortly before; Meidner and Lotz had plans at that time of putting out their own literary journal in Dresden.[140] Finally, both Benn and Schickele were traveling abroad during most of the first half of 1914.[141]

Given the conditions in the Meyer circle just described, the outbreak of the war, which Meyer considered "the most horrible caesura" in the history of Expressionism, was merely the final, fatal blow to the circle and its activities.[142] If, instead of having been a way of putting off the ultimate end of *Die Bücherei Maiandros,* the wide spacing of the publication of the last three supplements of it had been rather an indication of the editors' intention of eventually reviving the journal after a financial breathing spell, this intention was rendered virtually hopeless by the political events of August, 1914. Most of the associates or friends who had remained close to Meyer to this date now either volunteered immediately for military service or were drafted almost as soon. Meyer himself remained at home for a time, however, and continued to issue his *Lyrische Flugblätter.*

In the fall of 1914 three volumes of mostly patriotic and prowar verse appeared in the series, the first of which was an anthology entitled *Der Krieg* with contributions by numerous Expressionists and others, including Elsa Asenijeff, Dehmel, Herbert Eulenberg, Gerhart Hauptmann, Klabund, Leonhard, Lichtenstein, Scher, Rudolf Alexander Schröder, and Hermann Stehr.[143] The mixture of quite disparate literary directions in the latter volume, as represented by its contributors, seemed to suggest that Meyer, like the Kaiser, had suddenly become nonpartisan in the face of the war.[144] The second of the three volumes came out in October, 1914, with the title *Helden: Ein lyrisches Flugblatt aus den August- und Septembertagen 1914* and was authored by Meyer himself.[145] The verse in the third volume, Leonard's *Über den Schlachten* (pub. October or November, 1914) is often fanatic in its bellicosity; the opening poem, "Europa," for example, closes with the unabashedly sinister line: "We love war, we desire evil."[146] Such publications as this are known to have further alienated from Meyer at least Hermann-Neisse, but no doubt others in his circle as well, and certainly the most outspoken pacifist of the group, Schickele.[147]

After those three publications in the fall of 1914, only one more installment was made in the *Lyrische Flugblätter* before it became inactive for the remainder of the war; this was a volume of verse by Meyer with a title drawing by Meidner, which appeared in January, 1915.[148] Thus, when Meyer himself finally entered the war as a correspondent in 1916, his publishing company had already been dormant for over a year.[149]

When the war ended, Meyer returned to Berlin and very soon reopened his publishing company. The reactivation of the *Lyrische Flugblätter* in January, 1919, was marked by the publication of a volume whose appearance had originally been planned for the end of the prewar era: *Der neue Frauenlob,* an anthology of poems eulogizing certain women and written by young Expressionist poets.[150] The literary affiliation of the latter volume made it an exception in the *Lyrische Flugblätter* in this phase, however, for the series only harked back sporadically now, in the authors it published, to the literary direction which had dominated it in the latter prewar years.

The direction the series was following after the war was apparently reflecting, as it had before, the interests of its publisher. There is no evidence that a circle of supporters or associates, of significant size or note and connected with Expressionism, again developed around Meyer after the war. He did have some contacts with the *Sturm* circle in the 1920s, reading on occasion at its "Sturm-Abende"; but these contacts with former Expressionist friends appear to have been superficial and exceptional.[151] There is similarly little indication that the new spirit of political involvement and awareness, which dominated postwar Expressionism, in any tangible way affected either Meyer or his publishing company. Meyer, it would appear, went his own, individual way in this period, neither joining his former Expressionist friends and associates in their political pursuits after the war, nor taking up the cudgels again, with any noteworthy degree of dedication, for Expressionist literature or art.

Meyer continued the *Lyrische Flugblätter* until about the mid-1920s in much the same way in which he had reinitiated the series right after the war; and then, in 1929, after a few years of inactivity and in accordance with a new conception, he resumed the series one last time for a very brief period.[152]

8

Paul Cassirer and *Pan*

In 1898 two young cousins named Bruno and Paul Cassirer, the first fresh from university studies in Berlin and Munich and the other with more than one uneventful career already behind him, opened together an art salon with affiliated publishing company in Berlin.[1] This event took place in a year that was crucial in the development of German Impressionism in painting, a fact which was in no small part due to the Cassirers.[2] Since the beginning of the 1890s and with its centers in Munich and Berlin, Impressionism, as the new, as yet unrecognized style of the era, had begun energetically to assert itself through the work of Max Liebermann, Walter Leistikow, Lovis Corinth, Max Slevogt and others. Its opponent was the official, court-sanctioned school of Realism, which was represented, for example, by Anton von Werner, Adolf von Menzel, and Paul Meyerheim.[3] The division that was developing between the representatives of these two styles first surfaced prominently in Berlin in the "Verein Berliner Künstler" in a controversy amongst the members over the premature closing of a showing of the very unconventional work of Edvard Munch in the organization's exhibition rooms in 1892.[4] This first major confrontation between the progressive artists in the organization, who took the side of Munch, and the Old Guard, which was led by Anton von Werner and advocated the closing, ended in a standoff. When, however, a painting by Walter Leistikow was refused for the annual "Grosse Berliner Kunst-Ausstellung" in 1898, the original progressive faction of the "Verein Berliner Künstler," which had already quit the organization in 1892 and formed the relatively ineffectual group "XI," now banded together with renewed vigor and strength and, under the leadership of Max Liebermann, reorganized and renamed itself the "Berlin Sezession."[5]

Bruno and Paul Cassirer, arriving on the scene in Berlin in the same year, were both young and enterprising men, and it is, therefore, not surprising that they elected to make common cause with the Impressionists and the new "Berlin Sezession." As it happened, the Cassirers had made a fortunate choice, for in the following years, beginning quite notably with the first exhibition of the "Berlin Sezession" in 1899, for which Paul Cassirer served as business director, German Impressionism scored repeated victories over the official style.[6] The two cousins who had supported and helped secure these victories, on the other hand, had in the meantime proved to be incompatible business partners; as a result of a falling out, they dissolved their partnership just three years after it had been formed, with Bruno retaining the publishing company and Paul taking sole control over the art dealership.[7]

Under Paul Cassirer, the progressive tendency of the Cassirer dealership was intensified, for he not only continued to support the Impressionists in Germany, but also sponsored, from 1901 on, exhibitions of artists of related directions from other parts of Europe, including Cézanne (1901), van Gogh (1904), and Matisse (1907).[8] In addition, as a result of Cassirer's patronage of the German Impressionists, the "Salon Cassirer" became a gathering place for most of the leading representatives of the style in Germany in the approximate decade and a half that followed Cassirer's takeover.[9]

What attracted under one patron's wing so many painters and, later, the many poets, too, whom Cassirer sponsored during his career, was without doubt in large part the obvious dedication to the encouragement and support of artistic endeavor of originality and quality which was combined in the figure of Cassirer with an extremely shrewd business sense. Cassirer brought financial success both to himself and to the artists whom he sponsored, but he accomplished this feat by means of, and to the benefit of, new, unconventional, unrecognized, and contested styles in painting and literature; thus, he was, as his biographers tell us, a combination of art dealer and art enthusiast, of businessman and would-be artist in one person.[10] Cassirer's contemporaries recognized well these two sides to his character, but they often interpreted them as at constant odds with each other: they describe him as a sensitive, high-mettled individual, the one moment selfless in his unrestrained enthusiasm for an artist's work, the next tyrannical and dogmatic in the assertion of his own person; now sensitive and dedicated to high artistic achievement, now ruthlessly and opportunistically market-conscious.[11] Thus, to Ernst Barlach, a Cassirer artist for many years, it seemed that the businessman Cassirer was the "evil brother" of the artist in Cassirer; and Wilhelm Herzog, who was a close literary associate of Cassirer for a time, considered him, in a typical description, as an "extremely captivating figure," but read him as a man "full of contradictions":

> He was a mixture of artist, clever businessman, and imaginative, yet also frequently malicious and unruly child. A vital and yet sentimental person of unusual qualities. Full of contradictions. Capable of a naive degree of enthusiasm, but critical to the point of provocative offense. With an extremely receptive sense for lasting art and literature, always *cupidus rerum novarum*, ambitious and power-hungry, ruthless and opportunistic, bold and cowardly, often extravagant and unbalanced in his judgment, but never boring or doctrinaire.[12]

Whether at odds with one another or not, the combination of businessman and art enthusiast in Cassirer was at the root of much of the success of the "Salon Cassirer" and the later Paul Cassirer Verlag, for the dominance of the latter side in his character would no doubt have narrowed the range of his abilities to help his artists to broad public recognition and, therewith, to true financial success. The dominance of the businessman in him would have induced him to avoid the risk involved in backing unrecognized art, the kind of art which, in the unforeseeable future, was ultimately to make possible the very success of Cassirer's earliest business ventures. What, therefore, Cassirer's biographers usually describe as a rivalry of the two sides to his character, might better be understood as an interaction, a complementary relationship. Cassirer himself, in fact, described the proper role of the art dealer as he saw it as involving just such a dual aspect in a series of articles which appeared in *Pan* in May and July of 1911 under the lead title "Kunst und Kunsthandel."[13] These articles were occasioned by the appearance of Carl Vinnen's notorious brochure attacking the influx of French art into Germany; however, they carry Cassirer well afield of a mere reply to Vinnen, and in doing so reveal that by the time of their appearance in *Pan* Cassirer had already worked out very carefully and consciously a specific philosophy of his profession and, consequently, that he took his role in the development of art quite seriously, feeling a strong sense of ethical responsibility in performing it.[14]

At the basis of Cassirer's philosophy of the art dealer, as he sets forth in this article, is the view that the most healthy atmosphere for the artist and the development of his work is one in which there is a large and powerful art market directed by the professional dealer.[15] Only the latter kind of atmosphere is capable of providing the artist with the proper "protection" and "control" necessary for him and his art to prosper.[16] Prior to the nineteenth century, Cassirer states, the artist had been forced, for the sake of his livelihood, to serve the will of the individual patron; this condition had, naturally, robbed the artist of most of his creative freedom, for the patron had determined not only the quality, but also the style and content of the artist's work.[17] The contemporary era, however, can offer the artist a far more favorable alternative to the older condition, one which Cassirer calls "the flight into the public sphere," or, more specifically, the opportunity for the artist to show his work in public exhibitions, have it reviewed in the newspapers, to offer it for sale in the salons of the art dealers and have it hung in the art galleries.[18] In the public sphere, therefore, the artist can find both economic and artistic protection; through the wide exposure which this sphere provides, he can sell his work more easily and, in addition, create it without thought of the narrow interests of the individual patron.[19] The contemporary patron, in turn, ought, in Cassirer's view, to reverse the relationship he has had in the past to art and, rather than asking the artist to serve him, he should strive himself to serve the development of art. Moreover, he should assume a new sense of responsibility towards the artist's work and, on the model of the collector-curator Karl Osthaus, extend beyond the small circle of his own friends the audience permitted to share in the appreciation of the works of art which he himself has purchased.[20]

First and foremost, Cassirer emphasizes, the work of art must be sold, so that the artist may make his livelihood; but, at the same time, there must exist indirect controls, not over style and content, but over the quality of the artist's work.[21] As the artist began freeing himself from the very narrow controls of the individual patron in the course of the last century or so, he found his first great refuge within the public sphere in the exhibitions organized by the government and official artist organizations; from the latter institutions and their juries or selecting committees came new, but generally much less inhibiting controls.[22] Initially, the controls of such institutions stressed solely quality; yet, Cassirer maintains, such organizations inevitably begin in time to ossify aesthetically and then to resist and reject new tendencies in art, stifling, in the process, the talent struggling for recognition which represents these new tendencies.[23] The crucial counterbalance to the official institutions needed at this stage has come to be provided in the contemporary era by the art dealer, who now offers an alternative means of public exposure to the artist.[24] Through his salon, the art dealer provides support and recognition for young talent, especially when this talent has found refusal elsewhere, and provides the artist's work with a secondary form of exposure by inviting the critics to review the exhibition of the artist's work in the newspapers.[25] The art dealer, on the other hand, is himself a critic; he, too, is duty bound by the ethics of his profession to exercise his own aesthetic judgement in selecting the paintings to be shown in his salon.[26] Thus, the art dealer, in counterbalancing the controls of the official artist organizations, as well as the academies, by recognizing new, often unorthodox talent and, simultaneously, exercising his own form of indirect control over quality, is, as Cassirer terms him, an "active critic," and the showings he sponsors are "criticism become deed."[27]

The competence of Cassirer's own critical judgement and understanding of painting, which he claimed as a prerequisite of his profession in "Kunst und Kunsthandel," was well established by the beginning of the Expressionist decade; and painting was to remain a major interest of Cassirer throughout his career. However, Cassirer was far from being intellectually one-sided, as Tilla Durieux tells us.[28] Durieux claims that she owed to Cassirer her general intellectual development, an infinite inner enrichment and her increasing success on the stage during her marriage to him.[29] Cassirer, as Durieux attests, was well informed on literature and its contemporary manifestations.[30] In fact, while associating with Munich bohemian circles before the turn of the century, he had himself had at that time a brief career as a poet and as an assistant editor ("Mitredakteur") for the then avant-garde publication *Simplicissimus*.[31] Thus,

Cassirer can be said to have been qualified to play a key role, as he did, in the publishing activities which later became a part of his business ventures, even though he was to receive considerable assistance from others in the initial stages of these new activities.[32] Furthermore, Cassirer's idealistic philosophy of the art dealer was to be adapted to his work as an editor and publisher as well, for he brought to this work the same kind of dedication, direction of thrust, enthusiasm and seriousness of purpose which he brought to his art dealership. This is a fact which is corroborated by, among others, Wilhelm Herzog's first-hand report on the founding and beginnings of the Paul Cassirer Verlag, and by Heinrich Mann, who was a Cassirer author during the early phase of Expressionism.[33] Mann, for example, wrote of Cassirer the publisher:

> In reality he retained his pleasure in the remarkable works of peace until the outbreak of war. The only self-interest in his efforts was the honor he enjoyed in having participated. For five years, from 1910 to 1914, he generously paid for my works, which had been published long before that time, without regard for profit or compensation.[34]

Durieux first met Cassirer, whom she was to marry in 1910, through her first husband, the painter Eugen Spiro, and through the art critic Julius Meier-Graefe about 1905.[35] Following her divorce from Spiro in 1906, the actress became Cassirer's almost constant companion and was introduced by him into his circle of friends and associates in the fall of that year.[36] At this time, as Durieux reports, the circle around Cassirer was composed almost solely of German Impressionist painters, most of them also members of the "Berlin Sezession."[37] The circle was divided, according to Durieux, into two distinct and usually separate phalanxes, the one representing the younger, and the second the older generation of Impressionists.[38] The younger phalanx included, amongst others, the painters Fritz Klimsch, Konrad von Kardorff, George Mosson, Fritz Rhein, Ulrich and Heinrich Hübner, Theo von Brockhusen, Rudolf Grossmann, Leo von König, Karl Walser, and at least one poet, the latter's brother, Robert Walser.[39] To the older segment of the circle, which was relatively sedate and tended generally to maintain a certain reserved distance between itself and the younger, less restrained artists, belonged some of the most noted Impressionists in Germany of the time: Max Liebermann, Max Slevogt, Lovis Corinth, and Walter Leistikow.[40] Both segments of the Cassirer circle gathered in the art dealer's home, which was situated just a very short distance away from the art gallery (Viktoriastrasse 35). The younger segment was apparently that "boisterous band" which Durieux recalls participating in numerous clownish antics in front of Cassirer's residence.[41] One meeting place for a few of the older and younger painters in the circle, namely Corinth, George Mosson, Glevogt, Konrad von Kardorff, and often Liebermann as well, was Cassirer's regular table in Frederichs Restaurant in the Potsdamer Strasse, where the participants drank and engaged in debates from evening to the early hours of the following morning.[42]

The basic composition of the main body of Cassirer's circle remained as described above on into the early period of Expressionism, as we learn from Wilhelm Herzog who joined the group in 1909.[43] For 1906/07 the name of Frank Wedekind must be added to the list of Cassirer's friends; during that year or more Wedekind was residing in Berlin and spending most of his evenings with Cassirer (who was one of Wedekind's staunchest supporters), with Durieux and on occasion with the art dealer's circle.[44] Finally, Cassirer could also number among his closer friends during the approximate ten years that lie across 1910 the painter August Gaul and the editor Theodor Wolff (of the *Berliner Tageblatt*); the critics Max Osborn, Julius Meier-Graefe, Julius Elias, Georg Bernhard (all of them advocates of Impressionism), and the poets Alfred Walter Heymel, Carl Ludwig Schleich, and Rudolf Alexander Schröder.[45] With three of the friends just mentioned, Meier-Graefe, Heymel, and Schröder, Cassirer and Durieux often formed a party of madcap revelers who made merry together in the night spots of Berlin.[46]

None of the painters, poets and writers mentioned thus far as Cassirer's close friends and associates was to be intimately involved in the Expressionist movement. However, I have sketched in the outlines in the preceding pages of Cassirer's association with German Impressionism in order to illustrate the progressive propensities of his literary and artistic tastes well before the Expressionist period, and to identify the foundation of his later connections with the newer movement; for Cassirer's progressive bias was never to wane or ossify and his personal and professional association with German Impressionism was eventually to lead him (after 1910) into a similar relationship with German Expressionism. By the beginning of the Expressionist period, the once progressive Impressionists had become the Old Guard, the representatives of the current established style. Wishing to enjoy the security of this position indefinitely, they found themselves resisting, just as they themselves had once been resisted, the new faction of rebels now coming of age in their own "Berlin Sezession," a faction representing a style which was soon to be called "Expressionism."

While Cassirer's old revolutionaries were thus turning into reactionaries, Cassirer himself remained tenaciously liberal aesthetically and persistently open to fresh developments and talent. He had, perhaps unknowingly, already demonstrated his readiness to accept Expressionism as early as 1904 when he exhibited in that year an artist who is generally held to be a major forerunner of the movement: Vincent van Gogh.[47] When the "Berlin Sezession" split up in 1910 and the new progressive faction in it seceded and formed the "Neue Sezession," Cassirer's sympathies became divided; he remained associated with the older group until it finally came to an end in 1913, but began, in the meantime, to establish close contacts with the younger Expressionists, painters and poets alike.

Cassirer's support of Expressionist graphic artists became apparent already around the beginning of the new decade. In 1907, through August Gaul, Cassirer had met the sculptor and poet Ernst Barlach, much of whose later art and literary work has been interpreted by historians as Expressionist. In the following years, Cassirer was to become a close friend and strong supporter of the artist; and in 1910 and 1911, and again in 1920, Barlach was a house guest of the Cassirers.[48] Cassirer met Oskar Kokoschka in 1910 and in June of the same year sponsored the first one-man exhibition of his work, therewith launching the painter's career and establishing a friendship with him that was to last until Cassirer's death.[49] Cassirer was also associated with Max Beckmann, whom he gave a large one-man show in his gallery in 1913, and with Jules Pascin, who was seen in Cassirer's company as early as 1909 and who, like the other three Expressionists just referred to, also had his work published under the imprint of the Paul Cassirer Verlag.[50] Of the four Expressionist painters just mentioned, only Kokoschka and Pascin are known to have had extensive personal connections with the movement.[51]

Cassirer's ties with Expressionist literature and literary figures were facilitated in large part by his association with Herzog. After his association with Cassirer was to come to an end, Herzog was to go on to become one of the key figures, primarily as an editor-publisher, of the movement.[52] However, his first decisive start both as a writer and editor was given him by Cassirer. Thus, in 1909, at the recommendation of the German-Hungarian writer Ludwig Hatvany, who was a habitué of the Café des Westens before the war and, as mentioned earlier, was by now becoming popular amongst the literary circles that convened there because of his diatribe against the university philologists (*Die Wissenschaft des Nicht Wissenswerten:* Berlin, 1908, sec. ed. 1911), Cassirer hired Herzog as reader and organizer of the publishing company he established that same year.[53] The following year, Herzog cofounded with Cassirer, and from 1910-11 was coeditor with him of the journal *Pan.*[54] Cassirer and Herzog dissolved their partnership in 1911; and, after a brief sojourn in Paris, Herzog moved on to Munich and assumed the editorship there of the weekly *März* (1913), for which he recruited a number of Expressionist contributors. Shortly thereafter, he began editing and publishing his own, predominantly Expressionist journal, *Das Forum* (1914-15, 1918-29).[55] What Herzog was to do for *März* and for his own *Das Forum,* he had also accomplished for Cassirer's literary ventures, for it was largely through Herzog's instigation that several authors, closely connected with the Expressionist movement, appeared under the Cassirer imprint founded in 1909; these authors included Heinrich Mann, Schickele, Flake, Mühsam, Hermann Essig (a friend of Walden and contributor to *Der Sturm*), and Sternheim.[56] Of the latter, Mann and Schickele in particular were close friends of the Cassirers and frequent guests in the Cassirer home before the war.[57] The publication of *Pan* brought Cassirer into a close personal as well as literary association with Alfred Kerr, who was both a regular contributor to, and very briefly a coeditor of, the journal during the time that Cassirer sponsored its appearance; but their collaboration on *Pan,* as will be discussed later, also led to the rupture of their friendship.[58]

In two additional ways Cassirer was linked on a personal level with Expressionism before the war. First of all, Cassirer, and now and then Durieux as well, were habitués in this period of the Café des Westens, where Cassirer most often kept company with Walden and Lasker-Schüler, and on occasion even sponsored the couple financially here.[59] Cassirer and Walden had a common bond professionally also in their mutual support—Cassirer, of course, as an art dealer and Walden as a critic in the pages of *Der Sturm*—of the "Neue Sezession," the progressive faction which split off from the "Berlin Sezession" in 1910 and was composed mostly of young Expressionist painters, including the Munich "Neue Künstlervereinigung" and the "Brücke."[60] Lasker-Schüler is reported by Durieux to have been in love with Cassirer at one time and to have showered him with letters during the apparently one-sided romance; and the poetess was eventually to become a Cassirer author at the end of the Expressionist decade.[61] Cassirer's own personal tie with the movement was through his art salon, whose rooms he made available before the war for the recital evenings of numerous Expressionist circles in Berlin, such as "Der neue Club," *Der Sturm, Die Aktion,* the Meyer circle and the group called "Die feindlichen Brüder."[62] Throughout the Expressionist decade, he also sponsored such evenings under his own name, at which most often Durieux read from the works of the authors appearing at the time in his publishing company.[63]

Cassirer's major literary link with the Expressionist movement in the early phase was through his journal *Pan.* This journal represented a revival by Cassirer of a highly esoteric, *fin-de-siècle* publication founded in 1895 by members of the group that had gathered at that time around August Strindberg in the tavern Zum Schwarzen Ferkel.[64] However, Cassirer's *Pan* differed in one very decisive respect from the original journal, differed in a way which was simultaneously indicative of a crucial distinction aesthetically between the two eras from which the two journals came. It was a difference which, nonetheless, one of the chief editors of the first *Pan,* Meier-Graefe, encouraged and which Kerr helped to identify as a program in their contributions to the opening installment of the 1910 Cassirer revival.[65] This basic difference between the two journals involved very simply an endorsement by the new *Pan* of the Expressionist aesthetic of a "littérature engagée" and a rejection of the *fin-de-siècle* aesthetic of "l'art pour l'art," which the old journal had very consistently manifested.[66] Since the contributions by Meier-Graefe and Kerr to the first issue of Cassirer's *Pan* do outline, in the manner just suggested, the editorial policy and aesthetic position to be followed by the journal, and are given prominent positions in that issue, they are worth considering here in detail.

Meier-Graefe's article, entitled "Der Pan," opens that first issue, which came off the press on November 1, 1910; the article was written implicitly in response to a request from the editors for Meier-Graefe's blessing on the Cassirer revival—which Meier-Graefe gives, but it includes, in the main, the author's analysis of the failings of the old *Pan* and his recommendations for the new.[67] Most decisively, the original *Pan* came to a premature end, according to Meier-Graefe, because of its excessive exclusiveness, its overemphasis on purely artistic considerations in content and form, on the decorative element, or, as Meier-Graefe puts it at one point, on the paper and the type.[68] The journal had been founded originally on the basis of certain, more humanly inclusive ideals, which Meier-Graefe, offering them to the new journal as one salvable feature of the old, summarizes somewhat vaguely as a belief in a kind of monism or Pandean "cosmic harmony":

> Moreover, perhaps one or another of the old ideals of *Pan* can still be of use. We envisioned something vaguely mutual, universal. Scheerbart, I think, had christened it "cosmic harmony."[69]

However, these ideals were, because of a lack of agreement and cooperation on the part of the editors of the old journal, not manifested consistently throughout and were, in addition, largely overshadowed by the decorative element; there was, in short, too large an admixture of art in their journal.[70] Thus, Meier-Graefe advises the editors of the new edition of *Pan* to enforce more consistently throughout a specific editorial and philosophical position; they should, he stresses, take a precise stand:

> Our universalism, our versatility was too—nebulous. For God's sake, don't be nebulous. And beware of versatility. It was the blight of *Pan* and is the blight of all journals. There is nothing worse than being unpartisan, no matter how sublimely and nobly it might be managed; there is nothing more stupid.... Be one-sided, partisan, unjust to the point of excess and if possible somewhat plucky.[71]

More significantly, Meier-Graefe continues, this stand should be based on more than just artistic ideals; it should follow rather ideals which involve a moral, perhaps at times a political, as well as artistic commitment, so that a better balance might be achieved between art and life: "There was too much art in our basically praiseworthy thoughts. Art should be tied to life. We thought up all manner of ties, but they were all too artistic, which is not to say: artificial."[72]

Kerr's statement, "Brief an die Herausgeber," is ostensibly a written reply to conversations with the editors; it is fundamentally a reaffirmation of Meier-

Graefe's position, but at the same time in stronger, more radical and programmatic terms, with, on the whole, considerably greater stress placed on the need for extra-artistic commitment.[73] On another level, Kerr's statement offers some especially clear insight into the reasons behind the mutual attraction which existed between him and the prewar Expressionists, for we can see in the position he takes here a number of parallels with both the aesthetic and ideological position of those artists as it has been encountered in the course of this study.

Kerr begins by expressing his general approval of the plans for *Pan* as they were discussed with the editors in conversation, namely for a journal which is not esoteric either in interests or format:

> Moreover, you know from our conversations that I like your other plans for creating a journal which will not publish cultural rubbish in fancy dress, but will provide space for all sorts of work (it seems this sentence will never end) rich in experience of life and cheerful individualism.[74]

His approval is based upon his notions of what such a journal should properly be, which he sets forth in the remainder of his statement in the form of a series of recommendations. First of all, Kerr advocates a journal which, as he claims he has always done in his own criticism, "meets life face to face," i.e., confronts itself with life's totality, honestly and squarely. Moreover, this kind of confrontation with life must involve an aggressive literary posture which seeks to arouse or provoke the reader's response:

> Literature fills only one corner of my life and I therefore hope it will do the same for your journal. It should face life. The most brilliant piece of theater criticism seems wretched to me if it is not informed by a battlecry heard beyond the theater. He is a wretched critic who does not make people tremble or cry out with his words, guidance, sounds, in which the (mostly very insignificant) poetic egos do not share. Criticisms are pretexts. Beyond the theater.... I know you sense that.[75]

Secondly, in assuming such an aggressive, provocative aesthetic posture, the editors should, in keeping with Kerr's preference for a journal of wide interests, not shrink from becoming "prosaic" at times, i.e., from dealing with commonplace issues, and, in particular, political ones:

> Enter politics head-on with fanfare and flags unfurled. I do not see your journal as a sensation monger, whose aim it will be to overcome its own measure of stupidity by means of contradictions, gossip, and wild boasts.... I hope you would agree with something I wrote once in a critique: "Morally progressive regional associations are, of course, an abomination. Worse abominations, however, are the fools who reject their ideas.... Fools confuse the heralds of ideas with the ideas themselves..." Gentlemen, no false shame—of the sort that derives from an intellectual insufficiency. Don't have any of the writer's fear of appearing in print every day.[76]

Thus Kerr advocates a journal which is morally, socially, and politically committed, but one committed not to a fixed philosophy or ideology, rather to seeking change actively, change on any level, political, social, economic, moral, etc., as the need for such change is noticed from instance to instance, and committed to inducing the readers to follow suit: "I long for a journal which will not publish appeals, but will organize them. Which will not look for the approval of its readers, but will educate them to act . . . "[77] The general policy of the journal, on the other hand, should be anti-bourgeois, i.e., the journal should aim to censure the "wretchedness of the contemporary middle class," more specifically its materialism, hypocrisy, feudalism:

> I long also for a journal which will give a sound flogging to the contemporary middle class because of its baseness. A baseness which calls every five an even number as long as a profit is being made. . . . A radical baseness which, after one one-eighth of a generation, sees the sum total of happiness in feudalistic family ties.[78]

Those who shrink from committing or openly declaring themselves in the manner Kerr has recommended, and prefer instead to smile ironically in submission, are lacking in what Kerr interprets as essential human qualities: "the talent for being coarse" ("die Gabe des Rüdigseins"), "the strength to participate" ("die Macht des Mittuns"), "originality" (Ursprünglichkeit"), "the joy in a vigorous beginning" ("die Lust des Loslegens") and "the resoluteness for a fight" ("die Entschlossenheit zur Schlacht").[79] Therefore, as a counterinfluence to the kind of moral indolence and cowardice which established society considers "proper," a journal should activate its readers and offer them the ideal of individuals who, beneath their hypercultured, hyperurbanized, hyperartistic exterior, have, nonetheless, retained an elementally human aspect in their character:

> Help to drive home to decent people the fact that their cultured passivity is an obscenity. Perhaps they will then get over their irony, intolerance and their great progressive cowardice. . . .
> Offer them the following as an ideal: those who, along with a high degree of culture and fine artistic powers, have a bit of the rabble in them; who, along with their refined urbanity, have a bit of the wild beast in them, are ready to leap on their prey. Those are the types we need.[80]

The parallels which we can draw between Kerr's program and the Expressionist position are quite obvious. The two coincide in the espousal of an aggressive, provocative, antibourgeois literature (cf., e.g., the program of "Der neue Club," Kurtz's programmatic essay for the first issue of *Der Sturm* and Hardekopf's "Erste Proklamation des Aeternismus" written for the Pfemfert prose series—all discussed in earlier chapters). They both espouse a "littérature engagée," both in the broad sense of a literature committed to the support of some specific cause and seeking to realize the cause by using the word as deed, according to which all Expressionist literature can be defined, and in the more narrow sense of politically committed literature, in which the concept was manifested by *Die Aktion.* Finally, both espouse an attitude of mind which confronts life honestly and seeks to acknowledge and respect all forms of human endeavor and all sides of human character.

Considered together in their broadest implications, the recommendations of Meier-Graefe and Kerr were both intended to point *Pan* in the direction of a relatively all-inclusive editorial policy in relation to man's activities and experiences. The title of the journal itself was obviously borrowed from the older journal because of its capacity to connote such a policy; and Kerr, in a short commentary on an article published in the issue which opened the second year of *Pan* (October 1, 1911), reaffirmed the philosophical position of the journal in just such a way.[81] The article in question was by Willem van Wulfen and, as its title, "Der Genussmensch," implied, espoused a philosophy of hedonism. Kerr, however, in an editorial comment prefacing the essay, declared that Wulfen's essay was only being published in the pages of *Pan* in order to stimulate a "testing" and "confirming" of the kind of thinking for which the journal actually stood.[82] Kerr then added, by way of explaining the more catholic perspective of the journal opposite Wulfen's:

> I believe that we are both summer and winter creatures. Both tasters and cooks.... I believe that mankind should not cast aside any opportunity....[83]

Kerr's program, and along with it the fractionally related position of Meier-Graefe, was to have to face an unusually large number of changes in editorial staff during about the first year and a half of the journal, the period during which it came out under the Cassirer imprint.[84] During the first full year of publication, from November 1, 1918, to October 1, 1911 (vol. 1, nos. 1-22; vol. 2, no. 1), *Pan* appeared semimonthly, with Cassirer signing as publisher and founder (on the title page: "begründet von Paul Cassirer") and Herzog as editor ("Verantwortlich für die Redaktion").[85] About the middle of the same period, beginning with the June 16, 1911, issue, Kerr officially joined the journal as an independent contributing editor ("Alfred Kerr zeichnet verantwortlich für die von ihm verfassten Beiträge") ("Alfred Kerr assumes responsibility for the contributions signed by him."). He remained in this capacity until November 1, 1911 (vol. 2, no. 3), and, after briefly assuming the post Herzog had held for one single issue (November 16, 1911; vol. 2, no. 4), he left *Pan* altogether for the time being over what were described in a note published in the journal as "differences of opinion" between editor and publisher.[86] Following Herzog's departure from the staff of the journal in October, 1911, and throughout the remainder of Cassirer's ownership (until the end of March, 1912), *Pan* was continued at first as a semimonthly and then as a weekly (beginning January 4, 1912; vol. 2, no. 7). During this same six-month period the editorship of the journal changed hands several times: October 15, 1911, to November 1, 1911 (vol. 2, nos. 2-3): Cassirer ("Begründer") and Albert Damm ("Verantwortlich für die Redaktion"); November 16, 1911 (vol. 2, no. 4): Cassirer ("Begründer") and Kerr ("Verantwortlich für die Redaktion"); December 1, 1911, to January 25, 1912 (vol. 2, nos. 5-10): Cassirer ("Begründer" and "Redakteur"), W. Fred (pseud. for Alfred Wechsler; "Redakteur") and Damm ("Verantwortlich für die Redaktion"); February 1, 1912, to March 28, 1912 (vol. 2, nos. 11-19): Cassirer ("Herausgeber") and Damm ("Verantwortlich für die Redaktion").[87]

The "differences of opinion" which had come become between Cassirer's and Kerr's association on *Pan* in November, 1911, had, according to Durieux, stemmed from the Kerr-Jagow-*Pan* affair of the spring of that year. This affair and its ramifications had sufficiently soured Cassirer on the journal by March, 1912, again according to Durieux, to induce him to sell it to another publisher.[88] The new publisher, the Hammer-Verlag of Berlin, immediately engaged Kerr as sole editor ("Herausgeber" and "Verantwortlicher Leiter": April 4, 1912; vol. 2, nos. 20ff.).[89] While Kerr was to retain his new post on *Pan* to the end (April 1, 1915; vol. 4, no. 2/3), the publishing rights were to change hands once more—a full twelve months, but just *one* issue, prior to the final cessation of publication, when the Hyperionverlag of Berlin took over the journal "on commission," beginning with the May 13, 1914, issue (vol. 4, no. 1).[90] Kerr was able to continue the journal as a weekly through the first year of his term of editor; but then, probably as a result of financial difficulties, the subtitle ("Wochenschrift") was dropped altogether with the June 1, 1913, issue (vol. 3, no. 28) and the journal continued henceforth on an extremely sporadic basis through the remaining four numbers, put out in the course of two full calendar years.[91]

In spite of the journal's very checkered publishing and editorial life, the overlapping of Cassirer and Kerr's terms of association with *Pan* provided sufficient continuity for it to reflect the program of Kerr and Meier-Graefe in the overall contents of each issue. Herzog recalled in a memoir on Kerr, written many decades later, that he in particular had felt in 1910 that Kerr's "Brief an die Herausgeber" represented his intentions with *Pan* "exactly"; and Herzog added, claiming to speak for the other editors of *Pan* during his association with the journal, that they had attempted to abide by Kerr's program. After citing the key points from Kerr's "Brief an die Herausgeber," Herzog wrote: "That was exactly what I wanted. That was the note I wanted to strike in *Pan,* and we tried to maintain it."[92]

That Herzog was, indeed, speaking in a broad sense for the other editors of *Pan* is made clear by the contents of the journal's issues from the very start. Beginning with the first issue, there were to be, in addition to sections devoted regularly to imaginative literature, to literary, music, and art criticism and occasionally to the reproduction of graphic arts, also regular sections which published essays on political, social, moral, and related themes. Although the term "littérature engagée" cannot be used to characterize all of the imaginative literature published in *Pan* during especially the Cassirer period, the term does apply very much to the great bulk of the type of essays just mentioned. However, that first issue, again, is dominated by what can be read in context as three clear responses—in literary and sociopolitical form both—to the Kerr-Meier-Graefe program outlined in the same pages: a diatribe against the Wilhelminian university by Herzog ("Universitätsjubel," pp. 4-7); an essay by Frank Wedekind arguing for the sexual enlightenment of especially the young ("Aufklärungen," pp. 11-16); and a one-act social comedy by Heinrich Mann, exposing the unscrupulousness of an actress who, surrounded mostly by others of similar moral fiber, seeks theatrical success at any and all costs necessary ("Variété," pp. 16-30; continued in vol. 1, no. 2, pp. 51-59).

   Throughout Cassirer's ownership, there were to appear, as a regular part of *Pan*, articles and short marginal glosses, penned by various hands (occasionally by Cassirer's) similar to those contributed to that first issue by Herzog and Wedekind. Thus, in November, 1910, Herzog argued in an article entitled "Moabit" for a more humane legal system. The opening of this treatise reflects Kerr's program very directly:

> Still, the social set which pursues all the sensations of the theater and art would do well to pause in their mindless pursuit, to restrain their delight in the theater for a while and to attend to affairs which affect them pretty damned deeply.[93]

In December of the same year, Ludwig Frank, a member of the Reichstag, opposed Wilhelminian politics in "Politische Skizzen"; and later the same month René Schickele contributed a discussion of the politics of the French statesman Aristide Briand ("Briand").[94] *Pan* opened the new year (January 1, 1911; vol. 1, no. 5) with an issue containing an article by Herzog, "Die kommende Demokratie" (pp. 150-153), which advocates the full democratization of German political life. The second January issue was dominated by a series of statements on capital punishment, introduced by a strong proposal for abolishment of the practice by Hermann Bahr ("Todesstrafe"; vol. 1, no. 6, pp. 177-80). The next several issues (February 1, 1911, to March 16, 1911; vol. 1, nos. 7-10) featured Kerr's polemics against the Berlin Police Chief Traugott Jagow, initially for his banning of an issue of *Pan* because it contained a translation of sections from the diary of the young Flaubert, and then, later, for his behavior in connection with the Berlin première of Sternheim's comedy *Die Hose*.[95] In April of 1911 Herbert Eulenberg added his voice in *Pan* to the argument in favor of sexual enlightenment of the young with his "Brief eines Vaters unserer Zeit," which, as much for its political overtones (the authorship of this fictional letter to a son, which advocates a very liberal approach to sex education, is attributed to a diplomat!) as for its moral position, brought another censor's ban on the journal.[96] Kerr wrote several political pieces for *Pan* during 1911, including an attack on the chancellor ("Wanderungen mit Bethmann"), a discussion of German colonial possessions and their relationship to the Third Moroccan Crisis ("Kolonialdämmerung") and some recommendations to the German voter for a forthcoming election ("Was ist zu tun?").[97]

In January, 1911, *Pan* also sponsored in its essay section one of the most important politico-literary manifestoes of the Expressionist decade: Heinrich Mann's "Geist und Tat."[98] This essay is in large part a restatement of Kerr's *Pan* program, but at the same time a further radicalization of Kerr's already very aggressive position; the basic differences between the two essays, therefore, involve only factors of stress, degree, and detail. Mann, like Kerr, calls for change in Wilhelminian Germany in the direction of greater justice and humanity, and Mann, like Kerr, seeks to enlist the help of the intellectual, the "Literat," in the struggle for change; however, Mann identifies more precisely the specific goals and the enemy in the struggle, stresses to a greater degree the need for action, for militancy, and advocates, by implication, change on a broader scale, on the scale of a revolution.

The goal in the struggle for change, Mann suggests in "Geist und Tat," is a democratic form of government, a system in which the people rule, and through which the ideals of "freedom," "justice," and "human dignity" can be achieved.[99] The enemy in this struggle is, therefore, tyranny, the monarchy, the small privileged class which seeks to rule the majority, all of which Mann paraphrases with "the man of authority and might" ("Our enemy must be the men of authority and power.")[100] The leader in the fight for change must be the intellectual or "Literat," for he is the representative of "Geist" which, in turn, embodies the ideals in the fight: "His nature is: to define the word; the luminous perfection of the word is his commitment to disdain the oppressive imperfection of power. The mind places in his charge the dignity of the human race."[101] The intellectuals are to be the new rulers of Germany, so that through them the people may rule.[102]

The participation of the intellectual in the struggle to realize the political ideal involves, as Mann sees it, a conversion of the intellect ("Geist") from its isolation, which allows tyranny to obtain, into the active service of deed ("Tat"); the intellectual must, in other words, unite intellect with action by becoming an agitator of the people through the use of the literary word:

> The times require and their honor desires that the intellectuals in this country also once and for all ensure the realization of the demands of the mind, that they become agitators, join the people against power, that they devote the full force of the word to the fight, for it is also the mind's fight.[103]

In his political struggle and in seeking to achieve the prerequisite for it, i.e., the union of "Geist" and "Tat," the German can look to the French as a model. In Rousseau and Zola, and especially in those who fought in the Revolution of 1789, the French embodied the "Ratio militans" which results from that ideal union of intellect and deed; but even the French people as a whole represent the proper base for creating Rousseaus and Zolas and the men of 1789, for they are in temperament the "synthesis of Europe," the synthesis of the Nordic man of intellect with the Southern man of passion:

> The intellectuals of France, from Rousseau to Zola, who opposed established power, have had an easy time of it: they had a nation behind them. A nation with literary instincts which questions power, and so warm-blooded that power becomes intolerable the moment it is refuted by reason. How many things had to conjoin for such warriors of the mind to appear. A Nordic people, informed by the blood of the race and even more by the culture of the South. The synthesis of Europe. The race as strong as in the South, but all of the artistry which it confers dependent on the mind. The mind for us is not that familiar ethereal specter—and down below life lumbers on. The mind is life itself; it shapes life at the risk of abridging it.[104]

It is difficult to measure the direct impact which this essay had on the Expressionists, or to separate its influence on them from that of the many other similar statements in the period; but "Geist und Tat," as was much of Mann's other work, was widely received with great favor in the Expressionist camp. Herzog, who was editor of *Pan* when the essay was published, stressed, in a memoir on Mann, its far-reaching influence on his own life as on that of others: "Here [in *Pan*] his great manifesto "Geist und Tat" appeared; for many of us young writers it was a program which became a veritable model for our future lives and work."[105] The essay was greeted most enthusiastically amongst the prewar Expressionists in the circle around *Die Aktion,* which could already then readily appreciate its political implications. The leader of that circle hailed the essay in his journal as "a radical, courageous, sparkling manifesto."[106] Rubiner, who wrote a defense of Mann in *Die Aktion* and described him as a political revolutionary with his novel *Der Untertan,* published in the same journal, beginning in 1912, a series of theoretical pieces (put out collectively in 1917 as *Der Mensch in der Mitte*) in which he develops a line of thinking very closely related to that in Mann's "Geist und Tat." Rubiner's concept of "Intensität" ("Intensität = gleich: Platzen vor Geistes-Gegenwart"[107]), for example, which forms a key part of his philosophy of political activism, is roughly equivalent to Mann's "Ratio militans"; and the potential embodiment of "Intensität" and the leader in a political struggle is for Rubiner, too,[108] the "Literat" ("The poet breaks into the political arena."[109]) Hiller, another associate of Pfemfert, also developed a philosophy of political activism ("die Philosophie des Ziels") very similar to Mann's in his *Ziel-Jahrbücher* (1915ff.), the first volume of which opened with a reprint of Mann's manifesto.[110]

Of course, it was not only the politically committed among the prewar Expressionists who could welcome Mann's manifesto; there was much here that most Expressionists of the time could sympathize with: most obviously, Mann's strongly antiauthoritarian, his implicit anti-Wilhelminian position, but also his espousal of the ideal of a synthesis of Nordic and Mediterranean man, of the man of intellect and the man of action, of mind and body, which is at the center of the artistic program of, for example, "Der neue Club" and as well as of the circle around *Der Sturm*.[111] With the advent of wide-scale political involvement after the war amongst the majority of Expressionists, it was appropriate that Herzog once again sponsor the publication of "Geist und Tat" in an Expressionist journal (*Das Forum*, vol. 6, February, 1922, no. 5, pp. 215-23).

The literature published in *Pan* during Cassirer's term of ownership did not always express as strong a political, social, or moral commitment as had Mann's play "Variété" in that first issue. A number of representatives of pre-Expressionist styles, whose work could hardly be characterized as "littérature engagée," were published in the pages of *Pan* in this period: Peter Altenberg, Jakob Wassermann, Max Dauthendey, Richard Dehmel, Hugo von Hofmannsthal, et al.[112] However, the work of authors associated with the Expressionist camp or related tendencies are prominently represented with imaginative prose, poetry and literary criticism: Brod, Hiller, Schickele, Franz Blei, Heym, Rubiner, Hardekopf, Musil, Ehrenbaum-Degele, Essig, Ruest, Friedlaender, Blass, Einstein, Scheerbart, Flake, Leonhard, and many others.[113] There were also frequent critiques or glosses, most often written by authors of the same literary direction, dealing with the new Expressionist literature. Thus, Heinrich Mann the dramatist was studied in an essay in the December 1 issue of 1910; and in the same number there appeared a very appreciative review of Herbert Eulenberg's notorious Schiller talk given the previous month in Leipzig, which played a crucial role in coalescing that same winter the circle of young Expressionists in Leipzig around Kurt Wolff and Ernst Rowohlt.[114] In the summer of the next year, Hiller wrote an enthusiastic study of the work of his friend Heym for the journal; and Kurtz contributed in the same season a defense of the (at that time) little-recognized dramatic work of Lasker-Schüler.[115]

While there occurred no major changes in the general editorial policy and contents of *Pan* after Kerr assumed exclusive editorship of the journal, nevertheless, under his direction, the reader of *Pan* very soon began to detect, to a much stronger degree than ever before, the distinct signature of one firm and consistent editorial hand at work throughout all departments—political as well as literary, determining now in depth both the specific contents and the specific direction of each issue.

In the section devoted to nonliterary essay, there now still appear, of course, articles by a variety of contributors; but most represent very much the same kind of thinking as that of writers published in this section under previous editors. Sigmund Freud, for example, contributed a study on sexuality in primitive man ("Der Inzestscheu der Wilden") to the second April issue of 1912; and Otto Rank, a student of Freud, was represented by a related study ("Der Inzest") in July of the same year.[116] A lawyer, Dr. J. Werthauer, wrote a number of essays dealing with legal questions and the need for certain reforms in the law for issues of *Pan* under Kerr; and again, as had happened under other editors, there are published in this period numerous articles on the politics of Wilhelminian Germany, written on occasion by a professional politician.[117] The wide-ranging interest of *Pan* under Kerr, as under previous editors, is illustrated by an article by a magistrate, Dr. Ludwig Herz, on the shortage of meat in Germany ("Die Fleischteuerung"), which was published in the issue for November 29, 1912.[118] Kerr's own voice remains constantly in the forefront in this period, however; articles from his pen, covering almost any topic in this subject area which might strike his interest—the parliament, war, the army, the police, the courts, censorship, psychology, morality, prominent personalities of the period, etc.—constitute a regular and dominant feature of most issues of *Pan.*[119]

Equally perceptible now is the editor's hand in the literary sections of *Pan,* and for the most part not directly, but indirectly in the selections made for inclusion in each issue. Kerr himself only occasionally applies his pen to literary criticism, as, for instance, in his reaction to the appearance of Marinetti in Berlin in February, 1913 ("Der Futurist").[120] Most of the literary criticism and glosses on literature are contributed by other writers; yet—and here we perceive the effect of Kerr's tastes and interests—most of these pieces deal with, and are written by, Expressionists or those closely associated with the Expressionist camp. The very first issue edited in this period by Kerr (April 4, 1912; vol. 2, no. 20) includes excerpts from both the main text of, as well as from Hiller's programmatic foreword to, the Expressionist anthology *Der Kondor,* which came off the press at the end of the following month.[121] Hiller was one of the most frequent contributors of literary critiques and glosses, most of them dealing with the work of his fellow Expressionists, throughout the remaining volumes of *Pan.* In February, 1913, for example, he contributed a review of Franz Jung's *Das Trottelbuch* and in April of the same year some notes on Carl Einstein's *Bebuquin.*[122] Two other contributions to *Pan* under Kerr are of particular note in this context. Emil Faktor contributed in May, 1912, a very positive review of Benn's *Morgue,* which had just appeared two months before in Meyer's *Lyrische Flugblätter.*[123]

The November 1 issue of that year brought some lengthy excerpts, just in advance of publication, from Blass's foreword to the collection of his verse entitled *Die Strassen komme ich entlanggeweht.* This foreword is of more than passing interest because of the very clear echoes it contains of the thinking of both Blass's friend and associate Hiller and of Kerr. Thus, Blass also defines the ideal poet as a fighter for truth and the betterment of man's lot on earth ("Auch der Lyriker wird nächstens ein Erkennender sein, ein Kämpfer; einer, der haltbare Grundlagen sucht, um ein Steigen der Glückschancen für Menschen zu berechnen. . . . ") ("The lyric poet will also soon be a person of perception, a fighter, one who is looking for solid foundations on which to plan out an increase in mankind's chances for happiness . . . "), as a man of both thought and passion ("Der erkennende Kämpfer allerdings wird auch ein Lyriker sein. Das ist nichts gewissenhafter Vernunfttätigkeit Entgegengesetztes, sondern etwas, das sie beflügelt.... Der Denker wird ganz sorgfältig und voll Verantwortungsgefühl, dennoch feurig sein.") ("Our perceptive fighter will, of course, also be a poet. That is not something opposed to the scrupulous use of reason, but something which inspires reason.... Our thinker will be cautious and full of a sense of responsibility, but still fiery.") Blass, too, envisions the new poet as one who acknowledges all sides of human life, the high and the low ("Weil er ehrlich ist und bewusst, wird er eins auch im Traume nie vergessen: dass er nicht immer ein Engel ist, nicht immer ein Urwesen, nicht immer schwebend und alltagsfern... Das wird in seinen Klängen liegen: das Wissen um das Flache des Lebens, das Klebrige, das Alltägliche.... ") ("Because he is honest and aware, he will also not forget one thing in his dreams: that he is not always an angel, not always a primordial being, not always soaring and remote from reality... We will hear this in his songs: his awareness of the vapidity of life, the viscous, quotidian side of life.... "), and as one who is an observer of life with a critical eye ("Der neue Dichter... wird gegen künstlerisches Schaffen überhaupt, soweit es unkritisch ist, etwas skeptisch sein,—dennoch wird er eine Melodie haben... ") ("The new poet... will be somewhat sceptical about all artistic creations that are uncritical—nonetheless, his verse will be melodious... "). Finally, he also sees the ideal poet as a man of the modern metropolis ("The lyricist of the future... will, however, not render portraits of the great metropolis, but metropolitan portraits.")[124]

The most significant change to come out of Kerr's takeover of *Pan* involved a shift in emphasis in the department devoted to imaginative literature. Under Cassirer, the reader had been able to discern no special preference on the part of the editor in literary styles; under Kerr a clear dominant thrust of support in the direction of Expressionist literature very soon becomes noticeable. The reader encounters only infrequently now the work of representatives of pre-Expressionist styles, such as Hermann Conradi, Richard Dehmel, Otto Erich Hartleben, Gerhart Hauptmann, Wilhelm Lehmann.[125] Expressionist literature, on the other hand, gradually becomes a regular part of most issues of the journal after March, 1912. Kerr publishes some Expressionist prose from time to time, by, for example, Heinrich Eduard Jacob, Hermann Essig, Leonhard Frank; and in May, 1912, a section from Reinhard Sorge's play *Der Bettler* appears just before the complete work comes out in book form.[126]

Kerr's dominant interest clearly lay in the Expressionist lyric, for in the May 2 issue of 1912—less than a month, therefore, after he had assumed sole editorship of the journal—he inaugurated a special, continuing section devoted to the lyric of young, unrecognized poets, which in the following two years was to publish, with only rare exceptions, poetry emanating from the Expressionist camp.[127] Kerr gave this new section a permanent heading, "Fortgeschrittene

Lyrik"—a term which, shortly after its appearance in *Pan,* was to be adopted by some of the Expressionists themselves as a designation for their style of verse.[128] Kerr's explanation of the purpose of the new section, which prefaces its introduction in that May 2 issue, indicates that Kerr, like Hiller and many other literary theorists among the Expressionists, equated in his mind, too, the new, progressive lyric largely with the experience or background of the modern metropolis:

> Young poets, unknown to each other, send their verses to *Pan.* The desire has often been voiced by critics and been implicit in exemplary poems to find the progressive lyric of the metropolises. Not everything can be published: as long as the police are stalking art. You will receive an outline of the tendency here.[129]

The poets published in the ensuing issues under the rubric "Fortgeschrittene Lyrik" included Klabund (very often; both under his pseudonym and his real name, Alfred Henschke), Herrmann-Neisse (very often), Robert Schmidt, Benn, Friedrich Wilhelm Wagner, Werfel, Hardekopf, Blass, Hiller, Hasenclever, Lichtenstein, Schickele, Emmy Hennings, and others.[130]

Clearly, in the minds of both Cassirer and Kerr, *Pan* was conceived of as a primarily politico-literary journal. Even taking art criticism into account, the graphic arts, in spite of Cassirer's very active career in the field, played a decidedly secondary role in *Pan* throughout all of its four volumes of publication. Reproductions of art work in particular constituted a very insignificant ingredient in its overall typographical image in comparison with *Der Sturm* or *Die Aktion.* During Cassirer's ownership, art work decorated the pages of the journal only occasionally, and, with few exceptions, it was executed by artists of clearly Impressionist tendency in style; most such contributors were also associated with Cassirer's art dealership: Corinth, Rudolf Grossmann, Slevogt, Ernst Matthes, Karl Walser, Benno Berneis, and others.[131] Critically, the journal gave roughly equal support to both Impressionist and Expressionist art under Cassirer, but Cassirer's series of articles on the art market and the profession of the art dealer, which were discussed above, and the Marc-Beckmann controversy which took place in the pages of *Pan* in the early spring of 1912, were the only noteworthy contributions in the area of art criticism in the same period.[132]

Kerr exhibited especially small interest as an editor in having *Pan* take a prominent stand on the graphic arts. Reproductions of art work in the pages of the journal during his editorship were very rare, and thus allow the reader to remark no particular preference in styles on the part of the editor; the few artists whose work appeared in the journal in this period included Käthe Kollwitz, Liebermann, Oppenheimer, and Pechstein.[133] While *Pan* tended to favor Expressionist art in criticism under Kerr, outside of a series of articles by the critic Max Deri on progressive trends in contemporary art ("Die absolute

Malerei," "Die Futuristen" and "Die Kubisten und der Expressionismus"), which appeared in the second half of 1912, less coverage of this sort was given the graphic arts in the journal between April 4, 1912, and April 1, 1915, than had been given previously.[134]

The end of *Pan* came slowly and haltingly, in the manner described earlier in this chapter, between March 28, 1913, and April 1, 1915, with the last actual weekly issue appearing on the former date.[135] The manner in which the end came suggests most obviously two possible causes for the cessation of publication: financial difficulties or failing interest, or both, on the part of the editor; but the real causes are not known. The contents of the last three issues of the journal to appear (vol. 3, no. 31 for December 23, 1913; vol. 4, nos. 1 and 2/3 for May 13, 1913, and April 1, 1915) suggest that Kerr had, no doubt as a result of the increasing irregularity and unpredictability of the journal's appearance, forfeited most of the support he had been receiving regularly from other contributors: the first two of these last three issues were filled mostly with Kerr's own contributions, and the last of the three exclusively with the editor's work.[136] A good fourth (pp. 25-32) of the contents of the final number, put out towards the end of the first year of the war, was taken up by the kind of jingoistic verse which, as remarked in a previous chapter, cost Kerr in this period most of the favor he had once enjoyed amongst the Expressionists.[137] A footnote to that final issue tells us that Kerr was still entertaining plans at the time it went to press of continuing *Pan* through three numbers and more: "*Pan* will appear as long as its editor is alive—at intervals which he himself will decide. The three issues still due in this series will appear shortly."[138]

Two other activities were sponsored by Cassirer under the name "Pan": the "Pan-Presse" and the "Pan-Gesellschaft." Under the rubric of "Pan-Presse," which was established in 1909, the Verlag Paul Cassirer put out a series of bibliophile volumes printed with carefully selected type on special paper.[139] Between 1909 and 1914, thirteen volumes were put out in the series in fairly regular succession; and, then, after a four-year interruption, a final six volumes were issued between 1919 and 1921.[140] All of the nineteen volumes in the series published graphic arts, some of them original works, and all but four of them with accompanying text taken from classical world literature (James Fenimore Cooper, the Old Testament, Heinrich Heine, Voltaire, Heinrich von Kleist, et al.) or from original sources.[141] Most of the artists whose work was included represented Impressionism, although now and then, both before the war and after, an artist is represented in the series who played a role in Expressionism: 1909-14: Slevogt, Corinth, Beckmann, Jules Pascin, Willi Geiger, Emil Potterer, Grossmann, Barlach, Marcus Behmer, and Otto Hettner; 1919-21: Gaul, Pechstein, Barlach, and Slevogt.[142] The tenth volume in the series, published in 1912, is the only one of textual interest in the context of literary Expressionism: Barlach's play *Der tote Tag* with twenty-seven original lithographs by the poet.[143]

Of much greater significance for literary history was the Cassirer "Pan-Gesellschaft." According to Durieux, this organization was a product of Cassirer's friendship with Heinrich Mann, although Herzog claims he was the one who instigated the founding of it in 1910.[144] The "Pan-Gesellschaft" was a theater group established for the special purpose of producing plays by dramatists otherwise largely ignored or refused production by the established theaters.[145] Each play selected for production was to be given only one performance before a small circle of invited guests and staged by actors working for no other compensation than the pleasure of helping further the career of a talented, but unrecognized playwright.[146] The organization appears to have sponsored a total of only two productions. The first of these was a production of Wedekind's (until then) seldom-performed *Die Büchse der Pandora* (1893/94), which was given sometime in 1910 in the Berlin Hebbel-Theater; the performance was put on by Munich actors and directed with the assistance of Wedekind himself.[147] The second production was presented on November 21 of the same year in the Kleines Theater in Berlin and was devoted to three one-act plays by Heinrich Mann, the first two of which had been performed once before: *Der Tyrann* (1907), *Variété* (1910) and *Die Unschuldige* (1910).[148] There was also at least one recital evening sponsored by the same organization; it took place on November 10, 1910, and featured Wedekind reading his essay "Aufklärung," which had just appeared a few days before in Cassirer's journal, and reciting his one-act play *Totentanz* (1905).[149]

In July, 1914, the Cassirers went to Paris, primarily so that Durieux could realize a wish she had harbored for a long time of sitting for a portrait by Auguste Renoir.[150] They had planned on a lengthy sojourn in Paris; however, only a couple of weeks after having arrived in the French city, with the Renoir portrait finished, the political crisis in Europe which was soon to erupt into a full-scale global war had assumed a sufficiently ominous aspect to induce the Cassirers to abbreviate their Paris trip and return to Germany immediately.[151] They had gotten no farther than Düsseldorf on their way to Berlin when the news broke of the German declaration of war on France (August 3, 1914).[152]

Up to this time, Cassirer, like most of his friends—the content and policy of the journal he had sponsored two years before notwithstanding—had taken little real interest in political issues himself. Herzog wrote of Cassirer and his circle and the range of their interests as he knew them in 1909-11:

> It was a business setting without any business overtones. A motley confusion of aesthetic, literary, and art-critical opinions which often opposed each other. Political and economic issues were seldom touched on. In Cassirer's galleries you talked more of the beauty of the pictures on exhibition... than of their monetary value.[153]

The war was to force on Cassirer a complete transformation of attitude, as it was on most of his friends and associates. In Cassirer's case this transformation also began in a fashion typical for someone from his kind of art-oriented milieu, namely with the experiencing of the conflagration on a direct, personal level. When he heard the news of war in Düsseldorf, Cassirer was seized by the same sort of patriotic fervor which he and Durieux saw expressed in the streets of that city; although Cassirer was then well beyond draft age, he determined without hesitation to enlist.[154] Thus, the Cassirers rushed directly on to their place of residence so that Cassirer could carry out his plan. Arriving in Berlin, they found the city in an even greater state of excitement and jubilation over the news than Düsseldorf, as Durieux describes in her autobiography:

> We found Berlin surging with excitement. Everywhere were crowds of people and departing soldiers, to whom the people threw flowers. Every face glowed with joy: it's war!—In cafés and restaurants they kept on playing "Heil dir im Siegerkranz" and "Die Wacht am Rhein." Everyone had to stand until the music stopped; their dinners got cold, their beer warm. What did it matter: it's war! People stood in line to offer their automobiles for service. Soon enlistments were only possible if you knew someone. At the train station soldiers were given piles of sandwiches, sausages, and chocolate. There was a surplus of everything, people, food, and enthusiasm.[155]

In order to be able to offer the military a useful service, since he was much too old for the infantry, Cassirer had his chauffeur teach him to drive his own car, and then he enlisted.[156] Most of Cassirer's friends followed suit, including even his wife, who enlisted in the nurse corps.[157] Thus, Cassirer was sent to serve at the Western front, while Durieux began the war working as a nurse's aide in a military hospital in Buch near Berlin.[158]

Durieux remained in the nurse corps until the summer of 1915, when she was forced to return to the life of a private citizen and actress for reasons of health; but this time, no doubt largely under the impression of the mutilated bodies of the soldiers she had been caring for in the hospital in Buch, Durieux had already changed her thinking on the war and on politics in general and was now, as she relates in her autobiography, leaning towards pacifism and socialism.[159] Cassirer, on the other hand, continued to be a supporter of the war and to lean more to the right on the political spectrum throughout, it would seem, most of his term of service, which lasted until the spring of 1916; his original political position was, at any rate, still firm as late as the second half of 1915, when he made his only extended visit to Berlin on leave from the army, during which he took his wife to task for her "political derailment" ("politische Entgleisung"), as he termed it at the time.[160]

One of the reasons Cassirer took a leave from the service in the second half of 1915 in order to visit Berlin involved his business; he came to liquidate most of the holdings of his publishing company and to put the direction of his art salon in other hands for the remainder of his absence.[161] One segment of the Verlag Paul Cassirer remained active, however, throughout the rest of that year and on into the next, for during that time it continued to put out a periodical series of "Künstler-flugblätter" under the title *Kriegszeit*, which had been initiated just a few weeks after the outbreak of the war.[162] Although this series of broadsheets was devoted primarily to the graphic arts, it is instructive to consider it briefly in the context of this literary study, for it reflects and illustrates quite clearly the political persuasion of Cassirer, his publishing company and of members of his circle during the first approximate year and a half of the war.

Kriegszeit was initially a weekly (August 31, 1914, to August 5, 1915; first series, nos. 1-50), later a semimonthly (August 17, 1915, to January, 1916; new series, nos. 51-60), edited by Cassirer ("Herausgeber") and the poet-journalist-art historian Alfred Gold ("Verantwortlicher Redakteur").[163] The format of the series is large: each issue consists of two, unnumbered folio sheets, with, in two instances, supplemental sheets (first series, nos. 13 and 18/19). The vast majority of the space of each issue is, as just mentioned, devoted to the graphic arts, all of which take the form of original black-and-white (in one instance, color: May 5, 1915; first series, no. 38) lithographs ("Original-Steindrucke"). Most of the literary text is in the form of captions to, or commentary on, the lithographs, with, in addition, an occasional prose piece or poem. Graphically, *Kriegszeit* is, with few exceptions, an Impressionist publication; and, as expected, most of the regular contributors to this department of each issue come from Cassirer's prewar circle of Impressionist painters, some of whom are now contributing from the field of battle: Otto Hettner, Liebermann (first series, no. 6 [for September 30, 1914] is a "Sonderausgabe" for Max Liebermann), Gaul, Ulrich Hübner, Erich Büttner, Wilhelm Trübner, Willy Jaeckel, Barlach, Hedwig Weiss, Oskar Nerlinger; and, only occasionally or with one appearance alone, Fritz Rhein, Karl Walser, Max Unold, Ottomar Starke, Grossmann, Beckmann, and others.

Most of the graphic arts expresses, either by means of its narrative factor or the literalness of its connotations, aided often by the captions, obvious patriotism and strong support of the German cause in the war; there is, in addition, a not infrequent anti-British, anti-Russian, or anti-French lithograph. The sentiments of most of the lithographers is perhaps best illustrated by the many flattering portraits of the heroes of the moment which decorate the covers of several numbers: of the Kaiser (January 27, 1915; first series, no. 24: by Büttner), of the Bavarian crown prince (February 3, 1915; first series, no. 25: by Trübner), of Generalleutnant von Ludendorff (March 3, 1915; first series, no. 29: by Büttner), of General von Scheffer-Boyadel (November 1, 1915; new series, no. 56), etc. The literary texts in *Kriegszeit* express, either directly or indirectly, the same political sentiments; these contributions are also, again with few exceptions, by representatives of pre-Expressionist styles: Alfred Gold, Hans Meid, Christian Morgenstern, Camill Hoffmann, Gabriele Reuter, Gerhart Hauptmann, Wilhelm von Scholz, Richard Dehmel, et al. One poet closely associated with the Expressionist camp throughout the decade, Paul Zech, has his work included in three issues in the series (April 28, June 2, August 31, 1915; first series, nos. 37, 42, 52). Zech was later to compose antiwar poetry and to be, in both word and deed, a supporter of the left-wing revolutionary movement of 1918, as demonstrated by the poetry he contributed to Rubiner's anthology *Kameraden der Menschheit* (1919).[164] In *Kriegszeit,* however, he is represented in the August 31 issue of 1915 by a poem, entitled "Aufbruch der Flotte," which glorifies the German naval fleet leaving its North Sea harbor.

For Cassirer, the war ended in the spring of 1916, when, because of poor health, he was declared "unfit for military service" and released from the army.[165] He did not leave the military with regrets, for, as Durieux reports, his original enthusiasm for the war had been converted by this time to pacifism.[166] After spending the summer in Bavaria with his wife, recuperating from the effects of military duty, Cassirer returned to Berlin with Durieux and began expressing his new political philosophy openly. In the fall of 1916, Cassirer reinstated the practice he had sponsored before the war of giving literary evenings in his salon. Durieux again recites from the works of poets associated with the reactivated Verlag Paul Cassirer, including now some new poets, such as Bruno Schönlank and Adolf von Hatzfeld.[167] At one of these evenings, Durieux read a pacifist *novelle* by Leonhard Frank which had been offered the Cassirer company for publication. The recital was given, as usual, before invited guests, numbering in this instance about three hundred, in a hall in the "Salon Cassirer."[168] The evening was opened by the actress Gertrud Eysoldt, reading selected poetry, and concluded by Durieux's performance. The reaction of the audience to Frank's short story illustrates the extent to which disenchantment with, or simply weariness of, the war had already begun to spread abroad by the first half of the second year of the conflict. The spectators were moved to a passionate demonstration for peace, which some of the more sober-minded members of the audience only just managed to keep from taking to the streets of Berlin:

> First, Gertrud Eysoldt recited some poems and then I read a short story. The spectators, who were tired of war, were carried away by the story. I read with great emotion. Thus, when the readings had ended, the entire audience stood up in the same moment and shouted "Peace! Peace!" A few hotheads wanted to rush into the street and organize a demonstration, but, fortunately, they were prevented from doing so by the more sober-minded members of the audience.[169]

Cassirer's political philosophy on the war is again clearly reflected and illustrated in this period, as it was at the outbreak of the war, by the major activity sponsored now by his publishing firm. Again, it involves the publication of a periodical, *Der Bildermann: Steinzeichnungen fürs deutsche Volk,* which was begun in April, 1916—therefore, about the time Cassirer was released from active military duty—and represents in format, but definitely not in spirit, a continuation of *Kriegszeit.*[170] We note in *Der Bildermann* that not only Cassirer, but also some of the contributors to *Kriegszeit* who continue in the new periodical, have changed political horses.

Der Bildermann was a semimonthly publication edited by Cassirer ("Herausgeber") and Leo Kestenberg ("Leitung") in Berlin, with Hugo Heller acting as editor for Austria ("Verantwortlicher Leiter für Österreich") beginning with the fourth number (May 20, 1916; vol. 1, no. 4).[171] The journal put out a total of eighteen issues between April 1 and December 20 of 1916, each consisting of six unnumbered quarto pages and, occasionally, a supplement.[172] Like *Kriegszeit, Der Bildermann* is, as the subtitle suggests, devoted mainly to the graphic arts, and again in the form of lithographs; however, literature, prose and poetry, is in much stronger representation in the new periodical than it was in the old. A second, more significant change for the present study, is remarked in the list of contributors: while in *Kriegszeit* the work of artists or poets associated with Expressionism was seldom met with, in *Der Bildermann* representatives of this movement are given equal favor with other artists in the graphic arts and a predominant position over other poets in the literary sections of each issue. Thus, alongside the same kind of relatively subdued lithographs of Impressionists, such as Gaul, Jaeckel, Liebermann, and Slevogt, which the reader had already encountered in *Kriegszeit,* is now found the pictorially more startling work of Heckel, Kirchner, Kokoschka, and Mueller.[173] In the literature of *Der Bildermann,* the work of Brod, Hasenclever, Lasker-Schüler, Lotz, Mühsam, Klabund, and other Expressionists overshadows that of more conventional poets, such as Peter Altenberg, Christian Morgenstern, and Robert Walser.[174]

The most pronounced change in *Der Bildermann* as opposed to *Kriegszeit* occurs in the political sentiments which the new publication manifests. The portraits of military heroes, the drawings glorifying battle, the xenophobia—the general patriotic and bellicose fervor which had dominated both the pictorial and literary image of the earlier *Kriegszeit* are all totally missing from its successor; their place has been taken in *Der Bildermann* by lithographs and literary texts which emphasize the effects of war at home: the loss of loved ones, grief for the dead, hunger from the shortage of food, the greed of the war profiteers, the flowing of blood. The range of dominant sentiments in the graphic arts is exemplified on the one hand by Barlach's variation on the theme of the dance of death, brought to bear on the present by the suggestive title "Aus einem neuzeitlichen Totentanz" (September 5, 1916; vol. 1, no. 11); and on the other by Ottomar Starke's series of six lithographs, spread out through six different issues (August 5, August 20, September 5, September 20, October 20, December 5, 1916; vol. 1, nos. 9, 10, 11, 12, 14, 17) and given the main heading of "Die neue Gesellschaft," all of which caricature the nouveaux riches, i.e., the war profiteers. The similar sentiments, which dominate the literature in *Der Bildermann*, are given their strongest and most aggressive expression in two poems by Hasenclever in the October 20 issue (no. 14). The first, entitled "Jaurès' Tod," is a eulogy to the murdered French socialist-pacifist, Jean Jaurès, which concludes with a prophecy of his return, i.e., of the return of the spirit of peace he embodied: "Er ist uns nah. Er wird uns auferstehn." "He is at hand. He will be resurrected for us." The second poem, as its title suggests, "Jaurès' Auferstehung," carries further the theme of the first: it begins with both a call for, and a vision of, the return of the spirit of Jaurès, then exhorts the military to lay down its arms and the princes to come down from their thrones; it concludes with a call to the masses to rise up and take possession of the earth:

> Du aber, mächtiges Volk, geläuterte Menschheit:
> goldene Banken, Magnatengüter
> fallen Dir zu.
> Heraus aus Kasernen, Galeeren,
> Engbrüstige, Traumlose!
> Die Erde liegt vor Euch.
>
> Aufwärts, Freunde, Menschen!
>
> But you, mighty nation, ennobled race:
> banks of gold, the riches of tycoons
> are your lot.
> Leave your barracks and galleys,
> Frail and dreamless creatures!
> The earth is yours.
>
> Onward, friends, my people!

In summary: *Kriegszeit* had taught hatred for the enemy, the necessity of human sacrifice for the cause, a taste for victory; *Der Bildermann* teaches the brotherhood of all men, the preservation of life, a desire for peace.

The Cassirer recital at which Durieux read Frank's pacifist *novelle* in the fall of 1916 had some negative consequences for the Cassirers. The evening was attacked in the newspapers, which cast political suspicion on the sponsor, and the Cassirer house was searched by the authorities.[175] At that same recital Cassirer also made his own political position known openly and candidly; this fact, Durieux had reason to believe at the time—and we can assume in retrospect that his sponsorship of *Der Bildermann* in the same period was an additional cause—was responsible for Cassirer's being recalled to military service twice before the end of 1916, in spite of his recent release for poor health.[176] In both instances, however, Cassirer was able to secure a rerelease, the first time by going on a hunger strike and the second by being declared physically unfit again.[177] In the early part of 1917, he was saved for a time from another possible recall to duty by his friend Harry Graf Kessler, who took Cassirer with him to Switzerland to work in the German Foreign Office, which was in need of Cassirer's French connections in putting out unofficial peace feelers.[178] However, on Cassirer's return to Berlin three months later, he learned that his reinduction into the army was again imminent.[179] This time, he and his wife decided to move to Switzerland where Cassirer would be in a stronger position to avoid or stall off a fate which he could not meet either physically or emotionally.[180] They settle at first in Zürich, where Cassirer is again engaged by Kessler, who is now being aided by Schickele as well, to carry out unofficial political business on behalf of the German Foreign Office.[181] The Cassirers reside here in the "Hotel Schwert," where they are soon joined or visited by their many friends—painters, poets, critics—from Berlin and other parts of Germany, including Werfel, Lasker-Schüler, Meier-Graefe, Stefan Zweig, Karl Walser, Henri van de Velde, Annette Kolb, Gaul and others.[182] Besides the company of many of their old friends, the Cassirers were also able to enjoy literary evenings again, sponsored here in particular by the Zürich publisher Max Rascher.[183] The Cassirers moved in the spring of 1918 to Spiez on Lake Thun and resided in the "Hotel Spiezerhof."[184] Here, where they were again joined by many of the same friends they had seen in the "Hotel Schwert" in Zürich, their evenings "were filled with political and literary conversations."[185]

Before the end of the war, Cassirer was successful in warding off two more attempts to recall him to the military, the first time at the end of 1917 and the second at the beginning of the next year.[186] He was forced to go to Berlin about the middle of September, 1918, and report to the military authorities there in order to prevent legal action being taken against him and his property.[187] Finally, after one more brief visit to his former residence during the November Revolution at the end of the same year, he and his wife moved back there permanently in January, 1919, stopping off on the way in Munich where they were able to witness some of the conflicts already developing in the government of the new Bavarian Republic headed by their friend Kurt Eisner.[188]

Having once settled again in Berlin, Cassirer resumed personal direction of his art dealership and began rebuilding and expanding his publishing company beyond its prewar level of activity; and he began once again now to gather around himself in Berlin a circle of friends and associates. At the same time, as the streets of the city, like many others throughout Germany, continued to echo with revolutionary gunfire, Cassirer began to undertake an even more intense interest and involvement in politics than he had when last residing here in 1916, or than he had when working under Kessler in Switzerland for a French-German peace; politics, in fact, became, for the next approximate two years, the real axis of all his activities as an art dealer, as a publisher, and as a private citizen.

A look at Cassirer's circle of friends and associates in this period will illustrate the tight meshing of politics with his other interests and activities, for his circle represents now a fairly balanced mixture of professional politicians, political essayists, painters and (most of them politically committed) poets.

According to Durieux, the "Old Guard"—i.e., the group of painters, poets and critics, most of whom had identified with Impressionism, which had gathered around Cassirer before the war—now joined him again in Berlin.[189] However, all of the poets who are known to play a prominent role in his circle now have close ties with the younger movement of Expressionism: Däubler, Schönlank, Hasenclever, Hiller, Hatzfeld, Kokoschka, Schickele, and Edschmid.[190] Cassirer had also been in personal touch with Ernst Toller in Berlin near the end of the war; and Cassirer had perhaps been one of those "friends" of Toller whom the poet cites in *Eine Jugend in Deutschland* as responsible for introducing him to Kurt Eisner during a brief visit Eisner had paid to Berlin about that time.[191] Cassirer continued to maintain contact with Toller by mail after the poet had joined Eisner in Munich in order to participate in the revolutionary movement which was beginning to gain momentum there in the last months of the war; and just after the murder of Eisner on February 21, 1919, Cassirer arranged to have Toller "protect" his wife, who had gone to Munich the month before under contract to Albert Steinrück's "National-theater" there, during the political chaos that followed the assassination.[192] Cassirer was himself a member of the same party as that of Eisner and Toller, and, thus, as was to be expected, his artist-friends we have just mentioned and, most conspicuously, the many politicians and political writers with whom he was personally associated in the same period were all supporters of the socialist movement in Germany.[193] His political friends after the war included the socialist theorists Karl Kautsky and Eduard Bernstein; the Independent Social Democrats Hugo Haase and Hugo Simon; and the prosocialist diplomat Harry Graf Kessler and the pianist Leo Kestenberg, who was active in the Ministry of Culture in the Weimar Republic.[194] Cassirer's contacts with the latter figures, as well as with some of the poets listed earlier, were often occasioned by his participation in two quasi-political organizations which are known to have convened in his home or in the rooms of his art salon in this period: the pacifist group "Neues Vaterland," which had been founded during the war by, amongst others, Herzog, the Munich professor of pedagogy Friedrich Wilhelm Foerster, and the physicist Albert Einstein; and what Kessler describes in his journal as a "'revolutionary' club," an apparently informally constituted organization in which "open-minded individuals" could meet, outside of any sort of party affiliation, and converse and exchange ideas on, most especially, contemporary political questions.[195]

Cassirer's circle of friends represented the primary source after the war, as it had in the years before, of the publications sponsored by the Verlag Paul Cassirer. Two almanacs were put out by the company after the war to illustrate, as the title used for both was to suggest *(Unser Weg)*, the direction it was taking in this period; and the crucial factor in fixing that direction was a distinct political bias, which was enunciated unequivocally in a short editorial note in the second of the almanacs, *Unser Weg 1920*, published at the end of 1919:

Faithful to our tradition, we will serve the art of literature. We will attempt to support the ethical note, which for some time now has been struck with increasing stress in the work of our youth and which is intimately related to the socialist concept of regeneration, by publishing the literary works of leading socialists in fine editions.[196]

The socialist idea, which, that editorial note claims, informs the literature of the Verlag Paul Cassirer now, is espoused most directly in the political works which were published by the company. The authors of these works included some of the leading contemporary German socialist theorists, such as Bernstein (e.g., *Ferdinand Lassalle: Eine Würdigung des Lehrers und Kämpfers*, Berlin: Verlag Paul Cassirer, 1919), Gustav Landauer (*Aufruf zum Sozialismus, Revolutionsausgabe*, Berlin: Verlag Paul Cassirer, 1919), and Eisner (e.g., *Gesammelte Schriften*, 2 vols., Berlin: Verlag Paul Cassirer, 1919).[197] In addition, besides a twelve-volume edition (edited by Bernstein) of the collected writings and speeches of the nineteenth-century founder of the German Social Democratic movement, Ferdinand Lassalle, Cassirer also sponsored the publication of a series of reprints of selected writings of other early socialist thinkers under the heading *Wege zum Sozialismus*.[198]

Much of the imaginative prose and poetry which appeared after the war under the Cassirer imprint identifies as well, often very directly, with the same political direction. Moreover, this literature is now dominated by one literary direction, too. While the "Salon Cassirer" had continued to hold, since the close of the prewar era, exhibitions of the work of painters representing both Impressionism and Expressionism (e.g., Heckel, 1916; Meidner, 1918; Mueller, 1919; Kirchner, 1923), the Verlag Paul Cassirer was devoted in its literary department after the war almost exclusively to poets with close ties with the younger movement, including Edschmid, Hasenclever, Hatzfeld, Kokoschka, Lasker-Schüler, Toller, Meidner, Schickele, and Schönlank.[199] In especially the work of the last three poets named socialist thought is central: cf. e.g., Schickele's *Schreie auf dem Boulevard* (Berlin: Verlag Paul Cassirer, 1913, 1920), Schönlank's *Blutjunge Welt: Revolutionsgedichte* (Berlin: Verlag Paul Cassirer, 1919), and Meidner's *Septemberschrei* (Berlin: Verlag Paul Cassirer, 1920).

Beginning in January, 1919, Cassirer took over the publication of one of the three leading journals of Expressionism: *Die weissen Blätter*.[200] This monthly revue, which over the years had consistently lived up to its original promise of being "not only the artistic expression of the new generation, but also its ethical and political voice," continued to be edited, as it had since January, 1915 (vol. 2, no. 1), by Schickele on into its second year of appearance under the Cassirer imprint; then, during the first half of 1920, Cassirer himself replaces Schickele.[201] Shortly thereafter, at the beginning of 1921, the journal suspended publication altogether, following an abortive attempt to start a New Series, under the editorship of Emil Lederer, the first and only issue of which bore the special subtitle "Soziologische Probleme der Gegenwart."[202] With the exception of a possible change in contents in the direction of more practical concerns, as seemed to be projected by that last issue, neither Cassirer's publication, nor his later editing of *Die weissen Blätter,* brought about any significant changes in its editorial policy, in its general contents or in its list of contributors. The prominent role played by political issues, the clear pacifist image and the socialist tendencies of the bulk of the literature published in this journal were the features which made it an appropriate addition to the Cassirer publishing company after the war, but they were, none the less, features Schickele had begun introducing into the journal, in ever increasing degree, shortly after he had originally become its editor back in 1915.[203] A more detailed treatment of *Die weissen Blätter* properly belongs, therefore, in a study of the Leipzig circle of Expressionism, from which it originally emanated.[204]

The postwar inflation in Germany hit Cassirer's business ventures hard. The effects of the instability of the German mark on especially Cassirer's art dealership had become sufficiently serious by the beginning of the 1920s to induce Cassirer to seek to circumvent the crisis by establishing a branch firm, in partnership with a Munich art dealer, in New York.[205] This effort took Cassirer and his wife out of Europe for several months in 1921 and again in 1922.[206] Shortly after their return to Europe from the second trip to New York, some stability was restored to the financial structure of Germany by the establishment of the "Rentenbank" and the introduction in November, 1923, of the "Rentenmark." By this time, however, Cassirer was faced with a problem less easily solved, for his interest in his firm was now beginning to wane. He had begun to grow disenchanted with his profession for reasons which many of his colleagues could well appreciate who, like Cassirer, had allied themselves as sponsors with the Expressionist movement in literature and art before its great postwar success had come.

First of all, the function of the art dealer in the art market had greatly changed as a result of the postwar success of Expressionism and related tendencies. The success of the movement naturally removed the necessity for the struggle for recognition, in which the art dealer, as both patron and merchant, had participated with the artist. Modern art had now become a good financial investment, tantamount to stock in a market which virtually guaranteed an increase in value; the sale of modern art was, therefore, conducted effortlessly, while great expertise was now required to sell the work of the old masters.[207] Secondly, the buying public was now dominated by the nouveaux riches of postwar German society, i.e., the class which had attained affluence quickly and, in large part, by profiting off of the war and the economic chaos which followed it.[208] Few members of this new class, as Durieux claims, seemed to have the same genuine interest in the art they were buying that they had in the kind of financial investment it represented.[209] These changes brought financial success for the art dealer; at the same time, they meant that he was reduced to playing the role of mere merchant, and this was a role which, according to Durieux, Cassirer, who had always enjoyed the fight for recognition most and the earning of money the least, found difficult to accept.[210] Moreover, he was unable to establish a congenial rapport with the newest generation of artists, just beginning to appear on the scene in the 1920s, who might otherwise, in their efforts to be recognized, have had need of Cassirer.[211] Although Durieux only describes in her autobiography, *Eine Tür steht offen,* the change in Cassirer's attitude towards his art dealership in this period, we can assume, given the similar popularity of Expressionist literature after the war, that he could scarcely satisfy his appetite for opposition through his publishing or editorial activities either.

Finally, one last factor which Durieux cites as contributing to Cassirer's feeling of dissatisfaction in this period stemmed from his circle of friends. He continued to maintain some interest in, and contacts with, political issues and events after his return from the second trip abroad; and he was still seeing some of his political friends from the revolutionary period, such as Karl Kautsky and, less frequently, Rudolf Hilferding.[212] However, his circle of friends as a whole changed again in the course of the early 1920s, and he and his wife both no longer had any real close ties with the new friends who subsequently surrounded them in Berlin; this new circle seemed merely to be an amorphous "whirlpool of people."[213]

In Cassirer's case, the difficulties in adjusting to the many changes in German life after the war found a more tragic solution than in the case of most of his colleagues. At the beginning of 1926, in a state of increasing mental depression precipitated most directly by a crisis in his marriage with Durieux and greatly exacerbated by his disenchantment with his profession and his new circle of friends, Cassirer shot himself, dying several hours later, on January 7, in a Berlin hospital.[214] His funeral, which took place three days later, began with a tribute to Cassirer held in a hall in his art salon. Kessler, who gave the second commemorative speech after Liebermann's at the ceremonies, recorded in his journal in an entry for the same day that the "entire artistic community of Berlin" was in attendance.[215]

Following Cassirer's death, the activeness of both the "Salon Cassirer" and the Verlag Paul Cassirer quickly declined. The final, official liquidation of the holdings of both firms, which resulted in 1933 from Hitler's coming to power in Germany, was, for all practical purposes, no more than a belated post-mortem.[216]

9

Ludwig Meidner

In an autobiographical statement published in 1919, the painter and poet Ludwig Meidner briefly records the small, short-lived Expressionist phalanx which he founded with two other painters in Berlin in the summer of 1912 and then alludes to the overriding importance which that event had in his subsequent career: "I founded the club 'Die Pathetiker' with two comrades, and we held an exhibition under this banner in the fall of that same year in Berlin. The years that followed were full of unrest and insatiable work executed at a frantic pace."[1] The importance of the founding of "Die Pathetiker" for Meidner lay, therefore, in two major contributions it made to his career which are alluded to in that last sentence quoted: a great creative stimulus to his work and the impetus to the development of a large circle of friends around him, surrounding him with a constant source of excitement and inspiration in the following years.

Meidner, born in 1884 in Bernstadt (Silesia) and having spent two tortuous years (1903-4) at the Breslau Art Academy "drawing pots, skulls and stuffed birds," moved "almost penniless" to Berlin in 1905.[2] Here he remained, except for a few interruptions (in Paris, 1906 to the summer of 1907; in Dresden, from the spring of 1914 to January, 1915; in the army, 1916 to 1918), throughout the Expressionist decade.[3] Since 1909 he had been regularly spending long evenings in work and discussion in the Berlin Café des Westens, which, as Meidner confessed in conversations with his biographer decades later, had a decisive influence on his life.[4] During the Expressionist decade, Meidner was to make many friendships in this café with its regular guests, including Schickele, Flake, Ulrich Rauscher, Emil Faktor, Walden, Blümner, Scheerbart, Lasker-Schüler, Oppenheimer, Däubler, and George Grosz.[5] However, it was the founding of "Die Pathetiker" in 1912 which, as Meidner himself was later to admit, led to Meidner's close association with many painters and poets from Expressionist circles all over Europe.[6]

Meidner established "Die Pathetiker" with Richard Janthur, who was to become an occasional contributor to *Die Aktion* during the war, and with Jakob Steinhardt, a member of Lasker-Schüler's circle in the Café des Westens before the war whose work appeared from time to time in the same period in

Expressionist journals.[7] The name which these three young painters gave their phalanx was apparently chosen in order to suggest some ideological kinship with the circle of "Neopathetiker" around Hiller in "Der neue Club."[8]

"Die Pathetiker" had their first group showing in the eighth exhibition sponsored by *Der Sturm* in Berlin, which opened in the first half of November, 1912.[9] This remained the sole appearance of the group, for it promptly broke up shortly thereafter as a result of jealousy amongst its members.[10] The object of the jealousy was Meidner, who had stolen the show at that exhibition. The established press reacted as a whole to the show with the kind of denunciation it usually cast upon progressive art in the early phase of Expressionism; and the little praise that came from other quarters, as illustrated by Hiller's review of the exhibition in *Die Aktion,* was showered almost exclusively on Meidner's work.[11] Meidner benefited significantly from that exhibition in more than one way; it not only brought him considerable notoriety and, in the process, launched his career as a painter, but also put him into much closer contact with the Expressionists, thus bringing him many new friendships amongst them and many opportunities for collaborating with them.[12]

In the *Sturm* gallery where the exhibition was taking place, Meidner met three of the "Brücke" painters: Kirchner, Heckel, and Mueller, the latter of whom subsequently became a close friend.[13] Beckmann was prompted by what he saw in the *Sturm* gallery to visit Meidner's Berlin studio; Beckmann apparently benefited more from this visit than Meidner, for, as Beckmann himself admitted, it brought him new impulses for his work.[14] His reaction to the exhibition of Meidner's work was to be a typical one for the artist-spectator, for Meidner's studio was soon to develop into a favorite gathering place for painters and poets in Berlin, in particular those associated with *Der Sturm* and *Die Aktion;* and for some of the same artists this studio was to become a regular meeting place on Wednesday evenings in the following years.[15] Of the many artists who visited his studio or attended the Wednesday evening gatherings, Meidner later recalled especially Herrmann-Neisse, Grosz, Hasenclever, Hoddis, and Becher.[16] Hoddis was one of Meidner's most frequent visitors and closest friends in the prewar period, visiting Meidner's studio particularly in order to read to the painter his latest poetic efforts.[17] They also frequently went on long nocturnal hikes across Berlin, often continued through the dawn, during which the two shared what Meidner calls "the great experience" of that era for large numbers of their generation, namely the great awakening to the fascination and excitement possessed by the modern metropolis.[18] Meidner wrote in a memoir on Hoddis and their long hikes together across Berlin, which usually had their starting point at the Café des Westens:

> I have fond memories of the hours-long treks which we often took across Berlin at night. This great metropolis was the major experience of those days, and not only for me, born and raised in a small city, but also for Hoddis who was from Berlin. We left the Café des Westens

after midnight and marched right off, smartly and somewhat briskly, through the streets, always following our noses. While I, the painter, sniffed about and enjoyed the busy early morning of the city, Hoddis seemed not to take notice of his surroundings; yet, he did, indeed, take notice of them and saw things which a painter actually had to notice, for he did not see the world as a writer would. It was the same with his style of walking. Hoddis's stride was not that of the feminine aesthete; he jogged and stamped along the pavement—we avoided the sidewalk—like a musketeer. Now and then he would stop, remain silent for a moment, and then would laugh and say something witty or funny, but also clever things, for he was very intelligent. Then he continued on at a quick pace. We were 28 years old then and had a lot of endurance, which had not even run out by the time the sun came up....
   We were so much in love with this city.[19]

The date of the exhibition of "Die Pathetiker" also marks, as just mentioned, the beginning of Meidner's close collaboration with the Expressionists. In that month and year, Meidner launched a career, which was to last throughout the rest of the Expressionist era, as a contributor—at first only as a graphic artist, but eventually as a poet, too—to publications associated with the movement, including *Der Sturm* (November, 1912f.), *Die Aktion* (1913ff.), *Die Bücherei Maiandros* (1913), *Lyrische Flugblätter* (1913ff.), *Die weissen Blätter* (1915ff.), and many others.[20] In addition, the following year Meidner was briefly both coeditor of (May-June, 1913; vol. 1. nos 1-2: along with Zech, Ehrenbaum-Degele, and Robert R. Schmidt), and contributor to, *Das neue Pathos* (1913-14, 1920).[21] His most productive period as a poet also followed November, 1912, so that by the end of the Expressionist decade he was able to put together two collections of stylistically very unconventional "poems in prose" (his own term)[22], some of which had previously appeared in Expressionist publications: *Im Nacken das Sternemeer: Rufe eines Malers* (Leipzig: Kurt Wolff Verlag, 1918), *Septemberschrei: Hymnen, Gebete, Lästerungen* (Berlin: Verlag Paul Cassirer, 1920).
   In the spring of 1914, Meidner and his close friend, the poet Ernst Wilhelm Lotz, having grown tired for a time of the noise and confusion of Berlin, moved to the more quiet surroundings of Dresden with the intention of spending some time in "undisturbed" introspection and in working together, each at his own particular form of artistic expression.[23] The two artists had already successfully collaborated on an edition of Lotz's poetry with accompanying drawings by Meidner, inspiring each other's work at times in the process in the way they hoped to do again in Dresden.[24] In Dresden they shared three rooms, working in them a few feet from each other, took walks through the city together and frequented the favorite café amongst Dresden's intellectuals, the Café König.[25] As Meidner describes his time with Lotz in a memoir on the period published a few years later, the two artists were able to achieve for a short time the kind of congenial, communal, mutually inspiring atmosphere that they had come seeking here:

We were of the same mind in everything. We sparked each other's excitement constantly with our raptures—encouraged each other in all our daring exploits; and day after day we consented lightheartedly to each other's foolishness.—Poets and painters do not have to worry about working together. There is only luminous enrichment and life in spiritual profusion.[26]

Their communal life in Dresden very soon began to show promise of bearing tangible fruit, as they developed their plans for putting out a monthly journal together.[27] Lotz was in Berlin in April, from where he wrote to Meidner in Dresden of his intentions of visiting Hiller and the Café des Westens in order to recruit contributors for their journal; and, according to Meidner, Lotz also journeyed to Berlin in July for the same purpose.[28] However, these plans and their apparently ideal living and working arrangement in Dresden were both cut short by the outbreak of the war. Lotz was enthusiastic about the war and immediately volunteered (as a postcard addressed to Meidner documents, he is already in the field of military service by August 7, 1914![29]), leaving Meidner alone in Dresden.[30] He was killed the very next month, on September 26; and Meidner remained in Dresden only a few months longer, moving back to Berlin in January, 1915.[31]

Meidner returns again to his friends in the Café des Westens: and once the painter had set himself up again in new quarters in the city, his studio once more quickly became a gathering place for artists in Berlin, most regularly, as before, on Wednesday evenings.[32] As we learn primarily from Herzfelde, who began his very important friendship with Grosz in Meidner's studio in the summer of 1915, Meidner's visitors in this period included, besides the two artists just mentioned, Hasenclever and the painters Felixmüller and Heinrich Davringhausen.[33] The year 1915 was also the time of Meidner's intensive association, as a contributor, with *Die Aktion.*[34] This productive period was also cut short very soon, however, when his call to military duty finally came in 1916.[35]

He had to remain in uniform for the remainder of the war; yet, even prior to his return to Berlin in 1919—following a brief sojourn after the war in the city of his birth—Meidner's career, as both a painter and a poet, had kept pace with the flowering success of Expressionism in art and literature in that period. Thus, while still in uniform, he had signed a contract with Cassirer's art dealership and had been given a comprehensive exhibition of his work in the "Salon Cassirer" in January, 1918; and, indicative of the reversal of public opinion on modern art now, this showing, in contrast to that of "Die Pathetiker" in 1912, was received very enthusiastically by the majority of the press.[36] In 1918, as pointed out earlier, Meidner also began to establish himself with success as a poet.[37]

Like most of his fellow Expressionists, Meidner was driven to political commitment by the war and the events that immediately followed it. There are no records of this postwar period which indicate that his studio once again, as it had before and during the war, became a regular meeting place for artists in

Berlin; but this was only to be expected. His time, like that of his friends, was no doubt too much occupied, and his natural needs for social contacts were probably too often satisfied now, by politico-artistic activities to permit time for other interests or involvement as well. Thus, he became an active member of the "Novembergruppe" in Berlin on his return to the city, and was also associated with the revolutionary "Arbeitsrat für Kunst" there in this period.[38] He collaborated with other Expressionist painters and poets in espousing socialism and the socialization of art (primarily in the sense of making art accessible to, and allying the artist politically with, the masses) in politico-artistic statements, such as the pamphlet *An alle Künstler!* (Berlin, 1919). Meidner authored the pamphlet along with several other painters and poets, most of whom were associated with the "Novembergruppe" also (Pechstein, Klein, Richter-Berlin, Becher, Hasenclever, Zech, et al.).[39] As pointed out in the previous section on Cassirer, Meidner's own, independent literary efforts in this period also reflect a commitment to the socialist idea.[40] In a manifesto published in 1919 in *Das Kunstblatt,* for example, he exhorted "all artists, poets and composers" to actively support the socialist cause:

> If we do not want to be ashamed to face the firmament, we will have to begin helping the establishment of justice in government and society.
> We artists and poets must be in the forefront. There must not be any exploiters and exploited!
> ...Socialism shall be our new creed!
> ...Painters, poets, composers, be ashamed of your independence and cowardice and join forces with the outcast, disenfranchised, poorly paid slaves![41]

At the beginning of the 1920s, once the "failure" of the Revolution was sealed, he withdrew from political activism and turned his back in disillusionment on the socialist dream.[42] Ideologically, he now begins to look to established religion to fill the void left in his thinking by the loss of his recent "Glaubensbekenntnis," and, artistically, he begins to abandon Expressionism in favor of a more representational style, dealing often, as appropriate to his new faith, with Biblical subject matter.[43] He wrote in 1923: "I like doing nothing more than creating compositions on large sheets of paper of the figures and events of the Bible."[44] Many years later, he gave his biographer three reasons for these changes in his thinking and his art: a weakening of his health, the effects which the experiencing of the war had had on him and a simple tiring of Expressionism.[45]

By 1923, when Meidner writes the essay *Eine autobiographische Plauderei,* the changes mentioned in his thinking and his art have become firmly established; this short essay is at one and the same time a passionate testament to his new religious faith, with a pledge to strive to serve this new faith through his art, and a direct, sometimes polemical, recanting of his political past and the work of his Expressionist period.[46] Once, in 1914, when still a devout painter and fledgling poet of the cities, its streets, its houses and especially its cafés, looking as a model for his art to the cubist painting "La Tour Eiffel" (1910 version) by Robert Delaunay (whom he had met in the company of Apollinaire in the Café Josty in Berlin in 1913[47]), Meidner had exhorted his fellow painters to record on canvas the modern metropolis:

> We must finally begin to paint our native land, the metropolis, which we love immensely. On innumerable, fresco-sized canvases our feverish hands should sketch all the splendid and unusual, monstrous and dramatic things we see in the avenues, train stations, factories, and towering structures.[48]

Now, in 1923 in *Eine autobiographische Plauderei,* he scorns as "heathen" the painters of the "world of the senses" and the recent trends in art which glorify that world, and holds up as the new model painters of an older era, such as Peter von Cornelius and Philipp Otto Runge, for they "honor and serve God by praising his power and beauty on canvas":

> The artists, however, who are of the kingdom of God, have more quiet and less magnificent works to create. Their works radiate, instead, a great feeling of love which moves all of God's children in miraculous ways and strengthens them in their service and perseverance. The greater gain of their makers is that they honor thereby their merciful creator and serve him by praising the power of his name on their painted panels.
>   ... And the last centuries were in every respect a loud and clamoring age of heathenry. The rationalistic and completely irreligious world of Impressionism and everything that painting has achieved recently will, as I said, be found wanting on the Day of Judgment.[49]

Meidner's literary views reflect a similar change in this period. Thus, as recently as 1920 in *Im Nacken das Sternemeer,* he had written a prose panegyric to poets of all ages, but especially to his many fellow Expressionists, including Hardekopf, Werfel, Schickele, Becher, Benn, Boldt, Lichtenstein, Hasenclever, and many others.[50] However, again in 1923, he writes with regret and embarrassment of his literary work from the Expressionist period just ended, written in the style of many of the poets he had hailed just three years before, and finds his sole consolation now in two religious books he has recently completed:

> And he [the Holy Spirit] has blessed me in such generous and extravagant ways and I have gained so much thereby that I believe my small works have extinguished the meanness which I created with my earlier prose writings and with my ugly, demagogic pamphlets, which were published in the first few months of the Revolution. I have left far, far behind me the caprices, the madness, and the shamelessness which dominated my earlier prose; faith in God has so purified and sobered me that I can only read those youthful works now with a deep sense of shame.[51]

Neue Jugend (I)

In the last few months of Wilhelminian peace, a small group of freshman poets—most, if not almost all, of whom belonged to the youngest age group of the Expressionist generation (viz. to that born around the mid-1890s or later), put out together in Berlin a literary journal with a title typical of the Expressionist press in its double-pronged connotation of a break with the past: *Neue Jugend.*[1] The journal's progressive tendency connoted by its title was reinforced by its subtitle, "Zeitschrift für moderne Kunst und jungen Geist," and by its editorial policy. The initial editors, the Berlin *gymnasium* student Heinz Barger and the music student Friedrich Hollaender, pledged in the foreword to their first issue to address their journal to "young writers" and "to those interested in modern art and the spirit of youth, to those who are unburdened by Philistinism and prudery."[2] Still more typical of the Expressionist press, as of literary Expressionism in general, *Neue Jugend* was to assume as a whole an aggressive posture editorially, for its editors pledged in that same statement also to engage their journal in the "fight" against "oppressive 'tradition.'"[3]

The original founders of the journal, besides Barger and Hollaender, are also known to have included the student-poets Fritz Taendler and Martin Gumpert.[4] Their journal made a very modest and unprofessional beginning, for the first issue, which appeared in March, 1914, was printed hectographically and, by necessity, therefore, in a very limited edition (200 copies).[5] They managed, however, to consign the printing of the subsequent issues to a professional printer; these issues, running to a total of only five, were put out under the journal's own imprint between April and December of the same year.[6] During the latter months of publication, Barger and Hollaender were joined by two additional editors, the young students Rudolf Börsch (nos. 3-5) and Hans Jacob (signing under his pseudonym Jean Jacques for nos. 4-6).[7]

Very little more than the journal it produced is known about the circle around *Neue Jugend.* Two of the poets who worked on the journal, Jacob and Gumpert, report in their autobiographies that the group associated with the journal had social ties with one another as well; but neither Jacob's nor Gumpert's report on either activity is detailed.[8] Of the little over two dozen contributors to *Neue Jugend,* there is detailed biographical information available on only three: Gumpert, Oskar Maria Graf, and Jacob.[9] Furthermore, only eight of the contributors were to be met with again in Expressionist publications: Börsch, Taendler, Graf, Gumpert, Jacob, Hermann Plagge, Friedrich Wilhelm Wagner, and Otto Erich Schmidt; the others were to remain almost as obscure as poets as they had been when their work first appeared in the pages of *Neue Jugend.*[10]

Gumpert reports that he and Taendler spent the money they made on the sale of issues of *Neue Jugend* on visits to the Café des Westens; and these visits naturally brought them into some degree of contact with the Expressionist movement.[11] However, the circle around this journal appears to have been most closely tied biographically with the Expressionist camp before the war through Börsch, Graf, and Jacob. Thus, Herzfelde encountered Börsch on March 24, 1914, in Frankfurt am Main in the company of Lasker-Schüler, Werfel, and certain other poets, immediately following a reading by Lasker-Schüler and Werfel in the "Frankfurter Loge"; Börsch's presence at that gathering may very well point to more extensive contacts on his part with Expressionism.[12] Graf's personal ties with Expressionist circles in Munich and Berlin have been mentioned before in this study; they are described in detail in his autobiography *Wir sind Gefangene* (München, 1927).[13] Jacob had many friendships before the war in the circles that convened in the Café des Westens in Berlin.[14] He had originally been introduced to this side of Berlin literary life by his uncle, the lawyer Hugo Caro.[15] It was to this same uncle that Jacob also owed his first introductions to German literature of the sort produced by that same side of Berlin literary life; he had read the authors in his uncle's library and had also read with special interest there the issues of the journals which were soon to publish his own, first literary efforts, *Der Sturm* and *Die Aktion.*[16] Caro represented many of the progressive or avant-garde artists of Berlin in litigations, and, thus, not unexpectedly, his home in a suburb of the city became a gathering place before the war for some of them. As a result, Caro's nephew not only first heard the names and read the works here of such artists as Peter Hille, Victor Hadwiger, Walden, and Lasker-Schüler, but also first met them here in person.[17] Moroever, Caro himself presided over a regular table in the Café des Westens in the same period, at which Lasker-Schüler, Döblin, Victor and Else Hadwiger, Lena Amsel, and Hans Adalbert von Maltzahn sat.[18] Jacob's introduction to this milieu was, therefore, inevitable; he became a regular in the café in the last approximate two years before the war, which corresponded to his last years in the Königliches Französisches Gymnasium in Berlin and to the period of his most intensive association with publications of early Expressionism.[19]

If Jacob's report in his autobiography that he and his friends enlisted for military service at the outbreak of the war was meant to apply to his friends in the circle around *Neue Jugend*—we know that this was the fate of at least

Börsch, Graf, Wagner, and, evidently about the same time, of Plagge (Gumpert does not enter the service until the beginning of 1916[20]), then the abrupt end of the journal after the beginning of August, 1914, is not surprising.[21] The fifth issue of *Neue Jugend* came off the press on the very day of mobilization in Germany, i.e., August 1, 1914, and was, apparently according to an agreement reached in concert by the editors, to be the last issue.[22] However, in December of the same year one more issue was put out, billed as the sixth issue and as the first of a special war edition ("Kriegs-Sonderausgabe") of the journal.[23] The contributors to this final installment had, in most instances, been represented in previous issues of the journal as well; but one significant change had been made in the editorial staff—significant as one more illustration, in addition to the many others already encountered in this study, of the division of opinion on the question of the war from the outset amongst young intellectuals of that era. Number six of *Neue Jugend*, as an editorial note in it explained, was brought out "without" and "against the will" of one of the former editors—Börsch— who, himself already serving in the military by this time, had declared his opposition to the prowar sentiments dominating the text of the number.[24] An ironic footnote to the conflict in the staff of *Neue Jugend* is added a few months later by the report of Börsch's death in the field of battle at the end of June, 1915.[25]

Of the original members of the circle around *Neue Jugend*, only Graf, Gumpert, Jacob and Wagner are to maintain some noteworthy connections with Expressionism in later years. Graf spends approximately the first year and a half in the service and then, on psychological grounds, is released and allowed to return to Munich; here he spends most of the remainder of the war, at the end of which he becomes involved in the Revolution led by Eisner in the city.[26] After his term in the service (1914-18), Jacob also goes to Munich; he studies briefly here at the university, but soon returns to a career as a writer and translator and establishes some contacts with the Expressionists in the city (Kaiser, Wolfenstein, Ottomar Starke, Rudolf Levy, Heinrich Davringhausen, Georg Schrimpf, Graf, Heinrich Mann, Franz Blei, and Marietta).[27] Gumpert is in the military in the field from the beginning of 1916 to the early fall of 1918; around the end of the war he establishes personal contact with the circle around Wolf Przygode and *Die Dichtung* (1918-23), to which Gumpert had begun contributing in the previous winter (1917/18).[28] Finally, although Wagner is reported to have spent 1914-18 in uniform, Emil Szittya claims to have spotted Wagner in the Café Astoria in Zürich during the war.[29] Following a brief sojourn in Munich at the end of the fighting, Wagner moves on to Hannover in the summer of 1919 and coedits there, with Christof Spengemann, the monthly *Der Zweemann* (November 1919-August, 1920).[30]

11

"Die Feindlichen Brüder"

The March 21, 1914, issue of *Die Aktion* carried the following, largely cryptic announcement:

'DIE FEINDLICHEN BRÜDER'

Under this title a recital evening, organized by Paul Boldt, Gottfried Benn, Mathias [*sic:* for Leo Matthias], Egmont Seyerlen-Farussi, and Alfred Wolfenstein, will take place on March 24 in the Cassirer Galleries. Tickets at 3 marks each are available in the Café des Westens or at the box office on performance night.[1]

This appears to have been the sole public announcement put out by a group called "Die feindlichen Brüder"; and much of the mystery which surrounded the group in that announcement still remains. It is learned from an incidental reference to "Alfred Wolfensteins 'Feindliche Brüder'" by C.F.W. Behl in a recent memoir on Expressionism, and from a posthumous tribute to Benn by one of the participants scheduled for that March 24, 1914, recital, the poet Leo Matthias, that such a group did make at least one public appearance, presumably on the date just mentioned.[2] Matthias's tribute to Benn provides a few more details on the group and its activities.

Matthias claims that the name for the group originated with him and was a "nom de guerre," as much in the older, military sense (i.e., a name assumed by soldiers on entering the service) as in the contemporary meaning of "pseudonym" or "stage name," for it was a name denoting the dissimilarities of the group's members which were so great as to have made it impossible to bring them together under one flag:

The name "Die feindlichen Brüder' was my idea and was a *nom de guerre faute de mieux,* since it had been impossible to reconcile the participants, who included such diverse minds as Gottfried Benn, Paul Boldt who died young, the self-effacing novelist Egon [*sic*] Seyerlen, and Alfred Wolfenstein of whom Rilke thought so much.[3]

Thus, as Matthias continues, what united the members of this group, and what presumably was the precipitating factor to its founding, was their rejection of the programs of others: "What united all of these authors was less a program than the rejection of the programs of others; thus, our name covered very well what did not exist."[4] There was, however, one other factor, not cited by Matthias, which can be seen as providing a true common bond between all, especially four members of the group—Boldt, Benn, Wolfenstein, and Matthias: their mutual association with the literary life of Expressionism. The latter four poets were all represented in several publications of the movement during the decade, were habitués of the movement's converging center in Berlin, the Café des Westens, and, in the case of the first three mentioned, had close personal ties with one or more of the Expressionist circles that convened in that café.[5]

Behl's reference to this group to the contrary, it was not Wolfenstein, but Benn—at least by virtue of the wide reputation brought him by his recently published *Morgue und andere Gedichte* (March, 1912)—who was the leading member of "Die feindlichen Brüder," according to Matthias.[6] Matthias also reports that Benn was, at the same time, the most "restive" of these "hostile brothers," whose identification with a specific group here was scarcely more than an act of "courtesy" on his part.[7] The latter fact was demonstrated by Benn's behavior at the performance of the group reported on by Matthias, which was held in the Salon Cassirer in Berlin sometime before the war (Matthias gives no exact date).[8] Boldt, who was scheduled to read first on that evening, was late, and Benn, growing impatient, suggested Boldt either be scratched from, or moved to last place on, the program; when the others present dissented, Benn threatened to leave.[9] Seyerlen's attempt to appease Benn, by telling him that most of the audience had only come to hear the author of the *Morgue* poems, only succeeded in making Benn more angry. Boldt's arrival at the last minute saved the day.[10]

Benn's performance that evening, which involved a reading of selections from *Morgue* and of some unpublished poems, was a noteworthy success; and Matthias's description of Benn's style of recitation is interesting as an indication of the way in which the aggressive, provocative tone of Expressionist literature could be reinforced by the manner of its oral presentation:

> Benn had already found his recital style by then. He recited a few poems from *Morgue* and some unpublished poems in that sober, almost indifferent tone of voice which often gave one the impression that he was throwing his verses at the audience's feet. His tone of voice was not without a tinge of protest or polemics. But his success was lasting and genuine; Benn had quite obviously won the battle.[11]

Matthias reports on only one recital of "Die feindlichen Brüder," and it would appear to have been the only one given under that name.

12

Hugo Ball and Richard Huelsenbeck

As mentioned earlier in this study, the coming of the war had meant an abrupt end to, or at least a severe inhibiting of, the activities of most of the circles of Expressionists. The war had also strongly lessened, for the time being, the possibilities for the further expansion of the movement which had been promised by the last two years of the prewar period. Nonetheless, there were three important exceptions in Berlin to the general lag in the development of the movement during the four years that followed the summer of 1914: the activities organized by Hugo Ball and Richard Huelsenbeck in the first half of 1915; the circle which began developing around Wolf Przygode and Hermann Kasack in 1916; and the phalanx of Berlin Dadaists which was active from 1916 until the beginning of the 1920s.

The prewar Expressionist center of the Café Stephanie in Munich was the scene of Ball's and Huelsenbeck's first meeting in 1912.[1] Ball was at that time a "Dramaturg" in the "Münchener Kammerspiele," while Huelsenbeck had come to the city to study medicine.[2] Huelsenbeck, as he wrote several years later, was immediately impressed by the "far superior intelligence" and the "deeper knowledge of things" possessed by Ball, who was Huelsenbeck's senior by six years; and, thus, the younger poet "attached" himself to Ball.[3] The two soon became close friends, and also collaborated with their mutual friend Hans Leybold in the second half of 1913 on the Expressionist journal *Revolution* (1913).[4]

By the second half of 1914, Ball and Huelsenbeck are both discovered residing in Berlin.[5] Ball was working here as an assistant editor on *Zeit im Bild,* was privately studying politics and was in close contact with the circle around *Die Aktion;* Huelsenbeck had come here to continue his medical studies at Berlin University; but the two friends were also able to spend much time again in each other's company[6] (Ball in a letter to a friend of November 23, 1914: "...am often with Huelsenbeck.").[7] They shared especially at this time, as Helsenbeck reports, a mutual, intense opposition to the war and to the state that had helped to foster it.[8] Furthermore, as we learn from a letter written by Huelsenbeck in this period, he and Ball were also drawn together by their mutual, total commitment to Expressionism, which, according to

Huelsenbeck, stood in their minds for the "new life," for the "free style of life," both morally and politically, that they were seeking to achieve:

> Ball and I, and in particular Ball, were interested in nothing but Expressionism....
>
> We are whoring around the Tauentzienstrasse here; we drink and we often sit for two days at a time in the pubs and bars until the police throw us out. We consider everything Expressionism, since we pay less attention to the paintings than the life style. We want a new style of life; we want a new kind of activity; we want a new skin color, perhaps a new crease in our trousers, perhaps even a new tax law. We hate the government, the Kaiser, our decrepit minister—what's his name anyway?—the officers with high collars and high voices, the slaves who stand at attention, the firing canons (which we dream about), artificial honey, turnips, and everything else. Only the women stay the same. Thank God for the whores and their free life style; they are the real people.
>
> Sexuality, as we have found, is a playful form of life and very closely related to Expressionism.[9]

Ball stated his ideological and artistic position in this period in similar terms in his journal *Die Flucht aus der Zeit.*[10]

In the first half of 1915, shortly before Ball, and not long thereafter Huelsenbeck as well, were to move on to Zürich where they would both participate in the Swiss Dada movement, they sponsored two evenings of lectures and recitals. Judging from the very superficial information provided by Huelsenbeck and Ball on the content of these evenings, the second of them in particular, entitled "Expressionistenabend," was an expression of the thinking of their sponsors about this time as described above.[11] The first of the evenings was held on February 12, 1915, in the Berlin "Architektenhaus" and was designed as a memorial service for some of the poets recently killed in action: Walter Heymann, Leybold, Lotz, Charles Péguy and Stadler.[12] The evening was opened by Ball with a eulogy on his Munich friend Leybold (d. September 9, 1914) and a reading of selected poems by the poets being honored.[13] Huelsenbeck spoke at this evening on Péguy. The rest of the participants, although they are not mentioned by name by Ball in his report on the performance, included some others who also were reported to have been associated by reputation with Munich.[14] The evening was held, according to Ball, over a public protest against the inclusion of a Frenchman in the list of the dead being honored.[15]

The "Expressionistenabend" was given on May 12 of the same year in the "Harmoniumsaal" in Berlin, and was, according to separate reports by both Ball and Huelsenbeck, the "first" such evening (they probably mean the first under the name of "Expressionism") to be held in Berlin.[16] The content of the evening's program included poetry readings, and, it would appear from Ball's letters from this period, lectures of an at least partly political nature.[17] Besides Ball and Huelsenbeck, who read some of his "Negergedichte," the participants at this performance included the sponsors' mutual friend from this period in Berlin, the cabaret performer Resi Langer, also Wolfenstein and two others (the one identified by Huelsenbeck as an author of poetry "more Expressionist than Stramm" and the other as a Reinhardt actress) whose exact identities are not known.[18] There was also a hostile reaction from the public to this evening on similar grounds, for the allegedly strong presence of the Italian Futurism of Marinetti in the evening's activities was felt by some to be unpatriotic.[19]

Their "Expressionistenabend" was the last event which Ball and Huelsenbeck could have staged in Berlin together. As Ball's letters and the entries in his journal from this period show, his thoughts centered very much around politics at this time, around the desire to seek to achieve by political means some of the things which he had earlier only thought of striving for artistically. At the same time, and in letters from the very same months, he was also expressing the desire to be free of the gloom, the oppressive atmosphere created by the war, whose presence was so tangibly felt in Berlin.[20] Thus, in search of more peaceful surroundings unhaunted by the specter of the war, and also hoping to be able to avoid induction into the service, Ball left for Zürich shortly after that May 12, 1915, recital[21] (his first Zürich journal entry is dated May 29, 1915).[22] Huelsenbeck soon missed his friend's companionship in Berlin; attracted by the activities in Zürich which his friend began describing in letters written shortly after his arrival there, he followed Ball to Zürich on February 8 of the following year.[23]

13

Wolf Przygode and *Die Dichtung*

Present at the February 12, 1915, recital given by Ball and Huelsenbeck in Berlin was a young Berlin University student and aspiring poet by the name of Hermann Kasack.[1] Shortly after that date, Kasack was himself to begin identifying as a poet with the same literary movement represented that evening by Ball and Huelsenbeck, becoming in the course of the next few months a contributor to *Die Aktion* and then, over the next several years, to numerous other journals of related tendency.[2] Also in the winter of 1914/15, Kasack met a fellow student at the University in Berlin, Wolf Przygode, who was, as Kasack recalled, extraordinarily well read in modern literature and very much amenable to the new literary impulses, such as those originating most notably at that time in Expressionism.[3] Drawn together by their mutual interest in contemporary literature, the two students soon became close friends and, before much longer, literary associates as well.[4] In the course of the next few years, a small circle of friends developed around Przygode and Kasack, as they were joined, at first, by the writers Felix Emmel and Moritz Seeler and by the painter Walter Gramatté.[5] As their literary activities expanded at the end of the war and following, they were also to include in their circle of closer friends and associates principally the poets Paul Baudisch, Martin Gumpert, Simon Kronberg, Edlef Köppen, Georg Kulka, and Oskar Loerke, all of whom, with perhaps the sole exception of Kronberg, were closely associated with Expressionism.[6]

At the end of the spring of the year following their first meeting, and after thorough and careful planning, Przygode and Kasack initiated a series of literary recitals of their own in Berlin.[7] The general purpose of these evenings is explained by Kasack in a memoir on his friend Przygode as having been a means of spreading abroad their conception of poetry:

> Under his [Przygode's] initiative and after thorough preparations, we began to hold private recital evenings in May, 1916, in order to make clear to others, and to keep an account for ourselves of, our conception of the meaning of poetry.[8]

It was apparently not until the winter of 1916/17, in a statement of program delivered by Przygode at an evening opening a second series of recitals, that the group's particular conception of poetry was elucidated in detail.[9] Przygode declared in this statement that poetry represented for them man's means of giving expression to "the infinite," "the cosmic," "the divine":

> At these evenings we are interested in only one extremely important thing: to bring together people who, like ourselves, believe that art is not a medium of entertainment, not a means for relaxing one's nerves, but the ultimate human expression of something which you will not hesitate to acknowledge as the only important theme: "the eternal," "the cosmic," "the divine," if you want to give it a name.[10]

Such a conception of poetry was, of course, much too broad to be able to mark any alliance of the Przygode circle with a specific literary direction, aesthetically or ideologically—although Przygode's rejection here of poetry as "a means of entertainment" at least fulfilled a very general prerequisite for identification with a literature committed, either aesthetically, morally or politically, to some serious purpose, as Expressionism claimed to be.[11] However, in the next passage in Przygode's statement, it becomes clear that he and his followers were determined to throw the main thrust of their support behind the kind of literature represented, in most minds in that period, first and foremost by Expressionism. While Przygode here refuses to commit his group to a specific "direction," he does, none the less, pledge it to assisting the new or "emerging elements" in contemporary literature to recognition:

> We believe that the inexpressible flowering of Great Poetry can not emanate from infertile rock which chance has created. We want to do our part to help prepare the way for the poet of the future; we have accepted this as our duty and have no right to shirk it. You have understood that there cannot very well be any "modern art" or any "direction" for us. Our sole yardstick is the most intrinsic form of contemporaneity. . . . [12]

That the Przygode group did, in fact, identify most strongly, and from the outset, with Expressionism is indicated most unequivocally by the content of their recitals. The list of authors from whose work selections were read at these evenings, generally by Przygode and Kasack in alternation, was dominated far and away by poets prominently associated with the latter movement: Stadler, Heinrich Mann, Ehrenstein, Werfel, Edschmid, Frank, Blei, Lasker-Schüler, Heym, Schickele, Däubler, Trakl, Benn, Klabund, Herrmann-Neisse, Einstein, and others.[13]

Five recitals were given by the group in Berlin between May 29 and mid-July of 1916 in the first series, and presumably an approximately equal number in the second series in the following winter.[14] Kasack further reports, giving no details, however, on the dates or the programs, that the Berlin series were later continued in Munich, where Kasack was to continue to pursue his university studies at the end of the war and where, we can assume, Przygode was also residing at the time.[15] All of the Berlin recitals were held before an audience of invited guests, numbering around forty or fifty persons, who, according to Kasack, left each time following the readings without discussion.[16]

Kasack reports that the recitals in Berlin and Munich formed the preliminary or preparatory work to the journal which he began editing, singlehandedly, in the spring of 1918: *Die Dichtung.*[17] This journal, which, as the title was meant to indicate, was devoted exclusively to literature (rather than to certain ideas or causes which might happen to make use of literature as their means of expression), was issued in two series.[18] The First Series appeared in four "Books" ("Bücher") between the winter of 1917/18 and the fall of 1919 in the Roland-Verlag of Munich, and the second in two "Books" between 1920 and 1923 under the journal's own imprint, Verlag der Dichtung, which was a subsidiary of the Gustav Kiepenheuer Verlag (Potsdam) that had been established by Przygode with the financial help of a few friends.[19]

During the period of the appearance of the Second Series of *Die Dichtung,* i.e., in the first half of the 1920s, Kassack and Przygode were both also active in the general operations of the Gustav Kiepenheuer Verlag, which had recently become a major publisher of Expressionist literature. They were also at this time members of Kiepenheuer's circle of friends and associates who visited or gathered around him in Potsdam, including many of the poets that had been associated with the Expressionist camp in the decade past: Köppen, Kulka, Einstein, Goll (visiting from Paris), Sternheim, Starke, Urzidil, Blei, and others.[20] The work of several of the key contributors to *Die Dichtung* also appeared under the imprint of the Kiepenheuer company after the war: Kasack, Gumpert, Kulka, Baudisch, Kronberg, and Loerke.[21]

Przygode was to place great stress in his program for *Die Dichtung,* which will be discussed below, on selecting for publication only those works considered by the editor to be of lasting value.[22] This discriminating feature of the journal's editorial policy is already expressed typographically in the journal's bibliophilic format, a format which forces the reader to direct as much attention to the journal's physical appearance as he does to its contents. *Die Dichtung* was printed on large, quarto sheets, using a very large antique boldface type and very wide margins (in the sections devoted to the lyric, for example, there is usually only one short poem or a few stanzas of a longer work on a page). The cover, which simultaneously serves as the title page, creates, in design, the effect of a book rather than of a journal—as Kasack states, this fact accounts for the use of the term "Buch" instead of "Heft" for the issues—with all editorial information but the title and the series numbers removed to a succeeding page (the covers of the two "Books" of the Second Series have, in addition, a colophon, of extremely simple design, by Lyonel Feininger.)[23]

One of the ultimate aims of the recitals, as Przygode explained in the address given at the first evening of the second series, was to create "an intellectual community" through the communicating of the poetic work to an audience with common goals and perspectives:

In our work—which I must stress once more is only preparatory—we are counting as far as possible only on all of those who share our goal and approach. Let us help each other to leave unproductive isolation behind us and to form an intellectual community.[24]

This philosophy in particular also determined the character of *Die Dichtung*.[25] The effort to create such a "community" was also to be the "ultimate" purpose of the journal as well, as Przygode explained it in a programmatic statement opening the first issues.[26] Refusing to define poetry in a specific manner, he explains his conception of poetry in very broad terms here in much the same way he had in his earlier address. Poetry, more specifically (true) "contemporary poetry," has a serious moral commitment to seek to express in valid form the essence of the poetic object ("der gültig geformte Ausdruck des geschauten wesentlichen Gehalts"). This form of expression is achieved by the poet by seeking to speak, not through his arbitrary personal vision, but through a higher, more universal element, termed by Przygode "Geist":

It is time; let us consider this: the justification for creating and enjoying art without commitments gave way to a strong obligation to make choices and take a stand, once art had reassessed its role. In his own creative core the individual searches out the inviolable responsibilities of that Third Realm where things obey only their own laws; from a personal sense of concern he aims to bestow a sense of convincing universality on his observations through his structuring vision. Thus, he composes freely and, transcending his own limited experiences, he follows an innermost compulsion to create unfortuitious life. Freed of all of the limitations of subordinate factuality, the mind can create now less inhibited by the body than it otherwise would be.[27]

The "ultimate" function of *Die Dichtung* lies in communicating such poetry, which has a "universal validity," to the readership and therewith laying the ground for the kind of "intellectual community" of men that was sought through the group's literary recitals: "Because personal things of necessity lose their significance here, an objectively established relationship can be transformed into a very deep sense of community, pure in spirit: to lay the groundwork for this is the ultimate purpose of *Die Dichtung*.[28]

The themes of "Geist" and "Gemeinschaft" sounded above echo themes which run through much of Expressionist literature published during the decade—see especially the programs of *Der Sturm* and *Pan* discussed earlier, Hiller's essays "Philosophie des Ziels" (1915)[29] and *Geist werde Herr* (Berlin, 1920), Rubiner's *Der Mensch in der Mitte* (Berlin-Wilmersdorf, 1917), Edschmid's manifestoes in *Über den Expressionismus in der Literatur und die neue Dichtung* (Berlin, 1919), Wilhelm Michel's manifesto *Der Mensch versagt* (Berlin, 1920). However, Przygode's program for *Die Dichtung* taken as a whole—this applies only to a limited degree to the contents of the journal as well—reveals a problematical and sometimes equivocal relationship to Expressionism.

First of all, while Przygode pledges *Die Dichtung* to the publication of new literature, of contemporary literature, he rejects the polemical position often taken by Expressionist theorists in opposition to the literary movements of the recent past and defines the "new art" as the result of the "true synthesis" of the two "movements" of the last decade of the nineteenth century (he seems to be referring here especially to such post-Naturalist trends as Neo-Romanticism and Neo-Classicism[30]), which combined strains of idealism ("Sehnen nach traumhafter Unwirklichkeit") and realism ("Sucht nach handfester Wirklichkeit") with a "newly awakening sense of responsibility" ("mit wieder-erwachendem Verantwortungs-Bewusstsein"):

> No one can want us to explain what poetry is: terminology has become vague and there is seldom a desire now to understand. None the less, we will say the following in the hope of communicating with those of like mind: the truly viable elements, which those two movements (wrongly equated with each other) of the last, decisive decade of the past century have handed down to us, fused in a genuine synthesis to form a new form of art. A longing for visionary irreality—a form of flight from a shallow world—helped lend the rigor of significant objectivity to the law of formal beauty in a new, necessary relationship; a strong desire for concrete reality—counterbalanced by personal experiences—together with a reawakening sense of responsibility, placed a highly unstable artistic truth within the limits of valid structures.[31]

Die Dichtung will, therefore, attempt to illustrate the continuity in the literature which has appeared in the last approximate three decades, rather than the differences:

> The most essential task of *Die Dichtung,* particularly in the beginning, is ... to capture the typical cohesive elements of the periods—bases and developments—as they are felt directly to be contemporary, to combine established forms with those just created, to identify intrinsic relationships.[32]

Secondly, Przygode rejects extremes of literary style, on the one hand in the direction of hyperclassicism ("einwandfreie und gepflegte Syntax") and on the other in the direction of hyperunconventionality ("Perversion der kritisch-analytischen [Syntax]"), especially where such extremes of style are not justified by an acceptable content. Thus, he would apparently be inclined to reject the highly unconventional style of such poets as Stramm and other members of the *Sturm* circle (as he does, in fact, by name later in the afterword to an anthology of contemporary verse which he put together in 1919 under the title of *Buch der Toten*[33]). He states in the *Dichtung* program:

> ... we accept as contemporary poetic art the valid expression of observed, intrinsic matter. We dispense with questionable definitions, because we believe that we will therewith provide poetry with limits to protect it from spurious realms in which meager experience sagely (and in infinite exclusivity) leads a paltry existence with the help of a flawless and refined syntax

or, conversely, unabashedly covers up its deficiencies, for example, with poetic language in a perversion of critical-analytical syntax. In such spurious realms hypnosis and psychic suggestion are easily confused, and the proper discipline and will are lacking that are needed to make an all-encompassing form of beauty or the most cherished eruptions of ethic sentiments glow with the fervor of life.[34]

Finally, Przygode's position regarding Expressionism becomes particularly equivocal in his criticism of both mystical and political art. He rejects "mystical art," which attempt to replace religion with art; he may have in mind here the espousal of just such an approach to art, more specifically the lyric, in Zech's programmatic essay published in his journal *Das neue Pathos.*[35] He also rejects tendentious literature, in particular the political sort, which attempts to equate art, politics, and life; thus, it would seem, he does not accept a very large amount of post-1914 Expressionist literature which is dominated by sociopolitical concerns. In Przygode's view all art is mystical, in the sense that it is a "symbol of the infinite," and all art is political, in the sense that it seeks to influence the reader and arouses him to action:

Although art is without question for us the ultimate means of expressing creative spirituality, we none the less unequivocally reject the misuse of art as tendentious propaganda by means of references to a highly questionable form of reality. We especially consider the art which calls itself "political art," "poetry of the state," as apostasy; it is made possible by a dangerous form of confusion of concepts: art, politics . . . and above all life can not be equated with one another. Only brief mention need be made here of the related case of "mystical art" and its basis in the shift in the true relationship between art and religion. All art is implicitly a symbol of the eternal and final prophecy; the aim of all true art, of course, must be called political in a less tangible sense, as is suggested by the dual meaning of the concept of artistic "composition": art shows mankind its origins and aims, and calls mankind to action through the tension between real experience and observed truth.[36]

Przygode wrote an afterword to the First Series of *Die Dichtung,* which appeared at the end of the last volume of the series.[37] Here he once again summarizes the position of the journal editorially. This statement takes an even more implicitly hostile stand against Expressionist literature, for Przygode rejects vigorously now a contemporary form of literature which, like Expressionism at this time, espouses "Menschlichkeit" and which he identifies (as Expressionism consistently was throughout the decade) as "die 'jüngste deutsche Dichtung'": " . . . the 'youngest generation of German poets' therefore, who are in truth neither young, nor German, nor poets: they are our enemies."[38]

As suggested earlier, the problematical nature of the relationship of *Die Dichtung* to Expressionism was to be more a question of its program than of its contents. The journal was, as Przygode promised, to attempt to bridge the last thirty years literarily by illuminating the continuity of the present era with the recent past; but most of this task was to be confined to bibliographical appendixes, appearing under the headings "Das Werk" and "Das Buch" at the end of the issues of the two series in which the literature of the past thirty years, esteemed by the journal, is cited.[39] The basic literary contents of the journal, which consists, with few exceptions, of imaginative prose, poetry and drama, shows, on the other hand, an overwhelming preference for the new literature of Expressionism. The work of only three poets was published who were very clearly identified with a previous literary era: von Hofmannsthal, Rudolf Borchardt, and Rilke. The rest of the list of contributors was filled chiefly by poets who had maintained ties, in most cases very close ties, with the Expressionist camp: Paul Baudisch, Peter Baum, Benn, Blass, Paris Gütersloh, Gumpert, Hatzfeld, Herrmann-Neisse, Heynicke, Kaiser, Kasack, Köppen, Kornfeld, Kronberg, Kulka, Loerke, Lotz, Heinrich Mann, Przygode, Friedrich Schnack, Stadler, Trakl, Urzidil, et al.[40]

In addition, it can easily be argued that the contents of *Die Dichtung* did not faithfully reflect either Przygode's rejection of tendentious or political literature or his similar position on literature composed in a highly unconventional style. One of the most blatant examples of the former kind of literature in *Die Dichtung* is Kaiser's play *Hölle Weg Erde*, which appears here in the only form it feasibly could, in excerpt ("Erster Teil: Hölle/Zweites Bild"[41]); but the publication of that small excerpt nonetheless constituted, in effect, a commitment to the whole. Walter Sokel rightly calls this work an "activist drama," for the fact of its espousal of a radical transformation of society, economically and politically, cannot be denied, in spite of the play's failure to offer any concrete politico-economic solutions at its conclusion and in spite of its insinuation that the desired changes in society have their beginning in a change in the structure of man's ethics.[42] That same excerpt from *Hölle Weg Erde*, and, more prominently, much of the poetry of Kulka published in the journal (see, e.g., the poems "Charisma," "Die Städte," "De Profundis," "Für ein Pferd," "Budapest," "Die Station," "Allerheiligen"[43]), represent stylistically as radical literature as that written by Stramm. Przygode could, of course, have argued, within the flexibility allowed him by his statements on style cited earlier, that the content of the work of Kaiser and Kulka justified the extreme features of their style.[44]

The ancillary publications sponsored by *Die Dichtung* also were closely allied with Expressionism. The anthology *Buch der Toten*, mentioned above, opens with introductory poems by contributors to the journal (Kasack, Hatzfeld, Heynicke, and Herrmann-Neisse), which are dedicated to Expressionist poets lost to the war. The work of the latter then constitutes the main part of the text of the volume: Baum, Gustav Sack, Lichtenstein, Lotz, Stadler, and Trakl.[45] To demonstrate what Przygode considered the "unity" of all forms of contemporary art that represent the ideal, two volumes of graphic arts, both devoted to the work of Expressionist painters, were published under the imprint of the Verlag der Dichtung: *Die Erste Mappe* (Potsdam, 1921), with graphic arts by Feininger, Heckel, Wilhelm Lehmbruck, Marc, Meidner, Kirchner, Kokoschka, Macke, and Nolde; *Die Zweite Mappe* (Potsdam,

1923), with drawings by Marc.[46] The journal's imprint also appeared after the war on individual volumes of some of its contributors, including Baudisch, Gumpert, Kasack, Kronberg, Kulka, and Loerke.[47]

Kasack relates in a memoir on this group that he was himself either well or slightly acquainted on a personal basis with most of the contributors to *Die Dichtung;* and we know from other sources that this was true, to at least some degree, of Przygode as well.[48] However, Kasack emphasizes, recalling that Przygode also emphasized this same point "vigorously," that Przygode and the contributors to his journal did not form a tightly knit "literary circle" of which *Die Dichtung* was, in turn, the literary organ, in the way that, for example, *Der Sturm* and *Die Aktion* were the unofficial organs of a specific coterie of painters and poets.[49]

In 1923, with the appearance of the second volume of the Second Series of *Die Dichtung,* Przygode ended his editing and publishing career. This event, as Kasack explains, was the final outcome of Przygode's loss of faith in the effectiveness and significance of the poetic word.[50] He had not sought political change through the poetic word, as most Expressionists were doing by the end of the war (although, according to Kasack, Przygode had supported the November Revolution personally); but, nonetheless, like the Expressionists, he had sought to move his audiences at his recitals and to move the readers of his journal to action through the poetic word—the action, in this instance, being conceived of as taking place on an aesthetic-metaphysical level.[51] By about the beginning of the 1920s, however, as Kasack gathered from Przygode's statements to an increasing degree around this time, Przygode was experiencing a kind of literary disillusionment which the Expressionists as a whole were passing through on both a political as well as literary level.[52] Przygode, moreover, was induced to carry his loss of faith in the power of the poetic word much further than most of the Expressionists did, who merely altered the direction of their literary pursuits as they altered that of their political thinking; Przygode, in contrast, abandoned literature altogether, beginning, after the conclusion of *Die Dichtung,* to devote himself totally to an entirely new career in business and industry.[53] This new career was then abruptly cut short even sooner than the first had been, for Przygode died just three years later, on November 8, 1926.[54]

14

Neue Jugend (II) and the Berlin Dadaists

In April of 1914, a *gymnasium* student from Wiesbaden named Wieland Herzfelde, having, like most young, aspiring poets in that era of great artistic excitement, little else on his mind but literature, went for the first time to Berlin to visit the Café des Westens and look up there the poetess Lasker-Schüler.[1] The beginning of what was to be a long-standing and mutually profitable friendship between Herzfelde and Lasker-Schüler had already been made in the preceding months. Herzfelde had been corresponding with the poetess since a reading of her novel *Mein Herz* had first inspired him to write to her in November of the previous year; and just two months after she had provided him with a pen name in a reference to him in the January 24 issue of *Die Aktion* for 1914, Herzfelde had gone to Frankfurt am Main to hear her read from her work and to meet her for the first time.[2] Herzfelde already had one additional contact in Berlin. His brother, the painter Helmut Herzfeld (later to be known under the pseudonym of John Heartfield), had moved there at the end of 1913.[3] Thus, no doubt through both his brother and Lasker-Schüler, Herzfelde was able to establish some not insignificant contacts with the avant-garde artist life in Berlin on his first visit, in spite of its being a very short one.[4]

That visit had tentatively marked the real beginning of a literary career for Herzfelde. Nonetheless, just four short months after his return to Wiesbaden he had already put virtually all notions of such a career out of mind. An era of peace which had lasted over four decades had suddenly come to an end, and Herzfelde's thoughts were now joined with those of most other Europeans in concentrating on the earliest reports from the battlefields of World War One.[5] With some vague, but very strong visions of the glories of soldiery filling his head, and some equally vague, but much weaker misgivings about the righteousness of the cause troubling his conscience, he very soon enlisted in the medical corps, and was subsequently sent off to the Belgian front in October, 1914.[6]

In Belgium, while caring for the German wounded in an army hospital in Thourout, Herzfelde began to see most vividly the horrible face of modern war, its brutality and inhumanity. Within the space of a few months, he underwent a radical change of heart.[7] He even gave vent to this new attitude while still in uniform in Thourout through an act of insubordination on Christmas day, 1914, an act which led, in the end, to his discharge ("as unfit to wear the Kaiser's uniform") from the service on January 27 of the following year.[8] The day after his discharge, now a confirmed pacifist and committed within himself to active opposition to the war, he found himself sitting in a train that would take him to Berlin.[9] He later described the feelings he experienced while en route to Berlin that day from the front as "high-spirited" but nonetheless "more serious than during the trip to the front":

> The very next day I was sitting in the train which would take me back to Berlin. I was in high spirits, but more serious than on the way to the front. For I had been shown mercy: now I was headed for a real war, no longer as a first-aid corpsman but as a soldier. It was a good war which had begun for me on Christmas eve.[10]

On his arrival in Berlin, he immediately returned to the Café des Westens where he joined the many poets and painters who were able to continue gathering here in this period. Amongst the poets he saw now were some he had encountered here on his first visit: Lasker-Schüler, Däubler, Becher, Ball, Walter Benjamin, Ruest, Ehrenstein, Boldt, Jung, Curt Corrinth, Hardekopf, Huelsenbeck, Mynona (Salomo Friedlaender), Meidner, Davringhausen, Grosz, Oppenheimer, Martin Buber, Hedwig Lachmann, Carlo Mense, and Paul Gangolf.[11] As mentioned in the chapter on Meidner's circle of friends, Herzfelde also became a frequent visitor to Meidner's studio in this period.[12] His acquaintances and friends listed above were, like Herzfelde himself "all desirous of doing 'something' against the war."[13] However, in their work as artists they had continued to write, draw, and paint as in the preceding era of peace, ignoring political issues, ignoring the war, for art, as they had felt, could well enough express their opposition to the dominant society.[14] As Herzfelde and his friends surveyed the journals currently appearing in Germany, such as *Der Sturm* and *Die Aktion*, they perceived that they were being too closely watched by the censor to be able to serve effectively as voices of opposition to the European holocaust. They also remarked that the strongest such voice being heard in German at that time, the voice of *Die weissen Blätter*, was speaking from Switzerland, where Schickele had had to shift its seat of activity and publication in order to prevail.[15] As Herzfelde and his friends felt, however, for the voice of pacifism to be heard clearly, it had to speak from within the boundaries of Germany.[16] It was therefore decided that what was needed was a Berlin journal that could function as such a voice. "The decisive impetus" to the founding of one was not long in coming, as Herzfelde reports.[17]

In the summer of 1915, at one of the gatherings in Meidner's studio, Herzfelde first met the painter Grosz.[18] Not long thereafter, he saw Grosz again in the Café des Westens and was invited to his studio to see his work.[19] Both Grosz's work and his personality immediately made a strong impression on Herzfelde; soon a close friendship between them developed, a friendship which was also to include Herzfelde's brother, Helmut Herzfeld, who was still residing in Berlin.[20] On that first visit to Grosz's studio, Herzfelde won from the incredulous Grosz the promise to allow him, if he should be able to realize his desire of establishing a journal, to feature Grosz's work in it.[21]

One, almost insurmountable obstacle confronted Herzfelde's desire, however, for a new law stipulated that no new periodical publications could be established during the war without the license of the military authorities; clearly, as Herzfelde was well aware, no journal of pacifist tendency could hope to obtain such a license.[22] Then, about the beginning of 1916, Herzfelde and his brother learned of the existence of a journal which had appeared before the war under the name *Neue Jugend* and had been edited by a group of young poets who had voluntarily chosen to suspend publication after just six issues.[23] Herzfelde recalled at the time having met one of the editors of the journal, Rudolf Börsch, during a poetry reading given by Lasker-Schüler and Werfel in Frankfurt in March, 1914. He also recalled having encountered Börsch a few times shortly thereafter during his visit to Berlin that same spring. However, on inquiring after Börsch, it was learned that his name had already been added to the list of war dead.[24] Herzfelde succeeded, nevertheless, in tracking down one of the surviving editors, Heinz Barger, who was then still a *gymnasium* student in Berlin.[25] After several discussions with Herzfelde and his brother, Barger agreed to sell them the publishing rights to revive *Neue Jugend,* continuing it from where it had left off (issue six), and to sign as editor *pro forma* only, i.e., for the sake of the military authorities.[26]

Having by this maneuver circumvented the necessity of applying to the authorities for a publishing license, and having, in the meantime, collected money from friends to finance their project, the two brothers were ready to begin publishing their own journal.[27] Besides Grosz, who had committed his support to the journal well before its founding, their circle of friends and associates around the journal in Berlin was to include also Becher, Lasker-Schüler, Däubler, and Jung (who had recently returned to Berlin after his discharge from military service).[28] During the final stages of the journal's appearance, the group was further joined by Huelsenbeck, who moved back to Berlin in January, 1917, following the closing of the "Cabaret Voltaire" in Zürich.[29] All of the members of this circle were regular visitors to the Café des Westens in this period.[30]

Neue Jugend appeared in five monthly issues, printed in a very plain, modest octavo format and put out between July, 1916, and March, 1917, with Barger signing as head editor ("Herausgeber") for the first four issues (nos. 7-10), Herzfelde as associate editor ("Schriftleiter"; for no. 11/12: "Herausgeber") and, for all but the first issue, Helmut Herzfeld as assistant editor ("Verantwortlich für den gesamten Inhalt").[31] The first issue began on p. 123, so as to give the impression that it merely continued the older journal of the same name; but a poem by Becher opening the issue, and an editor's afterword closing it, both of which, according to Herzfelde, set forth the program of the new journal, clearly distinguished it in spirit from the older.[32]

The interests of the older version of *Neue Jugend* had been limited to literature, while this new one had political ambitions as well. Of course, since they were pacifist and ran counter to the thinking of the censor, they had to be, at most, implied, if the revival of *Neue Jugend* was to survive beyond a first installment. Thus, the afterword to the first issue, rather than boldly proclaiming, merely insinuates the journal's intentions. The first such insinuation is made at the opening of the statement, in which the editors declare the contents of the earlier issues of the journal as incongruent with their plans for the continuation:

> After an intermission of a year and a half, we are publishing the seventh issue of *Neue Jugend* with the declaration that the contents of the earlier issues are incongruent with our present plans. We are adopting only the title of *Neue Jugend* and one of its aims: to publish the work of young poets, intellectuals, artists, and composers. We intend to side with everyone who encounters public opposition and disapproval, especially with the youngest generation of artists who have not yet found their place in contemporary literature.[33]

The last sentence just quoted made it clear that the new journal, like the old, had the intention of supporting especially Expressionist literature. This intention is reinforced and stated more directly in the second half of the afterword: "All liberal-minded artists (Expressionists, the adherents of the Youth Movement...) shall be heard in *Neue Jugend*."[34] However, the editors place emphasis on their rejection of the older journal's "purely literary" interests and on their intention of setting as much store by cultural-historical, philosophical, and political contributions as by artistic ones, and in this sense to carry on—by association, the direction of the journal's politics is suggested most clearly now—the ideas on which were based the journals *Die neue Kunst, Revolution* (here very circumspectly alluded to as "the second journal of the former Verlag Bachmair"), *Das Forum, Der Aufbruch* and *Der Anfang:*

> Since we value cultural-historical, philosophical, and political contributions as much as artistic ones, *Neue Jugend* is a continuation of the ideas which underlay, on the one hand, *Neue Kunst* and the second journal published by the Bachmair Publishing Company, and, on the other, *Das Forum, Der Aufbruch,* and *Der Anfang.*"[35]

The editors become most aggressive when, as they underscore their rejection of "a purely literary sheet," they exhort (in phrasing which seems to echo intentionally the words of Heinrich Mann's manifesto "Geist und Tat") "all intellectuals" to unite in opposition to an "enemy" which, in the context of this statement, would be associated with those in power: "We cast aside our earlier plan to be a purely literary journal for the youngest generation: it is time for all intellectuals to oppose in concert our greatest enemy!"[36]

The title page poem by Becher, "An den Frieden," seems much more explicit politically—even in spite of its use of obscurely emotive language—when compared with that generally cryptic afterword. "An den Frieden" is, as the title indicates, a hymn to peace ("O süssester Traum der streicht wie Sommer lind!") ("Oh, most pleasant dreams, like a gentle summer breeze!"); but, more especially, it is a vision of the coming of peace ("Doch bald musst du wohl mehr sein als ein Ahnen/ Da blüht er auf wie kleinster Duft von Wind/ Ein Engel durch der Leichen Schlucht sich bahnend/ Dein Tag—: er wölbt! Die Stadt birst vor Geläut.") ("Yet, soon you must be more than just a presentiment / It bursts into bloom like the faintest fragrance of the wind / An angel forces its way through the trenches of the dead / Your day! It looms up! The city is shattered by the pealing of the bells."), and an activist exhortation to all to help prepare its way in word and deed:

> My fellow men: let us talk of eternal peace!
> Yes, knowing well that it is assuming form
> Still only the sweetest of dreams. Our hands uproot
> The weeds that cover our path.
> Let the words resound that drive us on to deeds!
> Our words must inspire! Therefore let us speak!![37]

The artistic contents of the five monthly issues of *Neue Jugend* never again reached the level of political boldness which informed Becher's "An den Frieden." There were to be frequent contributions which were morally provocative, for example, the often highly erotic verse by Edschmid ("Dem Gedächtnis der Tänzerin Angelique Holopainen"[38]), Herzfelde ("An Niobe," "Daisy," "Colombine"[39]) and Grosz ("Die Artisten"[40]). Poems with tangible political overtones, however, were to be rare exceptions and always far more tame than Becher's "An den Frieden." The first issue again contains the most explicit of these exceptions: Ehrenstein's "Frage," which asks when man, leaving the "clouds of blood" of the warring armies of lacerated men behind him, will finally attain to humanity ("When will the humanization of man / Blossom forth in the blue sky / Beyond the bloodred clouds?").[41] Later that year appears Becher's "Klänge aus Utopia," which envisions a land where all, even father and son ("No more sons who clash with their fathers."), live together in peace, harmony and freedom.[42] In a 1917 issue Grosz's exuberant paean to the new world of Australia, Africa and America, "Aus den Gesängen: Welten! Gluten...," concludes with a provocative equation of the trinity with a joint-stock company ("Gott, Vater, Sohn-Aktiengesellschaft.").[43]

Neue Jugend kept its promise of bringing cultural-historical and philosophical essays; and many of the contributions in these categories were implicitly antiestablishment. Thus, Hans Blüher contributed to the July issue of the journal a defense of the youth movement as led by Gustav Wyneken ("Die Jugendbewegung vor der geistigen Entscheidung"[44]); and Däubler began in the same issue, with a study of the painter Marc Chagall, a series of art critiques which was to be completed in the October issue ("Theodor Däubler-Sonderheft") by studies of van Gogh and Georges Seurat.[45] Gustav Landauer's article "Strindberg," which appeared in the July issue, is as much a defense of the Swedish poet as a study of him. Landauer interprets Strindberg here from a perspective peculiar to Expressionist program, for he sees Strindberg's life and work as centering around the struggle in life between passion and intellect ("Denken und Trieb, zwischen Geist und Natur"), a struggle which, as Landauer suggests, is resolved through insight into the basic complementary relationship of these two forces in human nature.[46] Finally, Friedlaender is represented in this department of *Neue Jugend* by two of his prose "Grotesken," which appeared under his pseudonym "Mynona" in the August and September issues, and by the philosophical essay "Eigne Göttlichkeit" in the journal's last monthly issue. In the latter essay Friedlaender sets forth in his theory of polar perspective a thesis closely paralleling the major theme in Landauer's study of Strindberg.[47]

An editorial note in the September issue explained the "almost exclusively artistic contents" of that particular issue as due to a "paucity of critical and philosophical contributions of the same quality"; and, as Herzfelde suggests in a later memoir, this explanation could have been applied to the overall absence of political contributions through all five monthly issues of *Neue Jugend*.[48] Herzfelde ascribes this absence to the persisting isolation of most German artists and writers at that time from the political world.[49] Whatever the reason, the very small amount of political commentary indulged in in the pages of *Neue Jugend* was published in the same form in which such commentary was appearing now in *Die Aktion*, namely in the form of marginal glosses ("Mitteilungen"). In these glosses the political position of the journal is at most insinuated by innuendo, the use of irony and by the context of statements relating to the war that are culled from the established press and republished here with a brief commentary by the editors.[50]

Neue Jugend did, on the other hand, as the editors had pledged to do, throw the bulk of its support behind the literature of "die Jüngsten," of Expressionism. As the list of contributors illustrates, it was devoted, with only a few exceptions, to the work of poets closely allied with the Expressionist camp: Becher, Däubler, Edschmid, Ehrenstein, Friedlaender, Grosz, Herzfelde, Huelsenbeck, Jung (under the pseudonym of Johannes Reinelt[51]), Landauer, Lasker-Schüler, Trakl, and others.[52] The graphic arts (drawings and reproductions from oil paintings) which are scattered throughout the five monthly issues are executed, with one exception, by painters with similar ties: Chagall, Davringhausen, James Ensor, Grosz, Lasker-Schüler, Carlo Mense, and the French Impressionist Georges Seurat.[53] One musical score is published by Werner Richard Heymann with text by Rainer Maria Rilke.[54]

In October, 1916, Herzfelde was suddenly recalled to military duty and subsequently returned to the western front; he was, therefore, not able to participate directly in the final stages of editing of the October and the February/March issues of the journal.[55] Barger, who all along had not been in accord with the basic political position of the Herzfelde circle, seized upon Herzfelde's absence as an opportunity to undermine it.[56] Barger first directed his attention at the October issue and attempted to counteract what he probably saw as its internationalist flavor (the issue is opened by Däubler's "Ode an Florenz," includes drawings by Marc Chagall and Georges Seurat and studies of Seurat and van Gogh by Däubler[57]) by appending to it a very nationalistic declaration by a recently formed German peace group called "Völkerrecht" ("Deutsche Zentrale für dauernden Frieden und Völkerverständigung"), which argues for a peace plan decidedly favorable to Germany.[58] He next became involved, apparently with similar aims in mind, in the final stages of the editing of *Der Almanach der Neuen Jugend auf das Jahr 1917*, which was to come off the press in November, 1916.[59] This volume had originally been put together by Herzfelde before his departure for the front, and was intended both to embody the basic spirit of *Neue Jugend* as well as to be a sampling of the work of its contributors.[60] However, Barger eventually signed himself as editor after making certain changes in the contents of the volume and adding some extraneous material to it in an attempt to mollify its originally very strong pacifist tone.[61] His tampering was not extensive enough to disguise fully the original political position of the contents: the volume was banned by the authorities even before it could reach the bookstores.[62] The other editors responded to Barger's moves by applying to the authorities for a license to establish their own publishing company, independent of Barger's Verlag Neue Jugend.[63] Helmut Herzfeld, who drafted the application on the advice of Jung, claimed that they wished to establish a new company solely for the purpose of bringing out, in complete book form, Lasker-Schüler's novel *Der Malik*, which had already begun to appear in serial form in issues of *Neue Jugend;* the new firm, as the applicants claimed, was, therefore, to be named Der Malik-Verlag.[64] This new maneuver was successful; and while the Lasker-Schüler novel was not finally to be published until after the war under a different imprint (Verlag Paul Cassirer), the new license allowed the Herzfelde circle to put out the next issue of *Neue Jugend,* a double number for February/March, 1917, under the imprint of Der Malik-Verlag and free of the interference of Barger.[65] This was to be the last monthly issue, however, for its appearance quickly brought the censor's ban, on unexplained grounds, over the entire journal.[66] This event might have spelled the end to the publishing activities of the Herzfelde circle if they had not once more, this time unwittingly, provided themselves with a means of outflanking the law.

The February/March number of *Neue Jugend* carried an announcement by the editors of their intention of initiating the following month a weekly edition which would publish work by the same circle of contributors and would supplement the monthly by fulfilling the need for the expression of a precise stand on more immediately current issues in literature, art, economics, and politics.[67] The weekly edition would reflect the policy and position of the monthly, but, the editors emphasized, it would be much more rigorous in its opposition to certain "established views and attitudes":

> As in the past, the monthly issues of *Neue Jugend* will continue to provide a medium of expression for the aims of its circle of artists. The second edition of the journal, however, will take a more rigorous stand on issues of the day, when that same circle needs to use its elbows in opposition to established views and attitudes, when it must defend itself and lay low the enemy, even if he should by chance be found in our own ranks.[68]

By taking advantage of the loophole in the law unexpectedly provided by that announcement when the ban was placed on the monthly edition of *Neue Jugend,* the Herzfelde circle was able to prolong the name of its journal through two more, weekly issues. Both of these came out under the imprint of Der Malik-Verlag and were printed in a large, multicolored, newspaper format. The first appeared on Wednesday, May 23, 1917, and bore the subtitle "Wochenausgabe: Nr. 1"; the second issue was dated "Im Juni 1917" and billed as a "Prospekt zur Kleinen Grosz Mappe."[69] Most of the contributions to these issues are unsigned. For the first issue, for which Helmut Herzfeld signs as editor ("Verantwortlich für den gesamten Inhalt") the contributors are listed collectively on the last page: Friedrich Markus Huebner, Johannes Reinelt [= Franz Jung], Herrmann-Neisse, and Helmut Herzfeld.[70] For the second issue, most of the articles of which are, again, unsigned, the contributors are no doubt those writers listed on the last page as "Mitarbeiter des Malik-Verlages": Herrmann-Neisse, Claire Öhring, Huelsenbeck, Grosz, Jung, and Helmut Herzfeld.[71]

The weekly issues are, as promised in the announcement for them, much more aggressively critical and much more politically oriented than the monthly issues were. However, the political commentary in these issues, although more prominent than such commentary was in the monthly edition, is still communicated more through insinuation than through direct statement; this fact is illustrated best by the column, appearing in both of the weekly issues, under the rubric "Chronik."[72] Although the column is unsigned, we learn from Wieland Herzfelde that it was penned by Jung; it is a critical record of current events, especially politico-economic events, whose antiestablishment and anti-war position is only partially disguised by the author's use of short, staccato sentences:

> It is not so much that the latest word on the war here at home is repeatedly (incessantly) "Don't give up." Because of this private matter? It is disguised as a horrible tragedy, a scourge, as an upheaval of the world, so that no one should pay it any attention! Not giving up is equated with living. Not yet hanging oneself is equated with war—and more war.... Defending oneself is growing in favor; acts of savagery, sentimentality are on the wane. They are exposed as fear, wanting to live, and—oh, what about the other people, etc. It is not, however, a question of wanting to live—here! But of living! Living!!"[73]

Besides political columns like those by Jung, these weekly issues also contain philosophical articles, quasi-literary contributions, critical and polemical commentary on literature, theater and other contemporary phenomena. The first issue is dominated by a long philosophical essay by Huelsenbeck entitled "Der neue Mensch."[74] This is Helsenbeck's contribution to the widely recurring theme in Expressionist literature of the New Man, whom Huelsenbeck defines in much the same way as in the other treatments of the subject in that period, namely as a man who synthesizes in ideal form within himself "all capabilities and qualities of man":

> We have to look deep down inside ourselves to understand what can be made of mankind and where the synthesis of all capabilities and qualities of man is to be found....
>
> The New Man must spread wide the wings of his soul; his inner ear must listen for the things to come; his knees must find their proper altar....
>
> His roots draw their strength from the Mycenaean age.... He lives one day like Lucian, one like Aretino, and one like Christ. He is everything and nothing, not today, not yesterday....
>
> The New Man believes there is only one battle, the battle against apathy, the fight against the obese.[75]

The second weekly issue was, according to Herzfelde, inspired by Grosz, Jung, and Zürich Dadaism.[76] The Dadaist tendency in literature towards hyperalogicality is, indeed, prominent throughout this issue, particularly in two articles written, as Herzfelde reports, by Grosz.[77] The first of these, entitled "Man muss Kautschukmann sein!" is the more conventionally lucid of the two; it exhorts the reader to assume, in the present state of affairs, a behavior like that of a "Kautschukmann," i.e., to be elastic and active, especially (as is insinuated most clearly in the seventh line quoted below) politically:

> As I've said, you have to be a rubberman
> all your bones elastic
> not merely dozing in your poet's chair
> or painting pretty little pictures at your easel.
> We have to disturb the after-dinner nap
> of the complacent
> to tickle his pacifistic rump,
> kick up a row! explode! blow up!—Or hang yourselves on the window frame...[78]

The typography of this issue, reportedly executed by Helmut Herzfeld, reflects Dadaist art clearly in the emphasis on disorder and accident in the arrangement of ingredients in the designs for the advertisements here for the volume of Grosz lithographs and poems, *Kleine Grosz-Mappe* (Berlin, 1917), forthcoming from Der Malik-Verlag.[79] The publication of a third weekly number was planned, but never materialized: it was to have been printed in white ink on black paper to remind the reader of the ubiquity of death in those times, but the printer, according to Herzfelde, refused to put the issue to press.[80]

Just prior to Herzfelde's recall to the military, the circle around *Neue Jugend* began sponsoring recital evenings. These evenings featured almost exclusively authors published in the journal, reading in most instances from their own works; but Herzfelde claims the recitals were intended to function "more as agitation against the war than as propaganda for the journal."[81] Seven recitals were held between the fall of 1916 and the spring of the following year: three in Berlin (September 13, September 22 and October 27, 1916, in the "Graphisches Kabinett I.B. Neumann"; and April 17, 1917), one in Dresden (November 7, 1916 in the Hotel Bristol), one in Munich (November 17, 1916, in the Café Luitpold under the direction of the "Kunstsalon Goltz") and one in Mannheim (December 7, 1916, in the Kunsthalle).[82] As Herzfelde reports, unlike the similarly antiwar recitals sponsored by Cassirer during the war for invited guests only, those given under the name of *Neue Jugend* were public.[83] Audience expression of sympathy with the content of the readings was no less passionate for their being public than at the Cassirer evenings: the wives and widows of soldiers are reported to have broken out into tears on occasion; cries of "Down with the war!" or "Down with the Kaiser!" were heard; and a few times the police intervened in order to put down tumults in the audience.[84] The most regular performers at the recitals included Däubler, Lasker-Schüler, Becher, Grosz, Herzfelde, and Ehrenstein.[85] Additional evenings were scheduled for Leipzig, Dresden, Berlin, Munich, Hamburg, Mannheim; but Herzfelde was at the front at the time they would have been held and is not able to provide any details on them.[86]

The publication of the weekly issues of *Neue Jugend* in the summer of 1917 and the *Kleine Grosz-Mappe* a few months later were the last signs of any concerted literary efforts on the part of this circle. According to Herzfelde, the group no longer felt further publications were in order at this time.[87] As Herzfelde claims, the appearance of the circle of poets and painters around *Neue Jugend* and their development in most cases in the course of their collaboration into politically committed individuals was representative of a development being undergone in the same general period by a whole class of artists and writers. It was the development described before in the present study, a development from a position of opposition to the status quo based upon certain largely inner-directed aesthetic-metaphysical views in early Expressionism to a position of political-activist opposition based on largely outer-directed sociopolitical ideals in the late phase.[88] Thus, as Herzfelde states, as long as there was still a war going on, the *Neue Jugend* circle felt that what was needed was not more publications, but action.[89]

When members of the original circle will join forces again with some additions to the group just before the end of the war and during the Revolution, it will be with as radical political aims in mind now as artistic ones and it will be under the dual banner of two almost equally stigmatized movements in

Germany in that period: Communism and Dadaism. In light of the group's espousal of Dadaism in this second stage, I should explain here why the discussion of this group is being continued in the context of the present study.

Dadaism, most obviously Dadaism as espoused in Berlin, was an offshoot of Expressionism.[90] Thus, although the members of this newly constituted *Neue Jugend* circle were to call themselves Dadaists and to attack Expressionism in name in their programmatic statements, none the less, they were all from the Expressionist camp originally and were, in most cases, still closely tied to it during the heyday of German Dadaism (1918-20). Moreover, the manifestoes and similar statements of the German Dadaists, as will become evident when they are discussed below, were scarcely distinguishable in their essential features from such statements issued in the name of Expressionism. The one feature of Dadaism that sets it in somewhat sharper focus within Expressionism as a whole is its tendency to carry the Expressionist break (as exemplified best by practitioners of the "Wortkunst" of *Der Sturm*) with conventional logic in both content and form to the extreme, so as to achieve an effect verging on nonsense or the absurd. However, this one feature was already to be remarked in the last weekly issue of *Neue Jugend,* thus, at a time when there was not yet any polemical division between Dadaism and Expressionism. Finally, although Herzfelde is anxious to minimize the extent of Dadaism's influence on *Neue Jugend* and reports that none of the members of the circle around the journal were calling themselves Dadaists at the time of its appearance, Jung characterizes the journal—which, it will be recalled, supported the Expressionists as such in its program—as the center of the Dada movement in Berlin in his autobiography.[91]

The regrouping of members of the circle and the simultaneous addition to their ranks of some new supporters under the banner of Dadaism in Berlin was sparked by an event staged by Huelsenbeck in February of 1918. As mentioned earlier, he had returned to Berlin from Zürich in January, 1917.[92] Although he had played an active role in the Dadaist activities in Zürich, by the time of his return to Berlin he had, according to Herzfelde, left Dadaism behind him for the time being (Herzfelde seems to mean here its tendency towards hyperalogicality in content).[93] Herzfelde's claim is corroborated by Huelsenbeck's contributions to the weekly issues of *Neue Jugend,* "Der neue Mensch" and "Dinge und Menschen," which bear no relationship to Dadaism in the sense implied above.[94] However, Huelsenbeck's apparent dissociation of himself from Dadaism was not to last long.

As he had during his previous stay in Berlin, he once again began frequenting the Café des Westens on his return from Zürich and was able to renew many of his old acquaintances here.[95] He saw Grosz in the café again and now met here for the first time Herzfelde and his brother.[96] He now became a close friend of Grosz; and through Grosz he met Grosz's friends Däubler and Herrmann-Neisse, the latter of whom had moved to Berlin from his hometown of Neisse in March, 1917.[97] With Grosz, Däubler, Herrmann-Neisse and the actor and writer Hans Heinrich von Twardowski, Huelsenbeck participated in a literary recital in Berlin on February 18, 1918.[98] The recital was held in a hall in the art salon of I.B. Neumann and was apparently planned originally as an independent effort; but Huelsenbeck, who gave the introductory talk, turned the evening, at least in name, into a declaration of support for Dadaism, much to the surprise and chagrin of some of the other participants.[99]

Two Dada talks by Huelsenbeck, both designated as having been given in the art salon of I.B. Neumann in February, 1918, have been published: the first one, entitled "Erste Daderede in Deutschland" and dated February, 1918, appeared in the 1920 *Dada Almanach* edited by Huelsenbeck; the second, entitled simply "Dadarede" and dated February 18, 1918, was recently (1964) published in another anthology of Dada writings edited by Huelsenbeck.[100] The exact relationship of these two talks to that February 18, 1918, recital is now known; but both are similar in contents. Both, especially the second one cited above, are written in a provocative tone clearly calculated to ruffle the spirits of the audience. They both declare that the evening about to begin is dedicated to Dadaism, make a brief reference to the beginnings of Dadaism in Zürich and conclude with some general and largely ambiguous remarks on the thinking behind the movement. The first talk defines Dadaism as an opponent of all international directions in art, as the means to a "new joy" in reality and hints at its potential for political commitment:

> [Dadaism] is the bridge to a new pleasure in reality. There are fellows who have grappled with life; there are odd fellows, people with destinies and the capacity to experience life. People with sharpened intellects, who understand that they are facing a turning point in time. We are but one step away from politics.[101]

The second talk declares sardonically that Dada is "nothing" and desires "nothing":

> Dada wanted to be more than culture and to be less; it did not really know what it wanted to be. Thus, if you ask me what Dada is, I would say it was nothing and wanted nothing. I therefore dedicate this reading by respected poets to nothingness. Please remain calm. No one will cause you any physical pain. The only thing that might happen to you is this: that you will have spent your money for nothing. With this in mind, ladies and gentlemen: Long live the Dadaist Revolution.[102]

Dadaism was, as Huelsenbeck has stated, a virtually unknown phenomenon in Berlin at this time; and, as illustrated by the two Dada talks just described, Huelsenbeck was not at the moment interested in enlightening the audience on the nature of the movement. He seemed more interested at this stage in provoking a reaction from the audience. He hit his apparent mark well, for his opening remarks caused such a furor both in the audience and amongst some of the participants that the host of the evening, Neumann, threatened to call the police.[103] The audience, however, demanded to hear the rest of the performance; thus, Huelsenbeck was able to prevail successfully upon

Neumann to allow the evening to continue.[104] Huelsenbeck's opening remarks were then followed by readings by the other participants from their own poetry and by Huelsenbeck reading from his Dadaist poems in the volume *Phantastische Gebete* (Zürich, 1916).[105]

In reviews of the evening the following day, the press generally reacted with hostility; but the recital as a whole was given much broader and more serious press coverage than had usually been accorded such an event in that period.[106] In addition, Däubler and Herrmann-Neisse, who had objected most vigorously to Huelsenbeck's unscheduled dedication of the recital to Dadaism in his opening remarks, dissociated themselves from the phenomenon of Dadaism the next day by publishing a public repudiation of it.[107] All of this notoriety amounted, of course, to a victory for Dadaism; and several young poets in Berlin, most of them from the earlier *Neue Jugend* circle, were enthusiastic about the new phenomenon.[108] Although they could have learned little from Huelsenbeck's talk about Dadaism, it was, as Huelsenbeck and Raoul Hausmann (who was himself one of the young poets in question) both have stated in separate reports, as if they had only been waiting for the word "Dada" as a cue for the creation of a rallying point for them in Berlin.[109]

As a direct result of that February 18 recital, and after a series of meetings and discussions, Huelsenbeck, Jung, Helmut Herzfeld, Grosz, and the Viennese poet Hausmann established the "Club-Dada" at the beginning of April, 1918, and made plans for the first activities under its sponsorship.[110] In the course of the next several months, the original founders of the club were to be joined by several other supporters in their various activities. Herzfelde was able to return to Berlin and join the club when he was released from active military duty shortly before the end of the war.[111] The poet Johannes Baader was introduced to the group by his friend Hausmann; and Walter Mehring established his first contacts with Grosz and Huelsenbeck through Grosz's friend Däubler, whom Mehring met in the circle around *Der Sturm* around the beginning of 1917.[112] Also active in the "Club-Dada" at the end of the war were Carl Einstein and the painter Hannah Höch.[113] Finally, Erwin Piscator met Herzfelde in Belgium in the military early in 1917 and then saw Herzfelde again in Berlin after the war; Piscator was introduced to the "Club-Dada" by Herzfelde at the beginning of 1919.[114] Piscator had only a brief, peripheral association with the group at this time, contributing to one of its journals, *Der Gegner*, and participating in at least one of its performances.[115]

Huelsenbeck wrote in a memoir on Dadaism published in 1920:

> I arrived in Berlin in January, 1917, and was confronted here with the greatest contrast imaginable with the situation in Zürich. The shortages had reached an extreme level. The German empire was shaken to its foundations; and the most resounding reports of victory could not banish the expression of worry and secret fears from the people's faces.[116]

The economic and sociopolitical conditions in Berlin described by Huelsenbeck were to a large degree to determine the face of Dadaism in that city in contrast to the form it had assumed in Zürich. For the Zürich Dadaists in the "Cabaret Voltaire," isolated as they were from any tangible contact with the war, literature could easily afford to be "purely artistic" or no more than an "artistic game."[117] Dadaism in Zürich was the embodiment of the absurd; it was, as Ball described it, "ein Narrenspiel aus dem Nichts."[118] In Zürich, again as Ball wrote of it, it was a vehicle for the denial and defiance of the contemporary epoch and the traditional European intellectual mind which had demonstrated its failure in the creation of the slaughter currently being carried out on the battle fields of Europe:

> Our cabaret is a gesture. Every word that is spoken and sung here says at least this one thing: that this humiliating age has not succeeded in winning our respect. What could be respectable and impressive about it? Its cannons? Our big drum drowns them. Its idealism? That has long been a laughing-stock, in its popular and its academic edition. The grandiose slaughters and cannibalistic exploits? Our spontaneous foolishness and our enthusiasm for illusion will destroy them.
> (Entry in Ball's journal for April 14, 1916)[119]

Zürich Dadaism was, therefore, in one sense, a form of escape from a contemporary European world of horror and collapse into a world of nonsense; Huelsenbeck's definition of Dadaism as representing "nothing" and desiring "nothing" in his first Berlin Dada speech—a definition based upon the form the movement had taken in Zürich—was, therefore, not far from the truth after all. When the movement took roots in Berlin, however, in the city where a revolution was soon to turn the streets into a new battleground, Dadaism could scarcely avoid confrontation with the kind of economic and political upheaval described by Huelsenbeck in his 1920 memoir. The very first manifesto to be issued by the Berlin Dadaists, in April of 1918, was already to make clear that Dadaism as propagated by this group did not, indeed, intend to attempt to escape from the realities of the contemporary world; like "the highest form of art" it was going to seek to come to terms with these realities and reflect them in its art:

> In its execution and direction, art is dependent on the times in which it lives, and the artist is a child of his age. The highest art will be one which presents the thousandfold problems of the times in its objects, which makes clear that it was influenced by last week's explosions, which attempts repeatedly to bear up under the impact of daily events. The best and most unprecedented artists will be those who gather together their battered bodies each hour from the chaos of life's deluge, firmly committed to the intellect of the times, bleeding in hand and heart.[120]

The Berlin Dadaists claimed in their first official manifesto of the "Club-Dada" that they were offering in Dadaism a means of coming to terms with the "brutal reality" of contemporary life. More precisely, at this early stage in their movement just prior to the Revolution, they were essentially offering (much like their counterparts in Zürich had) no more than a different metaphysical and aesthetic approach to contemporary life and art than that allegedly assumed by the conventional European mind.[121] They were themselves very soon to identify with Communism and therewith to begin proposing some specific economic and sociopolitical reforms of contemporary society; but as late as April, 1918, they were still attacking such proposals. Thus, in that month they rejected a form of Expressionism (they no doubt had in mind here most notably the "Activism" represented by Hiller and other contributors to his *Ziel-Jahrbücher* which were appearing in this period) that espouses a "melioristic" approach to the solutions of the problems of contemporary life; the Dadaists labeled such an approach "armchair politics."[122] They also rejected in their April, 1918, manifesto a form of Expressionism which offers a turn inward, "Verinnerlichung," as a means of coping with life; for the Dadaists this approach amounted to a withdrawal from reality.[123] However, the alternative which the Dadaists are offering at this time to meliorism and "Verinner-lichung" is certainly in essence as inner-directed as the latter position of the Expressionists, and is, furthermore, easily identified with the synthesis of human character and human experience espoused programmatically by large numbers of Expressionists encountered in the course of this study. Thus, the April, 1918, manifesto argues for the establishment of a new relationship between man and the reality which surrounds him, a relationship on a highly "primitive" or instinctual level at which all sensations of life blend into a "simultaneous maze of noises, colors and spiritual rhythms":

> The word 'Dada' symbolizes the most primitive relationship with the reality that surrounds us. With Dadaism a new reality begins to exercise its rights. Life assumes the appearance of a simultaneous confusion of noises, colors, and spiritual rhythms, which is appropriated by the art of Dada unwaveringly with all the sensational screams and passions of its audacious quotidian psyche and in all its brutal reality.[124]

The means to achieving this new relationship to reality was to be the aesthetic experience provided by any of the modes of the Dadaists poem, with its various forms of abstraction of language: "das bruitistische Gedicht": the poem of pure sound which Ball termed the "Lautgedicht"; "das simultanistische Gedicht": the poem in which time is telescoped, the conventional logic of chronology is disrupted; or "das statische Gedicht": the poem which ignores conventional logic in content and form. Through the medium one could overcome the historical, intellectualist, and scientific view of reality as it is propagated by the Dadaist's archenemy, the bourgeois or Philistine.[125] Especially once the Revolution had brought the promise of a new society, the smug German bourgeois ("der Spiesser") became a symbolical figure who stood for the attempt to revive "die gute alte Zeit" and the moral absolutism, the intellectual one-sidedness, the various social and political injustices for which that era stood in the Dadaist mind.[126]

With the coming of the end of the war and the November Revolution, the metaphysical and aesthetic radicalism of Berlin Dadaism was very quickly merged with the radical politics of Communism. According to Herzfelde, all of the Berlin Dadaists immediately joined the German Communist Party after it was founded on December 31, 1918.[127] Thus, the Berlin Dadaists now became engaged in a political and economic struggle as well as an artistic one, a struggle in which they were seeking to change now both art and the world.[128] They were still artists at heart, as Huelsenbeck has written, but the political upheaval of those times gave politics the louder voice in their struggle:

> As grotesque as it may sound, in Berlin we projected our resentment into politics, but we were never real politicians. We continued to be the eternal revolutionaries. We also made our projections into art; but since there was more politics than art in Berlin in that period, art did not come off as well. It is a different matter whether you are sitting in the quiet of Switzerland or, as we were then in Berlin, on the top of a volcano.[129]

Characteristic for Berlin Dadaism in this period, as Herzfelde reports, were two slogans prominently displayed at the "Erste internationale Dada-Messe" held in Berlin in June, 1920: "Dadaist man is the radical opponent of exploitation"—"Dada is fighting on the side of the revolutionary proletariat."[130] An even more directly and precisely Communist stand than that implicit in those two slogans is taken in a manifesto which was published in the Berlin Dadaist journal *Der Dada* in 1919. It was signed by Hausmann, Huelsenbeck, and the painter Jehim Golyscheff in the name of "Der dadistische revolutionäre Zentralrat: Gruppe Deutschland" and entitled "Was ist der Dadaismus und was will er in Deutschland."[131] The first half makes a series of three, broad demands in the name of Dadaism as a whole: the unification of all creative and intellectual individuals of the world on the foundation of radical Communism, the introduction of progressive unemployment through the mechanization of all activity, the expropriation and socialization of all property and the providing of food for all people through Communism.[132] The second half of the statement advocates a series of more specific social and political changes in the name of the "Central Council" of Dadaism, including the daily, public feeding of all creative and intellectual individuals on the Potsdamer Platz in Berlin, the commitment of all intellectuals and teachers to the principles of Dadaism, the introduction of the "simultanistic poem" as the Communist state prayer, the requisitioning of the churches for the production of "bruitistic, simultanist and Dadaistic poems," etc.[133]

All during the developments described above, the "Club-Dada" was sponsoring recitals of Dadaist poetry and manifestoes in Berlin and other cities of Europe. The first, held on April 12, 1918, in the hall of the "Neue Sezession" in Berlin, marked the official, public launching of the Berlin Dadaist movement; included in the evening's events was a reading by Huelsenbeck of the first manifesto issued by the "Club-Dada" cited earlier, signed by, amongst others, Huelsenbeck, Jung, Grosz, Hausmann, and Mehring.[134] This was to be only the first of a series of twelve such evenings and matinées sponsored by the club between that date and March, 1920. Other performances took place in Berlin (June, 1918: Café Austria; April 30, 1919: "Graphisches Kabinett" of I.B. Neumann; May 24, 1919: Meister-Saal; December 7 and 13, 1919: Die Tribüne), Dresden (January, 1920), Leipzig (January, 1920), Teplitz-Schönau (March, 1920) and Prague (two evenings in March, 1920).[135] These performances were all held, according to separate reports by both Hausmann and Huelsenbeck, with specific aims in mind and making use of specific tactics.[136] By attacking the middle-class elements in their audiences energetically and directly in their manifestoes, i.e., by attacking these elements on the grounds outlined above in the discussion of the Dadaist manifestoes, the Berlin Dadaists sought to provoke the audience into abandoning its one-sided, intellectual approach to life in favor of the more primitive one manifested in the Dadaist poetry read at these recitals.[137] Huelsenbeck described the purpose of the Dada performances similarly in his 1920 memoir on the movement:

> We want to make them [the audience] aware of a new primitive form of life, in which the intellect has deteriorated and yielded ground to instinctive behavior, in which the complicated symbolism of melody is replaced by noises and life is a delightful, powerful confusion of numerous wills. To accomplish this aim, we used both the simultaneous poem and the bruitistic concert.[138]

The responses to the barrages of the vitriolic criticism of the manifestoes and the disquieting poetry read at these recitals was perhaps a little more intense than the Berlin Dadaists had bargained for; these performances became, in fact, according to Huelsenbeck, "dangerous events," in the manner of that evening staged by Huelsenbeck and his friends in Berlin on February 18, 1918.[139] At the recital given in Dresden, for example, the public stormed the stage and attempted to club the performers with chair legs; in Leipzig the performers had to be protected from the audience by soldiers; and in Prague the Dadaists were only able to prevent a riot breaking out in the audience by a stroke of good fortune.[140]

No doubt the most scandalous Dada event staged in this period was the one-man performance of Baader, the self-appointed "Oberdada" of the group, in February, 1919. Two months before this event, Baader had already proved his mettle well for creating scandal when, in the name of Dada, he shouted blasphemies from the choir of the Berlin Cathedral during a sermon given by the Court Preacher Dryander on November 16, 1918.[141] Then, shortly thereafter, at a gathering of the "Club-Dada" at its table in the Café des Westens, Baader promised his cohorts a stunt which was obviously intended to be as much for publicity as for political protest: "If you will pay for my meals and expenses I will do something so that the whole world and its presses will be talking about Dada."[142] On the historical evening of February 6, 1919, as the

National Assembly was meeting in Weimar for the first time to declare officially the establishment of the Weimar Republic, Baader barged into the National Theater where the meeting was taking place and distributed amongst the newly elected deputies Dada leaflets protesting the new Republic.[143] Baader lived up to the letter of the promise he had given his friends in the Café des Westens, for the following day the press reported the incident to the world.[144]

After the war, beginning in February, 1919, the "Club-Dada" members sponsored a total of five journals during the group's approximate two years of concerted activities; most of them were published under the imprint of the Der Malik-Verlag, which was reactivated by Herzfelde after the war and which brought out many of the books and other publications executed by members of the "Club-Dada" in this period.[145] Only two of these journals managed to last beyond the first few issues, and, therefore, they will only be discussed briefly here.

The first significant foothold gained by the "Club-Dada" in print in Berlin was in an independent literary-philosophical journal which appeared during the war under the title *Freie Strasse.*[146] This was a journal of fairly modest means that was put out by the Berlin circle around Jung and Gross, which also included the artists Oskar Maria Graf, Georg Schrimpf, Richard Oehring, and Claire Jung.[147] Six issues or "Series" of *Freie Strasse,* printed in broadsheet format, appeared at irregular intervals between 1915 and 1918, each of which was edited by a member of the group, with Claire Jung reportedly functioning as general edtior of the series with the assistance of Franz Pfemfert.[148] Berlin Dadaism entered the series with the sixth, and last, number, a slim volume edited by Jung's new friend Huelsenbeck and published sometime during 1918 (thus, after the founding of "Club-Dada" in April of that year) under the subtitle *Club Dada: Wunder der Wunder!*[149] The literary contents of the volume was by Huelsenbeck and Jung, while Hausmann contributed graphic arts.[150]

It is not until about the middle of the fourth month of the German Revolution that the "Club-Dada" is finally able to appear once again in a literary tribune of its own; and this time it is in a journal of its own creation, an "illustrated semimonthly" with the Dadaistically inscrutable title *"Jedermann sein eigner Fussball."*[151] The first installment of the new journal appeared on February 15, 1919, a date which simultaneously marked the official reactivation of Der Malik-Verlag, under whose imprint the journal was published.[152] The journal was edited by Herzfelde ("Herausgeber") and Helmut Herzfeld ("Verantwortlich für den gesamten Inhalt"), who is now consistently signing himself John Heartfield.[153] Contributors to the first issue included the club members Grosz, Heartfield, Herzfelde, Mehring, and a friend of the group, Salomo Friedlaender (Mynona).[154] An eccentric scheme for propagandizing the journal was conceived by Mehring; it involved a magazine-vending march across Berlin by the club's members behind a horse-drawn charabanc mounted by a small orchestra, both of which had been rented by the club.[155] They had already succeeded in selling all 7600 copies of the first edition of the first number on their march, and were returning home by way of the Wilhelmstrasse, when they were arrested and legal proceedings initiated against them for singing an "obscene" and antimilitaristic song outside the government offices in that street and for distributing allegedly immoral literature in the city.[156] Their escapade also resulted in the banning of their journal after only one issue.

However, the Berlin Dadaists could only be encouraged by such events and the obvious notoriety they brought them. Thus, the very next month they established a second "illustrated semimonthly" with the even more provocative title *Die Pleite*.[157] This publication had actually been planned a month prior to the appearance of *"Jedermann sein eigner Fussball"* in the course of a heated, night-long discussion in Grosz's studio, involving Grosz himself, Herzfelde, Heartfield, Mehring, Carl Einstein, and the humorist from *Simplicissimus* and *Jugend,* John Förste.[158] After a series of titles had been suggested for a journal of the group by others present, Einstein finally offered one which would take sardonic advantage—in light of what they considered the economic and political "bankruptcy" of those times—of the ban they expected the censor to place on the journal almost immediately: "'Die Pleite' [bankruptcy]. ... They will in any case forbid it. Then they will have to announce: Bankruptcy is forbidden!"[159] Einstein's suggestion was agreed upon. His prophecy on the fate of the journal was also to be right: issues of *Die Pleite,* which began appearing in March, 1919, were repeatedly banned throughout the first year of publication, until January, 1920, when the journal as a whole was forbidden further publication.[160] *Die Pleite* subsequently appeared as the satirical section of the Halle-based journal *Der Gegner* (see below), and then, for the period 1923/24, briefly resumed publication independently through four final issues.[161] *Die Pleite,* like its predecessor, appeared in Der Malik-Verlag, and included among its editors during its appearance Herzfelde, Grosz, and Heartfield; the contributors also came from the "Club-Dada": Einstein, Grosz, Heartfield, Herzfelde and Mehring.[162]

As *Die Pleite* continued publication in 1919, Hausmann added a second tribune to the movement in Berlin with the creation of the short-lived journal *Der Dada,* which he initially both edited and published by himself.[163] The first two issues appeared in June and the winter of 1919, under the journal's own imprint, with contributions by the editor and by Baader, Huelsenbeck, and the Zürich Dadaist Tristan Tzara.[164] With the third, and last, issue, *Der Dada* moved to Der Malik-Verlag, where the new editors are listed as "Groszfield, Hearthaus, Georgemann" (= Hausmann, Grosz, Heartfield).[165] This last issue gave broader representation to the "Club-Dada," consistent with its new editors and publisher: Grosz, Hausmann, Herzfelde, Huelsenbeck, Mehring, Heartfield, and the French poet-painter who was active in Dadaism in both Zürich and Paris, Francis Picabia.[166]

The last two journals to be used as organs of Berlin Dadaism were also taken over by members of the "Club-Dada" (in the case of the second also by the club's publisher) from other editors, who, in these instances, had little connection with the club. The first of these, *Der Blutige Ernst,* had begun appearing in September, 1919, in the Berlin Trianon-Verlag and was the creation of its first editor, John Höxter.[167] Höxter, a poet and painter who was a regular in the Café des Westens with close ties to Expressionist circles that convened there during the Expressionist period, has been described by Mehring as "ein auf eigene Faust dadaisierender Vagant."[168] Whether Höxter was, as Mehring would claim, actually allied in spirit with Dadaism, the two issues of *Der Blutige Ernst* edited by him did include contributions by three members and one friend of the "Club-Dada": Hausmann, Huelsenbeck, Mehring, and Friedlaender (Mynona).[169] Thus, it is not surprising that, with the third issue, the editorship of the journal passed to two other "Club-Dada" members, Einstein and Grosz, with the addition of a subtitle appropriate to the Dadaist bent for satire: "Satirische Wochenschrift."[170] It lasted through a total of six issues, all of which appeared in the second half of 1919 under the imprint of the Trianon-Verlag; but the list of contributors to the last four issues included only one poet who was not associated with the "Club-Dada": Einstein, Grosz, Hausmann, Herrmann-Neisse, Huelsenbeck, Mehring, and Heartfield.[171]

The second of these last two journals adopted by the "Club-Dada" was the journal begun in April, 1919, by the two Expressionists Karl Otten and Julian Gumperz: *Der Gegner: Blätter zur Kritik der Zeit.*[172] *Der Gegner* was already allied, indirectly, with postwar Berlin Dadaism by its outspoken support of Communism.[173] The journal first became associated directly with the "Club-Dada" in the spring of 1920 when Gumperz offered asylum in its pages to the club's just-banned *Die Pleite.*[174] The club's acceptance of Gumperz's offer resulted in Otten's withdrawal as editor; shortly thereafter the journal was transferred to Der Malik-Verlag.[175] At the beginning of the journal's second year of publication (June, 1920), Herzfelde joined Gumperz as coeditor for the remainder of the journal's publishing life (to September, 1922).[176] Besides functioning as an organ of Berlin Dadaism during its appearance (contributors from the "Club-Dada" included Grosz, Hausmann, Heartfield, Herzfelde, Jung), for a brief period during the coeditorship of Gumperz and Herzfelde, *Der Gegner* was also a tribune for the "Proletarisches Theater" in Berlin of the club's sometime associate Piscator.[177]

Mehring claims that the only "authoritative" and lasting work of the Berlin Dada movement was the *Dada Almanach* (1920) edited by Huelsenbeck ("Im Auftrag des Zentralamts der deutschen Dada-Bewegung") and (according to Mehring) designed by Baader.[178] However, two factors, in particular, speak against Mehring's claim. First of all, the volume was not published by Der Malik-Verlag as the other major organs of the "Club-Dada" usually were, but by the Erich Reiss Verlag of Berlin.[179] More significantly, while the volume does include statements put out in the name of the "Club-Dada," only four of the club's members are represented here: Baader, Hausmann, Huelsenbeck, and Mehring.[180] Again, if we consider the *Dada Almanach* in the context of Berlin Dadaism, then most conspicuously absent from the volume throughout, and especially from Huelsenbeck's introduction in which he interprets Dadaism for the reader, is the kind of whole-hearted identification with Communism that was characteristic of the Berlin movement.[181] Huelsenbeck explains quite clearly in his introduction that the *Dada Almanach* was, in fact, not intended to represent simply Berlin Dadaism, but to be a kind of literary retrospective of Dadaism as manifested all over Europe and throughout the last half decade.[182] While he does recognize here the different forms the movement took in its various European centers, he emphasizes that the almanac was intended to represent no specific theory, party or type of Dadaism:

> This book is a collection of documents of Dadaist experiences; it represents no theory. It speaks of the Dadaist man, but postulates no type; it describes, it does not investigate. The Dadaist conception of Dadaism is very diverse: that will be made clear in this book. In Switzerland, for example, abstract art was favored, in Berlin it is opposed. The editor, who hopes his endeavors were based on higher, nonpartisan principles, is not really afraid of being attacked, since resistance from all sides is a necessity and a joy in his Dadaist existence.[183]

The appearance of the *Dada Almanach* in 1920, representing as it did a retrospective and nonpartisan view of Dadaism, came at a significant time in the history of the Berlin movement, for the "Erste internationale Dada-Messe" held in June of the same year marked both its highpoint and climax.[184] The "Erste internationale Dada-Messe" was an exhibition of Dadaist art, staged by Grosz, Hausmann, and Heartfield in the art salon of Dr. Otto Burchard in Berlin, in which all of the Berlin Dadaists participated.[185] This event represented their last group effort, for shortly after this event, after only about two years of collaboration, the "Club-Dada" began breaking up.[186] The phenomenon of Dadaism was, of course, to remain very much alive in Europe for several years after 1920, and in Paris a Dadaist movement was to continue to show strong signs of life into the 1920s. In Berlin, however, the *movement* very quickly died after that 1920 exhibition.[187]

Two of the former literary organs of the "Club-Dada," *Die Pleite* and *Der Gegner,* and Der Malik-Verlag, which had also functioned primarily as a publishing arm of the club right after the war, were all to outlive the club itself.[188] They were also to continue to publish the work of former club members from time to time after 1920; but after that date, particularly in the case of Der Malik-Verlag, they can no longer be said to be literary organs of the "Club-Dada."[189] Der Malik-Verlag was to show the most vitality after 1920, and was to remain active for more than two more decades; but in the course of the 1920s it was to become primarily a home for the work of far left-wing writers from all over the world.[190]

Some Conclusions

Literary scholarship has succeeded so convincingly in establishing the thematic and stylistic disunity of Expressionist literature as to cast serious doubt on the justifiability of the continued use of the term "Expressionism" as a label for a specific phase in twentieth-century German literary history. Literary historians as a whole, however, seem little inclined to abandon the term; moreover, proposals to do so have failed to confront squarely the important fact that it was originally introduced, not by literary historians, but by the very authors who claimed to represent it.

While acknowledging the divergence in themes and style in Expressionist literature, the present study seeks primarily to help rescue the term from the climate of doubt that currently surrounds it by looking for a unity of the movement on an alternative level, namely on that of the literary life of its self-confessed representatives, especially as it was manifested in the artist circles they formed between about 1910 and 1920. Since the literary life of groups of authors, like that of a single author, can be expected to develop and change in time, this investigation of Expressionism has been conducted from a strictly historical standpoint regarding both the era of the movement and the movement's own life span.

The study began with a brief consideration of the ideological background of the Expressionist movement in its response to its own age. This response was seen to involve chiefly a revolt directed first and foremost against the Wilhelminian middle class on four fronts: the political, moral, social, and artistic. Next, Expressionist literary life, its nature and development during the central period 1910-20, was broadly surveyed. Constituting a secession from the dominant society of Wilhelminian Germany, it centered on certain circles of artists whose focal points were artist cafés in major cities of Germany, Austria-Hungary, and France; they were held together by personal and literary ties, and, in most instances, also by a collective support of a variety of literary forums devoted more or less exclusively to the work of the circles' members. The development of the movement falls into three, distinct phases conditioned most directly by contemporary political events: (1) a mostly inner-directed, apolitical, pre-World War One phase, (2) a transitional phase spanning the war years and leading into (3) a mostly outer-directed, postwar phase dominated by a political activism centering on the November Revolution. Following a closer survey of Expressionist literary life as manifested in Berlin and of the artist cafés of note for Berlin Expressionism, the study proceeded to a detailed analysis of the Berlin circles. The structure, membership, history, development, and the collective socioliterary and politico-literary activities of the circles were reconstructed on the basis of the large body of memoirs and other reports on the period published by the Expressionists and with the help of the periodical publications and other literature which emanated from the circles.

In the broadest sense, this study is a demonstration of the validity of Paul Raabe's thesis that the unity of the Expressionist movement lies above all else in the group activities of its representatives. Thus, in demonstrating that the representatives of the movement were allied, and as a rule very closely, through the individual circles to which they belonged and, by a complicated process of crossing over, interaction, and interchange, through the activities of the movement as a whole, this study justifies—admittedly on a somewhat superficial level—the use of the term "Expressionism" as a label for the writers involved in the Expressionist circles.

In demonstrating a unity on the level of the literary lives of the circle members, this study provides a preliminary basis on which to determine the appropriateness of applying the label "Expressionism" to any author of the period 1910-20.

The discovery of unity in the literary life of Expressionism helps to begin to account for the divergence established by scholarship in the style and themes of the literature. This divergence is thus traceable, in part, to the great differences or variations in the activities, the thrusts of interest, the extragroup contacts, the programmatic statements, the particular experience of the groups' members, and to the particular manner of involvement of the individual circles in the changing course of their contemporary history.

The group activities of the circles provide a frame or source for the mutual influence of the members. The medium of influence is multifarious: the individual work or ideas of a member shared with other members, the program sponsored by the group as a whole in its journal and other activities, etc. The documentary record of this influence is Expressionist literature. Some of the more obvious instances of such influence include these: (a) some involvement in political issues in the activities of the circles parallels a similar involvement in the literature which emanated from those same circles; (b) the emphasis on an aggressive or provocative posture in the literary lives of the groups is matched by the same kind of posture in the literature of their members; (c) a strongly anti-middle-class orientation in the literary lives of the groups coincides with the same kind of orientation in the literature of their members; (d) a desire to reconcile ideological and existential opposites and to expand the breadth and depth of the experience of the myriad modes of existence in their literary lives is echoed in a similar desire expressed in their literature; (e) a special preoccupation with urban life in their literary lives is reflected by a similar bias in their literature.

Since we know, especially through the programmatic statements of the Expressionists, that their revolution was as much existential as literary, an understanding of the manifestation of the revolution in their lives helps us to understand better the revolution in their literature.

A study of the whole spectrum of Expressionist literary life from a historical standpoint is also helpful in correcting and supplementing past scholarship. By avoiding the selective approach which characterizes so many of the studies of the movement (Walter Muschg advocates, for example, studying only the "major figures"), insight is gained into the conditioning background of the work of many of the leading figures of the movement in their cooperation with lesser known figures; the leading figures are thus discovered in the end to be products of the whole movement as well. The adherence to a historical perspective in this study helps, in addition, to appreciate especially shifts in dominant interests in the movement in the course of time, so that, for example, a better assessment is made of the significance of the role played by political thinking and commitment. Thus, Wolfgang Paulsen's temporally fractured perspective on the literature led him to conclude that the movement should be divided into two distinct groups, the Expressionists and the Activists. Such strict divisions, however, are not possible in light of the fact that, as demonstrated in this study, the vast majority of Expressionists became either politically aware or active, or both, during the course of the movement. An underestimation of the extent to which politics informed most of Expressionism has also resulted from an overemphasis in past research on lyricists of the early period, especially Trakl, Heym, and Stadler, and on the use of their work as a yardstick for all Expressionists (see above, the studies of Martini, F.J. Schneider, K.L. Schneider, Mautz, van Bruggen, et al.). Trakl, Heym, Stadler, above all, are seen to be typical of at most but one segment of the movement and of that in the early phase alone. Two major factors support the latter interpretation: (a) none of the poets just mentioned shared the strong political interests already present in the early phase of the movement in, for instance, the circle around *Die Aktion;* (b) none of them managed to outlive the year 1914 (Heym died in January, 1912; Stadler died in October, 1914; Trakl died in November, 1914) and, therefore, none of them was potentially able to undergo the conversion to political interest experienced by most Expressionists under the impact of the war and the events that attended its conclusion.

Thus, the Expressionists did, indeed, as several of them maintained themselves, constitute a "community" of artists. Like the circles in other centers of the movement, those in Berlin were united individually through bonds of friendship, uniformity of views on life and literature in their era, and through a significant degree of collectivity in their various activities. In addition, interchange and interaction between the circles in all centers of the movement in the context of such collective endeavors united all of Expressionism. As already suggested, what seem to be signs of disunity are seldom more than reflections of the ravages of time.

Figure 1.   Program for the April 3, 1912, performance of "Der
             Neue Club" in memory of Georg Heym (masthead:
             woodcut by Karl Schmidt-Rottluff, 1911)

9. Abend: Mittwoch den 3. April 1912.

Architektenhaus, Saal C, Wilhelm-Straße 92-93, pkt. 8 Uhr.

□

Hölderlin: Unveröffentlichte Gedichte und Briefe (R. J.)

Golo Gangi: Gedenkrede auf Georg Heym.

An Georg Heym (Gedichte von Robert Jentzsch, Fritz Koffka, W. S. Ghuttman.)

Martin Buber: Gleichnisse des Tschuang—Tse.

□

GEORG HEYM: Gedichte aus dem Nachlaß, ungedruckte (R. J.; Gh.)

□

Eduard Steuermann: Sechs Klavierstücke von Arnold Schönberg.

Ferdinand Hardekopf: Der Gedankenstrich.

Stanislaw Przybyszewski: Prosa (F. H.)

Robert Jentzsch: Hymnen.

Erich Unger: „Mit allen Wassern gewaschen" von Wedekind.

W. S. Ghuttman: Ein Herr.

Jakob van Hoddis: Gedichte (R. J.; Gh.)

Mynona. Novelle.

□ □ □

Billets à 2 Mk. (numeriert) und 1 Mk. (unnumeriert) im Café des Westens
und an der Abendkasse.

□ □ □

Geschäftsstelle des NEUEN CLUBS: Erich Unger, Sigmundshof 21.

□

Im Verlage Ernst Rowohlt erschien soeben: Georg Heym: Der ewige Tag. 2. Auflage.
Demnächst erscheint: Die nachgelassenen Gedichte, und im Herbst 1912: Der Dieb, (Novellen).

Wissenschaftliche Buchgesellschaft, Darmstadt, and C.H. Beck
Verlag, Munich

Figure 2.   Kurt Hiller (1930)

Rowohlt Verlag GmbH, Reinbek bei Hamburg

Figure 3.   Portrait in oil of Herwarth Walden by Oskar
             Kokoschka (1910)

Galerie Nelz, Salzburg

Figure 4.   Poster by Oskar Kokoschka for *Der Sturm*

Haus der Kunst, Munich

Figure 5.   Herwarth Walden and Oskar Kokoschka in the offices
             of *Der Sturm* (1916)

New York Graphic Society, New York

Figure 6.   Title page for an August, 1911, number of *Der Sturm*
with drawing by Ernst Ludwig Kirchner

Figure 7.   Title page for the October 4, 1913, number of *Die Aktion* with portrait of Alfred Lichtenstein by Max Oppenheimer

DieAktion

WOCHENSCHRIFT FÜR POLITIK, LITERATUR, KUNST

III. JAHR   HERAUSGEGEBEN VON FRANZ PFEMFERT   NR. 40

INHALT: Max Oppenheimer: Der Lyriker Alfred Lichtenstein (Titelbild) / Franz Blei: Blatt aus meinem Tagebuch / Franz Pfemfert: Massenstreik-Unsinn / Ludwig Rubiner: Manuskripte / Oskar Kanehl: Im Zeltgarten zu Breslau / D. Wensickendorf: Aus dem Leben Voltaires / Alfred Lichtenstein: Selbstkritik; 8 Gedichte / Henriette Hardenberg: Verse / Sylvester von Babenhausen: Ueber die Ehe / Glossen

VERLAG / DIE AKTION / BERLIN - WILMERSDORF

HEFT 30 PFG.

Wissenschaftliche Buchgesellschaft, Darmstadt

Figure 8.   Woodcut portrait of Franz Pfemfert by Georg Tappert (1920)

Figure 9.   Alfred Richard Meyer (1928)

Ullstein-Bilderdienst, Berlin

Figure 10.   Title page for Book 6 (Sept. 1, 1913) of *Die Bücherei
Maiandros* with drawing by Ludwig Meidner

DIE BUECHEREI MAIANDROS

eine Zeitschrift von 60 zu 60 Tagen

herausgegeben von

Heinrich Lautensack/Alfred Richard Meyer/Anselm Ruest

im Verlag von Paul Knorr / Berlin-Wilmersdorf

Das sechste Buch   1. September 1913

IN MEMORIAM LÉON DEUBEL

Figure 11.   Gottfried Benn (Brussels, 1916)

Schiller-Nationalmuseum, Deutsches Literaturarchiv, Marbach a.N.

Figure 12.   Title page for Gottfried Benn's *Söhne* (1913) with
drawing by Ludwig Meidner

S Ö H N E

Neue Gedichte von GOTTFRIED BENN, dem Verfasser der Morgue

A. R. MEYER VERLAG BERLIN - WILMERSDORF

Alfred Richard Meyer Verlag, Berlin

Figure 13.   Portrait in ink of Paul Cassirer by Rudolf Grossmann

Kurt Desch Verlag, Vienna

Figure 14.   Hugo Ball reciting "Karawane" (1916)

Figure 15.   Title page for Book One of *Die Dichtung*

DIE DICHTUNG

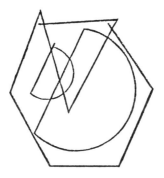

ZWEITE FOLGE / ERSTES BUCH

1920

Kraus Reprint, A Division of Kraus-Thomson Organization Limited

Notes

Introduction

1. Richard Brinkmann, *Expressionismus: Forschungs-Probleme 1952-1960,* Referate aus der *Deutschen Vierteljahrsschrift für Literaturwissenschaft und Geistesgeschichte,* ed. Richard Brinkmann, Hugo Kuhn, and Friedrich Sengle (Stuttgart, 1961). A substantially expanded and updated version of these reports was published after the completion of the present study. See Richard Brinkmann, *Expressionismus: Internationale Forschung zu einem internationalen Phänomen,* Sonderband der *Deutschen Vierteljahrsschrift für Literaturwissenschaft und Geistesgeschichte* (Stuttgart, 1980). Having reassessed older studies and reviewed those that had come out in the approximately twenty years since his previous reports, it is clear that Brinkmann rightly feels the major and most critical question still remains unanswered (see p. 1). He does, however, accept the validity of the present study's contribution to an answer to that question (see p. 133).

2. Brinkmann, *Expressionismus,* esp. pp. 1-2.

3. Ibid., p. 80.

4. Horst Denkler, *Drama des Expressionismus: Programm, Spieltext, Theater* (Munich, 1967), pp. 12-21; Annalisa Viviani, *Dramaturgische Elemente im expressionistischen Drama* (Bonn, 1970), pp. 1-6.

5. Armin Arnold, *Die Literatur des Expressionismus: Sprachliche und thematische Quellen* (Stuttgart, Berlin, Cologne, and Mainz, 1966), esp. pp. 9-15.

6. Peter Hohendahl, *Das Bild der bürgerlichen Welt im expressionistischen Drama* (Heidelberg, 1967), pp. 11-12; Gunter Martens, *Vitalismus und Expressionismus; Ein Beitrag zur Genese und Deutung expressionistischer Stilstrukturen und Motive* (Stuttgart, Berlin, Cologne, and Mainz, 1971), pp. 13-17; Armin Arnold, *Prosa des Expressionismus: Herkunft, Analyse, Inventar* (Stuttgart, Berlin, Cologne and Mainz, 1971), pp. 9-17, 56.

7. Wilhelm Emrich, "Die Struktur der modernen Dichtung," in Wilhelm Emrich, *Protest und Verheissung* (Bonn, 1963), pp. 111-22; Wilhelm Emrich, "Die Literaturrevolution 1910-1925," in Emrich, *Protest,* pp. 148-54; Wilhelm Emrich, "Arno Holz und die moderne Kunst," in Emrich, *Protest,* pp. 155-68; Wolfdietrich Rasch, *Zur deutschen Literatur seit der Jahrhundertwende* (Stuttgart, 1967), pp. 1-48; Wolfdietrich Rasch, "Was ist Expressionismus?" in Rasch, *Zur deutschen Literatur,* (Stuttgart, 1967), pp. 221-27; Herbert Lehnert, "Satirische Botschaft an den Leser: Das Ende des Jugendstils," in *Gestaltungsgeschichte und Gesellschaftsgeschichte: Literatur- kunst- und musikwissenschaftliche Studien,* ed. Käte Hamburger (Stuttgart, 1969), pp. 487-515; and Kreuzer, "Zur Periodisierung der 'modernen' deutschen Literatur," *Basis* 2 (1971): 7-32. See the criticism of

such proposals by Jost Hermand, "Über Nutzen und Nachteil literarischer Epochenbegriffe: Ein Vortrag," *Monatshefte* 58 (1966): 289-309.

8. Rasch, "Aspekte," p. 2; Kreuzer, "Zur Periodisierung," pp. 7ff.

9. Lehnert, "Satirische Botschaft," p. 487.

10. Arnold, *Die Literatur,* pp. 9ff.

11. Ibid., p. 7.

12. Albert Soergel, *Dichtung und Dichter der Zeit: Neue Folge: Im Banne des Expressionismus* (Leipzig, 1925). Cf. also the new edition: Albert Soergel and Curt Hohoff, *Dichtung und Dichter der Zeit: Vom Naturalismus bis zur Gegenwart,* vol. 2 (Düsseldorf, 1963).

13. Originally pub. in *Internationale Literatur* 1 (1934): 153-73; repr., e.g., in *Expressionismus: Der Kampf um eine literarische Bewegung,* ed. Paul Raabe (Munich, 1965), pp. 254-73.

14. On this polemical exchange, in which Alfred Kurella, Herwarth Walden, Klaus Berger, Kurt Kersten, Rudolf Leonhard, Ernst Bloch, Georg Lukacs, and others participated, see *Expressionismus: Der Kampf,* ed. Raabe, pp. 306-7.

15. Richard Samuel and R. Hinton Thomas, *Expressionism in German Life, Literature and the Theatre (1910-1924)* (Cambridge, 1939).

16. The same applies to *Der deutsche Expressionismus: Formen und Gestalten,* ed. Hans Steffen (Göttingen, 1965); *Aspekte des Expressionismus: Periodisierung, Stil, Gedankenwelt: Die Vorträge des ersten Kolloquiums in Amherst/Massachusetts,* ed. Wolfgang Paulsen (Heidelberg, 1968).

17. Sokel, *The Writer in Extremis: Expressionism in Twentieth-Century German Literature* (Stanford, 1959).

18. See above, p. 1.

19. See note 5, above.

20. See note 6, above.

21. See note 4, above.

22. See note 4, above.

23. See note 6, above.

24. See note 6, above.

25. Hohendahl, *Das Bild,* pp. 62-74.

26. See Hohendahl, *Das Bild,* pp. 62-74; also the large amount of documentary and bibliographical work being done in this field by the staff of the Schiller-Nationalmuseum in Marbach a.N., esp. *Expressionismus: Aufzeichnungen und Erinnerungen der Zeitgenossen,* ed. Paul Raabe (Olten and Freiburg im Breisgau, 1965).

27. We find it glossed only in such abbreviated handbooks as Karl Beckson and Arthur Ganz's *A Reader's Guide to Literary Terms: A Dictionary* (London, 1966); A.F. Scott's *Current Literary Terms: A Concise Dictionary of their Origin and Use* (New York, 1967); William Flint Thrall and Addison Hibbard's *A Handbook to Literature* (New York, 1960).

28. See, e.g., *Der Sprach Brockhaus: Deutsches Bildwörterbuch* (Wiesbaden, 1972); *Deutsches Wörterbuch,* ed. Lutz Mackensen (Munich, 1967); *Duden: Bedeutungswörterbuch: Der grosse Duden,* ed. Paul Grebe, et al. (Mannheim, Vienna, and Zürich, 1970); *Ullsteins Lexikon der deutschen Sprache,* ed. Rudolf Köster, et al. (Frankfurt and Berlin, 1969); *The*

Oxford English Dictionary (Oxford, 1933); *Webster's Third New International Dictionary of the English Language* (Springfield, 1963).

Chapter 1

1. See the Introduction where these studies are cited.

2. The source for the following description of German society in the Wilhelminian era, as for the description of Expressionist literary life in the same period, is the whole body of autobiographies, memoirs, and reminiscences left behind by those associated with the Expressionist movement in literature and the arts and cited in the course of this study. When a reference to a specific source for a point made in this study is considered appropriate, only an exemplary source or sources will be cited so as not to unnecessarily encumber the text or the notes.

3. See, e.g., Hans Reimann, *Mein blaues Wunder: Lebensmosaik eines Humoristen* (Munich, 1959), p. 53; Johannes Urzidil, "Im Anlauf der Epoche," in *Als das Jahrhundert jung war*, ed. by Josef Halperin (Zürich, 1961), p. 140; Herbert Jhering, *Begegnungen mit Zeit und Menschen* (Bremen, 1965), pp. 25, 180; Franz Jung, *Der Weg nach unten* (Neuwied a.R., 1961), p. 71; Otto Flake, *Es wird abend: Bericht aus einem langen Leben* (Gütersloh, 1960), pp. 242-43; Walter Mehring, *Die verlorene Bibliothek: Autobiographie einer Kultur* (Icking bei München, 1964), p. 45; Heinrich Mann, *Ein Zeitalter wird besichtigt* (Berlin, 1947), p. 192; Stefan Zweig, *Die Welt von gestern* (Stockholm, 1944), pp. 16ff; Ottomar Starke, *Was mein Leben anlangt* (Berlin-Grunewald, 1956), p. 16; Hans Jacob, *Kind meiner Zeit: Lebenserinnerungen* (Cologne and Berlin, 1962), p. 21; Max Krell, *Das alles gab es einmal* (Frankfurt a.M., 1961), p. 12.

   For the purposes of this study, no distinction will be made in the following description of pre-World War One society between Wilhelminian Germany and Hapsburg Austria of the same period. Only a relatively small number of Expressionists came from Austria, and those that did either traveled often between the two countries during the Expressionist decade or, as happened in most cases, soon moved to Germany to join circles there. In addition, the differences in social conditions between the two countries were, in the present context, negligible; Expressionist chroniclers from the Austro-Hungarian Empire, most notably Max Brod in *Streitbares Leben: Autobiographie* (Munich, 1960) and Stefan Zweig in the work cited above, draw no major distinctions between the manners and morals of Wilhelminian Germany and Hapsburg Austria, but treat the two societies as one continuous, virtually undiversified culture.

4. The Expressionist chroniclers as a whole stress especially this aspect of Wilhelminian society. Stefan Zweig, because of the age's very strong sense of security, labeled it "das goldene Zeitalter der Sicherheit." See Zweig, *Die Welt*, pp. 16ff.

5. Kurt Hiller, "Begegnungen mit Expressionisten," in *Expressionismus: Aufzeichnungen und Erinnerungen der Zeitgenossen*, ed. Paul Raabe (Olten and Freiburg im Breisgau, 1965), p. 27.

6. Richard Seewald, *Der Mann von gegenüber: Spiegelbild eines Lebens* (Munich, 1963), p. 63; Zweig, *Die Welt*, p. 51; Flake, *Es wird*, p. 200; Oskar Kokoschka, *Mein Leben* (Munich: 1971), pp. 56ff.

7. Seewald, *Der Mann*, pp. 56ff., 62ff.

8. Krell, *Das alles*, p. 207; Erwin Piscator, *Das politische Theater*, ed. Felix Gasbarra (Reinbek bei Hamburg, 1963), p. 43. The use of "Plüsch" or "Plüschmöbel" in this manner runs through Carl Sternheim's works. See also his autobiography, *Vorkriegseuropa im Gleichnis meines Lebens* (Amsterdam, 1936), p. 41.

9. Zweig, *Die Welt*, p. 51; Seewald, *Der Mann*, pp. 61ff; Martin Gumpert, *Die Hölle im Paradies: Selbstdarstellung eines Arztes* (Stockholm, 1939), p. 44.

10. See the program of the quarterly journal *Berliner Romantik* (1918-25), as cited in Raabe, *Die Zeitschriften*, p. 82.

"Es gilt die Wiedergeburt des Herzens."

11. Krell, *Das alles*, p. 207.

Der Protest galt der konventionellen Trägheit und illusionistischen Schönfärberei, die bis in das erste Jahrzehnt des Jahrhunderts so taten, als sei alles in unserer Welt wohlgeordnet und 'unter dem Schutz der Waffen' wohlbewahrt. Vor allem in der Literatur wiegte man sich bis dahin im Plüschsessel der guten Gesellschaft.

12. Karl Otten, as cited in Heinz Schöffler, "Karl Otten, Ego und Eros," afterword to *Ego und Eros: Meistererzählungen des Expressionismus*, ed. Karl Otten (Stuttgart, 1963), p. 547.

13. Seewald, *Der Mann*, pp. 70ff. See also Carl Zuckmayer, *Als wär's ein Stück von mir* (Vienna, 1966), pp. 147f.

14. Zweig, *Die Welt*, pp. 88-89.

Unser Jahrhundert ... empfand die Sexualität als ein anarchisches darum störendes Element, das sich nicht in die Ethik eingliedern liess, und das man nicht am lichten Tage schalten lassen dürfe, weil jede Form einer freien, einer ausserehelichen Liebe dem bürgerlichen 'Anstand' widersprach.... War die Sexualität schon nicht aus der Welt zu schaffen, so sollte sie wenigstens innerhalb ihrer Welt der Sitte nicht sichtbar sein. Es wurde also die stillschweigende Vereinbarung getroffen, den ganzen ärgerlichen Komplex weder in der Schule noch in der Familie noch in der Öffentlichkeit zu erörtern und alles zu unterdrücken, was an sein Vorhandensein erinnern konnte.

15. Tilla Durieux, *Eine Tür steht offen* (Berlin-Grunewald, 1954), p. 7; Zweig, *Die Welt*, pp. 70-99.

16. Durieux, *Eine Tür*, p. 99.

"'Gut erzogen' galt damals bei einem jungen Mädchen für vollkommen identisch mit lebensfremd..."

17. Ibid., pp. 81-88.

18. George Grosz, *A Little Yes and a Big No: The Autobiography of George Grosz*, trans. Lola Sachs Dorin (New York, 1946), p. 163. Unfortunately, only a translation of the latter work was available to the present author.

19. See the publication of this letter in *Briefe der Expressionisten*, ed. Kasimir Edschmid (Frankfurt a.M. and Berlin, 1964), p. 69. On the dating of the letter in 1915, see below, chapter 12, note 9.

"Danken wir Gott für die Huren und ihre freie Lebensart, sie sind die wirklichen Menschen."

20. See Raabe, *Die Zeitschriften*, pp. 33-37; also the chapter on *Die Aktion*, below.

21. See Raabe, *Die Zeitschriften*, pp. 32-33; also the chapter on *Pan*, below.

22. See Raabe, *Die Zeitschriften*, pp. 38-39.

23. Mann, *Ein Zeitalter*, p. 252; see also Brod, *Streitbares*, pp. 118-19.

"1910 durfte einer, der sich auf intellektuelle Politik verlegte, den Ernst seines Unternehmens wahrhaftig bezweifeln; so unverständlich wie damals war es in Deutschland weder früher noch später."

24. Jhering, *Begegnungen,* p. 25.

Es war Friede. Der Atem steht still beim Aufklingen dieses Wortes. Es war Friede. Friede im Glauben, im Bewusstsein und der Phantasie der Menschen. Friede aber auch in ihrer Blindheit. Weil sie glaubten, sahen sie nicht. Sie waren ergriffen von dem Gefühl, dass der Fortschritt in die Zivilisation ein Fortschritt alles Denkens sein, alles Leben, auch das politische und soziale, durchdringen und die finsteren Mächte der Gewalt und der rohen Leidenschaften vernichten oder auf produktive Leistungen ablenken müsste.

25. Urzidil, "Im Anlauf," p. 140; Jhering, *Begegnungen,* pp. 25, 65-66, 180; Karl Jakob Hirsch, *Heimkehr zu Gott: Briefe an meinen Sohn* (Munich, 1946), p. 11; Starke, *Was mein Leben,* p. 16.

26. Jhering, *Begegnungen,* pp. 65-66. See also Margarete Susman, *Ich habe viele Leben gelebt: Erinnerungen* (Stuttgart, 1964), p. 13.

Dass dieser sogenannte Boxer-Feldzug in China nicht als Krieg, nicht als Warnung vor jeder Hetze in der bürgerlichen Presse dargestellt wurde, sondern als Abenteuer mit patriotischem Stolz, das erklärte auch das falsche Sicherheitsgefühl der Zeit.

27. Susman, *Ich habe,* p. 83; Ludwig Marcuse, *Mein zwanzigstes Jahrhundert: Auf dem Weg zu einer Autobiographie* (Munich, 1960), p. 37.

28. Seewald, *Der Mann,* p. 61.

29. Ibid., pp. 61ff. See also Zweig, *Die Welt,* esp. the chapter "Die Schule im vorigen Jahrhundert," pp. 47ff.

30. Hirsch, *Heimkehr,* p. 13. See also Reimann, *Mein blaues,* p. 84; Zweig, *Die Welt,* pp. 47ff; Leonhard Frank, *Links wo das Herz ist: Roman* (Munich, 1952), p. 91 (Frank's autobiography in novel form); Gumpert, *Die Hölle,* pp. 45ff.

Und dann kam die Schulzeit. Es war nicht das fröhliche Lernenwollen, das eigentlich ein jeder Junge in sich spüren sollte, das mich in die Schule trug, es war der Zwang und nichts weiter als das.... Aber die Schule gehörte zu den Pflichten, denen sich ein deutscher Staatsbürger unterwerfen musste. Mein Bruder und ich besuchten das Lyzeum II, das später Goethe-Gymnasium hiess. Der Name des grössten deutschen Dichters war hier missbraucht, um einer Drill-Lehreranstalt den Anschein zu geben, als ob Humanität im Goetheschen Sinne dort zu Hause wäre. Dem war nicht so.

31. See John Höxter, *So lebten wir: 25 Jahre Berliner Boheme* (Berlin, 1929), p. 31.

32. On Werfel's case see Brod, *Streitbares,* pp. 12-42, 47ff; on Hasenclever see Kurt Pinthus, "Walter Hasenclever: Leben und Werk," introduction to Walter Hasenclever, *Gedichte, Dramen, Prosa,* ed. Kurt Pinthus (Reinbek bei Hamburg, 1963), pp. 9-12, 19; on Becher see his autobiographical novel *Abschied: Roman* (Berlin, 1958), passim; on Gross see Franz Jung, *Der Weg,* pp. 87ff. Brod felt that the father-son conflict was so crucial to Expressionism that he was induced to assert that he himself, although he felt he was an Expressionist, held an "isolated position" in the movement because of the absence of the latter conflict in his life. See Brod, *Streitbares,* p. 63.

33. Mann, *Ein Zeitalter,* p. 252.

Die Deutschen glaubten felsenfest an eine Macht, die 'das Reich' hiess,—dies, nachdem 'das Reich' zwanzig Jahre hindurch erschüttert worden war; wer nur selbst im Gleichgewicht gewesen wäre, musste es schaukeln fühlen. Niemand bemerkte es.
    Sie bildeten sich ein, noch immer wäre alles in Ordnung, nachdem so furchtbar lange die verhängnisvollen Entscheidungen einem Monarchen mit labilem Selbstgefühl, aber beständiger Unruhe, überlassen worden waren.

34. This is not to say, of course, that professional historians do not agree with much of the Expressionist interpretation of the Wilhelminian era. See, e.g., Arthur Rosenberg, *Die Entstehung der deutschen Republik: 1871-1918* (Berlin, 1928); Golo Mann, *Deutsche Geschichte des 19. und 20. Jahrhunderts* (Frankfurt a.M., 1966), pp. 396ff.

35. All of the painters and poets involved in the movement were born after 1871, except for Lasker-Schüler who was born in 1869. The vast majority were, however, born after the year 1880.

36. Mann states in *Ein Zeitalter*, p. 201, of *Der Untertan:* "Den Roman des bürgerlichen Deutschen unter der Regierung Wilhelms II. dokumentierte ich seit 1906. Beendet habe ich die Handschrift 1914, zwei Monate vor Ausbruch des Krieges—der in dem Buch nahe und unausweichlich erscheint."

37. In this work Thomas Mann takes special issue with the sociocritical and politically committed literature of the "Zivilisationsliterat," having in mind in particular his brother Heinrich; but he also employs the opportunity to attack "sociocritical Expressionism" as well. See, e.g., *Betrachtungen eines Unpolitischen* (Frankfurt a.M., 1956), pp. 556-59.

38. See, e.g., Hugo Ball, *Die Flucht aus der Zeit* (Lucerne, 1946), p. 8.

39. The term "Expressionism" did not become current and widespread as designating the literary movement until after 1914, although before this time certain labels with fixed connotations, such as "die Jungen," "die Jüngeren," "die Jüngsten," "die neuen Dichter," "die fortgeschrittenen Dichter," etc., did serve to identify what were later to be known as "Expressionists." Armin Arnold in *Die Literatur des Expressionismus: Sprachliche und thematische Quellen* (Stuttgart, Berlin, Cologne, and Mainz, 1966), pp. 9-15, covers the history of the term "Expressionism." The Expressionist journals and other publications designated their support of the movement either directly, by using the term "Expressionism" or "Expressionist," or, especially in the early phase, by emphasizing their support in their pages of "young" and "unrecognized" authors who, in one sense or another, represented revolutionary tendencies in style and thought. See the programmatic statements of these journals cited in Paul Raabe, *Die Zeitschriften und Sammlungen des literarischen Expressionismus: Repertorium der Zeitschriften, Jahrbücher, Anthologien, Sammelwerke, Schriftenreihen und Almanache: 1910-1921,* Repertorien zur deutschen Literaturgeschichte, vol. 1 (Stuttgart, 1964), passim.

40. C.F.W. Behl, "Begegnungen mit dem Expressionismus," in *Expressionismus: Aufzeichnungen,* ed. Raabe, p. 295; Kasimir Edschmid, *Lebendiger Expressionismus: Auseinandersetzungen, Gestalten, Erinnerungen* (Vienna, Munich, and Basel, 1961), p. 204; *Menschheitsdämmerung,* ed. Kurt Pinthus (Hamburg, 1959), p. 23; René Schickele, "Wie verhält es sich mit dem Expressionismus," reprinted from *Die weissen Blätter* (1920) in *Expressionismus: Der Kampf um eine literarische Bewegung,* ed. Paul Raabe (Munich, 1965), p. 178.

41. For source material on these circles see esp. *Expressionismus: Aufzeichnungen,* ed. Raabe, passim, and the source bibliography there, pp. 401-8. On the periodicals mentioned above, see Raabe, *Die Zeitschriften,* pp. 25ff.

42. Kreuzer, *Die Boheme: Beiträge ihrer Beschreibung* (Stuttgart, 1968), pp. 42-48.

43. Ibid., pp. 48-50. For the interpretation of the Bohemian life style as given by some of those associated with Expressionism see, e.g., Norbert Jacques, *Mit Lust gelebt* (Hamburg, 1950), p. 82; Erich Mühsam, *Unpolitische Erinnerungen* (Berlin, 1961), pp. 27-29; Hans Purrmann, "Erinnerungen an den Maler Rudolf Levy und an die mit ihm verlebten Jahre der Freundschaft," in Rudolf Levy, *Bildnisse, Stilleben, Landschaften* (Baden-Baden, 1961), p. 40; Karl Hirsch, *Heimkehr,* p. 28.

44.   *Die Aktion* 4 (1914): 320.

Alle Mitmenschen der Stadt
Waren nur staubige, blasse Laternen,
Wuchernd mit fremdem Licht.—
Nur hier fand ich Freunde,
Echte Wälder noch, verdornt und tief,
Oder Ebenen
Mit windreinem Fühlen.
Hier war Instinkt von schönen Tieren,
Hände hatten die Geste
Von knospenden Rosen.

Wie Musik
Schwebte, was sie sprachen,
Über dem Rauschen der Cyklopenstadt.

45.   Zweig, *Die Welt*, p. 58; Ferdinand Hardekopf, "Vorwort," in Ferdinand Hardekopf, *Lesestücke*, Aktions-Bücher der Aeternisten, (1) (Berlin-Wilmersdorf, 1916), p. 5.

46.   Wolfgang Goetz, *Im "Grössenwahn," bei Pschorr und anderswo... Erinnerungen an Berliner Stammtische* (Berlin, 1936), p. 14.

... dieses [Café des Westens] war eine Schule, eine sehr gute obendrein. Wir lernten sehen, erkennen, und lernten denken. Wir erfuhren, eindringlicher fast als auf der Universität, dass hinter dem Berge auch Leute wohnen und dass man ein Ding nicht nur von einer Seite ansehen soll, sondern von mindestens vier Seiten.

47.   Oskar Maria Graf, *Wir sind Gefangene: Ein Bekenntnis* (Vienna, Munich, and Basel, 1965), esp. pp. 86ff.; Frank, *Links*, p. 49.

48.   Purrmann, "Erinnerungen," p. 23.

Ort der Erziehung ist das Café für manchen geworden. Ich beleuchte dies zur Genüge, wenn ich erzähle, dass Paul Cassirer einmal in meiner Gegenwart der Witwe eines angesehenen Münchener Graphik-Händlers, die ihn besorgt wegen der Ausbildung ihres Sohnes befragte, den Rat gab: 'Schicken Sie ihn—lieber als zur Universität—drei Jahre in ein Künstlercafé, vielleicht das Dôme, und lassen Sie ihn Beziehung zu modernen Künstlern suchen.' So und ähnlich dürfte auch der Münchener Kunsthändler gedacht haben, als er seinen Sohn Justus einige Jahre zu uns ins Dôme schickte.

49.   Krell, *Das alles*, p. 18.

Unsere Heimat waren die Cafés. Die Cafés hatten damals noch eine Funktion, die verlorengegangen ist. Sie waren die Wechselstuben der Gedanken und Pläne, des geistigen Austausches, auch des Untergangs: ob im Pariser du Dôme, im Wiener Griensteidl, im Leipziger Merkur, im Römischen Greco. Hier wurde diskutiert und kritisch zerfetzt.

50.   Else Lasker-Schüler, *Lieber gestreifter Tiger: Briefe von Else Lasker-Schüler*, ed. Margarete Kupper (Munich, 1969), p. 104.

51.   Hugo Ball, *Briefe: 1911-1927*, ed. Annemarie Schütt-Hennings (Einsiedeln, Zürich, and Cologne, 1957), p. 28.

"Es ist eine verfluchte Sache. Ich gehe nicht mehr aus der Höhle, habe infolgedessen auch das Caféhaus aufgegeben, so wichtig es für mich ist. Denn dort kommen Bekannte, Zeitungen, neue Ideen."

52.   Hardekopf, "Vorwort," p. 5.

("Schnell rettete ich mich ins Café")

53. Ferdinand Hardekopf, "Ode vom seligen Morgen: Für Emmy Hennings," *Die Aktion* 5 (1915): 648. See also Hardekopf, *Lesestücke,* p. 23.

"Alles können wir entbehren, natürlich ausser dem/Kaffee (bezaubernder Oliven-Tinte, die Innenränder beschreibend) und dem Café."

54. See, e.g., Walter Mehring, "Berlin Avantgarde" and Ernst Blass, "Das alte Café des Westens," in *Expressionismus: Aufzeichnungen,* ed. Raabe, pp. 36-42, 116-21.

55. See, e.g., Marcuse, *Mein zwanzigstes,* pp. 25ff; Starke, *Was mein Leben,* p. 56.

56. Gottfried Benn, *Gesammelte Werke,* vol. 1 (Wiesbaden, 1962), p. 482.

Eigentlich hat alles, was meine Generation diskutierte, innerlich sich auseinanderdachte, man kann sagen: erlitt, man kann auch sagen: breittrat—alles das hatte sich bereits bei Nietzsche ausgesprochen und erschöpft, definitive Formulierung gefunden, alles Weitere war Exegese. Seine gefährliche stürmische blitzende Art, seine ruhelose Diktion, sein Sichversagen jeden Idylls und jeden allgemeinen Grundes, seine Aufstellung der Triebpsychologie als Dialektik—'Erkenntnis als Affekt,' die ganze Psychoanalyse, der ganze Existentialismus, alles dies ist seine Tat. Er ist, wie sich immer deutlicher zeigt, der weitreichende Gigant der nachgoetheschen Epoche.

57. Jung, *Der Weg,* p. 71.

58. See, e.g., the reports of Seewald, *Der Mann,* pp. 203-4; Blass, "Das alte," pp. 38, 39; Graf, *Wir sind,* p. 138; Erwin Loewenson, "Persönliches von Georg Heym," in *Georg Heym: Dokumente zu seinem Leben und Werk,* vol. 6 of Georg Heym, *Dichtungen und Schriften,* ed. Karl Ludwig Schneider and Gerhard Burkhardt (Darmstadt, 1968), p. 45.

59. See esp. Jung, *Der Weg,* pp. 87ff. See also Seewald *Der Mann,* p. 141; Emil Szittya, *Das Kuriositäten-Kabinett: Begegnungen mit seltsamen Begebenheiten, Landstreichern, Verbrechern, Artisten...*(Constance, 1923), pp. 150ff; Becher, *Abschied,* pp. 365ff, 375ff; Frank, *Links,* pp. 16-17; Karl Otten, "Die expressionistische Generation," introduction to *Ahnung und Aufbruch: Expressionistische Prosa,* ed. Karl Otten (Darmstadt, Berlin-Frohnau, and Neuwied am Rhein, 1957), p. 14. On Gross's relationship to Freud see Ernest Jones, *The Life and Work of Sigmund Freud,* vol. 2, *Years of Maturity, 1901-1919* (New York, 1955), pp. 29-30, 33.

60. Jones, *The Life,* p. 33.

61. See Gross's articles published in *Die Aktion* 3 (1913); 384ff, especially the essay "Zur Überwindung der kulturellen Krise," *Die Aktion* 3 (1913): 384-87.

62. Frank, *Links,* p. 31.

63. Blass, "Das alte," p. 38.

64. Mehring, "Berlin Avantgarde," p. 118; Nell Walden, "Aus meinen Erinnerungen an Herwarth Walden und die 'Sturmzeit,'" in *Der Sturm: Ein Erinnerungsbuch an Herwarth Walden und die Künstler aus dem Sturmkreis,* ed. Nell Walden and Lothar Schreyer (Baden-Baden, 1954), pp. 11, 14-15; Jacob, *Kind,* pp. 30ff; Alfred Richard Meyer, *die maer von der musa expressionistica: zugleich eine kleine quasi-literaturgeschichte mit über 130 praktischen beispielen* (Düsseldorf-Kaiserswerth, 1948), pp. 69ff.

65. Rosa Trillo Clough, *Futurism: The Story of a Modern Art Movement: A New Appraisal* (New York, 1961), p. 11. Marinetti's manifestoes were published in *Der Sturm* 2 (1912), pp. 828ff; they are reprinted in Paul Pörtner, *Literatur-Revolution: 1910-1925: Dokumente, Manifeste, Programme,* vol. 2, *Zur Begriffsbestimmung der "Ismen,"* Die Mainzer Reihe, Vol. 13/II (Neuwied am Rhein and Berlin-Spandau, 1961), pp. 35-63, 69-81.

66. Mehring, "Berlin Avantgarde," p. 118; Walden, "Aus meinen Erinnerungen," p. 15; Claire Goll, *Ich verzeihe keinem: Eine literarische Chronique scandaleuse unserer Zeit* (Bern and Munich, 1976), p. 30.

67. Nell Walden, "Aus meinen Erinnerungen," p. 14; *Der Sturm*, ed. Nell Walden and Lothar Schreyer, p. 258.

68. Meyer, *die maer*, pp. 6-7, 29-30; Johannes R. Becher, "Über Jakob van Hoddis," in Raabe, *Expressionismus: Aufzeichnungen*, pp. 50-55; Hiller, "Begegnungen," p. 31.

69. Lothar-Günther Buchheim, *Die Künstlergemeinschaft Brücke* (Feldafing, 1956), p. 39.

   Die erstrebte Einheit von Kunst und Leben wurde in dieser Friedrichstädter Boheme vollkommen verwirklicht. Man arbeitete mit besessenem Fleiss, steigerte sich gegenseitig zu höchster Intensität, half sich mit wechselseitiger, nichts beschönigender Kritik. Entdeckungen, die einer machte, teilten sich sofort den anderen mit. Man nutzte jede Stunde des Tags und arbeitete oft auch in den Nachtstunden, meist in rauschhafter Erregung.

70. Raabe, *Die Zeitschriften*, passim.

71. Walden, "Aus meinen Erinnerungen," p. 35; Frank, *Links*, p. 77; Seewald, *Der Mann*, p. 35; Brod, *Streitbares*, pp. 118-19; Hirsch, *Heimkehr*, p. 57.

72. Alfred Döblin, *Journal 1952/53*, unpub. typescript, p. 21, cited by Heinz Graber in Alfred Döblin, *Briefe*, ed. Heinz Graber (Olten and Freiburg i.B., 1970), p. 667.

   "Damals galt uns Politik gar nichts. Sie war der Alltag. Sie war eine Angelegenheit der Spiesser. Gegen Musik und Literatur kam sie nicht auf."

73. "Note," *Die Aktion* 1 (1911): 23. The same statement was reprinted from time to time in subsequent issues as well. See *Die Aktion* 1 (1911): 58, 152, 182, 264, 343, 505, 537.

74. Kurt Hiller, "Litteraturpolitik," *Die Aktion* 1 (1911): 138-39.

75. Georg Heym, *Tagebücher, Träume, Briefe*, vol. 3 of Georg Heym, *Dichtungen und Schriften*, ed. Karl Ludwig Schneider (Hamburg and Munich, 1960), pp. 128, 135, 138-39, 164-65; see Stadler's poem "Aufbruch," in Ernst Stadler, *Dichtungen*, ed. Karl Ludwig Schneider (Hamburg, n.d.), pp. 128-29; see Heym's poem "Der Krieg," which aroused nightmarish visions in the minds of those who heard it read in Berlin before the war, in Georg Heym, *Lyrik*, vol. 1 of Georg Heym, *Dichtungen und Schriften*, ed. Karl Ludwig Schneider (Hamburg and Munich, 1964), pp. 346-47; see Hoddis's poem "Weltende," which had similar effects on the audiences of Berlin in the same period, in *Menschheitsdämmerung*, p. 39; Behl, "Begegnungen," pp. 294-95; Hirsch, *Heimkehr*, p. 45; Karl Otten, "1914—Sommer ohne Herbst," in *Expressionismus: Aufzeichnungen*, ed. Raabe, p. 155, "Die Aktion: Stimmen der Freunde," ed. Roland H. Wiegenstein (unpub. MS of a radio broadcast commemorating the fiftieth anniversary of the founding of Pfemfert's journal, Feb. 25, 1961), pp. 14-18.

76. Brod, *Streitbares*, p. 118.

   Wer hatte denn 1914 an die Möglichkeit eines Krieges gedacht!... Man dachte daran als an etwas Historisch-Abgetanes, an etwas Phantastisches, etwas, woran frühere Geschlechter der Menschen (die Unglücklichen!) geglaubt hatten—nicht aber wir, die vernunftbegabten Realisten.

77. Hirsch, *Heimkehr*, p. 57.

   Ich war das Opfer einer bürgerlichen Erziehung, die damals nichts weiter von den Kindern forderte, als den Gesetzen der Klasse, zu der man gehörte, zu gehorchen.

78. Stefan Zweig, "Das neue Pathos," in *Das Literarische Echo* 11 (1909): 1701-9; reprinted in Stefan Zweig, *Emile Verhaeren* (Leipzig, 1910), pp. 107-9; reprinted again in *Das neue Pathos*

1 (1913): 1-6; reprinted also in *Expressionismus: Der Kampf um eine literarische Bewegung,* ed. Paul Raabe, vol. 41 of Sonderreihe, Deutscher Taschenbuch Verlag (Munich, 1965), pp. 15-22.

79.   Zweig, "Das neue Pathos," in *Expressionismus: Der Kampf,* ed. Raabe, pp. 16-17.

80.   Peter Scher, "Das Zeitalter der Lyrik," *Die Aktion* 3 (1913): 715. On the floodtide of artistic activities in other countries in the same period see, e.g., Roger Shattuck, *The Banquet Years: The Arts in France: 1885-1918: Apollinaire* (Garden City, 1961), pp. 28ff.

81.   Hugo Kersten, "Leo Matthias: *Der Jüngste Tag,*" *Die Aktion* 4 (1914): 465-66. See also Herbert Kuhn, "Das Gegenständliche des expressionistischen Dramas," *Die neue Schaubühne* 1 (1919): 205f.

82.   See, e.g., Raabe, *Die Zeitschriften,* passim.

83.   See the programs of the various Expressionist journals cited in Raabe, *Die Zeitschriften,* pp. 25ff.

84.   Paul Raabe, "Das literarische Leben im Expressionismus: Eine historische Skizze," in Raabe, *Die Zeitschriften,* pp. 1-2.

85.   Ball, *Die Flucht,* p. 8.

86.   Johannes R. Becher, *Auf andere Art so grosse Hoffnung: Tagebuch 1950: Mit Eintragungen 1951* (Berlin, 1952), p. 467.

Wir waren leidenschaftlich unserer Sache ergeben, einzig und allein von ihr erfüllt, ja, wir waren Besessene. In Cafés auf den Strassen und Plätzen, in den Ateliers, Tag und Nacht waren wir 'auf dem Marsch,' setzten uns selbst in rasende Bewegung, um das Unergründliche zu ergründen und um, als Dichter, Maler, Musiker vereint, die 'Kunst des Jahrhunderts' zu schaffen, die unvergleichliche, die alle Künste aller vergangenen Jahrhunderte zeitlos überragende. Wir—Unsere Zeit, das zwanzigste Jahrhundert! So traten wir vor das Forum der Jahrhunderte hin, sie zum Wettkampf herausfordernd. Und—'es ist eine Lust zu leben,' so 'heilig-ergriffen' von dieser Lebenslust waren wir, dass wir keinen Augenblick gezögert hätten, uns dieses herrlichen Lebensaufgangs wegen eine Kugel durch den Kopf zu jagen, als Zeichen, dass wir, wenn dieses *unser* Leben uns nicht lebensmöglich ist, auf jedes andere 'Am-Leben-Sein' verzichteten.

87.   Hans Arp, *Unsern täglichen Traum . . . Erinnerungen, Dichtungen und Betrachtungen aus den Jahren 1914-1954.*

Die Menschen, die nicht unmittelbar an der ungeheuerlichen Raserei des Weltkrieges beteiligt waren, taten so, als begriffen sie nicht, was um sie her vorging. Wie verirrte Lämmer blickten sie aus glasigen Augen in die Welt.

88.   Seewald, *Der Mann,* pp. 33-34; Marcuse, *Mein zwanzigstes,* pp. 37ff; Zweig, *Die Welt,* p. 232; Susman, *Ich habe,* p. 83; A.H. Kober, *Einst in Berlin: Rhapsodie 14,* ed. Richard Kirn (Hamburg, 1956), pp. 30ff.

89.   Brod, *Streitbares,* p. 119; Zweig, *Die Welt,* pp. 231-32, 271.

Nie ist eine Generation so brutal von den Tatsachen überrannt worden. Wir waren ganz einfach dumm, und alles, was wir im Gymnasium gelernt und in den Weltgeschichten gelesen hatten, hielten wir, ohne viel darüber nachzudenken, für Märchenliteratur.

90.   Hanna Höch, "Brief," in Walter Mehring, *Berlin Dada: Eine Chronik mit Photos und Dokumenten* (Zürich, 1959), p. 91; see the similar statement by Susman, *Ich habe,* p. 82.

91.   Wieland Herzfelde, *Unterwegs: Blätter aus fünfzig Jahren* (Berlin, 1961), pp. 90-91; Mehring, *Berlin Dada,* p. 16; Susman, *Ich habe,* p. 83; Krell, *Das alles,* p. 32.

92. Ball, *Briefe*, pp. 17-34.

93. Ibid., pp. 34-35.

Kunst? Das ist nun alles aus und lächerlich geworden. In alle Winde zersprengt. Das hat alles keinen Sinn mehr. Ich kann Dir gar nicht sagen, wie mir zu Mut ist. Und man sieht ja noch gar nicht die Folgen ab... Lasst bitte oft von euch hören. Mir graust vor der Zukunft. Der Krieg ist noch das Einzige, was mich noch reizt. Schade, auch das wird nur eine halbe Sache sein.

94. Ball, *Briefe*, pp. 35ff; Ball, *Flucht*, p. xii; Richard Huelsenbeck, *Mit Witz, Licht und Grütze* (Wiesbaden, 1957), p. 8.

95. Ball, *Briefe*, p. 35; Ball, *Flucht*, pp. 10, 13.

96. Wilhelm Herzog, "Klärungen," *Das Forum* 1 (1915): 553-77.

97. Herzog, "Klärungen," 554.

Zur Kultur gehörte für einen grossen Teil der Intellektuellen, bis zum 4. August 1914, dass man sich um das politische Leben seines Volkes nur wenig kümmerte, dass man von den parlamentarischen Kämpfen leicht degoutiert war, um sich ganz seinen Geschäften hinzugeben oder um sich—in Erinnerung an berühmte Vorbilder—ungestört der Bemalung einer Leinwandfläche oder der Ausarbeitung einer Novelle zu widmen. Nicht nur der grösste Teil unserer Künstler, sondern auch die Mehrzahl unserer ästhetisch Gebildeten lebte innerhalb des Staates abseits aller öffentlichen Interessen. Ja, es gehörte zum guten Ton, sich mit Politik nicht zu befassen. Man las gute Bücher, sammelte gute Bilder, hörte gute Konzerte, man wurde Bibliophile, hielt mehrere Revuen für Kulturausdruck und verwandte Gebiete, pflegte Umgang mit Gelehrten und Künstlern,—kurz: man hatte Kultur.
  Für gerechtere Lebensformen kämpfen? Sozialdemokraten besorgten dies schon allzulaut. Haben ja in manchem recht, aber es kommt schliesslich alles zu seiner Zeit....
  Da brach der Krieg herein. Und aus kultivierten ichsüchtigen Ästheten wurden Politiker, Volksanbeter. Jetzt schwuren sie ihren Individualismus ab und wollten nur noch Masse sein.

98. Krell, *Das alles*, p. 32.

99. Kurt Pinthus, "Erinnerungen an Bechers Frühzeit," in Johannes R. Becher, *Lyrik, Prosa, Dokumente: Eine Auswahl*, ed. Max Niedermayer (Wiesbaden, 1965), p. xlii. See also Marietta, "Klabund," in *Expressionismus: Aufzeichnungen*, ed. Raabe, p. 94; Graf, *Wir sind*, p. 142.

100. Otten, "1914," pp. 137ff; Otto Flake, "Halbfertiges Leben" and Jacob Picard, "Ernst Blass, seine Umwelt in Heidelberg und *Die Argonauten*," in *Expressionismus: Aufzeichnungen*, ed. Raabe, pp. 155ff, 137ff; Purrmann, "Erinnerungen," pp. 41ff; Friedrich Ahlers-Hestermann, "Der deutsche Künstlerkreis des 'Café du Dôme' in Paris," in *Künstlerbekenntnisse: Briefe/Tagebuchblätter/Betrachtungen heutiger Künstler*, ed. Paul Westheim (Berlin, n.d.), p. 267; Ernst Zunker, "*Der Wiecker Bote:* Das Organ eines Expressionistenkreises an der Universität Greifswald," *Germanisch-Romanische Monatsschrift*, n.s. 11 (1961): 229.

101. *Expressionismus: Literatur und Kunst: 1910-1923: Eine Ausstellung des deutschen Literaturarchivs im Schiller-Nationalmuseum Marbach a.N*, cat. 7 of Sonderausstellungen des Schiller-Nationalmuseums, ed. Bernhard Zeller, Paul Raabe, and H.L. Greve (Marbach a.N., 1960), p. 112.

102. Hermann Kesten, "Einleitung," in René Schickele, *Werke in drei Bänden*, ed. Hermann Kesten (Cologne and Berlin, 1959), vol. 1, pp. 12-13; Schickele, *Werke*, vol. 1, p. 1272; René Schickele, "Autobiographische Notizen," *Werke*, vol. 1, p. 839.

103. Flake, *Es wird*, pp. 241ff; Friedrich Eisenlohr, *Das gläserne Netz* (Berlin-Grunewald, 1927), pp. 610ff; Paul Raabe, "Der frühe Benn und die Veröffentlichung seiner Werke," in Gottfried

Benn, *Den Traum alleine tragen,* ed. Paul Raabe and Max Niedermayer (Wiesbaden, 1966), pp. 27ff; Gottfried Benn, "Epilog und lyrisches Ich," in *Gesammelte Werke* 4 (Wiesbaden, 1961), pp. 7ff; Carl Sternheim, *Vorkriegseuropa im Gleichnis meines Lebens* (Amsterdam, 1936), pp. 172-213; Carl Sternheim, *Zeitkritik,* vol. 6 of *Gesamtwerk,* ed. Wilhelm Emrich (Neuwied a.R., 1966), pp. 500, 514-15, 528-29; Gottfried Benn, *Ausgewählte Briefe,* ed. Max Rychner (Wiesbaden, 1957), pp. 12-13.

104. Raabe, *Die Zeitschriften,* pp. 25-56ff.

105. See, e.g., H.H. Houben, *Verbotene Literatur: Von der klassischen Zeit bis zur Gegenwart* 1 (Dessau, 1925), 2 (Bremen, 1928), passim.

106. See the many expressions of sympathy with Wedekind's troubles with the censor in *Das Forum* 1 (1914), esp. 48-49, 173-77, 246-54. See also *Das Wedekindbuch,* ed. Joachim Friedenthal (Munich, 1914) which contains statements of support of Wedekind by artists of a variety of tendencies, including some by those associated with Expressionism.

107. Durieux, *Eine Tür,* p. 70; Edschmid, *Lebendiger,* pp. 97ff; *Die Aktion* 4 (1914), 445ff; *Pan* 1 (1911): 217-23, 396-98, 587-90, 740; *Pan* 2 (1911): 32-33, 34.

108. Durieux, *Eine Tür,* pp. 70ff; *Pan* 1 (1911), 287-290, 321-326.

109. See Hugo Ball's letter concerning the plans for such a volume written to Richard Dehmel on May 12, 1914, and published with other letters from the early phase of Expressionism as "'Morgenrot!—Die Tage dämmern.!' Zwanzig Briefe aus dem Frühexpressionismus 1910-1914," ed. Paul Raabe, *Der Monat* 16 (1964): 68.

110. Wieland Herzfelde, "Wie ein Verlag entstand," in *Expressionismus: Aufzeichnungen,* ed. Raabe, p. 224.

111. Raabe, *Die Zeitschriften,* p. 53; Wilhelm Herzog, *Menschen, denen ich begegnete* (Bern and Munich, 1959), pp. 16ff. The deletions by the censor from issues of *Das Forum* begin in Vol. 2, No. 2/3, pp. 57ff., and steadily increase until the total ban of the periodical announced by Herzog in a notice dated September 19, 1915. Herzog published correspondence he had with the censor in 1915 concerning the deletions and the ban in *Das Forum* 3 (1918): 21-29.

112. Hans Rothe, "Theater: Es begann mit Sorge und endete mit Unruh," in *Expressionismus: Aufzeichnungen,* ed. Raabe, pp. 238ff; Houben, *Verbotene Literatur,* 2 pp. 508-18.

113. On "Das junge Deutschland" see below, the chapter on Berlin.

114. On the Herzfelde circle and *Neue Jugend* see that chapter, below.

115. Pinthus, "Walter Hasenclever," p. 22; Kurt Pinthus, "Leipzig und der frühe Expressionismus," in *Expressionismus: Aufzeichnungen,* p. 83; Ball, *Die Flucht,* pp. 20-21; Walter Kiaulehn, *Mein Freund der Verleger: Ernst Rowohlt und seine Zeit* (Reinbek bei Hamburg, 1967), pp. 87f; Paul Meyer, *Ernst Rowohlt in Selbstzeugnissen und Bilddokumenten,* Sonderdruck, Rowohlt Monographien (Reinbek bei Hamburg, 1967), p. 60. Heinrich Eduard Jacob portrays the Weimar meeting in the poem "Elegie an Weimar" (1921). On other such meetings and demonstrations see Frank, *Links,* pp. 92, 99; Durieux, *Eine Tür,* p. 109.

116. Jacob, *Kind,* p. 45; Edschmid, *Lebendiger,* p. 115; Graf, *Wir sind,* p. 142.

117. Raabe, *Die Zeitschriften,* p. 117, 165.

118. Herzog, *Menschen,* pp. 403ff. For some examples of Kerr's patriotic verse see the last issue of *Pan,* ed. Kerr: *Pan* 4 (April 1, 1915), no 2/3, 25-32.

119. Frank, *Links,* pp. 92-93; Behl, "Begegnungen," p. 297.

120. Frank, *Links,* pp. 93ff.

121. Rudolf Leonhard, *Über den Schlachten,* Lyrische Flugblätter, (48) (Berlin-Wilmersdorf, 1914). See Raabe, *Die Zeitschriften,* p. 165.

122. Leonhard, *Über den Schlachten,* pp. (5), (12).

"Wir lernten in Wunden eine ruhige Geberde / Es gibt kein Paradies hienieden / aber für uns ist es besser Krieg zu haben als Frieden."

123. See Rudolf Leonhard, *Das Chaos* (Hannover, 1919), pp. 35-71, 81-102, 108.

124. Ibid., passim.

125. Ibid., p. 35.

Ich bin in die Schlachten herabgestiegen
und habe das Grauen aufgesucht:
mein Herz hat auch im wüstesten Lärmen nicht geschwiegen,
es hat gerast, geweint, geflucht—
und wenn mir nach dem Frieden noch zu leben beschieden ist,
will ich immer lauter aussagen, was dann zu sagen ist!

(Auf dem Marsche in Polen, Februar 1915.)

126. Fritz Max Cahén, "Der Alfred Richard Meyer-Kreis," in *Expressionismus: Aufzeichnungen,* ed. Raabe, pp. 114-15.

127. See *Das Chaos,* pp. 1-2. The forword is dated "Pyrmont, im August 1917."

128. Ibid., p. 1.

In einer Hinsicht glaubte ich nicht unentschuldigt zu sein: ich hatte mich, bis dahin ein empfindsamer Skeptiker, nur ausnahmsweise mit Politik abgegeben; ich kannte bei Kriegsausbruch die politische Lage nicht, ich sah sie falsch, und war nicht beeinflussbar, aber leichtgläubig. Inzwischen habe ich gelernt, dass es eine Schuld ist, politisch nicht unterrichtet zu sein; aber wie sollte ich damals das wissen, und um wie viele stand es anders? Ich habe damals nicht umgelernt, denn ich hatte—schlimm genug—noch nicht gelernt. Als der Krieg ausbrach, lebte ich nur im ungeheuren Gefühl, dass Krieg sei; nichts als das; ohne zu wissen oder zu denken, was gut sei und was böse. Ich fühlte—es steht im ersten Gedicht—er sei das Böse; aber ich glaubte, er sei damit eine Revolution gegen eine bösere und seiner würdige Welt. Ich glaubte alles; ich glaubte auch—es steht im zweiten Gedicht—dass Völker, nicht Menschen am Krieg Schuld hätten. Ich kam zu der Verblendung, dass der verrottete Zustand des letzten Friedens den Leidenden schlimmer gewesen sei als der Krieg—und schrieb das Gedicht 'Soldaten.' Ich hatte über den Krieg wohl mit Freunden in akademischem Tone diskutiert, ja ich habe das Unrecht psychologischer Betrachtung begangen—und dabei versäumt, seinen entsetzlichen Gedanken vor seiner Wirklichkeit zu erleben. So kam es, dass ich so Falsches glaubte—bis ich sah. Und wenig später hätte ich dies nicht sehn und nicht glauben können: nun erst verstand ich die Beziehung von Krieg und Frieden.

129. See "Verzeichnis der Mitarbeiter und Beiträge," in *Die Aktion,* ed. Raabe (Stuttgart, 1961), vol. 1, p. 77.

130. Graf, *Wir sind;* Frank, *Links.*

131. Graf, *Wir sind,* pp. 72ff., 138ff.

132. Ibid., pp. 143ff.

133. Ibid., pp. 143ff., esp. 165ff.

134. Ibid., pp. 185ff., 210, 320ff. See also Graf's revolutionary poetry from this period: Oskar Maria Graf, *Die Revolutionäre,* Das neuste Gedicht, 4 (Dresden, 1918).

135. Frank, *Links*, pp. 90ff.

136. Ibid., pp. 90-91.

137. Ibid., pp. 93ff., 101, 109-10. Leonard Frank, *Der Mensch ist gut* (Zürich, 1918).

138. Raoul Hausmann, "Club Dada: Berlin 1918-1920," in *Expressionismus: Aufzeichnungen*, ed. Raabe, p. 233. See Hugo Ball's definition of Dada in an entry in his journal from the time of the beginning of the Zürich "Cabaret Voltaire": "Was wir Dada nennen, ist ein Narrenspiel aus dem Nichts... Da der Bankrott der Ideen das Menschenbild bis in die innersten Schichten zerblättert hat, treten in pathologischer Weise die Triebe und Hintergründe hervor. Da keinerlei Kunst, Politik oder Bekenntnis diesem Dammbruch gewachsen scheinen, bleibt nur die Blague und die blutige Pose." *Die Flucht*, p. 92.

139. Hausmann, "Club Dada," pp. 232-34; Richard Huelsenbeck, "Die dadaistische Bewegung," *Die neue Rundschau* 31 (1920), 972-79.

140. See, e.g., the Dadaist manifesto "Was ist der Dadaismus und was will er in Deutschland?" reprinted in Paul Pörtner, *Literatur-Revolution*, vol. 2, pp. 503-4.

141. Huelsenbeck, "Die dadaistische Bewegung," passim; Richard Huelsenbeck, "Dada oder der Sinn im Chaos," introduction to *Dada: Eine literarische Dokumentation*, ed. Richard Huelsenbeck (Reinbek bei Hamburg, 1964), p. 10 and passim; Richard Huelsenbeck, *Mit Witz, Licht und Grütze: Auf den Spuren des Dadaismus* (Wiesbaden, 1957), p. 89 and passim; Jung, *Der Weg*, pp. 110ff.

142. See Erich Mühsam's foreword to his journal reprinted in Raabe, *Die Zeitschriften*, p. 38.

143. Raabe, *Die Zeitschriften*, pp. 32-33, 38-39. Here, on p. 38, Raabe prints Mühsam's open letter announcing the suspension of publication of *Kain* in 1914.

144. Raabe, *Die Zeitschriften*, pp. 50, 52-54. On *Revolution* see also Ball, *Briefe*, p. 22; Ball, *Die Flucht*, p. 7; Richard Huelsenbeck, "Zürich 1916, wie es wirklich war," in *Expressionismus: Aufzeichnungen*, ed. Raabe, pp. 174-75. On *Das Forum* see also Herzog, *Menschen*, passim.

145. Raabe, *Die Zeitschriften*, p. 50.

146. Ibid., p. 53.

147. See note 111.

148. See Raabe, *Die Zeitschriften*, p. 34 and the chapter below on *Die Aktion*.

149. Jung, *Der Weg*, pp. 125ff.

150. See Pfemfert's public appeal for funds for this purpose which was printed as a flier and circulated in November, 1915. The flier is republished in *Expressionismus: Literatur und Kunst*, ed. Zeller, et al., p. 120.

151. Erwin Piscator, "Die politische Bedeutung der *Aktion*," in *Expressionismus: Aufzeichnungen*, ed. Raabe, pp. 192ff.

Man lebte damals in einem merkwürdigen Zwischen- und Schwebezustand. Man kam nach den Kriegsjahren nur langsam zur Besinnung. Vierzig Jahre lang hatte man im tiefsten Frieden gelebt. Eine herrliche, unbeschwerte, paradiesische Jugend lag hinter uns. Nun war auf einmal das ganze Dasein höchst problematisch geworden, man fühlte sich unsicher, bedroht, womöglich bespitzelt und denunziert. Es gab wenig zu essen. Man fühlte sich unfrei, wie geschoben, und wusste nicht, von welcher Seite und in welche Richtung. Man hätte gern Ordnung in seine Gedanken gebracht und kam doch zu keinem Ergebnis. Damals begann ich mein Dasein als das eines Menschen zu empfinden, der in dem vertrauten Boden überlieferter, anerkannter und befriedigender Gegebenheiten wurzelte und gezwungen wurde, ein nebelhaftes, undeutliches Dasein zu führen, man gehörte keiner Vergangenheit mehr an und noch keiner Zukunft. Es gab auch keine Gutgläubigkeit mehr, sondern eine Art summarischen Zynismus, ein sehr gefährliches Laisser-aller, an dem viele Zeitgenossen zerbrachen.

152.   See Rosenberg, *Die Entstehung,* pp. 215-57; Arthur Rosenberg, *Geschichte der Weimarer Republik* (Frankfurt a.M., 1961), pp. 125ff.

153.   Starke, *Was mein Leben,* p. 78. See also Piscator, *Das politische,* p. 35.

154.   This ideological blending of Expressionism and the Revolution is most prominent in the formulation of the Activist program. See esp. the essays in *Das Ziel,* ed. Kurt Hiller 1-2 (Munich and Berlin, 1916-18), 3-4 (Leipzig, 1919-20), 5 (Vienna, 1923). See also the manifestoes republished in Pörtner, *Literatur-Revolution,* pp. 393-472.

155.   See esp. *Kameraden der Menschheit: Dichtungen zur Weltrevolution,* ed. Ludwig Rubiner (Potsdam, 1919); *Die Gemeinschaft: Dokumente der geistigen Weltwende,* ed. Ludwig Rubiner (Potsdam, 1919).

156.   Hirsch, *Heimkehr,* p. 66.

157.   Ibid.; Armin T. Wegner, "Aufbruch: Berlin 1910," in *Expressionismus: Aufzeichnungen,* ed. Raabe, p. 21.

158.   Wegner, "Aufbruch," p. 21.

159.   Hirsch, *Heimkehr,* p. 68; Buchheim, *Brücke,* p. 81; Thomas Grochowiak, *Ludwig Meidner* (Recklinghausen, 1966), pp. 148-49; Bernard S. Myers, *The German Expressionists: A Generation in Revolt* (New York and Washington, 1966), pp. 217-23; Peter Selz, *German Expressionist Painting* (Berkeley and Los Angeles, 1957), pp. 312-13.

160.   Hirsch, *Heimkehr,* p. 68. See also the manifestoes of this group reprinted in *Manifeste: Manifeste: 1905-1933,* Schriften deutscher Künstler des zwanzigsten Jahrhunderts, vol. 1, ed. Diether Schmidt (Dresden, n.d.), pp. 156-59.

161.   Raabe, *Die Zeitschriften,* pp. 155-56; *Manifeste,* ed. Schmidt, pp. 243-45.

162.   Myers, *The German,* p. 220; Selz, *German Expressionist,* p. 313. Manifestoes issued by these groups are republished in *Manifeste,* ed. Schmidt, pp. 178-81.

163.   *Manifeste,* ed. Schmidt, p. 244.

        "Die Revolution hat uns die Freiheit gebracht, jahrelange Wünsche zu äussern und zu verwirklichen."

164.   Walden, "Aus meinen Erinerunge," pp. 61ff.

165.   See the chapter below on *Der Sturm.*

166.   Paul Raabe, "*Die Aktion:* Geschichte einer Zeitschrift," introduction to the reprint of Pfemfert's journal *Die Aktion,* ed. Paul Raabe (Stuttgart, 1961), vol. 1, p. 19.

167.   Raabe, *"Die Aktion,"* p. 19. See *Die Aktion* 8 (1918): 613ff.

168.   Franz Pfemfert, "Kleiner Briefkasten," *Die Aktion* (1918): 364.

169.   Fritz Schlawe, *Literarische Zeitschriften: 1910-1933,* pt. 2, Sammlung Metzler, 24 (Stuttgart, 1962), p. 85.

170.   See Flake's description of Berlin around this time in *Es wird,* pp. 242-43.

171.   Raabe, *Die Zeitschriften*, pp. 62-85.

172.   See below, the chapter on Berlin.

173.   Krell, *Das alles*, pp. 259-60.

Mit dem Waffenstillstand hatte ein Aufatmen eingesetzt. Dass die Kanonen schwiegen, war schon eine Erleichterung. Man wollte aufräumen, nicht nur mit den Gesetzen des Krieges, sondern auch mit denen, die zu ihm geführt hatten. In aller Enge der Verhälnisse hatte man doch das Gefühl, die Freiheit des Wortes, der Künste, die dem Leben einen reicheren Inhalt geben sollten, des Theaters, der Dichtung seien gerettet.

Mit einem Bienenfleiss ohnegleichen ging man daran, zu zeigen, dass die Niederlage keineswegs die geistige und die moralische Widerstandskraft gebrochen hatte.

In der Tat, vor der immer wieder von Stürmen gebeutelten Schicksalskulisse spielte das kulturelle Leben ein grosses Spiel.

174.   Nico Rost, a Dutch newspaper correspondent stationed in Berlin after the war and a friend of Benn during the same period, reports that Benn sat most often now in a very "unpretentious" café located near Benn's medical practice and called Reichskanzlei, and was to be seen only rarely in Das Romanische Café. See Nico Rost, "Meine Begegnungen mit Gottfried Benn," in Benn, *Den Traum*, pp. 50-51.

175.   As Rost's reports make clear, Benn was still very close to Carl Einstein, for one, during the 1920s. See Rost, "Meine Begegnungen," pp. 39ff. Benn also saw Lasker-Schüler from time to time during this period. See Paul Raabe, "Gottfried Benns Huldigungen an Else Lasker-Schüler: Unbekannte Dokumente des Dichters 1931-1932," in Benn, *Den Traum*, pp. 61-79. On other contacts see, e.g., Jung, *Der Weg*, p. 160.

176.   See on the circles mentioned *Expressionismus: Aufzeichnungen*, ed. Raabe, passim and source bibliography there, pp. 401-8.

177.   See below, the chapters on Berlin and *Neue Jugend*.

178.   Harry Graf Kessler, *Tagebücher: 1918-1937*, ed. Wolfgang Pfeiffer-Belli (Frankfurt a.M., 1961), p. 130.

"Die Publikationen, zum Teil interessante, schiessen wie die Pilze empor."

179.   Raabe, *Die Zeitschriften*, pp. 25-113.

180.   Ibid., pp. 180-97.

181.   Ibid., pp. 163ff.

182.   Ibid., pp. 126-29, 140-50, 154-59, 203-5.

183.   See below, the chapter on Berlin.

184.   See *Die Aktion* during the war years, 4-8 (1914-18), esp. the series of "Verse vom Schlachtfeld" by Wilhelm Klemm, *Die Aktion* 4 (1914): 834ff.

185.   See, e.g., the political verse in *Kameraden der Menschheit: Dichtungen zur Weltrevoltuion*, ed. Ludwig Rubiner (Potsdam, 1919).

186.   Behl, "Begegnungen," pp. 298-99; Rothe, "Theater," pp. 238ff; Jung, *Der Weg*, pp. 302-14; Krell, pp. 259-60; Marcuse, *Mein zwanzigstes*, pp. 68ff; Kuhn, "Das Gegenständliche," p. 205f; Ball, *Briefe*, p. 36; Jhering, *Begegnungen*, pp. 128-129. See also Raabe, "Das literarische Leben," p. 18; Hans Knudsen, *Deutsche Theater-Geschichte* (Stuttgart, 1959), pp. 341ff.

187.   Huelsenbeck, "Die dadaistische Bewegung," p. 972; Friedrich Markus Huebner, "Der Expressionismus in Deutschland," in *Expressionismus: Der Kampf*, ed. Raabe, pp. 142-43, 145-46.

188. Durieux, *Eine Tür*, p. 145.

189. Jung, *Der Weg*, pp. 303-4; Rothe, "Theater," pp. 238ff.

190. Lothar Schreyer, *Erinnerung an Sturm und Bauhaus: Was ist des Menschen Bild?* (Munich, 1956), pp. 81ff; Starke, *Was mein Leben*, p. 70.

191. Rosenberg, *Die Entstehung*, pp. 242ff.

192. Hasenclever, *Gedichte*, ed. Pinthus, pp. 502-3; Pinthus, "Walter Hasenclever," pp. 26-28ff.

193. The indirect statement of this loss of political faith comes in Hasenclever's political comedy *Die Entscheidung* (Berlin, 1919). See Pinthus, "Walter Hasenclever," pp. 26-28ff.

194. René Schickele, *Der neunte November*, Tribüne der Kunst und Zeit, vol. 8 (Berlin, 1919), pp. 21-22. This essay is reprinted without the "Nachwort" and "Anhang" of the original edition in René Schickele, *Werke in drei Bänden*, ed. Hermann Kesten (Cologne and Berlin, 1959), vol. 3, pp. 459-90.

   "Die neue Welt hat begonnen. Das ist sie, die befreite Menschheit... Jetzt! Beginnen wir, befreit vom Gepäck des Mittelalters, den Marsch in die Neuzeit! Los!"

195. Schickele, *Der neunte November*, p. 86.

   Heute, noch nicht ein Jahr später, müsste ich eine namenlose Enttäuschung bekennen, hätten nicht die inneren Kämpfe, die ich während des Krieges ausgetragen habe, mich auf diese Enttäuschung vorbereitet.

196. Ibid., 86-99. Schickele already had forebodings of this development and was already warning against the possibility of it in the main text of this essay. See pp. 33ff.

197. See, e.g., political circulars put out by the latter government and signed by Toller, reprinted in *Appelle einer Revolution: Dokumente aus Bayern zum Jahr 1918/1919: Das Ende der Monarchie, Das revolutionäre Interregnum, Die Rätezeit*, ed. Karl-Ludwig Ay (Munich, 1968), appendixes 64, 66, 68, 70, 72. See also Ernst Toller, *Eine Jugend in Deutschland*, reprinted in Ernst Toller, *Prosa, Briefe, Dramen, Gedichte* (Reinbek bei Hamburg, 1961), pp. 81ff., 99-140.

198. Toller, *Briefe aus dem Gefängnis*, reprinted in Toller, *Prosa*, p. 196.

199. Raabe, *Die Zeitschriften*, pp. 133ff.

200. See *Kameraden der Menschheit: Dichtungen zur Weltrevolution*, ed. Ludwig Rubiner (Potsdam, 1919), pp. 173-76; *Die Gemeinschaft: Dokumente der geistigen Weltwende*, ed. Ludwig Rubiner (Potsdam, 1919), pp. 5-6.

201. *Verkündigung: Anthologie junger Lyrik*, ed. Rudolf Kayser (Munich, 1921). The first printing, a special edition for bibliophiles, came out in the summer of 1920. See Raabe, *Die Zeitschriften*, pp. 147-48.

202. *Verkündigung*, pp. v-vi.

   Diese Zeit—es ist Herbst 1920, und die Atmosphäre sehr müde und verbraucht—ist alles Andere als Aufstieg oder Vollendung. . . . Nach Jahren jugendlichen Brausens, aufflammender Rufe und Revolutionen müssen wir heute bekennen: uns ward keine Erfüllung; wir sind Gejagte und Suchende, wartend zwischen Sohnes- und Vater-schaft. . . . Zum ersten Male in unseren Tagen ist hier eine Jugend versammelt, die kein übertreibender Optimismus anführt.

203. *Die Aktion* 8 (1918): 613-20.

204. Carl Sternheim, *Berlin oder Juste Milieu* (Munich, 1920).

205. *Briefe der Expressionisten,* ed. Kasimir Edschmid (Frankfurt a.M. and Berlin, 1964), pp. 66-67. See also Goll, *Ich verzeihe,* pp. 105ff.

206. The essay was originally published in *Zenit* 1 (1921): 8-9, and is reprinted in *Expressionismus: Der Kampf,* ed. Raabe, pp. 180-81.

   Was aller Orten gemunkelt, belächelt, geahnt wird, bestätigt sich: wieder stirbt eine Kunst an der Zeit, die sie verrät. Ob die Schuld an der Kunst liegt oder an der Zeit, ist ohne Belang. Wollte man kritisch sein, so wäre allerdings nachweisbar, dass der Expressionismus an jenem Revolutionsaas krepiert, dessen mütterliche Pythia er sein wollte....
   Und: Expressionismus war eine schöne, gute, grosse Sache. Solidarität der Geistigen. Aufmarsch der Wahrhaftigen.
   Aber das Resultat ist leider, und ohne Schuld der Expressionisten, die deutsche Republik, 1920....
   Jawohl, mein guter Bruder Expressionist: das Leben zu *ernst* zu nehmen, ist heute die Gefahr. Kampf ist zur Groteske geworden. Geist in dieser Schieberepoche Ulk....
   Der 'gute Mensch' mit einer verzweifelten Vergeugung begibt sich in die Kulisse.

207. *Menschheitsdämmerung,* ed. Pinthus (1959), pp. 33-35.

208. See below, the chapter on *Der Sturm.*

209. See Herwarth Walden, "Vulgär-Expressionismus," *Das Wort* 3 (1938), 89-100.

210. Franz Pfemfert, "Kleiner Briefkasten," *Die Aktion* 8 (1918): 364.

   Als es notwendig schien, dem jungen Deutschland die Öffentlichkeit zu erzwingen, fand jeder, in dem ich auch nur einen Funken Begabung zu spüren glaubte, hier ein Wirkungsfeld. Es macht mir nichts aus, dass ich bisweilen missgriff, dass für viele "Junge" die *Aktion* bloss das Sprungbrett in den Journalismus war. Ich schüttelte solche Burschen eben wortlos ab und hatte dann das Vergnügen, "Absagen" zu erhalten von den Weggejagten. Ich nahm nichts übel, denn es waren Zeitprodukte. Nur durch die völlige Kulturlosigkeit unserer Literatur konnte es möglich werden, was wir immer wieder erlebten: dass ein Pubertätsepigone Hasenclever sich als ein Dramatiker auftun durfte, dass ein grober Unfug wie die *Seeschlacht* als Theatersensation ausgerufen, ein Edschmid, ein Kornfeld usw, als Dichter angesprochen werden konnten. Das alles ist gewiss beschämend, aber gefährlich wurde es erst seit dem August 1914. Das 'Junge Deutschland' verkroch sich hinter dem breiten goldnen Rücken der Bourgeoisie, um gut zu verdienen. Jugend ist ein Geschäft geworden, und nie waren Geschäfte geistige Angelegenheiten. Zur Zeit vermag ich gegen diese Gesellschaft nichts anderes zu tun, als sie rücksichtslos von meiner Schwelle zu jagen, damit sie uns nicht kompromittiere.

211. Kasimir Edschmid, "Stand des Expressionismus," originally in *Deutscher Expressionismus* (Darmstadt, 1920), pp. 18-25, reprinted in *Expressionismus: Der Kampf,* ed. Raabe, pp. 173-76.

212. Johannes R. Becher to Walter Rheiner, Haar b. München May 24, 1920, published in *Briefe der Expressionisten,* ed. Edschmid, pp. 20-22.

   "ich sehe unergriffen dem vollständigen Verfall und der blamablen Pleite alles dessen entgegen, was sich das Wörtchen 'Expressionismus' umhängte."

213. Jung, *Der Weg,* p. 302.

   "Der Expressionismus hatte sich verflacht, war unter die Kontrolle der Lektorate der grossen Verlagsanstalten geraten."

214. On the S. Fischer Verlag see, e.g., the yearbooks ed. by Alfred Wolfenstein: *Die Erhebung* 1 (Berlin, 1919), 2 (Berlin, 1920); and the series *Dichtungen und Bekenntnisse aus unserer Zeit*

in 24 volumes (Berlin, 1919-20). On the Gustav Kiepenheuer Verlag see, e.g., its publication of *Das Forum* (1919-20), and of the volumes ed. by Ludwig Rubiner: *Kameraden der Menschheit* (Potsdam, 1919), *Die Gemeinschaft* (Potsdam, 1919). See Raabe, *Die Zeitschriften*, pp. 52-54, 76, 127-28, 141-43, 188, 193-94; Hermann Kasack, "Erinnerung an Gustav Kiepenheuer," in Hermann Kasack, *Mosaiksteine: Beiträge zu Literatur und Kunst* (Frankfurt a.M., 1956), pp. 289-296; *Die Erhebung* 1, p. 424; 2, pp. 388-89; Paul Westheim, "Wie *Das Kunstblatt* entstand," in *Expressionismus: Aufzeichnungen,* ed. Raabe, pp. 210-14.

215. In March, 1918, Edschmid's noted essay "Über den dichterischen Expressionismus," was published in *Die neue Rundschau* 29 (1918): 359-74, under the title "Expressionismus in der Dichtung," but it was not allowed to stand alone without editorial comment. A preface was added to it, without Edschmid's knowledge, in which the editor made clear the journal's lack of sympathy for the literature the essay represented:

> Wir brauchen nicht zu betonen, dass eine programmatische Bindung in dieser Zeitschrift damit nicht nur nicht gegeben ist, sondern dass wir die ästhetische und literar-historische Rangordnung der Werte, soweit sie sich auf die Produktion der letzten dreissig Jahre bezieht, durchaus ablehnen.

In the June, 1918, issue of *Die neue Rundschau* 29 (1918): 838-43, 843-50, appeared replies to the Edschmid essay by Hermann Hesse, "Zu 'Expressionismus in der Dichtung,'" and by Alfred Döblin, "Von der Freiheit eines Dichtermenschen." *Die neue Rundschau* had further published in September, 1915, a much more critical essay on Expressionism by Otto Flake under the title "Von der jüngsten Literatur," *Die neue Rundschau* 26 (1915): 1276-87. See also Edschmid, *Lebendiger Expressionismus*, p. 325f. The essays by Edschmid, Hesse, and Döblin just cited are reprinted in *Expressionismus: Der Kampf,* ed. Raabe, pp. 90-121.

214. Walter Mehring, "Die neue Form," *Die neue Rundschau* 31 (1920): 124-27. See also Walter Mehring, *Die verrufene Malerei: Von Malern, Kennern und Sammlern* (Zürich, 1958), pp. 7-16.

217. See, e.g., Friedrich Markus Huebner, "Der Expressionismus in Deutschland" (1920), reprinted in *Expressionismus: Der Kampf,* ed. Raabe, pp. 133-46; Walter von Molo, "Bekenntnis zum Expressionismus" (1920), reprinted in *Expressionismus: Der Kampf,* ed. Raabe, pp. 157-60; Max Krell, *Über neue Prosa,* Tribüne der Kunst und Zeit, vol. 7 (Berlin, 1919); various articles, e.g., Paul Hatvani, "Der Expressionismus ist tot . . . es lebe der Expressionismus" (1919), reprinted in *Expressionismus: Der Kampf,* ed. Raabe, pp. 273-77; Rudolf Kayser, "Das Ende des Expressionismus" (1920), reprinted in Pörtner, *Literatur-Revolution,* pp. 318-24; Wilhelm Worringer, *Künstlerische Zeitfragen* (Munich, 1921), pp. 7-8.

218. See the other numerous obituaries of the movement from this period which are reprinted in *Expressionismus: Der Kampf,* ed. Raabe, pp. 189ff., and in Pörtner, *Literatur-Revolution,* pp. 368ff.

"Der Expressionismus ist tot."

Chapter 2

1. Mühsam, *Unpolitische Erinnerungen,* pp. 51ff; Seewald, *Der Mann,* pp. 135ff; Albert Soergel and Curt Hohoff, *Dichtung und Dichter der Zeit: Vom Naturalismus bis zur Gegenwart,* vol. 1 (Düsseldorf, 1961), pp. 630ff.

2. Mühsam, *Unpolitische Erinnerungen,* pp. 8-9, 30ff., 51ff; Heinrich Hart, *Gesammelte Werke,* ed. Julius Hart, vol. 3 (Berlin, 1907), pp. 64ff., 95-96; Soergel, *Dichtung,* vol. 1 p. 238.

3. Mühsam, *Unpolitische Erinnerungen,* pp. 8-9, 30ff., 50; Else Lasker-Schüler, *Wo ist unser buntes Theben, Briefe von Else Lasker-Schüler,* ed. Margarete Kupper, vol. 2 (Munich, 1969), p. 13.

4. Mühsam, *Unpolitische Erinnerungen,* pp. 68ff; Zweig, *Die Welt,* pp. 139ff.

5. Mühsam, *Unpolitische Erinnerungen,* p. 68.

6. Ibid., pp. 68ff; Zweig, *Die Welt,* pp. 139ff; Lasker-Schüler, *Wo ist,* p. 15 and footnote 306 on p. 334.

7. Rudolf Kayser, "Literatur in Berlin, " *Das junge Deutschland* 1 (1918/19): 41-42, reprinted in *Expressionismus: Der Kampf,* ed. Raabe, pp. 130-132.

8. Kayser, "Literatur in Berlin," p. 130.

Als europäische Stadt erstand sie auf der Grenze zweier Welten, die beide keine Beziehung zum Geist haben: der korrekten Nüchternheit des alten Preussens und der schrankenlosen Gewinngier der Gründerjahre. Darum mangelte dem neuen Berlin: Eindeutigkeit, Gesinnung, Stil. Der Bewohner ward eine groteske Mischung eckigen Beamtentums und waghalsiger Unternehmerlust. Die Stadt, die sich um ihn emportürmte, schien ihm ein Produkt von Polizeiverordnungen, Geschäften und Operetten zu sein. In ihr blieben die Menschen liebeleer, ihren privaten Zwecken hingegeben, auch keinem Gewitter politischer Leidenschaft unterstellt.

9. Mehring, *Die verlorene Bibliothek,* p. 141.

10. Lasker-Schüler, *Wo ist,* p. 39.

11. The first signs of Expressionism in Germany apparently appeared in painting in the work of the "Brücke" artists residing in Dresden around 1905, and then, a few years later around 1909, in the work of the members of the "Neue Künstlervereinigung" in Munich. The "Brücke" group, however, moved practically *en masse* to Berlin in 1911, and then began dispersing. See Buchheim, *Brücke,* pp. 60ff; Huebner, "Der Expressionismus in Deutschland," pp. 137-38. On the move of the center of the avant-garde to Berlin see also Erwin Alexander-Katz, "Zukünftler," *B.Z. am Mittag* (6 May 1912), no. 106, first supplement.

12. See Raabe, *Die Zeitschriften,* pp. 25-119.

13. Ibid., pp. 47-50.

14. The major houses are indexed in Raabe, *Die Zeitschriften,* pp. 261-63.

15. See the chapters below on these groups.

16. See Mehring, "Berlin Avantgarde," p. 118; also chapter 1, notes 64, 65.

17. See the chapters below on these groups.

18. Flake, *Es wird,* p. 200.

Arp war in Paris gewesen und berichtete von den Experimenten der Maler; eine Unruhe ging durch die künstlerische wie durch die geistige Welt. Das Exotische trat ins Blickfeld und war nicht nur, wie vor hundert Jahren, ein romantischer Reiz; es verkörperte neue Denkimpulse, Erkenntnismotive. Die Sicherheit des Europäers, die führende Rasse zu sein, die Zivilisation schlechthin geformt zu haben, wankte. Es gab Kulturen, die nicht auf seinen Ideen aufgebaut waren, nicht auf Fortschritt, Bewusstsein, Steigerung der technischen Energie, und sie wussten vielleicht mehr vom Magischen, Bedeutsamen als er. Man dünkte sich nicht erhabener als die Primitiven; die Literaten waren sogar bereit, die Negerplastik über die ganze Antike zu stellen.

19. Walden, "Aus meinen Erinnerungen," p. 13; Buchheim, *Brücke*, pp. 62, 373; Grochowiak, *Meidner*, p. 224; Shattuck, *The Banquet Years*, p. 280.

20. Guillaume Apollinaire, "Realité, peinture pure," *Der Sturm* 3 (1912): 224-25. Subsequent to this article, other publications by Apollinaire appeared in succeeding issues of *Der Sturm*, in 1913 and 1914.

21. See list of exhibitions in *Der Sturm: Ein Erinnerungsbuch an Herwarth Walden und die Künstler aus dem Sturmkreis*, ed. Nell Walden and Lothar Schreyer (Baden-Baden, 1954), p. 257.

22. Buchheim, *Brücke*, p. 379.

23. Friedrich Burschell, "Zwischen München und Berlin," *Deutsche Rundschau* 89 (1963): 33.

24. See Raabe, *Die Zeitschriften*, pp. 86, 90; Friedrich Burschell, "*Revolution* und *Neue Erde:* München 1918/19: Aus meinen Erinnerungen," in *Expressionismus: Aufzeichnungen*, ed. Raabe, pp. 251-57.

25. Grosz, *A Little Yes*, p. 137.

26. Jung, *Der Weg*, p. 83.

27. Raabe, *Die Zeitschriften*, pp. 41ff.

28. See list in *Die Aktion*, ed. Raabe (Stuttgart, 1961), vol. 1, p. 123.

29. See list in *Der Sturm*, ed. Nell Walden and Lothar Schreyer, pp. 257-260.

30. Ball, *Briefe*, p. 33.

    "Das Leben hier ist grandios und überstürzt mich mit Eindrücken und Neuem."

31. See Durieux, *Eine Tür*, pp. 93-93; also Flake, *Es wird*, p. 205.

32. See list in *Die Aktion*, ed. Raabe (Stuttgart, 1961), vol. 1, p. 123.

33. See Meyer, *die maer*, pp. 32ff. An example of poetry from this circle associated with popular dancing is the lyrical broadsheet published by the Alfred Richard Meyer Verlag entitled *Ballhaus: Ein lyrisches Flugblatt von Ernst Blass, Max Brod*...(Berlin-Wilmersdorf, 1912). See description of it in Raabe, *Die Zeitschriften*, p. 134. See also Alfred Richard Meyer, "Paris" and "Drei Mädchenporträts aus dem Türkischen Zelt zu Charlottenburg," *Der Sturm* 4 (1913): 85-86 and 199, respectively.

34. Durieux, *Eine Tür*, pp. 93-93. See similar descriptions in Flake, *Es wird*, pp. 204ff; Meyer, *die maer*, pp. 32ff; Grosz, *A Little Yes*, pp. 137ff.

    In Halensee hatte man den Lunapark, auf den einst die Fenster meiner bescheidenen Wohnung schauten, zu einem grossartigen Vergnügungsetablissement umgebaut, mit allen Überraschungen und Erfindungen, die man damals kannte. Überall gab es Geschrei, Gelächter und Fröhlichkeit. Ein grosser Tanzsaal wimmelte Abend für Abend von Menschen, die es vorzogen, im Strassenanzug zu tanzen. Hier war der Treffpunkt der Bohème, der Maler, der Schriftsteller, hier traf man würdige Träger bekannter Namen, die sich plötzlich vergnügten und mit einem hübschen Mädel unermüdlich bis zum Morgen tanzten. Die Bars und das 'Palais de Dance' stellten schon andere Ansprüche an den äusseren Menschen und an das Portemonnaie. Der One-step war eben aufgekommen, und nach dem Schlager 'Boby, wo hast du deine Haare' tanzte man 'Holzbein,' das heisst man hüpfte mit einem lahmen Bein den Saal entlang. Ein Rausch hatte ganz Berlin erfasst.
    ...
    Arbeitslust, Lebensfreude füllte Berlin bis zum Platzen, und kein Mensch ahnte, dass in unserem tollen Reigen das Kriegsgespenst drohend mittanzte. Wohl gab es einige Stimmen,

die sich warnend erhoben, aber die Ohren waren verstopft. Es war, als ob jeder noch in einer unbewussten Angst drängte, das Leben zu geniessen, zu lachen, zu tollen, bevor das Entsetzliche hereinbrach.

35. Krell, *Das alles,* p. 32; Wolfgang Goetz, *Im "Grössenwahn," bei Pschorr und anderswo... Erinnerungen an Berliner Stammtische* (Berlin, 1936), pp. 37-38; Walden, "Aus meinen Erinnerungen," p. 38.

36. See Raabe, *Die Zeitschriften,* pp. 25-55.

37. Raabe, *Die Zeitschriften,* p. 60. See also Jung, *Der Weg,* p. 109. Hausmann, "Club Dada," p. 232.

38. Jung, *Der Weg,* p. 109.

39. See below, the chapter on the Berlin Dadaists.

40. Raabe, *Die Zeitschriften,* pp. 60-61, 62-63.

41. See Durieux, *Eine Tür,* pp. 118ff., and below, the chapter on Cassirer.

42. See below, the chapter on the Berlin Dadaists.

43. See below, the chapters on these circles.

44. See below.

45. See Raabe, *Die Zeitschriften,* pp. 67-68, 73, 79-80, 80-82, 82-83, 84-85.

46. See Ibid., pp. 175-59.

47. Heinz Herald, "Das junge Deutschland: Erstes Jahr," *Das junge Deutschland* 1 (1918): 193. On "Das junge Deutschland" see also Knudsen, *Deutsche Theater-Geschichte,* pp. 336ff; Behl, "Begegnungen," pp. 298-99; Rothe, "Theater," pp. 239-40; *Max Reinhardt: 25 Jahre Deutsches Theater: Ein Tafelwerk,* ed. Hans Rothe (Munich, 1930), p. 56.

    Was wollte das junge Deutschland? Eine Tribüne sein der jungen Generation, die sich zu regen begann, aber überall auf Widerstand stiess, die verlacht und nicht ernst genommen wurde, gerade weil sie ernst genommen werden wollte, weil sie anders war und sein musste als die Generation der Väter. Diese junge Generation verlangte herauszukommen aus der Passivität der herrschenden Kunstanschauung, sie verlangte nach Weite, Freiheit, Wirkung. Sie wollte durchgesetzt werden.

48. Herald, "Das junge Deutschland," p. 193.

49. See Herald's descriptions of the production in Herald, "Das junge Deutschland" p. 194; Heinz Herald, "Notiz zur Bettler-Aufführung," *Das junge Deutschland* 1 (1918): 30; Heinz Herald, *Max Reinhardt: Bildnis eines Theatermannes* (Hamburg, 1953), p. 43. See also Felix Hollaender, "Das junge Deutschland und Reinhard Sorge," *Das junge Deutschland* 1 (1918); 18-21.

50. See Franz Horch, *Die Spielpläne Max Reinhardts* (Munich, 1930), pp. 42, 45, 46, 49. See also *Expressionismus: Aufzeichnungen,* ed. Raabe, footnotes 2 and 3, pp. 358-59.

51. See Herald, "Das junge Deutschland," pp. 194; Rothe, "Theater," pp. 239-40; Behl, "Begegnungen," p. 298.

52. Herald, *Max Reinhardt,* p. 43.

53. See Herald, "Das junge Deutschland," pp. 193-94.

54. See Edschmid, *Lebendiger Expressionismus,* pp. 319ff.

55. Ibid., pp. 310ff.

56. Ibid., p. 310.

57. See Chapter 1, note 215. The talk was published under the title "Über den dichterischen Expressionismus," in Kasimir Edschmid, *Über den Expressionismus in der Literatur und die neue Dichtung,* Tribüne der Kunst und Zeit, vol. 1 (Berlin, 1919), pp. 39-78.

58. See Edschmid, *Lebendiger Expressionismus,* pp. 328-40. The lecture was published with the one given in Germany in 1917 in Edschmid *Über den Expressionismus,* pp. 11-38.

59. Flake, *Es wird,* pp. 242-43.

Es gab nicht nur die Annexionisten; die Sozialisten spalteten, die Geister erhitzten sich. Wie der Krieg auch ausging, die alte Zeit würde nicht wiederkehren. Man erfasste die Änderung im Unterbewussten, noch nicht mit Benennungen.

Ich selbst spürte eine seltsame Nötigung, die Sprache aufzulösen, die Sätze zu verdichten, für den Ausdruck neue Formen zu suchen. Der Expressionismus hatte damit angefangen; zum erstenmal fühlte ich mich von der Zeitströmung erfasst und mitgerissen.

60. Flake, *Es wird,* pp. 242ff.

61. Will Grohmann, *Bildende Kunst und Architektur,* vol. 3, *Zwischen den Kriegen* (Berlin, 1953), p. 32.

62. Grohmann, *Bildende Kunst,* vol. 3, p. 32.

63. See Raabe, *Die Zeitschriften,* pp. 25-119.

64. Ibid., pp. 25-119.

65. Ibid., pp. 163-97.

66. See below, the chapter on the Berlin Dadaists.

67. Kurt Pinthus, "Ernst Rowohlt und sein Verlag," introduction to *Rowohlt Almanach 1908-1962,* ed. Maria Hintermeier and Fritz J. Raddatz (Reinbek bei Hamburg, 1962), p. 20; Walther Kiaulehn, *Mein Freund der Verleger: Ernst Rowohlt und seine Zeit* (Reinbek bei Hamburt, 1967), pp. 48ff; Paul Meyer, *Ernst Rowohlt in Selbstzeugnissen und Bilddokumenten,* Sonderdruck, Rowohlts Monographien (Reinbek bei Hamburg, 1967), pp. 47ff; Arthur Seiffhart, *Inter folia fructus: Aus den Erinnerungen eines Verlegers* (Berlin, 1948), p. 15.

68. Mayer, *Rowohlt,* p. 67.

69. Ibid., pp. 62-67; Pinthus, "Rowohlt," pp. 24-25; Kiaulehn, *Rowohlt,* pp. 90f.

70. Pinthus, "Rowohlt," p. 25; Kiaulehn, *Rowohlt,* p. 90; Mayer, *Rowohlt,* p. 64.

71. Mayer, *Rowohlt,* p. 67; Pinthus, "Rowohlt," p. 25; Kiaulehn, *Rowohlt,* p. 90.

72. Mayer, *Rowohlt,* p. 67; Pinthus, "Rowohlt," p. 25.

73. Mayer, *Rowohlt,* p. 66; Pinthus, "Rowohlt," p. 25; Kiaulehn, *Rowohlt,* p. 92.

74. Pinthus, "Rowohlt," pp. 25-26; Kiaulehn, *Rowohlt,* pp. 91, 93ff.

75. Pinthus, "Rowohlt," pp. 25-26; Kiaulehn, *Rowohlt,* pp. 91, *Rowohlt,* p. 69. See also Raabe, *Die Zeitschriften,* pp. 143-45, 184-85; Kurt Pinthus, "Die Geschichte der *Menschheitsdämmerung,*" in *Gedichte der "Menschheitsdämmerung,"* ed. Horst Denkler (Munich, 1971), pp. vii-xxviii.

76. Pinthus, "Walter Hasenclever," p. 24.

77. See Knudsen, *Deutsche Theater-Geschichte,* pp. 342ff; PEM (Paul Erich Marcus), *Heimweh nach dem Kurfürstendamm: Aus Berlins glanzvollsten Tagen und Nächten* (Berlin, 1952), pp.

121ff. See the unsigned "Programm" of the theater published in its prospectus, repr. in *Literatur im Klassenkampf: Zur proletarisch-revolutionären Literaturtheorie 1919-1923: Eine Dokumentation,* ed. Walter Fähnders and Martin Rector (Munich, 1971), pp. 166-68.

78. Knudsen, *Deutsche Theater-Geschichte,* pp. 343f.

79. See Hasenclever, *Gedichte,* ed. Pinthus, pp. 27, 510, 511.

80. Pinthus, "Walter Hasenclever," pp. 21-27ff.

81. Herbert Jhering, *Von Reinhardt bis Brecht: Eine Auswahl der Theaterkritiken von 1909-1932,* ed. Rolf Badenhausen (Reinbek bei Hamburg, 1967), pp. 46-49.

82. Jherings, *Von Reinhardt,* pp. 51-54. See also Rudolf Bernauer, *Das Theater meines Lebens: Erinnerungen* (Berlin, 1955), p. 366; Siegfried Jacobsohn, *Das Jahr der Bühne,* vol. 9 (Berlin, 1920), pp. 16-22, repr. in *Deutsche Literaturkritik im zwanzigsten Jahrhundert,* ed. Hans Mayer (Stuttgart, 1965), pp. 322-28; Jürgen Rühle, *Das gefesselte Theater: Vom Revolutionstheater zum Sozialistischen Realismus* (Cologne and Berlin, 1957), p. 316; PEM, *Heimweh,* pp. 124-25.

83. See Knudsen, *Deutsche Theater-Geschichte,* pp. 344ff; PEM, *Heimweh,* pp. 125ff.

84. See below, the chapter on Cassirer.

85. See below, the chapter on *Die Aktion.*

86. See Raabe, *Die Zeitschriften,* pp. 25-119.

87. See Ibid., pp. 95-96, 96-97, 105, and the chapter on the Berlin Dadaists.

88. See Raabe, *Die Zeitschriften,* pp. 99-100, 110; and below, the chapter on the Berlin Dadaists.

89. See Raabe, *Die Zeitschriften,* pp. 25-119. The article by Walden on Expressionism from 1938, cited in note 209 of chapter 1, is a clear indication of his adherence to Expressionism well beyond its era.

90. Mühsam, *Unpolitische Erinnerungen,* pp. 30-31.

91. See, e.g., Walther Kiaulehn, *Berlin: Schicksal einer Weltstadt* (Munich and Berlin, 1958), pp. 532-65; Hermann Kesten, *Dichter im Café* (Vienna, Munich, and Basel, 1959), pp. 419-20; PEM, *Heimweh,* passim.

Chapter 3

1. Flake, *Es wird,* p. 192.

2. Blei had his own circle of friends in the Expressionist meeting place in Munich, the Café Stephanie, and was also close to Expressionist circles in Berlin, Leipzig and, during the war, in Switzerland. He was the editor of three journals associated with Expressionism: *Der lose Vogel, Summa, Die Rettung.* See Raabe, *Die Zeitschriften,* pp. 41-42, 64-65, 86-87. On Blei see below, the chapter on *Die Aktion,* and his autobiography: Franz Blei, *Erzählung eines Lebens* (Leipzig, 1930), passim. On Flake and Jacques see their autobiographies: Flake, *Es wird,* passim; Norbert Jacques, *Mit Lust gelebt: Roman meines Lebens* (Hamburg, 1950), passim.

3. Kesten, *Dichter,* p. 7.

4. Ibid., passim.

5. Szittya, *Das Kuriositäten-Kabinett* (Constance, 1923), p. 246. Evert Sprinchorn describes this group in detail in his lengthy "Introduction" to August Strindberg, *Inferno, Alone and*

other Writings, ed. Evert Sprinchorn (Garden City, 1968), pp. 10-47. See also Carl Ludwig Schleich, *Besonnte Vergangenheit: Lebenserinnerungen (1859-1919)* (Berlin, 1921), pp. 259-88. On *Pan* (1895-1900), later revived by the Expressionists, see Fritz Schlawe, *Literarische Zeitschriften: 1885-1910,* Sammlung Metzler, vol. 6, [pt. 1] (Stuttgart, 1961), pp. 48-50.

6. Schleich, *Besonnte Vergangenheit,* pp. 259-288; Sprinchorn, "Introduction," pp. 10-47; Julius Meier-Graefe, "Der Pan," *Pan* 1 (1910): 1-4.

7. Scheerbart was a member of the *Sturm* circle. See chapter on that circle below. Schleich was later a Rowohlt author. See Schleich, *Besonnte Vergangenheit,* esp. pp. 327ff. See also Mühsam, *Unpolitische Erinnerungen,* passim; Szittya, *Kuriositäten-Kabinett,* passim; Wolfgang Goetz, *Begegnungen und Bekenntnisse,* ed. Tilla Goetz (Berlin, 1964), passim. Julius Meier-Graefe was a friend of Franz Blei, Carl Sternheim, et al., had contacts with the circle of Expressionists in Dresden, and contributed to Expressionist periodicals. See Sternheim, *Vorkriegseuropa,* pp. 133-34; Alfred Günther, "Dresden im Expressionismus," in *Expressionismus: Aufzeichnungen,* ed. Raabe, p. 246.

8. See Mühsam, *Unpolitische Erinnerungen,* p. 129, 133-34; Jacques, *Mit Lust,* p. 190.

9. See Mühsam, *Unpolitische Erinnerungen,* pp. 133-34.

10. Schickele, *Werke,* vol. 3, p. 1272.

11. Heym, *Heym: Dokumente,* pp. 409-10.

12. Durieux, *Eine Tür,* pp. 46-48.

13. Mühsam, *Unpolitische Erinnerungen,* pp. 81ff.

14. See *Die Aktion,* ed. Raabe (Stuttgart, 1961), pp. 122-23.

15. See Heym, *Heym: Dokumente,* pp. 406-7.

16. Else Lasker-Schüler, *Mein Herz: Ein Liebesroman mit Bildern und wirklich lebenden Menschen,* reprinted in Else Lasker-Schüler, *Gesammelte Werke: Prosa und Schauspiele,* vol. 2, ed. Friedhelm Kemp (Munich, 1962), p. 327.

17. Meyer, *die maer,* p. 29.

18. Hausmann, "Club Dada," pp. 233-34; *Das war Dada: Dichtungen und Dokumente,* ed. Peter Schifferli, Sonderreihe, Deutscher Taschenbuch Verlag, vol. 18 (Munich, 1963), p. 173. On the Café Austria see also Szittya, *Das Kuriositäten-Kabinett,* p. 246.

19. Mühsam, *Unpolitische Erinnerungen,* p. 85. Mühsam claims here that Tilke's cabaret was Berlin's first. It has been established, however, that Ernst von Wolzogen's "Überbrettl," "Die bunte Bühne," established in Berlin in 1901, was both Berlin's and Germany's first literary cabaret. See Albert Soergel and Curt Hohoff, *Dichtung und Dichter der Zeit: Vom Naturalismus bis zur Gegenwart* (Düsseldorf, 1961), vol. 1, pp. 275-76; Gero von Wilpert, *Sachwörterbuch der Literatur* (Stuttgart, 1959), pp. 273-74; Mühsam, *Unpolitische Erinnerungen,* pp. 65, 78-79.

20. Mühsam, *Unpolitische Erinnerungen,* p. 87.

21. Julius Bab, *Richard Dehmel* (Leipzig, 1926), pp. 286ff.

22. Bab, *Dehmel,* pp. 286f.; Alfred Döblin's report in his *Journal 1952/53,* unpub. typescript, p. 18, cited by Heinz Graber in Alfred Döblin, *Briefe,* ed. Heinz Graber (Olten and Freiburg i.B., 1970), p. 505n.

23. Alfred Döblin, "Epilog," reprinted in Alfred Döblin, *Aufsätze zur Literatur,* ed. Walter Muschg (Olten and Freiburg i.B., 1963), p. 385; Flake, *Es wird,* p. 117.

24.   Alfred Döblin, e.g., first met and talked with Marinetti here, probably in the company of the *Sturm* circle, in the spring of 1913. See Alfred Döblin, "Futuristische Worttechnik: Offener Brief an F.T. Marinetti," reprinted in Pörtner, *Literatur-Revolution,* vol. 2, p. 63. See also Walden, "Aus meinen Erinnerungen," pp. 14-15.

25.   See Nell Walden, "Begegnung mit Else Lasker-Schüler," in Nell Walden, *Herwarth Walden: Ein Lebensbild* (Berlin and Mainz, 1963), p. 37; Nell Walden, "Kokoschka und der *Sturm*-Kreis," in *Expressionismus: Aufzeichnungen,* ed. Raabe, p. 133.

26.   Rudolf Leonhard reviewed this talk in a May 1, 1913, supplement to *Die Bücherei Maiandros* 4/5 (1913): 6-7. See also Rudolf Leonhard, "Marinetti in Berlin 1913," in *Expressionismus: Aufzeichnungen,* ed. Raabe, pp. 121-24. Marinetti also held lectures in Berlin under the auspices of *Der Sturm* in connection with "Der erste deutsche Herbstsalon" on November 27 and 30. See Walden, "Aus meinen Erinnerungen," p. 30; *Der Sturm,* ed. Nell Walden and Lothar Schreyer, p. 258.

27.   Else Lasker-Schüler, *Essays,* reprinted in Lasker-Schüler, *Gesammelte Werke,* vol. 2, pp. 277-79.

28.   See *Die Aktion* 2 (1914): 1456.

29.   Hans Erman, *Berliner Geschichten: Geschichte Berlins: Historien, Episoden, Anekdoten* (Rastatt, 1966), pp. 387-88; Mühsam, *Unpolitische Erinnerungen,* pp. 78ff; Hart, *Gesammelte Werke,* vol. 3, pp. 94-95.

30.   René Schickele, "Wie verhält es sich mit dem Expressionismus," reprinted in *Expressionismus: Der Kampf,* ed. Raabe, p. 178.

       "Wir waren, ausserhalb unseres Kreises, das Gesindel aus dem Café Grössenwahn [= Das Café des Westens]."

31.   Else Lasker-Schüler, *Essays,* reprinted in *Gesammelte Werke* vol. 2, p. 240. Here Lasker-Schüler reports that Hugo Caro, often a defender of Berlin Bohemian artists in Berlin court cases, considered the Café des Westens as "der Garten unter den Strassen Berlins." See also Krell, *Das alles,* pp. 18-19.

32.   Jacob, *Kind,* p. 27.

33.   See, e.g., Durieux, *Eine Tür,* p. 65; John Höxter, *So lebten wir: 25 Jahre Berliner Boheme* (Berlin, 1929), p. 44.

34.   Trust, "Der Sumpf von Berlin," *Der Sturm* 2 (1911): 652. See a similar account from the burgher's perspective in Zivier, *Das Romanische,* pp. 7-8.

       Scheu und geängstet hastet der schlichte Bürger am Höllenpfuhl vorbei. Der ehrbare Kaufmann, der sparsame Rentier, der mutige Offizier, der tiefe Gelehrte, der berufene Theaterdirektor, der standesbewusste Schauspieler, der sich Zeit lassende Handwerker, der herkömmliche Maler, der klassische Dichter, der rasende Fuhrmann, der treue Dramaturg, der tennisverdammte Demi-Jüngling, die handkoffertragende Jungfrau und, last not least, der bescheidene Lumpensammler werfen einen scheuen Blick durch die revolutionären Scheiben und empfehlen ihre Seele Wildenbruch und allen guten Geistern der grossen Kunstausstellung. Bleicher Schauer rieselt durch ihr normales Gebein, durch ihr gesundes Blut. Tief im Innern haben sie dämonische Gestalten sitzen sehen. Männer mit langen Haaren, schlangenhaft geringelten Locken, wildflatternden Krawatten, sezessionistischen Socken und alkoholfreien Unterhosen leben sich aus.

35.   Trust, "Der Sumpf," p. 651.

36. Trust, "Der Sumpf," p. 652; Höxter, *So lebten wir,* pp. 22, 26; Erman, *Berliner Geschichten,* p. 387; Blass, "Das alte," p. 37. Seewald reports that the equivalent of the Café des Westens in Munich, the Café Stephanie, was known popularly by the same nickname. See Seewald, *Der Mann,* p. 138.

37. See Trust, "Der Sumpf," p. 652; Goetz, *Begegnungen,* p. 103; Claire Jung, "Erinnerung an Georg Heym und seine Freunde," in *Expressionismus: Aufzeichnungen,* ed. Raabe, p. 49; Krell, *Das alles,* p. 19.

38. Krell, *Das alles,* pp. 19ff; Mehring, *Berlin Dada,* pp. 16, 23; Jhering, *Begegnungen,* p. 120.

39. Meyer, *die maer,* p. 12.

Man kann sich heute beim besten Willen nicht mehr vorstellen, mit welcher Erregung wir abends, im Café des Westens oder auf der Strasse vor Gerold an der Gedächtniskirche sitzend und bescheiden abendschoppend, das Erscheinen das *Sturms* oder der *Aktion* erwarteten, nicht so sehr auf den Rausch des Gedrucktseins bedacht als vielmehr scharf nach der Möglichkeit lugend: mit Worten angegriffen zu sein, die wie Ätzkalk oder Schwefelsäure wirken konnten.

40. Frank, *Links,* p. 77; Krell, *Das alles,* pp. 21ff.

41. Blass, "Das alte," p. 37.

42. Ibid., pp. 27-28.

Das war das Café meiner Schmerzen und Ahnungen, meiner Menschenscheu und meiner Ruhmsucht, meiner Freunde und Verächter, später auch meiner ersten Leidenschaft. Und was ich da unter Schmerzen mitmachte, war literarische Bewegung, Kampf gegen den enormen Spiesser.... Ja, es war schon ein seelenvoller Kampf gegen die Erlebnislosigkeit, gegen die Stumpfheit, Trägheit, Gemeinheit der Philisterwelt. Im Café, da war noch die Seele etwas wert. Ja, es war eine Erziehung zum Künstler in dieser Institution, an die ich wie an eine herbe Schule zurückdenke, nicht ohne ein Gefühl des Stolzes, sie durchgemacht zu haben.
Es war ein Zufluchtsort und ein unparlamentarisches Parlament. Auch der Furchtsame, Schweigsame lernte das Reden und den Ausdruck. Man lernte sich auf das zu besinnen, was einem wirklich am Herzen lag. Es war eine Erziehung zur Gefühlswahrheit.

43. Krell, *Das alles,* pp. 21ff; Claire Jung, "Erinnerung," p. 49; Walden, "Kokoschka," p. 133; Ball, *Briefe,* p. 25. See also, e.g., Ernst Wilhelm Lotz in a letter from Berlin to Ludwig Meidner, dated April 27, 1914, concerning Lotz's plans for soliciting contributors in this café for a journal which he and Meidner were planning to publish. The letter is published in *Briefe der Expressionisten,* ed. Edschmid, p. 18. See also there p. 17, and also above, note 38.

44. Lasker-Schüler, *Lieber gestreifter Tiger,* p. 67.

Weisst Du, das [Café des Westens] ist unsere Börse, dort muss man hin, dort schliesst man ab. Dorthin kommen alle Dramaturgen, Maler, Dichter...

45. Goll, *Ich verzeihe,* pp. 91ff.

46. Exactly when this change occurred is not clear. Lasker-Schüler was still going to the old café in November, 1920. See Lasker-Schüler, *Lieber gestreifter Tiger,* p. 82. Szittya says that he found the Café des Westens closed to the Bohemian artists when he returned to Berlin in 1921 after a year's absence from the city. See Szittya, *Das Kuriositäten-Kabinett,* p. 256. Georg Muche, *Blickpunkt: Sturm, Dada, Bauhaus, Gegenwart* (Munich, 1961), p. 177, reports on artists meeting in the Café des Westens as late as September, 1919. There are numerous reports besides Szittya's on the closing of the old café to the Bohemian clientele after the war.

See Walden, "Kokoschka," p. 133; Jacques, *Mit Lust,* p. 370f; PEM, *Heimweh,* pp. 77-78; Grochowiak, *Meidner,* p. 137; Frank, *Links,* p. 117. Krell dating this move to the Romanische Café in 1913 (*Das alles,* p. 25) is clearly a confusion of time. The Expressionists were definitely still meeting in the Café des Westens during the war. See Grosz, *A Little Yes,* p. 149; Frank, *Links,* pp. 92-93; Wieland Herzfelde, "Aus der Jugendzeit des Malik-Verlages: Zum Neudruck der Zeitschrift *Neue Jugend,*" introduction to reprint of *Neue Jugend: 1916/17* (Zürich, 1967), pp. 5-6; Else Lasker-Schüler, *Briefe an Karl Kraus,* ed. Astrid Gehlhoff-Claes (Cologne and Berlin, 1959), p. 77; Jung, *Der Weg,* p. 105; Hiller, "Begegnungen," p. 29; Georg Zivier, *Das Romanische Café: Erscheinungen und Randerscheinungen rund um die Gedächtniskirche* (Berlin, 1965), pp. 18-19.

47. See PEM, *Heimweh,* pp. 77-83; Walden, "Kokoschka," p. 133; Jacques, *Mit Lust,* p. 370f; Frank, *Links,* p. 117; Szittya, *Das Kuriositäten-Kabinett,* p. 256f; Starke, *Was mein Leben,* pp. 131-32. Zivier, *Das Romanische,* p. 19, disagrees with most chroniclers on this point.

48. See chapter 1.

49. Szittya, *Das Kuriositäten-Kabinett,* p. 256.

50. Szittya, *Das Kuriositäten-Kabinett;* PEM, *Heimweh,* p. 79.

51. PEM, *Heimweh,* pp. 77-93.

52. Walden, "Kokoschka," p. 133; PEM, *Heimweh,* pp. 77-93; Sylvia von Harden, "Erinnerungen an einst ...," in *Expressionismus: Aufzeichnungen,* ed. Raabe, p. 200; Grochowiak, *Meidner,* p. 137; Mühsam, *Unpolitische Erinnerungen,* pp. 29-31; Starke, *Was mein Leben,* pp. 126ff., 131ff; Schreyer, *Erinnerungen,* pp. 35ff; Jacques, *Mit Lust,* p. 370ff; Krell, *Das alles,* p. 25ff; Frank, *Links,* pp. 117ff; Szittya, *Das Kuriositäten-Kabinett,* pp. 256ff; Purrmann, "Erinnerungen," p. 41; Else Lasker-Schüler, *Ich räume auf!* (Zürich, 1925), reprinted in Lasker-Schüler, *Gesammelte Werke,* vol. 2, pp. 509ff; Becher, *Auf andere Art so grosse Hoffnung,* pp. 51-52; Zivier, *Das Romanische,* pp. 9ff.

53. Starke, *Was mein Leben,* p. 132; PEM, *Heimweh,* pp. 80ff; Krell, *Das alles,* p. 25f; Harden, "Erinnerungen," p. 200.

54. Rost, "Meine Begegnungen," pp. 53ff. On *Die neue Bücherschau* see Raabe, *Die Zeitschriften,* pp. 100-101.

55. Rost, "Meine Begegnungen," pp. 52ff.

56. Starke, *Was mein Leben,* p. 126; Mühsam, *Unpolitische Erinnerungen,* pp. 30-31; Frank, *Links,* p. 173.

Chapter 4

1. Hiller, "Begegnungen," p. 31; Gunter Martens, "Georg Heym und der 'Neue Club,'" in Heym, *Heym: Dokumente,* pp. 392-92; Kurt Hiller, "Notiz über ein Gespräch mit Dr. Kurt Hiller über Jakob van Hoddis," in Jakob van Hoddis, *Weltende: Gesammelte Dichtungen,* ed. Paul Pörtner (Zürich, 1958), p. 92.

2. Hiller, "Begegnungen," p. 31; Martens, "Heym," p. 393.

3. Hiller, "Begegnungen," p. 31; Erwin Loewenson, "Jakob van Hoddis: Erinnerungen mit Lebensdaten," in van Hoddis, *Weltende,* p. 100.

4. Hiller, "Begegnungen," p. 31; Martens, "Heym," p. 393; Kurt Hiller, *Die Weisheit der Langenweile: Eine Zeit- und Streitschrift* (Leipzig, 1913), I, p. 235; Loewenson, "Jakob van Hoddis," p. 100; Heinrich Eduard Jacob, "Zur Geschichte der deutschen Lyrik" in *Verse der*

Lebenden: Deutsche Lyrik seit 1910, ed. Heinrich Eduard Jacob (Berlin, 1924), p. 15. See also Thomas B. Schumann, "Geschichte des 'Neuen Clubs' in Berlin als wichtigster Anreger des literarischen Expressionismus: Eine Dokumentation," *Emuna* 9 (1974): 55-70.

5. Martens, "Heym," p. 393; Friedrich Schulze-Maizier, "Frühexistentialist unter Frühexpressionisten: Erlebnisse im Neuen Club," *Deutsche Rundschau* 88 (1962): 331; Blass, "Das alte," pp. 37f; Heinrich Eduard Jacob, "Georg Heym: Erinnerung und Gestalt," in Heym, *Heym: Dokumente,* p. 74; Jacob, "Zur Geschichte," p. 15.

6. Schulze-Maizier, "Frühexistentialist," pp. 331-32; Martens, "Heym," p. 393.

7. Martens, "Heym," p. 393.

8. Ibid., pp. 394f; Schulze-Maizier, "Frühexistentialist," pp. 332-33; Jacob, "Heym: Erinnerung," pp. 73f.

9. Martens, "Heym," pp. 395-396; Schulze-Maizier, "Frühexistentialist," pp. 332-333.

10. Jacob, "Heym: Erinnerung," p. 74; Schulze-Maizier, "Frühexistentialist," pp. 332ff; Blass, "Das alte," pp. 37ff; Martens, "Heym," p. 396.

11. Martens, "Heym," p. 396; Armin T. Wegner, "Aufbruch: Berlin 1910," in *Expressionismus: Aufzeichnungen,* ed. Raabe, pp. 20ff; Lasker-Schüler, *Mein Herz,* reprinted in *Gesammelte Werke,* vol. 2, p. 319; Jacob, "Heym: Erinnerung," pp. 63ff. Jacob and Kurtz performed at recitals of "Das neopathetische Cabaret." See Heym, *Heym: Dokumente,* pp. 403, 410.

12. Hiller, "Begegnungen," pp. 28ff; Wegner, "Aufbruch," pp. 20ff; Blass, "Das alte," p. 37; Höxter, *So lebten wir,* p. 38.

13. Höxter, *So lebten wir,* p. 38; Erwin Loewenson, "Aus einem Brief vom April 1946," in Heym, *Heym: Dokumente,* p. 92; Horst Lange, 36ff; Claire Jung, "Erinnerung," p. 49; Hiller, "Begegnungen," pp. 28ff; Lasker-Schüler, *Mein Herz,* reprinted in *Gesammelte Werke,* vol. 2, pp. 295-96, 319; Jhering, *Begegnungen,* p. 121; Mehring, *Berlin Dada,* p. 16. On the founding of "Der neue Club" see also Kurt Hiller, *Leben gegen die Zeit,* vol. 1: *Logos* (Reinbek beit Hamburg, 1969), pp. 62ff, 80ff; Jacob, "Zur Geschichte," p. 15.

14. Wegner, "Aufbruch," pp. 20-21; Jacob, "Heym: Erinnerung," p. 74; Max Brod, "Der junge Werfel und die Prager Dichter," in *Expressionismus: Aufzeichnungen,* ed. Raabe, p. 60; Kurt Pinthus, "Leipzig und der frühe Expressionismus," *Expressionismus: Aufzeichnungen,* p. 80.

15. Wegner, "Aufbruch," pp. 20-21; Jacob, "Heym: Erinnerung," p. 74; Pinthus, "Leipzig und der frühe Expressionismus," *Expressionismus: Aufzeichnungen,* ed. Raabe, p. 80; Hiller, *Die Weisheit,* 1, pp. 119-37; Kurt Hiller, foreword to *Der Konder,* ed. Kurt Hiller (Heidelberg, 1912) pp. 5-9.

16. Edschmid, *Lebendiger Expressionismus,* p. 193.

Kurt Hiller ist, mag man ihn aus der Entfernung betrachten, wie man will, nicht aus dem literarischen Leben vor dem Krieg herauszudenken. Die vorausgegangene Literatur stand stöhnend unter dem Hagel von Ohrfeigen, die er austeilte—mit einer Frische und einer Frechheit, mit einer Gescheitheit und einer Widerlichkeit, die ihr Ziel richtig trafen.

17. See Hiller, "Begegnungen," pp. 28-34; Wegner, "Aufbruch," pp. 20-21; Lasker-Schüler, *Mein Herz,* reprinted in *Gesammelte Werke,* vol. 2, pp. 295ff. and passim.

18. Kurt Hiller, *Die Weisheit der Langenweile: Eine Zeit- und Streitschrift* (Leipzig, 1913), 2 vols.

19. Schulze-Maizier, "Frühexistentialist," p. 333.

20. Hiller, "Notiz über ein Gespräch," p. 93.

21. Hiller, "Begegnungen," p. 31; Franz Pfemfert, "Die Verse des Alfred Lichtenstein," *Die Aktion* 3 (1913), 942; Johannes R. Becher, "Über Jakob van Hoddis," in *Expressionismus: Aufzeichnungen,* ed. Raabe, pp. 50-55. See also *Expressionismus: Aufzeichnungen,* p. 317 n. l; Kurt Hiller, "Notiz über ein Gespräch," p. 93; Kurt Pinthus, "Georg Heym: Nachgelassene Gedichte," in Heym, *Heym: Dokumente,* pp. 140ff.

22. See note 68, chapter 1.

23. *Menschheitsdämmerung,* ed. Pinthus (1959), p. 39.

24. See Hiller, "Begegnungen," p. 31; *Der Demokrat* 3 (1911): 43.

25. See Becher, "Über Jakob van Hoddis," pp. 50-55.

26. Ibid., p. 51-52.

Meine poetische Kraft reicht nicht aus, um die Wirkung jenes Gedichtes wiederherzustellen, von dem ich jetzt sprechen will. Auch die kühnste Phantasie meiner Leser würde ich überanstrengen bei dem Versuch, ihnen die Zauberhaftigkeit zu schildern, wie sie dieses Gedicht 'Weltende' von Jakob van Hoddis für uns in sich barg. Diese zwei Strophen, o diese acht Zeilen schienen uns in andere Menschen verwandelt zu haben, uns emporgehoben zu haben aus einer Welt stumpfer Bürgerlichkeit, die wir verachteten und von der wir nicht wussten, wie wir sie verlassen sollten. Diese acht Zeilen entführten uns. Immer neue Schönheiten entdeckten wir in diesen acht Zeilen, wir sangen sie, wir summten sie, wir murmelten sie, wir pfiffen sie vor uns hin, wir gingen mit diesen acht Zeilen auf den Lippen in die Kirchen, und wir sassen, sie vor uns hinflüsternd, mit ihnen beim Radrennen. Wir riefen sie uns gegenseitig über die Strasse hinweg zu wie Losungen, wir sassen mit diesen acht Zeilen beieinander, frierend und hungernd, und sprachen sie gegenseitig vor uns hin, und Hunger und Kälte waren nicht mehr. Was war geschehen? Wir kannten das Wort damals nicht: Verwandlung.

27. Ibid., p. 54; trans. J.M. Ritchie in *The Era of German Expressionism,* trans. J.M. Ritchie (Woodstock, 1974), p. 44.

28. See Klaus Kanzog, "Nachwort" to Alfred Lichtenstein, *Gesammelte Gedichte,* ed. Klaus Kanzog (Zürich, 1962), p. 102; Meyer, *die maer,* p. 13; Pfemfert, "Die Verse," p. 942.

29. See Alfred Lichtenstein, "Die Dämmerung," in *Gesammelte Gedichte,* p. 44. The poem was first published on March 18, 1911, in *Der Sturm* 1 (1910/11): 439, and then in *Simplizissimus* 16 (1911/12): 450. It also appeared in *Menschheitsdämmerung,* ed. Pinthus (1959), p. 47.

30. Kurt Mautz, *Mythologie und Gesellschaft im Expressionismus: Die Dichtung Georg Heyms* (Frankfurt am Main and Bonn, 1961), pp. 8, 225ff; Georg Heym, *Dichtungen und Schriften,* ed. Karl Ludwig Schneider, vol. 1, *Lyrik* (Hamburg, München, 1964), pp. 192, 346-47, 358-60, 462-63.

31. Blass, "Das alte," p. 31.

32. Ibid., pp. 40-42.

33. Blass, "Das alte," p. 37; trans. J.M. Ritchie in *The Era,* p. 28.

Die Klubmitglieder verkehrten im Café des Westens.... Ich kam nun auch dahin, sass mit den anderen zusammen, wurde von Dr. Hiller zur Mitgliedschaft aufgefordert. Ich nahm sehr erfreut an, obwohl ich mich sehr jung und sehr unsicher fühlte und die anderen als älter, urteilsfähiger und philosophisch fundierter empfand, vielleicht weil sie es waren, vielleicht weil sie allerhand Behauptungen aufstellten.

Wie ich zu mir selbst kam, weiss ich kaum. Man machte mir Mut, liess mich Gedichte machen, Kritiken schreiben. Ich begann zu rollen. Man fragte: 'Haben Sie in der letzten

Woche etwas Neues geschrieben?' Es waren dann Blasssche Gedichte, erst spielend und imitatorisch, dann aber gefühlter und bewusster. Aber wie ich dazu kam, davon habe ich sowenig Ahnung wie der Baron im *Nachtasyl.* Es vollzog sich, ich machte das ängstlich und auf gutes Glück.

34.   Erwin Loewenson, *Georg Heym oder Vom Geist des Schicksals* (Hamburg and Munich, 1962), pp. 69ff.

35.   Loewenson, *Heym,* p. 60; Martens, "Heym," pp. 390-91.

36.   See Georg Heym, *Dichtungen und Schriften,* ed. Karl Ludwig Schneider, vol. 2, *Prosa und Dramen* (Hamburg and Munich, 1962), pp. 335-63. This is the first version of *Atalanta oder Die Angst,* Heym, *Dichtungen und Schriften,* vol. 2, pp. 366-91.

37.   Loewenson, *Heym,* p. 60; Martens, "Heym," p. 391; Friedrich Schulze-Maizier, "Begegnung mit Georg Heym," in Heym, *Heym: Dokumente,* pp. 13-14.

38.   Martens, "Heym," p. 391.

39.   Loewenson, *Heym,* pp. 11f., 60ff., and passim.

40.   Jacob, "Heym: Erinnerung," p. 81; *Die Aktion,* ed. Raabe (Stuttgart, 1961), vol. 1, p. 81.

41.   See program for the evening reprinted in Heym, *Heym: Dokumente,* p. 403.

42.   Jacob, "Heym: Erinnerung," pp. 76ff.

43.   Ibid., pp. 78-81. The two poems by Heym published were "Laubenkolonie" and "Vorortbahnhof." See Georg Heym, *Dichtungen und Schriften,* ed. Karl Ludwig Schneider, vol. 1, *Lyrik* (Hamburg and Munich, 1964), pp. 102, 108-9. In the latter volume "Laubenkolonie" is published in two versions, both of which differ from the one cited by Jacob, "Heym: Erinnerung," p. 79.

44.   See *Die Aktion,* ed. Raabe (Stuttgart, 1961), vol. 1, pp. 59-60; *Die Aktion* 1 (1911): 18-19.

45.   See letter from Ernst Rowohlt to Georg Heym in Heym, *Tagebücher,* p. 222; Georg Heym, *Der ewige Tag* (Leipzig, 1911).

46.   See the many memoirs, reminiscences, posthumous tributes, commemorative articles published in Heym, *Heym: Dokumente,* pp. 8-190. See also Loewenson, *Heym,* pp. 60ff. and passim.

47.   Kurt Hiller, "Aus einem Brief vom 16.2.1942," in Heym, *Heym: Dokumente,* pp. 87-88.

     Er war wirklich *ganz Faust;* (nicht Heinrich, sondern geballte Hand). Just das Faustische im Goethesinn fehlte ihm völlig. Gewiss, seelisch war er, ich sagte es wohl schon, gerad so rechtwinklig wie leiblich; immer offen und redlich, schroff oft, aber nie intrigant, ein durch und durch *gerader* Kerl; aber er war philosophiefern, er war, bei aller, wenn man will, Tiefe seiner Visionen, imgrunde *ungeistig*—zumindest von dor logizistischen, begrifflichen Form der Geistigkeit so weit ab wie nur irgendein Bürger. Er war unproblematisch.

48.   Hiller, "Aus einem Brief," p. 88.

49.   See Loewenson, "Aus einem Brief vom April 1946," in Heym, *Heym: Dokumente,* pp. 92-95; Loewenson, "Heym," pp. 84-85 and passim; David Baumgardt, "Erinnerungen an Georg Heym," in Heym, *Heym: Dokumente,* pp. 8-13; Claire Jung, "Erinnerung an Georg Heym," p. 49.

50.   Hiller, "Aus einem Brief," p. 88; Ernst Blass, "Georg Heym: Zu seinem zwanzigsten Todestage," in Heym, *Heym: Dokumente,* pp. 173-79; Ernst Blass, "Georg Heym," in

Heym, *Heym: Dokumente,* pp. 196-98; Ernst Blass, "Georg Heym," *Die Aktion* 2 (1912): 882-85.

51. David Baumgardt, "Erinnerungen an Georg Heym," p. 8. Schulze-Maizier does not report in his memoirs on this period on any such special friendship with Heym and Baumgardt. He does, however, recall being particularly close to Heym and later corresponded with Baumgardt and was visited by Baumgardt after the war in Erfurt. See Schulze-Maizier, "Begegnung mit Georg Heym," pp. 17, 21; Schulze-Maizier, "Frühexistentialist," pp. 331, 332, 335, 336.

52. Baumgardt, "Erinnerungen," p. 8.

Thema unserer Gespräche war vor allem die Empörung gegen den Mangel an Leidenschaft in der Dichtung und dem bürgerlichen Denken der Zeit, die Solidarität mit Loewensons Programm, der 'Phalanx eines neuen, eines zweiten Pathos' nach der geistigen Sattheit und Skepsis der älteren Zeitgenossen.

53. Loewenson, *Heym,* pp. 60-63.

54. Ibid., pp. 62-63.

Heym wird sofort darin aufgenommen. Sein reflexschnelles Reagieren verändert seine Dichtung nach Inhalt und Form und verändert ihn selbst. Die 'Maske' des 'Naturburschen,' mit der er sich hier einführt und die er von lächelnder Freude begrüsst sieht, hört auf, blosse Maske zu sein: die grelle Robustheit, gemildert durch die Miene der Selbstironie, wird ihm zur zweiten Natur.

55. Ibid., pp. 63.

56. Heym, *Tagebücher,* p. 135; Loewenson, *Heym,* p. 63.

Ich eröffne ein drittes Tagebuch unter vielleicht günstigeren Auspizien. Ich beabsichtige eigentlich, keines mehr zu beginnen. . . .
    Im allgemeinen Sinne bin ich jetzt glücklicher, ruhiger, wie in den früheren Jahren. Ich lebe mich auf den robusten Stil ein, der mich wie eine Festung umschanzt.

57. Heym, *Heym: Dokumente,* pp. 173-79.

"Warum macht man keine Revolution?"

58. Loewenson, *Heym,* pp. 64ff; Martens, "Heym," p. 390.

59. Martens, "Heym," p. 390.

60. Jacob Picard, "Ernst Blass, seine Umwelt in Heidelberg und *Die Argonauten,*" in *Expressionismus: Aufzeichnungen,* ed. Raabe, p. 137.

61. Schulze-Maizier, "Frühexistentialist," p. 332.

62. Martens, "Heym," pp. 394-96. Loewenson's talk is as yet unpublished. On Hiller's see below, note 97.

63. See above note 8, chapter 1.

64. Loewenson, *Heym,* p. 61. See also pp. 57ff.

Unser 'neues Pathos' war zunächst wie jedes ein Ergriffensein, aber nicht nur des Gefühls, wie die alte, geistig-unselbständige, daher um so hohler dröhnende 'Pathetik.' . . . Aber auch ein neu-artiges, das den Intellekt nicht ausschaltete, ihn aber auch nicht, wie wir es als Studenten gelernt hatten, nur im Rahmen einer Theorie und umständlichen, historisch wohlbegründeten Doktrin gelten liess.

Wir stellten uns mit dem Selbstvertrauen der jungendlichen Verve dem Leben selbst, wie es uns auf allen Gebieten, mehr oder weniger erfreulich, begegnete.

65. Loewenson, *Heym*, pp. 61-67. See also Erwin Loewenson, "Bemerkungen über das 'Neopathos,'" in Georg Heym, *Gesammelte Gedichte*, ed. Carl Seelig (Zürich, 1947), pp. 241-46.

66. See Wegner, "Aufbruch," pp. 20ff.

67. See, e.g., Loewenson, *Heym*, p. 65; Schulze-Maizier, "Frühexistentialist," pp. 332-33; Schulze-Maizier, "Begegnung mit Georg Heym," p. 20; Baumgardt, "Erinnerungen an Georg Heym," p. 9; Jacob, "Heym," p. 73; Blass, "Das alte," p. 38; Martens, "Heym," p. 394. Nietzsche was frequently read at recitals in "Das neopathetische Cabaret." See Heym, *Heym: Dokumente*, pp. 402, 403, 405.

68. The talk is printed in Hiller, *Die Weisheit der Langenweile*, pp. 236-39. See there, p. 238.

69. See esp. *Die Geburt der Tragödie*, chapter 21, in which Nietzsche outlines in greatest detail the ideal condition of a balance of the Apollinian and Dionysian.

70. Loewenson, *Heym*, p. 11. David Baumgardt had a strong interest in Freud's psychoanalysis, dating from 1910, as he reports himself in David Baumgardt, "Brief über Jakob van Hoddis," in Hoddis, *Weltende*, p. 91. See also Baumgardt, "Erinnerungen an Georg Heym," p. 8.

71. Blass, "Das alte," pp. 38ff; Jacob, "Heym: Erinnerung," p. 75.

72. See the advertisement for this evening in *Der Sturm* 1 (1910): 306. The performance was reviewed by Else Lasker-Schüler in *Der Sturm* 1 (1910): 319-20. Brod's poetry had been read prior to this time in "Das neopathetische Cabaret" by Kurt Hiller at the July 6, 1910 meeting. See the program reprinted in Heym, *Heym: Dokumente*, p. 403. Brod's books were very enthusiastically received by members of the club. See Hiller, *Die Weisheit der Langenweile*, vol. 1, pp. 143-51; Kurt Hiller, "Zu Brods 'Beer,'" *Die Aktion* 2 (1912): 973-977; Ernst Blass, "Über Brods neuere Bücher," *Die Aktion* 2 (1912): 1073-76. See also Blass, "Das alte," pp. 41f.

73. Blass, "Das alte," p. 42.

74. See Loewenson, "Jakob van Hoddis," pp. 101-2; Carl Seelig, "Leben und Sterben von Georg Heym," in Georg Heym, *Gesammelte Gedichte*, ed. Carl Seelig (Zürich, 1947), p. 229; Martens, "Heym," p. 400. The "Brücke" artists had all moved to Berlin by 1911. Schmidt-Rottluff also did the title-heads for the announcements for the last two performances of "Das neopathetische Cabaret," December 16, 1911, and April 3, 1912. See reprint of these programs in Heym, *Heym: Dokumente*, pp. 410-11.

75. Loewenson, "Jakob van Hoddis," pp. 101-2; Seelig, "Leben," p. 229; Martens, "Heym," p. 400.

76. Paul Zech, "Brief vom 16.3.1946 aus Buenos Aires," published in Heym, *Heym: Dokumente*, pp. 97-100. See also letters written by Zech to Heym between October and November, 1911, published in Heym, *Tagebücher*, pp. 269-70, 272-73, 275-76.

77. See Zech, "Brief vom 16.3. 1946," pp. 97-98. See also Heym's letter to Ernst Rowohlt from the end of August, 1911, published in Heym, *Tagebücher*, p. 262. Here Heym suggests to Rowohlt the idea of a journal whose contributors should include Loewenson, Hoddis, Guttmann, Jentzsch, Koffka, and Heym.

78. Zech, "Brief vom 16.3. 1946," pp. 98-99.

79. Zech, "Brief vom 16.3.1946," p. 100; Seelig, "Heym," p. 229. See also Raabe, *Die Zeitschriften*, pp. 44-45.

80. Raabe, *Die Zeitschriften*, pp. 44-45.

81. The programs of meetings of "Das neopathetische Cabaret" are reprinted in Heym, *Heym: Dokumente*, pp. 402-11.

82. Heym, *Heym: Dokumente*, pp. 402-11.

83. Loewenson, "Bemerkungen über das 'Neopathos,'" p. 243.

84. Ibid.

   In diesem 'Neopathetischen Cabaret' sollte eine Synthese-Einheit zwischen künstlerisch-intuitiven und zentrales erkennenden und wollenden Intentionen in jedem Produkt zu Tage treten.

85. Ibid., pp. 243-44; Loewenson, *Heym*, p. 65.

86. See the reviews of the performances reprinted in Heym, *Heym: Dokumente*, pp. 412-28.

87. Martens, "Heym," p. 398; Heym, *Tagebücher*, p. 229; Loewenson, "Jakob van Hoddis," pp. 102-3.

88. Behl, "Begegnungen," pp. 293-95.

89. See Hiller, "Aus einem Brief," pp. 87-89. See also letters written to Heym by Ghuttmann and Hiller at the end of 1910 which already point to the development of divisions in the club over questions or events relating to Heym, published in Heym, *Tagebücher*, pp. 281-324.

90. Hiller, "Aus einem Brief," pp. 87-89; Hiller, *Die Weisheit der Langenweile*, p. 235.

91. See above, pp. 79-80.

92. Hiller, "Aus einem Brief," pp. 88-89.

93. Martens, "Heym," pp. 396, 399.

94. Ibid., p. 399.

95. Ibid., pp. 394-96.

96. Hiller's essay was first published in August, 1910, in *Der Sturm* 1 (1910): 187-88, 196-97, 203-4, and then in 1913 in *Die Weisheit der Langenweile*, pp. 49-72.

97. See above, pp. 81-82.

98. Loewenson, *Heym*, pp. 60-61.

99. Ibid.

   Er [= Heym] findet einen neuartigen Totalitätsaspekt als Programm und Kriterium für das Niveau, in wöchentlichen Debatten wie in den dichterischen und theoretischen Darbietungen; einen Totalitätsaspekt, der von der produktiven Vitalität ausgeht, sich der unbefangenen Gefühlsäusserung nicht mehr schämt, den lebensbejahenden Humor einschliesst, die unheimlichen und grotesk-tragikomischen Züge des Daseins verbindet. Er findet in dem turbulenten, dem witzig-ernsten und polemischen Durcheinander des 'Neopathetischen Cabarets'... eine eklatante Gesinnungs- und Willenseinheit. Er fühlt sich angeregt zur zentralisierenden Vereinigung seiner dichterischen, politisch-republikanischen und seiner naturreligiösen Neigungen.

100. Loewenson, "Bemerkungen über das 'Neopathos,'" p. 244.

Schon das Neopathos-Manifest wollte über das Persönlich-Geistige hinaus die Einleitung einer ausnahmsweise sachlich durchdachten und methodisch einsetzenden Regenerationsbewegung sein. Für diese eben galt als unumgängliche Vorbedingung eine allmählich instinktiv- und organisch-werdende Gesamtsynthese, die in den offensichtlichen Phänomenen selber den rationalüberzeugenden Zugang zum überrationalen aufschliesst. Nur mit ihrer Hilfe kann die in unserem Zeitalter ausgeschaltete 'Zentralität' des Menschen wieder in Kraft treten.

101.   Loewenson, *Heym*, pp. 8ff., 60ff. See a similar view in Oskar Maurus Fontana, "Georg Heym," in Heym, *Heym: Dokumente*, pp. 117-24.

102.   Hiller, "Aus einem Brief," pp. 88-89.

Schon damals lebte in mir, wenn auch noch stark ins Unbewusste verstrickt, das *hellenische* Ideal der Harmonie zwischen leiblicher und geistiger Vollkommenheit. Jedenfalls war mir schon damals, au delà de la littérature, der (sagen wir) *turnerische* Typus Mensch kein Objekt des ressentiment, sondern eines der Sympathie; wie sollte er innerhalb der Literatur mir ablehnenswert erschienen sein—gesetzt nur, die philosophische Röhre kommunizierte mit der gymnastischen!

103.   Hiller, "Über Kultur," in *Die Weisheit der Langenweile*, pp. 49ff; Georg Simmel, *Philosophie des Geldes* (Berlin, 1900); Roy Pascal, *From Naturalism to Expressionism: German Literature and Society 1880-1918* (New York, 1973), 24-25.

104.   Hiller, "Über Kultur," p. 53.

105.   Ibid.

Mir scheint das vehemente Auseinanderfallen von vergegenständlichtem Geist und individualer Kultur zu den widerwärtigsten Mängeln unseres Zeitalters zu gehören. Was frommt der Pomp von Differenzierung und Fülle, wenn kein Einzelner seiner teilhaftig werden kann.

106.   Ibid., p. 54.

107.   Ibid., p. 56.

So bleibt denn 'Kultur,' dieser so oft und arg missbrauchte Ausdruck, uns übrig als die Bezeichnung für einen logisch kaum fassbaren, aber gefühlsmässig doch recht bestimmten Verfeinerungsgrad der Bewegungen und Funktionen.

108.   Ibid., pp. 56, 63.

Erfüllt sich so die Idee des 'kultivierten' Menschen mit der neben dem blossen Ethos des Raffinements bestehenden Forderung, dass dies Raffinement Eigentümlichkeit allen Erlebens werde; *allen* Betätigens; das es in den Charakter eingehe; dass, anstatt sich auf das Denken allein oder auf das Empfinden allein oder auf das soziologische Verhalten allein oder auf sonst ein besonderes Vermögen zu erstrecken, es *universal* sei -: so verwandelt sich damit die Formel 'Kultur' in eine Bezeichnung für das höchste Lob, das wir, ausser dem Lobe der schöpferischen Kraft, einem Menschen spenden können....
        Kunst und Erkenntnis, Erlebnis und Problem, Gefühl und Gedanke umfassen, durchsetzen und zerschmelzen einander mit einer so ruhelosen Intensität, mit solchem Chemismus, dass die sogenannte 'Klassizistische' Forderung, wie sie besonders deutlich Leonard Nelson (im zweiten Band der Fries'schen Schule) erhoben hat: beide Funktionen streng getrennt auszubilden, in friedlicher Nebenordnung, ohne, 'Übergriffe' der einen in das Gebiet der anderen,... als ein Zwang erscheint... insofern er ein Stadium psychisch-anthropologischer Entwicklung zurückschrauben, einen Zustand der Kompliziertheit und

Verfeinerung in einen Zustand der Einfachheit und Robustität verwandeln, Armut für Reichtum einsetzen will.

109. Ibid., pp. 65-67. Hiller repeats this attack in the talk with which he opened "Gnu" in October, 1912. See *Die Weisheit der Langenweile*, pp. 247-48.

110. Hiller, "Über Kultur," pp. 69-70.

111. Hiller, *Die Weisheit der Langenweile*, p. 237.

Dies ist das Kennzeichen einer höher gestimmten Lebendigkeit und des neuen Pathos: das alleweil lodernde Erfülltsein von unserem geliebten Ideelichen, vom Willen zur Erkenntnis und zur Kunst und zu den sehr wundersamen Köstlichkeiten dazwischen. Das neue Pathos ist weiter nichts als: erhöhte psychische Temperatur.

112. Martens, "Heym," p. 396.

113. Hiller's opposition to a perceptually one-sided approach to experience and his advocacy of a synthesis of the various modes of perception and sensation run through his writings. In the essay "Gegen Lyrik," for example, which appeared in *Der Sturm* 1 (1911): 314-15, Hiller defines the new lyric, as he envisions it, in the form of such a synthesis:

... Komplex von Worten, der ein geordnet holdes Vagieren ist und worin die allerhand irdischen Sensationen—von den optischen bis zu den tastnervösen—, das allerhand Cerebrale, die allerhand Wollungen ineinanderschmilzen und einig zusammenfliessen mit dem Weltgefühl, das unsere Seele kennt. All dies kraft einer Vision gemischt und gefasst in das Gesetz einer Form -: das Gedicht ist da.

(p. 315)

Similarly, in his memoir on Hoddis, "Notiz über ein Gespräch," Hiller says of Hoddis and his relationship to the club:

Der dichterisch stärkste Vertreter unserer Anschauungen war Jakob van Hoddis, dessen Gedichte weitgehend meiner Theorie von der Gehirnlyrik genauer: von einer lyrischen Synthesis aus sensualen, sentimentalen und mentalen Elementen, entsprachen.

(p. 93)

See also *Die Weisheit der Langenweile*, pp. 247-48; Kurt Hiller, *Geist werde Herr*, Tribüne der Kunst und Zeit, vol. 16/17 (Berlin, 1920), pp. 116-17.

114. See esp. Erich Unger, "Nietzsche," *Der Sturm* 1 (1911): 380. See also Erich Unger, "Vom Pathos," *Der Sturm* 1 (1910): 316. See also Blass; foreword to his verse *Die Strassen komme ich entlanggeweht* (Heidelberg, 1912), discussed below in the section on Paul Cassirer. pp. 000-00.

115. Hiller, "Aus einem Brief," pp. 87-88; Hiller, "Notiz über ein Gespräch," p. 93.

116. David Baumgardt, "Brief über Jakob van Hoddis," in Hoddis, *Weltende*, p. 90; Loewenson, "Jakob van Hoddis," pp. 100-101.

117. Martens, "Heym," p. 399.

118. Hiller, "Notiz über ein Gespräch," p. 93; Loewenson, "Jakob van Hoddis," p. 101; Baumgardt, "Brief über Jakob van Hoddis," p. 90.

119. *Die Aktion* 1 (1911): 118.

Unser Mitarbeiter *Dr. Kurt Hiller* teilt uns mit, dass er aus dem 'Neuen Club,' den er seit seiner Gründung geleitet hat, vor kurzem ausgetreten ist, gelangweilt durch das taktlose Verhalten einiger Mitglieder; er legt Wert darauf, für künftige Taten dieser Vereinigung nicht mehr verantwortlich gemacht zu werden.

120. Martens, "Heym," p. 399.

121. Hiller, *Die Weisheit der Langenweile,* p. 235; Baumgardt, "Brief über Jakob van Hoddis," p. 90; Loewenson, "Jakob van Hoddis," p. 101; Martens, "Heym," p. 399.

122. The following performances of "Gnu" were preannounced to the public in *Der Sturm* and *Die Aktion:*

> November 2, 1911, *Der Sturm* 2 (1911): 658.—"First Evening."
> November 23, 1911, *Der Sturm* 2 (1911): 681.—"Second Evening."
> December 14, 1911, *Der Sturm* 2 (1911): 705.—"Third Evening."
> January 15, 1912, *Der Sturm* 2 (1912): 738.—"Fourth Evening."
> October 31, 1912, *Die Aktion* 2 (1912): 1367.—NS "First Evening."
> November 1, 1912, *Die Aktion* 2 (1912): 1367.—NS repeat of "First Evening."
> January 28, 1913, *Die Aktion* 3 (1913): 119.—NS "Third Evening."
> February 6, 1913, *Die Aktion* 3 (1913): 183.—NS repeat of "Third Evening."
> May 24, 1913, *Die Aktion* 3 (1913): 520.—NS "Fifth Evening."

Hiller announced further evenings for the fall/winter of 1913/14 in *Revolution* 1 (1913/14): no. 1, 7. Blass's program for the premiere evening of the cabaret is published in *Herder-Blätter* 1 (1913), no. 3, 49-50.

123. See the note above. The announcement for this evening in *Der Sturm* states that Brod will read from his works and from Franz Werfel's. Blass, Drey and Hiller are also scheduled to read. Broad first read publicly in Berlin for "Der neue Club" on November 17, 1910. See note 72, above. This evening was attended by Werfel who, as Brod puts it, "had escaped from his Hamburg exile" to attend the meeting. (Brod means Werfel had slipped away from the business position in Hamburg which he had been forced to take by his father.) See Brod *Streitbares Leben,* p. 47; Blass, "Das alte," p. 41f. Brod's third Berlin recital, on December 15, 1911, was sponsored by *Die Aktion.* The announcement for the evening in *Die Aktion* 1 (1911): 1333, schedules Brod to read "exclusively from his own unpublished works." However, a review of the evening by Ruest in *Die Aktion* 1 (1911): 1425-26, notes that Brod read from Werfel's works. Brod, *Streitbares Leben,* p. 49, mentions reading from Werfel's verse in Berlin ("some" months after the recital for "Der neue Club") on only *one* occasion. See also Blass, "Das alte," p. 42, for a similar reference to a reading "some months" after that on Nov. 17, 1910, at which Brod read Werfel's verse. See also *Die Aktion,* ed. Raabe (Stuttgart, 1961), vol. 1, p. 122; *Expressionismus: Aufzeichnungen,* ed. Raabe, p. 316 n. 5.

124. See Brod, *Streitbares Leben,* p. 50; Blass, "Das alte," p. 42. See also pp. 329-30.

125. Meyer, *die maer,* pp. 6, 23-24.

126. Lasker-Schüler, *Mein Herz,* in *Gesammelte Werke,* vol. 2, p. 327.

127. See the letters from the second half of 1913 written by Hiller and Blass to the Heidelberg publisher Richard Weissbach, published in "'Morgenrot!—Die Tage dämmern!' Zwanzig Briefe aus dem Frühexpressionismus 1910-1914," ed. Paul Raabe, *Der Monat* 16 (1964), 64-65.

128. See "'Morgenrot,'" p. 65; Picard, "Ernst Blass," pp. 138ff. See also Blass's letter to the Kurt Wolff Verlag from May 13, 1915, published in Kurt Wolff, *Briefwechsel eines Verlegers,* ed. Bernhard Zeller and Ellen Otten (Frankfurt a.M., 1966), pp. 220-21.

129. See *Expressionismus: Aufzeichnungen,* ed. Raabe, p. 313 n. 7. One of the postcards is published in "'Morgenrot! Die Tage dämmern!'" p. 68. See also Pinthus, "Walter Hasenclever," pp. 19-21.

130. Pinthus, "Walter Hasenclever," p. 19.

131. Hiller, "Begegnungen," p. 29; Lasker-Schüler, *Briefe an Karl Kraus,* p. 78; Flake, *Es wird,* p. 281; Wolff, *Briefwechsel,* pp. 310-20.

132. See Raabe, *Die Zeitschriften,* p. 226, for index for periodicals to which Hiller contributed.

133. See Raabe, *Die Zeitschriften,* pp. 125-26.

134. See, e.g., Hiller's revolutionary tracts "Wer sind wir? Was wollen wir?" (December 2, 1918) and "Ein Ministerium der Köpfe" (April, 1919), published in Hiller, *Geist werde Herr,* pp. 71-92, 125-47. See also Flake, *Es wird,* p. 281.

135. Seelig, "Georg Heym," p. 229; Martens, "Heym," p. 400; Loewenson, "Jakob van Hoddis," pp. 101-2.

136. Lasker-Schüler, *Mein Herz,* in *Gesammelte Werke,* vol. 2, p. 319. Mostly internal evidence dates this reference at about the early fall of 1911.

137. See programs of "Das neopathetische Cabaret," in Heym, *Heym: Dokumente,* pp. 409-11, and those of "Gnu" published in *Der Sturm* and *Die Aktion,* listed above, note 113.

138. Martens, "Heym," p. 399. On Heym's death, see reports in Heym, *Heym: Dokumente,* pp. 455-74.

139. Program reproduced in Heym, *Heym: Dokumente,* p. 411.

140. Martens, "Heym," pp. 399-400; Georg Heym, *Umbra Vitae: Nachgelassene Gedichte* (Leipzig, 1912).

141. Schulze-Maizier, "Begegnung mit Georg Heym," p. 21; Heym, *Tagebücher,* pp. 167, 174.

142. See, e.g., Loewenson, "Jakob van Hoddis," pp. 106ff; Schulze-Maizier, "Frühexistentialist," p. 335; Baumgardt, "Brief über Jakob van Hoddis," p. 90; Hiller, "Notiz über ein Gespräch," p. 94.

143. Baumgardt, "Brief über Jakob van Hoddis," p. 90.

144. Martens, "Heym," p. 400. Schulze-Maizier reports that he was a "member" of the club until 1914. See Schulze-Maizier, "Frühexistentialist," p. 336.

Chapter 5

1. Nell Walden, "Aus meinen Erinnerungen an Herwarth Walden und die 'Sturmzeit,'" in *Der Sturm: Ein Erinnerungsbuch an Herwarth Walden und die Künstler aus dem Sturmkreis,* ed. Nell Walden and Lothar Schreyer (Baden-Baden, 1954), pp. 9-63; Nell Walden, "Der Mensch Herwarth Walden," in Nell Walden, *Herwarth Walden: Ein Lebensbild* (Berlin and Mainz, 1963), pp. 15-34; Nell Walden and Hans Bolliger, "Biographische Daten," Nell Walden, *Herwarth Walden,* pp. 67-80; Lothar Schreyer, *Erinnerung an Sturm und Bauhaus: Was ist des Menschen Bild?* (Munich, 1956), passim; Lothar Schreyer, "Das war *Der Sturm,*" in *Minotaurus: Dichtung unter den Hufen von Staat und Industrie,* ed. Alfred Döblin (Wiesbaden, 1953), pp. 112-30; Else Lasker-Schüler, *Mein Herz* (Munich and Berlin, 1912), reprinted in Else Lasker-Schüler, *Prosa und Schauspiele,* vol. 2 of *Gesammelte Werke,* ed. Friedhelm Kemp (Munich, 1962), pp. 289-391; Else Lasker-Schüler, *Der Malik* (Berlin, 1919), reprinted, Lasker-Schüler, *Gesammelte Werke,* vol. 2, pp. 393-489; Else Lasker-Schüler, *Gesichte* (Berlin, 1920), reprinted, Lasker-Schüler, *Gesammelte Werke,* vol. 2, pp. 137-216; Else Lasker-Schüler, *Essays* (Berlin, 1920), reprinted in Lasker-Schüler, *Gesammelte Werke,* vol. 2, pp. 217-87; Else Lasker-Schüler, *Lieber gestreifter Tiger,* vol. 1 of *Briefe,* ed. Margarete Kupper (Munich, 1969), passim; Else Lasker-Schüler, *Wo ist unser buntes Theben,* vol. 2 of *Briefe,* ed. Margarete Kupper

(Munich, 1969), passim; Else Lasker-Schüler, *Briefe an Karl Kraus,* ed. Astrid Gehlhoff-Claes (Cologne and Berlin, 1959), passim; Peter Scher, "Als Kokoschka mich malte," in *Oskar Kokoschka: Ein Lebensbild in zeitgenössischen Dokumenten,* ed. Hans Maria Wingler (Munich, 1956), pp. 20-24; Paul Raabe, "Der frühe Benn und die Veröffentlichung seiner Werke," in Gottfried Benn, *Den Traum alleine tragen: Neue Texte, Briefe, Dokumente,* ed. Paul Raabe and Max Niedermayer (Wiesbaden, 1966), pp. 12-14; Alfred Döblin, *Briefe,* ed. Heinz Graber and Walter Muschg (Olten and Freiburg im Breisgau, 1970), pp. 21-127 and notes, pp. 503-43; see also there Heinz Graber, "Nachwort des Herausgebers," pp. 663ff; Salomo Friedlaender [Mynona], "Ich: Autobiographische Skizze (1871-1936)," in: Salomo Friedlaender [Mynona], *Rosa, die schöne Schutzmannsfrau und andere Grotesken,* ed. Ellen Otten (Zürich, 1965), pp. 227ff.

2.   See Döblin, *Briefe,* pp. 21ff; Alfred Döblin, "Epilog," reprinted in Alfred Döblin, *Aufsätze zur Literatur,* ed. Walter Muschg (Olten and Freiburg im Breisgau, 1963), p. 385; *Expressionismus: Literatur und Kunst,* ed. Zeller, et al., pp. 145, 155, 162; Nell Walden, "Biographische Daten," p. 67.

3.   On the journals edited by Walden prior to *Der Sturm* and Friedlaender's connections with them see below. Friedlaender, who used the synonym "Mynona" (anagram for "Anonym") for his nonphilosophical writings, esp. (as he termed them) his "Grotesken," was one of the signatories of the 1909 pamphlet published in Walden's defense (see below). See on Friedlaender *Expressionismus: Literatur und Kunst,* ed. Zeller, et al., pp. 165-66; *Die Aktion,* ed. Raabe (Stuttgart, 1961), pp. 48-49. On Wauer see Schreyer, *Erinnerungen,* esp. pp. 102-13; Else Lasker-Schüler, "William Wauer," in Lasker-Schüler, *Essays,* pp. 265-67.

4.   Scher, "Als Kokoschka mich malte," pp. 335-36. See also Raabe, "Der frühe Benn," pp. 12-14. Benn's first contribution to *Der Sturm:* "Nocturno," *Der Sturm* 3 (January, 1913), no. 144/45, p. 254. He is then represented by only one more contribution in the journal: "Gedichte," *Der Sturm* 4 (May, 1913), no. 160/161, p. 26.

5.   See note 1, above.

6.   See note 1, above.

7.   See esp. Nell Walden, "Kokoschka und der *Sturm*-Kreis," in *Expressionismus: Aufzeichnungen,* ed. Raabe, pp. 128ff; Schreyer, *Erinnerungen,* pp. 98f. Kokoschka depicts his experience living with Blümner in Berlin during this period in the tale "Geschichte von der Tochter Virginia," reprinted in Oskar Kokoschka, *Schriften: 1907-1955,* ed. Hans Maria Wingler (Munich, 1956), pp. 60-68. See also there, pp. 448-449; Kokoschka, *Leben,* pp. 107-20.

8.   Kokoschka is first listed in *Der Sturm* as the editor for Austria in vol. 1, no. 33 (October, 1910): 266, and so listed for the last time in vol. 2, no. 77 (September, 1911): 616. This corrects Schreyer, "Das war *Der Sturm,*" p. 123, who dates Kokoschka's editorship November, 1910, to September, 1911. See also Kokoschka, *Leben,* pp. 108ff.

9.   Nell Walden, "Kokoschka," pp. 129ff. See also below, p. 96.

10. *Menschheitsdämmerung,* ed. Pinthus (Hamburg, 1959), p. 368; Oskar Maurus Fontana, "Expressionismus in Wien: Erinnerungen," in *Expressionismus: Aufzeichnungen,* ed. Raabe, p. 187; Paul Raabe, "Bio-Bibliographischer Anhang zu den Jahrgängen 5-8 (1915-1918)," in *Die Aktion: 1917/1918,* ed. Paul Raabe (Munich, 1967), p. 18; Kokoschka, *Leben,* pp. 122-25; Oskar Maria Fontana, "Jugend" in Albert Ehrenstein, *Gedichte und Prosa,* ed. Karl Otten (Neuwied am Rhein and Berlin-Spandau, 1961), p. 28.

11. René Radrizzani, "Lebensgeschichte," in August Stramm, *Das Werk,* ed. René Radrizzani (Wiesbaden, 1963), pp. 426, 429ff.

12. For the effect of the association on Stramm and his work see Radrizzani, "Lebensgeschichte," pp. 430ff. Its effect on Walden and *Der Sturm* will be discussed below. See also, on the meeting of Stramm and Walden, Nell Walden and Hans Bolliger, "Biographische Daten," p. 71; Nell Walden, "Der Mensch," p. 37.

13. Radrizzani, "Lebensgeschichte," pp. 442ff.

14. See note 1; also Walter Mehring, *Berlin Dada* (Zürich, 1959), pp. 28-30; Walter Mehring, *Die verlorene Bibliothek: Autobiographie einer Kultur* (Icking bei München, 1964), pp. 145-49; *Das war Dada: Dichtungen und Dokumente,* ed. Peter Schifferli (Munich, 1963), p. 181; Nell Walden and Hans Bolliger, "Biographische Daten," p. 69, report: "1911 stossen die Künstler der 'Brücke' nach ihrer Übersiedlung von Dresden nach Berlin zum *Sturm...*" Nell Walden apparently means here that the "Brücke" artists supported, and contributed to, *Der Sturm* and not that they became members of the circle itself. There is no indication in other sources that would justify, at any rate, the latter interpretation of her statement. Thomas Grochowiak, *Ludwig Meidner* (Recklinghausen, 1966), p. 138, reports that Meidner claimed that the "Brücke" group did not frequent the Café des Westens, the meeting place of the *Sturm* in its first two years. However, see Max Pechstein, *Erinnerungen* (Wiesbaden, 1960), p. 41.

15. Höxter, *So lebten wir,* p. 39.

16. Nell Walden, "Der Mensch," p. 20; Nell Walden, "Biographische Daten," p. 70; Nell Walden, "Kokoschka," p. 133; Nell Walden, "Begegnung mit Else Lasker-Schüler," in Nell Walden, *Herwarth Walden,* p. 37; Krell, *Das alles,* p. 21; Mehring, *Berlin Dada,* pp. 15-16, 23; Mehring, *Die velorene Bibliothek,* pp. 145ff; Walter Mehring, "Berlin Avantgarde," in *Expressionismus: Aufzeichnungen,* ed. Raabe, p. 117; Lasker-Schüler, *Mein Herz,* passim; Lasker-Schüler, *Gesichte,* passim; Lasker-Schüler, *Essays,* passim; Lasker-Schüler, *Briefe an Karl Kraus,* passim; Lasker-Schüler, *Der Malik,* passim; Lasker-Schüler, *Lieber gestreifter Tiger,* passim; Lasker-Schüler, *Wo ist,* passim; Durieux, *Eine Tür,* p. 65; Hiller, *Begegnungen,* p. 29; Meyer, *die maer,* passim; Wieland Herzfelde, "Fremd und Nah: Über meinen Briefwechsel und meine Begegnungen mit Else Lasker-Schüler," in *Nachrichten aus dem Kösel-Verlag: Sonderheft für Else Lasker-Schüler Dezember 1965,* ed. Dr. Heinrich Wild and Friedrich Pfäfflin (München, 1965), pp. 43, 45; Hans Jacob, *Kind meiner Zeit: Lebenserinnerungen* (Cologne and Berlin, 1962), p. 27; Grosz, *A Little Yes,* p. 149; Fritz Max Cahén, "Der Alfred Richard Meyer-Kreis," in *Expressionismus: Aufzeichnungen,* ed. Raabe, p. 114; Raabe, "Der frühe Benn," pp. 12-13; Höxter, *So lebten wir,* pp. 38ff; Jhering, *Begegnungen,* pp. 119-20; Grochowiak, *Meidner,* p. 137; Kober, *Einst in Berlin,* p. 104; Zivier, *Das Romanische,* pp. 9ff.

17. Nell Walden, "Begegnung mit Else Lasker-Schüler," pp. 36-37.

18. Nell Walden, "Begegnung mit Else Lasker-Schüler," p. 37; Nell Walden, "Aus meinen Erinnerungen," pp. 11-13.

19. Nell Walden, "Begegnung mit Else Lasker-Schüler," p. 37.

20. Ibid.

21. See *Expressionismus: Literatur und Kunst,* ed. Zeller, et al., pp. 39, 82, 152, 155, 184; Nell Walden, "Der Mensch," p. 27; Paul Raabe, "Bio-Bibliographischer Anhang zu den Jahrgängen 5-8 (1915-1918)," in *Die Aktion* 7-8 (1917-1918), ed. Paul Raabe (Munich, 1967), p. 18; *Die Aktion,* ed. Raabe (Stuttgart, 1961), vol. 1, pp. 34, 35; Oskar Maurus Fontana, "Jugend," in Albert Ehrenstein, *Gedichte und Prosa,* ed. Karl Otten (Neuwied am Rhein and Berlin-Spandau, 1961), p. 28; Döblin, *Briefe,* pp. 61ff.

22. See *Expressionismus: Literatur und Kunst*, ed. Zeller, et al., p. 162; *Die Aktion*, ed. Raabe (Stuttgart, 1961), vol 1, pp. 95-96.

23. Nell Walden, "Der Mensch," p. 27.

24. Mehring *Die verlorene Bibliothek*, pp. 145ff; Mehring, "Berlin Avantgarde," pp. 116ff; Schreyer, *Erinnerungen*, pp. 35ff.

25. Nell Walden, "Der Mensch," p. 27; Schreyer, *Erinnerungen*, pp. 131-34; *Expressionismus: Literatur und Kunst*, ed. Zeller, et al., p. 157.

26. Nell Walden, "Der Mensch," p. 27; Georg Muche, *Blickpunkt: Sturm, Dada, Bauhaus, Gegenwart* (Munich, 1961), pp. 191-98 and passim; Georg Schrimpf, "Der Künstler über sich," in Oskar Maria Graf, *Georg Schrimpf*, Junge Kunst, vol. 37 (Leipzig, 1923), pp. 15-16; Georg Schrimpf, "Erinnerung an Maria Uhden," in Oskar Maria Graf, *Maria Uhden*, Junge Kunst, vol. 20 (Leipzig, 1921) pp. 12-13.

27. Schreyer, *Erinnerungen*, pp. 7ff.

28. *Der Sturm* 7 (1916): 40-44.

29. Schreyer, *Erinnerungen*, pp. 9-12.

30. Ibid., pp. 12-13.

31. Ibid., pp. 13, 19-20. Schreyer is first given as editor of *Der Sturm* with 8 (August, 1917), no. 5, p. 79, and last so given with 15 (1924), no. 4, p. 236.

32. Nell Walden, "Kokoschka," pp. 131ff; Nell Walden, "Der Mensch," p. 27; Schreyer, "Erinnerungen," p. 99; Kokoschka, *Leben*, pp. 165-66.

33. Nell Walden, "Kokoschka," p. 131. Kokoschka's drawings from this period are published in *Der Sturm* 7 (October, November, December, 1916), nos. 7, 8, 9, pp. 74, 77, 79, 85, 86, 87, 88, 97, 101, 103.

34. Nell Walden, "Der Mensch," p. 27. On "Sturm-Bühne" see below.

35. Schreyer, *Erinnerungen*, pp. 131-32.

36. Nell Walden, "Der Mensch," p. 27; Muche, *Blickpunkt*, pp. 205ff; Schrimpf, "Der Künstler über sich selbst," p. 16; Schrimpf, "Maria Uhden," pp. 12-13.

37. Nell Walden, "Aus meinen Erinnerungen," pp. 42ff; Nell Walden, "Der Mensch," pp. 29ff; Nell Walden, "Biographische Daten" pp. 77ff; Schreyer, *Erinnerungen*, passim.

38. See esp. Schreyer, *Erinnerungen*, pp. 114ff.

39. See esp. Ibid., pp. 275ff; also Nell Walden, "Biographische Daten," p. 77.

40. See esp. Schreyer, *Erinnerungen*, p. 7.

41. Ibid.; Mehring, "Berlin Avant-garde," p. 119; Mehring, *Die verlorene Bibliothek*, p. 146; Muche, *Blickpunkt*, p. 191; Sophie van Leer, "Aus zwei Briefen von Sophie van Leer," in Nell Walden, *Herwarth Walden*, pp. 111-17.

42. Nell Walden, "Der Mensch," p. 15; Sophie van Leer, "Aus zwei Briefen," pp. 111-17; Mehring, *Die verlorene Bibliothek*, p. 145; Mehring, "Berlin Avantgarde," p. 119.

Es ist auch nicht leicht, diesen komplizierten Charakter zu verstehen, der aus so vielen Elementen zusammengesetzt war: aus Härte, Schroffheit, Abwehr, Angriffslust und Kampfgeist, dabei—allerdings ängstlich verborgen—innerlich sehr sensibel und empfindsam. Seine Grenzen waren scharf gezogen: dunkel oder hell—es gab keine Zwischentöne; immer kompromisslos, wie er es auch im Leben war. Walden war eine Kämpfernatur; gewiss nicht im soldatischen, aber im geistigen Sinn. Aggressiv und unermüdlich trat er für seine Ansichten und Ideen ein. Dynamisch und energiegeladen, rastlos, in gewissem Sinne grenzenlos, lag ihm nur am Kampf. Polemik und Propaganda waren seine Waffen.

43. Mehring, *Die verlorene Bibliothek,* p. 145; Muche, *Blickpunkt,* p. 191.

44. Nell Walden, "Aus meinen Erinnerungen," p. 45.

45. Schreyer, *Erinnerungen,* p. 7.

46. Mehring, *Die verlorene Bibliothek,* p. 146; Mehring, "Berlin Avantgarde," p. 119.

47. Nell Walden, "Begegnung mit Else Lasker-Schüler," pp. 35, 37; Astrid Gehlhoff-Claes, "Else Lasker-Schüler: Versuch einer biographischen Darstellung," in Lasker-Schüler, *Briefe an Karl Kraus,* pp. 144, 154; Margarete Kupper, "Else Lasker-Schüler," in *Nachrichten aus dem Kösel-Verlag,* ed. Wild, pp. 7ff; Lasker-Schüler, *Lieber gestreifter Tiger,* p. 10; Lasker-Schüler, *Wo ist,* p. 231; Döblin, "Epilog," p. 385.

48. See esp. Benn's description of her in "Rede auf Else Lasker-Schüler," reprinted in Gottfried Benn, *Gesammelte Werke,* ed. Dieter Wellershoff, vol. I (Wiesbaden, 1959, 1962), pp. 537ff.

49. Gehlhoff-Claes, "Else Lasker-Schüler," p. 151.

50. See above, p. 53; also Lasker-Schüller, *Wo ist,* pp. 9ff. and p. 334, note to letter no. 306.

51. Lasker-Schüler's first appearance in *Die Gesellschaft* was in 15 (1899), vol. 3, pp. 243-44. See Lasker-Schüler, *Lieber gestreifter Tiger,* p. 10; Lasker-Schüler, *Wo ist,* p. 244, note to letter no. 2.

52. Lasker-Schüler, *Briefe an Karl Kraus,* pp. 64ff. and passim; Cahén, "Der Alfred Richard Meyer-Kreis," p. 114. See also below, the chapter on the Meyer circle.

53. See esp. Lasker-Schüler's "Essay" on Caro, in Lasker-Schüler, *Essays,* pp. 239-41; also Lasker-Schüler, *Mein Herz,* pp. 293, 304, 316. Caro was, according to Lasker-Schüler, her lawyer. See Lasker-Schüler, *Lieber gestreifter Tiger,* pp. 93-95, 97, 99; also Lasker-Schüler, *Der Malik,* p. 407; Jacob, *Kind,* pp. 25ff.

54. See above, chapter 3, pp. 69-70.

55. Lasker-Schüler, *Briefe an Karl Kraus,* pp. 35ff; Lasker-Schüler, *Lieber gestreifter Tiger,* 85, 87, 88, 90; Lasker-Schüler, *Wo ist,* pp. 40, 54, 55, 60, 62, 82 and p. 269, note to letter no. 63; Lasker-Schüler, *Essays,* pp. 227-229; Lasker-Schüler, *Der Malik,* passim; Raabe, "Der frühe Benn," pp. 11, 12; Paul Raabe, "Gottfried Benns Huldigungen an Else Lasker-Schüler," in Benn, *Den Traum,* ed. Raabe and Niedermayer, pp. 61-79; Gehlhoff-Claes, "Else Lasker-Schüler," p. 157; Benn, "Rede an Else Lasker-Schüler," pp. 437ff.

56. See above, chapter 3, pp. 69-70.

57. See, e.g., Ball, *Briefe,* p. 95; Durieux, *Eine Tür,* pp. 122, 123; Jacques, *Mit Lust gelebt,* p. 305; Szittya, *Das Kuriositäten-Kabinett,* pp. 281-82; Hans Arp, "Dadaland," in *Expressionismus: Aufzeichnungen,* ed. Raabe, p. 184.

58. Lasker-Schüler, *Briefe an Karl Kraus,* pp. 78-79; Hiller, "Begegnungen," p. 29; Jung, *Der Weg,* p. 106; Lasker-Schüler, *Lieber gestreifter Tiger,* p. 92; Lasker-Schüler, *Wo ist,* pp. 66-69; Herzfelde, "Fremd und Nah," pp. 42-46.

59. See, e.g., Lasker-Schüler's efforts on behalf of Benn, Boldt, and Herzfelde, and her effort to bring together Ehrenbaum-Degele and Zech for literary purposes, recorded in Lasker-Schüler, *Lieber gestreifter Tiger,* pp. 79, 87-90, 92, 101.

60. See again esp. Benn. "Rede an Else Lasker-Schüler," pp. 537ff; also Raabe, "Gottfried Benns Huldigungen," pp. 61-79; Nico Rost, "Meine Begegnungen mit Gottfried Benn" in Benn, *Den Traum,* ed. Raabe and Niedermayer, p. 46; "Else Lasker-Schüler im Urteil ihrer Zeitgenossen," in *Nachrichten aus dem Kösel-Verlag,* ed. Wild, pp. 23-38.

61. Many of her recitals are recorded in Lasker-Schüler, *Lieber gestreifter Tiger,* passim; Lasker-Schüler, *Wo ist,* passim; Lasker-Schüler, *Briefe an Karl Kraus,* passim. See also under many of the recitals of the circles mentioned and discussed in this study.

62. See the index of her contributions to Expressionist publications in Raabe, *Die Zeitschriften,* pp. 231-32, 253.

63. See below under Walden's earlier journals. For a handy index to Lasker-Schüler's contributions to *Der Sturm* see *Der Sturm,* ed. Nell Walden and Lothar Schreyer, pp. 230-31.

64. See "Die Sturm-Dichter: Eine Auswahl der Gedichte," in *Der Sturm,* ed. Nell Walden and Lothar Schreyer, p. 168.

65. Döblin, "Epilog," p. 385.

66. Ibid.

67. Ibid.

68. The founding date of the "Verein für Kunst" is variously reported as 1903 or 1904. However, Nell Walden, who is usually very accurate on such details, gives 1903. See Nell Walden, "Biographische Daten," p. 67. 1903 is, at the same time, the most frequently given date for this event. The "Verein für Kunst" was also a publishing company, "Verlag des Vereins für Kunst" in Berlin. The company published, amongst other volumes, Lasker-Schüler's *Der siebente Tag* in 1905.

69. Peter Altenberg, Hermann Bahr, Hermann Bang, Oskar Baum, et al., *Der neue Weg der Genossenschaft Deutscher Bühnenangehöriger: Ein Protest in Sachen Herwarth Walden* (Berlin, n.d. 1909), pp. 8-10. This pamphlet is reprinted in part in Nell Walden, *Herwarth Walden,* pp. 118-30.

70. Nell Walden, *Herwarth Walden,* pp. 8-9. See also there the similar statements on the "Verein für Kunst" by Hermann Bang, Kurtz, Karl Larsen, Samuel Lublinski, Alfred Mombert, Hermann Muthesius, and Schickele, pp. 3, 14, 16, 19, 20, 22.

    Er schuf den Verein für Kunst, dessen organisatorische und aesthetische Leistung in der Kulturgeschichte sehr sorgsam aufgezeichnet werden wird: als unerbittliche Dokumentierung aristokratischer Geistigkeit innerhalb der 'zeitgemässen' Verblödung, als Kriegserklärung des künstlerischen Europäertums an eine deutsche Welt, die bei asphalt-materialistischen Plattheiten oder heimatskünstlerischen Kochbuch-Rührungen (wenns hoch kommt: Sonntagsglocken über dem Ährenfeld) erbärmlichste Ergötzungen findet. Der Verein für Kunst leistete sich den Luxus, Geschmack zu haben und die neuen, die nicht approbierten Werte fanatisch zu lieben. Immer waltete dort 'Selektion': jener edel-karge Kritizismus, jene Selbstzucht, die nicht auf alle Reize reagiert, sondern nur auf die unvorhergesehenen, gefährlichen, auf die Meisterschaft der Hirne, die sich sehr weit vorgewagt hatten.... Diese Zelle war ganz reinlich; in diese Abende drang kein

Pöbelinstinkt. Und jedem Dichter, der hier eintrat, bereitete Herr Walden, mit ein paar arrangierenden Handbewegungen, das seiner Art geziemende Bild.

71. Nell Walden, "Biographische Daten," p. 67; O.E., "Herwarth Walden," *Der Sturm* 19 (1928): 282. Heinz Graber has been able to establish the dates and programs of many of these evenings by locating reviews of them published in the contemporary Berlin press. See the notes to Döblin, *Briefe,* pp. 508-15.

72. In addition to the journals discussed in the following pages, Walden is reported in *Expressionismus: Literatur und Kunst,* ed. Zeller, et al., p. 142, as having been editor of *Nord und Süd.* However, there is no indication of such an association in the pages of *Nord und Süd.* On the other hand, Schickele, Walden's close friend at the time, was a coeditor of the journal from February to April, 1909. See *Nord und Süd* 33 (1909), vols. 128, 129, the issues for February, March, April. Also, *Morgen,* which Walden edited before 1910, was merged with *Nord und Süd* at the end of Walden's period of editorship. Nell Walden, "Biographisches Daten," p. 68, reports that Walden also edited the journal *Komet* before *Der Sturm.* However, Schlawe, *Literarische Zeitschriften,* vol. 2, p. 36, lists *Der Komet* as having appeared under the editorship of Paul L. Fuhrmann, initially with the assistance of Frank Wedekind, in Munich from the spring of 1911 to the spring of 1912.

73. From July, 1904, to January, 1905, under the ownership of the Jakob Hegner Verlag, Schickele had edited this journal. Its title during his editorship was changed to *Das neue Magazin für Literatur, Kunst und soziales Leben.*

74. *Das Magazin* 77 (1908), nos. 4, 5, 6, January, February, March.

75. *Das Magazin* 77 (1908), 49, 73, 97. This corrects Fritz Schlawe, *Literarische Zeitschriften: 1885-1910,* pt. 1; Sammlung Metzler, 6 (Stuttgart, 1961), p. 20, who erroneously gives the date for the subtitle change as July, 1906.

76. *Das Magazin* 77 (1908): 49, 73, 97.

77. Ibid., pp. 71, 95, 119.

78. Ibid., nos. 7/8ff.

79. *Morgen: Wochenschrift für deutsche Kultur* 2 (1908), nos. 36-51/52. See Schlawe, *Literarische Zeitschriften,* pt. 1, pp. 72-74; Paul Raabe, "Kafka und Franz Blei," in Jürgen Born, Ludwig Dietz, Malcolm Pasley, Paul Raabe, Klaus Wagenbuch, *Kafka-Symposium* (Berlin, 1965), p. 15 and pp. 19-20, n. 19.

80. Schlawe, *Literarische Zeitschriften,* pt. 1, pp. 72-73.

81. Raabe, "Kafka und Franz Blei," pp. 19-20, n. 19.

82. See note 79, above.

83. See Altenberg, et al., *Der neue Weg: Ein Protest,* pp. 1, 4-5 and passim.

84. Quoted by Raabe, "Kafka und Franz Blei," p. 16.

Der neue Weg ist das Blatt der freien Geister, der guten Europäer. Nichts weiter soll im Voraus hier gekündet werden. Die Tat soll zeigen was wir wollen und ob wirs können. Der deutsche Schauspieler hatte den Mut zur Tat. Den Neuen Weg, den er beschreiben will, er wandert ihn gemeinsam mit den freien Geistern aller Künste und aller Kulturen. Seinen Interessen seien diese Blätter besonders gewidmet.

85. Ibid. By special and personal arrangement with Walden, the Nietzsche Archives in Weimar were to have participated in *Der neue Weg* by contributing unpublished letters of Nietzsche and reports relating directly to the archives. See Elisabeth Förster-Nietzsche's statement to

this effect in Altenberg, et al., *Der neue Weg: Ein Protest,* pp. 7-8. See also in the latter volume, pp. 1-2, for a list of the contributors acquired for *Der neue Weg* by Walden during his editorship.

86. Altenberg, et al., *Der neue Weg: Ein Protest,* pp. 1, 4-6 and passim.

87. See above, note 69.

88. *Das Theater: Illustrierte Halbmonatsschrift für internationale Bühnenkunst,* 1909/1910, nos. 1-10, for September, 1909, to January, 1910.

89. See Rudolf Blümner, Alfred Döblin, Salomo Friedlaender, et al., "Erklärung," *Der Sturm* 1 (1910): 6; Nell Walden, "Biographische Daten," p. 68. Under Walden's editorship the contributors to *Das Theater* included Blei, Blümner, Brod, Döblin, Hardekopf, Siegmund Kalischer, Kurtz, Lasker-Schüler, Rubiner, Scheerbart, and Schickele. See Raabe, "Kafka und Franz Blei," p. 16 and p. 20 n. 22; Döblin, *Briefe,* pp. 517-18.

90. Rudolf Blümner, et al., "Erklärung," p. 6.

91. See esp. Nell Walden, "Biographische Daten," p. 70.

92. Nell Walden, "Der Mensch," p. 18. For an example of other members of the circle following the same pattern, see, e.g., Schreyer, *Erinnerungen,* pp. 40ff.

93. Nell Walden, "Aus meinen Erinnerungen," p. 16.

94. "Zwei Worte," *Der Sturm* 1 (1910): 1.

Zum vierten Mal treten wir mit einer neuen Zeitschrift in die Öffentlichkeit. Dreimal versuchte man, mit gröbsten Vertragsbrüchen unsere Tätigkeit zu verhindern, die von den Vielzuvielen peinlich empfunden wird. Wir haben uns entschlossen, unser eigener Verleger zu sein. Denn wir sind noch immer so glücklich, glauben zu können, dass an die Stelle des Journalismus und des Feuilletonismus wieder Kunst und die Künste treten können.

95. Schreyer, *Erinnerungen,* p. 8.

Unter diesem Zeichen hat alles gestanden, was nun zwangsläufig geschah. Der Sturm reinigt, entwurzelt, zerstört. Aber er braust auch als der Heilige Geist durch die Welt. Er ist die immerwährende Verwandlung, die Erneuerung von Grund auf, das Signal, in dem die geistige Wirklichkeit des Vollkommenen sich mit der Hinfälligkeit und der Hoffnung des irdischen Lebens begegnet.

96. Rudolf Kurtz, "Programmatisches," *Der Sturm* 1 (1910): 2-3.

97. Ibid., p. 2.

98. Ibid.

99. Ibid.

100. Ibid.

101. Ibid.

102. Ibid.

In jener glücklichen Epoche deutschen Daseins, als logische Begeisterung mit einer tiefen ästhetischen Intuition sich durchdrang, spiegelte sich dieses Gefühl in dem Begriff der Ironie und einer der wenigen ebenbürtigen Nachfahren jenes Geschlechtes, Nietzsche, predigte einem dumpfen Ernst zwecklos die frohe Botschaft des 'Tanzes.'

103. Ibid.

Der Intellektualismus kann nur gedämpft werden von der lärmvollen Betonung der Instinkte, der dunklen Kräfte, die er organisierend im Dienst des Lebens stellen sollte und zu denen er längst alle Beziehungen verloren hat.

104. Ibid.

105. Ibid.

106. Ibid.

107. Ibid.

Mit der provokantesten Geste werden wir jede Äusserung dieser Kultur verhöhnen, die statt auf Ausschöpfung des Lebens auf Erhaltung ihrer Konventionen abzielt. Jede liberale Schüchternheit, inhaltlose Gebräuche zu erhalten, werden wir mit radikaler Sorgfalt ausrupfen.

108. Ibid.

109. Kurt Hiller, "Über Kultur," *Der Sturm* 1 (1910): 187-88, 196-97, 203-4; Kurt Hiller, "Das Cabaret und die Gehirne," *Der Sturm* 1 (1910): 351; Kurt Hiller, "Gegen 'Lyrik,'" *Der Sturm* 1 (1911): 314-15; Erich Unger, "Vom Pathos," *Der Sturm* 1 (1910), 316; Erich Unger, "Nietzsche," *Der Sturm* 1 (1911): 380-81; 388-89; Salomo Friedlaender, "Polarität," *Der Sturm* 2 (1911): 732; Salomo Friedlaender, "Die Mitte zwischen Extremen," *Der Sturm* 4 (1913): 22-23; Salomo Friedlaender, "Nochmals Polarität," *Der Sturm* 6 (1915): 88-89; Umberto Boccioni, Carlo Carra, Luigi Russolo, Giacomo Galla, and Gino Severini, "Manifest der Futuristen," *Der Sturm* 2 (1912): 822-24; Filippo Marinetti, "Manifest des Futurismus," *Der Sturm* 2 (1912): 828-29; Umberto Boccioni, Carlo Carra, Luigi Russolo, Giacomo Balla, and Gino Severini, "Futuristen: Die Aussteller an das Publikum," *Der Sturm* 3 (1912): 3-4; Filippo Marinetti, "Tod dem Mondschein!," *Der Sturm* 3 (1912): 50-51, 57-58; Filippo Marinetti, "Die futuristische Literatur: Technisches Manifest," *Der Sturm* 3 (1912): 194-95; Filippo Marinetti, "Supplement zum technischen Manifest der futuristischen Literatur," *Der Sturm* 3 (1913): 279-80. On the "Wortkunst" theory see below.

110. The caricatures and other illustrations in a related, pre-expressionistic style begin in the April issue of 1910. *Der Sturm* 1 (1910): 61, and continue regularly thereafter. The artists are Samuel Fridolin, Max Fröhlich, Harry Jaeger-Mewe, Joe Loe, and others. See, e.g., in the first half year of *Der Sturm* 1 (1910): 61, 69, 70, 77, 86, 97, 105, 115, 123, 131, 135, 139, 147, 151, 159, 167, 171, 179, 183, 195, 211, 219, 223, 240, 247. Kokoschka's drawings in that first half year of 1910 were "Karl Kraus," "Adolf Loos," three illustrations for his play "Mörder Hoffnung der Frauen," "Herwarth Walden," "Himmlische und irdische Liebe," "Wintergarten," "Paul Scheerbart," "Gesindel in der Sternennacht," "Schlangenzeichnung." See *Der Sturm* 1 (1910): 91, 141, 155, 163, 189, 175, 203, 207, 213, 227, 235, respectively. That first half year Kokoschka also contributed two literary pieces to *Der Sturm:* "Mörder Hoffnung der Frauen" and a short cabaret critique. See *Der Sturm* 1 (1910): 155-56, 207.

111. The "Brücke" artists and their *first* drawings to appear in *Der Sturm* are: Max Pechstein, "Das Lager," Emil Nolde, "Tingeltangel," *Der Sturm* 1 (1911): 371, 443, respectively; Ernst Ludwig Kirchner, "Panamagirls," Erich Heckel, "Das schwarze Tuch," Karl Schmidt-Rottluff, "Mädchen," Otto Mueller, "Am Nachmittag," *Der Sturm* 2 (1911): 484, 499, 580, 695, respectively.

112. Kirchner's first woodcut to appear in *Der Sturm* was entitled "Ball." See *Der Sturm* 2 (1911): 548. The first appearances in *Der Sturm* by the others listed were: Artur Segal, "Holzschnitt," Jules Pascin, "Zeichnung," Moriz Melzer, "Grablegung, "César Klein, "Originalholzschnitt," Heinrich Richter-Berlin, "Die Brüstung," Georg Tappert, "Der

Clown," *Der Sturm* 2 (1911/12): 707, 751, 775, 783, 791, 799; Wilhelm Morgner, "Holzschnitt," Franz Marc, "Versöhnung," Wassily Kandinsky, "Originalholzschnitt," *Der Sturm* 3 (1912): 37, 133, 157.

113. See *Der Sturm* 3 (1912): 156.

114. See above, note 109.

115. See index to Walden's contributions to *Der Sturm* from that period in *Der Sturm*, ed. Nell Walden and Lothar Schreyer, pp. 250-54.

116. See announcement in *Der Sturm* 5 (1914), 80. *Der Sturm* had, several months before that event, already been reduced to a semimonthly; this had been made official, without any editorial announcement to the effect, by changing the subtitle of the journal to "Halbmonatsschrift für Kultur und die Künste." See its first appearance in the March, 1913, issue: *Der Sturm* 4 (1913) no. 152/153.

117. The first appearances in *Der Sturm* of these artists were: Maria Uhden, "Originalholzschnitt," *Der Sturm* 6 (1915): 91; Georg Schrimpf, "Linoleumschnitt," *Der Sturm* 7 (1916): 7; Fritz Stuckenberg, "Zeichnung," Lyonel Feininger, "Zeichnung," Georg Muche, "Marc Chagall gewidmet," *Der Sturm* 8 (1917): 65, 81, 129, respectively.

118. Heynicke's poetry first appeared in *Der Sturm* in the July, 1914, issue. See Kurt Heynicke, "Gedichte," *Der Sturm* 5 (1914): 55. However, the vast majority of his poetry was contributed to the journal during and after the war. Knoblauch made an appearance in *Der Sturm* before the war with a piece of literary criticism. See Adolf Knoblauch, "L'oeuvre Péladan," *Der Sturm* 1 (1911): 47. He did not appear again until September, 1914, and then began contributing poetry. See Adolf Knoblauch, "Besinnung," *Der Sturm* 5 (1914): 76. Sophie van Leer premiered in Walden's journal in June, 1915. See Sophie van Leer, "Freude," *Der Sturm* 6 (1915): 32. Runge made one contribution to *Der Sturm* before the war. See Wilhelm Runge, "Gedicht," *Der Sturm* 3 (1912): 130. He did not reappear until January, 1916. See Wilhelm Runge, "Lieder," *Der Sturm* 6 (1916): 114. Runge fell in battle in March, 1918. Quartner made three appearances in *Der Sturm* in 1913. See Isidor Quartner, "Gedichte," "Liebeslied," "Sinnlichkeit," *Der Sturm* 4 (1913): 10, 20, 59, respectively. Quartner died in October, 1915. Subsequently, his poetry appeared in only one more issue, the June number for 1916, where it assumed the most prominent place in that issue. See Isidor Quartner, "Gedichte," *Der Sturm* 7 (1916): 26-27. Ring's poetry first began appearing in the journal in August, 1916. See Thomas Ring, "Gedichte," *Der Sturm* 7 (1916): 9.

119. Lothar Schreyer, "Expressionistische Dichtung," *Sturm-Bühne* Ser. 4-6 (1918/19), reprinted in Paul Pörtner, *Literatur-Revolution: 1910-1925: Dokumente, Manifeste, Programme*, vol. 1, *Zur Aesthetik und Poetik*, Die Mainzer Reihe, vol. 13/1 (Darmstadt, Neuwied am Rhein, and Berlin-Spandau, 1960), p. 437. Schreyer further developed and elucidated the theory of the "Wortkunst" in several contributions to the *Sturm* publications. See, besides the essays cited in the following pages, esp. Lothar Schreyer, "Die neue Kunst," *Der Sturm* 10 (1919): 118-22; and Lothar Schreyer, "Das Wort," *Der Sturm* 13 (1922): 125-28, 141-50, 168-72.

120. Schreyer, "Expressionistische Dichtung," pp. 436-37; Lothar Schreyer, "Das Drama," *Der Sturm* 7 (1916): 119; Herwarth Walden, "Das begriffliche in der Dichtung," in *Expressionismus: Die Kunstwende*, ed. Herwarth Walden (Berlin, 1918), reprinted in Pörtner, *Literatur-Revolution*, vol. 1, p. 411; Rudolf Blümner, "August Stramm," *Der Sturm* 16 (1925): 122, 123, 124; Kurt Schwitters, "Selbstbestimmungsrecht der Künstler," *Der Sturm* 10 (1920), 140; Otto Nebel, "Vorworte zur Dichtung UNFEIG," *Der Sturm* 15 (1924): 131; Kurt Liebmann, "August Stramm," *Der Sturm* 12 (1921): 41-42.

121. Walden, "Das begriffliche," p. 411.

122. Schreyer, "Expressionistische Dichtung," p. 437.

    Das Wortkunstwerk, das Kunstwerk bildet uns ein in den Kosmos. Der Eingebildete ist der Gebildete der Gegenwart. Die Bildung der Vergangenheit ist tot. Räumen wir die tote Bildung fort, dass Raum wird für die lebendige Einbildung des Eins ins All, des Menschen in die Welt.

123. Nebel, "Vorworte," p. 131.

    Das LOS der Dichtung ist ein FEST im All, und alles Reine ist *Gedicht* im Licht.

124. Herwarth Walden, "Einblick in die Kunst," *Der Sturm* 6 (1916): 122-23; Walden, "Das begriffliche," pp. 404, 405, 409; Liebmann, "Stramm," p. 41; Schreyer, "Expressionistische Dichtung," pp. 437, 441; Nebel, "Vorworte," pp. 130-31; Otto Nebel, "GELEIT- und BEGLEIT-ERSCHEINUNGEN zur absoluten Dichtung," *Der Sturm* 15 (1924): 210-22; Rudolf Blümner, "Die absolute Dichtung," *Der Sturm* 12 (1921): 122; Blümner, "Stramm," pp. 122, 123.

125. Walden, "Das begriffliche," p. 405; Walden, "Einblick," p. 123; Schreyer, "Expressionistische Dichtung," p. 437.

126. Schreyer, "Expressionistische Dichtung," pp. 437, 442; Walden, "Einblick," p. 123.

127. Walden, "Einblick," p. 123.

128. Walden, "Das begriffliche," p. 410; Herwarth Walden, "Kritik der vorexpressionistischen Dichtung," *Der Sturm* 11 (1920): 98-99; Schreyer, "Expressionistische Dichtung," p. 436; Nebel, "Vorworte," p. 131; Nebel, "...zur absoluten Dichtung," p. 212; Liebmann, "Stramm," p. 42.

129. Schreyer, "Expressionistische Dichtung," p. 442.

130. Ibid., p. 437ff; Walden, "Das begriffliche," pp. 405, 409; Blümner, "Stramm," p. 123; Rudolf Blümner, "Die Dichtung als Wortkunst," in Rudolf Blümner, *Der Geist des Kubismus und die Künste* (Berlin, 1921), reprinted in Pörtner, *Literatur-Revolution,* vol. 1, pp. 443-44; Blümner, "Die absolute Dichtung," p. 449; Schwitters, "Selbstbestimmungsrecht," p. 140; Nebel, "Vorworte," pp. 130-31; Nebel, "...zur absoluten Dichtung," pp. 210ff; Liebmann, "Stramm," p. 42.

131. Schreyer, "Expressionistische Dichtung," pp. 439-41; Walden, "Das begriffliche," p. 410; Blümner, "Die absolute Dichtung," p. 122; Blümner, "Stramm," pp. 122-23; Nebel, "Vorworte," pp. 130-31; Nebel, "...zur absoluten Dichtung," pp. 210ff.

132. Schreyer, "Expressionistische Dichtung," pp. 439-41.

133. Ibid., pp. 437, 441, 442; Blümner, "Die absolute Dichtung," p. 122; Walden, "Einblick," p. 123; Walden, "Das begriffliche," p. 405.

134. Richard Brinkmann, "'Abstrakte' Lyrik im Expressionismus und die Möglichkeit symbolischer Aussage," in *Der deutsche Expressionismus: Formen und Gestalten,* ed. Hans Steffen, Kleine Vandenhoeck-Reihe, 208 (S) (Göttingen, 1965), p. 90.

135. See esp. Schreyer, Erinnerungen, p. 91.

136. See above, note 109, for a list of the Futurist manifestoes which appeared in *Der Sturm* in 1912 and 1913.

137. Schreyer, *Erinnerungen,* pp. 78-80; Blümner, "Stramm," pp. 121ff; Blümner, "Die absolute Dichtung," p. 121; Walden, "Einblick," p. 124; Liebmann, "Stramm," pp. 41-42; Schreyer,

"Expressionistische Dichtung," p. 443. On Stramm and the influence on him of the Futurists see Radrizzani, "Lebensgeschichte," pp. 432-33. Radrizzani quotes from a letter written by Stramm to his wife on December 29, 1914, in which Stramm suggests this influence himself. See Radrizzani, "Lebensgeschichte," p. 433. See also the investigation of this influence in Armin Arnold, *Die Literatur des Expressionismus: Sprachliche und thematische Quellen*, Sprache und Literatur, 35 (Stuttgart, Berlin, Cologne, and Mainz, 1966), pp. 28ff.

138. The letter cited by Radrizzani, "Lebensgeschichte," p. 433, suggests this also. See also the similar suggestion in the passage from a letter written by Stramm on the same date, quoted from by Radrizzani, "Lebensgeschichte," p. 431.

139. Radrizzani, "Lebensgeschichte," p. 432. Stramm's initial appearance in Walden's journal was in April, 1914. See August Stramm, "Gedichte," *Der Sturm* 5 (1914): 10-11. Stramm first met Walden personally at the beginning of 1914, see Radrizzani, "Lebensgeschichte," pp. 426, 432.

140. Schreyer premiered in *Der Sturm* in July, 1916, with the play *Nacht*. See above, note 28. Behrens's first contribution came in February, 1916. See Franz Richard Behrens, "Expressionist-Artillerist," *Der Sturm* 6 (1916): 130. Mehring first appeared in April, 1918. See Walter Mehring, "Deri," *Der Sturm* 9 (1918): 14. Allwohn's verse first appeared in *Der Sturm* in the June, 1918, issue. See Adolf Allwohn, "Um Gott," *Der Sturm* 9 (1918): 34-35. Liebmann contributed his first verse in August, 1918. See Kurt Liebmann, "Roter Tanz Kreuz Bären Ich," *Der Sturm* 9 (1918): 72. On Mürr see below.

141. Günther Mürr, "Hamburg," *Der Sturm* 3 (1912): 758, 766, 773, 784, 790, 801, 808, 813; Günther Mürr, "Marie," "Gedicht," "Irischer Abend," "Marienlied," "Gedichte," *Der Sturm* 3 (1912/1913): 85, 161, 222, 238, 283, respectively; Günther Mürr, "Vergottung in Maria," "Gedicht," *Der Sturm* 4 (1913): 75, 140, respectively; Günther Mürr, "Gedichte," "Gedichte," "Wir," *Der Sturm* 9 (1918): 8, 60, 84, respectively; Günther Mürr, "Raumfahrt," *Der Sturm* 10 (1919): 98-99.

142. See, e.g., the announcements of the deaths of the following: of Macke in *Der Sturm* 5 (1915): 138; of Stramm in *Der Sturm* 5 (1915): 74; of Marc in *Der Sturm* 5 (1916): 133.

143. August Stramm, *Tropfblut* (Berlin, n.d. [1919]). This edition did not conform in part to the wishes of the author for a collection with the title "Tropfblut," according to the editor of Stramm's works, René Radrizzani. Stramm, Radrizzani points out, intended such a title for a collection of exclusively the poetry which he wrote during the war from the field of battle, November, 1914ff. Radrizzani has corrected the 1919 edition of *Tropfblut* to bring it in line with Stramm's wishes in Stramm, *Das Werk*, pp. 65-99. See also the editorial notes there, pp. 461-64.

144. The last poetry to appear in *Der Sturm* was in the second to the last issue of the journal. One of the two poems in that issue is a posthumous publication of one of August Stramm's war poems, "Krieggrab." See *Der Sturm* 21 (1932), no. 2, p. 36.

145. See Hugo Ball, *Die Flucht aus der Zeit* (Lucerne, 1946), pp. 98-99.

146. Blümner, "Die absolute Dichtung," pp. 121-23; Nebel, "Vorworte," pp. 130-31; Nebel, "...zur absoluten Dichtung," pp. 210-13; Rudolf Blümner, "Angolaina," *Der Sturm* 12 (1921): 123; Otto Nebel, "Unfeig," *Der Sturm* 15 (1924): 129-38, *Der Sturm* 16 (1925): 22-23, 34-36, 78-80, 90-92, 111-12.

147. Stramm's and Runge's verse continued to appear in *Der Sturm* in this phase occasionally, but posthumously; both had been killed in battle before the end of the war.
      Poems by Ring from this phase, such as "Kreis" or "1914," represent full-fledged "Wortkunst." See *Der Sturm* 16 (1925): 108, *Der Sturm* 19 (1929): 313-15, respectively.

"1914" is also an overtly political poem of leftist sympathies. Some of Heynicke's verse from this phase also exhibits clear tendencies towards condensation of language. See Kurt Heynicke, "Gedichte," *Der Sturm* 15 (1924): 26-28; Kurt Heynicke, "Die Sappe," *Der Sturm* 17 (1926): 75.

148.   Herwarth Walden, "Kunst und Leben," *Der Sturm* 10 (1919): 2-3; Herwarth Walden, "Künstler Volk und Kunst," *Der Sturm* 10 (1919): 10-13.

149.   Walden, "Kunst und Leben," pp. 2-3.

150.   Ibid.; Walden, "Künstler," p. 12.

151.   Walden, "Kunst und Leben," pp. 2-3.

152.   Ibid.

153.   Ibid., p. 3.

Wir wollen nicht Politik treiben, wir wollen die Politik treiben, dass Leben sich zum Leben gestalte. Wir wollen Politik machen, sachlich und nüchtern. Denn auch die Kunst ist sachlich und nüchtern, das heisst organisch.

154.   Lothar Schreyer, "Der neue Mensch," *Der Sturm* 10 (1919): 18-20.

155.   Ibid., pp. 18-19.

156.   Ibid., pp. 19-20.

157.   Ibid., p. 20.

Sie [= die Güte] ist die Hingabe des Eins an das All.

158.   Since the journal's inception in March, 1910, the publishing year of *Der Sturm* had cut across the calendar year. A notice in the eleventh year of the journal announced that, beginning in its twelfth year, the publishing year of *Der Sturm* would follow the calendar year. See *Der Sturm* 11 (1920): 93. This remained the practice until the seventeenth year (1926/1927).

159.   See "Mitteilung an die Leser des *Sturm,*" *Der Sturm* 11 (1920): 141.

160.   William Wauer, "Gold Währung Kapital: Eine Studie," *Der Sturm* 11 (1920): 146-48.

161.   R.B. [Rudolf Blümner], "An die Leser des *Sturm!*" *Der Sturm* 14 (1923): 191-92.

162.   Another side effect, no doubt, of the inflation was the resumption in the thirteenth year (1922) of picture advertisements for business firms, etc. See *Der Sturm* 13 (1922), no. 11, last unnumbered sheet.

163.   Blümner, "An die Leser des *Sturm!*" p. 191.

164.   Ibid.

165.   On Walden's postwar ideological development see below.

166.   See Nell Walden, "Biographische Daten," p. 78. Nell Walden records here that Walden's visit to Russia was undertaken as the director of the "Bund der Freunde der Sowjetunion."

167.   Herwarth Walden, "USSR 1927," *Der Sturm* 18 (1927): 73-75. See also Herwarth Walden, "Sowjet-Russland," *Der Sturm* 18 (1927): 105-12; Herwarth Walden, "Vom Bolschewismus," *Der Sturm* 19 (1928), 207-9.

168.   "Sonderheft: Sowjet-Union," *Der Sturm* 20 (December, 1929-January, 1930), no. 5/6.

169. "Sonderheft: Junge slovenische Kunst," *Der Sturm* 19 (January, 1929), no. 10; "Sonderheft: Junge bulgarische Kunst," *Der Sturm* 20 (October-November, 1929), no. 2/3; "Sonderheft: Rumänische Literatur," *Der Sturm* 20 (August-September, 1930), no. 8.

170. See "Anmerkung," *Der Sturm* 21 (1932): 32.

171. See *Der Sturm* 21 (1932): nos. 1-3.

172. See note to this effect in Trust, "Furchtbar dräut der Erbfeind," *Der Sturm* 2 (1911): 500.

173. See announcements of such evenings in *Der Sturm* 1 (1910): 8; *Der Sturm* 2 (1911/1912): 618, 626, 642, 665, 681, 697, 705, 713, 745, 753, 770, 806.

174. See notice of the reorganization in *Der Sturm* 7 (1916): 60. See also Nell Walden, "Biographische Daten," p. 72.

175. See the announcement of the Stramm memorial evening in *Der Sturm* 7 (1916): 60. See also *Sturm-Abende: Ausgewählte Gedichte* (Berlin, n.d. [1918]). The latter volume is a collection of verse read at the "Sturm-Kunstabende." See Raabe, *Die Zeitschriften,* p. 140.

176. See Schreyer, *Erinnerungen,* p. 80; Nell Walden, "Aus meinen Erinnerungen," pp. 30, 40. See also the announcements for the series of evenings in the winter of 1916/17 in *Der Sturm* 7 (1916): 60, and the series announced in succeeding issues.

177. See Schreyer, *Erinnerungen,* pp. 78ff; Herwarth Walden, "Rudolf Blümner zum fünzigsten Geburtstag," *Der Sturm* 14 (1923): 113-14.

178. See announcements of programs of the evenings in *Der Sturm* 7 (1916): 60, and the announcements given regularly in the issues that followed.

179. See Schreyer, "Das war *Der Sturm,*" pp. 124-25. See also announcements of evenings abroad in *Der Sturm* 7 (1916), passim, and in subsequent volumes of the journal.

180. Nell Walden, "Der Mensch," p. 28; Nell Walden, "Kokoschka," p. 133; Schreyer, *Erinnerungen,* p. 85.

181. Schreyer, *Erinnerungen,* p. 81.

182. See *Der Sturm* 17 (March, 1927), no. 12, p. II.

183. Schreyer, "Das war *Der Sturm,*" p. 123. Nell Walden, "Der Mensch," p. 34, claims that the last *Sturm* exhibitions took place in 1929. However, in "Biographische Daten," p. 79, where she lists some of those last exhibitions, she implies that there is some uncertainty concerning them. Schreyer, *Erinnerungen,* p. 16, describes his last meeting with Walden before he left on a trip to Russia; and, although he does not make clear the date of this meeting, the context of Schreyer's report on it seems to point to Walden's permanent move to Moscow in June, 1932. During that last meeting, Schreyer notes, he and Walden toured Walden's "last exhibition."

184. See, e.g., Nell Walden, "Aus meinen Erinnerungen," p. 11; Schreyer, "Das war *Der Sturm,*" p. 123.

185. See Schreyer, "Das war *Der Sturm,*" pp. 123-24. There is a list of the exhibitions sponsored by *Der Sturm* from 1912 to 1921 in *Der Sturm,* ed. Nell Walden and Lothar Schreyer, pp. 257-68.

186. Nell Walden, "Aus meinen Erinnerungen," pp. 10-11.

187. Schreyer, "Das war *Der Sturm,*" p. 124.

188. See above, chapter 1, p. 27.

189. See contents of these exhibitions in *Der Sturm,* ed. Nell Walden and Lothar Schreyer, pp. 257-58.

190. See Nell Walden, "Aus meinen Erinnerungen," p. 13; *Der Sturm,* ed. Nell Walden and Lothar Schreyer, p. 258. See Elisabeth Erdmann-Macke, *Erinnerung an August Macke* (Stuttgart, 1962), pp. 204-5.

191. Schreyer, "Das war *Der Sturm,*" p. 125.

192. See Nell Walden, "Aus meinen Erinnerungen," passim; Nell Walden, "Biographische Daten," pp. 69ff; Nell Walden, "Kokoschka," passim.

193. See *Der Sturm,* ed. Nell Walden and Lothar Schreyer, p. 257; Peter Selz, *German Expressionist Painting* (Berkeley and Los Angeles, 1957), pp. 265ff; Jean-Paul Crespelle, *The Fauves,* trans. Anita Brookner (Greenwich, 1962), pp. 11ff., 27; Jean Leymarie, *Fauvism: Biographical and Critical Study* (Paris, 1959), pp. 22-23.

194. Nell Walden, "Aus meinen Erinnerungen," pp. 13ff.

195. Ibid., p. 13.

196. Ibid., pp. 21-22; Hans Arp, *Unsern täglichen Traum . . . Erinnerungen, Dichtungen und Betrachtungen aus den Jahren 1914-1954* (Zürich, 1955), pp. 7-8.

197. Nell Walden, "Aus meinen Erinnerungen," pp. 13-22.

198. Ibid., pp. 30-31.

199. Ball, *Die Flucht,* pp. 10-13; Ball, *Briefe,* pp. 29-31.

200. Ball, *Die Flucht,* pp. 11-12.

201. Ibid.

202. Ibid.

203. Ibid., p. 12.

204. Ibid.

205. Ibid., p. 13; Ball, *Briefe,* pp. 29-31.

206. Ball, *Briefe,* p. 33.

207. Ball, *Die Flucht,* pp. 142-162; Ball, *Briefe,* pp. 78-81.

208. Ball, *Die Flucht,* p. 142.

209. Ibid., pp. 142-62.

210. Ibid.

211. Ibid., p. 150.

212. Kandinsky, Klee, Marc had been included in several of the *Sturm* exhibitions from 1912 through 1917. See *Der Sturm,* ed. Nell Walden and Lothar Schreyer, pp. 257-63. Kandinsky and Marc were contributing to *Der Sturm* from 1912 on with both art work and essays; Klee began contributing to the journal with art work in 1913. See *Der Sturm,* ed. Nell Walden and Lothar Schreyer, pp. 226, 234. Klee, in addition, was listed as one of the teachers in the "Sturm-Schule" founded in March, 1917. See below. Marc and his wife were especially good friends of the Waldens. On contacts between the Waldens and the Marcs, Kandinsky and Klee see Nell Walden, "Aus meinen Erinnerungen," passim; Nell Walden, "Der Mensch," passim. See also August Macke and Franz Marc, *Briefwechsel,* ed. Wolfgang Macke (Cologne, 1964), passim.

213. Herwarth Walden, "Theater," *Der Sturm* 5 (1915): 147.

214. *Der Sturm* 7 (March, 1917), no. 12, p. 144. Nell Walden gives the date of the establishment of the "Sturm-Kunstschule" as September 1, 1916. See Nell Walden, "Biographische Daten," p. 72. However, the first notice on it appears in *Der Sturm* in the issue just cited.

215. Schreyer, *Erinnerungen,* pp. 78ff.

216. *Der Sturm* 7 (1917): 144.

217. Ibid.

218. Schreyer, *Erinnerungen,* pp. 19ff; Nell Walden, "Biographische Daten" pp. 72, 77; Nell Walden, "Aus meinen Erinnerungen," p. 40. The first announcement of the "Sturm-Bühne" comes in "Aufruf," *Der Sturm* 8 (September, 1917), no. 6, p. 94.

219. "Aufruf," p. 94; Nell Walden, "Biographische Daten," p. 77.

220. Lothar Schreyer, "Das Bühnenkunstwerk," *Der Sturm* 7 (August, 1916), no. 5, pp. 50-51; Lothar Schreyer, "Das Drama," *Der Sturm* 7 (January, 1917), no. 10, p. 119; Lothar Schreyer, "Das Bühnenkunstwerk: Die Wirklichkeit des Geistes," *Der Sturm* 8 (May, 1917), no. 2, pp. 18-20, 22. Schreyer's series of six lectures in this period, under the title "Das Bühnenkunstwerk," were given at "Sturm-Kunstabende" held between April 11 and June 20, 1917. See announcement of them in *Der Sturm* 7 (1917), p. 144. Two more series of five lectures each, entitled "Der Expressionismus" and "Das Bühnenkunstwerk," were given by Schreyer between October 7 and December, 1917. See *Der Sturm* 8 (1917), p. 123.

221. See esp. Lothar Schreyer, *Expressionistisches Theater: Aus meinen Erinnerungen,* Hamburger Theaterbücherei, vol. 4 (Hamburg, 1947), passim; Schreyer, "Das Bühnenkunstwerk," passim; Schreyer, "Das Drama," passim; Schreyer, "Das Bühnenkunstwerk: Die Wirklichkeit," passim; Schreyer, *Erinnerungen,* pp. 21ff.

222. Schreyer, *Expressionistisches Theater,* pp. 202f.

223. See esp. Ibid., the chapter entitled "Wortgestalt," pp. 96ff.

224. Ibid., pp. 124ff., 167ff. and passim; Schreyer, "Das Bühnenkunstwerk," pp. 50-51; Schreyer, "Das Drama," 119; Schreyer, "Das Bühnenkunstwerk: Die Wirklichkeit," p. 18.

225. "Aufruf," *Der Sturm* 8 (1917): 94.

    Wir wissen, dass der Mensch der Gegenwart sich sehnt nach einer geistigen Wirklichkeit, in der er die Einheit des Seins erlebt. Die geistige Wirklichkeit kündet sich in der Kunst. Das Erlebnis der Kunst füllt unsere Sehnsucht.

226. Schreyer, *Erinnerungen,* pp. 32-33.

    Uns ging es um den Menschen in der Gemeinschaft und um die Möglichkeit im Schaffen und Spielen des Bühnenkunstwerks, das ein kosmischer Spiegel der Einheit des Lebens sein wollte, die Gemeinschaft des natürlich-übernatürlichen Lebens in ihrem Erleiden der Vereinigung zu verkünden, indem wir diese Vereinigung unter uns selbst vollzogen und ihr eine wahrnehmende Gestalt im Sinnbild des Kunstwerks aus allen Mitteln der Kunst geformt, gaben.

227. Schreyer, "Das war *Der Sturm,*" p. 125; *Der Sturm* 9 (1918): 88.

228. Schreyer, *Erinnerungen,* p. 24. Schreyer does not give a date here for the premiere. The announcements in *Der Sturm* 9 (1918): 88, 100, give October 15, 18, 19, 26 and December 3, 1918, as the dates for the first scheduled performances of the "Sturm-Bühne." The actual date of the premiere of the theater and of Stramm's play as October 16, 1918, is provided by the date on Herbert Jhering's review of the performance. See Herbert Jhering, *Von*

Reinhardt bis Brecht: Eine Auswahl der Theaterkritiken von 1909-1932, ed. Rolf Badenhausen, Rowohlt Paperback, 55 (Reinbek bei Hamburg, 1967), pp. 32-34.

229. Schreyer, *Erinnerungen,* pp. 24-25; Schreyer, *Expressionistisches Theater,* p. 197.

230. See the announcements of original dates in *Der Sturm* cited in note 228, above. See also description of the performance of *Sancta Susanna* in the fall of 1918 as a single performance, *Expressionistisches Theater,* p. 197.

231. See Raabe, *Die Zeitschriften,* p. 73; Nell Walden, "Biographische Daten," p. 77.

232. Raabe, *Die Zeitschriften,* p. 73; Nell Walden, "Biographische Daten," p. 7.

233. Raabe, *Die Zeitschriften,* p. 73.

234. Schreyer, *Erinnerungen,* p. 25; Schreyer, *Expressionistisches Theater,* p. 198.

235. Schreyer, *Erinnerungen,* pp. 25ff; Schreyer, *Expressionistisches Theater,* pp. 198ff.

236. Schreyer, *Erinnerungen,* p. 26; Schreyer, *Expressionistisches Theater,* p. 199.

237. Schreyer, *Erinnerungen,* p. 26; Schreyer, *Expressionistisches Theater,* p. 198.

238. See note 236, above. Since Schreyer claims that the "Kampf-Bühne" made only one guest appearance in Berlin (see below), then the production of Stramm's play *Haidebraut* in Berlin in the fall of 1920 can, indeed, as the announcement in *Der Sturm* indicates, be assumed to have been given by the "Sturm-Bühne" and not Schreyer's "Kampf-Bühne." See *Der Sturm* 11 (1920): 48, 80. The production of Lothar Schreyer's play *Mann* under the name of the "Sturm-Bühne," announced in *Der Sturm* for May 16, 1920, in the "Kammerspiele des Deutschen Theaters" in Berlin, is without question the guest appearance of Schreyer's "Kampf-Bühne" about that time (see below). Franz Horch, *Die Spielpläne Max Reinhardts: 1905-1930* (Munich, 1930), p. 50, also lists the 1920 performance of Schreyer's *Mann* in the Reinhardt theater as done by the "Sturm-Bühne, Theater der Expressionisten."

239. Schreyer, *Expressionistische Theater,* p. 199.

240. Ibid., p. 201; Schreyer, *Erinnerungen,* p. 29.

241. Schreyer, *Expressionistisches Theater,* pp. 201-2; Schreyer, *Erinnerungen,* pp. 29-30.

242. Schreyer, *Expressionistisches Theater,* p. 202; Schreyer, *Erinnerungen,* p. 30.

243. Schreyer, *Expressionistisches Theater,* p. 206; Schreyer, *Erinnerungen,* p. 33.

244. See, e.g., announcements in *Der Sturm* 11 (1920): 15, 31, 119. See also Nell Walden, "Biographische Daten," p. 78.

245. *Der Sturm* 21 (1932): 62.

246. Nell Walden, "Aus meinen Erinnerungen," p. 16. *Der Sturm,* from 1912 on especially, contains numerous answers, written mostly by Walden, to criticisms of the *Sturm* exhibitions and of *Der Sturm* itself from the established press. On the troubles of *Der Sturm* with the censor before the war, especially over the publication in the journal's pages of drawings of female nudes, see the glosses in *Der Sturm:* e.g., *Der Sturm* 1 (1911): 424; *Der Sturm* 2 (1911): 472, 515, 576. See also Schreyer, *Erinnerungen,* p. 81.

247. Nell Walden, "Aus meinen Erinnerungen," p. 38; Nell Walden, "Biographische Daten," p. 71.

248. Nell Walden, "Biographische Daten," p. 40.

249. Ibid.

250. Schreyer, "Das war *Der Sturm,*" p. 124.

251. Schreyer, *Erinnerungen,* pp. 111-12.

252. Nell Walden, "Der Mensch," p. 23.

253. Schreyer, *Erinnerungen,* pp. 33, 136-37.

254. *Expressionismus: Literatur und Kunst,* ed. Zeller, et al., pp. 150, 149; Muche, *Blickpunkt,* p. 229.

255. Essays indicating such interest on the part of Schreyer and Wauer have already been cited. See above. For other examples, see Thomas Ring, "Die Krise des Imperialismus," *Der Sturm* 17 (1926): 106-12, 124-48; Rudolf Blümner, "Spezialbehandlung," *Der Sturm* 21 (1932): 21-24; Otto Nebel, "Doktor Sport," *Der Sturm* 21 (1932): 44-46.

256. Schreyer, *Erinnerungen,* p. 17.

257. Ibid.

258. Nell Walden, "Aus meinen Erinnerungen," p. 61.

259. Schreyer, *Erinnerungen,* p. 15.

260. Nell Walden, "Aus meinen Erinnerungen," p. 61.

    Kunst und Politik haben nichts miteinander zu tun.

261. Ibid., p. 35.

262. Ibid., p. 61.

263. Nell Walden, "Der Mensch," p. 32. On the presence and activities of the Russian émigrés in Berlin after the war see Ilya Ehrenburg, *Memoirs: 1921-1941,* trans. Tatania Shebunna (Cleveland and New York, 1964), pp. 18ff; Otto Friedrich, *Before the Deluge: A Portrait of Berlin in the 1920's* (New York, 1972), pp. 79ff.

264. Nell Walden, "Der Mensch," p. 32; Schreyer, *Erinnerungen,* pp. 54ff.

265. Nell Walden, "Der Mensch," p. 32; Schreyer, *Erinnerungen,* pp. 54ff. See also Walden's review of Jushny's cabaret: Herwarth Walden, "Der Blaue Vogel," *Der Sturm* 15 (1924): 37-39.

266. For Walden's positive interest in Russian culture see, e.g., the gloss in *Der Sturm* 13 (1923): 66; Herwarth Walden, "Zum Film *Potemkin,*" *Der Sturm* 17 (1926): 100-101. In September, 1927, with the essay "USSR 1927," Walden's positive interest in Russian politics begins to come to the fore. See note 167, above.

267. Nell Walden, "Der Mensch," p. 32.

268. Nell Walden, "Biographische Daten," p. 78. Nell Walden, "Der Mensch," p. 34, reports that Walden began making extended visits to Russia after 1929.

269. Herwarth Walden, "Auf!" *Der Sturm* 19 (February-March, 1929), no. 11/12, pp. 345-47.

270. Nell Walden, "Der Mensch," p. 34; Nell Walden, "Biographische Daten," p. 80.

271. Nell Walden, "Biographische Daten," p. 80.

272. Herwarth Walden, "Vulgär-Expressionismus," *Das Wort* 3 (1938): 89-100. See esp. the concluding sentences, p. 100:

    Das grosse politische Ziel der Volksfront ergibt die Konsequenz, die Künstlerishe Avantgarde zu stützen, sie ist ein aktiver Teil der Volksfront. Je mehr sich die Künstler

politisch und sozial schulen, je mehr sie also die Zeit erkennen, in der sie leben, je mehr sie
sich unvoreingenommen mit dem Aufbau der Sowjetunion befassen, um so mehr wird
jeder einzelne zu dem kommen, um was es geht: zum Stil der Zeit.

See also Schreyer, *Erinnerungen,* p. 17.

273.   Nell Walden, "Der Mensch," p. 34; Nell Walden, "Biographische Daten," p. 80; Schreyer,
Erinnerungen, p. 17.

274.   Kurt Pinthus, "Erinnerungen an Bechers Frühzeit," in Johannes R. Becher, *Lyrik, Prosa,
Dokumente: Eine Auswahl,* ed. Max Niedermayer (Wiesbaden, 1965), p. xl.

Es wird einst schwierig sein, die Geschichte der literarischen Gruppen zu schreiben, die sich
zwischen 1910 und 1920 zugleich in Prag, Berlin, Wien, Leipzig, Dresden, München und
anderen Städten entwickelten—oft im Zusammenhang mit ähnlichen Bestrebungen in den
bildenden Künsten—und sich trotz individueller Verschiedenheiten als Gemeinsamkeit, als
Gemeinschaft empfanden.

275.   Richard Brinkmann, *Expressionismus: Forschungs-Probleme 1952-1960,* Sonderdruck:
Deutsche Vierteljahrsschrift für Literaturwissenschaft und Geistesgeschichte, vol. 33, 1959;
vol. 34, 1960 (Stuttgart, 1961). See also the Introduction to the present study, above.

276.   Mehring, "Berlin Avantgarde," pp. 118ff; Heinrich Eduard Jacob, "Berlin—
Vorkriegsdichtung und Lebensgefühl," in *Expressionismus: Aufzeichnungen,* ed. Raabe,
pp. 15f; Peter Scher, "Als Kokoschka mich malte," reprinted in *Expressionismus:
Aufzeichnungen,* ed. Raabe, p. 336, n. 1.

277.   See below on the Cassirer circle.

278.   Franz Pfemfert, "Der kleine Kraus ist tot," *Die Aktion* 1 (April 10, 1911), no. 8, pp. 242-43.

279.   Trust, "Zeitgeschichte: Der geopferte Gott," *Der Sturm* 2 (April 29, 1911), no. 61, p. 484.

280.   Franz Pfemfert, "Pressepranger: Der ausgebleichte Somali-Neger," *Die Aktion* 1 (May 8,
1911), no. 12, p. 363; Herwarth Walden, "Der Name," *Der Sturm* 2 (May 13, 1911), no. 62, p.
492; Franz Pfemfert, "Pressepranger: Herr Herwarth Walden," *Die Aktion* 1 (May 22,
1911), no. 14, p. 424; Trust, "Zeitgeschichte: Bubenstreiche," *Der Sturm* 2 (July, 1911), no.
68, pp. 539-40; Franz Pfemfert, "Glossen: Herr Herwarth Walden," *Die Aktion* 1 (July 31,
1911), no. 24, p. 746.

281.   Nikodemus (pseud. of Franz Blei), "Eine ästhetische Entdeckung," *Die Aktion* 5 (1915):
472-73; Paul Lasker-Schüler, "Der Triumphator" (drawing with caption), *Die Aktion* 5
(1915): 654; Franz Pfemfert, "Kleiner Briefkasten," *Die Aktion* 8 (May 18, 1918), no. 19/20,
p. 257; Herwarth Walden, "Gute Kritik: Die Vossische Aktion," *Der Sturm* 9 (June, 1918),
no. 3, p. 46; Libori (pseud. for Franz Pfemfert), "Brief an den Lewin-Walden," *Die Aktion* 8
(July 27, 1918), no. 29/30, pp. 386-87.

282.   See Scher, "Als Kokoschka mich malte," p. 336; Raabe, "Der frühe Benn," pp. 13-14.

283.   See *Die Aktion,* ed. Raabe (Stuttgart, 1961), vol. 1, p. 122. On contacts of those listed with
both Walden's and Pfemfert's circle see above, the list of members and guests of Walden's
circle, and below, the similar list for the Pfemfert circle.

284.   See Meyer, *die maer,* p. 12; Benn, "Rede auf Else Lasker-Schüler," p. 537; Ball, *Die Flucht,*
p. 7. See also Mehring, "Berlin Avantgarde," p. 17.

Chapter 6

1. Else Lasker-Schüler, *Briefe an Karl Kraus,* ed. Astrid Gehloff-Claes (Cologne and Berlin, 1959), pp. 64, 68; Alexandra Pfemfert, "Die Gründung der *Aktion,*" in *Expressionismus: Aufzeichnungen,* ed. Raabe, p. 43; Walter Mehring, *Berlin Dada: Eine Chronik mit Photos und Dokumenten* (Zürich, 1959), p. 15; Walter Mehring, "Berlin Avantgarde," in *Expressionismus: Aufzeichnungen,* ed. Raabe, pp. 117ff; Walter Mehring, *Die verlorene Bibliothek: Autobiographie einer Kultur* (Icking bei München, 1964), pp. 144ff; Max Krell, *Das alles gab es einmal* (Frankfurt a.M., 1961), p. 13. Sources which cite the members and friends of Pfemfert's circle individually as habitués of the Café des Westens are lacking only for Otten, Wetzel, Gross: see the memoirs just cited, passim; also Else Lasker-Schüler, *Lieber gestreifter Tiger,* vol. 1 of *Briefe,* ed. Margarete Kupper (Munich, 1969), passim; Else Lasker-Schüler, *Wo ist unser buntes Theben,* vol. 2 of *Briefe,* ed. Margarete Kupper (Munich, 1969), passim; Else Lasker-Schüler, *Mein Herz* (Munich and Berlin, 1912), passim, reprinted in Else Lasker-Schüler, *Prosa und Schauspiele,* vol. 2 of *Gesammelte Werke,* ed. Friedhelm Kemp (Munich, 1962), pp. 289-391; Else Lasker-Schüler, *Der Malik* (Berlin, 1919), passim, reprinted Lasker-Schüler, *Gesammelte Werke,* vol. 2, pp. 393-489; Else Lasker-Schüler, *Gesichte* (Berlin, 1920), passim, reprinted Lasker-Schüler, *Gesammelte Werke,* vol. 2, pp. 137-216; Else Lasker-Schüler, *Essays* (Berlin, 1920), passim, reprinted Lasker-Schüler, *Gesammelte Werke,* vol. 2, pp. 217-87; Alfred Lichtenstein, *Gesammelte Gedichte,* ed. Klaus Kanzog (Zürich, 1962), pp. 101ff; Emil Szittya, *Das Kuriositäten-Kabinett* (Constance, 1923), p. 246ff; Wieland Herzfelde, "Aus der Jugendzeit des Malik-Verlages: Zum Neudruck der Zeitschrift *Neue Jugend,*" in *Neue Jugend 1916/17* (Zürich, 1967), pp. 5-6; Wieland Herzfelde, "Fremd und Nah: Über meinen Briefwechsel und meine Begegnungen mit Else Lasker-Schüler," in *Nachrichten aus dem Kösel-Verlag: Sonderheft für Else Lasker-Schüler Dezember 1965,* ed. Dr. Heinrich Wild and Friedrich Pfäfflin (Munich, 1965), pp. 43, 45; Kurt Hiller, "Begegnungen mit 'Expressionisten,'" in *Expressionismus: Aufzeichnungen,* ed. Raabe, p. 28ff; John Höxter, *So lebten wir: 25 Jahre Berliner Boheme* (Berlin, 1929), passim; René Schickele, *Werke in drei Bänden* (Cologne and Berlin, 1959), vol. 3, p. 1272; Thomas Grochowiak, *Ludwig Meidner* (Recklinghausen, 1966), p. 137; Ferdinand Hardekopf, "Wir Gespenster," *Die Aktion* 4 (1914), 80; Erich Mühsam, *Unpolitische Erinnerungen* (Berlin, 1961), passim; Franz Jung, *Der Weg nach unten* (Neuwied a.R., 1961), pp. 83ff; Georg Heym, *Tagebücher, Träume, Briefe,* vol. 3 of *Dichtungen und Schriften,* ed. Karl Ludwig Schneider (Hamburg and Munich, 1960), p. 231; Leonhard Frank, *Links wo das Herz ist* (Munich, 1952), pp. 78ff; Claire Jung, "Erinnerung an Georg Heym und seine Freunde," in *Expressionismus: Aufzeichnungen,* ed. Raabe, pp. 44ff; Ernst Blass, "Das alte Café des Westens," in *Expressionismus: Aufzeichnungen,* ed. Raabe, pp. 36ff; Friedlaender, "Ich," pp. 227ff; Kober, *Einst in Berlin,* pp. 104-5.

2. Sources on individual members will be cited in the following notes; for general source material on the composition of Pfemfert's circle see esp. Alexandra Pfemfert, "Die Gründung der *Aktion,*" pp. 43-44; Franz Jung, *Der Weg,* pp. 84ff; Claire Jung, "Erinnerung an Georg Heym," pp. 44-50; Walter Mehring, *Die verlorene Bibliothek,* pp. 144ff; Walter Mehring, "Berlin Avantgarde," pp. 117ff; C.F.W. Behl, "Begegnungen mit dem Expressionismus," in *Expressionismus: Aufzeichnungen,* ed. Raabe, pp. 294ff. See also under the names of members of the circle in "Verzeichnis der Mitarbeiter und der Beiträge in den Jahrgängen 1911 bis 1914," in *Die Aktion: 1911-1914,* reprint ed. Paul Raabe (Stuttgart, 1961), vol. 1, pp. 29-112. Some additional information on the members included in the "Verzeichnis" for *Die Aktion* 1911-14 in the latter reprint has been collected recently and published in the reprint of the years 1915-18: "Bio-Bibliographischer Anhang zu den

Jahrgängen 5-8 (1915-1918)," in *Die Aktion: 1917/18,* reprint ed. Paul Raabe (Munich, 1967), pp. 4-75; *"Die Aktion:* Stimmen der Freunde," ed. Wiegenstein, passim.

An indispensable study of especially *Die Aktion* but also of Pfemfert and the activities of his circle of associates, on which the present study has drawn heavily, is Paul Raabe, *"Die Aktion:* Geschichte einer Zeitschrift," in *Die Aktion,* reprint ed. Raabe (Stuttgart, 1961), vol. 1, pp. 7-21.

3. See note 2, above.

4. Alexandra Ramm, "Die Gründung der *Aktion,"* pp. 43-44; *Expressionismus: Aufzeichnungen,* ed. Raabe, p. 316 n. 1; Hiller, "Begegnungen," pp. 24-35; Heym, *Tagebücher,* pp. 218, 224, 229, 240-42, 244, 249; Heinrich Eduard Jacob, "Georg Heym— Erinnerung und Gestalt," reprinted in Georg Heym, *Dokumente zu seinem Leben und Werk,* vol. 6 of *Dichtungen und Schriften,* ed. Karl Ludwig Schneider and Gerhard Burkhardt (Darmstadt, 1968), p. 81; Hans Peter Renz, "Bericht vom Tode Georg Heyms," in Heym, *Dokumente,* p. 469; "Verzeichnis der Mitarbeiter," in *Die Aktion,* ed. Raabe (Stuttgart, 1961), vol. 1, pp. 45, 48-49, 59-62, 86, 90-91, 93-95; Ernst Nef, "Carl Einstein: Vorwort," in Carl Einstein, *Gesammelte Werke* (Wiesbaden, 1962), pp. 8ff. On Alexandra Pfemfert's role in *Die Aktion* see, e.g., Pfemfert's comment in "Kleiner Briefkasten," *Die Aktion* 8 (1918): 338.

There were close connections between Pfemfert and "Der neue Club," in the prewar phase of Expressionism. Several of the members of the club were published in *Der Demokrat;* these included, besides Hiller, Hoddis, and Heym, also Jentzsch, Ghuttmann, and Loewenson. Except for Loewenson, the members of the club just mentioned, in addition to Unger, Blass, Drey, Kurtz, and Jacob, all of whom were associated with the group, were published in *Die Aktion* before the war. See "Verzeichnis der Mitarbeiter," in *Die Aktion,* ed. Raabe (Stuttgart, 1961), vol. 1, pp. 36-37, 43, 50, 59-62, 65-66, 74, 106; Heym, *Dokumente,* pp. 430-37.

5. Heym, *Tagebücher,* p. 153.

6. Claire Jung, "Erinnerung an Georg Heym," pp. 44ff; Jung, *Der Weg,* pp. 83ff; "Verzeichnis der Mitarbeiter," in *Die Aktion,* ed. Raabe (Stuttgart, 1961), p. 67.

7. See Paul Raabe, "Der frühe Benn und die Veröffentlichung seiner Werke," in Gottfried Benn, *Den Traum alleine tragen: Neue Texte, Briefe, Dokumente,* ed. Paul Raabe and Max Niedermayer (Wiesbaden, 1966), pp. 12ff; *Briefe der Expressionisten,* ed. Kasimir Edschmid (Frankfurt a.M. and Berlin, 1964), pp. 163-64; "Verzeichnis der Mitarbeiter," in *Die Aktion,* ed. Raabe (Stuttgart, 1961), vol. 1, p. 35; Gottfried Benn, *Ausgewählte Briefe,* ed. Max Rychner (Wiesbaden, 1957), pp. 180, 208; Walter Lennig, *Gottfried Benn: In Selbstzeugnissen und Bilddokumenten,* Rowohlts Monographien, 71 (Reinbek bei Hamburg, 1962), p. 58.

8. Heinrich F.S. Bachmair, "Bericht eines Verlegers 1911-1914," in *Expressionismus: Aufzeichnungen,* ed. Raabe pp. 96ff; "Verzeichnis der Mitarbeiter," in *Die Aktion,* ed. Raabe (Stuttgart, 1961), vol. 1, pp. 34-35; *Briefe der Expressionisten,* ed. Edschmid, pp. 19-20; Johannes R. Becher, *Auf andere Art so grosse Hoffnung: Tagebuch 1950* (Berlin, 1952), pp. 433-434; Johannes R. Becher, "Wiederanders: Aus dem Romanfragment," in *Sinn und Form: Zweites Sonderheft Johannes R. Becher* (Berlin, 1960), pp. 528ff.

9. Bachmair, "Bericht eines Verlegers," p. 104; *Briefe der Expressionisten,* ed. Edschmid, pp. 19-20; Becher, *Tagebüch,* pp. 522-523.

10. Jung, *Der Weg,* pp. 87ff; "Verzeichnis der Mitarbeiter," in *Die Aktion,* ed. Raabe (Stuttgart, 1961), pp. 52, 67.

11. The special Gross numbers were *Die Aktion* 3 (December 20, 1913), no. 51; *Die Revolution* 1 (December 20, 1913), no. 5 (ed. Franz Jung). See Jung, *Der Weg*, pp. 87ff; Richard Seewald, *Der Mann von gegenüber* (Munich, 1963), pp. 141, 170ff. See also *Die Aktion* 4 (1914), pp. 23-25, 44, 67, 92-93, 110, 139-140, 242. Jung based a short story on the Gross case. See Franz Jung, "Der Fall Gross," reprinted in *Ego und Eros: Meistererzählungen des Expressionismus,* ed. Karl Otten (Stuttgart, 1963), pp. 201-20.

12. Jung, *Der Weg*, p. 91. Becher's autobiographical novel *Abschied* generally follows historical chronology. He has Gross (in the novel called "Dr. Hoch") in Munich amongst the Expressionists again at the time of the outbreak of World War One. See Johannes R. Becher, *Abschied* (Berlin, 1958), pp. 365ff., 407ff.

13. Carl Sternheim, *Zeitkritik,* vol. 6 of *Das Gesamtwerk,* ed. Wilhelm Emrich (Neuwied a.R. and Berlin, 1966), p. 517; "Verzeichnis der Mitarbeiter," in *Die Aktion,* ed. Raabe (Stuttgart, 1961), vol. 1, p. 103; Carl Sternheim, *Vorkriegseuropa im Gleichnis meines Lebens* (Amsterdam, 1936), pp. 208f; Franz Blei, *Erzählung eines Lebens* (Leipzig, 1930), pp. 435ff; Karl Ludwig Schneider, "Das Leben und die Dichtung Ernst Stadlers," in Ernst Stadler, *Dichtungen,* ed. Karl Ludwig Schneider (Hamburg, n.d.), vol. 1, pp. 30, 32.

14. See under these names in "Verzeichnis der Mitarbeiter," in *Die Aktion,* ed. Raabe (Stuttgart, 1961), vol. 1, pp. 29ff. See also *Briefe der Expressionisten,* ed. Edschmid, p. 163; Blass, "Das alte Café des Westens," pp. 36ff; Nef, "Carl Einstein," p. 8; Heinz Schöffler, "Karl Otten, Ego und Eros: Ein Nachwort in zwei Teilen," in *Ego und Eros,* ed. Otten, p. 572; *Menschheitsdämmerung: Ein Dokument des Expressionismus,* ed. Kurt Pinthus (Hamburg, 1959), pp. 355-56; "Veranstaltungen und Veröffentlichungen des Verlags der Wochenschrift *Die Aktion,*" in *Die Aktion,* ed. Raabe (Stuttgart, 1961), vol. 1, pp. 122-26; letter from Hardekopf to Schickele of November 18, 1922, pub. in "'Morgenrot!—Die Tage dämmern!' Zwanzig Briefe aus dem Frühexpressionismus 1910-1914," ed. Paul Raabe, *Der Monat* 16 (1964): 59. On Boldt see Wolfgang Minaty, "Ein preussischer Proteus" in Paul Boldt, *Junge Pferde! Junge Pferde! Das Gesamtwerk,* ed. Wolfgang Minaty (Olten and Freiburg i. Br., 1979), 215-29.

15. Jung, *Der Weg*, p. 86; Hugo Ball, *Die Flucht aus der Zeit* (Luceren, 1946), pp. 20, 27; *Briefe der Expressionisten,* ed. Edschmid, p. 163. On Landauer's life and work see, e.g., Gustav Landauer, *Zwang und Befreiung: Eine Auswahl aus seinem Werk,* ed. Heinz-Joachim Heydorn (Cologne, 1968), pp. 9-44.

16. See above, "Der neue Club."

17. See "Verzeichnis der Mitarbeiter," in *Die Aktion,* ed. Raabe (Stuttgart, 1961), vol. 1, p. 61; Franz Pfemfert, "Der Karriere-Revolteur," *Die Aktion* 3 (1913): 1129-36. See Pfemfert's later attacks on Hiller in *Die Aktion* 5 (1915): 103-6; *Die Aktion* 7 (1917): 468 *Die Aktion* 8 (1918): 234, 605, 628.

18. See above, "Der neue Club." See also "Verzeichnis der Mitarbeiter," in *Die Aktion,* ed. Raabe (Stuttgart, 1961), vol. 1, p. 36.

19. See "Verzeichnis der Mitarbeiter," p. 96; Lichtenstein, *Gesammelte Gedichte,* p. 123. For Pfemfert's attacks on Scher see *Die Aktion* 6 (1916): 476, 658; *Die Aktion* 8 (1918): 539, 628. See also "Bio-Bibliographischer Anhang," in *Die Aktion: 1917/18,* ed. Raabe (Munich, 1967), p. 59.

20. See above, "Der neue Club." See also "Verzeichnis der Mitarbeiter," in *Die Aktion,* ed. Raabe (Stuttgart, 1961), vol. 1, pp. 61-62; Erwin Loewenson, "Jakob van Hoddis: Erinnerungen mit Lebensdaten," in Jakob van Hoddis, *Weltende: Gesammelte Dichtungen,* ed. Paul Pörtner (Zürich, 1958), p. 111.

21. See "Verzeichnis der Mitarbeiter," in *Die Aktion,* ed. Raabe (Stuttgart, 1961), vol. 1, pp. 82-83.

22. See "Verzeichnis der Mitarbeiter," in *Die Aktion,* ed. Raabe (Stuttgart, 1961), vol. 1, pp. 38, 48-49, 75-76, 87, 90-91, 109-10; Raabe, "*Die Aktion:* Geschichte einer Zeitschrift," op. cit., pp. 15ff; "Bio-Bibliographischer Anhang," in *Die Aktion: 1917/18,* ed. Raabe (Munich, 1967), pp. 11, 23, 42, 48-49, 54, 73; Claire Jung, "Erinnerung an Georg Heym," pp. 49-50; Lasker-Schüler, *Briefe an Karl Kraus,* pp. 77ff; Lasker-Schüler, *Lieber gestreifter Tiger,* passim; Lasker-Schüler, *Wo ist unser buntes Theben,* pp. 62ff; Herzfelde, "Aus der Jugendzeit des Malik-Verlages," pp. 5-6; Wieland Herzfelde, "Wie ein Verlag entstand," in *Expressionismus: Aufzeichnungen,* ed. Raabe, p. 226; Jung, *Der Weg,* pp. 104ff; Ball, *Die Flucht,* p. 20; Max Brod, *Streitbares Leben: Autobiographie* (Munich, 1960), pp. 145-46.

23. Lichtenstein, *Gesammelte Gedichte,* pp. 96-100, 123-25; "Verzeichnis der Mitarbeiter," in *Die Aktion,* ed. Raabe (Stuttgart, 1961), vol. 1, p. 78; *Expressionismus: Literatur und Kunst: 1910-1923: Eine Ausstellung des Deutschen Literaturarchivs im Schiller-Nationalmuseum, Marbach a.N.,* cat. no. 7 of Sonderausstellungen des Schiller-Nationalmuseums, ed. Bernhard Zeller, Paul Raabe, and H.L. Greve (Marbach a.N., 1960), p. 34.

24. See above, chapter 1, note 102. See also "Verzeichnis der Mitarbeiter," in *Die Aktion,* ed. Raabe (Stuttgart, 1961), vol. 1, pp. 34-35, 37-40, 45, 71, 79-80; "Bio-Bibliographischer Anhang," in *Die Aktion: 1917/18,* ed. Raabe (Munich, 1967), pp. 7-8, 10, 12-13, 18-19, 36-38, 44-45; Brod, *Streitbares Leben,* pp. 135ff; Nef, "Carl Einstein," pp. 8-9; Ball, *Briefe,* p. 83; Herzfelde, "Aus der Jugendzeit des Malik-Verlages," pp. 5-6, 11.

25. *Menschheitsdämmerung,* ed. Pinthus (Hamburg, 1959), p. 356. See also Karl Otten's autobiographical novel, covering his Expressionist years, *Wurzeln* (Neuwied a.R., Berlin, 1963), pp. 155ff.

26. "Verzeichnis der Mitarbeiter," in *Die Aktion,* ed. Raabe (Stuttgart, 1961), vol. 1, pp. 51, 93-94; *Menschheitsdämmerung,* ed. Pinthus (Hamburg, 1959), pp. 341, 357; Frank, *Links wo das Herz ist,* p. 104; Norbert Jacques, *Mit Lust gelebt* (Hamburg, 1950), p. 305; Nell Walden, "Aus meinen Erinnerungen an einst..," in *Expressionismus: Aufzeichnungen,* ed. Raabe, pp. 201-2; Ball, *Briefe,* pp. 51, 55; Schickele, *Werke in drei Bänden,* vol. 3, p. 1024; Hans Arp, "Dadaland," in *Expressionismus: Aufzeichnungen,* ed. Raabe, pp. 184-85; Kasimir Edschmid, *Lebendiger Expressionismus* (Vienna, Munich, and Basel, 1961), p. 146; *Das war Dada: Dichtungen und Dokumente,* ed. Peter Schifferli (Munich, 1963), p. 179.

28. René Schickele, *Der neunte November,* Tribüne der Kunst und Zeit: Eine Schriftensammlung, 3, ed. Kasimir Edschmid (Berlin, 1919), pp. 22ff; Schickele, *Werke in drei Bänden,* vol. 3, pp. 1015-24, 1272; Otto Flake, *Es wird Abend* (Gütersloh, 1960), p. 258; Tilla Durieux, *Eine Tür steht offen* (Berlin-Grunewald, 1954), pp. 119-21, 123-24; Frank, *Links wo das Herz ist,* p. 103; Jacques, *Mit Lust gelebt,* pp. 305, 350; Schad, "Zürich/Genf," p. 173; Arp, "Dadaland," pp. 184-85; Herzfelde, "Aus der Jugendzeit das Malik-Verlages," p. 6; Edschmid, *Lebendiger Expressionismus,* pp. 146, 148ff; Raabe, *Die Zeitschriften,* p. 48. For Pfemfert's attacks on Schickele at this time see *Die Aktion* 6 (1916): 711; *Die Aktion* 7 (1917): 52, 207-8; *Die Aktion* 8 (1918): 284-85, 539.

29. See above, note 19. See also "Verzeichnis der Mitarbeiter," in *Die Aktion,* ed. Raabe (Stuttgart, 1961), vol. 1, pp. 94-96: "Bio-Bibliographischer Anhang," in *Die Aktion: 1917/18,* ed. Raabe (Munich, 1967), pp. 57, 59.

30. See "Verzeichnis der Mitarbeiter," in *Die Aktion,* ed. Raabe (Stuttgart, 1961), vol. 1, pp. 37-38, 55-56, 110-111; "Bio-Bibliographischer Anhang," in *Die Aktion: 1917/18,* ed. Raabe (Munich, 1967), pp. 10, 28, 73-74; *Menschheitsdämmerung,* ed. Pinthus (Hamburg, 1959),

p. 366. The special no. for Wolfenstein was *Die Aktion* 7 (June 2, 1917), no. 22/23. By February, 1918, however, this patronage was reversed. See *Die Aktion* 8 (1918), 78, 172. Pfemfert's break with Blei is implicit in the note appended to Blei's last contribution in the war: *Die Aktion* 7 (1917): 670.

31. It seems that Pfemfert found it hardest to forgive Hasenclever for allowing his work to be produced in Max Reinhardt's "Das junge Deutschland." See *Die Aktion* 6 (1916): 398; *Die Aktion* 7 (1917): 704; *Die Aktion* 8 (1918): 336, 364, 567. See also "Verzeichnis der Mitarbeiter," in *Die Aktion,* ed. Raabe (Stuttgart, 1961), p. 56; "Bio-Bibliographischer Anhang," in *Die Aktion: 1917/18,* ed. Raabe (Munich, 1967), pp. 28-29.

32. See "Verzeichnis der Mitarbeiter," in *Die Aktion,* ed. Raabe (Stuttgart, 1961), p. 32.

33. Ibid., pp. 54, 77-78. See also Ball's posthumous tribute to Hans Leybold: Hugo Ball, "Totenrede," *Die weissen Blätter* 2 (April, 1915): 525-27.

34. Ball, *Briefe,* p. 25-33.

35. Ibid., pp. 35-42; Ball, *Die Flucht,* pp. 13-23.

36. Ball, *Die Flucht,* pp. 13ff; Ball, *Briefe,* pp. 35ff.

37. Sylvia von Harden, "Erinnerungen an einst...," pp. 198ff.

38. Ibid., pp. 200-201.

39. Ibid., pp. 201-3.

40. For an index to the Expressionist publications to which she contributed see Raabe, *Die Zeitschriften,* p. 225.

41. Jung, *Der Weg,* pp. 99ff.

42. Ibid., pp. 104ff; Raabe, *Die Zeitschriften,* p. 60; Szittya, *Das Kuriositäten-Kabinett,* p. 278; "Verzeichnis der Mitarbeiter," in *Die Aktion,* ed. Raabe (Stuttgart, 1961), p. 67; "Veranstaltungen und Veröffentlichungen des Verlags der Wochenschrift *Die Aktion,*" in *Die Aktion,* ed. Raabe (Stuttgart, 1961), pp. 124-26; Raabe, *Die Zeitschriften,* pp. 175-79.

43. There is no indication of Claire Otto's part in *Freie Strasse* given in the pages of the journal itself. See Jung, *Der Weg,* p. 109; Raabe, *Die Zeitschriften,* p. 60; Claire Jung, "Erinnerung an Georg Heym," pp. 44ff; Raoul Hausmann, "Club Dada," p. 232.

44. Karl Jakob Hirsch, *Heimkehr zu Gott* (Munich, 1946), pp. 53ff; Karl Jakob Hirsch, "Novembergedanken," in *Zehn Jahre Novembergruppe* (Berlin, 1928), repr. in *Manifeste, Manifeste: 1905-1933,* Fundus-Bücher, 15/16/16, ed. Diether Schmidt (Dresden, n.d.), pp. 378-379.

45. Hirsch, *Heimkehr zu Gott,* pp. 30ff.

46. Ibid., p. 53; "Bio-Bibliographischer Anhang," in *Die Aktion: 1917/18,* ed. Raabe (Munich, 1967), p. 32.

47. Hirsch, *Heimkehr zu Gott,* pp. 59ff.

48. The special Hirsch number of *Die Aktion* was no. 24/25, vol. 6 (June 17, 1916). For a listing of the Hirsch exhibition see "Veranstaltungen und Veröffentlichungen des Verlags der Wochenschrift *Die Aktion,*" in *Die Aktion,* ed. Raabe (Stuttgart, 1961), vol. 1, p. 123. See also the volume of poetry and graphic arts pub. in Pfemfert's series *Der rote Hahn:* Karl Jakob Hirsch, *Revolutionäre Kunst, Der rote Hahn,* 31/32 (Berlin, 1919). See Raabe, *Die Zeitschriften,* p. 178.

49. See "Verzeichnis der Mitarbeiter," in *Die Aktion*, ed. Raabe (Stuttgart, 1961), vol. 1, pp. 69-70; "Bio-Bibliographischer Anhang," in *Die Aktion: 1917/18*, ed. Raabe (Munich, 1967), p. 37; Szittya, *Das Kuriositäten-Kabinett*, pp. 278, 281.

50. See "Verzeichnis der Mitarbeiter," in *Die Aktion*, ed. Raabe (Stuttgart, 1961), vol. 1, p. 70.

51. "Verzeichnis der Mitarbeiter," p. 58.

52. Jung, *Der Weg*, pp. 33ff; Rosemarie Lorenz, *Max Hermann-Neisse*, Germanistische Abhandlungen, 14 (Stuttgart, 1966), pp. 3ff.

53. Lorenz, *Hermann-Neisse*, p. 7. See also Jung, *Der Weg*, p. 68.

54. Lorenz, *Herrmann-Neisse*, pp. 7ff.

55. Ibid., pp. 13ff. Herrmann-Neisse was apparently able to make at least one visit to the circles of exiled German Expressionists in Zürich during the war, for Jacques reports seeing him there in the spring of 1915. See Jacques, *Mit Lust gelebt*, p. 305. For Herrmann-Neisse's contributions to Pfemfert's publications in this period see "Bio-Bibliographischer Anhang," in *Die Aktion: 1917/18*, ed. Raabe (Munich, 1967), p. 31. See also his letters, mostly from Neisse, Sept., 1914-1916, to Friedrich Grieger, in Max Herrmann-Neisse, *Eine Einführung in sein Werk und eine Auswahl*, Verschollene und Vergessene, ed. Friedrich Grieger (Wiesbaden, 1951), pp. 67-73.

56. See "Bio-Bibliographischer Anhang," in *Die Aktion: 1917/18*, ed. Raabe (Munich, 1967), pp. 4-75.

57. See Raabe, *Die Zeitschriften*, p. 175; "Veranstaltungen und Veröffentlichungen des Verlags der Wochenschrift *Die Aktion*," in *Die Aktion*, ed. Raabe (Stuttgart, 1961), vol. 1, p. 125.

58. See Stefan Wronski (Ferdinand Hardekopf), "Die Aeternisten: Erste Proklamation des Aeternismus" (dated April, 1916), reprinted in *Expressionismus: Literatur und Kunst*, ed. Zeller et al., pp. 124-25.

(Hier wird, auf einem Kap, Extremes geformt. Unsere Bücher werden euch unfasslich sein, Bürger.)

(Durchwühlt haben wir die Eingeweide der Millionenstädte und phosphoreszierender Seelen. Lustig zu Hause sind wir auf macabren Redouten und bei scabreusen Dérouten, in geschminkten Katakomben und clair-obscuren Cafés, in subcutanen Bars und auf ogivalen Stil-Spitzen, in Rasta-Tavernen und bei Eusapia-Séancen, in syndikalistischen café-concerts und detektivischen Schlafwagen, bei Somn- und Noktambulen, Bistros, Erdarbeitern und Deputierten, in morphinistischen Boudoirs und Korruptions-Automobilen, Spielhöllen und Betthimmeln, in Disciplin und Spleen.)

(In uns ist alle Vergangenheit Gegenwart Zukunft. Alles muss durch uns hindurch.)

(Unsere Psychologie wird euch skandalisieren, Unsere Syntax wird euch asphyxiieren. Wir werden eure grossen Konfusionen belächeln, abstrakt und augurisch. Erhabene Konjunktive werden zerstäuben, Futura exacta narkotisch verdampfen, und je-m'enfichistisch zergehen schaumige Duftbälle von Quintessenz.)

59. See above, note 57.

60. See Raabe, *Die Zeitschriften*, pp. 176, 177; "Veranstaltungen und Veröffentlichungen des Verlags der Wochenschrift *Die Aktion*," in *Die Aktion*, ed. Raabe (Stuttgart, 1961), vol. 1, p. 125.

61. "Veranstaltungen und Veröffentlichungen des Verlags der Wochenschrift *Die Aktion*," in *Die Aktion*, ed. Raabe (Stuttgart, 1961), pp. 125-26; Raabe, *Die Zeitschriften*, pp. 177-79.

62. "Veranstaltungen und Veröffentlichungen des Verlags der Wochenschrift *Die Aktion,*" in *Die Aktion,* ed. Raabe (Stuttgart, 1961), vol. 1, p. 123.

63. See the short note prefacing the "Aufruf der Antinationalen Sozialisten Partei (A.S.P.) Gruppe Deutschland," *Die Aktion* 8 (1918): 583. See also Raabe, "*Die Aktion:* Geschichte einer Zeitschrift," p. 19.

64. See "Aufruf der Antinationalen Sozialisten Partei (A.S.P.) Gruppe Deutschland," *Die Aktion* 8 (1910): 583-86; Franz Pfemfert, "Freunde der *Aktion,*" *Die Aktion* 8 (1918): 610.

65. See the advertisement for the meetings of the A.S.P. in *Die Aktion* 8 (1918): 666, 688. See also "Veranstaltungen und Veröffentlichungen des Verlags der Wochenschrift *Die Aktion,*" in *Die Aktion,* ed. Raabe (Stuttgart, 1961), vol. 1, p. 123.

66. See "Verzeichnis der Mitarbeiter," pp. 58, 68, 90-91, 95; "Bio-Bibliographischer Anhang," in *Die Aktion: 1917/18,* ed. Raabe (Munich, 1967), pp. 31, 36, 49-50, 54, 59, 81-84; Lorenz, *Herrmann-Neisse,* pp. 20ff., 41ff; Raabe, "*Die Aktion:* Geschichte einer Zeitschrift," pp. 19ff; Otten, *Wurzeln,* pp. 270ff.

67. See Conrad Felixmüller, "Erinnerungen eines Malers an seinen Kunstfreund Carl Sternheim," *Neue Texte* 4 (1964): 454-72.

68. Ibid., p. 459 and passim.

69. See "Verzeichnis der Mitarbeiter," in *Die Aktion,* ed. Raabe (Stuttgart, 1961), vol. 1, p. 55; "Bio-Bibliographischer Anhang," in *Die Aktion: 1917/18,* ed. Raabe (Munich, 1967), pp. 28, 81-83.

70. See Arthur Rosenberg, *Die Enstehung der deutschen Republik 1871-1918* (Berlin, 1928), p. 43; "Verzeichnis der Mitarbeiter," in *Die Aktion,* ed. Raabe (Stuttgart, 1961), vol. 1, p. 55.

71. "Bio-Bibliographischer Anhang," in *Die Aktion: 1917/18,* ed. Raabe (Munich, 1967), pp. 44, 81-84; Raabe, "*Die Aktion:* Geschichte einer Zeitschrift," p. 19; Claire Jung, "Erinnerung an Georg Heym," p. 50.

72. See under these names in "Verzeichnis der Mitarbeiter," in *Die Aktion,* ed. Raabe (Stuttgart, 1961), vol. 1, pp. 29-126; "Bio-Bibliographischer Anhang," in *Die Aktion: 1917/18,* ed. Raabe (Munich, 1967), pp. 4-84; Lasker-Schüler, *Briefe an Karl Kraus,* pp. 85ff; Lasker-Schüler, *Lieber gestreifter Tiger,* passim; Lasker-Schüler, *Wo ist unser buntes Theben,* pp. 71ff; *Menschheitsdämmerung,* ed. Pinthus (Hamburg, 1959), p. 357; Benn, *Ausgewählte Briefe,* p. 13ff; Raabe, "Der frühe Benn," pp. 29f; Nico Rost, "Meine Begegnungen mit Gottfried Benn," in Benn, *Den Traum,* pp. 39-60; *Briefe der Expressionisten,* ed. Edschmid, pp. 111, 163-64; Kurt Pinthus, "Erinnerungen an Bechers Frühzeit," in Johannes R. Becher, *Lyrik Prosa, Dokumente: Eine Auswahl,* ed. Max Niedermayer (Wiesbaden, 1965), pp. xlii-xliv; also there, p. 180; Hirsch, *Heimkehr zu Gott,* pp. 65ff; Hirsch, "Novembergedanken," pp. 378-79; Jung *Der Weg,* pp. 106ff. On Einstein's activities after the war see below, the section on *Neue Jugend* (II) and the Dadaists; also Nef, "Carl Einstein," pp. 9f. Otten was still contributing to *Die Aktion* in 1919, but he states himself in his autobiographical contribution to *Menschheitsdämmerung,* ed. Pinthus (Hamburg, 1959), p. 356, that after the war he lived in Vienna where he edited the journal *Der Friede;* then, he states, he was back in Berlin from 1924-33. See however, Paul Raabe, "Schlusswort," in *Die Aktion: 1917/18,* ed. Raabe (Munich, 1967), p. 87. Raabe, *Die Zeitschriften,* pp. 73-74, has *Der Friede* edited in Vienna from 1918-19 by Benno Karpeles, not Otten. Otten is, nevertheless, listed as a contributor to the journal. Pfemfert had broken with Blei and with Mühsam in the war, but had apparently become reconciled with them sometime after the war when they both reappear in the pages of *Die Aktion.* On Pfemfert's

break with Mühsam see *Die Aktion* 5 (1915): 215; *Die Aktion* 7 (1917): 468, 571-72; *Die Aktion* 8 (1918): 104, 466, 493-94; Minaty, "Ein preussischer Proteus," p. 228.

73. René Schickele, "Wie verhält es sich mit dem Expressionismus," reprinted in *Expressionismus: Der Kampf um eine literarische Bewegung,* ed. Paul Raabe (Munich, 1965), p. 178.

74. Karl Otten, "Die expressionistische Generation," in *Ahnung und Aufbruch: Expressionistische Prosa,* ed. Karl Otten (Darmstadt, Berlin-Frohnau, and Neuwied a.R., 1957), p. 34.

75. Raabe, "*Die Aktion:* Geschichte einer Zeitschrift," p. 9; Kurt Pinthus, "*Die Aktion:* Zum 50. Jubiläum ihrer Gründung" (unpub. ms. of a radio talk given on Feb. 25, 1961, in commemoration of the 50th anniversary of the founding of *Die Aktion*), pp. 6-7.

76. Raabe, "*Die Aktion:* Geschichte einer Zeitschrift," p. 9.

77. Ibid.; Szittya, *Das Kuriositäten-Kabinett,* pp. 137-38.

78. Szittya, *Das Kuriositäten-Kabinett,* pp. 137-38; "Verzeichnis der Mitarbeiter," in *Die Aktion,* ed. Raabe (Stuttgart, 1961), vol. 1, pp. 63, 89.

79. "Verzeichnis der Mitarbeiter," pp. 63-64. The special Senna Hoy number was: *Die Aktion* 4 (May 9, 1914), no. 19. See esp. there the essay by Pfemfert, "Senna Hoy ist gestorben," pp. 399-403.

80. See "Verzeichnis der Mitarbeiter," in *Die Aktion,* ed. Raabe (Stuttgart, 1961), vol. 1, pp. 90-91; Raabe, "*Die Aktion:* Geschichte einer Zeitschrift," p. 9; *Expressionismus: Aufzeichnungen,* ed. Raabe, p. 316; Hirsch, *Heimkehr zu Gott,* pp. 54-55.

81. See "Verzeichnis der Mitarbeiter," in *Die Aktion,* ed. Raabe (Stuttgart, 1961), pp. 89, 49-50; Raabe, "*Die Aktion:* Geschichte einer Zeitschrift," p. 9.

82. *Expressionismus: Literatur und Kunst,* ed. Zeller et al., p. 120.

Das 'grosse,' das 'öffentliche,' das 'soziale' Leben ist nur Böses, Kleines, Wahnsinniges. Dagegen gibt es nur Arbeit und rücksichtslosen Kampf. Ich wünschte, ich brauchte das nicht, das heisst: dieses Leben wäre weniger von allem Draussen provoziert. Aber ich bin es gewesen, so lange ich politisch denke.

83. Alexandra Pfemfert, "Die Gründung der *Aktion,*" p. 44; "*Die Aktion:* Stimmen der Freunde," ed. Wiegenstein, p. 7.

84. *Das Aktionsbuch,* ed. Franz Pfemfert (Berlin, 1917). See Raabe, *Die Zeitschriften,* pp. 138-39.

85. Franz Pfemfert, "Schlussbemerkung für Fernstehende," in *Das Aktionsbuch,* p. 342.

Dieses *Aktionsbuch* ist kein Werbe-Almanach eines Verlagsunternehmens.
Ich verlege nicht Bücher, um Geschäfte zu machen, sondern um Geschäfte zu erschweren, wie ich bei der Herausgabe meiner völlig unzeitgemässen, zeitfeindlichen Wochenschrift die technischen Mittel der Presse verwende, um gegen das Pressegeschäft zu wirken. Ich habe das *Aktionsbuch* unter den denkbar ungünstigsten Verhältnissen zusammengestellt und drucken lassen; nicht, damit ihr interessante Lektüre erhalten solltet; mich leitete nur dieser Wunsch: das Buch möge euch lehren, menschlichen Angelegenheiten gegenüber die heilige deutsche Indolenz abzulegen.

86. See Raabe, "*Die Aktion:* Geschichte einer Zeitschrift," pp. 11ff; Franz Pfemfert, "Die Jugend und die Schlittenbauer," *Die Aktion* 4 (1914): 155-56. See also Pfemfert's editorials and essays, which run throughout *Die Aktion* 1911-14.

87. See Claire Jung, "Erinnerung an Georg Heym," p. 44. See also Ludwig Rubiner, *Kameraden der Menschheit* (Potsdam, 1919), p. 170.

88. Becher, *Auf andere Art so grosse Hoffnung*, p. 434.

89. Jung, *Der Weg*, p. 85. See also Karl Otten, "*Die Aktion:* Eine Zeitschrift gegen die Zeit" (unpub. ms. of a radio talk given on Feb. 25, 1961, in commemoration of the 50th anniversary of the founding of *Die Aktion*), p. 15.

90. Jung, *Der Weg*, p. 85.

91. See above, chapter 1.

92. Jung, *Der Weg*, pp. 84ff.

93. Sylvia von Harden, "Erinnerungen an einst...," pp. 200-201.

    Wenn meine Gedanken weiter in die Vergangenheit schweifen, denke ich an den immensen Eindruck, den Franz Pfemfert auf mich machte, dessen Bekanntschaft ich auch Hardy [= Ferdinand Hardekopf] zu verdanken hatte. Pfemfert, der zähe Mann mit den glitzernden Mäuseaugen, der spitzen Nase in dem eigenwilligen Gesicht, mit seiner singenden Stimme, aber vor allem seine politische Persönlichkeit bedeutete mir unsagbar viel.

94. Hirsch, *Heimkehr zu Gott*, p. 54.

95. Ibid., pp. 65ff; Hirsch, "Novembergedanken," pp. 378-79.

96. Hirsch, "Novembergedanken," p. 378.

    Novemberstürme. Novembergruppe. Das begann, als wir noch in rissigen Soldatenmänteln durch das dunkle Berlin liefen, als wir im Regen auf einer Leiter standen, und mit blau-weiss-roten Buchstaben das aufreizende Wort 'Aktion' über die neue Buchhandlung in der Kaiserallee malten, bis ein pickelhelmiger Schutzmann herbeieilte und es uns untersagte, weil in einer 'Prachtstrasse' Plakatschilder verboten seien. Als in die nächtliche Stille der königlichen Fliegerinspektion ein Geheimtelegramm hineinplatze, das lautete: 'Revolutionsgefahr—Ausgangsverbot für Mannschaften.' Das begann im atelierhaften Büro der königlichen Inspektion der Fliegertruppen, wo als Soldaten kostümierte Maler Abbildungen von Flugzeugen zeichnen mussten, aber unter dem Tische lagen revolutionäre Zeichnungen für die *Aktion* des Tapferen Pfemfert, auf kgl. preussischem Papier mit kgl. preussischer Tusche gezeichnet. Da wurde *Die schöne Rarität* geboren und manch *Roter Hahn*. Da winkte man vorsichtig mit den Augen den demonstrierenden Arbeitern im Januar 1918 Sympathie zu, sass da und wartete auf die Stunde der Befreiung, denn das Licht schien im Osten!

97. Alexandra Pfemfert, "Die Gründung der *Aktion*," pp. 43-44; Raabe, "*Die Aktion:* Geschichte einer Zeitschrift," p. 10. See also Kurt Hiller's "Offener Brief an Dr. Georg Zepler" in that first issue: *Die Aktion* (February 20, 1911), no. 1, pp. 10-12.

98. Alexandra Pfemfert, "Die Gründung der *Aktion*," p. 43; Raabe, "*Die Aktion:* Geschichte einer Zeitschrift," p. 10.

99. See Jakob van Hoddis, "Weltende," *Der Demokrat* 3 (1911): 43; *Expressionismus: Aufzeichnungen*, ed. Raabe, p. 313 n. 5, and p. 317 n. 1; Heym, *Tagebücher*, pp. 222ff; Becher, "Wiederanders," p. 533.

100. Alexandra Pfemfert, "Die Gründung der *Aktion*," pp. 43-44.

101. See above, note 82.

102. "Note," *Die Aktion* 1 (1911), 24.

103.   Ibid.

    "*Die Aktion* tritt, ohne sich auf den Boden einer bestimmten politischen Partei zu stellen, für
    die Idee der Grossen Deutschen Linken ein."

104.   Ibid.

    In den Dingen der Kunst und der Literatur sucht *Die Aktion* ein Gegengewicht zu bilden zu
    der traurigen Gewohnheit der pseudoliberalen Presse, neuere Regungen lediglich vom
    Geschäftsstandpunkt aus zu bewerten, also sie totzuschweigen.

105.   Ibid. See also Pinthus's remarks on the program in Pinthus, *"Die Aktion,"* p. 3.

    Die Aktion hat den Ehrgeiz, ein Organ des ehrlichen Radikalismus zu sein.

106.   Paul Raabe, "Einleitung," in *Ich schneide die Zeit aus: Expressionismus und Politik in
    Franz Pfemferts Aktion: 1911-1918,* ed. Paul Raabe (Munich, 1964), p. 11.

    Das war das Neue. *Die Aktion* wurde das Forum für eine im Aufbrechen begriffene
    Literatur vor dem Hintergrund einer radikalen politischen Gesinnung.

107.   Some of the changes in *Die Aktion* described in the pages that follow were first pointed out
    by Paul Raabe, in Raabe, *"Die Aktion:* Geschichte einer Zeitschrift," pp. 11ff.

108.   The last connections with "Das Komitee Konfessionslos" were in the May 1 issue, no. 11, of
    1911. See *Die Aktion* 1 (1911): 345. The subtitle "Publikationsorgan der Organisation der
    Intelligenz" was dropped after the June 5 issue, no. 16, for 1911. See *Die Aktion* 1 (1911):
    481. No reports for the organization had been published since March 27, 1911. See *Die
    Aktion* 1 (1911): 181-84.

109.   See under these names in "Verzeichnis der Mitarbeiter," in *Die Aktion,* ed. Raabe
    (Stuttgart, 1961), pp. 29-112.

110.   See "Verzeichnis der Mitarbeiter," pp. 45, 97, for page numbers of these installments.

111.   For a complete listing of the series see "Verzeichnis der Mitarbeiter," pp. 123-24.

112.   See above, chapter 1, notes 80 and 81.

113.   For drawings in 1912 see *Die Aktion* 2 (1912): 643/644 (by Max Oppenheimer), 785/786 (by
    Rudolf Grossmann), 1009/1010 (by Max Oppenheimer), 1075 (by Lucien Bernhard),
    1135/1136 (by Rudolf Grossmann), 1265/1266 (by John Höxter), 1297/1298 (anon.)
    1457/1458 (by John Höxter), 1489/1490 (by Max Oppenheimer), 1553/1554 (by Max
    Oppenheimer), 1585/1586 (by Max Oppenheimer), 1617/1618 (by Max Oppenheimer).

114.   *Die Aktion* 3 (1913): 595/596.

115.   For the first title-page drawing, which was executed by Wilhelm Morgner, see *Die Aktion* 3
    (April 16, 1913), no. 16.

116.   Franz Pfemfert, *"Die Aktion* und der Staatsanwalt," *Die Aktion* 4 (May 23, 1914), no. 21,
    445-47. On the development of the use of the term "Expressionismus" see Armin Arnold,
    Die Literatur des Expressionismus, Sprache und Literatur, 35 (Stuttgart, Berlin, Cologne,
    and Mainz, 1966), pp. 9-15. On instances of the use of the terms employed by Pfemfert in his
    letter to the prosecutor see, e.g., the programs of the journal and other Expressionist
    publications cited by Raabe in *Die Zeitschriften,* passim.

117.   Raabe, *Die Zeitschriften,* pp. 445-46. *Die Aktion* 4 (March 28, 1914), no. 13 was officially
    confiscated because of a poem pub. on p. 267 by Ball and Hans Leybold (under pseud. Ha.
    Hu. Baley). *Die Aktion* 4 (April 4, 1914), no. 14 was included in the obscenity charges lodged
    against the journal officially because of two poems trans. from the Old Provençal by

Edschmid and because of two prose pieces, the one by Hardekopf and the second by Kurt Striepe. See *Die Aktion* 4 (1914), pp. 303-6. However, it is evident that the main reason for confiscating these two issues was because of Franz Pfemfert's and Hugo Kersten's championing, in the same two issues, of Madame Caillaux. Madame Caillaux, the wife of the French minister Joseph Caillaux, had shot to death the head editor of the Paris newspaper *Le Figaro* for publishing her love letters to her husband without her consent. See Franz Pfemfert, "Revolver und Journalismus," *Die Aktion* 4 (March 28, 1914), no. 13, 265-66; Hugo Kersten, "Madame Caillaux," *Die Aktion* 4 (April 4, 1914), no. 14, 293-94. Edschmid, who had to appear in court in Berlin with Pfemfert and Ball, reports that he himself was acquitted, while Pfemfert and Ball had to pay nominal fines. See Edschmid, *Lebendiger Expressionismus,* pp. 97-98; Kasimir Edschmid, *Tagebuch 1958-1960* (Vienna, Munich, and Basel, 1960), pp. 312-14. See also on this case *Die Aktion* 4 (1914): 466, 467-68, 513, 532-33, 538-39, 766, 894, 918; *Die Aktion* 5 (1915): 119. Pfemfert reports on the results of the trial, which had been postponed numerous times and had finally been held on March 9, 1915, in a short note in his marginal column "Kleiner Briefkasten." See *Die Aktion* 5 (1915): 168.

Hören Sie, Herr Staatsanwalt! *Die Aktion* ist eine Wochenschrift für Politik, Literatur, Kunst. Für menschlichste Politik. Für (Verzeihung, Leser und Mitarbeiter) erstklassige jüngste Literatur. Für jüngste, heiligste Kunst. . . . Was in drei vergangenen Jahren in meiner Zeitschrift gedruckt worden ist, es ist so werterreich, so voll heissen Lebens, so (Gott, ein populäres Wort noch!) pyramidal, dass kommende Historiker der Literatur, der Kunst, der Politik die Geschichte des heutigen Deutschlands nicht schreiben werden, ohne *Die Aktion* studiert zu haben. Der Literarhistoriker z.B. wird dann feststellen: Das wichtigste, temperament-vollste, mutigste, moralischste Wochenblatt der jungen Literatur um 1910 war die Berliner *Aktion.* Hier (wird der Geschichtsschreiber sagen) haben die besten Köpfe des Jungen Deutschland ihre ersten Schlachten geschlagen . . .

118. See "Verzeichnis der Mitarbeiter," in *Die Aktion,* ed. Raabe (Stuttgart, 1961), vol. l, pp. 29-112.

119. *Die Aktion* 4 (1914): 693. The announcement was repeated in *Die Aktion* 4 (1914): 742. See also *Die Aktion* 4 (1914): 822, 846.

Freunde der *Aktion,* Leser, Mitarbeiter!

Die Aktion wird in den nächsten Wochen nur Literatur und Kunst enthalten.

Soweit es von meiner Kraft abhängt, von meinem Wollen, wird unsere Zeitschrift ohne Unterbrechung *weitererscheinen.*

120. That the political department of *Die Aktion* was specifically being discarded for the duration of the war is stated directly in Pfemfert's marginal column "Kleiner Briefkasten." See *Die Aktion* 4 (November 21, 1914), no. 46/47, p. 894. See also *Die Aktion* 6 (1916): 286.

121. The column "Ich schneide die Zeit aus" first appeared in the April 17 issue of 1915. See *Die Aktion* 5 (1915): 214.

122. *Die Aktion* 5 (1915): 214.

123. See *Die Aktion* 4 (1914): 834.

124. Ibid.

Mein Herz ist so gross wie Deutschland und Frankreich zusammen,
Durchbohrt von allen Geschossen der Welt.

Die Batterie erhebt ihre Löwenstimme,
Sechsmal hinaus in das Land. Die Granaten heulen.

Stille. In der Ferne brodelt das Feuer der Infanterie,
Tagelang, wochenlang.

125. See under these names in "Bio-Bibliographischer Anhang," in *Die Aktion: 1917/18*, ed. Raabe (Munich, 1967), pp. 4-75.

126. The first prose piece to appear in *Die Aktion* which was composed on the battlefield—the author's own words, cited by Pfemfert in the prefatory note to the piece, verify this fact— and dealt with the war experience, was Hans Koch's short story "Die Weinrebe und der Pflaumenbaum." See *Die Aktion* 4 (November 7, 1914), no. 44/45, pp. 847-50.

    Ludwig Meidner did two additional drawings on the battlefield theme. See the title-page drawing for *Die Aktion* 5 (January, 2, 1915), no. 1/2; also "Schlachtfeld," *Die Aktion* 5 (1915), 58.

127. See Erwin Piscator, "Die politische Bedeutung der *Aktion*," in *Expressionismus: Aufzeichnungen*, ed. Raabe, pp. 192-96; Erwin Piscator, *Das politische Theater*, ed. Felix Gasbarra (Reinbek bei Hamburg, 1963), pp. 27ff.

    On *Die Aktion* being sent to soldiers in the field see Pfemfert's open letter, calling for financial support of his journal and for the sending of free copies of it to the fields of battle, dated November, 1915, reprinted in *Expressionismus: Literatur und Kunst*, ed. Zeller et al., p. 120. See also similar requests in *Die Aktion* 4 (1914): 766, 798, 822.

128. See under these names in "Bio-Bibliographischer Anhang," in *Die Aktion: 1917/18*, ed. Raabe (Munich, 1967), pp. 4-75.

129. See in this connection Pfemfert's note in "Kleiner Briefkasten," *Die Aktion* 4 (1914): 766, in which he expresses the intention of returning to weekly publication "as soon as all technical obstacles are removed"—an intention which he was never able to realize throughout the remainder of the journal's publishing life.

130. See under these names in Raabe, "Bio-Bibliographischer Anhang," in *Die Aktion: 1917/18*, ed. Raabe (Munich, 1967), pp. 4-75.

131. See the table of contents on the title page of *Die Aktion* 8 (1918), no. 45/46.

    Der Kapitalismus, der das werktätige Volk zur Schlachtbank hetzte und entrechtete, schreit, um weiter entrechten und ausplündern zu können, nach der 'Nationalversammlung.'

132. "Aufruf der Antinationalen Sozialisten Partei (A.S.P.) Gruppe Deutschland," *Die Aktion* 8 (1918): 583, 586.

133. See *Die Aktion* 8 (1918): 583-610.

134. Franz Pfemfert, "Nationalversammlung *ist* Kontrerevolution," *Die Aktion* 8 (November 30, 1918), no. 47/48, pp. 611-612.

135. Carl Sternheim, "Die deutsche Revolution," *Die Aktion* 8 (1918): 613-20.

136. Franz Pfemfert ("namens der Antinationalen Sozialisten-Partei Gruppe Deutschland"), "Erklärung," *Die Aktion* 8 (1918): 637-38.

    The other article in the second postwar issue, besides additional glosses by Pfemfert, was N. Lenin's "Kautskys' Diktatur des Proletariats," 620-24.

137. "Die Verfassung der russischen sozialistischen föderativen Sowjetrepublik," *Die Aktion* 8 (1918): 642-51.

138. See Raabe, "*Die Aktion:* Geschichte einer Zeitschrift," p. 19.

139. *Die Aktion* 8 (1918): 172.

Wenn ich es doch endlich allen Ahnungslosen einhämmern könnte, dass es mir nicht um Literatur, jüngste oder älteste Dichtung geht!

140. *Die Aktion* 8 (1918): 364.

141. See title page of *Die Aktion* 8 (November 16, 1918), no. 45/46.

142. See complete list of these special numbers in "Veranstaltungen und Veröffentlichungen des Verlags der Wochenschrift *Die Aktion,*" in *Die Aktion,* ed. Raabe (Stuttgart, 1961), vol. 1, p. 124.

143. Ibid.

144. Raabe, "Einleitung," in *Ich schneide die Zeit aus,* p. 14.

145. See Raabe, "*Die Aktion:* Geschichte einer Zeitschrift," p. 20. There is an outline of the contents of these latter years of *Die Aktion* in Raabe, "Bio-Bibliographischer Anhang," in *Die Aktion: 1917/18,* ed. Raabe (Munich, 1967), pp. 81-84.

146. For a complete list of those evenings that have been verified and documented see "Veranstaltungen und Veröffentlichungen des Verlags der Wochenschrift *Die Aktion,*" in *Die Aktion,* ed. Raabe (Stuttgart, 1961), vol. 1, pp. 122-23.

147. See *Die Aktion* 1 (1911): 118.

148. Ibid.

149. See *Die Aktion* 6 (1916), 286.

150. See above, note 146.

151. See above, note 146.

152. See "Veranstaltungen und Veröffentlichungen des Verlags der Wochenschrift *Die Aktion,*" in *Die Aktion,* ed. Raabe (Stuttgart, 1961), vol. 1, pp. 122. Pfemfert also dedicated a special number to Franz Blei. See *Die Aktion* 3 (August 2, 1913), no. 31. On these three poets and *Die Aktion* see "Verzeichnis der Mitarbeiter," in *Die Aktion,* ed. Raabe (Stuttgart, 1961), vol. 1, pp. 37-38, 39-40, 95-96.

153. For a review of this recital see Anselm Ruest, "Der Max Brod-Abend," *Die Aktion* 1 (1911): 1425-26. On Brod's previous Berlin recitals see p. 199 and p. 597 n. 123.

154. See "Veranstaltungen und Veröffentlichungen des Verlags der Wochenschrift *Die Aktion,*" in *Die Aktion,* ed. Raabe (Stuttgart, 1961), vol. 1, pp. 23. Pfemfert wrote a posthumous tribute to Senna Hoy in which he expressed his own grief over the poet's death and angrily lashed out at the brutality of Russian prisons. See Franz Pfemfert, "Senna Hoy ist gestorben," *Die Aktion* 4 (1914): 399-403. On Senna Hoy and Pfemfert see above; also "Verzeichnis der Mitarbeiter," in *Die Aktion,* ed. Raabe (Stuttgart, 1961), vol. 1, pp. 63-64.

155. Five letters have been published, written by Lasker-Schüler from Russia between November 5 and November 11, 1913, to her son Paul Lasker-Schüler. See Lasker-Schüler, *Wo ist unser buntes Theben,* pp. 54-56. See also ibid., p. 280 n. 95; Lasker-Schüler, *Der Malik,* repr. *Gesammelte Werke,* vol. 1, pp. 432ff; Lasker-Schüler, *Briefe an Karl Kraus,* pp. 62-75, where she mentions Pfemfert's doubts about her visit to Russia, and p. 134 n. 141. Senna Hoy wrote an essay on Lasker-Schüler, pub. posthumously in *Die Aktion.* See Senna Hoy, "Essay," *Die Aktion* 5 (1915), 193-99 (dated Moscow, 1912).

156. See above, note 146.

157. See above, note 147.

158. Heinrich Lautensack, "Das Heimliche Theater: Ein Weg zu Überwindung des Zensors," *Die Aktion* 2 (January 22, 1912), no. 4, 97-101. On Lautensack see "Verzeichnis der Mitarbeiter," in *Die Aktion,* ed. Raabe (Stuttgart, 1961), vol. 1, p. 76. Lautensack apparently withdrew from the project while it was in the planning stages. See *Die Aktion* 2 (March 11, 1912), no. 11, p. 325.

159. Lautensack, "Das Heimliche Theater," pp. 97-100.

160. See *Die Aktion* 2 (1912): 140-44, 169-70, 204-6, 237-38, 298, 308-10.

161. See *Die Aktion* 2 (1912): 101, 216, 238, 278, 328.

162. See *Die Aktion* 2 (1912): 328, 367, 399.

163. See *Die Aktion* 2 (1912): 399, 437.

164. For a list of these publications see "Veranstaltungen und Veröffentlichungen des Verlags der Wochenschrift *Die Aktion,*" in *Die Aktion,* ed. Raabe (Stuttgart, 1961), vol. 1, pp. 123-26; also Raabe, *Die Zeitschriften,* pp. 138-39, 175-79.

165. See "Veranstaltungen und Veröffentlichungen des Verlags der Wochenschrift *Die Aktion,*" in *Die Aktion,* ed. Raabe (Stuttgart, 1961), vol. 1, pp. 125-26; Raabe, *Die Zeitschriften,* pp. 177-79.

166. See preceding note. A peripheral activity of the *Aktion* circle before the war were its "Revolutions-Bälle." Two were held in 1913, on February 4 and February 13; and two in 1914, on February 4 and February 23. The organizing committee for the first two consisted of Gertrud Eysoldt, Else Berna, Blei, Schickele, Oppenheimer, and (for the February 13 ball only) Scher. See *Die Aktion* 3 (1913): 90, 216, 233-35. For the second series of balls the committee included Berna, Eysoldt, Blei, Heinrich Mann, Oppenheimer, and (for the February 23 ball only) Erik-Ernst Schwabach. See Die Aktion 4 (1914): 66, 88. The costumes for all of the balls were to be based on the dress of the "Revolutions of 1789-1889." See *Die Aktion* 3 (1913): 90; *Die Aktion* 4 (1914): 88.

167. Raabe, "*Die Aktion*: Geschichte einer Zeitschrift," p. 19; Rosenberg, *Geschichte der Weimarer Republik,* pp. 50ff.

168. Raabe, "*Die Aktion:* Geschichte einer Zeitschrift," p. 19.

169. Ibid.

170. Ibid.

171. Piscator, *Das politische Theater,* p. 31.

172. Raabe, "*Die Aktion:* Geschichte einer Zeitschrift," p. 20.

173. See Isaac Deutscher, *The Prophet Outcast: Trotsky: 1929-1940* (New York, Toronto, and London, 1963), pp. 356-509. On Pfemfert's publication of Trotsky's works see "Verzeichnis der Mitarbeiter," in *Die Aktion,* ed. Raabe (Stuttgart, 1961), vol. 1, p. 125; Raabe, *Die Zeitschriften,* p. 177; "Bio-Bibliographischer Anhang," in *Die Aktion: 1917/18,* ed. Raabe (Munich, 1967), pp. 81-84; Raabe, "*Die Aktion:* Geschichte einer Zeitschrift," pp. 19-20.

174. Raabe, "*Die Aktion:* Geschichte einer Zeitschrift," p. 20.

Chapter 7

1. Alfred Richard Meyer, *die maer von der musa expressionistica* (Düsseldorf-Kaiserswerth, 1948), p. 105; "Verzeichnis der Mitarbeiter und der Beiträge in den Jahrgängen 1911 bis 1914," in *Die Aktion: 1911-1914,* reprint ed. Paul Raabe (Stuttgart, 1961), vol. 1, pp. 83-84; Raabe, *Die Zeitschriften,* p. 163.

2. Meyer, *die maer*, p. 105.

3. Raabe, *Die Zeitschriften*, p. 163.

4. Meyer, *die maer*, p. 105; Raabe, *Die Zeitschriften*, p. 163.

5. Raabe, *Die Zeitschriften*, p. 163.

6. Meyer, *die maer*, pp. 11, 34ff; Fritz Max Cahén, *Der Weg nach Versailles: Erinnerungen 1912-1919: Schicksalsepoche einer Generation* (Boppard a.R., 1963), pp. 23ff; Fritz Max Cahén, "Der Alfred Richard Meyer-Kreis," in *Expressionismus: Aufzeichnungen*, ed. Raabe, pp. 111-16; Paul Raabe, "Der frühe Benn und die Veröffentlichung seiner Werke," in Gottfried Benn, *Den Traum alleine tragen: Neue Texte, Briefe, Dokumente*, ed. Paul Raabe and Max Niedermayer (Wiesbaden, 1966), pp. 14-24; Gottfried Benn, *Ausgewählte Briefe*, ed. Max Rychner (Wiesbaden, 1957), p. 12; Alfred Richard Meyer, "Paris," *Der Sturm* 4 (1913): 85-86; "Verzeichnis der Mitarbeiter und der Beiträge," in *Die Aktion*, ed. Raabe (Stuttgart, 1961), vol. 1, p. 83.

7. Meyer, *die maer*, pp. 34, 35. Herrmann-Neisse is known to have made a total of four brief visits to Berlin and the Meyer circle between November, 1912, and the outbreak of the war in 1914. See Rosemarie Lorenz, *Max Hermann-Neisse*, Germanistische Abhandlungen, 14 (Stuttgart, 1966), pp. 9-14. Fritz Max Cahén further claims that Meyer and Herrmann-Neisse were actively corresponding with each other. See Cahén, "Der Alfred Richard Meyer-Kreis," p. 113.

8. Meyer, *die maer*, p. 34; Heinrich F.S. Bachmair, "Bericht eines Verlegers 1911-1914," in *Expressionismus: Aufzeichnungen*, ed. Raabe, p. 101; Cahén, "Der Alfred Richard Meyer-Kreis," p. 114; Lorenz, *Herrmann-Neisse*, pp. 11f; Else Lasker-Schüler, *Lieber gestreifter Tiger*, pp. 78, 87, 88, 106; Cahén, *Der Weg nach Versailles*, p. 29.

9. Meyer, *die maer*, pp. 32-33.

10. Alfred Richard Meyer, "Paris" and "Drei Mädchenporträts aus dem Türkischen Zelt zu Charlottenburg," *Der Sturm* 4 (1913), 85-86 and 199; Alfred Richard Meyer, *Der grosse Munkepunke: Gesammelte Werke* (Hamburg and Berlin, 1924), pp. 7, 54-57, 110-112.

11. Meyer, *die maer*, p. 33.

12. Ibid., p. 34; Raabe, *Die Zeitschriften*, pp. 134, 164.

13. See note 12, above.

14. Cahén, *Der Weg*, p. 24; Cahén, "Der Alfred Richard Meyer-Kreis," p. 111.

15. Cahén, *Der Weg*, pp. 5ff; Cahén, "Der Alfred Richard Meyer-Kreis," p. 111.

16. Cahén, *Der Weg*, pp. 23-25; Cahén, "Der Alfred Richard Meyer-Kreis," p. 111.

17. Cahén, *Der Weg*, pp. 25ff; Cahén, "Der Alfred Richard Meyer-Kreis," pp. 111ff.

18. Cahén, *Der Weg*, p. 28; Cahén, "Der Alfred Richard Meyer-Kreis," p. 112; Meyer, *die maer*, pp. 24ff.

19. Cahén, "Der Alfred Richard Meyer-Kreis," p. 112; Victor Hadwiger, *Wenn unter uns ein Wandrer ist: Ausgewählte Gedichte*, selected from the literary remains of Hadwiger and edited by Ruest (Berlin-Wilmersdorf, n.d. [1912]), p. 16; Meyer, *die maer*, p. 24; "Verzeichnis der Mitarbeiter und der Beiträge," in *Die Aktion*, ed. Raabe (Stuttgart, 1961), vol. 1, pp. 53-54, 94.

    Victor Hadwiger, whom Paul Raabe considers a "forerunner of Expressionism" most notably in the poems in the posthumous collection just cited, was born in Prague in 1878, had associated in that city with the members of the group called "Jung-Prag," including

Gustav Meyrink, Paul Leppin, Oskar Wiener, Alexander Moissi, Richard Teschner; he later moved to Berlin, in 1903, where he appeared on the stages of the cabarets of Max Tilke ("Der Hungrige Pegasus") and Hans Hyan ("Die Silberne Punschterrine"). He died in Berlin on October 4, 1911, having made many close friendships in the Expressionist community in the city. Besides in publications sponsored by Meyer, Hadwiger also appeared in a few others associated with Expressionism. See *Die Aktion*, vol. 1, pp. 53-54, 94; Raabe, *Die Zeitschriften*, pp. 36, 44, 94, 134, 136, 141. On Hadwiger in Prague see espec. Max Brod, *Der Prager Kreis* (Stuttgart, Berlin, Cologne, and Mainz, 1966), pp. 38, 73-74, 82. See also *Expressionismus: Aufzeichnungen*, ed. Raabe, p. 381.

20. Cahén, *Der Weg*, p. 28; Cahén, "Der Alfred Richard Meyer-Kreis," p. 112.

21. Cahén, *Der Weg*, pp. 27-28; Cahén, "Der Alfred Richard Meyer-Kreis," p. 113.

22. Cahén, *Der Weg*, p. 25; Cahén, "Der Alfred Richard Meyer-Kreis," p. 112.

23. Cahén, "Der Alfred Richard Meyer-Kreis," p. 112.

24. Alfred Richard Meyer, "Paris," *Der Sturm* 4 (August, 1913), no. 174/175, pp. 85-86. The poem is reprinted in Meyer, *Der grosse Munkepunke*, pp. 54-57. The latter version lacks the dedication. See also *Expressionismus: Aufzeichnungen*, ed. Raabe, p. 332 n. 1.

25. Meyer, "Paris," *Der Sturm*, p. 85.

26. See note 24, above.

27. Cahén, *Der Weg*, p. 25; Cahén, "Der Alfred Richard Meyer-Kreis," p. 112.

28. Cahén, *Der Weg*, p. 27; Cahén, "Der Alfred Richard Meyer-Kreis," p. 113.

29. Cahén, "Der Alfred Richard Meyer-Kreis," p. 113.

30. Ibid.

31. Cahén, *Der Weg*, pp. 27-28.

32. See note 28, above. See also Kurt Pinthus, "Ernst Rowohlt und sein Verlag," in *Ernst Rowohlt Almanach: 1908-1962*, ed. Mara Hintermeier and Fritz J. Raddatz (Reinbek bei Hamburg, 1962), pp. 20-21.

33. See note 28, above.

34. Cahén, "Der Alfred Richard Meyer-Kreis," p. 113.

35. Ibid.; Raabe, *Die Zeitschriften*, p. 165.

36. Cahén, "Der Alfred Richard Meyer-Kreis," p. 113.

37. Ibid., pp. 111, 114; Cahén, *Der Weg*, pp. 30ff. For documentation of the individual presence of members of the Meyer circle in the Café des Westens see Leonhard Frank, *Links wo das Herz ist* (Munich, 1952), p. 89; Emil Szittya, *Das Kuriositäten-Kabinett* (Constance, 1923), p. 255; John Höxter, *So lebten wir: 25 Jahre Berliner Boheme* (Berlin, 1929), p. 41; Max Krell, *Das alles gab es einmal* (Frankfurt a.M., 1961), pp. 21, 23; Meyer, *die maer*, pp. 12, 44; Else Lasker-Schüler, *Briefe an Karl Kraus*, ed. Astrid Gehlhoff-Claes (Cologne and Berlin, 1959), passim; Else Lasker-Schüler, *Lieber gestreifter Tiger*, passim: Else Lasker-Schüler, *Wo ist unser buntes Theben*, passim; Else Lasker-Schüler, *Essays*, passim; Else Lasker-Schüler, *Mein Herz*, passim; Else Lasker-Schüler, *Der Malik*, passim; Kober, *Einst in Berlin*, p. 105.

38. Cahén, *Der Weg*, pp. 30ff.

39. Ibid., p. 30.

Das eigentliche Berliner Erlebnis, das von ausschlaggebender Bedeutung für meine spätere Entwicklung wurde, war jedoch das Caféhaus.

40. Cahén, "Der Alfred Richard Meyer-Kreis," p. 111.

41. See, e.g., Walter Graeser, "Dichter-Verleger," *Die Aktion* 1 (1911): 435-38. See also below, note 127.

42. "Verzeichnis der Mitarbeiter und der Beiträge," in *Die Aktion,* ed. Raabe (Stuttgart, 1961), vol. 1, pp. 83-84.

43. Raabe, "Der frühe Benn," p. 14.

44. See Meyer, *die maer,* passim; Bachmair, "Bericht eines Verlegers," p. 101; Kurt Pinthus, "Leipzig und der frühe Expressionismus," in *Expressionismus: Aufzeichnungen,* ed. Raabe, p. 79. On Meyer's ties with other Berlin circles see above, the circle around *Der Sturm* and "Der neue Club."

45. See Cahén, "Der Alfred Richard Meyer-Kreis," p. 114; Szittya, *Das Kuriositäten-Kabinett,* p. 159.

46. See above, note 42; also Cahén, "Der Alfred Richard Meyer-Kreis," p. 111; Raabe, "Der frühe Benn," p. 14.

47. Anselm Ruest, "Ein Vorleseabend," *Die Aktion* 1 (1911): 1328.

48. Gottfried Benn, "Lebensweg eines Intellektuellen," in Gottfried Benn, *Autobiographische und vermischte Schriften,* vol. 4 of *Gesammelte Werke in vier Bänden,* ed. Dieter Wellershoff (Wiesbaden, 1961), pp. 27-29; Walter Lennig, *Gottfried Benn in Selbstzeugnissen und Bilddokumenten* (Reinbek bei Hamburg, 1962), pp. 20ff; Meyer, *die maer,* p. 14.

49. See Harald Steinhagen, "'Herbst': Ein frühes Gedicht Gottfried Benns," in Benn, *Den Traum alleine tragen,* pp. 7-10; Gottfried Benn, *Gedichte,* vol. 3 of Gottfried Benn, *Gesammelte Werke in vier Bänden,* ed. Dieter Wellershoff (Wiesbaden, 1960 and 1963), pp. 349-50; Gottfried Benn, *Autobiographische und vermischte Schriften,* pp. 179-87. See also Raabe, "Der frühe Benn," pp. 14-16.

50. Meyer, *die maer,* p. 14.

51. Ibid.

52. Ibid., p. 15.

53. Ibid.; Raabe, *Die Zeitschriften,* p. 164.

54. Meyer, *die maer,* pp. 15-16.

55. Benn, "Lebensweg eines Intellektuellen," p. 29.

Schon diese erste Gedichtsammlung brachte mir von seiten der Öffentlichkeit den Ruf eines brüchigen Roués ein, eines infernalischen Snobs und des typischen—heute des typischen jüdischen Mischlings, damals des typischen—Kaffeehausliteraten, während ich auf den Kartoffelfeldern der Uckermark die Regimentsübungen mitmarschierte und in Döberitz beim Stab des Divisionskommandeurs im englischen Trab über die Kiefernhügel setzte.

56. Kurt Hiller, e.g., was negative. See Kurt Hiller, *Die Weisheit der Langenweile* (Leipzig, 1913), vol. 1, p. 121. For examples of positive voices see Rolf Wolfgang Martens, "Klinische Lyrik," *Die Aktion* 2 (1912): 1106-9; Emil Faktor, "Fortgeschrittene Lyrik," *Pan* 2 (1912): 710-11; Ernst Stadler, "*Der Kondor . . . ,*" review repr. in Ernst Stadler, *Dichtungen,* ed. Karl Ludwig Schneider (Hamburg, n.d.), pp. 21-22; Else Lasker-Schüler, "Doktor Benn," in *Essays,* pp. 227-28; Rudolf Kurtz, "Bei Gelegenheit Benns," *Pan* 2 (1912): 1059-62.

57. Stadler, "Kondor...," p. 22.

58. Benn, "Lebensweg eines Intellektuellen," p. 45.

59. See Raabe, *Die Zeitschriften*, pp. 163ff.

60. Meyer, *die maer*, passim; Cahén, "Der Alfred Richard Meyer-Kreis," p. 116; Cahén, *Der Weg*, pp. 5ff.

61. Meyer, *die maer*, p. 8.

62. Ibid., see also Alfred Richard Meyer, "Leon Deubel," *Die Aktion* 1 (1911): 1114-5.

63. Meyer, *die maer*, pp. 54-57; Cahén, *Der Weg*, p. 29; Roger Shattuck, *The Banquet Years: The Arts in France: 1885-1918* (Garden City, 1961), pp. 252ff.

64. Otto Flake, *Es wird Abend* (Gütersloh, 1960), p. 155 and passim; René Schickele, *Werke in drei Bänden*, ed. Hermann Kesten (Cologne and Berlin, 1959), vol. 3, pp. 1271-72; "Verzeichnis der Mitarbeiter und der Beiträge," in *Die Aktion*, ed. Raabe (Stuttgart, 1961), vol. 1, pp. 96-97.

65. See esp. René Schickele, *Schreie auf dem Boulevard* (1913), repr. in René Schickele, *Werke in drei Bänden*, vol. 3, pp. 275-411.

66. Karl Ludwig Schneider, "Das Leben und die Dichtung Ernst Stadlers," in Stadler, *Dichtungen*, vol. 1, pp. 23ff.

67. Stadler's translations of Jammes's poetry, samples of which appeared in Expressionist periodicals, were collected and published as the ninth volume of the Kurt Wolff series *Der jüngste Tag*. See Francis Jammes, *Die Gebete der Demut*, trans. Ernst Stadler, *Der jüngste Tag*, vol. 9 (Leipzig, 1913). See Raabe, *Die Zeitschriften*, p. 169.

68. Raabe, *Die Zeitschriften*, pp. 163-68.

69. Ibid.

70. Ibid., pp. 163-64.

71. Meyer, *die maer*, pp. 5ff.

72. Ibid., p. 7.

73. Ibid., pp. 8ff.

74. Ibid., pp. 8, 54ff.

75. Alfred Richard Meyer, "Interieur," *Der Sturm* 1 (February 11, 1911), no. 50, p. 398; Alfred Richard Meyer, "Karneval," *Die Aktion* (May 29, 1911), no. 15, pp. 467-68. At the beginning of the next month appeared in *Die Aktion* a translation by Meyer of a poem by Albert Giraud, which was perhaps done on arrival in Paris. See Albert Giraud, "Madrigal in Rot," trans. Alfred Richard Meyer, *Die Aktion* 1 (June 5, 1911), no. 16, p. 500. Meyer's next contribution to Pfemfert's journal does not come until September, 1911; it is again a poem and is, by title, clearly a product of Meyer's Paris trip. See Alfred Richard Meyer, "Aus meinem Pariser Tagebuch," *Die Aktion* 1 (September 25, 1911), no. 32, p. 1010.

76. Raabe, *Die Zeitschriften*, pp. 45-47.

77. Ibid., p. 164.

78. Ibid. On Hoddis's literary influence on Lichtenstein see the discussion of this question in the section on "Der neue Club" above.

79. Raabe, *Die Zeitschriften*, p. 164.

80. Kurtz's foreword is reprinted in *Expressionismus: Literatur und Kunst: 1910-1923: Eine Ausstellung des Deutschen Literaturarchivs im Schiller-Nationalmuseum, Marbach a.N.,* cat. no. 7 of Sonderausstellungen des Schiller-Nationalmuseums, ed. Bernhard Zeller, Paul Raabe, H.L. Greve (Marbach a.N., 1960), p. 49; also repr. in Paul Pörtner, *Literatur-Revolution 1910-1925: Dokumente, Manifeste, Programme,* Die Mainzer Reihe, 13, vol. 2 (Neuwied a.R. and Berlin-Spandau, 1961), p. 89. The foreword was also pub. in *Der Sturm* in November, 1912. See Rudolf Kurtz, "Futuristische Dichtungen," *Der Sturm* 3 (November, 1912), no. 136/137, p. 218.

81. Kurtz, "Futuristisches," 218.

> Er ist ... ein Lobsinger des ewigen Meers, der ruhmvollen Sonnenuntergänge, des kühnen Sterbens.
>
> Aus den Explosionsmotoren des zwanzigsten Jahrhunderts, aus Dampfwolken und elektrischen Wirbeln steigt senkrecht ein melancholisch-weisser Mond empor—der Mond Jean Jacques Rousseaus, der Mond Jules Laforgues.... Ein Begeisterter, vom äussersten Kap seiner Zeit schauend; vorgedrungen zur Schönheit der Eisenkonstruktion und keineswegs zurückschreckend vor dem Hymnus auf das Automobil.
>
> Es gilt die unfassbare Allheit des Augenblicks zu spiegeln.
>
> Dreitausend Jahre Kunst ziehen sich lautlos in den Orkus zurück.

82. Raabe, *Die Zeitschriften,* pp. 164-65.

83. Ibid., p. 164.

84. Ibid.; Meyer, *die maer,* p. 8.

85. Raabe, *Die Zeitschriften,* p. 165. On a discussion of the importance of this poem and others published with it in Apollinaire's *Alcools* (1913) see Roger Shattuck *The Banquet Years,* pp. 280-81, 306, 308-10, 314-16. In April of the same year the poem had already appeared in the original French in *Der Sturm* 4 (April, 1913), no. 154/155, 4-5.

86. Iwan Goll, *Die drei guten Geister Frankreichs,* Tribüne der Kunst und Zeit, 5 (Berlin, 1919), p. 73.

87. See *Der Sturm,* ed. Nell Walden and Lothar Schreyer, p. 13; Meyer, *die maer,* pp. 54-57; Cahén, *Der Weg,* p. 29; Walter Mehring, "Berlin Avantgarde," in *Expressionismus: Aufzeichnungen,* ed. Raabe, p. 117. Prior to November, 1913, only a few pieces of art criticism and theory in prose by Apollinaire had appeared in one other publication associated with Expressionism outside of the Meyer circle. See *Der Sturm* 3 (1912/13): 224, 272, 283.

88. On Apollinaire's "Zone" and the stylistic features just mentioned see Roger Shattuck, *The Banquet Years,* pp. 306, 308-10, 314-16.

89. Raabe, *Die Zeitschriften,* pp. 163-64.

90. Ibid., 164-165.

91. Artur Segal, *Vom Strande: Acht Original-Holzschnitte mit Nachwort von Rudolf Leonhard,* Lyrische Flugblätter, 32 (Berlin-Wilmersdorf, May, 1913), 8 sheets. See Raabe, *Die Zeitschriften,* p. 164.

92. Alfred Döblin, *Das Stiftsfräulein und der Tod: Novelle,* Lyrische Flugblätter, 41 (Berlin-Wilmersdorf, December, 1913), 8 sheets. See Raabe, *Die Zeitschriften,* p. 165.

93. *Die Bücherei Maiandros: Eine Zeitschrift von 60 zu 60 Tagen,* ed. Heinrich Lautensack, Alfred Richard Meyer, and Anselm Ruest (Berlin-Wilmersdorf: Paul Knorr Verlag, 1912-

14), books 1-6 and 8 supplements. See Raabe, *Die Zeitschriften*, p. 44. See Meyer, *die maer,* p. 31. On Beckmann and Expressionism see Peter Selz, *German Expressionist Painting* (Berkeley and Los Angeles, 1957), pp. 238-40, 284-87; Bernard S. Myers, *The German Expressionists* (New York and Washington, 1966), pp. 242-54.

94. Meyer, *die maer,* p. 11.

95. See note 93, above.

96. See note 93, above.

97. See note 93, above. See also Ida Lublinski, "Einleitung," in Samuel Lublinski, *Nachgelassene Schriften* (München, 1914), p. xi.

98. See Mühsam, *Unpolitische Erinnerungen* (Berlin, 1961), p. 98; Alfred Döblin, *Briefe,* ed. Walter Muschg and Heinz Graber (Olten and Freiburg i.B., 1970), pp. 23, 27, 29, 30, 41, 46; Else Lasker-Schüler, "S. Lublinski," in Else Lasker-Schüler, *Essays,* pp. 241-45; Else Lasker-Schüler, *Wo ist unser buntes Theben,* p. 16.

99. Alfred Richard Meyer and Heinrich Lautensack, "Ekstatische Wallfahrten," *Die Bücherei Maiandros,* Book 1 (December 1, 1912), pp. 1-32.

100. Alfred Richard Meyer, "Semilasso in Afrika," *Die Bücherei Maiandros,* Book 1 (December 1, 1912), pp. 1-21.

101. Heinrich Lautensack, "Via Crucis: Der Text zu einer Kantate," *Die Bücherei Maiandros,* Book 1 (December 1, 1912), pp. 22-32.

102. Anselm Ruest, "Apollodorus: Über Lyrik ein Dialog," *Die Bücherei Maiandros,* Book 3 (February 1, 1913), pp. 1-38; Anselm Ruest, "Vorwort zum 'Apollodorus,'" *Die Bücherei Maiandros,* Supplement to Book 3 (February 1, 1913), p. 1.

103. Ruest, "Apollodorus," p. 1.

104. Heym can be identified as "Oikos" on the basis of the poetry cited and attributed to "Oikos": "Wolken," "Die Dämonen der Städte," "Louis Capet." See Ruest, "Apollodorus," pp. 4ff; Georg Heym, *Lyrik,* vol. 1 of Georg Heym, *Dichtungen und Schriften,* ed. Karl Ludwig Schneider (Hamburg and Munich, 1964), pp. 51-52, 87, 186-87, 678-79.

105. Ruest, "Apollodorus," p. 3.

War doch sein [= Socrates'] ganzes Streben, wie ich oft von ihm gehört habe, das Streben nach der feinsten Mischung überhaupt, nach Mitte, nach mathematischer Ehe von Wollust und Einsicht.

106. Ibid.

Und sollte er [= Socrates] da nicht an seinem Todestage noch Zeugnis haben ablegen wollen, dass er der nüchternen Vernunft und der begrifflichen Fassung nicht mehr die Führerrolle durch das dunkle Leben zuerkenne, sondern dass die Worte der Dichtung möglicherweise einzig die so grausam gesuchte Mitte des Weltwesens zu treffen im stande wären?

107. Ibid., pp. 8ff.

108. Ibid., p. 13.

...sehe ich, mein Kebes, die viel weiterreichende, kraftvollere Wirkensmöglichkeit solcher Kunst der Worte eben darin, dass sie einer spezielleren, deutlicheren Bewusstseins- und Vorstellungstätigkeit der Seele zunächst einmal den Anstoss geben, dadurch aber auch die tausend vielleicht sonst nie geweckten, schon dem kleinsten Teilchen der Begriffswelt verketteten Gefühls- und Empfindungstöne zu ungeahnter Mitarbeit aufrufen kann!

109. Ibid., pp. 12-14.

110. Ibid., pp. 15-20.

111. Ibid., pp. 4-8, 33ff. Lautensack ("Die Apotheose der Zahnbürste"), Schickele ("Vorortballade") and Benn ("Blinddarm," "Mann und Frau gehn durch die Krebsbaracke") can also be identified on the basis of their poetry. See Meyer, *die maer*, p. 17; *Die Aktion* 1 (1911): 1424-25; Benn, *Gedichte*, pp. 14-15, 351-52.

112. Ruest, "Apollodorus," pp. 32-38.

113. Ibid., p. 37.

114. Ibid., pp. 37-38.

Langsam, langsam entwinden sich die Neueren und Jüngeren einem Fluche, der ihnen tausend und abertausend Jahre den *Leib* verekelt hat, aber erst die wirklich Jungen und Jüngsten bleiben ganz frei, ganz unberührt von jedem vererbten, überkommenen 'Gut' oder 'Böse' hinsichtlich seiner; sie stehen auch vor seinen das 'Schönheitsgefühl' (diesen grossen Götzen, nicht Gott der Jahrhunderte!) verletzenden Erbärmlichkeiten als wahre Dichter, als solche die seinen *Gott* eben entdecken und verehren! Sie sehen das neugeborene Kind, in der schwülstigen Sprache der Nur-Geist-Anbeter die 'zarte Hoffnung der Geschlechter,' das 'Unterpfand der Liebe' und ähnlich genannt: sie aber sehen erst genauer und klarer, sie sehen seinen Ursprung, seine Eileithyia wieder, und sie sagen: so sind wir wenn wir ankommen— 'bläulich und klein, von Urin und Stuhlgang eingesalbt'; und sie sehen auch die rauhen Männer mit der Zange, die dabei gewesen. Sie stehen auch nicht wie die Neugierigen bloss bei den furchtbaren Operationen der Ärzte, sondern weil sie die grässliche Notwendigkeit der schmerz-bereitenden Hände und Instrumente tief durchschauen, darum rufen sie nicht dabei nach dem falschen Gotte der Rührung und des Mitleids, der diese Hände bloss verwirren und tödlich machen könnte; aber sie bemerken plötzlich, wie nebenher, in der rechten Sekunde des Atemholens und Aufseufzens ein einzelnes linderndes göttliches Zeichen des Blühens und Hoffens und Genesens....

115. See e.g., Paul Pörtner, *Literatur-Revolution: 1910-1925: Dokumente, Manifeste, Programme,* Die Mainzer Reihe, 13/1 (Darmstadt, Neuwied a.R. and Berlin-Spandau, 1960), 13/2 (Neuwied a.R. and Berlin-Spandau, 1961), passim.

116. "Der Mistral: Eine lyrische Anthologie," ed. Heinrich Lautensack, Alfred Richard Meyer, and Anselm Ruest, *Die Bücherei Maiandros,* Books 4/5 (May 1, 1913), pp. 1-70.

117. See Friedrich Nietzsche, *Werke in drei Bänden,* ed. Karl Schlechta, vol. 3 (Munich, 1955), pp. 272-74.

118. See the section on "Der neue Club," above.

119. *Der Kondor,* ed. Kurt Hiller (Heidelberg, May, 1912), p. 7.

120. Alfred Richard Meyer, "An Stelle eines Vorwortes," *Die Bücherei Maiandros,* Supplement to Books 4/5 (May 1, 1913), p. 1.

121. For a list of contributors to the anthology see "Der Mistral," pp. 70-71.

122. See note 120, above.

Der Mistral soll als ständiges Jahrbuch erscheinen und wird für die Folge weniger die Zusammenhänge der Dichterjahrgänge 1862 und 1882 dartun, vielmehr in erster Linie ein Vorkämpfer für die Jugend sein.

123. See note 120, above.

    Schon heute ergehe unsere Einladung an alle, die sich stark genug wissen, der Lyrik wirklich neue Werte zuzuführen.

124. "In memoriam Leon Deubel," ed. Heinrich Lautensack, Alfred Richard Meyer and Anselm Ruest, *Die Bücherei Maiandros,* Book 6 (September 1, 1913), pp. 1-48. See also Meyer, *die maer,* p. 9.

125. Anselm Ruest, "Ein Vortragsbend," *Die Aktion* 1 (December 4, 1911), no. 42, 1328-29.

126. Ruest, "Ein Vortragsabend," pp. 1328-29.

127. Ernst Blass, "A.R. Meyer-Abend," *Die Aktion* 2 (November 13, 1912), no. 46, 1453.

128. Blass, "A.R. Meyer-Abend," p. 1453.

129. See *Der Sturm* 3 (October, 1912), no. 129, p. 164; *Die Aktion* 2 (September 25, 1912), no. 39, p. 1238.

130. *Der Sturm* 3 (1912): 164.

131. *Die Aktion* 2 (1912): 1238. See also the announcement in *Die Bücherei Maiandros,* Supplement to Book 1 (October 1, 1912), p. 14.

132. See Lorenz, *Herrmann-Neisse,* p. 9. Here Lorenz reports that on the same evening Langer read Herrmann-Neisse's poem "Das elektrische Klavier." On the second appearance of Herrmann-Neisse see C.F.W. Behl, "Begegnungen mit dem Expressionismus," in *Expressionismus: Aufzeichnungen,* ed. Raabe, pp. 295-96. See also announcements in *Die Bücherei Maiandros,* Supplements to Book 6 (February 1, 1914), p. 14, and (May 1, 1914), p. 14.

133. Raabe, "Der frühe Benn," p. 16; Meyer, *die maer,* p. 38. See also Behl, "Begegnungen," pp. 295-96.

134. See, e.g., Cahén, "Der Alfred Richard Meyer-Kreis," p. 112; Klabund, *Briefe an einen Freund,* ed. Ernst Heinrich (Köln, Berlin, 1963), p. 80 and footnote to letter of December 15, 1913, pp. 156-57; R.K. [Rudolf Kurtz], "Vortragsabend Resi Langer," *Die Aktion* 2 (February 5, 1912), no. 6, pp. 176-77; Rudolf Leonhard, "Über einen Vortragsabend," *Die Aktion* 2 (December 25, 1912), no. 52, 1649-50; Rudolf Leonhard, "Resi Langer," *Die Bücherei Maiandros,* Supplement to Books 4/5 (May 1, 1913), p. 7.

135. Cahén, "Der Alfred Richard Meyer-Kreis," p. 115.

136. Benn, *Briefe,* p. 12.

    Maiandros rüstet also schon ab.

137. Kurt Pinthus, "Vorwort zur Neu-Ausgabe (1963)," in *Das Kinobuch,* ed. Kurt Pinthus (1913/14; rpt. Zürich, 1963), pp. 14-16; Cahén, *Der Weg,* pp. 34-36.

138. See Rudolf Kurtz, *Expressionismus und Film,* Filmwissenschaftliche Studientexte, vol. 1 (1926; rpt. Zürich, 1965), p. 137.
    Kurt Pinthus, *Das Kinobuch,* pp. 13-14, 155, reports that another Meyer associate, Lautensack, was the first poet to work for the film professionally; Lautensack had written for the German film "secretly," according to Pinthus, even before the appearance of *Das Kinobuch* at the end of 1913.

139. See Raabe, *Die Zeitschriften,* pp. 45-46; Ernst Zunker, "*Der Wiecker Bote:* Das Organ eines Expressionistenkreises an der Universität Greifswald," *Germanisch-Romanische Monatsschrift* n.s. 11 (1961), 226-29.

140. Thomas Grochowiak, *Ludwig Meidner* (Recklinghausen, 1966), pp. 99ff; *Briefe der Expressionisten*, ed. Kasimir Edschmid (Frankfurt a.M. and Berlin, 1964), pp. 17-18.

141. Lennig, *Benn*, pp. 38-40; Schickele, *Werke in drei Bänden*, vol. 3, p. 1272.

142. Meyer, *die maer*, p. 14.

143. *Der Krieg: Ein Flugblatt*, with contributions by Elsa Asenijeff, Richard Dehmel, Herbert Eulenberg, et al., Lyrische Flugblätter, 46 (Berlin-Wilmersdorf, September, 1914), 8 sheets. See Raabe, *Die Zeitschriften*, pp. 158, 165.

144. On the statement of William II at the outset of the war: "Ich kenne keine Parteien mehr: ich kenne nur noch Deutsche"—see, e.g., Kurt F. Reinhardt, *Germany 2000 Years* (New York, 1950, 1961), vol. 2, pp. 636ff.

145. Alfred Richard Meyer, *Helden: Ein Lyrisches Flugblatt aus den August- und Septembertagen 1914*, Lyrische Flugblatter, [47] (Berlin-Wilmersdorf, 1914), 16 pp. See Raabe, *Die Zeitschriften*, p. 165.

146. Rudolf Leonhard *Über den Schlachten: Gedichte*, Lyrische Flugblätter, [48] (Berlin-Wilmersdorf, 1914), p. [3].

     Wir lieben den Krieg, wir wollen das Böse!

147. See Herrmann-Neisse's letters from this period to Friedrich Grieger in Max Herrmann-Neisse, *Eine Einführung in sein Werk und eine Auswahl*, ed. Friedrich Grieger (Wiesbaden, 1951), pp. 67-71.

148. Alfred Richard Meyer, *"Und ich sahe das Tier,"* Lyrische Flugblätter, [49] (Berlin-Wilmersdorf, 1915), 8 sheets.

149. See "Verzeichnis der Mitarbeiter und der Beiträge," in *Die Aktion*, ed. Raabe (Stuttgart, 1961), vol. 1, p. 84.

150. *Der neue Frauenlob,* [ed. Alfred Richard Meyer], Lyrische Flugblätter, 50 (Berlin-Wilmersdorf, 1919), 12 sheets. See Raabe, *Die Zeitschriften*, pp. 137-38, 165.

151. Meyer, *die maer*, pp. 82, 91. See also announcements of "Sturm-Abende" in which Meyer was scheduled to participate in *Der Sturm*, Prospectus for no. 1, January, 1925, p. [2]; *Der Sturm* 19 (October, 1925), no. 7, 282. Meyer also appears to have sought out a regular table in quarters in Berlin not regularly frequented by former fellow Expressionists after the war, for he was often seen in this period, according to Nell Walden, in the establishment run by Aenne Maenz in the Augsburger Strasse, where mostly actors and actresses gathered. See Nell Walden, "Kokoschka und der *Sturm*-Kreis," in *Expressionismus: Aufzeichnungen*, ed. Raabe, p. 133.

152. See Raabe, *Die Zeitschriften*, pp. 165-68.

Chapter 8

1. Tilla Durieux, *Eine Tür steht offen* (Berlin-Grunewald, 1954), p. 34; Karl H. Salzmann, "Die Verlage Paul und Bruno Cassirer, ein Stück Berliner Kulturgeschichte," *Berliner Hefte für das geistige Leben* 4 (1949): 503-8; *Neue deutsche Biographie,* ed. Die Historische Kommission bei der Bayrischen Akademie der Wissenschaften, vol. 3 (Berlin, 1957), pp. 167-68, 169-70.

2. Richard Hamann and Jost Herman, *Impressionismus* (Berlin, 1960), p. 127.

3. Werner Doede, *Berlin: Kunst und Künstler seit 1870: Anfänge und Entwicklungen* (Recklinghausen, 1961), pp. 12ff., 52ff; Peter Selz, *German Expressionist Paintings*

(Berkeley and Los Angeles, 1957), pp. 32ff; Bernard S. Myers, *The German Expressionists: A Generation in Revolt* (New York and Washington, 1966), pp. 18ff.

4. Doede, *Berlin,* pp. 13, 53; Selz, *German Expressionist Painting,* pp. 36f; Myers, *The German Expressionists,* p. 19.

5. Doede, *Berlin,* p. 73; Selz, *German Expressionist Painting,* pp. 36-38; Myers, *The German Expressionists,* p. 19.

6. Doede, *Berlin,* pp. 52ff.

7. Durieux, *Eine Tür,* p. 34; Salzmann, "Die Verlage," pp. 503, 505; *Neue deutsche Biographie,* vol. 3, pp. 167, 169.

8. Doede, *Berlin,* pp. 80, 92, 98.

9. Durieux, *Eine Tür,* pp. 41f; Wilhelm Herzog, *Menschen, denen ich begegnete* (Bern and Munich, 1959), pp. 462ff. and passim; Salzmann, "Die Verlage," pp. 502ff.

10. Durieux, *Eine Tür,* passim; Herzog, *Menschen,* pp. 462ff; Ernst Barlach, *Ein selbsterzähltes Leben* (Munich, 1948), pp. 41-44; Kasimir Edschmid, *Lebendiger Expressionismus* (Vienna, Munich, and Basel, 1961), pp. 215ff; René Schickele, "Abschied von Paul Cassirer" (1926), reprinted in Schickele, *Werke,* vol. 3, pp. 914-15; Lovis Corinth *Selbstbiographie* (Leipzig, 1926), pp. 149ff; Rudolf Bernauer, *Das Theater meines Lebens: Erinnerungen* (Berlin, 1955), p. 277; Ernst Barlach, *Die Briefe,* vol. 1 (Munich, 1968), passim; Ernst Barlach, *Die Briefe,* vol. 2 (Munich, 1969), passim.

11. See note 10, above.

12. Barlach, *Ein selbsterzähltes Leben,* p. 43; Herzog, *Menschen,* p. 462.

Er selbst eine Mischung von Künstler, schlauem Händler und einem phantasievollen, aber zugleich oft bösartigen, schwer zu behandelnden Kind. Ein vitaler und doch empfindsamer Mensch mit ungewöhnlichen Eigenschaften. Voller Widersprüche. Naiv begeisterungsfähig und kritisch bis zur provokatorischen Kränkung. Mit empfänglichsten Sinnen für Wertvolles in der Kunst und in der Literatur, immer cupidus rerum novarum, ehrgeizig und machtliebend, rücksichtslos und opportunistisch, kühn und feig, oft im Urteil ausschweifend und ohne Gleichgewicht, aber nie langweilig oder doktrinär.

13. Paul Cassirer, "Kunst und Kunsthandel," *Pan* 1 (1911): 457-469, 558-573.

14. *Ein Protest deutscher Künstler,* ed. Carl Vinnen (Jena, 1911). The first of Cassirer's articles cited in the footnote above was also published, under the same title, as Cassirer's contribution to the group reply to Vinnen's brochure. See *Im Kampf um die Kunst; Die Antwort auf den "Protest deutscher Künstler"* (Munich, 1911), pp. 154-67.

15. Cassirer, "Kunst und Kunsthandel," p. 572.

16. Ibid., p. 563.

17. Ibid., p. 561.

18. Ibid.

19. Ibid., p. 561ff.

20. Ibid., p. 565.

21. Ibid., pp. 566-67, 569-70.

22. Ibid., pp. 567-69.

23. Ibid., p. 568.

24. Ibid., pp. 568-71.
25. Ibid., p. 569.
26. Ibid.
27. Ibid., pp. 570-71.
28. Durieux, *Eine Tür,* p. 40.
29. Ibid., p. 32.
30. Ibid., p. 40ff.
31. *Neue deutsche Biographie,* vol. 3, p. 169.
32. See Herzog, *Menschen,* pp. 464ff. See below on *Pan* and other journals published by Cassirer.
33. Herzog, *Menschen,* pp. 462ff; Heinrich Mann, *Ein Zeitalter wird besichtigt* (Berlin, 1947), p. 222. See also Durieux, *Eine Tür,* passim.
34. Mann, *Ein Zeitalter,* p. 222.

    In Wirklichkeit behielt er bis zum Kriege das Vergnügen an den auffallenden Werken des Friedens. Seine eigennützige Arbeit war allein der Ruhm, an ihnen teilzuhaben. Fünf Jahre, von 1910 bis 1914, bezahlte er meine längst vorliegenden Leistungen reichlich, ohne auf Gewinn oder nur Ersatz zu achten.

35. Durieux, *Eine Tür,* p. 32.
36. Ibid., p. 41.
37. Ibid., pp. 41f.
38. Ibid., p. 41.
39. Ibid.
40. Ibid.
41. Ibid., pp. 41-42.
42. Ibid., p. 42.
43. Herzog, *Menschen,* pp. 173, 203, 459, 462, 465.
44. Durieux, *Eine Tür,* pp. 41-48.
45. Ibid., pp. 49, 64-65, 90, 139.
46. Ibid., p. 90.
47. See above, p. 174.
48. Durieux, *Eine Tür,* p. 139; Herzog, *Menschen,* p. 465; Barlach, *Ein selbsterzähltes Leben,* p. 41; Barlach, *Briefe,* passim.
49. Durieux, *Eine Tür,* p. 130; Herzog, *Menschen,* p. 465; Selz, *German Expressionist Painting,* p. 253; Edith Hoffmann, *Kokoschka: Life and Work* (London, n.d.), pp. 84-85; Myers, *The German Expressionists,* pp. 52-53; Kokoschka, *Leben,* pp. 115-16.
50. Herzog, *Menschen,* pp. 459, 465; Selz, *German Expressionist Painting,* p. 239.
51. On Kokoschka's association with Expressionism see the section on *Der Sturm,* above. On Jules Pascin, who was associated with the circles of German Expressionists that gathered in

the Munich Café Stephanie and in the Café du Dôme in Paris, see esp. Hans Purrmann, "Erinnerungen an den Maler Rudolf Levey und an die mit ihm verlebten Jahre der Freundschaft," in Rudolf Levy, *Bildnisse, Stilleben, Landschaften* (Baden-Baden, 1961), p. 24; Edschmid, *Lebendiger Expressionismus,* pp. 88, 90, 358; Rudolf Grossmann, "Schöpferische Konfession," in *Schöpferische Konfession,* ed. Kasimir Edschmid, Tribüne der Kunst und Zeit, 13 (Berlin, 1920), p. 25; Mühsam, *Unpolitische Erinnerungen,* pp. 169, 171, 173, 178-79; Herzog, *Menschen,* p. 460.

52.   See Herzog, *Menschen,* passim.

53.   Ibid., p. 462; Höxter, *So lebten wir,* p. 31; "Verzeichnis der Mitarbeiter und Beiträge," in *Die Aktion,* ed. Raabe (Stuttgart, 1961), p. 56.

54.   See Herzog, *Menschen,* passim. On *Pan,* cf. below.

55.   See Herzog, *Menschen,* pp. 208-211 and passim. On *Das Forum,* see also chapter 1, above.

56.   Herzog, *Menschen,* pp. 464-65.

57.   See Durieux, *Eine Tür,* passim; Schickele, "Abschied von Paul Cassirer," pp. 914-15.

58.   Durieux, *Eine Tür,* pp. 63-74.

59.   Ibid., pp. 65ff; Lasker-Schüler, *Lieber gestreifter Tiger,* pp. 87, 122, 148; Lasker-Schüler, *Wo ist unser buntes Theben,* pp. 29, 71, 78, 79, 80, 87, 92, 94, 112, 114; Else Lasker-Schüler, *Ich räume auf! Meine Anklage gegen meine Verleger* (Zürich, 1925), reprinted in Lasker-Schüler, *Prosa und Schauspiele,* pp. 505-55.

60.   On Walden and the "Neue Sezession," see Nell Walden, "Biographische Daten," p. 69. On Cassirer and this group, see below.

61.   Durieux, *Eine Tür,* pp. 65-66.

62.   See under the sections devoted to these circles in this study.

63.   Durieux, *Eine Tür,* p. 90; Lasker-Schüler, *Briefe an Karl Kraus,* p. 88; Lasker-Schüler, *Gesichte,* pp. 208-9.

64.   See Fritz Schlawe, *Literarische Zeitschriften: 1885-1910,* Sammlung Metzler, vol. 6, no. 1 (Stuttgart, 1961), pp. 48-50. See also Julius Meier-Graefe, "Der Pan," *Pan* 1 (1910): 1-4.

65.   Meier-Graefe, "Der Pan," pp. 1-4. Alfred Kerr, "Brief an die Herausgeber," *Pan* 1 (1910): 7-10. Kerr's letter is dated "October, 1910."

66.   See Meier-Graefe, "Der Pan," pp. 1-4; Schlawe, *Literarische,* vol. 1, pp. 48-49.

67.   Meier-Graefe, "Der Pan," pp. 1-4.

68.   Ibid., pp. 2-3.

69.   Ibid., p. 2.

Im übrigen lässt sich vielleicht noch dieses und jenes von den alten PAN-Idealen benutzen. Es schwebte uns so etwas Gemeinsames, Universelles vor. Scheerbart hatte es, glaube ich, kosmische Harmonie getauft.

70.   Ibid., p. 3.

71.   Ibid.

Unser Universalismus, unsere Vielseitigkeit war zu—duftig. Um Gotteswillen, seien Sie nicht duftig. Und hüten Sie sich vor der Vielseitigkeit. Sie war der Krebsschaden des PAN und ist der Krebsschaden jeder Zeitschrift. Nichts Schlimmeres als das Unparteiische, auch wenn es noch so hoch und edel gehandhabt wird, nichts Dümmeres. . . . Werden Sie einseitig, parteiisch, ungerecht bis zum Exzess und womöglich etwas zackig.

72.   Ibid., pp. 3-4.

Wir trugen zu viel Kunst in unseren an sich lobenswerten Gedanken hinein. Die Kunst sollte mit dem Leben verbunden werden. Wir erdachten alle möglichen Verbindungen, aber sie waren alle zu künstlerisch, um nicht zu sagen: künstlich.

73.   Kerr, "Brief," pp. 7-10.

74.   Ibid., p. 7.

Sie wissen ferner, aus unseren Gesprächen, dass der andre Plan, eine Zeitschrift zu schaffen, die nicht gemustert und geblümt ein Kulturgesabber macht, sondern einen Raum öffnet für allerhand Daseinsvolles und Freiheitlich-Frohes (dieser Satz kommt nie zu Ende)—dass dieser Plan mir gefällt.

75.   Ibid., p. 8.

Ich wünsche, weil in meinem Dasein die Literatur bloss eine der Ecken ausfüllt,—ich wünsche der Zeitschrift ein ähnliches Dasein. Dem Leben zugewandt. Arm erscheint mir noch die glänzendste Theaterkritik: wenn ein Kampfruf nicht hindurchschwillt—über das Theater hinaus. Ein elender Kritiker, der nicht Menschen erzittern oder kreischen macht mit Worten, Weisungen, Klängen, woran die (vorwiegend so unbedeutenden) Dichteriche keinen Teil haben. Kritiken bleiben Vorwände. Über das Theater hinaus. . . . Ich weiss, Sie empfinden das.

76.   Ibid., pp. 8-9.

Gehen Sie dennoch mit Fahnen und Fanfaren hart ins Politische. Ich denke mir die Zeitschrift nicht als ein Sensationsgeschöpf, das durch Widerspruch, Personalklatsch, Kilometerschwadronieren das eigene Mass an Dummheit zu überwinden trachtet. . . . Ich wünsche Sie da einverstanden mit dem, was ich in einer Kritik schrieb: 'Ein Greuel sind zwar sittlich-vorwärtsgehende Bezirksvereine. Tiefere Greuel aber die Affen, welche darum ihre Ideen verwerfen. . . . Affen verwechseln Ideenverkünder mit Ideen . . . ' Meine Herren, haben Sie keine falsche Scham: als welche dem Intellektmangel entspringt. Keine Literatenfurcht, alltäglich zu erscheinen.

77.   Ibid., p. 9.

Ich sehne mich nach einem Blatt, das nicht Aufrufe schreibt: sondern das organisiert. Das nicht auf Zustimmung der Leser läuft: sondern sie zu Handelnden ausbildet . . .

78.   Ibid., p. 10.

Ich sehne mich auch nach einem Blatt, welches die Erbärmlichkeit des gegenwärtigen Bürgertums zerpeitscht. Erbärmlichkeit, die jede Fünf gerade sein lässt, solange verdient wird. . . . Erbärmlichkeit eines Radikalismus, der nach einer Achtel-Generation sämtliches Glück in einer feudalen Familienverbindung sieht.

79.   Ibid.

80.   Ibid.

Helfen Sie: die gebildete Tatlosigkeit der anständigen Menschen als etwas Unanständiges ihnen einzubläuen. Vielleicht kommen sie dann über Ironie, Kopfschütteln und hochstehend fortschrittliche Feigheit hinweg. . . .
    Stellen Sie denen als Ideal solche vor: die bei letzter Kultur, bei klingender Künstlerkraft ein Stücke Pöbel in sich tragen; ein Stück Waldtier bei aller verfeinten Stadthaftigkeit, sprungmächtig. Die brauchen wir.

81. Willem van Wulfen, "Der Genussmensch," *Pan* 2 (1911): 12-13.

82. Van Wulfen, "Der Genussmensch," pp. 12-18.

83. Van Wulfen, "Der Genussmensch," p. 13.

Ich bin des Glaubens: dass man zugleich ein Sommer- und ein Wintermensch ist. Zugleich ein Koster und ein Koch. . . . Ich bin des Glaubens: dass für Menschen keine Möglichkeit ins Korn zu werfen ist. . . .

84. The bibliographical data that follow complete Raabe's brief description in Raabe, *Die Zeitschriften*, p. 32.

85. Ibid.

86. Ibid. See *Pan* 2 (1911): 131. See also Durieux, *Eine Tür*, p. 74.

87. Raabe, *Die Zeitschriften*, p. 32.

88. Durieux, *Eine Tür*, pp. 70-74. This incident had its roots in the banning and confiscation by Traugott von Jagow, the Chief of Police and censor in Berlin, of the January 16, 1910, issue (no. 6) of *Pan* for its publication of allegedly morally objectionable selections from Gustave Flaubert's diaries of his youth. See Gustave Flaubert, "Tagebuch des jungen Flaubert," 1 (1911): 181-88, continued in the next issue, no. 7, pp. 226-34. Kerr responded to Jagow's action in the latter issue: Alfred Kerr, "Jagow, Flaubert, *Pan,*" 1 (1911): 217-23. Kerr also attacked Jagow in a satirical poem, published in the next issue, no. 8, for confiscating the seventh issue of *Pan* on the same grounds as he did the sixth. See Alfred Kerr, "Ballade vom Alexanderplatz," *Pan* 1 (1911): 255-56. These incidents set Kerr and Jagow at odds and prepared for an encounter between the two which immediately followed.

   At the end of 1910, Cassirer had published Carl Sternheim's play *Die Hose* (bearing the pub. date: Berlin, 1911). This play was subsequently produced by Max Reinhardt in the "Berliner Kammerspiele" under the direction of Felix Hollaender. Jagow had initially placed his ban over the production; however, Sternheim and Reinhardt convinced the Chief of Police to attend a special dress rehearsal in order to judge at first hand the propriety of the production. With the cooperation of Cassirer, it was arranged that Tilla Durieux would sit with Jagow during the performance and distract him by conversation and charm at possibly objectionable points in the play. The maneuver was largely successful; Jagow lifted his ban over the production, although only after certain deletions and a change in title (*Die Hose* to *Der Riese*) were agreed to. Jagow, however, had obviously been charmed by Tilla Durieux and, shortly after the performance, wrote her a private note, in which he asked for a second meeting with her in order "to continue the conversation" they had begun earlier that day. Cassirer, on learning of the note, protested to Jagow, who, in turn, immediately sent a captain on his force to apologize. While Cassirer therewith considered the matter closed— and continued to think in these terms in spite of a revival of the affair in the established press, Kerr was not satisfied. Seeing an opportunity to strike back at Jagow for his actions earlier that year against *Pan,* Kerr exposed Jagow and the text of his note to Durieux to ridicule in *Pan.* See Alfred Kerr, "Vorletzter Brief an Jagow," *Pan* 1 (March 1, 1911), no. 9, pp. 287-90. Cassirer's position on Kerr's handling of the affair in the latter articles was made clear in his disavowal of Kerr's article in the same issue. See Paul Cassirer, "Erklärung," *Pan* 1 (1911): 320. The next issue of *Pan* saw a continuation of Kerr's attack on Jagow and a reiteration by Cassirer of his position. See Alfred Kerr, "Nachlese," *Pan* 1 (March 16, 1911), no. 10, pp. 321-26; Paul Cassirer, untitled article in *Pan* 1 (March 15, 1911), no. 10, see also Carl Sternheim, *Gesamtwerk,* vol. 1 (Neuwied am Rhein and Berlin, 1963), pp. 564-71.

   Pan was banned again the very next month, perhaps as Jagow's way of responding to Kerr's attacks, for the publication of Herbert Eulenberg's "Brief eines Vaters unserer Zeit." See *Pan* 1 (April 1, 1911), no. 11, 358-63. See Eulenberg's and Wilhelm Herzog's replies to the confiscation and ban in the next issue: Herbert Eulenberg, "Ein Protest," *Pan* 1 (April 16, 1911), no. 12, pp. 393-95; Wilhelm Herzog, "Der denunzierte Dichter," *Pan* 1 (April 16, 1911), no. 12 pp. 396-98. Trials against the journal, its contributors, editors, and its publisher, over issue 11 and the earlier issues banned (nos. 6 and 7), followed later that year and ended in both instances in acquittals. See reports on these trials in *Pan:* Wilhelm Herzog, "Die unzüchtige No. 7," *Pan* 1 (July 16, 1911), no. 18, pp. 587-90; K [Kerr?], "Freisprechung," *Pan* 2 (October 1, 1911), no. 1, p. 34.

Cassirer's ultimate reaction to all of these incidents was, as Tilla Durieux claimed, to become so soured on the journal that he decided to sell it. His decision was no doubt also influenced by his difficulties with his editorial staff after Kerr's departure from the journal in November, 1911. See esp. Paul Cassirer, untitled article in *Pan* 2 (January 25, 1912), no. 10, p. 316; W. Fred, "Abschied des Journalisten," *Pan* 2 (January 25, 1910), no. 10, pp. 312-16. On the Kerr-Jagow-*Pan* affair, see also Herzog, *Menschen,* pp. 399-400.

89. Raabe, *Die Zeitschriften,* p. 32.

90. Ibid.

91. Ibid.

92. Herzog, *Menschen,* p. 396.

Das war haargenau was ich wollte. Das war der Ton, den ich im *Pan* anschlagen wollte, und wir haben versucht, ihn durchzuhalten.

93. Wilhelm Herzog, "Moabit," *Pan* 1 (1910): 40.

Immerhin: die Gesellschaft, die allen Sensationen des Theaters und der Kunst nachläuft, täte gut, einmal in ihrem besinnungslosen Lauf einzuhalten, ihre Theaterfreude für eine Weile zu unterdrücken, und sich um Angelegenheiten zu kümmern, die ihr verdammt nahe gehen.

94. Ludwig Frank, M.D.R., "Politische Skizzen," *Pan* 1 (1911): 75-79; René Schickele, "Briand," *Pan* 1 (1911): pp. 113-14.

95. See note 88, above.

96. See note 88, above.

97. Alfred Kerr, "Wanderungen mit Bethmann," *Pan* 1 (1911): 423-30; Alfred Kerr, "Kolonialdämmerung," *Pan* 1 (1911): 679-85; Alfred Kerr, "Was ist zu tun?" *Pan* 1 (1911): 69-74.

98. Heinrich Mann, "Geist und Tat," *Pan* 1 (1911): 137-43.

99. Ibid., pp. 138-40.

100. Ibid., pp. 140-41.

Der Faust- und Autoritätsmensch muss der Feind sein.

101. Ibid., pp. 142-43.

Seine Natur: die Definition der Welt, die helle Vollkommenheit des Wortes verpflichtet ihn zur Verachtung der dumpfen, unsauberen Macht. Vom Geist ist ihm die Würde des Menschen auferlegt.

102. Ibid., p. 143.

103. Ibid.

Die Zeit verlangt und ihre Ehre will, dass [die Literaten] endlich, endlich auch in diesem Lande dem Geist die Erfüllung seiner Forderungen sichern, dass sie Agitatoren werden, sich dem Volk verbinden gegen die Macht, dass sie die ganze Kraft des Wortes seinem Kampf schenken, der auch der Kampf des Geistes ist.

104. Ibid., pp. 138-39.

Sie haben es leicht gehabt, die Literaten Frankreichs, die, von Rousseau bis Zola, der bestehenden Macht entgegentraten: sie hatten ein Volk. Ein Volk mit literarischen Instinkten, das die Macht bezweifelt, und von so warmem Blut, dass sie ihm unerträglich wird, sobald sie durch die Vernunft widerlegt ist. Was alles musste zusammenkommen, damit dem Geist Krieger erstanden! Nordische Menschen, vom Blut und noch mehr von der Kultur des Südens durchdrungen. Die Synthese Europas. Das Geschlecht mächtig wie im Süden, aber die ganze Künstlerschaft, die es verleiht, auf den Geist geworfen. Der Geist ist hier nicht das luftige Gespenst, das wir kennen,—und drunten trottet plump das Leben weiter. Der Geist ist das Leben selbst, er bildet es, auf die Gefahr, es abzukürzen.

105. Herzog, *Menschen*, p. 231. That Herzog understood Mann's essay in the manner in which it has been interpreted by the present author is made clear by a passage from an essay on Mann by Herzog, originally published in 1929, cited in Herzog, *Menschen*, p. 241.

Hier [in *Pan*] erschien u.a. sein grossartiges Manifest 'Geist und Tat,' das einigen von uns Jüngeren geradezu zum vorbildlichen Programm für unser künftiges Leben und Arbeiten wurde.

106. Franz Pfemfert, "Die Presse," *Die Aktion* 2 (1912): 453-54. See also Franz Pfemfert, "Glossen: Geist und Tat," *Die Aktion* 1 (1911): 425; Rudolf Kurtz, "Heinrich Manns politische Ideologie," *Die Aktion* 2 (1912), 1605-6.

107. Ludwig Rubiner, "Intensität," *Die Aktion* 3 (1913): 511; Ludwig Rubiner, *Der Mensch in der Mitte*, Politische Aktions-Bibliothek, 2 (Berlin-Wilmersdorf, 1917), p. 35.

108. Ludwig Rubiner, "Heinrich Manns *Untertan*," *Die Aktion* 4 (1914): 335-37. For a list of the essays, collected in Rubiner, *Der Mensch*, and first published in *Die Aktion*, see "Verzeichnis der Mitarbeiter und Beiträge," in *Die Aktion*, ed. Raabe (Stuttgart, 1961), vol. 1, pp. 93-94; "Bio-Bibliographischer Anhang," in *Die Aktion: 1917/18*, ed. Raabe (Munich, 1967), p. 57.

109. Ludwig Rubiner, "Der Dichter greift in die Politik," *Die Aktion* 2 (1912): 645-52, 709-15; Rubiner, *Der Mensch*, pp. 17-32.

Der Dichter greift in die Politik.

110. See Heinrich Mann, "Geist und Tat," *Das Ziel: Aufrufe zum Tätigen Geist*, ed. Kurt Hiller (Munich and Berlin, 1926), pp. 1-8; Kurt Hiller, "Philosophie des Ziels," *Das Ziel*, pp. 187-217.

111. See above under these circles. The response among the Expressionists to Mann's work in general, not just to his noted manifesto, typically resembled a youthful response to the writer as dynamic inciter to energetic action. See, e.g., Heinrich Eduard Jacob's autobiographical novel *Der Zwanzigjährige* (Munich, 1918), p. 97.

112. See table of contents for vol. 1 of *Pan*: "Inhalts-Verzeichnis (Erster Jahrgang)," *Pan* 1 (1910/11), pp. [i-viii]. See also Raabe, *Die Zeitschriften*, pp. 32-33.

113. Raabe, *Die Zeitschriften*, pp. 32-33.

114. Lucia Dora Frost, "Heinrich Manns Einakter," *Pan* 1 (1910): 83-86; "Herbert Eulenberg über Schiller," *Pan* 1 (1910): 97-99.

115. Kurt Hiller, "Über Georg Heym," *Pan* 1 (1911), 597-99; Rudolf Kurtz, "Appell an ehrliebende Theaterdirektoren," *Pan* 1 (1911): 126-28.

116. Sigmund Freud, "Die Inzestscheu der Wilden," *Pan* 2 (1912): 624-30, 653-55; Otto Rank, "Der Inzest," *Pan* 2 (1912): pp. 952-53.

117. See table of contents for the second half of 1912: "Inhalts-Verzeichnis," *Pan* 2 (1912), pp. iii-x. See also Raabe, *Die Zeitschriften,* pp. 32-33.

118. Dr. Ludwig Herz, "Die Fleischteuerung," *Pan* 3 (1912): 207-11.

119. See note 117, above.

120. Alfred Kerr, "Der Futurist," *Pan* 3 (1913): 507.

121. "Der Kondor," *Pan* 2 (1912): 603-4.

122. Kurt Hiller, "Trottelglosse," *Pan* 3 (1913): 504-6; Kurt Hiller, "Bemerkungen zu *Bebuquin,*" *Pan* 3 (1913): 650-54.

123. Emil Faktor, "Fortgeschrittene Lyrik," *Pan* 2 (1912): 710-11.

124. Ernst Blass, "Mein Herz," *Pan* 3 (1912): 118-22.

Der kommende Lyriker...wird aber kein Schilderer der Weltstadt sein, sondern ein weltstädtischer Schilderer....

125. See, e.g., note 117, above.

126. Reinhold Sorge, "Des Dichters Aug'," *Pan* 2 (1912): 755-63. See also note 117, above.

127. "Stadtverse (Fortgeschrittene Lyrik)," *Pan* 2 (1912): 698-701.

128. See, e.g., Kurt Hiller, "Begegnungen mit 'Expressionisten,'" in *Expressionismus: Aufzeichnungen,* ed. Raabe, p. 31; Blass, "Mein Herz," p. 121.

129. "Stadtverse," p. 698.

Junge Dichter, untereinander nicht bekannt, schicken dem *Pan* ihre Strophen. Vielfach zeigt sich der durch Kritik und Beispiel oft geäusserte Wunsch, die fortgeschrittene Lyrik der grossen Städte zu finden. Nicht alles geht zu veröffentlichen: so lange Polizisten wider die Kunst lauern. Einen Umriss der Strömung erhält man.

130. These selections appeared in the following issues of *Pan:* vol. 2, nos. 24, 28, 29, 34; vol. 3, nos. 2, 4, 5, 7, 9, 15, 18, 19, 20, 21, 23, 24, 25, 26, 27, 28, 29/30, 31; vol. 4, no. 1.

131. See note 112, above.

132. See Franz Marc, "Die neue Malerei," *Pan* 2 (1912): 468-71; Max Beckmann, untitled article in *Pan* 2 (1912): 485; Franz Marc, "Die konstruktiven Ideen der neuen Malerei," *Pan* 2 (1912): 527-31; Franz Marc, "Anti-Beckmann," *Pan* 2 (1912): 556. See also Selz, *German Expressionist Painting,* pp. 238-40.

133. See *Pan* 2 (1912): 581, 637, 667, 738, 743.

134. Max Deri, "Die Futuristen" *Pan* 2 (1912): 817ff; Max Deri, "Die Kubisten und der Expressionismus," *Pan* 2 (1912): 872-78; Max Deri, "Die absolute Malerei," *Pan* 2 (1912): 1201ff.

135. Raabe, *Die Zeitschriften,* p. 32.

136. Ibid.

137. See above, chapter 1. See also Herzog, *Menschen,* pp. 400-404.

138. Untitled article in *Pan* 4 (1915): 55.

> Der *Pan* erscheint bei Lebzeiten des Herausgebers immer. In selbstgewählten Zwischenräumen. Die drei noch fälligen Nummern des jetzigen Bezuges folgen binnen kurzem.

139. See Julius Rodenberg, *Deutsche Pressen: Eine Bibliographie* (Zürich, Vienna, and Leipzig, 1925), pp. 452-54. See also Herzog, *Menschen,* p. 459.

140. Rodenberg, *Deutsche,* pp. 452-54.

141. Ibid.

142. Ibid.

143. Ibid., p. 453.

144. Durieux, *Eine Tür,* p. 64; Herzog, *Menschen,* p. 207; Salzmann, "Die Verlage," p. 505; *Neue deutsche Biographie,* vol. 3, p. 169.

145. Durieux, *Eine Tür,* p. 64; Herzog, *Menschen,* p. 207.

146. Durieux, *Eine Tür,* p. 64.

147. Herzog, *Menschen,* p. 207.

148. Herzog, *Menschen,* p. 230; Ulrich Weisstein, *Heinrich Mann: Eine historisch-kritische Einführung in sein dichterisches Werk* (Tübingen, 1962), pp. 232ff., and p. 252, nn. 3-5. See also excerpts from contemporary reviews of the production in *Pan:* "Die erste Vorstellung der Gesellschaft *Pan:* Heinrich Mann und die Kritik," *Pan* 1 (1910): 99-100. The title of the latter article suggests that Herzog's recollection in *Menschen,* p. 207, that the "first" production of this organization was Wedekind's *Büchse der Pandora* may be erroneous!

149. See the review of this performance in *Pan:* "Wedekind in Berlin und München," *Pan* 1 (1910): 69.

150. Durieux, *Eine Tür,* pp. 94ff.

151. Ibid., pp. 97-98.

152. Ibid., p. 98.

153. Herzog, *Menschen,* pp. 465-466.

> Es war ein geschäftliches Milieu ohne geschäftlichen Anstrich. Ein buntes Durcheinander von ästhetischen, literarischen und kunstkritischen Meinungen, die oft einander befehdeten. Probleme der Politik und der Wirtschaft wurden selten berührt. Man sprach im Kunstsalon Cassirer mehr von der Schönheit der ausgestellten Bilder ... als von ihrem Geldwert.

154. Durieux, *Eine Tür,* p. 98.

155. Ibid., p. 99.

> In Berlin fanden wir die Stadt in tosender Aufregung. Überall Knäuel von Menschen, dazu abmarschierende Soldaten, denen die Leute Blumen zuwarfen. Jedes Gesicht glänzte freudig: Wir haben Krieg!—In den Cafés, in den Restaurants spielte die Musik unablässig 'Heil dir im Siegerkranz' und 'Die Wacht am Rhein,' jeder hatte es stehend anzuhören, das Essen wurde dabei kalt, das Bier warm, was schadete es: Wir haben Krieg! Die Menschen standen Schlange, um ihre Autos zum Hilfsdienst anzumelden. Freiwillige wurden bald nur noch auf dem Wege der Protektion angenommen. Die Soldaten bekamen an den Stationen Berge von Butterbroten, Würsten und Schokolade. An allem war Überfluss, an Menschen, Nahrung und Begeisterung.

156. Ibid.

157. Ibid.

158. Ibid.

159. Ibid., pp. 99-104.

160. Ibid., p. 104.

161. Ibid., pp. 104-5.

162. *Kriegszeit: Künstlerflugblätter* (Berlin: Verlag Paul Cassirer, Berlin W 10, Viktoriastr. 35, August 31, 1914-January, 1916), nos. 1-60. Since this publication is not described in detail in any bibliographical source available to me, its bibliographical data will be given in detail below. Raabe, *Die Zeitschriften*, p. 61, mentions this publication only in passing, in connection with its sequel, *Der Bildermann*, and states incorrectly that it ran to only twenty-three issues.

163. On Alfred Gold, a contributor to *Die Aktion*, see "Verzeichnis der Mitarbeiter und Beiträge," in *Die Aktion*, ed. Raabe (Stuttgart, 1961), vol. 1, pp. 50-51.

164. See *Menschheitsdämmerung*, ed. Pinthus (Hamburg, 1959), pp. 367-71; *Kameraden der Menschheit: Dichtungen zur Weltrevolution*, ed. Ludwig Rubiner (Potsdam, 1919), pp. 16-17, 33, 74-75, 98, 109-11, 152-53.

165. Durieux, *Eine Tür*, p. 107.

166. Ibid., p. 109.

167. Ibid.

168. Ibid.; Leo Kestenberg, *Bewegte Zeiten: Musisch-musikalische Lebenserinnerungen* (Wolfenbüttel and Zürich, 1961), pp. 38-39.

169. Kestenberg, *Bewegte*, pp. 38-39.

   Zuerst trug Gertrud Eysoldt Gedichte vor, dann las ich die Novelle. Die kriegsmüden Zuhörer wurden von dem Inhalt hingerissen. Ich las mit grosser Hingabe, und so kam es, dass sich nach Beendigung der Vorlesung der ganze Saal wie ein Mann erhob und 'Friede! Friede!' schrie. Einige Hitzköpfe wollten auf die Strasse eilen, um einen Demonstrationszug zu machen, aber glücklicherweise wurden sie von Besonneneren daran gehindert.

170. See Raabe, *Die Zeitschriften*, pp. 60-61.

171. Ibid., p. 60; Kestenberg, *Bewegte*, pp. 35ff.

172. Kestenberg, *Bewegte*, pp. 60-61.

173. Ibid., p. 61.

174. Ibid.

175. Durieux, *Eine Tür*, p. 109.

176. Ibid., pp. 109-17.

177. Ibid., pp. 109, 116-17.

178. Ibid., pp. 117-18.

179. Ibid., p. 118.

180. Ibid.

181. Ibid., pp. 120ff.

182. Ibid., pp. 121-23.

183. Ibid., p. 123.

184. Ibid., pp. 125-26.

185. Ibid., p. 126.

186. Ibid., pp. 123, 124-25.

187. Ibid., p. 127.

188. Ibid., pp. 128-30; Harry Graf Kessler, *Tagebücher*, pp. 23-29.

189. Durieux, *Eine Tür*, p. 130.

190. Ibid.; Harry Graf Kessler, *Tagebücher*, pp. 23-222; Edschmid, *Lebendiger Expressionismus*, pp. 215-29, 327, 400.

191. Durieux, *Eine Tür*, p. 131; Ernst Toller, *Eine Jugend in Deutschland* (1933), reprinted in Ernst Toller, *Prosa, Briefe, Dramen, Gedichte*, ed. Kurt Hiller (Reinbek bei Hamburg, 1961), p. 82.

192. Durieux, *Eine Tür*, pp. 131-38; Toller, *Eine Jugend*, pp. 83ff.

193. Durieux, *Eine Tür*, p. 138.

194. Durieux, *Eine Tür*, p. 130; Harry Graf Kessler, *Tagebücher*, pp. 23-222.

195. Harry Graf Kessler, *Tagebücher*, pp. 23, 122, 125, 144, 155, 163, 168, 172-73, 175. On "Neues Vaterland," see Herzog, *Menschen*, pp. 80, 238. This organization published a series of political pamphlets under its own name and authored by members of the "Bund," beginning in 1915. See the listings in *Deutsches Bücherverzeichnis* 4 (1915-20): 758; 7 (1921-25): 996.

196. *Unser Weg 1920: Ein Jahrbuch des Verlags Paul Cassirer: Mit Beiträgen von...*(Berlin, 1919), p. 124. The first almanac was: *Unser Weg 1919: Ein Jahrbuch des Verlags Paul Cassirer: Mit Beiträgen von...*(Berlin, 1918). See Raabe, *Die Zeitschriften*, pp. 204-5.

Unserer Tradition getreu, dienen wir der schönen Literatur, durch das handwerklich schöne Buch versuchen wir die in den Werken unserer Jungen seit geraumer Zeit verstärkt tönende ethische, dem sozialistischen Erlösergedanken nahestehende Note durch Herausgabe der literarischen Werke führender Sozialisten zu unterstüzen.

197. See *Unser Weg 1920*, pp. 124-36.

198. Ibid., pp. 128, 132.

199. Ibid., pp. 124-31; see also *Unser Weg 1919*, pp. 106-12. On the Cassirer exhibitions mentioned, see Myers, *The German Expressionists*, pp. 61, 79, 149; Lothar-Günther Buchheim, *Die Künstlergemeinschaft Brücke* (Feldafing, 1956), pp. 381, 384, 389.

200. See Raabe, *Die Zeitschriften*, pp. 47-50; *Unser Weg 1920*, p. 132.

201. Raabe, *Die Zeitschriften*, pp. 47-48.

202. Ibid., p. 48.

203. Ibid.

204. See, e.g., Kurt Wolff, *Autoren, Bücher, Abenteuer: Betrachtungen und Erinnerungen eines Verlegers* (Berlin, 1965), p. 105.

205. Durieux, *Eine Tür*, p. 142.

206. Ibid., pp. 142-45.

207. Ibid., p. 145.

208. Ibid.

209. Ibid.

210. Ibid.

211. Ibid.

212. Ibid., pp. 145-46.

213. Ibid., p. 146.

214. Ibid., pp. 146-47.

215. Harry Graf Kessler, *Tagebücher*, p. 448.

216. Salzmann, "Die Verlage," p. 505.

Chapter 9

1. Ludwig Meidner, "Mein Leben" (1919), reprinted in *Manifeste: Manifeste*, ed. Schmidt, p. 178.

   Ich gründete mit zwei Kameraden den Klub 'Die Pathetiker' und wir stellten unter dieser Fahne im Herbst desselben Jahres zum ersten mal in Berlin aus. Die folgenden Jahre waren voller Unruhe und nimmersatter Arbeit im Sturmesschritt.

2. Ibid., p. 177.

3. Ibid., pp. 177-78; Thomas Grochowiak, *Ludwig Meidner* (Recklinghausen, 1966), pp. 23-115, 224.

4. Grochowiak, *Meidner*, p. 137.

5. Ibid., pp. 137-38.

6. Ibid., pp. 38-39, 140.

7. Ibid., p. 38; "Bio-Bibliographischer Anhang," in *Die Aktion: 1917/18*, ed. Raabe (Munich, 1967), p. 34; Szittya, *Das Kuriositäten-Kabinett*, p. 248. Steinhardt contributed to *Der Sturm, Saturn, Das neue Pathos*. See Raabe, *Die Zeitschriften*, pp. 28, 41, 45.

8. See Hiller's assumption to this effect in his review of the group's exhibition: Kurt Hiller, "Ausstellung der Pathetiker," *Die Aktion* 2 (1912), 1514-16.

9. Grochowiak, *Meidner*, p. 38; Meidner, "Mein Leben," p. 178; *Der Sturm*, ed. Nell Walden and Lothar Schreyer, p. 257.

10. Grochowiak, *Meidner*, p. 39.

11. Ibid., pp. 39, 115. For Hiller's review see note 8, above.

12. Grochowiak, *Meidner*, pp. 38ff.

13. Ibid., p. 38.

14. Ibid.

15. Ibid., p. 140.

16. Ibid., pp. 140-44, 150; Ludwig Meidner, *Im Nacken das Sternmeer: Rufe eines Malers* (Leipzig, 1918), p. 77. See also Hasenclever's letter to Meidner of March 11, 1917, published in *Expressionismus: Literatur und Kunst*, ed. Bernhard Zeller, et al., p. 296; Herrmann-Neisse's letter to Friedrich Griegor of December 14, 1914, published in Max Herrmann-Neisse, *Eine Einführung in sein Werk und eine Auswahl*, ed. Friedrich Grieger (Wiesbaden, 1951), pp. 68-69; Ludwig Meidner, "Erinnerungen an Jakob van Hoddis," in Jakob van Hoddis, *Weltende: Gesammelte Dichtungen*, ed. Paul Pörtner (Zürich, 1958), pp. 88-89.

17. Hoddis, *Weltende*, p. 88.

18.   Ibid., pp. 88-89.

19.   Ibid. For an example of a similar reaction to the city see the statement by Becher in *Wiederanders,* pp. 530-31.

> Gern erinnere ich mich an die stundenlangen Fussmärsche durch das nächtliche Berlin, die wir häufig unternahmen. Diese Weltstadt Berlin war damals das grosse Erlebnis, und nicht nur für mich, den geborenen Kleinstädter, sondern auch für van Hoddis, der Berliner war. Wir verliessen nach Mitternacht das 'Café des Westens' und marschierten stramm, ziemlich rasch, geradeaus durch die Strassen, immer der Nase nach. Während ich als Maler umherspähte und das belebte Hell-Dunkel genoss, schien van Hoddis die Umwelt nicht zu beachten; aber er beachtete sie doch und nahm Dinge wahr, die eigentlich dem Maler auffallen mussten, denn er schaute die Welt nicht wie ein Literat an. Und so wars auch mit dem Marschieren. Van Hoddis wandelte mit seinen Beinen nicht den femininen Ästhetengang, sondern trottete und stampfte den Fahrdamm wie ein Musketier, denn wir vermieden den Bürgersteig. Zuweilen blieb er stehen, eine Weile schweigend, dann lachte er und sagte etwas Witziges oder Komisches, aber auch kluge Sachen, denn er war sehr intelligent. Dann ging er weiter in rascher Gangart, wir waren damals achtungzwanzig Jahre und bewiesen grosse Ausdauer im Marschieren, das nicht aufhörte, als der Morgen graute....
> So verliebt waren wir in diese Stadt.

20.   See Raabe, *Die Zeitschriften,* pp. 234, 253, for complete index to Meidner's contributions of this sort.

21.   Ibid., pp. 44-45.

22.   See Meidner's letter to Kurt Wolff Verlag of January 28, 1917, published in Kurt Wolff, *Briefwechsel eines Verlegers: 1911-1963,* ed. Bernhard Zeller and Ellen Otten (Frankfurt am Main, 1966), p. 191.

23.   Ludwig Meidner, "Erinnerung an Dresden," in Ludwig Meidner, *Septemberschrei: Hymnen, Gebete, Lasterungen* (Berlin, 1920), pp. 11-14; reprinted in *Expressionismus: Aufzeichnungen,* ed. Raabe, pp. 145-50. See also Grochowiak, *Meidner,* p. 99; *Briefe der Expressionisten,* ed. Edschmid, pp. 17-18.

24.   See Meidner's letter to the Hyperion-Verlag of February 27, 1914, published in Wolff, *Briefwechsel,* p. 190.

25.   See note 21, above.

26.   Meidner, "Erinnerung an Dresden," in *Expressionismus: Aufzeichnungen,* ed. Raabe, p. 146.

> Eines Sinnes waren wir in allen Dingen. Rissen uns immer abwechselnd an unsern Entzückungen hoch—ermunterten uns in allen Wagnissen, und Tag für Tag gaben wir unbekümmert unsern süssen Kindereien recht.—Dichter und Maler können getrost zusammen arbeiten. Da gibts keine Feindschaft noch Neid. Da gibt es nur helle Bereicherung und Leben in geistiger Fülle.

27.   See note 23, above.

28.   *Briefe der Expressionisten,* ed. Edschmid, pp. 17-18; Grochowiak, *Meidner,* p. 99.

29.   The postcard is published in *Expressionismus: Literatur und Kunst,* ed. Bernhard Zeller, et al., p. 110.

30.   Grochowiak, *Meidner,* pp. 105-6.

31. Ibid., p. 106; *Expressionismus: Literatur und Kunst,* ed. Bernhard Zeller, et al., p. 35.

32. Grochowiak, *Meidner,* pp. 106-7.

33. See Wieland Herzfelde, *Unterwegs: Blätter aus fünfzig Jahren* (Berlin, 1961), pp. 114-32.

34. See "Bio-Bibliographischer Anhang," in *Die Aktion: 1917/18,* ed. Raabe (Munich, 1967), p. 46.

35. Grochowiak, *Meidner,* p. 108; Meidner, "Mein Leben," p. 178.

36. Grochowiak, *Meidner,* p. 115.

37. See above, p. 000.

38. Grochowiak, *Meidner,* pp. 148-49.

39. See Raabe, *Die Zeitschriften,* pp. 155-56.

40. See above, p. 000.

41. See Ludwig Meidner, "An alle Künstler, Dichter, Musiker," *Das Kunstblatt* 3 (1919), 29ff; reprinted in *Manifeste: Manifeste,* ed. Schmidt, pp. 245-46.

    Damit wir uns nicht mehr vor dem Firmament zu schämen haben, müssen wir uns endlich aufmachen und mithelfen, dass eine gerechte Ordnung in Staat und Gesellschaft eingesetzt werde.
    Wir Künstler und Dichter müssen da in erster Reihe mittun. Es darf keine Ausbeuter und Ausgebeuteten geben!
    ... Der Sozialismus soll unser neues Glaubensbekenntnis sein!
    ... Maler, Dichter, Musiker, schämt euch eurer Abhängigkeit und Feigheit und verbrüdert euch mit dem ausgestossenen, rechtlosen, gering bezahlten Knecht.

42. Grochowiak, *Meidner,* p. 149.

43. Ibid., pp. 179-80.

44. Ludwig Meidner, *Eine autobiographische Plauderei,* Junge Kunst, vol. 4 (Leipzig, 1923), p. 8.

    Nichts tu ich lieber als grosse Blätter komponieren mit Gestalten oder Begebnissen der heiligen Schrift.

45. Grochowiak, *Meidner,* p. 180.

46. See note 43, above.

47. Grochowiak, *Meidner,* p. 224.

48. Ludwig Meidner, "Anleitung zum Malen von Grossstadtbildern," *Kunst und Künstler* 12 (1914): 312; see also reprint of this essay in Pörtner, *Literatur-Revolution,* vol. 2, pp. 164-65.

    Wir müssen endlich anfangen, unsere Heimat zu malen, die Grossstadt, die wir unendlich lieben. Auf unzähligen, fresken-grossen Leinwänden sollten unsre fiebernden Hände all das Herrliche und Seltsame, das Monströse und Dramatische der Avenüen, Bahnhöfe, Fabriken und Türme hinkritzeln.

49. Meidner, *Eine autobiographische Plauderei,* p. 11.

    Die Gestalterer aber, die dem Reiche Gottes zugehören haben stillere und weniger glanzvolle Werke darzubringen. Dafür geht von ihnen ein Strom der Liebe aus, der alle Gotteskinder wundersam berührt und sie bestärkt im Dienst und im Ausharren, und der höhere Nutzen für ihre Hervorbringer ist der, dass sie dem barmherzigen Schöpfer Ehre antun und ihm dienen, indem sie auf gemalten Tafeln seines Namens Macht und Schönheit preisen.

   ... Und vollends, die letzten Jahrhunderte, sind eine laute und schreiende Heidenzeit geworden, und die rationalistische und gänzlich entgotterte Welt der Impressionisten und alles das, was jüngsthin die Malerei geleistet hat, wird, wie ich sagte, zu leicht befunden werden am Tage des letzten Gerichts.

50.   Meidner, *Im Nacken,* pp. 74-77.

51.   Meidner, *Eine autobiographische Plauderei,* p. 13.

   Und er [= der heilige Geist] hat mich dazu so reich und überschwänglich gesegnet und ich habe innerlich so viel dabei gewonnen, dass ich glaube mit jenen kleinen Werken die Gemeinheit getilgt zu haben, welche ich mit meinen früheren Prosaschriften und mit hässlichen demagogischen Pamphleten anstiftete, die in den ersten Revolutionsmonaten in die Welt gingen. Den Spleen, die Übergeschnapptheit und Schamlosigkeit, welche in meiner früheren Prosa walteten, habe ich weit, weit hinter mir gelassen und so sehr hat mich der Gottesglaube geklärt und nüchtern gemacht, dass ich heute nur noch mit tiefer Schamröte in jenen jugendlichen Arbeiten lesen kann.

Chapter 10

1.   See Raabe, *Die Zeitschriften,* pp. 51-52. Dates of birth are available only for the following: Oskar Maria Graf (1894), Martin Gumpert (1897), Friedrich Hollaender (1896), Hans Jacob (1896), and Friedrich Wilhelm Wagner (1892). See "Verzeichnis der Mitarbeiter und Beiträge," in *Die Aktion,* ed. Raabe (Stuttgart, 1961), pp. 51, 65, 90, 97, 105, 107; Ingrid Bode, *Die Autobiographien zur deutschen Literatur, Kunst und Musik 1900-1965: Bibliographie und Nachweise der persönlichen Begegnungen und Charakterisken,* Repertorien zur Deutschen Literaturgeschichte, ed. Paul Raabe, vol. 2 (Stuttgart, 1966), p. 47; "Bio-Bibliographischer Anhang," in *Die Aktion: 1917/18,* ed. Raabe (Munich, 1967), p. 27. In addition, it is known that Borsch died in battle at the end of June, 1915, at the age of 20; thus we can place his birth at approximately 1895. See "Bio-Bibliographischer Anhang," p. 12. Also, Herzfelde reports visiting Barger in 1916 in Berlin and discovering that he was still a *gymnasium* student, living with his parents; this report would, therefore, place Barger's birth after 1895. See Wieland Herzfelde, "Über den Malik-Verlag," in *Der Malik-Verlag: 1916-1947,* ed. Wieland Herzfelde (Berlin and Weimar, n.d.), pp. 9-10. Finally, Gumpert's reminiscences on his friendship with Taendler around the time of the appearance of *Neue Jugend* make it clear that Taendler was about the same age as Gumpert then. See Martin Gumpert, *Hölle im Paradies: Selbstdarstellung eines Arztes* (Stockholm, 1939), pp. 48ff. Gumpert also reports here that Taendler committed suicide "under the pressure of the war years." See Gumpert, *Hölle* p. 48.

2.   *Neue Jugend* 1 (March, 1914), no. 1; also cited in Raabe, *Die Zeitschriften,* p. 52.

3.   Raabe, *Die Zeitschriften,* p. 52.

4.   Gumpert, *Hölle,* p. 48; Hans Jacob, *Kind meiner Zeit: Lebenserinnerungen* (Cologne and Berlin, 1962), p. 35.

5.   Raabe, *Die Zeitschriften,* p. 52; Herzfelde, "Über den Malik-Verlag," p. 9; Gumpert, *Hölle,* pp. 48-49.

6.   Raabe, *Die Zeitschriften,* p. 51.

7.   Ibid.

8. Gumpert, *Hölle*, pp. 48ff; Jacob, *Kind*, p. 35.

9. See note 1, above; and the autobiographies of Gumpert, Jacob, cited in footnotes 1 and 4, above, also Oskar Maria Graf, *Wir sind Gefangene: Ein Bekenntnis aus diesem Jahrzehnt* (Munich, 1927).

10. See index to contributors in Raabe, *Die Zeitschriften*, pp. 215ff; on Taendler and *Die Aktion* see "Verzeichnis der Mitarbeiter und Beiträge," in *Die Aktion*, ed. Raabe (Stuttgart, 1961), p. 105.

11. Gumpert, *Hölle*, p. 49.

12. Wieland Herzfelde, *Unterwegs* (Berlin, 1961), pp. 278-80; Herzfelde, "Über den Malik-Verlag," p. 9.

13. See above, chapter 1, and below, the chapter on the Berlin Dadaists.

14. Jacob, *Kind*, pp. 26ff.

15. Ibid., pp. 22ff.

16. Ibid., pp. 22-25.

17. Ibid., pp. 22-24; Mühsam, *Unpolitische Erinnerungen*, p. 215. See also above, the chapter on *Der Sturm:* Lasker-Schüler's essay on Caro: Else Lasker-Schüler, "Unser Rechtsanwalt Hugo Caro," repr. in Lasker-Schüler, *Prosa und Schauspiele*, pp. 239-41.

18. Jacob, *Kind*, p. 27.

19. Ibid., pp. 26ff., 33.

20. Gumpert, *Hölle*, pp. 69-70.

21. See note 1, above, Jacob, *Kind*, p. 45.

22. See *Neue Jugend* 1 (December, 1914), no. 6; Herzfelde, "Über den Malik-Verlag," p. 10.

23. Raabe, *Die Zeitschriften*, p. 52.

24. See note 22, above.

25. Herzfelde, "Über den Malik-Verlag," p. 10; "Verzeichnis der Mitarbeiter und Beiträge," in *Die Aktion*, ed. Raabe (Stuttgart, 1961), p. 38.

26. Graf, *Wir sind*, pp. 143ff., 210ff.

27. Jacob, *Kind*, pp. 45ff., 50ff.

28. Gumpert, *Hölle*, pp. 125-26; see also below, the chapter on *Die Dichtung*.

29. Szittya, *Das Kuriositäten-Kabinett*, p. 280; "Verzeichnis der Mitarbeiter und Beiträge," in *Die Aktion*, ed. Raabe (Stuttgart, 1961), pp. 107-8.

30. "Verzeichnis der Mitarbeiter," pp. 107-8; Raabe, *Die Zeitschriften*, p. 112.

Chapter 11

1. *Die Aktion* 4 (1914): 264.

   'DIE FEINDLICHEN BRÜDER'
   Unter diesem Zeichen findet den 24. März im Salon Cassirer ein Vortragsabend statt, veranstaltet von Paul Boldt, Gottfried Benn, Mathias [*sic:* for Leo Matthias], Egmont Seyerlen-Farussi und Alfred Wolfenstein. Karten á M. 3,—im Café des Westens und an der Abendkasse.

2.   C.F.W. Behl, "Begegnungen mit dem Expressionismus," in *Expressionismus: Aufzeichnungen,* ed. Raabe, p. 295; L.L. Matthias, "Erinnerungen an Gottfried Benn," in Gottfried Benn, *Lyrik und Prosa, Briefe und Dokumente,* ed. Max Niedermayer (Wiesbaden, 1962), pp. xci-xcii.

3.   Matthias, "Erinnerungen," pp. xci-xcii.

Der Name 'Die feindlichen Brüder' stammte von mir und war ein *nom de guerre faute de mieux,* da es uns unmöglich gewesen war, die Mitwirkenden—zu denen so verschiedene Geister wie Gottfried Benn, der frühverstorbene Paul Boldt, der bedeutende, aber sich stets verleugnende Romancier Egon [*sic*] Seyerlen und der von Rilke geschätzte Alfred Wolfenstein gehörten—unter einen Hut zu bringen.

4.   Matthias, "Erinnerungen," p. xcii.

Was alle diese Autoren vereinte, war weniger ein Programm als die Verneinung von Programmen anderer, und so verdeckte der Name ganz gut, was nicht dawar.

5.   See under these poets in the sections on *Der Sturm, Die Aktion,* and Alfred Richard Meyer, above. See also the index to contributors in Raabe, *Die Zeitschriften,* pp. 215ff; "Verzeichnis der Mitarbeiter und Beiträge," in *Die Aktion,* ed. Raabe (Stuttgart, 1961), pp. 35, 38, 110-11. Seyerlen was also a contributor to *Die Aktion.* See "Verzeichnis," p. 100. On Matthias see also Wolff, *Briefwechsel,* pp. 310-12.

6.   Matthias, "Erinnerungen," pp. xci-xcii.

7.   Ibid., p. xcii.

8.   Ibid., p. xci.

9.   Ibid., p. xcii.

10.   Ibid.

11.   Ibid.

Benn hatte seinen Vortragsstil schon damals gefunden. Er las einige Gedichte aus *Morgue* und einige ungedruckte in jenem sachlichen, fast unbeteiligten Ton, der manchmal den Eindruck hervorrief, als ob er den Leuten Verse vor die Füsse werfen wollte. Sein Sprachton war nicht frei von Protest und Polemik. Aber der Erfolg war nachhaltig und ehrlich, und Benn hatte die Schlacht ganz offenbar gewonnen.

Chapter 12

1.   Richard Huelsenbeck, "Zürich 1916, wie es wirklich war," in *Expressionismus: Aufzeichnungen,* ed. Raabe, pp. 174-75; Richard Huelsenbeck, *Mit Witz, Licht und Grütze* (Wiesbaden, 1957), p. 9; Richard Huelsenbeck, "Dada oder der Sinn im Chaos," in *Dada: Eine literarische Dokumentation,* ed. Richard Huelsenbeck (Reinbek bei Hamburg, 1964), pp. 11-13.

2.   Huelsenbeck, "Zürich 1916," p. 174; Huelsenbeck, *Dada,* p. 343; Huelsenbeck, *Mit Witz,* p. 9; Ball, *Briefe,* pp. 19ff.

3.   Huelsenbeck, "Zürich 1916," p. 174.

4.   Ibid., pp. 174-75; Ball, *Briefe,* p. 22; Ball, *Die Flucht,* pp. 6-7; Hugo Ball, "Totenrede" *Die weissen Blätter* 2 (April, 1915), no. 4, 525-27; Gustav Sack, "Aus Schwabing," Gustav Sack, *Prosa, Briefe, Verse* (Munich and Vienna, 1962), pp. 380-84; Raabe, *Die Zeitschriften,* p. 50; "Verzeichnis der Mitarbeiter und Beiträge," in *Die Aktion,* ed. Raabe (Stuttgart, 1961), pp.

32, 77-78; Hans Leybold in letter of September 29, 1913, to Käthe Brodnitz, published in "'Morgenrot!—Die Tage dämmern!' Zwanzig Briefe aus dem Frühexpressionismus 1910-1914," ed. Paul Raabe, *Der Monat* 16 (1964), no. 191, pp. 66-67; Huelsenbeck, "Dada oder der Sinn im Chaos," p. 11.

5. Huelsenbeck, "Zürich 1916," pp. 175-76; Huelsenbeck, *Mit Witz*, pp. 7-8; Ball, *Briefe*, pp. 35ff; Ball, *Die Flucht*, pp. 13ff.

6. See note 5, above, also Emmy Hennings-Ball, *Hugo Balls Weg zu Gott* (Munich, 1931), p. 48; Huelsenbeck, "Dada oder der Sinn im Chaos," p. 13.

7. Ball, *Briefe*, p. 35.
    ... bin mit Huelsenbeck oft zusammen.

8. Huelsenbeck, "Zürich 1916," pp. 175-76. See also Ball, *Briefe*, p. 39; Ball, *Flucht*, pp. xii, 14ff.

9. See Richard Huelsenbeck's undated letter to a certain "N.F." printed in *Briefe der Expressionisten*, ed. Edschmid, pp. 68-69. Edschmid suggests 1918 here as a probable date for this letter; however, the events Huelsenbeck, describes here can all (except for the curious reference to the fact that Hans Leybold, who died on September 9, 1914, "is also here"—unless Huelsenbeck, means only *in spirit*) be placed quite precisely in the first half of 1915. Huelsenbeck also makes reference to the "Expressionistenabend" described in this letter in Huelsenbeck, "Dada oder der Sinn im Chaos," p. 13.

Ball und ich haben uns für nichts als für den Expressionismus interessiert, hauptsächlich Ball....
    Wir huren hier herum, um die Tauentzienstrasse, wir trinken, auch sitzen wir manchmal in den Tavernen und Liqueurstuben zwei Tage lang, bis uns die Polizei hinauswirft. Wir halten alles das für Expressionismus, da wir weniger auf die Bilder sehen als auf den Lebensstil. Wir wollen ein neues Leben, wir wollen eine neue Aktivität, wir wollen eine neue Hautfarbe, vielleicht eine neue Bügelfalte, vielleicht auch ein neues Steuergesetz. Wir hassen die Regierung, den Kaiser, diesen krachbeinigen Minister—wie ist doch sein Name—die Offiziere mit den hohen Kragen und der hohen Stimme, die stramm stehenden Sklaven, die schiessenden Kanonen (von denen wir träumen), den Kunsthonig, die Rüben und alles andere. Nur die Weiber bleiben dieselben. Danken wir Gott für die Huren und ihre freie Lebensart, sie sind die wirklichen Menschen.
    Sexualität, haben wir herausgefunden, ist eine spielerische Lebensform und dem Expressionismus sehr verwandt.

10. Ball, *Die Flucht*, pp. 5-12.

11. See Huelsenbeck's letter in *Briefe der Expressionisten*, ed. Edschmid, pp. 69-70; Huelsenbeck, "Dada oder der Sinn im Chaos" pp. 13, 16; Ball, *Briefe*, pp. 37-42; Ball, *Die Flucht*, pp. 21, 23.

12. Ball, *Briefe*, pp. 37-38; Ball, *Die Flucht*, p. 21. See a reference to the evening in *Die Aktion* 5 (1915), 96; Georg Muche, *Blickpunkt* (Munich, 1961), p. 205; Huelsenbeck, "Dada oder der Sinn im Chaos," p. 16.

13. Ball, *Briefe*, p. 37; Muche, *Blickpunkt*, p. 205. Ball's tribute to Leybold was published two months later in *Die weissen Blätter*. See Ball's "Totenrede" cited in note 4, above.

14. Huelsenbeck, "Dada oder der Sinn im Chaos," p. 16; Ball, *Briefe*, p. 37.

15. Ball, *Die Flucht*, p. 21.

16. Ibid., p. 23; Ball, *Briefe*, pp. 38-42; Huelsenbeck's letter in *Briefe der Expressionisten*, ed. Edschmid, pp. 69-70; Huelsenbeck, "Dada oder der Sinn im Chaos," p. 13.

17. Huelsenbeck, "Dada," p. 13; Ball, *Briefe*, pp. 38-42.

18. See Huelsenbeck's letter in *Briefe der Expressionisten*, ed. Edschmid, pp. 69-70.

19. *Briefe der Expressionisten*, ed. Edschmid, p. 70; Ball, *Die Flucht*, p. 23.

20. Ball, *Die Flucht*, pp. 13-23; Ball, *Briefe*, pp. 35-42.

21. Ball, *Briefe*, p. 45.

22. Ball, *Die Flucht*, p. 23.

23. Huelsenbeck, *Mit Witz*, pp. 11-12.

Chapter 13

1. Hermann Kasack, "Deutsche Literatur im Zeichen des Expressionismus," *Merkur* 15 (April, 1961), no. 4, p. 361.

2. Kasack, "Deutsche Literatur," pp. 353-63; "Bio-Bibliographischer Anhang," in *Die Aktion: 1917-18*, ed. Raabe (Munich, 1967); *Expressionismus: Literatur und Kunst*, ed. Bernhard Zeller, et al., pp. 272-73; index to contributors in Raabe, *Die Zeitschriften*, p. 229.

3. Kasack, "Deutsche Literatur," p. 359; Hermann Kasack, "Wolf Przygode und *Die Dichtung* (1918-1923)," in *Expressionismus: Aufzeichnungen*, ed. Raabe, p. 215; Herman Kasack, "Gedenkrede auf Wolf Przygode" (1926), in Hermann Kasack, *Mosaiksteine: Beiträge zu Literatur und Kunst* (Frankfurt a.M., 1956), pp. 207, 210.

4. Kasack, "Wolf Przygode," p. 215.

5. Kasack "Deutsche Literatur," p. 359. The exact time of the first meeting between Kasack and Przygode and the writers Emmel and Seeler is not recorded; nor is it known when they joined the Przygode circle. Kasack does record that he first met the painter Gramatté in 1917. See Hermann Kasack, "Walter Gramatté," in Kasack, *Mosaiksteine*, pp. 256-59.

6. See Kasack, "Wolf Przygode," pp. 215-24; Kasack, "Gedenkrede," pp. 207-30; Hermann Kasack, "Gruss an Georg Kaiser," in Kasack, *Mosaiksteine*, pp. 236-37; Hermann Kasack, "Erinnerung an Gustav Kiepenheuer," *Mosaiksteine*, pp. 289-96; Oskar Loerke, *Tagebücher: 1903-1939*, ed. Hermann Kasack, Veröffentlichungen der Deutschen Akademie für Sprache und Dichtung, 5 (Heidelberg und Darmstadt, 1956), pp. 77ff; Martin Gumpert, *Hölle im Paradies: Selbstdarstellung eines Arztes* (Stockholm, 1939), pp. 125-26. The exact times that the poets mentioned joined the Przygode circle are not known. Kasack, however, reports that he first met Loerke in 1917. See Loerke, *Tagebücher*, p. 12. See also, on the poets mentioned and their connections with Expressionism, the index to contributors in Raabe, *Die Zeitschriften*, pp. 215ff; *Expressionismus: Literatur und Kunst*, ed. Bernhard Zeller, et al., esp. pp. 96-100, 273-75; "Bio-Bibliographischer Anhang," in *Die Aktion: 1917/18*, ed. Raabe (Munich, 1967), pp. 27, 38-39, 40-41.

7. Kasack, "Wolf Przygode," pp. 215-18; Kasack, "Gedenkrede," p. 207; Kasack, "Deutsche Literatur," pp. 259-60.

8. Kasack, "Wolf Przygode," p. 215.

Unter seiner Initiative [= Przygode's] begannen wir nach gründlicher Vorbereitung im Mai 1916 Vorlesungsabende in privatem Kreise zu veranstalten, um unsere Auffassung von dem, was wir unter dem Sinn der Dichtung zu verstehen meinten, anderen deutlich zu machen und kontrollieren zu lassen.

9.   Ibid., pp. 217-18.

10. Kasack, "Wolf Przygode," p. 217.

Es handelt sich für uns bei diesen Abenden um gar nichts anderes als um dieses Wichtigste: Menschen zu sammeln, die wie wir glauben, dass Kunst nicht Mittel der Unterhaltung, nicht Annehmlichkeit entspannter Nerven ist, sondern dass Kunst der letzte menschliche Ausdruck ist für das, was Sie als einzig wichtigen Inhalt anzuerkennen nicht zögern werden: das 'Ewige,' das 'Kosmische,' das 'Göttliche'—wenn Sie es benennen wollen.

11. See Kasack's explanation of Przygode's attitude towards the role played by art in society in Kasack, "Gedenkrede," passim.

12. Kasack, "Wolf Przygode," pp. 217-18.

Wir glauben, dass die namenlose Blüte der Grossen Dichtung nicht aufbrechen kann aus unfruchtbarem Gestein, das der Zufall aneinandergefügt hat. Wir wollen, an unserem Teile, dem Kommenden den Weg bereiten helfen, wie wir es als unsere Pflicht erkannt haben, der uns zu entziehen wir kein Recht haben. Sie haben verstanden, dass es für uns füglich keine 'Moderne' und keine 'Richtung' geben kann. Innerste Aktualität ist einziger Massstab....

13. Ibid., pp. 216-18.

14. Ibid., pp. 215-18; Kasack, "Gedenkrede," p. 207; Kasack, "Deutsche Literatur," p. 359.

15. Kasack, "Gedenkrede," p. 207; Kasack, "Kiepenheuer," p. 290; Kasack, "Deutsche Literatur," p. 359. We can assume, with some degree of likelihood, that Przygode was in Munich c. 1918f., not only because Kasack says that the recitals were continued there, but also because that was the city in which *Die Dichtung* appeared 1918/19. See Raabe, *Die Zeitschriften*, p. 76; note 20, below.

16. Kasack, "Wolf Przygode," pp. 215, 1217; Kasack, "Deutsche Literatur," p. 359.

17. Kasack, "Wolf Przygode," p. 218.

18. Ibid., pp. 215, 218; Raabe, *Die Zeitschriften*, p. 76.

19. Kasack, "Wolf Przygode," p. 220; Kasack, "Gedenkrede," p. 220; Kasack, "Kiepenheuer," p. 293.

20. Kasack, "Kiepenheuer," pp. 289-96.

21. *Expressionismus: Literatur und Kunst,* ed. Bernhard Zeller, et al., pp. 272-75.

22. See P. [Wolf Przygode], "Die Dichtung," *Die Dichtung,* first series, 1 (1918): 4-6; Kasack, "Gedenkrede," pp. 214-17.

23. Kasack, "Wolf Przygode," p. 218; Raabe, *Die Zeitschriften*, p. 76.

24. Kasack, "Wolf Przygode," p. 218.

Wir rechnen bei unserer Arbeit, die—ich betone es wiederholend—eine Vorarbeit ist, nur, aber nach Möglichkeiten, auf alle die, mit denen wir Erkenntnis des Zieles und Weges gemein haben. Helfen wir uns aus fruchtlosem Fremdsein hinauf zu einer geistigen Gemeinschaft.

25. Kasack, "Wolf Przygode," p. 218; Kasack, "Gedenkrede," p. 214.

26. Przygode, "Die Dichtung," p. 6.

27. Ibid., p. 4.

Es ist Zeit, besinnen wir uns: Berechtigung, unverbindlich Kunst zu schaffen und zu geniessen, wich strenger Verpflichtung zu Wahl und Bekenntnis, seitdem sie ihrer Stellung neu sich bewusst ward. Im eigenen zeugenden Kern sucht der Mensch die unverbrüchlichen Bindungen jenes Dritten Reichs, in dem die Dinge ihren eigenen Gesetzen allein gehorchen, aus privatem Anteil will er das geschaute durch ordnende Gestaltung in überzeugend-allgemeine Gültigkeit erheben. So gestaltet er frei sich selbst, schwingt über gelebtes Leben ins unzufällig aus innerster Notwendigkeit geformte hinüber. Aller Gebundenheit an subalterne Tatsächlichkeit entfesselt, verwirklicht Geist sich hier vom Körper weniger gehemmt als irgend sonst.

28. Ibid., p. 6.

Hier, wo das persönliche notwendig abfällt, kann sachlich-begründete Verbundenheit zu tiefst-empfundener Gemeinschaft, im Geiste rein, sich wandeln: ihr Boden zu bereiten, ist letzter Sinn der *Dichtung.*

29. See Kurt Hiller, "Philosophie des Ziels," in *Das Ziel: Aufrufe zu tätigem Geist,* ed. Kurt Hiller (Munich and Berlin, 1916), pp. 187-217.

30. This assumption is substantiated by the authors who are cited from this period, i.e., from the pre-Expressionist era, in the appendixes to the issues of *Die Dichtung* headed "Das Werk" and "Das Buch." See *Die Dichtung,* first series, 1 (1917/18): 98-103; first series, 2 (1918): 68-71; first series, 3 (1918): 90-91; first series, 4 (1919): 62-68; second series, 1 (1920): 164-68; second series (1923): 161-63. Expressionists also dominate these appendixes. The pre-Expressionist authors listed here included some of the Naturalists as well: Hermann Bahr, Richard Beer-Hofmann, Rudolf Borchardt, Hermann Conradi, Max Dauthedley, Paul Ernst, Stefan George, Leo Greiner, Victor Hadwiger, Otto Erich Hartleben, Gerhart Hauptmann, Peter Hille, Hugo von Hofmannsthal, Richarda Huch, Eduard von Keyserling, Detlev von Liliencron, Heinrich Mann, Hermann Stehr, Emil Strauss.

31. Przygode, "Die Dichtung," p. 4.

Was 'Dichtkunst' sei, kann niemand hier erklärt wollen: Terminologie ist geblasst, und geneigter Wille zu verstehen selten. Immerhin sei gesagt, in einiger Hoffnung, gleiches denkenden sich zu verständigen: was an wahrhaft lebenswertem jene beiden (zu Unrecht gleich-gestellten) 'Bewegungen' im letzten, grundlegenden Jahrzehnt des abgelaufenen Jahrhunderts uns hinterliessen, schloss in echter Synthese zu neuer Kunst sich zusammen. Sehnen nach traumhafter Unwirklichkeit—Zuflucht aus schaler Welt—half das Gesetz der schönen Form in neuer, notwendiger Beziehung auf den bedeutenden Gegenstand verhärten, Sucht nach handfester Wirklichkeit—der gelebten neben-geordnet—bannte im Verein mit wieder-erwachendem Verantwortungs-Bewusstsein, eine höchst flackernde künstlerische Wahrheit in die Grenzen gültiger Gestaltung.

32. Ibid., p. 6.

Den Zusammenhang der Epochen—Grund und Aufbau—wie das unmittelbare Gefühl sie als heutig empfindet, im typischen zu erfassen, das schon-bestehende mit dem eben-gewordenen zu verknüpfen, innere Bezüge fest-zu-stellen..., ist, vornehmlich im Anfang, wesenlichste Aufgabe der *Dichtung.*

33. *Buch der Toten,* ed. Wolf Przygode (Munich, 1919). The afterword is cited in Raabe, *Die Zeitschriften,* pp. 156-57.

34. Przygode, "Die Dichtung," p. 5.

...bejahen wir als *heutige Dichtkunst den gültig geformten Ausdruck des geschauten wesentlichen Gehalts,* sei verzichtet auf fragwürdige Definition—im Glauben, hiermit immerhin der Dichtung die Grenzen zu stecken gegen jene unechten Bezirke, in denen karges Erlebnis mit Hilfe einwand-freier und gepflegter Syntax klug (und unendlich privat) vegetiert oder, umgekehrt, sein Unvermögen etwa mit Perversion der kritisch-analytischen in dichterische Sprache unverfroren deckt; wo Hypnose und Suggestion leicht verwechselt sind, und panischer Schönheit oder liebenswertesten Ethos' Explosionen in Glut zu wandeln Zucht und Wille fehlen.

35. See Paul Zech, "Die Grundbedingung der modernen Lyrik," *Das neue Pathos* 2 (1914): 2-3, excerpted in *Literatur-Revolution,* ed. Pörtner, vol. 1, pp. 245-47. See also Stefan Zweig, "Das neue Pathos," *Das neue Pathos* 1 (1913): 1-6, reprinted in *Expressionismus: Der Kampf,* ed. Raabe, pp. 15-22.

36. Przygode, "Die Dichtung," p. 5.

So entschieden uns also Kunst letzte Ausdrucks-Möglichkeit der schöpferischen Spiritualität ist, so deutlich weisen wir jenen Missbrauch der Kunst zurück, der sich ihrer bedient, durch Beziehung auf eine höchst fragwürdige Realität Tendenzen zu propagieren; vorzüglich in dem, was als 'Politische Kunst,' als 'Staats-Gedicht' auftritt, erblicken wir nichts als Apostasie—ermöglicht durch gefährlichste Verwirrung der Begriffe: Kunst, Politik...und gar 'Leben' kann keine Gleichung einen. Für den verwandten Fall der 'mystischen Kunst' und ihr zu Grunde liegende Verschiebung des echten Verhältnisses von Kunst und Religion kann hiernach blosser Hinweis genügen. Und wie dem nur entgegen-gesetzt sei, dass alle Kunst, ohne davon auszusagen, Symbol des Ewigen ist und letzte Prophetie, muss in einem weniger wirklichkeits-gebundenen Sinn freilich aller wahren Kunst Wille zur Wirkung politisch genannt werden, wie er in der doppeten Bedeutung künstlerischen 'gestaltens' beschlossen ist: Herkunft und Ziel des Menschen weist die Kunst, durch die Spannung zwischen gelebter Wirklichkeit und geschauter Wahrheit ruft zur Tat sie auf.

37. Wolf Przygode, "Nachbemerkung zur Ersten Folge," *Die Dichtung,* first series, 4 (1919): 69-72.

38. Ibid., p. 69.

39. See note 30, above. See also Kasack, "Gedenkrede," p. 217; Kasack, "Wolf Przygode," pp. 222-23.

40. See Raabe, *Die Zeitschriften,* p. 76. On the ties of these poets with Expressionism see, e.g., the index to contributors, Raabe, *Die Zeitschriften,* pp. 215ff; and the sections on the other Expressionist circles in which most of these poets were involved, above.

41. See *Die Dichtung,* first series, 4 (1919): 4-11.

42. Walter Sokel, *The Writer in Extremis: Expressionism in Twentieth-Century German Literature* (Stanford, 1959), p. 201.

43. See *Die Dichtung,* first series, 4 (1919): 55, 58-59, 100, 101, 107, 110, 114-15, respectively.

44. Przygode, "Die Dichtung," p. 5.

45. Raabe, *Die Zeitschriften,* pp. 156-57.

46. See Kasack, "Wolf Przygode," pp. 221-22; Kasack, "Gedenkrede," p. 219; Raabe, *Die Zeitschriften,* p. 76. See also Albert Rapp, "Die Bildende Kunst," *Die Dichtung,* first series, 1 (1918): 7-12.

47. Kasack, "Wolf Przygode," p. 222; *Expressionismus: Literatur und Kunst,* ed. Bernhard Zeller, et al., pp. 272-75.

48. Kasack, "Wolf Przygode," p. 224; Kasack, "Gedenkrede," pp. 207-30; Kasack, "Gruss an Georg Kaiser," pp. 236-42; Kasack, "Kiepenheuer," pp. 289-96; Loerke, *Tagebücher,* pp. 77ff; Gumpert, *Hölle,* pp. 125-26; *Expressionismus: Literatur und Kunst,* ed. Bernhard Zeller, et al., pp. 90, 199, 269, 279, 305.

49. Kasack, "Wolf Przygode," p. 224.

50. Kasack, "Gedenkrede," pp. 221ff.

51. Ibid.

52. Ibid., pp. 223ff.

53. Ibid., pp. 208, 226.

54. Ibid., p. 229; Kasack, "Wolf Przygode," p. 224.

Chapter 14

1. Wieland Herzfelde, "Fremd und Nah: Über meinen Briefwechsel und meine Begegnungen mit Else Lasker-Schüler," in *Nachrichten aus dem Kösel-Verlag: Sonderheft für Else Lasker-Schüler Dezember 1965,* ed. Dr. Heinrich Wild and Friedrich Pfäfflin (Munich, 1965), p. 45.

2. Herzfelde, "Fremd," pp. 42-46; Wieland Herzfelde, *Unterwegs, Blätter aus fünfzig Jahren* (Berlin, 1961), pp. 271-80; Else Lasker-Schüler, "Briefe," *Die Aktion* (January 24, 1914), no. 4, p. 86; Lasker-Schüler, *Lieber gestreifter Tiger,* pp. 92-93; Wieland Herzfelde über den Malik-Verlag," in *Der Malik-Verlag: 1916-1947: Ausstellungskatalog,* ed. Wieland Herzfelde (Berlin and Weimar, n.d.), pp. 5, 9.

3. Herzfelde, "Fremd," p. 43.

4. Herzfelde, "...über den Malik-Verlag," pp. 6, 9.

5. Herzfelde, *Unterwegs,* pp. 90ff., 286ff.

6. Ibid., pp. 90-93, 289-99. In an earlier memoir on this period, Herzfelde claimed that his enlistment in the army was "in no way due to enthusiasm for the war." See Wieland Herzfelde, "Wie ein Verlag enstand," originally pub. in *Das Wort* (1936), repr. in *Expressionismus: Aufzeichnungen,* ed. Raabe, p. 226. This version is, however, probably colored by its being written in the shadow of the Nazi era.

7. Herzfelde, *Unterwegs,* pp. 93-113.

8. Ibid., pp. 108-13.

9. Ibid., p. 113.

10. Ibid.

Bereits am nächsten Tage sass ich in dem Zug, der mich nach Berlin zurückbrächte. Ich war hochgestimmt. Aber ernster als während der Fahrt zur Front. Denn ich wusste, mir war Gnade widerfahren: jetzt fuhr ich wirklich in den Krieg. Nicht mehr als Sanitäter, sondern als Soldat. Und in einen guten Krieg, der für mich in der Weihnachtsnacht begonnen hatte.

11. Herzfelde, "...über den Malik-Verlag," p. 6; Wieland Herzfelde, "Aus der Jugendzeit des Malik-Verlags: Zum Neudruck der Zeitschrift *Neue Jugend,*" in *Neue Jugend: 1916/17* (reprint: Zürich, 1967), pp. 5-6; Wieland Herzfelde, "Wandelbar und stetig: Zum Werk Johannes R. Bechers," in *Sinn und Form: Zweites Sonderheft Johannes R. Becher* (Berlin, 1960), p. 50.

12. Herzfelde, *Unterwegs,* pp. 114-32.

13. Herzfelde, "...über den Malik-Verlag," p. 6.

14. Ibid.

15. Ibid.; Herzfelde, "Aus der Jugendzeit," p. 6.

16. Herzfelde, "Aus der Jugendzeit," p. 6; Herzfelde, "... über den Malik-Verlag," p. 6.

17. Herzfelde, "... über den Malik-Verlag," p. 6.

18. Herzfelde, *Unterwegs,* pp. 114ff.

19. Ibid., pp. 125ff.

20. Ibid., pp. 128-32; Herzfelde, "... über den Malik-Verlag," p. 7.

21. Herzfelde, *Unterwegs,* p. 131.

22. Herzfelde, "... über den Malik-Verlag," p. 9; Herzfelde, "Aus der Jugendzeit," p. 7.

23. Herzfelde, "Aus der Jugendzeit," p. 8; Herzfelde, "... über den Malik-Verlag," p. 9. On *Neue Jugend* (1914) see the section on this journal, above.

24. Herzfelde, "... über den Malik-Verlag," pp. 9-10; Herzfelde, "Aus der Jugendzeit," pp. 7-8; "Mitarbeiter und Beiträge," in *Die Aktion,* ed. Raabe (Stuttgart, 1961), p. 38.

25. Herzfelde, "Aus der Jugendzeit," p. 9; Herzfelde, "... über den Malik-Verlag," p. 10.

26. Ibid.; Herzfelde, "Aus der Jugendzeit," p. 9.

27. Herzfelde, "... über den Malik-Verlag," pp. 10-11; Herzfelde, *Unterwegs,* p. 131.

28. Herzfelde, "... über den Malik-Verlag," pp. 5-23; Herzfelde, "Aus der Jugendzeit," pp. 5-16; Herzfelde, "Wie ein Verlag," pp. 226-29; Lasker-Schüler, *Briefe an Karl Kraus,* pp. 78-84; Jung, *Der Weg,* pp. 105ff., 110ff; Meyer, *die maer,* p. 48; Hans Richter, *Dada-Profile* (Zürich, 1961), passim; Grosz, *A Little Yes,* pp. 146-49.

29. See note 28, above; also Richard Huelsenbeck, *Mit Witz Licht und Grütze* (Wiesbaden, 1957), pp. 81ff; Richard Huelsenbeck, "Die dadaistische Bewegung," *Die neue Rundschau* 31 (1920): 972-79.

30. See notes 28 and 29, above.

31. Raabe, *Die Zeitschriften,* pp. 62-63. Raabe here does not list Helmut Herzfeld's role in the editing of the journal and does not indicate the change in Herzfelde's position with the last issue. See, however, *Neue Jugend* 1 (1916/17): 166, 186, 210, 211, 248.

32. Johannes R. Becher, "An den Frieden," *Neue Jugend* 1 (1916): 123; "Nachwort," *Neue Jugend* 1 (1916): 146; Herzfelde, "... über den Malik-Verlag," pp. 12-15.

33. "Nachwort," p. 146.

  Nach eineinhalbjähriger Unterbrechung veröffentlichen wir das siebte Heft der *Neuen Jugend* mit der Erklärung, dass der Inhalt der früher erschienen Nummern unsern jetzigen Absichten nicht entspricht. Wir übernehmen lediglich den Titel der Neuen Jugend und die darin enthaltene Tendenz: die Arbeit junger Dichter, Intellektueller, Zeichner und Musiker zu veröffentlichen. Wir wollen eintreten für alle, die in der Öffentlichkeit auf Opposition und Verständnislosigkeit stossen, vor allem aber für die *Jüngsten,* die noch keinen Platz in der heutigen Literatur gefunden haben.

34. Ibid.

  Alle freiheitlich Gesinnten (Expressionisten, die Anhänger der Jugendbewegung...) sollen in der *Neuen Jugend* zu Worte kommen.

35. Ibid. On the first three journals mentioned, which emanated from Expressionist circles, see Raabe, *Die Zeitschriften,* pp. 46-47, 50, 52-54. *Der Aufbruch* (1915/16) and *Der Anfang* (1913/14) were publications of the "Jugendbewegungen" led by Gustav Wyneken. See, e.g., Harry Pross, *Jugend, Eros, Politik: Die Geschichte der Jugendverbände* (Bern, Munich, and Vienna, 1964), pp. 135ff., 513. *Der Anfang* was published in the Verlag der

Wochenschrift *Die Aktion.* See "Veranstaltungen und Veröffentlichungen des Verlags der Wochenschrift *Die Aktion,*" in *Die Aktion,* ed. Raabe (Stuttgart, 1961), p. 124.

Da wir auf kulturhistorische, philosophische und politische Beiträge denselben Wert legen wie auf künstlerische, bedeutet die *Neue Jugend* die Fortführung der Ideen, die einerseits der *Neuen Kunst* und der zweiten Zeitschrift des ehemaligen Verlags Bachmair, andrerseits dem *Forum,* dem *Aufbruch* und dem *Anfang* zugrunde lagen.

36. "Nachwort," p. 146. The phrase "...dem äussersten Feinde..." reads in the 1967 reprint of *Neue Jugend:* "...dem äusseren Feinde..." However, Herzfelde, "...über den Malik-Verlag," p. 12, indicates that the reading in the original printing of the journal was as cited in the present study. Since the reading "...dem äussersten Feinde..." is that which appears in the reprint of the "Nachwort" in the latter essay (see Herzfelde, "...über den Malik-Verlag," p. 15) and in Raabe, *Die Zeitschriften,* p. 63, both of which are presumably based on the original, the same reading has been cited in the present study. The reading "...dem äusseren Feinde..." was first used in the original announcement of the forthcoming appearance of the journal put out by the publishing company. See reprint of this announcement in *Expressionismus: Literatur und Kunst,* ed. Bernhard Zeller, et al., pp. 115-16. However, as Herzfelde reports (Herzfelde, "...über den Malik-Verlag," p. 12), when Becher read this announcement he was "incensed" at the possible misinterpretation of the phrase as referring to the French, English, etc., which nations were, in fact, being designated in contemporary war propaganda as "äussere Feinde." Thus, the editors of *Neue Jugend* decided to alter the reading for the "Nachwort." The new reading was, nonetheless, apparently also misinterpreted, for an editorial note in the eighth, August issue of *Neue Jugend* explained: "Hinweis für Ausländer: Im Nachwort des Juliheftes scheint folgender Satz verschiedentlich missverstanden worden zu sein: 'Es ist an der Zeit, dass alle Geistigen vereint ihrem äussersten Feinde entgegentreten' (bezw. im Prospekt 'dem äusseren Feind'). Um weiteren Missverständnissen vorzubeugen, sei erklärt, dass unter äusserstem (äusserem) Feind der Geistigen eine Menschenkategorie, nicht aber irgendwelche Völker und Nationen gemeint sind." See *Neue Jugend* 1 (1916): 167.

Unsern früheren Standpunkt, ein *rein literarisches* Blatt der Jüngsten zu sein, verwerfen wir: *es ist an der Zeit, dass alle Geistigen vereint dem äussersten Feinde entgegentreten!*

37. Becher, "An den Frieden," p. 123.

Ihr—: lasst uns gern vom ewigen Frieden reden!
Ja, wissend sehr, dass er Gestalt gewinnt
Noch süssester Traum nur. Unsere Hände jaten
Das Unkraut aus, das jenen Weg bespinnt.
Ertön o Wort, das gleich zur Tat gerinnt!
Das Wort muss wirken! Also lasst uns reden!

38. *Neue Jugend* 1 (1916): 147.

39. *Neue Jugend* 1 (1916/17): 161, 181, 216-18.

40. *Neue Jugend* 1 (1917): 237-38, 240.

41. *Neue Jugend* 1 (1916): 128.

Der Menschwerdung des Menschen/ Wann blüht es blau/ Über Blutwolken hin?

42. *Neue Jugend* 1 (1916): 175.

43. *Neue Jugend* 1 (1917): 243.

44. *Neue Jugend* 1 (1916): 124-26.

45. Theodor Däubler, "Chagall," *Neue Jugend* 1 (1916): 137-39; Theodor Däubler, "Georges Seurat," *Neue Jugend* 1 (1916): 199; Theodor Däubler, "Van Gogh," *Neue Jugend* 1 (1916): 200.

46. *Neue Jugend* 1 (1916): 135-36. See Herzfelde's interpretation of the work of Däubler in the very same manner in "Mitteilungen: Theodor Däubler, *Hesperien*, Georg Müller Verlag 1915," Neue Jugend 1 (1916): 185.

47. Mynona, "Der Stereograph oder die kinetische Automodellierung," *Neue Jugend* 1 (1916): 148-49; Mynona, "Ich verlange ein Reiterstandbild," *Neue Jugend* 1 (1916): 170-71; Dr. S. Friedlaender, "Eigne Göttlichkeit," *Neue Jugend* 1 (1917): 212-13.

48. *Neue Jugend* 1 (1916): 186; Herzfelde, "...über den Malik-Verlag," p. 16.

49. Herzfelde, "...über den Malik-Verlag," p. 16.

50. *Neue Jugend* 1 (1916): 142-44, 165-66, 186, 209-10; Herzfelde, "...über den Malik-Verlag," p. 16; Herzfelde, "Wie ein Verlag," p. 228.

51. Herzfelde, "...über den Malik-Verlag," p. 21.

52. See Raabe, *Die Zeitschriften*, p. 63; "Inhaltsverzeichnis," *Neue Jugend* 1 (1917): 247-48. On the ties of the authors mentioned with Expressionism see the circles above in which they were involved; also the index to contributors in Raabe, *Die Zeitschriften*, pp. 215ff.

53. See note 52, above.

54. Werner Richard Heymann, "Die Mädchen singen," *Neue Jugend* 1 (1916): 140-41.

55. Herzfelde, "...über den Malik-Verlag," pp. 16ff; Herzfelde, *Unterwegs*, pp. 133ff; Herzfelde, "Aus der Jugendzeit," p. 12.

56. Herzfelde, "...über den Malik-Verlag," p. 54; Herzfelde, "Aus der Jugendzeit," p. 13.

57. Theodor Däubler, "Ode an Florenz," *Neue Jugend* 1 (1916): 187-94; the drawings by Chagall and Seurat appear here on pp. 195, 198. See also note 45, above.

58. See *Neue Jugend* 1 (1916): 209-10; Herzfelde, "...über den Malik-Verlag," p. 17.

59. Herzfelde, "...über den Malik-Verlag," pp. 17-18; *Der Almanach der Neuen Jugend auf das Jahr 1917*, ed. Heinz Barger (Berlin, [1916]); Raabe, *Die Zeitschriften*, pp. 202-3.

60. Herzfelde, "...über den Malik-Verlag," pp. 17-18.

61. Ibid., pp. 18-19.

62. Ibid., p. 19.

63. Ibid., pp. 17, 19, 21; Herzfelde, "Aus der Jugendzeit," p. 13. Herzfelde's report on the founding of Der Malik-Verlag in "Wie ein Verlag," p. 229, contains some confusion of the facts which is no doubt due to the fact that this report was written during Herzfelde's exile from Germany when he, of course, would have had very limited access to original sources to refresh his memory.

64. See preceding note. Installments of Lasker-Schüler's *Der Malik* appeared in the July, August, September, and February/March issues. See *Neue Jugend* 1 (1916/17): 130-31, 157-59, 176-79, 219-25.

65. See note 63, above; also Raabe, *Die Zeitschriften*, p. 62.

66. Herzfelde, "...über den Malik-Verlag," p. 20; Herzfelde, "Aus der Jugendzeit," p. 14.

67. See inside front cover [p. ii] of *Neue Jugend* 1 (February/March, 1917), no. 11/12.

68. See preceding note.

   Das, was der Kreis der Neuen Jugend erstrebt, und wozu er Ausdrucksmittel zu sein wünscht, wird nach wie vor in den Monatsheften der Neuen Jugend enthalten sein. Wozu er aber in dem Gegensatz zu herrschenden Ansichten und Einstellungen Ellbogen gebrauchen muss, wo es darum handelt, sich zu wehren und einen Feind niederzuschlagen, soll er auch möglicherweise in unseren Reihen sein, wird die zweite Ausgabe, schärfer, auf den Tag gestellter eingreifen können.

69. This corrects Raabe, *Die Zeitschriften,* p. 63. See also Herzfelde, "...über den Malik-Verlag," p. 20.

70. See *Neue Jugend* (May 23, 1917), no. 1, p. 4.

71. See *Neue Jugend* (June, 1917), no. 2, p. 4.

72. [Franz Jung], "Chronik," *Neue Jugend* (May 23, 1917), no. 1, p. 1; [Franz Jung], "Chronik," *Neue Jugend* (June, 1917), [no. 2], p. 1. On the identification of Jung as the author of these columns see Herzfelde, "...über den Malik-Verlag," p. 21; Wieland Herzfelde, "Mein Bruder John Heartfield," in *Dada: Eine literarische Dokumentation,* ed. Richard Huelsenbeck (Reinbek bei Hamburg, 1964), p. 243.

73. [Jung], "Chronik," *Neue Jugend* (May 23, 1917), no. 1, p. 1.

   Nicht so sehr, dass auch hier im Land es immer wieder vom Krieg heisst: (immer wieder) durchhalten. Dieser Privatsache wegen?—als Schrecken, Geissel, Weltenverwirrung aufgemacht, niemand sollte darauf achten! Durchhalten gleich Dasein: Noch nicht sich aufhängen gleich Krieg—mehr Krieg...Das Sich-Wehren steigt endlich im Kurs, Roheitsdelikte, Sentimentalität fällt. Entblättert zu Angst, Leben-Wollen, oh—die anderen etc. Nicht aber wollen—hier! sondern leben! Leben!!

74. *Neue Jugend* (May 23, 1917), no. 1, pp. 2-3.

75. *Neue Jugend* (May 23, 1917), no. 1, p. 2.

   Wir haben ganz tief in uns hinein zu sehen, um begreifen zu können, was sich aus Menschlichem machen lässt und wo die Synthese aller Fähigkeiten und Dinge des Menschen zu suchen ist....
   Der neue Mensch muss die Flügel seiner Seele weit ausspannen, seine inneren Ohren müssen gerichtet sein auf die kommenden Dinge, seine Knie müssen sich einen Altar finden, vor dem sie sich beugen können....
   ...Seine Wurzel zieht Kräfte aus mykenischem Zeitalter...er lebt einen Tag wie Lukian, wie Aretin und wie Christus—er ist alles und nichts, nicht heute, nicht gestern...
   ...
   Der neue Mensch glaubt, nur einen Kampf zu kennen, den Kampf gegen die Trägheit, den Combat gegen die Dicken.

76. Herzfelde, "Mein Bruder," p. 243.

77. See [George Grosz], "Man muss Kautschukmann sein!" and "Kannst du radfahren?" *Neue Jugend* (June, 1917), [no. 2], p. 1. On the identification of Grosz as author of these articles see Herzfelde, "...über den Malik-Verlag," p. 21; Herzfelde, "Mein Bruder," p. 243.

78. [Grosz], "Man muss Kautschukmann sein!" p. 1.

   Wie gesagt, Kautschukmann sein
   beweglich in allen Knochen

nicht blos im Dichter-Sessel dösen
oder vor der Staffelei schön gepinselte Bildchen pinseln.

. . .

Den Bequemen gilts zu stören
beim Verdauungsschläfchen
ihm den pazifistischen Popo zu kitzeln,
rumort! explodiert! zerplatzt!—oder hängt euch ans Fensterkreuz...

79. See *Neue Jugend* (June, 1917), [no. 2], 4; Herzfelde, "... über den Malik-Verlag," pp. 20, 74; Herzfelde, "Mein Bruder," p. 243.

80. Herzfelde, "... über den Malik-Verlag," pp. 22; Herzfelde, "Mein Bruder," pp. 243-44; Herzfelde, "Wie ein Verlag," p. 230.

81. See listings of the evenings in *Neue Jugend* 1 (1916/17): 186, 210, 245-46; also Herzfelde, "... über den Malik-Verlag," p. 16; Herzfelde, "Wie ein Verlag," pp. 230-31; Herzfelde, "Aus der Jugendzeit," pp. 10-12.

82. See preceding note.

83. Herzfelde, "... über den Malik-Verlag," p. 16; Herzfelde, "Wie ein Verlag," pp. 230-31.

84. See preceding note.

85. See note 81, above.

86. See note 81, above.

87. Herzfelde, "... über den Malik-Verlag," p. 23.

88. Ibid.

89. Ibid.

90. See, e.g., Paul Pörtner, "Einführung," in *Literatur-Revolution,* ed. Pörtner, vol. 2, pp. 29-30; Paul Raabe, "Vorwort," in *Expressionismus: Aufzeichnungen,* ed. Raabe, p. 11; Goll, *Ich verzeihe,* pp. 47-48.

91. Jung, *Der Weg,* pp. 210ff; Herzfelde, "... über den Malik-Verlag," pp. 20-21.

92. See note 29, above.

93. Herzfelde, "... über den Malik-Verlag," pp. 20-21.

94. Richard Huelsenbeck, "Der neue Mensch," *Neue Jugend* (May 23, 1917), no. 1, 2-3; Richard Huelsenbeck, "Dinge und Menschen," *Neue Jugend* (June, 1917), [no. 2], 3-4.

95. Huelsenbeck, *Mit Witz,* p. 93; Goll, *Ich verzeihe,* p. 91.

96. Huelsenbeck, *Mit Witz,* p. 93; Grosz, *A Little Yes,* p. 181.

97. Huelsenbeck, *Mit Witz,* p. 93.

98. Ibid., pp. 93-95; Raoul Hausmann, "Club Dada: Berlin 1918-1920," in *Expressionismus: Aufzeichnungen,* ed. Raabe, p. 232; Hans Baumann, "Eine dadaistische Privatangelegenheit," in *Dada Almanach,* ed. Huelsenbeck, p. 29. On the exact dating of this recital see Richard Huelsenbeck, "Erste Dadarede in Deutschland, gehalten von R. Huelsenbeck im Februar 1918 (Saal der Neuen Sezession, I.B. Neumann)," *Dada Almanach,* ed. Huelsenbeck, pp. 104-8; Richard Huelsenbeck, "Dadarede, gehalten in der Galerie Neumann, Berlin, Kurfürstendamm, am 18. Februar 1918," in *Dada: Eine literarische Dokumentation,* ed. Huelsenbeck, p. 30.

99. See preceding note.

100. These are the two talks cited in note 98, above: Huelsenbeck, "Erste Dadarede," and Huelsenbeck, "Dadarede."

101. Huelsenbeck, "Erste Dadarede," p. 108.

   [Der Dadaismus] ist die Überleitung zu der neuen Freude an den realen Dingen. Da sind Kerle, die sich mit dem Leben herumgeschlagen haben, da sind Typen, Menschen mit Schicksalen und der Fähigkeit zu erleben. Menschen mit geschärftem Intellekt, die verstehen, dass sie an eine Wende der Zeit gestellt sind. Es ist nur ein Schritt bis zur Politik.

102. Huelsenbeck, "Dadarede," p. 20.

   Dada wollte mehr sein als Kultur und es wollte weniger sein, es wusste nicht recht, was es sein wollte. Deswegen, wenn Sie mich fragen, was Dada ist, würde ich sagen, es war nichts und wollte nichts. Ich widme deshalb diesen Vortrag der respektierten Dichter dem Nichts. Bitte bleiben Sie ruhig, man wird Ihnen keine körperlichen Schmerzen bereiten. Das einzige, was Ihnen passieren könnte, ist dies: dass Sie Ihr Geld umsonst ausgegeben haben. In diesem Sinne, meine Damen und Herren. Es lebe die dadaistische Revolution.

103. Huelsenbeck, *Mit Witz,* pp. 93-95.

104. Ibid.

105. Ibid., pp. 94-95.

106. Ibid., p. 95.

107. Ibid.; Baumann, "Eine dadaistische," pp. 29-30.

108. Huelsenbeck, *Mit Witz,* pp. 95ff; Raoul Hausmann, "Zwei dadaistische Persönlichkeiten: Huelsenbeck und Baader," in *Dada: Eine literarische Dokumentation,* ed. Huelsenbeck, pp. 217-24.

109. Huelsenbeck, *Mit Witz,* p. 93; Hausmann, "Zwei dadaistische," p. 221.

110. Huelsenbeck, *Mit Witz,* pp. 95ff; Hausmann, "Club Dada," pp. 232-33; Richard Huelsenbeck, "Dada oder der Sinn im Chaos," in *Dada: Eine literarische Dokumentation,* ed. Huelsenbeck, p. 19. Walter Mehring, *Berlin Dada: Eine Chronik mit Photos und Dokumenten* (Zürich, 1959), passim; Grosz, *A Little Yes,* pp. 181-82; Jung, *Der Weg,* pp. 110ff; Hans Richter, *Dada-Profile,* passim; Hans Richter, *Dada: Kunst und Antikunst: Der Beitrag Dadas zur Kunst des 20. Jahrhunderts* (Cologne, 1964), pp. 105-40.

111. See preceding note; also Herzfelde, "Mein Bruder."

112. See notes 110 and 111, above.

113. See footnote above; also Edouard Roditi, "Hannah Höch und die Berliner Dadaisten: Ein Gespräch mit der Malerin," *Der Monat* 12 (November, 1959), no. 134, pp. 60-68.

114. Huelsenbeck, *Mit Witz,* p. 118; Piscator, *Das politische Theater,* pp. 36-39; Herzfelde, "...über den Malik-Verlag," p. 20; Herzfelde, *Unterwegs,* p. 151; Herzfelde, "Aus der Jugendzeit," p. 14.

115. See preceding note. On *Der Gegner* see below.

116. Huelsenbeck, "Die dadaistische Bewegung," p. 976.

   Ich kam im Januar 1917 nach Berlin und fand hier in allem den denkbar grössten Gegensatz zu den Verhältnissen in Zürich. Der Mangel war aufs höchste gestiegen, das deutsche

Kaiserreich wackelte in seinen Fugen, und die tönendsten Siegesnachrichten konnten den Ausdruck der Sorge und der geheimen Angst nicht von den Gesichtern der Menschen bannen.

117. Ibid.; Hausmann, "Club Dada," p. 233; Jung, *Der Weg,* p. 110; Richard Huelsenbeck, "Aus der Geschichte des Dadaismus," *En Avant Dada* (1919), repr. in *Literatur-Revolution,* ed. Pörtner, p. 492.

118. Ball, *Die Flucht,* p. 91.

119. Ibid., p. 85. Trans. Ann Raimes in Hugo Ball, *Flight out of Time,* ed. John Elderfield and trans. Ann Raimes (New York, 1974), p. 61.

Unser Kabaret [= Cabaret Voltaire] ist eine Geste. Jedes Wort, das hier gesprochen und gesungen wird, besagt wenigstens das eine, dass es dieser erniedrigenden Zeit nicht gelungen ist, uns Respekt abzunötigen. Was wäre auch respektabel und imponierend an ihr? Ihre Kanonen? Unsere grosse Trommel übertönt sie. Ihr Idealismus? Er ist längst zum Gelächter geworden, in seiner populären und seiner akademischen Ausgabe. Die grandiosen Schlachtfeste und kannibalischen Heldentaten? Unsere freiwillige Torheit, unsere Begeisterung für die Illusion wird sie zuschanden machen.

(Entry in Ball's journal for April 14, 1916)

120. Richard Huelsenbeck,, "Dadaistisches Manifest (. . . vorgetragen auf der grossen Berliner Dada-Soirée im April 1918)." in *Dada Almanach,* ed. Huelsenbeck, p. 36. Also pub. in *Literatur-Revolution,* ed. Pörtner, p. 486.

Die Kunst ist in ihrer Ausführung und Richtung von der Zeit abhängig, in der sie lebt, und die Künstler sind Kreaturen ihrer Epoche. Die höchste Kunst wird diejenige sein, die in ihren Bewusstseinsinhalten die tausendfachen Probleme der Zeit präsentiert, der man anmerkt, dass sie sich von den Explosionen der letzten Woche werfen liess, die ihre Glieder immer wieder unter dem Stoss des letzten Tages zusammensucht. Die besten und unerhörtesten Künstler werden diejenigen sein, die stündlich die Fetzen ihres Leibes aus dem Wirrsal der Lebenskatarakte zusammenreissen, verbissen in den Intellekt der Zeit, blutend an Händen und Herzen.

121. Huelsenbeck, "Dadaistisches Manifest," in *Dada Almanach,* ed. Huelsenbeck, pp. 36-40.

122. Huelsenbeck, "Dadaistisches Manifest," p. 37. See also "Was wollte der Expressionismus?" *Dada Almanach,* pp. 35-36.

123. See preceding note.

124. Huelsenbeck, "Dadaistisches Manifest," in *Dada Almanach,* ed. Huelsenbeck, p. 38.

Das Wort Dada symbolisiert das primitivste Verhältnis zur umgebenden Wirklichkeit, mit dem Dadaismus tritt eine neue Realität in ihre Rechte. Das Leben erscheint als ein simultanes Gewirr von Geräuschen, Farben und geistigen Rhythmen, das in die dadaistische Kunst unbeirrt mit allen sensationellen Schreien und Fiebern seiner verwegenen Alltagspsyche und in seiner gesamten brutalen Realität übernommen wird.

125. Huelsenbeck, "Dadaistisches Manifest," in *Dada Almanach,* pp. 38-39; Huelsenbeck, *Mit Witz,* pp. 94-107, 122-23; Raoul Hausmann, "Manifest von der Gesetzmässigkeit des Lautes," *Der Blutige Ernst* (1919), repr. in *Literatur-Revolution,* ed. Pörtner, pp. 507-9; Raoul Hausmann, "Pamphlet gegen die Weimarische Lebensauffassung," *Der Einzige* (1919), repr. in *Dada: Eine literarische Dokumentation,* ed. Huelsenbeck, pp. 33-35; Herzfelde, " . . . über den Malik-Verlag," p. 27; Huelsenbeck, "Die dadaistische Bewegung," p. 978. The "bruitistic poem": had its roots in the Futurist "Geräusch Konzert" invented by Marinetti. See Huelsenbeck, "Die dadaistische Bewegung," p. 979. See also note 134, below.

126. Herzfelde, "... über den Malik-Verlag," p. 37. See the manifesto by Raoul Hausmann, "Der deutsche Spiesser ärgert sich," *Der Dada* (1919), repr. in *Literatur- Revolution,* ed. Pörtner, pp. 504-7; Huelsenbeck, *Mit Witz,* p. 114.

127. Herzfelde, "Mein Bruder," p. 245.

128. See esp. Herzfelde's conversations with Harry Graf Kessler, a patron of the Berlin Dadaists, from this period as recorded by Kessler in his *Tagebücher,* pp. 107-8, 114, 119, 120-21, 125, 130, 146, 151, 155, 157, 159, 161, 173, 182-83, 194-97, 198. See also Richard Huelsenbeck, "Erinnerung an George Grosz," in Richard Huelsenbeck, *Phantastische Gebete* (Zürich, 1960), pp. 85-86.

129. Huelsenbeck, *Mit Witz,* p. 89. See also Piscator, *Das politische Theater,* pp. 36-39.

So grotesk das Klingen mag, in Berlin projizierten wir unser Ressentiment in die Politik, aber wir waren niemals wirkliche Politiker. Wir blieben die ewigen Revolutionäre. Wir projizierten auch in die Kunst, da es aber damals in Berlin mehr Politik als Kunst gab, kam die Kunst weniger gut davon. Es ist etwas anderes, ob man ruhig in der Schweiz sitzt oder, wie wir damals in Berlin, seine Ruhestatt auf einem Vulkan sucht.

130. Herzfelde, "... über den Malik-Verlag," p. 27.

"Der dadaistische Mensch ist der radikale Gegner der Ausbeutung"—"Dada kämpft auf Seiten des revolutionären Proletariats."

131. *Der Dada* (1919), repr. in *Literatur-Revolution,* ed. Pörtner, pp. 503-4.

132. Ibid., p. 503.

133. Ibid., pp. 503-4.

134. Hausmann, "Club Dada," pp. 233-34; Richter, *Dada,* p. 132. The full program for this evening is reprinted in *Dada: Eine literarische Dokumentation,* ed. Huelsenbeck, p. 26. The evening's program included a reading by Else Hadwiger of Futurist poetry by Marinetti, Paolo Buzzi, Libero Altomare, et al. Other performers were Huelsenbeck, reading a treatise on Dadaism; Grosz, reading from his own verse; and Hausmann, speaking on "Das neue Material in der Malerei."

135. See preceding note.

136. Hausmann, "Club Dada," p. 233; Huelsenbeck, "Die dadaistische Bewegung," p. 979.

137. See preceding note.

138. Huelsenbeck, "Die dadaistische Bewegung," p. 979.

Wir wollten sie [= the audience] auf ein neues primitives Leben hinweisen wo der Intellekt zerfallen ist und einfachen Triebhandlungen Raum gegeben hat, wo die komplizierte Symbolik der Melodie durch Geräusche ersetzt und das Leben ein lustvolles mächtiges Durcheinander zahlreicher Willen ist. Wir benutzten dazu einmal das Simultangedicht und dann das bruitistische Konzert.

139. Ibid.

140. Ibid. See also Baumann, "Eine dadaistische," p. 34.

141. Mehring, *Berlin Dada,* p. 56; Hausmann, "Club Dada," p. 234; Richter, *Dada,* p. 130.

142. Mehring, *Berlin Dada,* p. 54. For documentation on ties in this period between the Berlin Dadaists and the Café des Westens see esp. Mehring, *Berlin Dada,* pp. 15, 23, 27-28; Huelsenbeck, *Mit Witz,* p. 93; Grosz, *A Little Yes,* p. 149; Hausmann, "Zwei dadaistische," p. 217.

Wenn ihr mir meine Konsommation und Spesen zahlt, werde ich etwas vollbringen, dass die ganze Welt und die ganze Weltpresse von Dada sprechen wird.

143. Mehring, *Berlin Dada*, pp. 54-60; Hausmann, "Club Dada," p. 234; Richter, *Dada*, p. 129; Huelsenbeck, *Mit Witz*, p. 113.

144. Mehring, *Berlin Dada*, p. 60; Richter, *Dada*, p. 129.

145. See *Der Malik-Verlag: 1916-1947*, pp. 75ff; Herzfelde, "...über den Malik-Verlag," pp. 24ff.

146. Jung, *Der Weg*, p. 109; Raabe, *Die Zeitschriften*, p. 60; Hausmann, "Club Dada," p. 232.

147. Hausmann, "Club Dada," p. 232.

148. Ibid.; Jung, *Der Weg*, p. 109.

149. Raabe, *Die Zeitschriften*, p. 60; *Dada: Eine literarische Dokumentation*, ed. Huelsenbeck, p. 280.

150. *Dada: Eine literarische Dokumentation*, ed. Huelsenbeck, p. 280.

151. Raabe, *Die Zeitschriften*, pp. 95-96; Herzfelde, "...über den Malik-Verlag," p. 24; *Dada: Eine literarische Dokumentation*, ed. Huelsenbeck, pp. 75-76; Mehring, *Berlin Dada*, pp. 67-70.

152. See preceding note.

153. See note 151, above.

154. See note 151, above.

155. Mehring, *Berlin Dada*, pp. 67-70; Herzfelde, "...über den Malik-Verlag," p. 24; Herzfelde, "Mein Bruder," p. 246.

156. See note 151, above. See also Kessler, *Tagebücher*, pp. 151, 155, 159.

157. See Raabe, *Die Zeitschriften*, pp. 96-97; Herzfelde, "...über den Malik-Verlag," p. 24; Kessler, *Tagebücher*, pp. 146, 157, 161, 173, 183; Mehring, *Berlin Dada*, pp. 63-67.

158. Mehring, *Berlin Dada*, pp. 63-66.

159. Ibid., p. 66.

Die Pleite.... Verbieten werden sie ja Euch auf jeden Fall. Und dann sollen sie mal bekanntmachen: Verboten—die Pleite!

160. Herzfelde, "...über den Malik-Verlag," p. 24.

161. Ibid., p. 27; Raabe, *Die Zeitschriften*, pp. 97, 99-100.

162. See note 157, above.

163. Raabe, *Die Zeitschriften*, p. 105; Hausmann, "Club Dada," p. 234. Huelsenbeck, *Mit Witz*, p. 101, claims both he and Hausmann established *Der Dada*.

164. Raabe, *Die Zeitschriften*, p. 105.

165. Ibid.; *Der Malik-Verlag: 1916-1947*, p. 76; Herzfelde, "Mein Bruder," p. 245.

166. See preceding note.

167. Raabe, *Die Zeitschriften*, p. 110.

168. Mehring, *Berlin Dada*, p. 64. See also Höxter, *So lebten wir*, passim.

169. See Raabe, *Die Zeitschriften,* p. 110; Mehring, *Berlin Dada,* pp. 63-64.

170. Raabe, *Die Zeitschriften,* p. 110.

171. Ibid.

172. Ibid., pp. 99-100; Herzfelde, "...über den Malik-Verlag," pp. 27-28; *Der Malik-Verlag,* pp. 76-77.

173. See preceding note.

174. Herzfelde, "...über den Malik-Verlag," p. 27.

175. Ibid.

176. See note 172, above.

177. Herzfelde, "...über den Malik-Verlag," p. 28; Piscator, *Das politische Theater,* pp. 39-54.

178. See Mehring, *Berlin Dada,* pp. 66-67; Raabe, *Die Zeitschriften,* p. 158.

179. Raabe, *Die Zeitschriften,* p. 158.

180. Ibid.

181. See Richard Huelsenbeck, "Einleitung," in *Dada Almanach,* ed. Huelsenbeck, pp. 3-9. This introduction shows most clearly the close parallels between Dadaist program and that of Expressionism. Thus, Huelsenbeck defines Dadaism here as (a) "der tänzerische Geist über den Moralen der Erde," i.e., as opposed to moral absolutism (this thesis derives, as does so much of Expressionist thinking, from Nietzsche: see Friedrich Nietzsche, *Jenseits von Gut und Böse,* repr. in Friedrich Nietzsche, *Werke in drei Banden,* ed. Karl Schlechtz, vol. 2, Munich, 1955, p. 686.); (b) as espousing a relativistic attitude of mind; (c) as opposed to all ossified elements in contemporary culture; (d) as opposed to the intellectually oriented bourgeois; (e) as able to assume the form of any artistic direction.

182. Huelsenbeck, "Einleitung," pp. 8-9.

183. Ibid.

Dies Buch ist eine Sammlung von Dokumenten des dadaistischen Erlebens, es vertritt keine Theorie. Es spricht vom dadaistischen Menschen, aber es stellt keinen Typus auf, es schildert, es untersucht nicht. Die Auffassung der Dadaisten vom Dadaismus ist eine sehr verschiedene: das wird in diesem Buch zum Ausdruck kommen. In der Schweiz war man z. B. für abstrakte Kunst, in Berlin ist man dagegen. Der Herausgeber, der von einem höheren Standpunkt parteilos verfahren zu sein hofft, scheut im einzelnen den Angriff nicht, da der Widerstand von allen Seiten eine Notwendigkeit und Freude seiner dadaistischen Existenz ist.

184. Herzfelde, "...über den Malik-Verlag," pp. 26-27; *Der Malik-Verlag,* p. 77; Hausmann, "Club Dada," p. 234; Richter, *Dada,* p. 137.

185. See preceding note.

186. Hausmann, "Club Dada," p. 234; Richter, *Dada,* pp. 137ff.

187. See, e.g., Richter, *Dada,* pp. 137ff., 171ff.

188. See Raabe, *Die Zeitschriften,* pp. 96-97, 99-100; *Der Malik-Verlag: 1916-1947,* pp. 76ff.

189. See note above; also Herzfelde, "...über den Malik-Verlag," pp. 28ff.

190. Herzfelde, "...über den Malik-Verlag," pp. 28ff; Herzfelde, "Wie ein Verlag," p. 231.

Some Conclusions

1.   Paul Raabe, "Das literarische Leben im Expressionismus: Eine historische Skizze," in Paul Raabe, *Die Zeitschriften und Sammlungen des literarischen Expressionismus* (Stuttgart, 1964), p. 1.

2.   Muschg, *Von Trakl,* pp. 18-19, 23.

3.   Denkler, *Drama des Expressionismus,* p. 15, offers this view as well.

Bibliography

Listed below are only those books and articles cited directly in the main text and footnotes of this study, with the exceptions of the journals, series publications, almanacs, and anthologies which are described in detail bibliographically in Paul Raabe, *Die Zeitschriften* (see below) and Fritz Schlawe, *Literarische Zeitschriften* (see below).

Ahnung und Aufbruch: Expressionistische Prosa. Ed. Karl Otten. Darmstadt, Berlin-Frouhnau, and Neuwied am Rhein, 1957.

Alexander-Katz, Erwin. "Zukünftler." *B.Z. am Mittag.* (6 May 1912), no. 106, First Supplement.

Als das Jahrhundert jung war. Ed. Josef Halperin. Zürich, 1961.

Altenberg, Peter, et al. *Der neue Weg der Genossenschaft Deutscher Bühnenangehöriger: Ein Protest in Sachen Herwarth Walden.* Berlin, n.d. [1909].

Appelle einer Revolution: Dokumente aus Bayern zum Jahr 1918/1919: Das Ende der Monarchie, Das revolutionäre Interregnum, Die Rätezeit. Ed. Karl-Ludwig Ay. Munich, 1968

Arnold, Armin. *Die Literatur des Expressionismus: Sprachliche und thematische Quellen.* Sprache und Literatur, 35. Stuttgart, Berlin, Cologne, and Mainz, 1966.

———. *Prosa des Expressionismus: Herkunft, Analyse, Inventar.* Sprache und Literatur,76. Stuttgart, Berlin, Cologne, and Mainz, 1971.

Arp, Hans. *Unsern täglichen Traum... Erinnerungen, Dichtungen, und Betrachtungen aus den Jahren 1914-1954.* Zürich, 1955.

Aspekte des Expressionismus: Periodisierung, Stil, Gedankenwelt: Die Vorträge des ersten Kolloquiums in Amherst/Massachusetts. Ed. Wolfgang Paulsen. Heidelberg, 1968.

Bab, Julius. *Richard Dehmel.* Leipzig, 1926.

Ball, Hugo. *Briefe: 1911-1927.* Ed. Annemarie Schütt-Hennings. Einsiedeln, Zürich, and Cologne, 1957.

———. *Die Flucht aus der Zeit.* Lucerne, 1946.

———. *Gesammelte Gedichte.* Ed. Annemarie Schütt-Hennings. Zürich, 1963.

Barlach, Ernst. *Die Briefe.* Ed. Friedrich Dross. vol. 1: Munich, 1968. Vol. 2: Munich, 1969.

———. *Ein selbsterzähltes Leben.* Munich, 1948.

Becher, Johannes. R. *Abschied: Roman.* Berlin, 1958.

———. *Auf andere Art so grosse Hoffnung: Tagebuch 1950: Mit Eintragungen 1951.* Berlin, 1952.

———. *Das poetische Prinzip.* Berlin, 1957.

———. *Lyrik, Prosa, Dokumente: Eine Auswahl.* Ed. Max Niedermayer. Wiesbaden, 1965.

———. *Macht der Poesie.* Berlin, 1955.

———. *Poetische Konfession.* Berlin, 1955.

———. *Verteidigung der Poesie.* Berlin, 1952.

Beckson, Karl and Arthur Ganz. *A Reader's Guide to Literary Terms: A Dictionary.* London, 1966.

Benn, Gottfried. *Ausgewählte Briefe.* Ed. Max Rychner. Wiesbaden, 1957.

———. *Den Traum alleine tragen: Neue Texte, Briefe, Dokumente.* Ed. Paul Raabe and Max Niedermayer. Wiesbaden, 1966.

———. *Gesammelte Werke in vier Bänden.* Ed. Dieter Wellershiff. Wiesbaden, 1959-61, 1962.

———. *Lyrik und Prosa, Briefe und Dokumente.* Ed. Max Niedermayer. Wiesbaden, 1962.

Bernauer, Rodolf. *Das Theater meines Lebens: Erinnerungen.* Berlin, 1955.

Blass, Ernst. *Die Strassen komme ich entlanggeweht.* Heidelberg, 1912.

Blei, Franz. *Erzählung eines Lebens.* Leipzig, 1930.

Blümner, Rudolf. *Der Geist des Kubismus und die Künste.* Berlin, 1921.

Bode, Ingrid. *Die Autobiographien zur deutschen Literatur, Kunst, und Musik 1900-1965: Bibliographie und Nachweise der persönlichen Begegnungen und Charakteristiken.* Repertorien zur deutschen Literaturgeschichte, ed. Paul Raabe, vol. 2. Stuttgart, 1966.

Boldt, Paul. *Junge Pferde! Junge Pferde! Das Gesamtwerk.* Ed. Wolfgang Minaty. Olten and Freiburg i. Br., 1979.

Born, Jürgen, et al. *Kafka-Symposium.* Berlin, 1965.

Briefe der Expressionisten. Ed. Kasimir Edschmid. Frankfurt am Main and Berlin, 1964.

Brinkmann, Richard. *Expressinismus: Forschungs-Probleme 1952-1960.* Referate aus der *Deutschen Vierteljahrsschrift für Literaturwissenschaft und Geistesgeschichte.* Ed. Richard Brinkmann, et al. Stuttgart, 1961.

———. *Expressionismus: Internationale Forschung zu einem internationalen Phänomen.* Sonderband der *Deutschen Vierteljahrsschrift für Literaturwissenschaft und Geistesgeschichte.* Stuttgart, 1980.

Brod, Max. *Der Prager Kreis.* Stuttgart, Berlin, Cologne, and Mainz, 1966.

———. *Streitbares Leben: Autobiographie.* Munich, 1960.

Bruggen, M.F.E. van. *Im Schatten des Nihilismus: Die expressionistische Lyrik im Rahmen und als Ausdruck der geistigen Situation Deutschlands.* Paris and Amsterdam, 1946.

Buchheim, Lothar-Güther. *Die Künstlergemeinschaft Brücke.* Feldafing, 1956.

Burschell, Friedrich. "Zwischen München und Berlin." *Deutsche Rundschau,* 89 (1963): 31-39.

Cahén, Fritz Max. *Der Weg nach Versailles: Erinnerungen 1912-1919: Schicksalsepoche einer Generation.* Boppard am Rhein, 1963.

Clough, Rosa Trillo. *Futurism: The Story of a Modern Art Movement: A New Appraisal.* New York, 1961.

Corinth, Lovis. *Selbstbiographie.* Leipzig, 1926.

Crespelle, Jean-Paul. *The Fauves.* Trans. Anita Brookner. Greenwich, 1962.

Dada: Eine Literarische Dokumentation. Ed. Richard Huelsenbeck. Reinbek bei Hamburg, 1964.

Das Kinobuch. Ed. Kurt Pinthus. 1913/14; rpt. Zürich, 1963.

Das war Dada: Dichtungen und Dokumente. Ed. Peter Schifferli. Sonderreihe, Deutscher Taschenbuch Verlag, vol. 18. Munich, 1963.

Das Wedekindbuch. Ed. Joachim Friedenthal. Munich, 1914.

Denkler, Horst. *Drama des Expressionismus: Programm, Spieltext, Theater.* Munich, 1967.

Der Blaue Reiter. Ed. Wassily Kandinsky and Franz Marc. Dokumentarische Neuausgabe. Ed. Klaus Lankheit. Munich, 1965.

Der deutsche Expressionismus: Formen und Gestalten. Ed. Hans Steffen. Kleine Vandenhoeck-Reihe, 208 (S). Göttingen, 1965.

Der Malik-Verlag: 1916-1947: Ausstellungskatalog. Ed. Wieland Herzfelde. Berlin and Weimar, n.d.

Der Sprach Brockhaus: Deutsches Bildwörterbuch. Wiesbaden, 1972.

Der Sturm: Ein Erinnerungsbuch an Herwarth Walden und die Künstler aus dem Sturmkreis. Ed. Nell Walden and Lothar Schreyer. Baden-Baden, 1954.

Deutsche Literatur-Kritik im zwanzigsten Jahrhundert. Ed. Hans Mayer. Stuttgart, 1965.

Deutscher, Isaac. *The Prophet Armed: Trotsky: 1879-1921.* New York and London, 1954.

———. *The Prophet Outcast: Trotsky: 1929-1940.* New York, Toronto and London, 1963.

Deutscher, Isaac. *The Prophet Unarmed: Trotsky: 1921-1929.* London, New York and Toronto, 1959.

Deutsches Wörterbuch. Ed. Lutz Mackensen. Munich, 1967.

Die Aktion: 1911-1914. Rpt. ed. Paul Raabe. 4 vols. Stuttgart, 1961.

Die Aktion: 1915-1918. Rpt. ed. Paul Raabe. 2 vols. Munich, 1967.

"*Die Aktion:* Stimmen der Freunde." Ed. Roland H. Wiegenstein. Unpubl. ms. of a radio broadcast commemorating the 50th anniversary of the founding of *Die Aktion,* Feb. 25, 1961. Schiller-Nationalmuseum, Marbach a.N.

Döblin, Alfred. *Aufsäftze zur Literatur.* Ed. Walter Muschg. Olten and Freiburg im Breisgau, 1963.

_____. *Briefe.* Ed. Walter Muschg and Heinz Graber. Olten and Freiburg im Breisgau, 1970.

Doede, Werner. *Berlin: Kunst und Künstler seit 1870: Anfänge und Entwicklung.* Recklinghausen, 1961.

Duden: Bedeutungswörterbuch: Der grosse Duden. Ed. Paul Grebe, et al. Mannheim, Vienna, and Zürich, 1970.

Durieux, Tilla. *Eine Tür steht offen.* Berlin-Grunewald, 1954.

Duwe, Willi. *Deutsche Dichtung des 20. Jahrhunderts: Die Geschichte der Ausdruckskunst.* Zürich, 1936.

Edschmid, Kasimir. *Lebendiger Expressionismus: Auseinandersetzungen, Gestalten, Erinnerungen.* Vienna, Munich, and Basel, 1961.

_____. *Tagebuch 1958-1960.* Vienna, Munich, and Basel, 1960.

Ego und Eros: Meistererzählungen des Expressionismus. Ed. Karl Otten. Stuttgart, 1963.

Ehrenburg, Ilya. *Memoirs: 1921-1941.* Trans. Tatania Shebunna. Cleveland and New York, 1964.

Ehrenstein, Albert. *Gedichte und Prosa.* Ed. Karl Otten. Neuwied am Rhein and Berlin-Spandau, 1961.

Ein Protest deutscher Künstler. Ed. Carl Vinnen. Jena, 1911.

Einstein, Carl. *Gesammelte Werke.* Wiesbaden, 1962.

Eisenlohr, Friedrich, *Das gläserne Netz.* Berlin-Grunewald, 1927.

Emrich, Wilhelm. *Protest und Verheissung.* Bonn, 1963.

Erdmann-Macke, Elisabeth. *Erinnerung an August Macke.* Stuttgart, 1962.

Erman, Hans. *Berliner Geschichten: Geschichte Berlins: Historien, Episoden, Anekdoten.* Rastatt, 1966.

Expressionismus als Literatur. Ed. Wolfgang Rothe. Bern and Munich, 1969.

Expressionismus: Aufzeichnungen und Erinnerungen der Zeitgenossen. Ed. Paul Raabe. Olten and Freiburg i.B., 1965. Trans: *The Era of German Expressionism.* Ed. Paul Raabe. Trans. J.M. Ritchie. Woodstock, 1974.

Expressionismus: Der Kampf um eine literarische Bewegung. Ed. Paul Raabe. Sonnderreihe, Deutscher Taschenbuch Verlag, vol. 41. Munich, 1965.

Expressionismus: Die Kunstwende. Ed. Herwarth Walden. Berlin, 1918.

Expressionismus: Gestalten einer literarischen Bewegung. Ed. Hermann Friedmann and Otto Mann. Heidelberg, 1956.

Expressionismus: Literatur und Kunst: 1910-1923: Eine Ausstellung des deutschen Literaturarchivs im Schiller-Nationalmuseum Marbach a. N. Kat. 7, Sonderausstellungen des Schiller-Nationalmuseums. Ed. Bernhard Zeller, et al. Marback a.N., 1960.

Felixmüller, Conrad. "Erinnerungen eines Malers an seinen Kunstfreund Carl Sternheim." *Neue Texte* 4 (1964): 454-72.

Flake, Otto. *Es wird Abend: Bericht aus einem langen Leben.* Gütersloh, 1960.

Frank, Leonhard. *Der Mensch ist gut.* Zürich, 1918.

_____. *Links wo das Herz: Roman.* Munich, 1952.

Friedlaender, Salomo [Mynona]. *Rosa, die schöne Schutzmannsfrau und andere Grotesken.* Ed. Ellen Otten. Zürich, 1965.

Friedrich, Otto. *Before the Deluge: A Portrait of Berlin in the 1920's.* New York, 1972.

Gedichte der "Menschheitsdämmerung." Ed. Horst Denkler. Munich, 1971.

Goering, Reinhard. *Prosa, Draman, Verse.* Munich, 1961.

Goetz, Wolfgang. *Begegnungen und Bekenntnisse.* Ed. Tilla Goetz. Berlin, 1964.

———. *Im "Grössenwahn" bei Pschorr und anderswo... Erinnerungen an Berliner Stammtische.* Berlin, 1936.

Goll, Claire. *Ich verzeihe keinem: Eine literarische Chronique scandaleuse unserer Zeit.* Bern and Munich, 1976.

Graf, Oskar Maria. *Georg Schrimpf.* Junge Kunst, vol. 37, Leipzig, 1923.

———. *Maria Uhden.* Junge Kunst, vol. 20. Leipzig, 1921.

———. *Wir sind Gefangene: Ein Bekenntnis.* Vienna, Munich, and Basel, 1965.

———. *Wir sind Gefangene: Ein Bekenntnis aus diesem Jahrzehnt.* Munich, 1927.

Grochowiak, Thomas, *Ludwig Meidner.* Rechlinghausen, 1966.

Grohamnn, Will. *Bildende Kunst und Achitektur.* vol. 3, *Zwischen den Kriegen.* Berlin, 1953.

Grosz, George. *A Little Yes and a Big No: The Autobiography of George Grosz.* Trans. Lola Sachs Dorin. New York, 1946.

Gumbert, Martin. *Hölle im Paradies: Selbstdarstellung eines Arztes.* Stockholm, 1939.

Haas, Willy. *Die literarische Welt: Erinnerungen.* Munich, 1957.

Hadwiger, Victor. *Wenn unter uns ein Wandrer ist: Ausgewählte Gedichte.* Ed. Anselm Ruest. Berlin-Wilmersdorf, n.d. [1912].

Hamann, Richard and Jost Hermand. *Impressionismus.* Berlin, 1960.

Hart, Heinrich. *Gesammelte Werke.* Ed. Julius Hart. Vol. 3. Berlin, 1907.

Hasenclever, Walter. *Der Retter.* Leipzig, 1916.

———. *Die Entscheidung.* Berlin, 1919.

———. *Gedichte, Dramen, Prosa.* Ed. Kurt Pinthus. Rowohlt Paperback, 8. Reinbek bei Hamburg, 1963.

———. *Irrtum und Leidenschaft: Roman.* Berlin, 1969.

Hatvany, Ludwig. *Die Wissenschaft des Nicht Wissenswerten.* 2nd. ed., Berlin, 1911.

Hausenstein, Wilhelm. *Lux perpetua: Summe eines Lebens aus dieser Zeit.* Vol. 1. Munich, 1947.

Hennings, Emmy. *Blume und Flamme: Geschichte einer Jugend.* Einsiedeln, 1938.

———. *Das Flüchtige Spiel: Wege und Umwege einer Frau.* Einsiedeln, 1940.

———. *Ruf und Echo: Mein Leben mit Hugo Ball.* Einsiedeln, 1953.

Hennings-Ball, Emmy. *Hugo Balls Weg zu Gott.* Munich, 1931.

Herald, Heinz. *Max Reinhardt: Bildnis eines Theatermannes.* Hamburg, 1953.

Hermand, Jost. "Über Nutzen und Nachteil literarischer Epochenbegriffe: Ein Vortrag." *Monatshefte* 58 (1966): 289-309.

Herrmann-Neisse, Max. *Eine Einführung in sein Werk und eine Auswahl.* Ed. Friedrich Grieger. Wiesbaden, 1951.

Herzfelde, Wieland. "Aus der Jugendzeit des Malik-Verlages: Zum Neudruck der Zeitschrift *Neue Jugend.*" *Neue Jugend 1916/17.* Rpt. ed. Wieland Herzfelde, pp. 5-18. Zürich, 1967.

———. *Unterwegs: Blätter aus Fünfzig Jahren.* Berlin, 1961.

Herzog, Wilhelm. *Menschen denen ich begegnete.* Bern and Munich, 1959.

Heym, Georg. *Dichtungen und Schriften.* Ed. Karl Ludwig Schneider and Gerhard Burkhardt. Vols. 1, 2, 3, and 6. Hamburg, Munich, and Darmstadt, 1960ff.

———. *Gesammelte Gedichte.* Ed. Carl Seelig. Zürich, 1947.

Hiller, Kurt. *Die Weisheit der Langenweile: Eine Zeit- und Streitschrift.* 2 vols. Leipzig, 1913.

———. *Leben gegen die Zeit.* Vol. 1: *Logos.* Reinbek bei Hamburg, 1969.

Hirsch, Karl Jakob. *Heimkehr zu Gott; Briefe an meinen Sohn.* Munich, 1946.

Hoddis, Jakob van. *Weltende: Gesammelte Dichtungen.* Ed. Paul Pörtner. Zürich, 1958.

Höxter, John. *So lebten wir: 25 Jahre Berliner Boheme.* Berlin, 1929.

Hoffmann, Edith. *Kokoschka: Life and Work.* London, n.d.

Hohendahl, Peter. *Das Bild der bürgerlichen Welt im expressonistischen Drama.* Heidelberg, 1967.

Horch, Franz. *Die Spielpläne Max Reinhardts: 1905-1930.* Muinich, 1930.

Houben, H.H. *Verbotene Literatur: Von der klassischen Zeit bis zur Gegenwart.* Vol. 1. Dessau, 1925. Vol. 2. Bremen, 1928.

Huelsenbeck, Richard. "Die dadaistische Bewegung." *Die neue Rundschau,* 31 (1920): 972-79.

―――. *Mit Witz, Licht und Grütz.* Wiesbaden, 1957.

―――. *Phantastische Gebete.* Zürich, 1960.

Ich schneide die Zeit aus: Expressionismus and Politik in Franz Pfemferts Aktion: 1911-1918. Ed. Paul Raabe. Deutscher Taschenbuch Verlag, 195/196. Munich, 1964.

Im Kampf um die Kunst: Die Antwort auf den "Protest deutscher Künstler." Munich, 1911.

Jacob, Hans. *Kind meiner Zeit: Lebenserinnerungen.* Cologne and Berlin, 1962.

Jacob, Heinrich Eduard. *Der Zwanzigjährige: Ein symphonischer Roman.* Munich, 1918.

Jacobsohn, Siegfried. *Das Jahr der Bühne.* Vol. 9. Berlin, 1920.

Jacques, Norbert. *Mit Lust gelebt: Roman meines Lebens.* Hamburg, 1950.

Jhering, Herbert. *Begegnungen mit Zeit und Menschen.* Bremen, 1965.

―――. *Von Reinhardt bis Brecht: Eine Auswahl der Theaterkritiken von 1909-1932.* Ed. Rolf Badenhausen. Reinbek bei Hamburg, 1967.

Jones, Ernest. *The Life and Work of Sigmund Freud.* Vol. 1. New York, 1953. Vol. 2. New York, 1955.

Jung, Franz. *Der Weg nach unten.* Neuwied am Rhein, 1961.

Kaiser, Georg. *Stücke, Erzählungen, Aufsätze, Gedichte.* Ed. Walther Huder. Cologne and Berlin, 1966.

Kandinsky, Wassily. *Über das Geistige in der Kunst.* Introduction by Max Bill. Bern-Bümpliz, 1963.

Kasack, Hermann. "Deutsche Literatur im Zeichen des Expressionismus." *Merkur,* 15 (April, 1961), no. 4 pp. 353-63.

―――. *Mosaiksteine: Beiträge zu Literatur und Kunst.* Frankfurt am Main, 1956.

Kessler, Harry Graf. *Tagebücher: 1918-1937.* Ed. Wolfgang Pfeiffer-Belli. Frankfurt am Main, 1961.

Kesten, Hermann. *Dichter im Café.* Vienna, Munich, and Basel, 1959.

Kestenberg, Leo *Bewegte Zeiten: Musisch-musikalische Lebenserinnerungen.* Wolfenbüttel and Zürich, 1961.

Kiaulehn, Walter. *Berlin: Schicksal einer Weltstadt.* Munich and Berlin, 1958.

Kiaulein, Walter. *Mein Freund der Verleger: Ernst Rowohlt und seine Zeit.* Reinbek bei Hamburg, 1967.

Klabund. *Briefe an einen Freund.* Ed. Ernst Heinrich. Cologne and Berlin, 1963.

Knudsen, Hans. *Deutsche Theater-Geschichte.* Stuttgart, 1959.

Kober, A.H. *Einst in Berlin: Rhapsodie 14.* Ed. Richard Virn. Hamburg, 1956.

Kokoschka, Oskar. *Mein Leben.* Munich, 1971.

―――. *Schriften: 1907-1955.* Ed. Hans Maria Wingler. Munich, 1956.

Kolinsky, Eva. *Engagierter Expressionismus: Politik und Literatur zwischen Weltkrieg und Weimarer Republik.* Stuttgart, 1970.

Krell, Max. *Das alles gab es einmal.* Frankfurt am Main, 1961.

Kreuzer, Helmut. *Die Boheme: Beiträge zu ihrer Beschreibung.* Stuttgart, 1968.

―――. "Zur Periodisierung der 'modernen' deutschen Literatur." *Basis* 2 (1971): 7-32.

Krispyn, Egbert. *Style and Society in German Literary Expressionism.* Gainesville, 1964.

Kühn, Herbert. "Das Gegenständliche des expressionistischen Dramas." *Die neue Schaubühne* 1 (1919): 204-6.

Künstlerbekenntnisse: Briefe/Tagebuchblätter/Betrachtungen heutiger Künstler. Ed. Paul Westheim. Berlin, n.d.

Kurtz, Rudolf. *Expressionisums und Film.* Filmwissenschaftliche Studientexte, vol. 1. 1926; rpt. Zürich, 1965.

Landauer, Gustav. *Zwang und Befreiung: Eine Auswahl aus seinem Werk.* Ed. Heinz-Joachim Heydorn. Cologne, 1968.

Lasker-Schüler, Else. *Briefe an Karl Kraus.* Ed. Astrid Gehlhoff-Class. Cologne and Berlin, 1959.

————. *Gesammelte Werke in drei Bänden.* Vols. 1-2. Ed. Friedhelm Kemp. Munich, 1959-62. Vol. 3. Ed. Werner Kraft. Munich, 1961.

————. *Lieber gestreifter Tiger.* Vol. 1. of *Briefe von Else Lasker-Schüler.* Ed. Margarete Kupper. Munich, 1969.

————. *Wo ist unser buntes Theben.* Vol. 2 of *Briefe von Else Lasker-Schüler.* Ed. Margarete Kupper. Munich, 1969.

Lehnert, Herbert. "Satirische Botschaft an den Leser: Das Ende des Jugendstils." *Gestaltungsgeschichte und Gesellschaftsgeschichte: Literatur-, kunst- und musikwissenschaftliche Studien,* ed. Käte Hamburger and Helmut Kreuzer, pp. 487-515. Stuttgart, 1969.

Lennig, Walter. *Gottfried Benn: In Selbstzeugnissen und Bilddokumenten.* Rowohlts Monographien, 71. Reinbek bei Hamburg, 1962.

Leonhard, Rudolf. *Das Chaos.* Hannover, 1919.

Levy, Rudolf. *Bildnisse, Stilleben, Landschaften.* Geleitwort und Nachruf von Genia Levy. Erinnerungen an den Freund von Hans Purrman. Baden-Baden, 1961.

Leymarie, Jean. *Fauvism: Biographical and Critical Study.* Paris, 1959.

Lichtenstein, Alfred. *Gesammelte Gedichte.* Ed. Klaus Kanzog. Zürich, 1962.

Literatur im Klassenkampf: Zur proletarisch-revolutionären Literaturtheorie 1919-1923: Eine Dokumentation. Ed. Walter Fähnders and Martin Rector. Munich, 1971.

Loerke, Oskar. *Tagebücher: 1903-1939.* Ed. Hermann Kasack. Veröffentlichungen der Deutschen Akademie für Sprache und Dichtung, 5. Heidelberg and Darmstadt, 1956.

Loewenson, Erwin. *Georg Heym oder Vom Geist des Schicksals.* Hamburg and Munich, 1962.

Lorenz, Rosemarie. *Max Herrmann-Neisse.* Germanistische Abhandlungen, 14. Stuttgart, 1966.

Lublinski, Samuel. *Der Ausgang der Moderne.* Dresden, 1909.

————. *Die Bilanz der Moderne.* Berlin, 1904.

————. *Nachgelassene Schriften.* Munich, 1914.

Macke, August and Franz Marc. *Briefwechsel.* Ed. Wolfgang Macke. Cologne, 1964.

Manifeste: Manifeste: 1905-1933. Ed. Diether Schmidt. Schriften deutscher Künstler des zwanzigsten Jahrhunderts, vol. 1. Fundus-Bücher, 15/16/17. Dresden, n.d.

Mann, Golo. *Deutsche Geschichte des 19. und 20. Jahrhunderts.* Frankfurt am Main, 1966.

Mann, Heinrich. *Der Kopf.* Vienna, 1925.

————. *Der Untertan.* Leipzig, 1918.

————. *Die Armen.* Leipzig, 1917.

————. *Ein Zeitalter wird besichtigt.* Berlin, 1947.

Mann, Thomas. *Betrachtungen eines Unpolitischen.* Frankfurt am Main, 1956.

Marcuse, Ludwig. *Mein zwanzigstes Jahrhundert: Auf dem Weg zu einer Autobiographie.* Munich, 1960.

Martens, Gunter. *Vitalismus und Expressionismus: Ein Beitrag zur Genese und Deutung expressionistischer Stilstrukturen und Motive.* Stuttgart, Berlin, Cologne, and Mainz, 1971.

Martini, Fritz. *Was war Expressionismus?* Urach, 1948.

Mautz, Kurt. *Mythologie und Gesellschaft im Expressionismus: Die Dichtung Georg Heyms.* Frankfurt am Main and Bonn, 1961.

Max Reinhardt: 25 Jahre Deutsches Theater: Ein Tafelwerk. Ed. Hans Rothe. Munich, 1930.

Mayer, Paul. *Ernst Rowohlt in Selbstzeugnissen und Bilddokumenten.* Sonderdruck, Rowohlts Monographien. Reinbek bei Hamburg, 1967.

Mehring, Walter. *Berlin Dada: Eine Chronik mit Photos und Dokumenten.* Zürich, 1959.

————. "Die neue Form." *Die neue Rundschau* 31 (1920): 124-127.

————. *Die verlorene Bibliothek: Autobiographie einer Kultur.* Icking bei München, 1964.

Meidner, Ludwig. *Eine autobiographische Plauderei.* Junge Kunst, vol. 4. Leipzig, 1923.

――――. *Im Nacken das Sternemeer: Rufe eines Malers.* Leipzig, 1918.

――――. *Septemberschrei: Hymnen, Gebete, Lästerungen.* Berlin, 1920.

Menschheitsdämmerung: Ein Dokument des Expressionismus. Ed. Kurt Pinthus. Hamburg. 1959.

Meyer, Alfred Richard. *Berlin: Ein impressionistischer Sonettenkranz.* Berlin, 1907.

――――. *Der grosse Munkepunke: Gesammelte Werke.* Hamburg and Berlin, 1924.

Meyer, Alfred Richard. *die maer von der musa expressionistica: zugleich eine kleine quasi-literaturgeschichte mit über 130 praktischen beispielen.* Düsseldorf-Kaiserswerth, 1948.

Minotaurus: Dichtung unter den Hufen von Staat und Industrie. Ed. Alfred Döblin. Wiesbaden, 1953.

"'Morgenrot!—Die Tage dämmern!' Zwanzig Briefe aus dem Frühexpressionismus 1910-1914." Ed. Paul Raabe. *Der Monat* 16 (1964), no. 191, pp. 52-70.

Muche, Georg. *Blickpunkt: Sturm, Dada, Bauhaus, Gegenwart.* Munich, 1961.

Mühsam, Erich. *Unpolitische Erinnerungen.* Berlin, 1961.

Muschg, Walter. *Von Trakl zu Brecht: Dichter des Expressionismus.* Munich, 1961.

Myers, Bernard S. *The German Expressionists: A Generation in Revolt.* New York and Washington, 1966.

Nachrichten aus dem Kösel-Verlag: Sonderheft für Else Lasker-Schüler Dezember 1965. Ed. Dr. Heinrich Wild and Friedrich Pfäfflin. Munich, 1965.

Neue deutsche Biographie. Ed. Die Historische Kommission bei der Bayrischen Akademie der Wissenschaften. Vol. 3. Berlin, 1957.

Nietzsche, Friedrich. *Werke in drei Bänden.* Ed. Karl Schlechta. Munich, 1955.

Oskar Kokoschka: Ein Lebensbild in zeitgenössischen Dokumenten. Ed. Hans Maria Wingler. Munich, 1956.

Otten, Karl. "*Die Aktion:* Eine Zeitschrift gegen die Zeit." Unpub. ms. of a radio talk given on Feb. 25, 1961, in commemoration of the 50th anniversary of the founding of *Die Aktion.* Schiller-Nationalmuseum, Marbach a.N.

――――. *Wurzeln.* Neuwied am Rhein and Berlin, 1963.

The Oxford English Dictionary. Oxford, 1933.

Pascal, Roy. *From Naturalism to Expressionism: German Literature and Society 1880-1918.* New York, 1973.

Paulsen, Wolfgang. *Expressionismus und Aktivismus: Eine typologische Untersuchung.* Bern and Leipzig, 1935.

Pechstein, Max. *Erinnerungen.* Wiesbaden, 1960.

PEM [Paul Erich Marcus]. *Heimweh nach dem Kurfürstendamm: Aus Berlins glanzvollsten Tagen und Nächten.* Berlin, 1952.

Pinthus, Kurt. *Der Zeitgenosse: Literarische Portraits und Kritiken.* Marbach a.N., 1971.

――――. "*Die Aktion:* Zum 50. Jubiläiiu

S

Schiller-Nationalmuseum, Marbach a.N.   Feb

Piscator, Erwin. *Das politische Theater.* Ed. Felix Gasbarra. Rowohlt Paperback, 11. Reinbek bei Hamburg, 1963.

Pörtner, Paul. *Literatur-Revolution: 1910-1925: Dokumente, Manifeste, Programme.* Die Mainzer Reihe, 13. Vol. 1. Darmstadt, Neuwied am Rhein, and Berlin-Spandau, 1960. Vol. 2. Neuwied am Rhein and Berlin-Spandau, 1961.

Pross, Harry. *Jugend, Eros, Politik: Die Geschichte der Jugendverbände.* Bern, Munich, and Vienna, 1964.

Pulver, Max. *Erinnerungen an eine europäische Zeit.* Zürich, 1953.

Raabe, Paul. *Die Zeitschriften und Sammlungen des literarischen Expressionismus: Repertorium der Zeitschriften, Jahrbücher, Anthologien, Sammelwerke, Schriftenreihen und Almanache: 1910-1921.* Repertorien zur deutschen Literaturgeschichte, 1. Stuttgart, 1964.

Rasch, Wolfdietrich. *Zur deutschen Literatur seit der Jahrhundertwende.* Stuttgart, 1967.

Reimann, Hans. *Mein blaues Wunder: Lebensmosaik eines Humoristen.* Munich, 1959.

Reinhardt, Kurt F. *Germany 2000 Years.* 2 vols. New York, 1950, 1961.

Richter, Hans. *Dada: Kunst und Antikunst: Der Beitrag Dadas zur Kunst des 20. Jahrhunderts.* Cologne, 1964.

———. *Dada-Profile.* Zürich, 1961.

Rodenberg, Julius. *Deutsche Pressen: Eine Bibliographie.* Zürich, Vienna, and Leipzig, 1925.

Roditi, Edouard. "Hannah Höch und die Berliner Dadaisten: Ein Gespräch mit der Malerin." *Der Monat* 12 (1959), no. 134, pp. 60-68.

Rosenberg, Arthur. *Die Entstehung der deutschen Republik: 1871-1918.* Berlin, 1928.

———. *Geschichte der Weimarer Republik.* Ed. Kurt Kersten. Frankfurt a.M., 1961.

Rowohlt Almanach: 1908-1962. Ed. Mara Hintermeier and Fritz J. Raddatz. Rowohlt Paperback, 9. Reinbek bei Hamburg, 1962.

Rühle, Gunther. *Theater für die Republik: 1917-1933: Im Spiegel der Kritik.* Frankfurt a.M., 1967.

———. *Das gefesselte Theater: Vom Revolutionstheater zum Sozialistischen Realismus.* Cologne and Berlin, 1957.

Sack, Gustav. *Prosa, Briefe, Verse.* Munich and Vienna, 1962.

Salzmann, Karl H. "Die Verlage Paul und Bruno Cassirer: Ein Stück Berliner Kulturgeschichte." *Berliner Hefte für das geistige Leben* 4 (1949): 503-8.

Samuel, Richard and R. Hinton Thomas. *Expressionism in German Life, Literature and the Theatre (1910-1924).* Cambridge, 1939.

Schickele, René. *Werke in drei Bänden.* Ed. Hermann Kesten. Cologe and Berlin, 1959.

Schlawe, Fritz. *Literarische Zeitschriften.* [Pt. 1.] *1885-1910.* Sammlung Metzler, 6. Stuttgart, 1961.

———. *Literarische Zeitschriften.* Pt. 2. *1910-1933.* Sammlung Metzler, 24. Stuttgart, 1962.

Schleich, Carl Ludwig. *Besonnte Vergangenheit: Lebenserinnerungen (1859-1919).* Berlin, 1921.

Schneider, Ferdinand Josef. *Der expressive Mensch und die deutsche Lyrik der Gegenwart.* Stuttgart, 1927.

Schneider, Karl Ludwig. *Der bildhafte Ausdruck in den Dichtungen Georg Heyms, Georg Trakls und Ernst Stadlers.* Heidelberg, 1954, 1961.

———. *Zerbrochene Formen: Wort und Bild im Expressionismus.* Hamburg, 1967.

Schönlank, Bruno. *Blutjunge Welt: Revolutionsgedichte.* Berlin, 1919.

Schrei und Bekenntnis: Expressionistches Theater. Ed. Karl Otten. Darmstadt, Berlin-Spandau, and Neuwied am Rhein, 1959.

Schreyer, Lothar. *Erinnerungen an Sturm und Bauhus: Was ist des Menschen Bild?* Munich, 1956.

———. *Expressionistisches Theater: Aus meinen Erinnerungen.* Hamburger Theaterbücherei, vol. 4. Hamburg, 1947.

Schulze-Maizier, Friedrich. "Frühexistentialist unter Frühexpressionisten: Erlebnisse im Neuen Club." *Deutsche Rundschau* 88 (1962): 331-38.

Schumann, Thomas B. "Geschichte des "Neuen Clubs" in Berlin als wichtigster Anreger des literarischen Expressionismus: Eine Dokumentation." *Emuna* 9 (1974), 55-70.

Scott, A.F. *Current Literary Terms: A Concise Dictionary of their Origin and Use.* New York, 1967.

Seewald, Richard. *Der Mann von gegenüber: Spiegelbild eines Lebens.* Munich, 1963.

Seiffhart, Arthur. *Inter folia fructus: Aus den Erinnerungen eines Verlegers.* Berlin, 1948.

Selz, Peter. *German Expressionist Painting.* Berkeley and Los Angeles, 1957.

Shattuck, Roger. *The Banquet Years: The Art in France: 1885-1918: Alfred Jarry, Henri Rousseau, Erik Satie, Guillaume Apollinaire.* Garden City, 1961.

Simmel, George. *Philosophie des Geldes.* Berlin, 1900.

Sinn und Form: Beiträge zur Literatur: Zweites Sonderheft Johannes R. Becher. Berlin, 1960.

Sinsheimer, Hermann. *Gelebt im Paradies: Erinnerungen und Begegnungen.* Munich, 1953.

Soergel, Albert. *Dichtung und Dichter der Zeit: Neue Folge: Im Banne des Expressionisumus.* Leipzig, 1925.

————, and Curt Hohoff. *Dichtung und Dichter der Zeit: Vom Naturalismus bis zur Gegenwart.* Vol. 1. Düsseldorf, 1961, Vol. 2. Düsseldorf, 1963.

Sokel, Walter. *The Writer in Extemis: Expressionism in Twentieth-Century German Literature.* Stanford, 1959.

Stadler, Ernst. *Dichtungen.* Ed. Karl Ludwig Schneider. 2 vols. Hamburg, n.d. [1954].

Starke, Ottomar. *Was mein Leben anlangt.* Berlin-Grunewald, 1956.

Steinke, Gerhardt Edward. *The Life and Work of Hugo Ball: Founder of Dadaism.* The Hague and Paris, 1967.

Sternheim, Carl. *Gesamtwerk.* Ed. Wilhelm Emrich. Vols. 1-9. Neuwied am Rhein, Berlin, 1963-70.

————. *Vorkreigseuropa im Gleichnis meines Lebens.* Amsterdam, 1936.

Stramm, August. *Das Werk.* Ed. René Radrizzani. Wiesbaden, 1963.

Strindberg, August. *Inferno, Alone and Other Writings.* Ed. Evert Sprinchorn. Garden City, 1968.

Stuyver, Wilhemina. *Deutsche expressionistische Dichtung im Lichte der Philosophie der Gegenwart.* Amsterdam and Paris, 1939.

Susman, Margarete. *Ich habe viele Leben gelebt: Erinnerungen.* Stuttgart, 1964.

Szittya, Emil. *Das Kuriositäten-Kabinett: Begegnungen mit seltsamen Begebenheiten, Landstreichern, Verbrechern, Artisten, religiös Wahnsinnigen, sexuellen Merkwürdigkeiten, Sozialdemokraten, Syndikalisten, Kommunisten, Anarchisten, Politikern und Künstlern.* Constance, 1923.

Thrall, William Flint, and Addison Hibbard. *A Handbook to Literature.* New York, 1960.

Toller, Ernst. *Prosa, Briefe, Dramen, Gedichte.* Ed. Kurt Hiller. Rowohlt Paperback, 1. Reinbek bei Hamburg, 1961.

Ullstein Lexikon der deutschen Sprache. Ed. Rudolf Köster, et al. Frankfurt and Berlin, 1969.

Verse der Lebenden: Deutsche Lyrik seit 1910. Ed. Heinrich Eduard Jacob. Berlin, 1924.

Viviani, Annalisa. *Dramaturgische Elemente im expressionistischen Drama.* vol. 21 of Bonner Arbeiten zur deutschen Literatur, ed. Benno von Wiese. Bonn, 1970.

Walden, Herwarth. "Vulgär-Expressionismus." *Das Wort* 3 (1938): 89-100.

Walden, Nell. *Herwarth Walden: Ein Lebensbild.* Berlin and Mainz, 1963.

Wassermann, Jacob. *Caspar Hauser oder Die Trägheit des Herzens,* Berlin, 1908.

Webster's Third New International Dictionary of the English Language. Springfield, 1963.

Weisstein, Ulrich. *Heinrich Mann: Eine historisch-kritische Einführung in sein dichterisches Werk.* Tübingen, 1962.

Willett, John. *Expressionism.* Toronto, 1970.

Wilpert, Gero von. *Sachwörterbuch der Literatur.* Stuttgart, 1959.

Wolff, Kurt. *Autoren, Bücher, Abenteuer: Betrachtungen und Erinnerungen eines Verlegers.* Berlin, 1965.

————. *Briefwechsel eines Verlegers: 1911-1963.* Ed. Bernhard Zeller and Ellen Otthen. Frankfurt am Main, 1966.

Worringer, Wilhelm. *Künstlerische Zeitfragen.* Munich, 1921.

Zehn Jahre Novembergruppe. Berlin, 1928.

Zivier, Georg. *Das Romanische Café: Erscheinungen und Randerscheinungen rund um die Gedächtniskirche.* Berlin, 1965.

Zuckmayer, Carl. *Als wär's ein Stück von mir.* Vienna, 1966.

Zunker, Ernst. "*Der Wiecker Bote:* Das Organ eines Expressionistenkreises an der Universität Griefswald." *Germanisch-Romanische Monatsschrift* n.s. 11 (1961): 226-29.

Zweig, Stefan. *Die Welt von gestern: Erinnerungen eines Europäers.* Stockholm, 1944.

Index

Hoffmann, Camill, 196
Hoffmann, Franz, 110
Hofmannsthal, Hugo von, 31, 68, 101, 166, 168, 189, 227
Hohendahl, Peter, 2, 7, 8, 11
Holitscher, Arthur, 115
Hollaender, Friedrich, 211
Holz, Arno, 53, 100, 102, 155, 168
Holzer, Marie, 143
Holzmann, Johannes. *See* Senna Hoy
Hotel Bristol, 238
Hotel Koschel, 63
Hotel Schwert, 200
Hotel Spiezerhof, 200
Hoy, Senna, 136-37, 149
Huebner, Friedrich Markus, 236
Hübner, Heinrich, 177
Hübner, Ulrich, 177, 196
Huelsenbeck, Richard, 14, 46, 58, 59, 73, 217-19, 221, 230, 231, 234, 236, 237, 239, 240-42, 244, 245, 247, 248, 249
Hyperion, 83, 128
Hyperionverlag, 185

Ilgenstein, Heinrich, 137
Impressionism, 2, 166, 173, 174, 177, 178, 198, 201, 234
"Internationale Vereinigung der Expressionisten, Futuristen, Kubisten und Konstruktivisten," 121
Itten, Johannes, 109

Jacob, Hans, 211-13
Jacob, Heinrich Eduard, 35, 76, 78, 79, 142, 191
Jacobowsky, Ludwig, 53, 98
Jacques, Jean. *See* Hans Jacob
Jacques, Norbert, 67, 102, 128
Jaeckel, Willy, 196, 198
Jagow, Traugott, 27, 34, 186
Jammes, Francis, 160
Janthur, Richard, 205
Jaurès, Jean, 199
"Jedermann sein eigner Fussball," 44, 65, 246-47
Jentzsch, Robert, 75, 76, 80, 84, 92, 140
Jessner, Leopold, 64
Jhering, Herbert, 15, 64
Joel, Hans Theodor, 73
Jugend, 105, 247
Jugendstil, 2, 105, 163
Jüngste Tag, Der, 20, 45
Jung, Claire. *See* Claire Otto
Jung, Franz, 7, 22, 26, 39, 40, 46, 49, 50, 51, 56, 58, 127, 128, 129, 131, 132, 133, 135, 138, 140, 146, 151, 190, 230, 231, 234, 235, 236, 237, 239, 241, 245, 246, 248
"Junge Deutschland, Das," 43, 60, 63, 64

"Junge Rheinland, Das," 42
Jungnickel, Max, 142
Jushny, 122

"Kabarett Grössenwahn," 72
Kadar, Béla, 109
Kafka, Franz, 128
Kain, 15, 39-40
Kaiser, Georg, 7, 18, 45, 47, 60, 213, 227
Kampf, 136
"Kampf-Bühne," 120
Kandinsky, Wassily, 20, 32, 105, 114, 116, 117
Kanehl, Oskar, 20, 46, 127, 129, 130, 134, 140, 143, 145, 148, 154, 156, 161, 170
Kant, Immanuel, 156
Kardoff, Konrad von, 177
Kasack, Hermann, 59, 218, 221-23, 227-28
Kássak, Ludwig, 109
Kautsky, Karl, 201, 204
Kayser, Rudolf, 47, 48, 143-44
Keller, Julius Talbot, 134, 146
Kellermann, Bernhard, 67
Kerr, Alfred, 14, 25, 36, 39, 83, 94, 95, 124, 180, 181, 182-85, 186, 187, 189-93
Kerr-*Pan*-Jagow affair, 124, 185
Kersten, Hugo, 30, 129, 132, 143
Kersten, Kurt, 135, 142
Kestenberg, Leo, 68, 198, 201
Kessler, Harry Graf, 44, 199, 200, 201, 204
Kesten, Hermann, 68, 127
Kesting, Edmund, 109
Kirchner, Ludwig, 164, 198, 202, 206, 227
Kisch, Egon Erwin, 73
Klabund, 34, 36, 46, 154, 171, 192, 198, 222
Klages, Ludwig, 4
Klee, Paul, 109, 114, 117, 121
Klein, César, 42, 105, 134, 209
Kleist, Heinrich von, 193
Klemm, Erna, 137, 140
Klemm, Wilhelm, 129, 130, 133, 137, 145, 146
Klimsch, Fritz, 177
Knoblauch, Adolf, 95, 106
Knoblauch, Anna, 95
Knoblauch, Willy, 110
Koch, Hans, 145, 146
König, Leo von, 177
Köppen, Edlef, 146, 221, 223, 227
Koffka, Friedrich, 60, 75, 76
Kokoschka, Oskar, 60, 63, 94, 95, 96, 105, 109, 114, 115, 117, 143, 179, 198, 201, 202, 227
Kolb, Annette, 67, 200
Kolinsky, Eva, 7-8
Kollwitz, Käthe, 192
"Komittee Konfessionslos, Das," 142
"Kommenden, Die," 53, 98
Kornfeld, Paul, 60, 227
Krapotkin, Peter, 32